ROUTLEDGE LIBRARY EDITIONS:
SOCIAL THEORY

Volume 89

TOWARDS THE SOCIOLOGY
OF KNOWLEDGE

TOWARDS THE SOCIOLOGY OF KNOWLEDGE

Origin and development of a sociological thought style

Edited by
GUNTER W. REMMLING

Routledge
Taylor & Francis Group
LONDON AND NEW YORK

First published in 1973

This edition first published in 2015
by Routledge
2 Park Square, Milton Park, Abingdon, Oxfordshire OX14 4RN

and by Routledge
711 Third Avenue, New York, NY 10017

Routledge is an imprint of the Taylor and Francis Group, an informa business

First issued in paperback 2015

British Library Cataloguing in Publication Data
A catalogue record for this book is available from the British Library

ISBN 978-0-415-72731-0 (Set)
eISBN 978-1-315-76997-4 (Set)
ISBN 978-1-138-78385-0 (hbk) (Volume 89)
ISBN 978-1-138-98585-8 (pbk) (Volume 89)

Publisher's Note
The publisher has gone to great lengths to ensure the quality of this reprint but
points out that some imperfections in the original copies may be apparent.

Disclaimer
The publisher has made every effort to trace copyright holders and would
welcome correspondence from those they have been unable to trace.

Towards the sociology of knowledge

Origin and development of a
sociological thought style

Edited by
Gunter W. Remmling

Routledge & Kegan Paul
London

First published in 1973
by Routledge & Kegan Paul Ltd
Broadway House, 68–74 Carter Lane,
London EC4V 5EL
Printed in Great Britain by
C. Tinling & Co. Ltd, London and Prescot
© Routledge & Kegan Paul Ltd 1973

ISBN 0 7100 7539 1

To Anita

Contents

CONTENTS

viii

CONTENTS

Preface

Professional and general interest in the sociology of knowledge is steadily increasing; every year new books and journal articles join the list of publications addressed to questions and problems which are germane to this sociological speciality. Waxing fascination with the sub-field is also reflected by the growing number of universities and colleges that add courses in the sociology of knowledge to their graduate and undergraduate curricula.

A major reason for this accumulation of interest in the United States has been identified by Robert K. Merton: the methods, concepts, and theories of sociologists of knowledge are assuming increasing relevance for the analysis of modern American life and its problems. U.S. society, according to Merton's presentation in *Social Theory and Social Structure*, 'has come to have certain characteristics of those European societies in which the discipline was initially developed.'

Many European intellectuals have contributed theoretical and conceptual insights during the long pre-history of the sociology of knowledge: the opposition of the Athenian Sophists to absolute standards of behavior and knowledge is as significant as Francis Bacon's theory of idols and Claude Helvétius's argument that our ideas are 'of necessity the consequences of the societies we live in.' The contribution of Karl Marx crystallized in the famous passage in his *Contribution to the Critique of Political Economy:* 'It is not the consciousness of men that determines their existence, but, on the contrary, their social existence determines their consciousness.' Marx never tired of relating the ideas of men to their social bases; his larger role as revolutionary theorist, however, eclipsed this aspect of his work promising the development of a 'sociology of consciousness.'

During the pre-history of the sociology of knowledge contributions usually originated in minds sensitized to the detection of social conflict and distrustful attitudes; intellectual workers of this type often lived during troubled times as witnesses to tumultuous social changes.

The systematic conceptualization of relevant issues took place when the seams of European civilization began to break; leading systematizers of the discipline were typically outsiders—men marked by cultural, ethnic and, often, personal marginality. After the turn of the century conceptualization of major themes occurred in rapid succession. In 1909, the Bohemian philosopher-sociologist Wilhelm Jerusalem introduced the term 'sociology of cognition' (*Soziologie des Erkennens*); in 1912 Émile Durkheim interpreted a 'sociological theory of knowledge' in the introduction to his *Elementary Forms of the Religious Life*; in 1924 Max Scheler used the concept of 'sociology of knowledge' (*Soziologie des Wissens*) in a book title; in 1925 Karl Mannheim worked with Scheler's concept which he was soon to contract into the more familiar *Wissenssoziologie*.

The movement of the sociology of knowledge from the periphery to the center of attention significantly correlates with a larger process of socio-cultural change that promises the elevation of knowledge and intellectual-psychic awareness to a position of central significance. Novel concepts have come into use which illuminate the transformations of the American experience: information explosion, campus revolt, search for new life styles, generation gap, black power, credibility gap, disaffiliation from the moneytheism of the plastic society, expansion of consciousness, liberation. . . .

The sociology of knowledge has special relevance for the emergent climate of opinion since the protagonists of this intellectual scenario remained steadfast in their opposition to the separation of theory and practice and the fragmentation of the intellect by fetishistic veneration of specialization. This intellectual attitude possesses importance both for social scientists and the intellectual community at large.

For the social scientist's universe of discourse the sociology of knowledge provides insights into the connections between social theory and social structure. The optic of the sociology of knowledge reveals social theories as reflections or emanations of a substratum of social forces and reality factors which possess—in comparison to thought products—a greater degree of ontic reality in the sense of constituting *ens realissimum*. The sociologist of knowledge offers and augments material evidence for the assumption that specific reality factors and their interplay affect the production, distribution, and consumption of social theories which appear as concretizations of the striving generated by reality factors or as reaction formations against a particular movement of social forces. Reality factors may be identified variously as confluences of forces in the direction of military dominance, political hegemony, economic power, and the psycho-physical affirmation of repressive senescence or youthful vitality.

The sociology of knowledge is significant for the intellectual community at large because of its heuristic and methodological potentials. The heuristic significance of the discipline stems mainly from extant efforts to discern and describe differences in mental production among diverse groups and at different historical times. Not unlike the art historian who differentiates varying styles of art the sociologist of knowledge distinguishes different styles of thought. As I suggested in *Road to Suspicion* the sub-field possesses additional methodological potential: 'The sociology of knowledge does not only aim at the discovery, analysis, and description of different thought-styles. The discipline is more than that; it is also a theory of the relation of ideas and reality asserting the primacy of reality and the determination of ideas by reality.'

The arrangement of the following essays is not haphazard—nor is it coincidental or faddish. On the contrary, each selection adds to the growth of an understanding of the theoretical, conceptual, and substantive development of the sociology of knowledge. Like other scientific and intellectual endeavours this special area of sociological inquiry is endowed with an overarching theoretical intent, a pre-history, methodological and conceptual presuppositions, classical varieties of systematization, and evolving attempts at interpretation and application.

This volume intends to foster systematic insights into the development, problems, and promises of the sociology of knowledge; such insights seem desirable and necessary in view of the growing interest in the discipline.

Acknowledgments and sources

The author and publishers would like to thank those listed below for their kind permission to reprint material in this volume:

From *Road to Suspicion* by Gunter W. Remmling, New York: Appleton-Century-Crofts, 1967, pp. 118–19, 120–1, 124–6, 129–30, 130–1, 136–41. Copyright © 1967. Reprinted by permission of Appleton-Century-Crofts, Educational Division, Meredith Corporation.
From *Sociological Quarterly*, vol. 1, no. 4 (October 1960), pp. 217–25. This article was slightly revised for publication in this volume. Reprinted with the permission of the *Sociological Quarterly*, the Midwest Sociological Society, and the author.
From *Kyklos*, vol. 13, no. 1 (1960), pp. 90–100. Reprinted by permission of *Kyklos* and the author.
From *Ethics*, vol. 51, no. 4 (July 1941), pp. 392–418. Reprinted by permission of the University of Chicago Press and the author.
From *Essays on the Sociology of Knowledge* by Karl Mannheim, London: Routledge & Kegan Paul, 1952; Oxford University Press, Inc., 1952, pp. 84–97. Reprinted by permission.
This is a revised version of a paper entitled, 'Some Social and Political Functions of Ideology', read at the 61st Annual Meeting of the American Sociological Association, 31 August 1966, Miami Beach, Florida. Originally published in *Sociological Quarterly*, vol. 10, no. 1 (Winter 1969), pp. 72–83. Reprinted by permission of the *Sociological Quarterly*, the Midwest Sociological Society, and the author.
From: 'Author's Preface' to Karl Marx, *A Contribution to the Critique of Political Economy* (trans. from the 2nd German ed. by N. I. Stone), Chicago: Charles H. Kerr and Company, 1904, pp. 10–15.
From *Road to Suspicion* by Gunter W. Remmling, New York: Appleton-Century-Crofts, 1967, pp. 23–31, 145–51, 160–2. Copy-

right © 1967. Reprinted by permission of Appleton-Century-Crofts, Educational Division, Meredith Corporation.

From *Road to Suspicion* by Gunter W. Remmling, New York: Appleton-Century-Crofts, 1967, pp. 11–21. Copyright © 1967. Reprinted by permission of Appleton-Century-Crofts, Educational Division, Meredith Corporation.

From *Philosophical Review*, vol. 29, no. 4 (July 1920), 319–39. Reprinted by permission of the *Philosophical Review*.

From *Essays on the Sociology of Knowledge* by Karl Mannheim, London: Routledge & Kegan Paul, 1952; Oxford University Press, Inc., 1952, pp. 154–69. Reprinted by permission.

From *Philosophy and Phenomenological Research*, vol. 2, no. 3 (March 1942), 310–22. Reprinted by permission of *Philosophy and Phenomenological Research* and the author.

From *Chaos or Planning: The Sociology of Karl Mannheim* by Gunter W. Remmling, London: Routledge & Kegan Paul (forthcoming). Reprinted by permission of Routledge & Kegan Paul.

From *Journal of Philosophy*, vol. 40, no. 3 (4 February 1943), pp. 57–72. Reprinted by permission of the *Journal of Philosophy* and the author.

Read at the 'Sociology of Knowledge' session of the Fifth World Congress of Sociology, Washington, D.C., 7 September 1962. Originally published in *Philosophy and Phenomenological Research*, vol. 25, no. 4 (June 1965), 560–71. Reprinted by permission of *Philosophy and Phenomenological Research* and the author.

From *Sociological Quarterly*, vol. 11, no. 1 (Winter 1970), 3–13. Reprinted with the permission of the *Sociological Quarterly*, the Midwest Sociological Society, and the author.

From *European Journal of Sociology*, vol. 7, no. 1 (1966), 105–15. Reprinted by permission of the *European Journal of Sociology* and the author.

From *American Sociological Review*, vol. 30, no. 5 (October 1965), 674–88. Reprinted by permission of the American Sociological Association and the author.

From *British Journal of Sociology*, vol. 19, no. 3 (September 1968), 334–42. Reprinted by permission of the author.

From *American Sociological Review*, vol. 19, no. 1 (February 1954), 42–8. Reprinted by permission of the American Sociological Association and the author.

From *British Journal of Sociology*, vol. 17, no. 3 (September 1966), 292–9. Reprinted by permission of the author.

From *Maxwell Review*, vol. 6, no. 2 (Spring 1970), 51–71. This article was revised for publication in this volume. Reprinted by permission of *Maxwell Review*, the Maxwell Graduate Student Association, and the author.

From *British Journal of Sociology*, vol. 14, no. 1 (March 1963), 59–76. Reprinted by permission of the author.
First presented to the Centennial Colloquium, 'Beyond Left and Right? The Sociology of the Future', held at Syracuse University, New York, during March 1970. The version here has been revised and enlarged.
The acknowledgements listed above refer to chapters 2 to 25.

part one

Introduction

1 Existence and thought

Gunter W. Remmling

Throughout history intellectuals have done more to obscure the relationship between human existence and thought than to reveal it. Although it may seem rather obvious to interpret mental activity as a reflection of the actor's bio-psychic and social life there has been a pronounced preference in intellectual history to claim or to assume different connections between the theoretical and the nontheoretical. In succession the most celebrated intellectuals correlated their theories with a 'higher' reality; this assumed reality appeared in various masks including such conceptual guises as guardian deities, immutable essences, the heavenly kingdom, monarchic wisdom, natural law, national destiny, supreme reason, popular will, folkish spirit, the law of history, social solidarity, the common good, truth and beauty, scientific progress, and corporate beneficence.

The leading intellectual spokesmen of any generation owed their success mainly to acquired skill in the elegant manipulation of a hidden, but vital procedure of combination: they convincingly thought their way into an interpretative paradigm which 'organically' fused the inevitable logic of their theories with the inexorable necessity of preserving the established social, political, and economic order.

By accepting dominant political and socio-economic arrangements intellectuals have deflected the analytical thrust of their cerebral power from the bedrock of existential reality; by correlating their activities and their productions with transtemporal spirit and values, ideas and ideals intellectuals have sanctified their failure as diagnosticians of socio-historical life situations. The defensive preoccupation of mainstream intellectuals with emanations from a fabricated 'higher' reality gave birth to a (conveniently) bewildering plethora of concepts which includes incantations such as structure, equilibrium, order, consensus, tradition, authority, beauty, gentility, rationality, objectivity, reliability, and validity. These concepts—rendered ridiculous by actual political, social, and economic behavior—have been dressed up in the musty robes of theology, the threadbare raiment of philosophy, and the mod costumes of mathematics. Some newer conceptual creations such as 'welfare capitalism' obscenely elevate a contradiction in terms to the rank of central explanatory principle; the plethora of traditional concepts constitutes a force field wherein intellectual activity cannot help but fetishize each socio-historical phenomenon. In this mental operation a living phenomenon is severed from its concrete historical and social context; subsequently the ghostly remains of the phenomenon are processed through the particularizing filter of abstract conceptualization and given the appearance of an entity allegedly capable of independent existence.

Analyses of the relationship between existence and thought which strike at the root of intellectual and social orthodoxy are, then, comparatively rare; their appearance usually indicates the presence of marginal men whose opposition to the existing order is partially manifested by their attempts to lay bare the sinews of power and privilege. The efforts of outsiders to denude insiders are commonly inspired by a simultaneous attempt to establish a new order of things which is capable of catering for the rebels' interests.

The disinterested student of the relationship between existence and thought is a rare bird, indeed, and the extent of his detachment will always remain debatable. Aside from the problematic aspects of motivation there are, however, the recognizable dimensions of systematic coherence and conceptual sophistication which permit us to view the sociology of knowledge as a meaningful research strategy in the struggle for insight into the relationship between existence and thought.

Apart from highly specialized or esoteric procedures two essential ways of introducing the sociology of knowledge may be distinguished: the *diffuse* and the *focused* approach.

The diffuse approach treats the field broadly and includes a large number of investigations in areas of inquiry sharing the overall sociology of knowledge orientation toward relating the mental sphere with the social realm. The diffuse approach, therefore, fuses the sociology of knowledge proper with related sub-fields such as historical sociology, socio-linguistics, sociology of art, sociology of culture, sociology of law, sociology of literature, sociology of occupations and professions, sociology of popular culture, sociology of public opinion and mass communication, sociology of religion, sociology of science, and the sociology of sociology. The diffuse approach has the merit of illuminating the wide applicability of the sociology of knowledge perspective and permits the inclusion of empirical research in the sociology of knowledge paradigm carried out by researchers who are informed by child psychology, cultural anthropology, demography, dissonance theory, ethno-methodology, human genetics, phenomenology, reference group theory, role theory, social exchange theory, symbolic interactionism, etc.

The focused approach treats the field more specifically with major emphasis on its origin, present state and further development; this approach reveals the confluence of intellectual and social forces which created, to begin with, the climate of opinion permitting the construction of the sociology of knowledge framework. The focused approach, then, has the merit of clearly delineating the origin of the field and permits the systematic demonstration of its methodological, conceptual, and substantive development.

Since the diffuse approach presupposes the focused approach—inasmuch as an intellectual tool cannot be applied without prior knowledge of its exact properties—this volume utilizes the focused approach to introduce the sociology of knowledge which may be provisionally defined as an area of sociological inquiry devoted to investigations of the reciprocal relations connecting cognitive processes and mental products with social processes and social structure.

Strictly speaking the sociology of knowledge originated during the years 1924–5, when first Max Scheler and then Karl Mannheim used the term to define and delimit the nature, purpose, and scope of the sub-discipline.[1] On the other hand, Mannheim realized that 'the sociology of knowledge actually emerged with Marx, whose profoundly suggestive *aperçus* went to the heart of the matter'.[2] Émile Durkheim's sociological theory of knowledge is of similar importance; therefore, the development of the sociology of knowledge proper will be traced from its actual points of departure in the Marxian and Durkheimian contributions.

As far as Scheler and Mannheim are concerned it should be noted that their efforts at conceptual clarification and methodological systematization led them to narrow the search for the tendons connecting existence and thought to the investigation of relations between social existence and knowledge.

With their self-imposed restrictions Scheler and Mannheim continued the scientific tradition of recognizing the utility of a division of labor. The dependence of mental activity on man's bio-psychic nature, on original impulses and drives, had been studied by Friedrich Nietzsche and Vilfredo Pareto; Sigmund Freud and other psychoanalytic researchers were rapidly pre-empting this area of inquiry.[3] French anthropologists, Émile Durkheim, Maurice Halbwachs, and other members of the Durkheim school were leading in the investigation of the influence which social existence exerts upon thought as a cognitive process with psychological and episte-mological variables.[4]

Scheler's and Mannheim's delimitation of the sociology of know-ledge also continues the philosophical tradition of German idealism. The emphasis on social existence at the expense of bio-psychic reality has distant, but significant roots in Immanuel Kant's opposi-tion to all attempts to psychologize epistemology.[5] The preoccupation with the products of thought, that is with knowledge, reflects the influence of Georg Wilhelm Friedrich Hegel who had achieved his most penetrating analyses in his confrontation with 'objective spirit' which Scheler interpreted as meaningful content embodied in matter or social activities.[6] Significant in this context are Wilhelm Dilthey's methodological considerations which establish the objec-tive manifestations of life as the subject matter for all human and social sciences; Mannheim in particular was keenly aware of Dilthey's interpretation of objective spirit as the sum of the objective manifestations of social existence and his companion claim that mental activities are best understood through the interpretation of their outward expressions in historical records, in social institutions, in artistic products, or in published works.[7]

In establishing the sociology of knowledge Scheler and, especially, Mannheim worked in proximity to Marxian methodology which is in many respects a sociological research strategy almost entirely devoid of psychological elements. The emphasis on social existence rather than bio-psychic existence reflects the narrower Marxian decision to single out the economic structure of society as the real basis on which develop legal, political, religious, artistic, and theoretical superstructures with their corresponding forms of social consciousness.[8] Marx and Engels viewed changes in the manner of intellectual production as reflections of alterations in the mode of material production: 'Does it require deep intuition to comprehend that man's ideas, views, and conceptions, in one word, man's con-sciousness, changes with every change in the conditions of his material existence, in his social relations and in his social life?'[9]

In view of their intellectual situation the founders of the sociology of knowledge did not act arbitrarily when they established the specific focus on the relationship between social existence and knowledge; nor were they whimsical in their emphasis on theoretical, systematic knowledge 'objectified' in world views, idea systems, and political theories. In the powerful force field of idealist philosophy, Hegelianism, and Marxism there was little room for the pre-theo-retical commonsense knowledge of everyday life and even less for 'knowledge' as mere private opinion; moreover as a result of the political and social revolutions of the nineteenth century and early twentieth century European societies were divided into huge, warring groups whose members acted collectively in response to 'objectified' world views, idea systems, and politico-social theories. In this real life situation there was nothing more practical, nothing more in the nature of daily routine than the theory and practice of 'ideas'.

Bearing in mind the social situation which propelled the sociology of knowledge into a position of centrality there is nothing odd about the fact that the preoccupation with the relationship between social existence and knowledge—traditionally the concern of marginal men—assumed the coherence and systematic force characteristic of the work of Scheler and Mannheim. The sociology of knowledge matured in the cultural climate of the Weimar Republic which permitted marginal artists and intellectuals to play a new role, that of the 'outsider as insider'. In the words of the historian Peter Gay, Weimar culture itself 'was the creation of outsiders, propelled by history into the inside, for a short, dizzying, fragile moment'.[10]

As social theory the German variant of sociology of knowledge reflects a social structure of peculiar fluidity: between 1919 and 1933, the German Reich, commonly referred to as the Weimar Republic, was a virtual laboratory of socio-cultural experimentation. In the streets of German towns and cities political armies competed for followers—a process punctuated by assassinations and advertised by street battles embroiling monarchists, imperial militarists, nihilistic war veterans, communists, socialists, anarchists, and national socialists. Parliamentary activity involved about twenty-five political parties whose shifting alliances produced twenty governmental cabinets with an average life-span of less than nine months. The political circus performed in an economic crazy house: the hungry postwar years skidded into an inflationary period during which the German mark—valued before the war at 4·2 per dollar—plummeted to the value of 42 hundred million to the dollar. At this point, in November 1923, individuals paid a billion marks to send a letter abroad and the German Republic verged on complete financial bankruptcy and political disintegration.

An era of political and economic reconstruction began in 1924; by 1929 Germany had become the leading industrial power on the European continent. The Great Depression, announced by the crash of the New York stock exchange in October 1929, brought the Weimar Republic to the brink of disaster: by the end of 1932, nearly half of the German labor force was unemployed. Many jobless men provoked arrest seeking shelter and food in prison—others swelled the ranks of the Red Front and, ominously, those of Hitler's Storm Troops; in his propaganda the budding dictator exploited the additional economic problem of reparations payments to the Western Allies which the Young Committee had finally set in such a way that the actual payments, including interest, were to total approximately 29 billion dollars from 1928 to 1988.[11]

The Weimar Republic was also a whirling carousel of personal experimentation with differing life-styles. Guitar-playing, poetry-reading, free-loving youngsters roamed the country giving expression to the anti-bourgeois sentiments of the youth movement; nudist colonies flourished; in Berlin nightclubs phallic symbols became part of interior decoration, naked girls swang from the ceiling, and the staged performance of the sexual act was incorporated in the routine of show business; prostitutes and transvestites took their place in the street scene along with proselytizers for exotic cults.[12]

In Weimar Germany intellectual and artistic innovations transformed science, philosophy, literature, music, painting, the theater, movies, and architecture into images expressing the dawn of a new consciousness. After the collapse of the Republic political refugees carried the productive spirit of Weimar culture into the four corners of the world merging it with the creative mainstream which brought forth the awareness of men in the twentieth century. The creative process of Weimar culture is rich in conspicuous examples such as expressionist painting, atonal music, Brechtian theater, Einsteinian physics, and revolutionized visual experiences commonly associated with the Bauhaus.[13] While cosmopolitan audiences cheered successive opening nights, exhibitions, and first editions, conservatives and, increasingly, Nazis reassured the provincial masses with warmed-over portions of traditional beer-and-sauerkraut culture.

Sociology of knowledge—precariously posted on the social science frontier of the Weimar experience—did not fail to attract its share of intellectuals who balanced their nervous brilliance on the instantaneity of the razor-edge present. The startling iridescence of their work reflects dissatisfaction with the solidified and a peculiar attraction to cerebral self-torment. The discipline has a stalwart anti-hero who hanged himself with the detachment of scientific experimentation: Alfred Seidel—author of *Consciousness as Fate*—chose this exit to consummate his compelling desire to nihilize nihilism which had been instilled by the enchanting perils of psychoanalysis and Max Weber's vast disenchantment of the world.[14] In the Marxist storm center of *Wissenssoziologie* we encounter the gift for penetrating social analysis which surrounds leading intellects such as Lukács with the sulphurous halo of the Lubyanka.

The characteristic alterations of the German experience during empire and republic are mirrored in the life and thought of Max Scheler who is the incarnation of the Mannheimian notion of the 'gliding of standpoints', who is, as it were, the embodiment of the intellectual and political experimentation in Weimar Germany. The ill-starred republic, this society suspended between the hell fires of global war and total dictatorship, found another anti-hero in Scheler: son of a Jewish mother and Protestant father, ardent Catholic, slanderer of religion, Germanic militarist, European pacifist, democrat; Scheler who tore through three marriages, who had love encounters in hotel rooms and flashes of insight in the no-man's-land of nightclubs; Scheler the chain-smoking exile from the middle-class respectability of academe; Scheler whose firstborn son went from small-time delinquency to Hitler's Brownshirts and from there to early death in streetfighting.[15]

Marginality in the sense of being marginal to the socio-cultural traditions of two or more groups or by virtue of personal estrangement from dominant ideas and values represents a quality common to most intellectuals who view the equation associating thought and existence as problematic. A comprehensive analysis of the complex prehistory of the sociology of knowledge has so far not been written, but extant preliminary studies suggest that the concepts of marginality and alienation are of central significance in understanding the existential factors which motivated forerunners, pioneers and practitioners of sociology of knowledge.[16]

Within the confines of Western thought the fifth century B.C. is a significant point of departure for a prehistory of the sociology of knowledge: surviving literary fragments, testimonia, Platonic dialogues such as *Gorgias, Hippias Minor, Protagoras, Sophist*, and Aristotle's *Rhetoric* reveal the pragmatic Sophists in ancient Athens as opposing absolute standards of behavior and courageously advocating ethical and epistemological relativism. The Sophists were wandering teachers—truly marginal intellectuals—who flocked to Athens from foreign cities to instruct young men in rhetoric and other subjects deemed useful for the pursuit of political, professional, and financial success.

The most famous of the Greek Sophists, Protagoras of Abdera (*c*. 490–410 B.C.), opened his work on *Truth* with the statement that 'man is the measure of all things' and proceeded to develop an epistemological relativism according to which an individual knows only what *he* perceives but not the *object* perceived; in the view of Protagoras all things are in flux and flow, all sensation is subjective, and there is no objective truth. In *Concerning the Gods* he assumed an agnostic stance, arguing that it is impossible to determine whether the gods exist or what they are like. Protagoras was forced to flee after a conviction of impiety terminated his successful career in Periclean Athens.

Another itinerant 'professor of wisdom' (*sophia*), Gorgias of Leontini (*c*. 483–376 B.C.), propagated a nihilistic style of thought: in a work entitled *On Nature, or on the Nonent*, he claimed (1) that nothing exists, (2) that, if anything exists, it cannot be known by man, (3) that, if anything exists and can be known, it cannot be communicated to others.

Hippias of Elis (*c.* fifth century B.C.), one of the company of Sophists introduced in Plato's *Protagoras* and depicted in his *Hippias Minor*, added to the early awareness of an existential determination of thought by defining religion as a man-made instrument used by the wealthy and powerful for the practical purpose of enforcing morality and docility through fear; Hippias reached across centuries with a claim repeated by protagonists of twentieth-century youth culture: 'Laws are the conventions of an older generation.'

The Sophists' penetrating insights into the socio-economic and political roots of traditional ethico-religious precepts and their keen understanding of the relative, man-made, ceaselessly changing nature of ideas, laws, and social norms were buried for centuries beneath the opposing doctrines of establishment intellectuals following the lead of Plato and Aristotle.[17] The significance of sophistry was not recognized until the nineteenth century; glimmerings of recognition appear in lectures of the German philosopher Hegel who recognized Gorgias' significant contributions to the development of dialectics. More generally Hegel admitted: 'The Sophists ... made dialectic, universal Philosophy, their object, and they were profound thinkers.'[18] The English historian and political radical George Grote (1794–1871) fully revealed the importance of the Greek Sophists whom he revalued as champions of intellectual progress.[19]

The philosophical tradition established by Plato and Aristotle was further developed and modified by dominant schools of thought such as Stoicism, patristicism, and scholasticism which continued the ancient emphasis on 'higher truths', and absolute standards and values. Beneath the grandiose thought structures erected by the 'official' theoretical imagination there were occasional echoes of small hammers wielded by subterranean intellectuals attempting to separate fact from fancy. In their search for earth-bound realities 'subversive' thinkers found the concealed links connecting ideas and theories with economic interest and political power as may be seen in the works of Marsilius of Padua (*c.* 1275–1342), Ibn Khaldun (1332–1406), and Niccolò Machiavelli (1469–1527). A systematic attack upon the Aristotelian-Christian intellectual establishment, however, was not undertaken until the seventeenth century when Francis Bacon turned the critical probe of philosophy and social theory inward and upon itself to reveal the biases distorting knowledge and clouding its objectivity. In the first book of his *Novum Organum* (1620) the English philosopher defined these distorting factors of social origin as the 'idols of the mind'.[20]

In the course of his work on the method of inductive research Bacon came to demand that the observer must approach the physical world free from all reality-distorting prejudices; at the same time he discovered that man's scientific endeavors are hindered by illusions and fallacies, both native and acquired. Bacon identified these cognitive obstacles as the 'idols of the mind' and proceeded to divide them into four species to bring them to light, to neutralize their negative influence on knowledge and the instauration of the sciences.

Bacon's efforts had the dual purpose of revealing the structure of knowledge and its connection with external reality; this antimetaphysical program was further developed by John Locke who analysed the nature and validity of knowledge in his *Essay Concerning Human Understanding* (1690). While Locke's work on epistemology grounded knowledge in experience, David Hume's essay, *The Natural History of Religion* (1757), extended the empirical approach to the analysis of religious life; at the same time Hume continued Bacon's social explanation of intellectual errors with his critical conceptualization of the four causes of idolatry as deification of the unknown (ignorance), power, fear, and the search for happiness.

The journeys of Voltaire and Montesquieu to England hastened the diffusion of British thought styles; empiricist and antimetaphysical interpretations of reality penetrated France and the Continent. Voltaire, who had been exiled to England from 1726–9, reported his English experience in the *Lettres philosophiques* (1734) and was promptly forced to leave Paris. Prison, exile, and banishment did not deter Voltaire from his relentless attack on the religious and social establishment of France. As a political intellectual he continued to employ the scientific theories of Newton and the philosophical ideas of other Englishmen such as Bolingbroke, Hume, Locke, Pope, Swift, Walpole, and Woolston.

Montesquieu spent two years in England and, soon after his return to France in 1731, he began to express his admiration for the island's political system and its social institutions. Montesquieu remained enamored of the social and political structure of England and critical of French conditions in *L'Esprit des lois* (1748). In his major work, he analyses the cultural variation of customs and laws and derives the principle of relativity; he proceeds to demonstrate how varying laws and governments are determined by different climatic, economic, geographical, moral, and racial conditions.

His systematic efforts to explain of the origin of ideas and social institutions in socio-cultural terms make the Baron de Montesquieu one of the foremost pioneers of the sociology of knowledge; but the philosophers of the French Enlightenment in general contributed significantly to the emerging search for the tendons connecting thought and existence. On the radical fringe of the Enlightenment in particular there appeared significant insights such as Helvétius' realization that our ideas are 'the consequences of the societies we live in'.

The Abbé de Condillac, head of the sensationalist school, augmented Locke's epistemological position in his *Essai sur l'origine des connaissances humaines* (1746); he claimed that all thought is derived from sensations and conceived of the senses and the apparatus of sensual receptivity as themselves being dependent upon experience.

Condillac, the friend of Diderot and Rousseau, represents the link connecting the French Enlightenment with the *idéologues*. Led by Destutt de Tracy, the *idéologues* developed the *science des idées* to discover the origin and formative principle of ideas. Their efforts to prevent the formation of false ideas attracted the wrath of Napoleon Bonaparte who, as a politician, thrived on the false consciousness of the masses.

The great heir of British empiricism and the French Enlightenment is Karl Marx who keenly absorbs the philosphical tradition based upon 'the healthy human senses'; in Marx's social theory the war against idols, idolatry, and the metaphysical-religious tradition continues within the framework of a revolutionary program which includes among its theoretical supports a systematized awareness of the existential determination of thought.[21]

Marx's understanding of the social determination of consciousness was deepened by his expertise in political economy derived from his extended studies of the British classical economists and socialist theorists including Claude Henri de Saint-Simon, the Saint-Simonians, Pierre Proudhon, and Johann Karl Rodbertus-Jagetzow.[22] Marx's knowledge of German critical and idealist philosophy, in particular his mastery of Hegelian dialectics, permitted him to transcend the naive, unilinear progressivism and often ahistorical temporo-centrism of the Enlightenment philosophers and to achieve the methodological subtlety and historical depth characteristic of his own brand of materialism.

Marx and all other students of the relation between thought and existence are indebted to Kant's critical philosophy which demonstrated that 'reality' was determined in its appearance by the structure of cognition: Kantian epistemology grounded the reality of experience in human subjectivity by equating reality with the lawful order of human consciousness. All attempts to establish the dependence of cognition and knowledge on social reality are epistemologically rooted in the Kantian assumption that the object of cognition is constituted by a creative act of the perceiving individual, who is—as Hegel would show—a denizen of the social world.[23] In the language of critical philosophy the unity which man sees in the universe is a quality given it by the instrumentalities of the mind, first by the forms of the sensibility—space and time—and second by the categories of the understanding, such as quantity, quality, relation and modality. These *a priori* instrumentalities enable human consciousness to give form to the world surrounding it, to make the world intelligible to itself and to establish the connections, necessities, unities, and laws which are the prerequisites for science.

German critical philosophy had argued convincingly that the universe owed all of its arrangements and connections—its very distribution in space and time—to the cognitive constitution of knowing man. Hegel's objective idealism argued as convincingly that this knowing man was an eminently social creature, a lesson which was not lost on Marx. Kant's thinking was oriented toward the mathematical physics of Kepler, Galileo, and Newton; the social philosophy of Hegel, from the start, concentrated on life and history and the alleviation of the contradictions and conflicts inherent in life and history.

In Hegel's *Early Theological Writings*, composed between 1795 and 1800, life is seen as unification of impressions and as contradiction. Life appears as a social concept—the result of intellectual labors reflecting disharmonious and contradictory socio-historical circumstances. His social awareness enables Hegel to forge the tool capable of conceptualizing the absurdities and contradictions of social reality: a dialectical logic which empowers vision to grasp the meaning of social processes taking place in a world unhinged by the historical conflicts engaging men and institutions.[24]

Equipped with the 'eye of the concept' it is above all the philosophy of history which promises discovery of the law of historical and social change; in Hegel's vision the philosophy of history figures prominently because it will reveal the universe in the perspective of reason and identify the meaningful content of the historical process as continuous progress in the consciousness of freedom. *The Phenomenology of Mind* (1807) represents an important milestone in Hegel's advance to *The Philosophy of History*, published posthumously in 1837, on the basis of lecture notes. Hegel analyses the phenomenological evolution of thought to demonstrate the close connection between knowledge and existence by equating intellectual development with the historical evolution of nature and society. In 1821 Hegel arrives at a conclusion which foreshadows the sociology of knowledge: 'Whatever happens, every individual is a child of his time; so philosophy too is its own time apprehended in thoughts. It is just as absurd to fancy that a philosophy can transcend its contemporary world as it is to fancy that an individual can overleap his own age.'[25]

With Hegel a significant intellectual tradition had grown old; there are well-known Hegelian formulations indicating the thinker's awareness of this process: 'When philosophy paints its grey in grey, then has a shape of life grown old ... The owl of Minerva spreads its wings only with the falling of the dusk.'[26] Hegel surmised a decline of European civilization in general, but, as Marx was soon to demonstrate, senility afflicted only the intellectual and social activities of certain segments of the population within this civilization.[27]

The intellectual and social force that had dried up in the fires of the abortive French Revolution may be termed the *bourgeois-revolutionary program*. This tradition emerged as a motor of social change in the debris of the crumbling feudal-theological order which had dominated medieval civilization. The bourgeois-revolutionary program was allied with analytical-scientific thought styles against myth and religious tradition and utilized progressive economic and political schemes of liberalization to combat the static and repressive policies of entrenched aristocracies; as an intellectual movement it had important roots in Bacon's instauration of the sciences, British empiricism, and the French Enlightenment. The bourgeois-revolutionary program appeared as an afterglow in the deliberations of Saint-Simon and the young Hegel.

The politically and economically victorious bourgeoisie failed to end the exploitation of man by man; it retreated into a mechanical, meaningless cycle of materialistic acquisition and military conquest benefiting steadily decreasing numbers of people. As the entrenched bourgeoisie began to use repressive tactics, Marx and his company of socialists decided to replace the defunct bourgeois-revolutionary program with a new motor of social change which may be termed the *proletarian-revolutionary program*; this program's main goal was to abolish the exploitation of man by man and restore human life in all its fullness and meaning.

The policies of Prince Metternich and his camarilla of restoration agents led to a political and economic rapprochement between dominant bourgeois elements and surviving elements of the aristocracy. This alliance, which grew closer with the successful unfolding of the proletarian-revolutionary program, was partially responsible for the emergence of a third paradigm of intellectual and social alteration which may be termed the *aristocratic-counterrevolutionary program*. The intellectual spokesmen for this program 'rediscovered' the virtues of medieval civilization; they postulated rules of conduct which were based, sometimes implicitly, on the shadowy deportment of disembodied aristocratic personalities moving through the social landscape of an essentially imaginary past.

The aristocratic-counterrevolutionary program relied on art, poetry, metaphysics, and religion to combat the base materialism spawned by the scientific-technological-industrial order. Its organicist, synthetic, holistic, intuitive thought styles surrounded diffuse political intentions to the restoration of simpler, pre-industrial social traditions. The program has important intellectual roots in the thinking of Edmund Burke, de Bonald, and Johann Gottfried Herder; it connects with currents such as *Sturm und Drang* and Romanticism. The aristocratic-counterrevolutionary program has been purposely or indeliberately supported by intellectuals such as Nietzsche, Scheler, and Heidegger whose glorification of elitist principles reflects ultimate admiration of the aristocracy as true-born leaders of society.

The three conflicting programs for alterations in social structure affected the formation of theories of society and consequently left their imprint on such specialized areas of inquiry as the sociology of knowledge.

Forerunners and pioneers

Part two of this volume opens with a selection which reveals how the bourgeois-revolutionary program for social change was connected with the intellectual development linking Francis Bacon, British empiricism, and the French Enlightenment philosophers. In the course of this intellectual development, triggered off as it was by the socio-economic and political transformations of Western civilization, there emerged theories and concepts of basic significance for the nascent sociology of knowledge perspective. This ideational process began with Bacon's typology of the idols and false notions which distort scientific understanding; it led via British empiricism and materialism to the theory of prejudices by means of which the French philosophers subjected all sciences to the suspicion of ideological distortion. British materialism was applied to social life by the radical philosophers Helvétius and Holbach who unmasked self-interest as the foundation of moral ideals and norms.

The bourgeois-revolutionary program gave a final flicker in the pseudo-socialism of the renegade count, Claude Henri de Saint-Simon, who propagated the Utopia of a peaceful society organized for productive labor by industrial leaders and guided spiritually by scientists. This society was to realize the core elements of Christianity by striving toward the 'amelioration of the moral and physical existence of the poorest class'. The insolent profiteering and brutal irresponsibility of the bourgeoisie turned Saint-Simon's mildhearted Utopia into a farce and the red banner of revolution was soon to pass into the hands of the socialist proletariat.

Saint-Simon's followers realized that the industrial chiefs exploited the workers who were only nominally free since they either had to accept the conditions dictated by their employers or starve. Without popular support the radicalized program of the Saint-Simonians was doomed to failure; the sect was split by internal dissensions and

15

Enfantin's remaining commune at Ménilmontant was broken up by the police in 1832.[28]

The paper by Georg G. Iggers shows that the Saint-Simonians precede Marx in formulating a theory of the social determination of knowledge. The Saint-Simonians analysed various types of mental productions, including aesthetics, historiography, jurisprudence, literature, political economy, science, theology and concluded that knowledge and all ideas were inseparable from their social context. More basically the positive scientific method itself was considered as related to a specific historic society rather than as universally valid.

The sociology of knowledge is rooted in bourgeois-revolutionary and proletarian-revolutionary world views; it also has roots in the aristocratic-counterrevolutionary world view. The paper by Werner Stark draws attention to the relevant contributions of conservative writers who were close to or central to the aristocratic-counter-revolutionary program. Stark shows the importance of the conservative tradition for the nascent sociology of knowledge perspective with special attention to Herder, Goethe, de Bonald, and Donoso Cortés; he also points to the subtle connection between conservatives and Marxists who often concur with their adversaries both in deprecating bourgeois capitalism and in calling for restoration of an organic, complete, free type of man.

Methodological and conceptual presuppositions

The major methodological premiss of the sociology of knowledge is the proposition that thought products may be viewed extrinsically and that this reveals them as phenomena which are functionally related to various facets of social reality hypostatized as the ontological absolute. This methodological premiss recommends itself because it promises to be a useful and timely guide to research; but the method of extrinsic interpretation collides with the traditional and established method of immanent interpretation which is politely limited to analysing the given theoretical content of mental products.

Much of the furor released by the methodological thrust of the sociology of knowledge reveals, not the scientific superiority of its enemies, but their unwillingness to accept the extratheoretical consequences of the extrinsic approach to the mental sphere. In his research the sociologist of knowledge debunks time-honored traditions, norms, 'truths', and modes of thought as so many masks concealing the vested interests of social groups. This process subverts shared beliefs, disrupts collective habits, spawns skepticism and has the extratheoretical potential of undermining established power positions.

The paper by Arthur Child shows the intensity of the theoretical controversy which erupted when the sociology of knowledge first appeared as a serious threat to other forms of humanistic and social scientific interpretation. Child also locates the sociology of knowledge in the larger methodological universe which affords tenancy to other disciplines which analyse thought within the force field of a social matrix. An important, though rarely admitted, insight is the realization that all methodological considerations are rooted in metaphysical assumptions, that is, in decisions to accept particular conceptions of reality. Child concludes that there are 'ultimate philosophical oppositions beyond which no additional analysis can avail. At such a point, indeed, the thinker must make a decisive and unambiguous choice as to the postulates from which his constructive reasoning will flow, as to his final—and only in that sense metaphysical—assumptions.' In this respect the methodological and theoretical legitimacy of the sociology of knowledge rests ultimately upon assumptions that are not open to further reduction such as the 'postulate of the intrinsic sociality of mind.'[29]

The basic postulates of the sociology of knowledge include conceptions of reality which emphasize the dynamic, historically flowing, relative nature of the world and its division into strata of unequal ontological significance. The concept of historicism expresses the relativistic desire to interpret the world as a dynamic unity undergoing constant sociohistorical changes; ideology conceptualizes the assumption that the ideal and ideational spheres are ontologically less real than the social stratum of existence.

The selection by Karl Mannheim reveals the central methodological and conceptual importance of historicism for the establishing of the sociology of knowledge perspective. In Mannheim's analysis historicism emerges not only as a methodological and conceptual tool, but as a modern world view which illuminates a socio-cultural reality characterized by all-pervading change. Historicism is an interpretative principle derived from the conscious experience of the world as forever changing; consequently historicism recommends itself as the fundament on which contemporary men may construct their observations and interpretations of the dynamic socio-cultural reality surrounding them.

Historicism is rooted in the historical consciousness of conservative thinkers such as Möser, Herder, Goethe, and von Ranke, who wanted to appreciate each historical period for its inherent, individual value; in the conservative paradigm history appeared as a process of organic development imparting significance and meaning to the succession of manifold historic phenomena which were to be enjoyed as colorful flashes revealing the beauty and wisdom that permeates the universe. Hegel, as well, saw the world as a unity engaged in a process of continual historic transformation. But in

Hegel's philosophy a new concern came to the forefront: the desire to deal with political ideas and the complex processes of social life.

Wilhelm Dilthey demolished the belief in the objective reality of a meaningfully ordered historical world when he demonstrated that only the subjective activity of the historian imparted 'meaning' to the historical world. Dilthey functionally related the unity of the world to the subjective intentions and interests of men living in the present for the future; he thereby encouraged the assumption that all ideas and knowledge are existentially determined. With Dilthey men 'do not carry any meaning from the universe into life . . . meaning and significance only originate in man and his history'.[30] While Dilthey relativized the historicist principle of interpretation, Marx moved it into the radical orbit with the assumption that modern life reveals itself most meaningfully in *social* existence. On the basis of Dilthey's relativism and Marx's socio-economic radicalism Mannheim developed his extreme historicism to express a novel attitude to the world. The new orientation expressed by extreme historicism summarizes methodological and conceptual presuppositions for the sociological construction of an interpretative paradigm evolving around supratheoretical realities represented by historical time, economic interest, social class, generational position, religious behavior, and political striving.

The methodological significance of historicism is matched by the conception of ideology which has both philosophical and political roots. The philosophical sources of ideology may be found in the development of a philosophy of consciousness replacing the classical and medieval-Christian objective ontological unity of the universe with the subjective epistemological unity of the perceiving subject celebrated by Locke, Berkeley, Hume, and Kant. Bacon's theory of idols had warned that this subjective unity represented by the perceiving individual was distorted; Hegel and Dilthey robbed it of supertemporal stature by submerging man in the flowing streams of dialectical history and bio-psychic life.

The political sources of ideology reach back to the theory of prejudices by which the philosophers of the French Enlightenment explained and alleviated the errors and deceptions which distort men's relations to the objects constituting their cognitive universe. The philosophers' emphasis on priestly fraud gave a political edge to this conceptual development since the people were encouraged to rebel against fraudulent rulers subjugating them with the help of religious and metaphysical distortions of social reality. The political element was present at the birth of the word ideology itself; Destutt de Tracy had barely coined 'ideology' to identify his science of ideas when Napoleon Bonaparte hurled the concept back at the troublesome intellectuals to defame them as fools. With Marx ideology took on a dual meaning which served to politicize the concept further: (1) ideology became coextensive with distorted ideas used by the ruling class as weapons against the deceived and exploited masses; (2) ideology came to explain the manifestation of false consciousness or the politically self-defeating refusal to see reality as it is.

Marx's *special* concept of ideology attacked only the ideas of the bourgeois class enemy; Mannheim widened ideology to refer to the thinking of all social actors and thereby came to operate with a *general* concept of ideology. This became the cornerstone for his attempts to transform the simple theory of ideology into sociological analysis. In the optic of Mannheim's general concept 'the thought of every group is seen as arising out of its life conditions'.[31]

Contemporary analysts of ideology frequently utilize the general conception which employs 'ideology' as a descriptive term referring to norms and ideas which channel observable behavior to help maintain a given social structure.[32] The general approach also allows the modern student of ideological behavior to augment his research design with social-psychological strategies.

The article by Rolf Schulze represents the contemporary emphasis on characteristics of ideology which may be discovered 'among all groups of people regardless of their specific affiliation and type of belief system'.[33] Schulze's social-psychological approach to the functions of ideology attends to quantitative dimensions; he observes and measures the behavior of individuals in their social milieu but, significantly, does not neglect larger social and political problems as evidenced by his criticism of the 'end of ideology' theme.

Karl Marx and the social determination of consciousness

Marx never systematized his investigations of the social roots of knowledge within a single work; conversely, he never ceased to confront the problem in his lifelong work on modern social structure and the dynamics of development. Marx's approach has a double significance: on the one hand, he achieves a creative synthesis of preceding theoretical and conceptual positions; on the other hand, he initiates theoretical clarifications and research strategies which coalesce into the first coherent sociology of knowledge.

Marx's sociology of knowledge perspective is part of his historical materialism and asserts that ideas are determined by socio-economic reality. The selection from the work of Karl Marx is his account of the theoretical progression leading to the materialist conception of history. Here he, furthermore, announces his decision to view consciousness as a phenomenon determined by social existence—a decision which has basic significance for all his subsequent work on the relations between thought and existence.

The next selection dealing with 'Marxism and Marxist sociology of knowledge' has a dual purpose: first, it relates Marx's sociology of knowledge perspective to his larger theoretical paradigm and, second, it traces the work of Marx's followers. The distinction between positivist and historicist branches of Marxist sociology of knowledge permits discussion of the work of theorists as different in orientation as Bogdanov and Lukács.

Émile Durkheim and the sociological theory of knowledge

The positivistic sociology of Émile Durkheim cloaked the opposition of bourgeois intellectuals to Marx's theory of social revolution with scientific respectability. In 1885–6, during his year's leave of absence in Germany, Durkheim studied the writings of Marx; this experience reinforced his fear of the violent features and the proletarian class character of socialism. According to Marcel Mauss, Durkheim 'desired change only for the benefit of the whole of society and not of one of its parts'.[34] In view of the unequal distribution of economic and political power this wish was about as effective as a nun's prayer for the abolition of social injustice.

Notwithstanding his disdain for various substantive aspects of positive philosophy Durkheim shares common ground with Saint-Simon and Comte when it comes to the glorification of social solidarity and the neglect of extant class cleavages, the emphasis on humanist ideals and the uninterest in the redistribution of wealth, power, and privilege.

Durkheim's 'organic solidarity' results from the industrial-capitalist division of labor;[35] in his *Catéchisme des Industriels* (1823–4), Saint-Simon celebrated the process of industrialization with similar enthusiasm because it guaranteed material as well as intellectual and moral progress. In *Le Nouveau Christianisme* (1825), Saint-Simon made it quite clear that the realization of the ideal of social solidarity presupposed the authoritarian rule of upper-class experts such as bankers, industrialists, and technocrats. In the four volumes of Comte's *Système de Politique Positive* (1851–4), social solidarity again emerged as the product of a mysterious, pseudo-religious unification of the intellectual and moral forces of a society ruled by businessmen and bankers. In the conservative style of his positivist predecessors Durkheim dismisses the Marxist search for social reconstruction as irrelevant. Fearful of disturbing the 'organic' capitalist-industrial order he resorts to the lofty spiritualism of Saint-Simon and Comte. Durkheim, as well, neglects questions of economic and political power in the belief that the state of the economy is less important than the state of morality to be enforced by the established ruling groups. In Durkheim's bourgeois vision there can be no social order unless the masses are compelled to be content with their fate. Moreover, Durkheim is not interested to find out whether the masses have more or less, but he wants to make sure that 'they be convinced they have no right to more. And for this, it is absolutely essential that there be an authority whose superiority they acknowledge and which tells them what is right.'[36]

Durkheim's sociological theory of knowledge is indebted to Saint-Simon's and Comte's attempts to see the correspondence between ideas and social structure.

In L'Industrie (1816–18), Saint-Simon claimed that men's ideas always correspond to their modes of social organization; specifically he suggested that there were correspondences between theological knowledge and military despotism, between scientific knowledge and industrialism. Comte also saw the progression of states of mind in relation to changes in social structure; he implied overlapping correspondences between primitive social organization and the theological state of mind, feudalism and the metaphysical stage of intellectual development, industrial society and positivism.[37] Comte knew that the origin, development and application of knowledge were determined by social conditions: 'The theological stage when paramount is always contingent upon the supremacy of military regimes. The gods and the generals go hand in hand. The metaphysical stage is marked by religious and political upheaval whereas the positive stage is marked by the beginning of the supremacy of industry and technology.[38]

Durkheim's sociological theory of knowledge further develops the Comtean realization that there are interdependent relations between social structure and social consciousness; Durkheim's major contribution to the sociology of knowledge consists of descriptions which show the interaction between primitive social structure, religious behavior, and the origin of basic logical categories.

As documented by the first selection in part five, Durkheim and his followers adopted a descriptive, general approach to the sociology of knowledge; while Marx emphasized the specific study of relationships between socio-economic reality and thought, Durkheim and his students observed various social influences on the intellectual life of men.

The paper by Edward L. Schaub questions the epistemological relevance of Durkheim's work. It also reveals the persistence of Durkheim's conservative stress on the maintenance of social order and solidarity: in their origin and functioning thought-processes reflect above all the needs of society for stability and perpetuation.

GUNTER W. REMMLING

Max Scheler and phenomenological sociology of knowledge

Nineteenth-century liberalism and positivism impressed many fin-de-siècle youths as disgusting amalgams of political impotence, social callousness, ethical hypocrisy, and intellectual irrelevance. The strutting burghers of Wilhelmian Germany became the symbol of the 'bourgeois human type' that many youthful individuals hated and despised; these emotions swelled the ranks of the youth movement and escalated to cults the admiration for Friedrich Nietzsche, Stefan George, and their company of counter-cultural gurus.

Ironically, the romantic armies of the counter culture were rapidly transformed into the armed forces of World War I; on the battlefields the young quoted Schiller and Dostoevsky who had taught them to embrace war as the flame that would cleanse the world of materialism and petty greed. The steely dialectics of machine guns quickly submerged the armies of the counter culture in the grey mass that had been forced to perform the dirty work for Europe's imperialist bourgeoisie.

Unimpressed by Marxist futurology and the patient reforms of revisionist Social Democrats, some anti-bourgeois intellectuals conjured up Utopias of their own. In Max Scheler's case disgust with the present inspired dreams of a mythical past represented by the romantic picture of medieval, Christian-corporate society, which had allegedly generated meaningful metaphysical and harmonious 'community building powers' under the leadership of its creative aristocracy.[39]

Scheler's world views and ideological commitments changed repeatedly during the course of his restless life; in the end he even accepted and defended the political liberalism of Weimar Germany. But he never renounced his idealistic vision of man as a spiritual being capable of subordinating his instinctual animal nature. Scheler's desire to preserve the dignity and independence of the human spirit motivated his opposition both to Comte's positivist-bourgeois Utopia and Marx's revolutionist-proletarian program which appeared to him as equally debasing and mechanical. On the other hand, Scheler felt a strong affinity with the conflicting social processes of the empirical world. Torn between otherworldliness and this-worldliness Scheler produced a sociology of knowledge held together by his philosophical anthropology and phenomenology. He pictured mind and life, spirit and nature as independent phenomenal essences and ontic states. This sociology of knowledge recognizes the importance of men's biological, economic, and political strivings which successively determine the dominance or decline of certain ideas and types of knowledge at given historical moments. At the same time Scheler's model retains the phenomenal independence of ideas since material interests only determine their passage from potentiality to actuality, but not their meaning, form, or content.

In opposition to myopic materialists Scheler argues that mind, finding its expression in 'ideal factors', determines what works and thoughts can be created in a society. Turning against one-sided idealists he maintains that historically prevalent material forces, finding their expression in 'real factors', determine what works and thoughts actually get created. Challenging the conformity and mechanical formalism of bourgeois and proletarian mass societies alike, Scheler finally underscores the role of the elite as a 'positive factor of realization'. The passage of knowledge from potentiality to actuality does not only depend on the 'negatively selective power' of real factors, but also on the 'free volitional causality' of the elite. Its mentally creative and socially aggressive members help to open the 'sluice gates' for the stream of mind by preparing the masses for novel ideas.[40]

The selection from Karl Mannheim shows the underlying assumptions of Scheler's phenomenological position; in particular he criticizes Scheler's sharp distinction between 'factual' and 'essential' knowledge which ultimately justifies the dualism of the temporal and eternal. This bifurcation of the cognitive universe reflects the assumptions of the traditional Catholic world view and supports intellectual efforts to construct intuitional metaphysics. Mannheim recognizes Scheler's affinity with the social realities of the modern world, but maintains that the structure of an argument is subject to perilous tensions if a *conservative* mode of thought and experience is forced to accommodate so strong a feeling of affinity with the temporal world. For the rest Mannheim analyses, in the terms of the sociology of knowledge, the structural problems of Scheler's theory; he is not concerned with detecting inaccuracies and errors on Scheler's part, but 'in tracing the line of historical determination which made this type of thought fatefully what it is'.[41]

The paper by Howard Becker and Helmut Otto Dahlke introduces an aspect of Scheler's thinking that Mannheim does not sufficiently deal with. This is his desire to synthesize Eastern salvation-knowledge and its spirit of self-liberation with those Western types of knowledge which serve scientific-technological and pragmatic-activistic purposes. Scheler's division of mind and nature is again seen as problematic, but Becker and Dahlke agree with his assertion that the validity of ideas lies outside the competence of sociologists of knowledge.

Karl Mannheim and historicist sociology of knowledge

The methodological radicalism and epistemological relativism of Mannheim's theory result from his decision to accept the full consequences of historicist principles and ideological analysis. In 1924 he formulated his extreme historicism which viewed all ideas as historically determined and changeable; moreover, extreme historicism stressed the element of commitment, of action, as the essence of the historical process.[42]

Ideological analysis systematizes the popular distrust of public statements and theoretical interpretations which became widespread at the time of the Italian Renaissance. The French Enlightenment philosophers transformed the probing of the credibility of 'official' ideas into the 'particular' conception of ideology. This unmasked intellectual distortions on the psychological level by revealing the personal roots of conscious or unconscious falsifications of reality. The French philosophers did not question man's basic ability to think correctly. While they assumed that material interests obscured truth they did not discredit the total structure of their opponent's consciousness; consequently their analysis of ideology did not reach into the cognitive sphere, but remained limited or 'particularized' to the psychic sphere.

The total conception of ideology appeared when Marx interpreted ideas as mere reflections of the thinker's position in the process of production; Marx ascribed a determining influence to social class position and accused the entire mind of being ideological. At the same time, however, the Marxist conception of ideology was 'special' since only the bourgeoisie was charged with that cognitive unreliability which Marx regarded as a function of the social situation. The interests of the proletariat were believed to coincide with the real life-process of history and consequently the ideas of proletarian intellectuals did not appear as ideological but 'true'.

It is Karl Mannheim who assumes that the ideas of *all* groups are ideological, in other words, that the mental productions of every group arise out of its life conditions.[43] This proposition leads to the total and general conception of ideology and, in Mannheim's opinion, transforms ideological analysis into sociology of knowledge.

Whereas Scheler stresses the contention that social reality does not determine the content of validity of knowledge, Mannheim views the cognitive act as an 'instrument for dealing with life-situations at the disposal of a certain kind of vital being under certain conditions of life'.[44] In contrast to Scheler's moderate perspective Mannheim's radical optic intends to penetrate the phenomenological surface of ontic differences and to reach the structural core of social reality. Mannheim's central concept of the 'socio-existential determination of knowledge' expresses the assumption that social life centered around socio-economic orders has actual relevance for all ideas; consequently social reality does not only determine the realization of knowledge, but also its content and validity. Mannheim's claim that all knowledge in the human and social sciences is existentially determined invites the charge of relativism; he answers this accusation with a series of defensive arguments including the well-known assertion that the 'socially unattached intelligentsia' has access to truth since its creative members are not attached to specific interest groups.[45]

Conservative critics attacked Mannheim as a subversive intellectual bent on undermining the dignity of mind and of spiritual values. Left-wing social theorists ridiculed his sociology of knowledge as a decadent bourgeois game which, much like existentialism, questioned everything and attacked nothing. In the opinion of the political left Mannheim withdrew behind the smoke screen of Husserl's presuppositionless philosophy and the empty pathos of Max Weber's rationalistic objectivity because of his inability to understand Marxist analysis. Whereas Marx attempted to distinguish between reality-adequate cognition and ideology, Mannheim's reinterpretation served the purposes of bourgeois idealism masking the material interests of capitalism; consequently Marx's concrete social contradictions and class war realities reappeared in Mannheim's theory as free-floating theoretical conflicts involving disembodied ideas, thought styles, and world views. Marx created a theory of social revolution to change the world; Mannheim fashioned exercises in academic futility devoted to interminable distinctions between finite and infinite truths.[46]

Ironically, Mannheim's critics, proceeding as they do from observable world view presuppositions, reinforce his central assumption that the existentially determined standpoint of thinking extends via an individual's shared perspective context into the content of a judgment, leaving its imprint on the entire body of knowledge.[47]

The first selection dealing with Mannheim's sociology of knowledge attempts to view his work in the larger context of his entire intellectual development; moreover it tries to locate his thought style in the universe of social theoretical discourse which he shares and which alone illuminates the ultimately personal and meta-empirical quest for the validation or rejection of his propositions.

The paper by Virgil G. Hinshaw returns to the more detailed, but methodologically significant question: what are the epistemological implications of the growing awareness of the relativity of historical and social phenomena? In Hinshaw's view a substantive sociology of knowledge with its self-contained empirical and procedural aspects is a legitimate scientific enterprise; on the other hand, sociologists are not legitimized to conduct epistemological inquiries concerned with the bearing of the interrelationship between society and knowledge upon the validity of thought.

Finally, the paper by Thelma Z. Lavine singles out the relationship between historically located social structures and mental structures which occupies a central position in Mannheim's paradigm. From this vantage point Lavine analyses his contributions to the functionalist viewpoint in sociology and differentiates between functionalist theory derived from biologistic organicism and Mannheim's functionalism which is rooted in an historicist-Romanticist orientation.

Contemporary sociology of knowledge: symbolic interactionism, phenomenology, quantitatism

Mannheim's historicist sociology of knowledge was not a mere exercise in theoretical sophistication: his ultimate goal was to achieve what Ernst Troeltsch conceptualized as the 'contemporary cultural synthesis' which would submit all the data of social science simultaneously to historical and systematic analyses.[48] This giant synthesis had the long-range purpose of revealing to the disillusioned denizens of the twentieth century the meaning of collective life and its history. In this respect Mannheim shared common ground with historical-cultural sociologists such as Lukács, Scheler, Sorokin, Toynbee, Troeltsch, and Alfred Weber.[49] But Mannheim was convinced that historical-cultural meanings could only be understood within a perspective of three-dimensional time fusing past, present, and future with modern man's action-oriented pragmatism: 'historical knowledge ... presupposes a subject harbouring definite aspirations regarding the future and actively striving to achieve them. Only out of the interest which the subject at present acting has in the pattern of the future, does the observation of the past become possible.'[50] Going beyond Troeltsch, Mannheim added his proposition that the 'historico-philosophically relevant subject is just that kernel of the human personality whose being and dynamism is consubstantial with the dominant active forces of history'.[51]

The historicist fusion of past, present, and future is formally similar to George Herbert Mead's symbolic interactionist interpretation of thinking as a process which occurs within the individual, but which has its external basis and origin in the experiential matrix of social relations and interactions among people.[52] According to Mead intelligence 'is essentially the ability to solve the problems of the present in terms of future consequences as implicated on the basis of past experience'.[53]

Historical-cultural sociology in general and sociology of knowledge in particular matured at a time when European society moved mainly to the rhythm of large collective processes. Therefore theorists such as Mannheim saw man predominantly as an agent performing intellectual and social roles which received their normative and valuative legitimacy from collectivistic processes. The macro-sociological emphasis on abstractly conceived social forces correspondingly de-emphasized man's role as an inter-personal agent. In the view of contemporary sociologists such as Peter Berger, Robert K. Merton, and John C. McKinney it is precisely the understanding of this role performance which promises to answer the neglected question: how do collectivistic-existential conditions actually infiltrate individualistic-discrete mentalities? Contemporary sociologists of knowledge who are concerned with this question suggest that the sub-discipline would benefit from symbolic interactionist theory—especially from George Herbert Mead's treatment of thinking, intelligence, and knowledge as processes which bind society and the individual together in a context of interaction made meaningful by shared, significant gestures and symbols. In Mead's behavioristic approach, mind, after all, functions as 'the internalization within the individual of the social process of communication in which meaning emerges'.[54]

The article by Harvey A. Farberman reflects the contemporary suggestion that the (European) sociology of knowledge needs an adequate social psychology, specifically a realistic social theory of mentality capable of fusing psychical and institutional process. In Farberman's analysis Mead's theory of mind and self, as symbolic interaction, emerges as an interpretative scheme capable of directing the necessary search for 'a sphere of experience which can support both the public and private and still be adequate to the methodological postulates of research science'.[55]

Berger's and Luckmann's sociology of knowledge perspective includes certain social-psychological presuppositions which permit analyses of the 'internalization of social reality'. These presuppositions 'are greatly influenced by George Herbert Mead and some developments of his work by the so-called symbolic-interactionist school of American sociology'.[56] The essay by Peter Berger focuses on the significant theoretical affinity between the sociology of knowledge perspective and a social-psychological perspective which Mead empowered with the vision that reveals psychic reality as 'an ongoing dialectical relationship with social structure'.[57]

A fusion of the sociology of knowledge with social psychology in the Meadian tradition would, however, have to accommodate various basic differences separating the two perspectives. Especially important is the realization that sociologists of knowledge are mainly concerned with the role of social groups in the construction of a cosmos of historical significance. Mannheim, in particular, developed an adequate concept of social structure, but failed to conceptualize personality structure. The symbolic interactionists, on the other side, are mainly concerned with the social construction of reality to explain the role of individuals in a given world; in pursuit of this interest

Mead and his company failed to conceptualize social structure adequately.[58]

The 'collectivism versus individualism dichotomy', setting the sociology of knowledge apart from symbolic interactionism, not only indicates basic divergences in thought styles, but reflects essential differences in the structure of European and American society. The sociology of knowledge was developed by men living in European societies where the emotionally and politically charged factor of social class greatly determined the lives of individuals. In this context social structure assumed a massive factuality compelling the theoretical imagination. Symbolic interactionism, as Leon Shaskolsky convincingly argues, is a uniquely American theory which mirrors the social and political circumstances of a society proclaiming the virtues of social mobility and democratic egalitarianism. Mead and the symbolic interactionists write in an optimistic spirit which expresses their faith in the 'uniqueness of each member of society and in his freedom to plan and perform his everyday actions in inter-relationship with others unencumbered by either the impinging rules of a structural society or the automatic responses of an uncontrolled personality'.[59]

Phenomenology is of European origin and has long-standing ties with the sociology of knowledge as documented by the thought of Mannheim and especially the work of Scheler. Therefore it could be expected that contemporary theorists interested in reorientating the sociology of knowledge along the lines of phenomenology would not have to cope with the particularistic, ethnocentric problems which confront those attempting to achieve such reorientation with the help of symbolic interactionist definitions and concepts.

As indicated by Berger's and Luckmann's work on *The Social Construction of Reality* contemporary efforts on behalf of a phenomenological sociology of knowledge rely to a large extent on the approach developed by Alfred Schutz. Significantly Schutz shares common ground with Mead both in accepting basic symbolic interactionist principles and in preferring a consensus model of society. Mead's social thought remained strangely untouched by the violent group conflicts of Chicago—birthplace of the Industrial Workers of the World; Schutz's paradigm is equally remote from the intense class struggles of his native Vienna, where prime minister Dollfuss, in 1934, resorted to artillery fire to silence the workers.

In opposition to a politically and socio-economically oriented sociology of knowledge—dismissed by Schutz as a misnomer—he focuses on 'common-sense thinking' and on the world of daily life as a social reality that is allegedly taken for granted and shared by all men.[60] From Edmund Husserl's phenomenology Schutz accepts the assumption that there is a 'world of the natural attitude' to be taken for granted 'exactly as it presents itself to us in our everyday experience'.[61] Schutz utilizes Dilthey's and Mead's insights into the nature of symbolic communication and Max Weber's notion of subjective meaning to support his central concept of intersubjectivity which claims that the activities and creations of my fellowmen can be understood by me. In the commonness of the world of everyday experience, I, in turn, take it for granted that others 'will take my actions in substantially the same way as I mean them'.[62] For Schutz this orientation through understanding is made possible by the basic fact of human co-operation: 'this world has meaning not only for me but also for you and you and everyone. My experience of the world justifies and corrects itself by the experience of the others with whom I am interrelated by common knowledge, common work, and common suffering'.[63]

The stress on the commonness of the world and on co-operation among meaningfully interrelated individuals has rendered Schutz's theory highly problematic since realistic analysis has uncovered a world torn and fragmented by numerous conflicts which pit the young against the old, women against men, the poor against the affluent, the untutored against the learned, the powerless against their overlords, the peaceful against the warlike, the lovers of nature against its despoilers, socialists against capitalists, the denizens of the Third World against white men, and ethical protesters against the faceless robots of riot police formations. Inevitably, therefore, the Husserl–Schutz tradition has stimulated the drift of the sociology of knowledge and of phenomenological sociology into the calm waters of micro-sociological studies which—as demonstrated by Harold Garfinkel's ethnomethodology—focus mainly on the formal properties of commonplace actions. Ethnomethodology further encourages the limitation of sociological activity to the study of the small world of the private—a tendency which leads to such ultimate places of withdrawal as the gynecologist's examining room.[64]

Ever since Sören Kierkegaard's dictum that 'subjectivity is truth' exponents of the existentialist variant of phenomenology have exhibited an individualistic bias. Heidegger, Jaspers and, especially, Sartre urge individuals to free themselves from the impersonal constraints of society so that they may realize their human potentials. Yet existentialist phenomenology seems capable of accommodating macro-sociological studies within its framework since the individual's liberation from the banal routines of social life carries with it responsible intersubjective social participation.

An existentially relevant macro-sociology of knowledge could begin by combining Mannheim's sociological intentions with the philosophical-psychological imagination of Sartre's existentialism. Mannheim and Sartre both interpret intellectual activity as cognitive

29

mapping of the experiential universe and both accept human experience as the source of all knowledge. They concur in the postulate that individual actors must accept their engagement with the social world, and they both see the ultimate test of meaning in action whereby they change human history into the history of man's active life. Sartre widens this paradigm by the addition of his skeptical, 'pessimistic humanism' and his psychological understanding of human irrationality. Sartre is in touch with the mood of the waning twentieth century; this is exemplified by his redefinition of social action which casts the existentially engaged individual in the role of an ethical protester who unmasks and opposes the flagrant injustices and callous abuses perpetrated by the icy, but brittle men of power. In this respect Sartre extends to all people a responsibility which Mannheim had settled on the shoulders of the socially unattached intellectuals, for it is the essential consequence of his existentialism 'that man being condemned to be free carries the weight of the whole world on his shoulders; he is responsible for the world and for himself as a way of being'.[65]

The paper by Edward A. Tiryakian maintains that 'truth is an existential relation between the social actor and his situation; seen phenomenologically, truth and reality are binding for the actor who is always *engaged* in his situation'.[66] Tiryakian's discussion of existential phenomenology reveals significant connections between this philosophical perspective and sociological research. Phenomenology not only informed sociologists of knowledge such as Scheler and Mannheim; it also sensitized the work of Alfred Vierkandt, Max Weber, Georg Simmel, Émile Durkheim, William I. Thomas, Pitirim Sorokin, and Talcott Parsons. Tiryakian demonstrates that this methodological convergence indicates the possibility of a more comprehensive theory of social existence. Existential awareness promises to revitalize sociology 'grounded in the sociological tradition, of utilizing its global knowledge for socially responsible ends'.[67]

The selection by David Martin critically summarizes the present status of phenomenological sociology; this Martin achieves by his reviews of Staude's work on Scheler and of relevant writings by Schutz, and Berger and Luckmann. The inclusion of Hayek's theories permits attention to an attitude which denies the legitimacy of the socio-analysis of ideas and the possibility of subjecting all social phenomena to phenomenological scrutiny.

Quantitatism refers to an intellectual attitude favoring statistical and mathematical descriptions of measured social phenomena and the use of quantified social indexes derived inductively from numerous observations; it implies the possibility of prediction from one set of variables to others. Reporting measured behavior is, therefore, not the only purpose of the quantitative analyst: he assumes that his type of social accounting provides knowledge which is germane to policy decisions. The success of quantitatism in the physical sciences inspired 'a general belief that one knows something only when it has been counted. Enumeration has become the corner-stone of knowledge. Though this epistemological assumption was first applied in the natural sciences, it has come to dominate Western man's thought concerning human affairs as well.'[68] Quantitative analysts use statistics as social reality from which they persuade others to act and accept policies. 'The man who uses statistics for the purpose of persuading someone else to adopt a particular policy or particular action is already convinced of the correctness of his position.'[69]

The discovery 'that the purpose of social indicators is not primarily to record historical events but to provide the basis of planning for future policies'[70] is important for all those who wish to study quantitatism through the sociology of knowledge. Investigations of this type have shown how the statistician's interest in the legitimating and persuasive powers of quantified data blunts his alertness to the technical correctness of his methods and their products.[71]

Quantitatism as an intellectual attitude is based on ontic and epistemological assumptions which include the proposition that social reality is qualitatively indistinct from and not more primary in experience than physical reality. In the opinion of the neopositivist George A. Lundberg 'nearly all empirically observed behavior of bodies from the point of view of their movement in space and time are "covered" by the general "principles" of physics. That is, events as "different" (from some points of view) as a man falling from a twentieth-story window, a bullet fired into the air from a rifle, or drops of water in a rain storm, are all "explained" by the same basic principle.'[72]

Most sociologists of knowledge have been favorably impressed by Wilhelm Dilthey's division of the sciences by subject matter and Max Weber's legitimation of 'understanding'. They consequently assume that the logical status of the physical sciences differs from that of the humanities and social sciences: the latter find their objects of inquiry in the mental products of an existentially situated human conscious-ness. For many sociologists of knowledge, such as Mannheim, the methods of the physical sciences are not appropriate 'because impor-tant items of knowledge are existentially determined in concrete historical situations, hence incapable of being measured quanti-tatively and interpreted on an absolute scale. We cannot assume that socio-cultural units are constant in space and time, and this raises the methodological problem of measurement.'[73]

The article by Franz Adler represents the relatively rare species

GUNTER W. REMMLING

of studies in the sociology of knowledge which employ a quantitative methodology under the assumption that there is no significant difference between socio-cultural activities and other forms of behavior. In Adler's opinion his study shows 'that the sociology of knowledge is accessible by the same methods as the other parts of sociology, provided that the questions asked are of a nature that is suitable for scientific investigation'.[74]

Applied sociology of knowledge

Studies in applied sociology of knowledge usually attempt to reveal the influence of socio-existential conditions upon cognitive processes and the production, distribution, and consumption of mental products such as logico-scientific systems, theories, beliefs, norms, values, motives, and attitudes.

The ethnographic style of the Durkheim school resulted in successful applications of the sociological theory of knowledge to cognitive processes and the formation of primitive attitudes and beliefs. Marx and Mannheim developed more radical, deterministic conceptions of the nature and extent of the socio-existential determination of mental production; in the course of their applied studies they came to illuminate mainly the process of intellectual production. This emphasis pervades Mannheim's most accomplished study in applied sociology of knowledge, that is, his essay on 'Conservative Thought'.[75] Scheler's moderate sociology of knowledge motivated greater attention to the processes of knowledge distribution and consumption as exemplified by the numerous analyses carried out by him and his followers.[76]

The general orientation of this volume—conceptualized as the focused approach—does not permit the inclusion of studies which only hindsight reveals as pertinent to the sociology of knowledge. The selections in part nine share a deliberate sociology of knowledge perspective because they accept the assumption that cognitive processes and mental productions reflect the influence of social conditions.

The article by Alex Simirenko applies Mannheim's conceptual differentiation among various generational groupings to the question concerning the persistence of minority communities in the United States. W. Lloyd Warner's studies of American ethnic groups emphasized economic attraction to support the proposition that each subsequent generation loses more and more of its ethnicity as it moves into the middle classes; more recent studies, such as *Beyond the Melting Pot* by Nathan Glazer and Daniel Moynihan, have provided new information on the descendants of immigrants which—

32

in opposition to Warner's assumptions—supports the notion of the persistence of minority sub-cultures.

Simirenko utilizes data obtained by his larger study of the Minneapolis Russian community and the conceptual distinctions provided by Mannheim's essay on 'The Problem of Generations' to explain 'the emergence of new cultural forms inadequately dealt with by Warner'.[77]

Thorstein Veblen's work, *The Higher Learning in America* (1918), generally alerted social scientists to view the production and distribution of knowledge in the academy as problematic; subsequent research efforts such as Florian Znaniecki's and Logan Wilson's studies of the role of scholars fostered more systematic insights into the dependence of intellectual activity upon the structural and functional properties of universities.[78] Since the late 1950s there have been intra-institutional studies of the intellectual's dependence on the social organization of academe; these have been augmented by inter-institutional analyses which show how the university depends on those economic, political, and military components of the social structure which C. Wright Mills called the 'power elite' and Dwight D. Eisenhower the 'military-industrial complex'.[79]

Within the framework of inter-institutional analysis the selection by Robert G. Snyder claims that the modern university 'has established an organization of knowledge which basically orients itself as a service industry to the government and business sectors'.[80] The dependence of the academic system upon the economic-political system imprisons the scholar in his limited area of competence which alone has the power of attracting a nonacademic clientele in search of specialized and marketable expertise.

Significantly the academic's dependence upon economic, political, and military interest groups keeps him from intellectual pursuits such as innovative thinking and social criticism which would benefit society at large. Since most academic experts parade an acquiescent 'end of ideology' orientation and the anti-historical logic of the scientific method they, furthermore, promote an intellectual stance which discourages all efforts to judge the quality of contemporary experience; instead academics are merely motivated to measure and manipulate its ability to foster order and stability and to insure the continued development of the established political-economic system.

Snyder concludes that the socio-economically determined impotence of scholars can only be terminated by the reorientation of the university toward an educated and critical public capable of protecting the intellectual 'from co-optation and abuse by powerful interest groups. *And it is only to the public, therefore, that the university owes any lasting allegiance.*'[81]

The paper by Kurt Danziger introduces the proposition that,

under present social conditions, the sociology of knowledge is best suited for the empirical analysis of 'underdeveloped' countries. This proposition is based on an interpretation of the sociology of knowledge as a research strategy the strength of which resided 'in its ability to analyse and assign a proper place to socially transcendent ideas, that is to say, ideas which went beyond the present, actually existing, framework of social relationships and pointed either towards the past or towards the future'. [82] Furthermore, situationally transcendent ideas, both in their ideological and in their Utopian forms, play a significant role only in societies suffering from unstable relationships between social classes which threaten the social system as a whole. Since class relations in the 'underdeveloped' countries 'retain a degree of instability which casts doubt on the continuation of the existing system of social relationships as a whole' [83] it is here that the sociology of knowledge perspective develops its greatest empirical strength.

For the purpose of testing this proposition Danziger singled out contemporary South Africa where extreme forms of racial and social injustice have caused the doubt in the continuation of existing social relations to assume unusually intense proportions. Danziger used several hundred essays written by students and assessed by several qualified raters to investigate cognitive styles in South Africa empirically. He found that the percentage frequency of various types of historical orientation conformed broadly to the social position of different groups. Thus, for example, the highest frequency of conservative types of historical orientation was found among the Afrikaans group which is at the top of the power hierarchy; conversely the highest frequency of revolutionary types of historical orientation was discovered among the indigenous African group which is situated at the bottom of society. On the basis of these and other correlations between social position and cognitive style Danziger concludes that position in the social structure apparently 'determines the range of available historical orientations for the members of each social group'. [84]

The paper on social classes in Ecuador also applies the sociology of knowledge perspective to a country suffering from retarded socioeconomic development. In the case of this South American republic the massively unequal distribution of political power and economic wealth causes an unreliability of social orientations which finds a particularly dramatic expression in the distortion of cognitive forms imposed on the system of social stratification. Observations in the field and data obtained from interviews indicate that the traditional and common division of the Ecuadorian population into Whites, mestizos, and Indians is not only misleading, but expressive of an ideological distortion of social reality in the classical manner of false consciousness.

In this selection the 'racial' distinctions are replaced by the differentiation of social classes; such differentiations initiate a more realistic approach to the understanding of the Ecuadorian social system which is representative of Latin American societies marked by an unsolved 'Indian problem' and the attendant retardation of socio-economic development.

The article by Manfred Stanley was especially written for this volume on the question of legitimacy which has repeatedly manifested itself as a problematic aspect of methodological and conceptual reflections on the sociology of knowledge.

Specifically, Stanley asks: how is it that in all societies certain aspects of the life-world are experienced by individuals as true, right, and proper and, furthermore, how do social scientists account for this universal ontic experience?

In contrast to many self-conscious social scientific reflections which politicize the discussion of legitimacy—often without separating it conceptually from legality and authority—Stanley argues that the legitimacy of anything, be it a norm, a social practice, or a command, can most fundamentally be understood as *the sense of its appropriateness* in a given context; this sense of appropriateness may be strong or weak, widely shared or restricted, qualified or unqualified. Phenomenologically, this sense of appropriateness is part of the cognition of an object itself, although this cognition may not be immediate. Legitimacy may have to be constructed through interpretation on the part of group members in a given situation, a process commonly referred to as justification. But justification, as a task of legitimation, will fail unless the object in question comes finally to be recognized by someone (even if not by the justifiers) as true, right, or proper in a given context. Therefore, the legitimacy of any object should be defined as part of its phenomenological structure for someone; otherwise processes such as polemicizing and propagandizing will replace the experience of legitimacy.

Stanley views social structure as an important medium through which ideas are refracted and diffused. However, his interest in the full range of explanations concerning the sources of legitimacy motivates attention to other factors such as situational contingencies, language, and the inherent logic of ideas.

In this paradigm the sociology of knowledge seems to take on the appearance of an intellectual enterprise concerned with the empirical investigation of the role of social structure as *a* variable affecting the itinerary of ideas.

GUNTER W. REMMLING

Notes

1 See Max Scheler, 'Probleme einer Soziologie des Wissens' in Max Scheler (ed.), *Versuche zu einer Soziologie des Wissens*, Munich and Leipzig: Duncker und Humblot, 1924, pp. 5–146; Karl Mannheim, 'Das Problem einer Soziologie des Wissens', *Archiv für Sozialwissenschaft und Sozialpolitik*, vol. 53, no. 3 (September 1925), pp. 577–652; and 'The Problem of a Sociology of Knowledge' in Karl Mannheim, *Essays on the Sociology of Knowledge* (ed. Paul Kecskemeti), London: Routledge & Kegan Paul, 1952, pp. 134–90. As a sociologist of knowledge Mannheim is best known for his work on *Ideology and Utopia*; see Karl Mannheim, *Ideologie und Utopie*, Bonn: Cohen, 1929; and *Ideology and Utopia: An Introduction to the Sociology of Knowledge* (trans. and ed. Louis Wirth and Edward Shils), New York: Harcourt, Brace, 1936. The Austrian philosopher-sociologist Wilhelm Jerusalem used the term 'sociology of cognition' as early as 1909, when he wrote an article attempting to reconcile the epistemological differences separating neo-Kantians from neopositivists. See Wilhelm Jerusalem, 'Soziologie des Erkennens', *Die Zukunft*, vol. 67 (May 1909), pp. 236–46.

2 Mannheim, *Ideology and Utopia*, p. 278. In contrast to Mannheim, Max Scheler opposed Marxist materialism from the position of phenomenological philosophy and tried to anchor the sociology of knowledge in his philosophical anthropology.

3 See Friedrich Wilhelm Nietzsche, *On the Genealogy of Morals* (trans. Walter Kaufmann and R. J. Hollingdale), New York: Vintage Books, 1967; Friedrich Wilhelm Nietzsche, *The Will to Power* (trans. Walter Kaufmann and R. J. Hollingdale), New York: Random House, 1967; Vilfredo Pareto, *The Mind and Society*, 4 vols (trans. A. Bongiorno and A. Livingston), New York: Harcourt, Brace, 1935; Sigmund Freud, *Civilization and Its Discontents* (newly trans. and ed. James Strachey), New York: Norton, 1961; Sigmund Freud, *The Future of an Illusion* (trans. W. D. Robson-Scott), London: Hogarth Press and Institute of Psychoanalysis, 1928. See also Gunter W. Remmling, 'Friedrich Nietzsche: Panegyrist of the Lie' in Gunter W. Remmling, *Road to Suspicion: A Study of Modern Mentality and the Sociology of Knowledge*, New York: Appleton-Century-Crofts, 1967, pp. 165–80; Gunter W. Remmling, 'Sigmund Freud: A Tortuous Epitaph for the Mind' in *ibid.*, pp. 181–98; and Brigitte Berger, 'Vilfredo Pareto and the Sociology of Knowledge', *Social Research*, vol. 34, no. 2 (Summer 1967), pp. 265–81.

4 See Lucien Lévy-Bruhl, *Primitive Mentality* (trans. Lilian A. Clare), London: Allen & Unwin, 1923; Émile Durkheim and Marcel Mauss, *Primitive Classification* (trans. Rodney Needham from 'De quelques formes primitives de classification', *Année sociologique*, 1902), University of Chicago Press, 1963; Émile Durkheim and Célestin Bouglé, 'Les conditions sociologiques de la connaissance', *Année sociologique*, vol. 11 (1906–9), pp. 41–8; Émile Durkheim, 'Sociologie religieuse et théorie de la connaissance', *Revue de Métaphysique et de Morale*, vol.

36

17, no. 6 (November 1909), pp. 733–58; Émile Durkheim, 'Subject of Our Study: Religious Sociology and the Theory of Knowledge', introduction to *The Elementary Forms of the Religious Life* (trans. Joseph Ward Swain), New York: Free Press, 1965, pp. 13–33; and 'Conclusion', *ibid.*, pp. 462–96. See also Maurice Halbwachs, *Les Cadres sociaux de la mémoire*, Paris: Alcan, 1925; Marcel Granet, *La Pensée chinoise*, Paris: La Renaissance du Livre, 1934.

5 See Gunter W. Remmling, 'Immanuel Kant: The Limitations of Reason' in Remmling, *Road to Suspicion*, pp. 53–62. In the twentieth century Ernst Cassirer was especially active in opposing all attempts to erode the formalistic purity of Kantian epistemology by way of historicistic, sociologistic, or psychologistic reinterpretations. See Ernst Cassirer, *Das Erkenntnisproblem in der Philosophie und Wissenschaft der neueren Zeit*, 3 vols, Berlin: Cassirer, 1922–3.

6 See G. W. F. Hegel, *Philosophy of Right* (trans. T. M. Knox), London: Oxford University Press, 1953. See also Hans Freyer, *Theorie des objektiven Geistes*, 3rd ed., Leipzig and Berlin: Teubner, 1934; Max Scheler, *Die Wissensformen und die Gesellschaft, Gesammelte Werke*, vol. 8 (ed. with commentaries by Maria Scheler), Berne and Munich: Francke, 1960, p. 24.

7 See Wilhelm Dilthey, *Die geistige Welt: Einleitung in die Philosophie des Lebens, Gesammelte Schriften*, vol. 5, Leipzig and Berlin: Teubner, 1924, pp. 4–5; Wilhelm Dilthey, *Der Aufbau der geschichtlichen Welt in den Geisteswissenschaften, Gesammelte Schriften*, vol. 7, Leipzig and Berlin: Teubner, 1927, p. 191. See also Gunter W. Remmling, 'Wilhelm Dilthey: The Fragmentary Nature of Life' in Remmling, *Road to Suspicion*, pp. 72–84.

8 See Karl Marx, *A Contribution to the Critique of Political Economy* (trans. N. I. Stone), Chicago: Kerr, 1904, pp. 11–12.

9 Karl Marx and Friedrich Engels, *The Communist Manifesto* (ed. Samuel H. Beer), New York: Appleton-Century-Crofts, 1955, pp. 29–30.

10 Peter Gay, *Weimar Culture: The Outsider as Insider*, New York: Harper & Row, 1968, p. xiv.

11 See Louis L. Snyder, *The Weimar Republic: A History of Germany from Ebert to Hitler*, Princeton, N.J.: Van Nostrand, 1966. See also Karl Dietrich Bracher, *Die Auflösung der Weimarer Republik: Eine Studie zum Problem des Machtverfalls in der Demokratie*, Stuttgart: Ring-Verlag, 1955; Erich Eyck, *A History of the Weimar Republic*, 2 vols (trans. Harlan P. Hanson and Robert G. L. Waite), Cambridge, Mass.: Harvard University Press, 1962–3; S. William Halperin, *Germany Tried Democracy: A Political History of the Reich from 1918–1932*, New York: Crowell, 1946.

12 See Harlan R. Crippen (ed.), *Germany: A Self-Portrait*, London: Oxford University Press, 1944. See also Walther Kiaulehn, *Berlin: Schicksal einer Weltstadt*, Munich: Biederstein, 1958; Waltzer Z. Laqueur, *Young Germany: A History of the German Youth Movement*, New York: Basic Books, 1962; Paul Erich Marcus (PEM), *Heimweh nach dem Kurfürstendamm: Aus Berlins glanzvollsten Tagen und*

Nächten, Berlin: Blanvalet, 1952; Stefan Zweig, *The World of Yesterday: An Autobiography*, New York: Viking Press, 1943.

13 See Martin Esslin, *Brecht: The Man and His Work*, Garden City, N.Y.: Doubleday, 1959; Walter Gropius, *The New Architecture and the Bauhaus* (trans. P. Morton Shand), New York: Museum of Modern Art; London: Faber & Faber, 1937; Siegfried Kracauer, *From Caligari to Hitler: A Psychological History of the German Film*, Princeton, N.J.: Princeton University Press, 1947; Bernard S. Myers, *The German Expressionists: A Generation in Revolt*, New York: McGraw-Hill, 1963; Erwin Piscator, *Das politische Theater*, Berlin: Schultz, 1929; Hans Richter, *Dada: Art and Anti-Art*, New York: McGraw-Hill, 1965.

14 See Alfred Seidel, *Bewusstsein als Verhängnis* (ed. Hans Prinzhorn), Bonn: Cohen, 1927.

15 See Gunter W. Remmling, review of '*Max Scheler: An Intellectual Portrait*, by John Raphael Staude, New York: Free Press, 1967', in *Social Forces*, vol. 46, no. 4 (June 1968), p. 553.

16 Apart from studies of individual thinkers see the following general works: H. Otto Dahlke, 'The Sociology of Knowledge' in Harry Elmer Barnes, Howard Becker and F. B. Becker (eds), *Contemporary Social Theory*, New York: Appleton-Century-Crofts, 1940, pp. 64–89; Gottfried Eisermann, 'Wissenssoziologie' in G. Eisermann (ed.), *Die Lehre von der Gesellschaft: Ein Lehrbuch der Soziologie*, Stuttgart: Enke 1969, pp. 481–535; Ernst Grünwald, *Das Problem der Soziologie des Wissens: Versuch einer kritischen Darstellung der Wissenssoziologischen Theorien*, Vienna and Leipzig: Braumüller, 1934; Irving Louis Horowitz, 'The Pre-History of the Sociology of Knowledge' in I. L. Horowitz, *Philosophy, Science and the Sociology of Knowledge*, Springfield, Ill.: Thomas, 1961, pp. 10–33; Remmling, *Road to Suspicion*, pp. 53–198; Werner Stark, 'The Antecedents of the Sociology of Knowledge' in W. Stark, *The Sociology of Knowledge: An Essay in Aid of a Deeper Understanding of the History of Ideas*, London: Routledge & Kegan Paul, 1958, pp. 46–98.

17 In the Seventh Book of the *Republic*, Plato develops a social theory of cognition claiming that only the privileged ruling elite of the 'true-born' can achieve knowledge of truth and insight into what is beautiful, just, and good. The aristocrat Plato, however, had little interest in further revealing the connections between the social reality of special interests and the intellectual irreality of grandiose concepts; on the contrary he advocated the 'noble lie' as mental fodder for the underlying population and the inculcation of superstition for reasons of state. It is not without interest to note that political condottieri and charlatans of power frequently find the trappings of idealist philosophy highly useful whenever they choose to perform their public acts as moral virtuosos. See for example Benito Mussolini, *Fascism: Doctrines and Institutions* (official translation), Rome: Ardita, 1935, pp. 8–9: 'Fascism sees individuals and generations bound together by a moral law ... which, suppressing the instinct for life closed in a brief circle of pleasure, builds up a higher life, founded on duty, a life free from the limitations of time and space, in which the individual, by self-sacrifice,

by the renunciation of self-interest, by death itself, can achieve that purely spiritual existence in which his value as a man insists. . . . The Fascist conception of life is a religious one, in which man is viewed in his immanent relation to a higher law, endowed with an objective will transcending the individual and raising him to conscious membership of a spiritual society.'

18 G. W. F. Hegel, *Lectures on the History of Philosophy*, vol. 1 (trans. E. S. Haldane), London: Routledge & Kegan Paul; New York: Humanities Press, 1963, p. 384.

19 See George Grote, *Greece*, vol. 8, New York: Collier, 1899, pp. 350–99.

20 See Gunter W. Remmling, 'Origin and Development of Sociology' in G. W. Remmling and R. B. Campbell, *Basic Sociology: An Introduction to the Study of Society*, Totowa, N.J.: Littlefield, Adams, 1970, esp. pp. 4–11.

21 See Karl Marx, *Selected Essays* (trans. H. J. Stenning), New York: International Publishers, 1926, p. 190.

22 See Franz Mehring, *Karl Marx: The Story of His Life* (trans. Edward Fitzgerald), Ann Arbor: University of Michigan Press, 1962, pp. 73–8.

23 See Immanuel Kant, *Critique of Pure Reason* (trans. Norman Kemp Smith), London: Macmillan, 1956, p. 22.

24 See G. W. F. Hegel, *Early Theological Writings* (trans. T. M. Knox and Richard Kroner), University of Chicago Press, 1948.

25 G. W. F. Hegel, *Philosophy of Right* (trans. with notes by T. M. Knox), New York: Oxford University Press, 1967, p. 11.

26 *Ibid.*, p. 13.

27 For an expression of Hegel's pessimism with regard to European civilization see Georg Wilhelm Friedrich Hegel, *The Philosophy of History* (trans. J. Sibree), rev. ed., New York: Colonial Press, 1899, p. 86: 'America is therefore the land of the future, where, in the ages that lie before us, the burden of the World's History shall reveal itself—perhaps in a contest between North and South America. It is a land of desire for all those who are weary of the historical lumber-room of old Europe.'

28 See Henri de Saint-Simon, *Social Organization, The Science of Man and Other Writings* (ed. and trans. with an introduction by Felix Markham), New York: Harper & Row, 1964, pp. xxxviii–xxxix.

29 Arthur Child, 'The Theoretical Possibility of the Sociology of Knowledge', *Ethics*, vol. 51, no. 4 (July 1941), pp. 417, 418.

30 Dilthey, *Der Aufbau der geschichtlichen Welt in den Geistewissenschaften*, p. 291 (my translation).

31 Mannheim, *Ideology and Utopia*, p. 69.

32 See Gunter W. Remmling, 'Ideology: The Twilight of Ideas', in Remmling, *Road to Suspicion*, p. 108.

33 Rolf Schulze, 'Some Social-Psychological and Political Functions of Ideology', *Sociological Quarterly*, vol. 10, no. 1 (Winter 1969), p. 72.

34 Marcel Mauss, 'Introduction to the First Edition' of Émile Durkheim, *Socialism* (ed. with an introduction by Alvin W. Gouldner; translated by Charlotte Sattler), New York: Macmillan, 1962, p. 34.

35 See Émile Durkheim, *The Division of Labor in Society* (trans. George Simpson), New York: Free Press, 1964, p. 131.

36 Émile Durkheim, *Socialism*, p. 242.

37 See Auguste Comte, *The Positive Philosophy* (freely translated and condensed by Harriet Martineau), New York: Blanchard, 1858, pp. 453–68.

38 George Simpson, introduction to *Auguste Comte: Sire of Sociology* (selections from his writings, with an introduction and commentaries by George Simpson), New York: Crowell, 1969, p. 10.

39 See Max Scheler, *Ressentiment* (trans. William W. Holdheim and edited with introduction by Lewis A. Coser), Chicago: Free Press, 1961.

40 See Gunter W. Remmling, 'Max Scheler: Quest for a Catholic Sociology of Knowledge' in Remmling, *Road to Suspicion*, esp. p. 37.

41 Mannheim, *Essays on the Sociology of Knowledge*, p. 156.

42 See Karl Mannheim, 'Historismus', *Archiv für Sozialwissenschaft und Sozialpolitik*, vol. 52, no. 1 (June 1924), pp. 1 ff.; and 'Historicism' in Mannheim, *Essays on the Sociology of Knowledge*, pp. 84–133. See also Gunter W. Remmling, 'Philosophical Parameters of Karl Mannheim's Sociology of Knowledge', *Sociological Quarterly*, vol. 12, no. 4 (Fall 1971), pp. 531–47.

43 See Mannheim, *Ideology and Utopia*, p. 69.

44 *Ibid.*, p. 268.

45 See Gunter W. Remmling, 'Karl Mannheim: Revision of an Intellectual Portrait', *Social Forces*, vol. 40, no. 1 (October 1961), pp. 23–30.

46 See Ernst Robert Curtius, *Deutscher Geist in Gefahr*, Berlin and Stuttgart: Deutsche Verlags-Anstalt, 1932; Theodor W. Adorno, 'Das Bewusstsein der Wissenssoziologie' in Th. W. Adorno, *Prismen: Kulturkritik und Gesellschaft*, Berlin and Frankfurt: Suhrkamp, 1955, pp. 32–50; Max Horkheimer, 'Ein neuer Ideologiebegriff?', *Archiv für die Geschichte des Sozialismus und der Arbeiterbewegung*, vol. 15 (1930), pp. 33–56; Georg Lukács, *Die Zerstörung der Vernunft*, *Georg Lukács Werke*, vol. 9, Neuwied am Rhein and Berlin-Spandau: Luchterhand, 1962, pp. 549–50.

47 See Mannheim, *Ideology and Utopia*, pp. 263–4.

48 See Ernst Troeltsch, *Der Historismus und seine Probleme*, vol. 1, Tübingen: Mohr, 1922.

49 See Alfred Weber, 'Fundamentals of Culture-Sociology' (trans. G. H. Weltner and C. F. Hirshman) in Talcott Parsons *et al.* (eds), *Theories of Society*, vol. 2, Chicago: Free Press, 1961, pp. 1274–83. For the nature of historical-cultural sociology and its relation to social theory see Remmling and Campbell, *Basic Sociology*, pp. 25–7, 38–42, 56, 345–6, and 349.

50 Mannheim, 'Historicism', p. 102.

51 *Ibid.*, p. 102.

52 See George Herbert Mead, *Mind, Self, and Society* (ed. Charles W. Morris), University of Chicago Press, 1934, p. 156.

53 John C. McKinney, 'The Contribution of George H. Mead to the Sociology of Knowledge', *Social Forces*, vol. 34, no. 2 (December 1955), p. 148.

54 Mead, *Mind, Self, and Society*, p. xxii.
55 Harvey A. Farberman, 'Mannheim, Cooley, and Mead: Toward a Social Theory of Mentality', *Sociological Quarterly*, vol. 11, no. 1 (Winter 1970), p. 7.
56 Peter L. Berger and Thomas Luckmann, *The Social Construction of Reality: A Treatise in the Sociology of Knowledge*, Anchor Books Edition, Garden City, N.Y.: Doubleday, 1967, p. 17.
57 Peter L. Berger, 'Identity as a Problem in the Sociology of Knowledge', *European Journal of Sociology*, vol. 7, no. 1 (1966), p. 106.
58 See Berger and Luckmann, *The Social Construction of Reality*, p. 194. See also Remmling, 'Philosophical Parameters of Karl Mannheim's Sociology of Knowledge', pp. 541–2.
59 Leon Shaskolsky, 'The Development of Sociological Theory in America: A Sociology of Knowledge Interpretation' in Larry T. Reynolds and Janice M. Reynolds (eds), *The Sociology of Sociology: Analysis and Criticism of the Thought, Research, and Ethical Folkways of Sociology and Its Practitioners*, New York: McKay, 1970, p. 17.
60 See Alfred Schutz, 'The Well-Informed Citizen: An Essay on the Social Distribution of Knowledge' in Arvid Broderson (ed.), *Collected Papers of Alfred Schutz*, vol. 2, The Hague: Nijhoff, 1964, p. 121.
61 Aron Gurwitsch, 'The Common-Sense World as Social Reality: A Discourse on Alfred Schutz', *Social Research*, vol. 29, no. 1 (Spring 1962), p. 51.
62 Richard M. Zaner, 'Theory of Intersubjectivity: Alfred Schutz', *ibid.*, vol. 28, no. 1 (Spring 1961), p. 75.
63 Alfred Schutz, 'The Social World and the Theory of Social Action' in *Collected Papers of Alfred Schutz*, vol. 2, p. 9.
64 See Harold Garfinkel. *Studies in Ethnomethodology*, Englewood Cliffs, N.J.: Prentice-Hall, 1967; and Joan P. Emerson, 'Behavior in Private Places: Sustaining Definitions of Reality in Gynecological Examinations' in Hans Peter Dreitzel (ed.), *Recent Sociology No. 2. Patterns of Communicative Behavior: Eight Articles That Demonstrate What Ethnomethodology Is All About*, New York: Macmillan, 1970, pp. 74–97.
65 Jean-Paul Sartre, *Being and Nothingness: An Essay in Phenomenological Ontology* (trans. Hazel E. Barnes), 5th ed., New York: Citadel Press, 1968, p. 529. See also Remmling, 'Philosophical Parameters of Karl Mannheim's Sociology of Knowledge', p. 544.
66 Edward A. Tiryakian, 'Existential Phenomenology and the Sociological Tradition', *American Sociological Review*, vol. 30, no. 5 (October 1965), p. 683 (emphasis in original).
67 *Ibid.*, p. 688.
68 Jack D. Douglas, *The Social Meanings of Suicide*, Princeton, N.J.: Princeton University Press, 1967, p. 163.
69 Raymond A. Bauer, *Social Indicators*, Cambridge, Mass.: M.I.T. Press, 1966, p. 26.
70 *Ibid.*, p. 19.
71 See for example Irwin Deutscher, 'Looking Backward: Case Studies on the Progress of Methodology in Sociological Research', *American*

Sociologist, vol. 4, no. 1 (February 1969), pp. 35–41; Thomas J. Duggan and Charles W. Dean, 'Common Misinterpretations of Significance Levels in Sociology Journals', *ibid.*, vol. 3, no. 1 (February 1968), pp. 45–6; Herbert Gamberg, 'Science and Scientism: The State of Sociology', *ibid.*, vol. 4, no. 2 (May 1969), pp. 111–16; James L. McCartney, 'On Being Scientific: Changing Styles of Presentation of Sociological Research', *ibid.*, vol. 5, no. 1 (February 1970), pp. 30–5; Hannan C. Selvin, 'A Critique of Tests of Significance in Survey Research', *American Sociological Review*, vol. 22, no. 5 (October 1957), pp. 519–27; Andrew J. Weigert, 'The Immoral Rhetoric of Scientific Sociology', *American Sociologist*, vol. 5, no. 2 (May 1970), pp. 111–19.

72 George A. Lundberg, *Foundations of Sociology*, rev. ed., New York: McKay, 1964, p. 2.

73 Tiryakian, 'Existential Phenomenology and the Sociological Tradition', p. 676.

74 Franz Adler, 'A Quantitative Study in the Sociology of Knowledge', *American Sociological Review*, vol. 19, no. 1 (February 1954), p. 48. For other examples of the quantitative approach see Pauline Bart, 'The Role of the Sociologist on Public Issues: An Exercise in the Sociology of Knowledge', *American Sociologist*, vol. 5, no. 4 (November 1970), pp. 339–44; Terry N. Clark *et al.*, 'Discipline, Method, Community Structure, and Decision-Making: The Role and Limitations of the Sociology of Knowledge', *ibid.*, vol. 3, no. 3 (August 1968), pp. 214–17; William Petersen, 'The Classification of Subnations in Hawaii: An Essay in the Sociology of Knowledge', *American Sociological Review*, vol. 34, no. 6 (December 1969), pp. 863–77; Melvin Seeman, 'Intellectual Perspective and Adjustment to Minority Status', *Social Problems*, vol. 3, no. 3 (January 1956), pp. 142–53; John Walton, 'Discipline, Method and Community Power: A Note on the Sociology of Knowledge', *American Sociological Review*, vol. 31, no. 5 (October 1966), pp. 684–9; Jules J. Wanderer, 'An Empirical Study in the Sociology of Knowledge', *Sociological Inquiry*, vol. 39, no. 1 (Winter 1969), pp. 19–26.

75 See Karl Mannheim, 'Conservative Thought' in Karl Mannheim, *Essays on Sociology and Social Psychology*, London: Routledge & Kegan Paul, 1953, pp. 74–164; see also Karl Mannheim, 'The History of the Concept of the State as an Organism: A Sociological Analysis' in *ibid.*, pp. 165–82; and Karl Mannheim, 'The Problem of the Intelligentsia: An Inquiry into its Past and Present Role' in Karl Mannheim, *Essays on the Sociology of Culture*, London: Routledge & Kegan Paul, 1956, pp. 91–170.

76 See Justus Hashagen, 'Ausserwissenschaftliche Einflüsse auf die neuere Geschichtswissenschaft' in Scheler (ed.), *Versuche zu einer Soziologie des Wissens*, pp. 233–55; Paul Honigsheim, 'Soziologie der Scholastik' in *ibid.*, pp. 302–7; Paul Honigsheim, 'Soziologie des realistischen und des nominalistischen Denkens' in *ibid.*, pp. 308–22; Paul Honigsheim, 'Soziologie der Mystik' in *ibid.*, pp. 323–46; Paul Luchtenberg, 'Übertragungsformen des Wissens' in *ibid.*, pp. 151–81; Helmut

Plessner, 'Zur Soziologie der modernen Forschung und ihrer Organisation' in *ibid.*, pp. 407–25.

77 Alex Simirenko, 'Mannheim's Generational Analysis and Acculturation', *British Journal of Sociology*, vol. 17, no. 3 (September 1966), p. 298.

78 See Thorstein Veblen, *The Higher Learning in America: A Memorandum on the Conduct of Universities by Businessmen*, New York: Huebsch, 1918; Florian Znaniecki, *The Social Role of the Man of Knowledge*, New York: Columbia University Press, 1940; Logan Wilson, *The Academic Man: A Study in the Sociology of a Profession*, New York: Oxford University Press, 1942. For examples of more recent research see Charles H. Anderson and John D. Murray (eds), *The Professors: Work and Life Styles Among Academicians*, Cambridge, Mass.: Schenkman, 1971; Theodore Caplow and Reece J. McGee, *The Academic Marketplace*, New York: Basic Books, 1958; George B. de Huszar (ed.), *The Intellectuals: A Controversial Portrait*, Chicago: Free Press, 1960.

79 See C. Wright Mills, *The Power Elite*, New York: Oxford University Press, 1956. See also Irving Louis Horowitz, 'Social Science Yogis and Military Commissars' in I. L. Horowitz, *Professing Sociology: Studies in the Life Cycle of Social Science*, Chicago: Aldine, 1968, pp. 340–54; Clark Kerr, *The Uses of the University*, Cambridge, Mass.: Harvard University Press, 1963; James Ridgeway, *The Closed Corporation*, New York: Random House, 1968; Theodore Roszak (ed.), *The Dissenting Academy*, New York: Pantheon, 1968; Harold L. Wilensky, *Organizational Intelligence: Knowledge and Policy in Government and Industry*, New York: Basic Books, 1967; Kenneth Winetrout, 'Mills and the Intellectual Default' in Irving Louis Horowitz (ed.), *The New Sociology*, New York: Oxford University Press, 1965, pp. 147–61.

80 Robert G. Snyder, 'Knowledge, Power and the University: Notes on the Impotence of the Intellectual', *Maxwell Review*, vol. 6, no. 2 (Spring 1970), p. 56.

81 *Ibid.*, p. 70 (emphasis in original).

82 K. Danziger, 'Ideology and Utopia in South Africa: A Methodological Contribution to the Sociology of Knowledge', *British Journal of Sociology*, vol. 14, no. 1 (March 1963), p. 59.

83 *Ibid.*, p. 60.

84 *Ibid.*, p. 70.

part two

Forerunners and pioneers

2 Francis Bacon and the French Enlightenment philosophers

Gunter W. Remmling

When Bacon equated the practical and theoretical with his announcement, whatever is most useful in practice is most correct in theory, he not only voiced an early pragmatism but also expressed the new spirit of the Renaissance which transformed the ideas of the Middle Ages.[1] His pragmatic assertion reflects the will to lord it over nature and to make its forces serve man's wants. In this he becomes the spokesman of the English Renaissance, the bold theorist of the Elizabethan Age. Bacon, peer of brazen navigators, adventurers, and daring scientists, wanted men to abandon the medieval wasteland of empty words and phantasies and to turn to the study of *things*; born in London in 1561, he labored to show men what power and advantage they could gain from a true knowledge of nature and worked out a method for the acquisition of this knowledge. A scholar to the end, he died in 1626, when an experiment to test the preservative properties of snow proved too much for his already feeble health.

Bacon explained the method by means of which he believed true knowledge of nature could be gained in his *Novum Organum*, first published in 1620. Aristotle's logical works had long borne the title of the *Organon* and Bacon chose his title to announce the end of the Aristotelian influence, which he blamed for what *he* considered the barren landscape of medieval intellectual life. In the *Novum Organum*, man is exhorted to interpret nature to discover the laws of nature. Bacon disdains the vain attempts to extract truth deductively by the use of syllogistic forms and advocates induction, the employment of systematic observation, experimentation, and reasoning about things and their modes of behavior. In brief, he sets out to analyze the inductive method and demonstrates what conditions must be fulfilled so true knowledge can be obtained.

In the course of this work—the analysis and illustration of the method of inductive research—Bacon 'discovered' obstacles in the path of true knowledge: the '*idols*,' or fallacies to which the mind is especially subject in the attempt to reach truth. He believed that man must reduce himself to a blank tablet, if he wants to understand nature correctly. The observer of nature must enter this realm free from all prejudices which distort reality; but man is hindered by various illusions, both native and acquired (*idola mentis*).

A typology of intellectual fallacies

The idols and false notions which have already preoccupied the human understanding, and are deeply rooted in it, not only so beset men's minds that they become difficult of access, but even when access is obtained will again meet and trouble us in the instauration of the sciences. To counteract their influence men must be warned so that they can guard themselves with all possible care against the idols. Bacon distinguishes four species of idols which beset the human mind and he calls the first *Idols of the Tribe*, the second *Idols of the Cave*, the third *Idols of the Market*, the fourth *Idols of the Theater*.

The idols of the tribe (*idola tribus*) are inherent in human nature and the very tribe or race of man; this Bacon attributes to the false claim that human intelligence is the measure of things. Actually *mankind* suffers from serious intellectual inadequacies, exemplified by the tendency to believe only what is pleasing and to disregard what is not.

The idols of the cave (*idola specus*) reflect *individual* prejudices and intellectual shortcomings. Errors arise because we are particular kinds of beings with limited ranges of experience and knowledge. We all interpret the world around us from the restricted, provincial viewpoint of the particular 'cave' we happen to occupy: all thoughts are affected by the personal situation of the thinker.

Other distortions stem from associated living and from the failure of language to properly communicate ideas. These twin problems find their conceptualization in the idols of the market (*idola fori*) which show that language and thus thought are socially determined: words are shaped by the aspirations and will of the majority which render them inexact and faulty. Therefore, men are endlessly plagued by confusion, vain controversies, and fallacies.[2]

Bacon ascribes the idols of the theater (*idola theatri*) to the influence of traditional theories. Aristotelianism is his hated example; but errors arising from received opinion and systems of philosophy are as general as all others. Without exception philosophers have failed to advance knowledge—they merely created 'fictitious and theatrical worlds.' In the exact sciences, as well, many theories and axioms gained acceptance simply because of the human tendency to set tradition and majority opinion above critical, independent inquiry.

The origin of idols

The idols of the tribe are caused by a number of elements; they arise from the alleged uniformity of the constitution of the human mind, from man's prejudices, and the limited intellectual faculties of man. Furthermore, they arise from the interference of human passions, from the incompetency of the senses, or the mode of their impressions.

The origin of the idols of the cave is seen in the particular nature of each individual's mind and body, and in education, habit, and personal circumstance. They are furthermore caused by some predominant pursuit, or by an excess in synthesis and analysis, by a bias in favor of certain periods, and by the scope of a researcher's subject matter.

The distortions caused by the idols of the cave call for the greatest caution. Here we are confronted by influences which exert formidable power in polluting our understanding: extreme specialization in scientific pursuits is a case in point. The bias in favor of certain periods was of special interest to Bacon, who himself was battling the rule of Aristotelianism, the authoritarian intellectual system of his own time. He argued that some scientists and philosophers betray an unlimited admiration for antiquity; others, however, make their mistakes by going too far in the opposite direction because of their uncritical and eager acceptance of novelty.[3]

The idols of the market are the most troublesome of all. Their distorting influence stems from the rule of words and names over reason —undoubtedly Bacon had an early semantic awareness concerning the tyranny of words over philosophy and science. The idols of the market are subdivided: one type stems from the practice to invent names for things which have no existence outside the fanciful imagination of certain thinkers. The *primum mobile* is such an empty word derived from false and futile theories. The second type is represented by the names of actual, ontically real objects which are, however, confused, badly defined, and hastily and inaccurately abstracted from things. The first type can be destroyed with relative ease by the refutation of the phantastic theories which gave rise to it. The idols of the second type, derived from faulty abstraction, are more deeply rooted in man's mind.[4]

The idols of the theater are numerous and Bacon foresees that there will even be more of them as time goes on. He derived the term from a comparison between the stage of philosophical speculation and the poetical stage; the plots enacted upon the stage of philosophy resemble those of the poetical and dramatic theater since both are invented for the sake of consistency, elegance, pleasure, and both differ from the less glittering but more accurate plots of real history.

Along with the term 'idols of the theater' Bacon uses the more obvious synonym 'idols of theories' to indicate that these obstacles in the path of knowledge originate in the fictitious theories and corrupted rules of demonstration of 'false philosophy.' Actually there are three sources of error giving birth to three types of false philosophy: the *sophistic*, the *empiric*, and the *superstitious*.

The 'sophistic' or 'theoretic' philosophers err by taking for the groundwork of their philosophy either too much from a few topics, or too little from many; their philosophy has an insufficient experimental basis and never attains to the certainty of results that only repeated observation can achieve.[5] Essentially their systems are founded on vulgar notions—the commonplace.

Similarly distorted are the systems of the empiric philosophers who have diligently and accurately attended to a few experiments. They left the path of realistic knowledge when they set out to deduce and invent systems of philosophy on this scanty basis. They did violence to the facts when they furthermore presumed to form everything to conformity with their insufficiently empirical systems of philosophy.

Faith and religious veneration have persuaded the superstitious philosophers to rely on theology and tradition; some of them have gone so far as to 'derive the sciences from spirits and genii.'

The significance of Bacon's philosophy

Bacon was not content with depicting the past and heralding the future; he also contributed to the advancement of science. First of all, he showed that man is the interpreter of nature, that truth is not derived from authority, that knowledge is the product of experience. He gave to logic the method of *ampliative inference* which employs analogy to infer from the properties of a single *datum* the characteristics of the larger group to which that *datum* belongs, leaving to subsequent experience the correction of evident errors. This technique constituted an advance over the older method of induction by simple enumeration, whereby general conclusions were derived from a number of particular data. The new technique of *ampliative inference* promoted greater boldness in the formulation of hypotheses—an important step in the direction of scientific progress had been taken.

In his *Novum Organum*, Bacon promulgated a new scientific spirit of more objective and exact observation and experimentation. His postulate to free the mind from all prejudices and preconceived attitudes—embodied in the various species of idols—represents an important milestone in the development of modern scientific method.

The English philosopher did not question the ability of the human mind to perceive the phenomena of nature. On the other hand, man has failed to utilize this perceptive potential because of a number of obstacles that have so far obscured his knowledge: the deductive method, the syllogism, and the *idola mentis* which dominate the human understanding.

Bacon accuses the Greek and medieval philosophers of having sacrificed the study of nature by wasting their energies on mere words and concepts. Against the deductive and syllogistic logic of the past he pits induction and experimentation. His critique of the human understanding is contained in his theory of idols which is to safeguard our understanding of nature. This precaution is necessary because of the properties of the human mind which Bacon compares to an 'uneven mirror' that changes the reflection of the objects because of its peculiar shape.

Bacon assumes that certain species of idols are learned while others are innate. In the first case, their destruction is difficult, but possible. In the second instance, however, the idols cannot be annihilated— man can only hope to bring the innate idols into his consciousness so that their hidden power may be known and overcome.

Our understanding is furthermore endangered because of the powerful influence of the human will. For Bacon the human mind is 'not a dry light' but subject to the influence of our will, our affections and feelings which sway the intellect in many different and often imperceptible ways; the idols are to a large extent products of the human will and of human feelings. Bacon's critique of the human understanding is, therefore, basically aimed at the analysis of the psychological preconditions of intellectual operations. He hopes to bring into consciousness the subjective elements of feeling and the social factors which hinder our understanding of nature. Once man knows the obstacles in the path of true knowledge he will be able to attack and remove the sources of error. Bacon's concept of truth is based on the idea that man is able to establish an adequate relation-ship between existence and consciousness.

Our understanding is also endangered by superstition. Bacon arrived at this argument probably under the impression which the religious struggle of the sixteenth century had made upon him. He favored a clear division between philosophy and theology, between knowledge and faith, to avoid the corruption of philosophy as evidenced by *scholasticism*. In the first book *Of the Proficience and Advancement of Learning*, Bacon attributes to superstition and religious fanaticism the same pernicious influence that he attributes to the *idola mentis* in his *Novum Organum*. The four species of idols are thus augmented by superstition—by perverted religion. Super-stition mainly results from the vested interests of the clergy, which pits itself as a social class against the rest of society.

The philosophers of the French Enlightenment were quick to

realize the dynamic potential of the theory of idols; because of the close connection between this theory and Bacon's critique of (religious) superstition, they could use it as a weapon in their attack upon religion.

Basically the theory of idols was only applicable to the physical sciences. But this limitation could not be maintained for very long.[6] Soon the philosophers of the eighteenth century were to develop Bacon's critique of idols into the *theory of prejudice*. Especially the philosophers of the French Enlightenment widened Bacon's theory by intensifying the critique of religion and by radically expanding the theory of idols that was henceforth to encompass state and society. Now all sciences were subject to the suspicion of ideological distortion. It must be realized, however, that Bacon had viewed the social order as something that was hopelessly subject to authority, tradition, and irrational opinions. In this realm, innovations could only endanger the existing balance.

In contrast, the philosophers of the Enlightenment maintained a far more optimistic view of the social world. They believed in a social order based on reason and natural law and interpreted the absence of such a rational order in state and society by reference to the prejudices which tend to obscure its existence. They were, however, intent upon the discovery of this rational order; the theory of idols assumed a definitely political character, as soon as it had been transformed into the theory of prejudices. The irrational basis of the existing state and of religion was now exposed as an idol, as a prejudice, that had to answer the summons of the tribunal of reason.

The destruction of metaphysics

The philosophers of the French Enlightenment—the *philosophes*—who made the Great French Encyclopedia a reality were to a large extent the intellectual heirs of Bacon, the progenitor of English materialism. Bacon, whose thinking anciently connects with the *homoiomeriae* of Anaxagoras and the atoms of Democritus, hypostatized the physical sciences and especially physics. With Bacon, all science rests upon experience and consists in subjecting the data furnished by the senses—the infallible source of all knowledge—to a rational method of investigation which has observation, experimentation, comparison, induction, and analysis for its instruments.

With Hobbes, knowledge based upon the senses becomes the abstract experience of the mathematician who reduces the movement of matter to mechanical or mathematical processes thereby losing track of the vital spirit which Bacon had emphasized in his description of the qualities inherent in matter movement. Hobbes's systematization of Baconian materialism, furthermore, failed to establish

Bacon's thesis concerning the origin of all knowledge in the senses on firm grounds.

It was not until John Locke investigated the nature and validity of human knowledge in his *Essay Concerning Human Understanding* (1690) that Bacon's and Hobbes's fundamental principle was provided with a firmer basis. Locke's ideas were to have special importance for the course of events on the other side of the English Channel: they provided the final blow to the metaphysical tradition which still held the seventeenth century spell-bound. Thus, Locke gave the signal for the attack of the *philosophes* upon all metaphysics, especially that of Descartes, Malebranche, Leibniz, and Spinoza, and the resulting fight against the extant political institutions and their supposed ally: theology and religion.

Thus France, where the old order of things had reached a greater degree of contemptuous definiteness than in England and Germany, was revolutionized *pace* English ideas. After Voltaire's and Montesquieu's visits to England the island's philosophical, political, religious, scientific, and aesthetic thought-styles found their way into France and the Continent generally. In 1734 the hangman burned as irreligious and subversive Voltaire's just-published synthesis of his English experience, the *Lettres philosophiques*. But after that Voltaire frequently based his sarcastic criticism of the Church's theology and the established order of things on English notions, such as Locke's principle that all our ideas proceed from experience, Hume's psychological approach to the history of religion, the critical deism of men like Woolston, and above all Newton's discovery of the uniformity of nature and his 'refusal to make hypotheses.' Montesquieu, enamored with the English form of constitution, criticized the French conditions incisively in his *Esprit des lois*, which he published in 1748.

The immediate follower and interpreter of Locke, however, was Condillac, who did not hesitate to turn the sensationalism of the English physician upon the metaphysics of the seventeenth century.

Condillac referred conscious experience to passive sensations when he tried to simplify Locke's epistemology in his *Traité des sensations* (1754). Furthermore, he augmented Locke's position in his *L'Essai sur l'origine des connaissances humaines*, in as much as he conceived of the senses and the apparatus of sensual receptivity as themselves being dependent upon experience. Now man's development was subject to external circumstances and education. Although Condillac, who was a priest and an abbé, never openly doubted theology, he, nevertheless, accepted Locke's scepticism as to the power of the mind to reveal the real nature of outer objects. Moreover, his *Traité des systèmes* clearly rejects the metaphysical assumptions of Descartes, Leibniz, Spinoza, and Malebranche. Helvétius demonstrated in his

De l'esprit that all the operations and contents of the mind originated in sense-perception and proceeded to establish an ethical and political theory that viewed moral ideals and norms as the outgrowth of the basic sensations of pleasure and pain. In Helvétius' *De l'homme*, English materialism, then, found its application to social life; the foundation of morality was now seen in sensual qualities and egotism, enjoyment and enlightened self-interest.

In 1770 Holbach (1723–89) published his *Système de la nature*, where materialism found its most systematic elaboration in the synthesis of English and French materialism as derived from Cartesian physics. Holbach's discussion of morals is based essentially on the ethics of Helvétius (1715–71).

Thought and existence

The question concerning the relationship between thinking and being is increasingly becoming a major concern of modern intellectual pursuits. This disturbing question dates back to medieval *scholasticism*, where the primacy of nature and mind was debated. At the close of the Middle Ages, the question appeared in sharper formulation: did God create the world or did it always exist?

Those philosophers who maintained the primacy of mind over nature assumed ultimately that the universe had somehow been created and, thus, formed the various schools of *idealism*. Other thinkers, however, claimed the primacy of nature and initiated the varieties of *materialism*.

According to a radically materialistic position—such as the one held by Holbach—man is born into the world with nothing but the capacity to register sensations. His intellectual abilities are only an outgrowth of these basic sensory capacities. Some sensations that man receives from the objects will be to his liking; others will cause him pain. Thus, man will call everything that causes pleasure, good, and everything that results in pain, he will call bad. From this materialistic position it follows that, should a person be the source of pain, he would be called bad. Or differently worded: a person who hurts his fellow creatures is bad; another, who does good for them, is good. These simple relationships in the epistemological as well as in the ethical realm are, however, disturbed and distorted through the operation of a number of factors. First of all, as Holbach teaches, man is only bad because he has an *interest* in being bad.

The philosophers worked with the conception that three *prejudices* operate to cause errors and deceptions which distort men's relations to the objects constituting their world: *idols, interests, priestly fraud.* They largely accepted Bacon's theory of idols as a conceptual model for dealing with the problems of distorted perception and error. They did not signally contribute, however, to the further advancement of the theory. The main contribution of the *philosophes* must be seen in the elaboration of the third source of error: priestly deceit. The emphasis upon the cunning of the priests is probably a result of the antireligious program of the French Enlightenment, which sets this strand of the European Enlightenment apart from the English and especially German movements which were less radical in their approach to religion. The attack upon religion is, furthermore, the only motive that the different representatives of the French school really share. In many other respects, especially with regard to methodology and philosophical outlook, one philosopher was often the worst antagonist of another. Holbach and Helvétius, for example, were actually *encyclopédistes* by mere association. They found no admirers among their associates for their cut and dried methodological premisses and they contributed little to the *Encyclopédie*. But in their criticism of religion they reflected the position of their contemporaries, although in its most radical and outspoken manner. Drawing upon these two men, therefore, means to get at the strongest statement of the Enlightenment attitude toward religion, which amounts to a declaration of open warfare. Driven by Voltaire's battle cry, *écrasez l'infâme*, the Encylopedists accused 'religion, of having been an eternal hindrance to intellectual progress and of having been incapable of founding a genuine morality and a just social and political order.'[7]

This antireligious theory divides mankind into two groups: a small elite, with access to truth, and the mass of people living in the darkness of superstition and error. The priests know truth but they deliberately keep it from the masses to maintain their powerful grip over them. Simultaneously, the *philosophes* inform the masses that they have exposed the cunning and deceit of the priests and encourage the people to rebel against the fraudulent rulers that have subjugated them for so long with the help of religion, metaphysics, and pseudo-scientific dogmas.

The theory of priestly deceit has rarely been used in this pure form. Most of the time it made its appearance in combination with the 'interest theory.' The priests were accused of exploiting their knowledge and power to advance their economic interests. In this combination the theory charged the ideological adversary with deliberate lying: the enemy was pictured as using the weapon of ideas to consciously falsify reality.

This, however, was only one variant of the interest theory. First, it must be understood that this theory constituted probably the most important thesis of Enlightenment philosophy. Basically, the interest theory represented the stubborn epistemological optimism of this intellectual movement, in as much as man was credited with the ability to conceive truth. The problem of distorted or ideological knowledge entered as a *psychological* phenomenon: man is able to see truth, but he rejects it because it conflicts with his interests. Thus man may block his own path to truth in following his interests. The source of ideology in this case is man's will. The therapy consists of making this voluntaristic element conscious. Once we are *conscious* of the falsifying power of our *will* we are able to hinder and paralyze it. This is the other variant of the interest theory which still credits man with good faith; it goes back into antiquity and also finds an appropriate formulation in the Hobbesian proposition that man will go against reason, as soon as reason goes against man.

The first-mentioned variant of the interest theory, however, does no longer credit the falsifier of truth with good faith; it indicts him as a *deliberate liar*. In this instance, man, principally equipped to see truth, keeps it away from others to further his selfish interests. Here the therapy must come from outside forces: enlightening education of the victims of the falsifiers of truth. In this connection the *philosophes* saw themselves as therapists. Their major target was the priests as falsifiers of truth; their patients were the people deliberately kept in superstition and ignorance by the representatives of religion. The plot against truth assumed even more sinister forms through the alliance between throne and altar. In the opinion of the philosophers, the priests were seeking additional power by drawing the representatives of the political order into their antitruth conspiracy; the intellectuals, therefore, constantly tried to drive a wedge between the monarch and the priests.

Among the philosophers, two especially stand out for their religious, political, and social criticism: Helvétius and Holbach. Throughout their writings we find the complaint that the prejudices work against man's attempts to realize his personal happiness and a rational social order.

The radicalism of Helvétius and Holbach

Bacon meant to safeguard our understanding of *nature* from the pernicious influence of the idols. Helvétius and Holbach wanted to establish the objective and independent understanding of *social reality*. The rational reconstruction of the social order begins for these authors with a 'sociological' interpretation of the ideas which guide men in their behavior and actions; ideas which men mistake for an objective reflection of social reality. This approach implies the analysis of society's influence upon the formation and the content of ideas.

Helvétius argues: 'our ideas are ... of necessity the consequences of the societies we live in.'[8] The reactions of people to different occurrences and facts change as we move from one standpoint to another. Men accept only the ideas and conceptual perspectives that correspond to their particular social position and occupation; they are products of society and their minds are quite passive. Consequently, the importance of education is paramount: *'L'éducation peut tout.'*[9] The progress of education, however, presupposes political progress. Under an enlightened and constitutional government, there develops a human type that is upright, courageous, frank, and loyal. A despotic government, in contrast, breeds men that are 'vile, without spirit and courage.' Helvétius attributes this difference in the character of people to the 'different education received under one or the other of these governments.'[10]

Ethical ideas are also socially determined. 'The sentiments of father-love, mother-love, and child-love merely result from reflection and habit. All ideas, all the concepts of men are acquired.'[11] What, then, is virtue? 'He is virtuous who does good for his fellow citizens. The word virtue always includes the idea of some public usefulness.' Saints therefore are not virtuous. They have done no good for the earthly life. They are as dishonest as the scoundrel who 'converts at the moment of death, he is saved; he is quite happy; but he is not virtuous. A person merits this name only through habitually just and noble conduct.'[12]

The ethical sphere is, furthermore, dominated by the relativism which characterizes all social action. The centuries lead, 'in both a physical and moral sense, to revolutions which change the face of Empires . . . in great confusion . . . the same actions can become successively useful and detrimental and consequently, can be called in turn both virtuous and vicious.'[13] Therefore, each nation 'esteems in others only those ideas which are analogous to its own; all contrary opinion is therefore a germ of contempt between them.'[14]

Holbach also claims that *existence determines thought*: 'Our ways of thinking are necessarily determined by the circumstances of our existence.'[15] Most philosophers have been unable to see the important influence which the environment exerts upon man's thinking and behavior, because of their one-sided fascination with the alleged freedom of the will.[16]

Ideas and values are socially determined, because thinking and acting are determined by interests which are always shaped by social conditions and needs. According to Helvétius, it is always personal interest which produces the astonishing diversity of opinion.[17] The different moral, political, and philosophical beliefs result from the fact that it is against man's interest to see things as they really are: 'the Public never takes advice unless to its interest;' it never esteems intellectual and artistic achievements with regard to quality but only with regard to the 'advantage which it reaps from them.'[18] In other

GUNTER W. REMMLING

words, we do not judge objects, ideas, or human actions by their inherent value but by the utility that they possess for ourselves or our group.[19]

In *De l'esprit*, Helvétius taught that self-love is the essence of man, the driving force behind his actions, and that it is necessarily one with love of power, since man can only fulfill his desires if he possesses the means to reach his goals. From here important political consequences follow:

Tyrants and fanatics have always 'felt that their power had only human ignorance and imbecility as its foundation: thus, they have always imposed silence on whoever, in uncovering the true principles of morals to the nations, would have revealed all their misfortunes and all their rights to them, and would have armed them against injustice.'[20]

Similarly, persecutions of defenseless people are triggered off by egotistical interests. *'L'intérêt est toujours le motif caché de la persécution.'*[21]

On this basis Helvétius developed his psychological theory and practice of unmasking and debunking. Now it becomes clear that the socially determined ideas, i.e. the prejudices, result from the love of power. The prejudices hide the love of power. The philosopher of the Enlightenment has the supreme task of unmasking this fact.[22]

Notes

1 Cf. Francis Bacon, *Advancement of Learning and Novum Organum*, New York: Wiley, 1944, p. 370.
2 Cf. *ibid.*, pp. 319–20.
3 Cf. *ibid.*, p. 323.
4 Cf. *ibid.*, p. 325.
5 Cf. *ibid.*, p. 326.
6 Cf. Hans Barth, *Wahrheit und Ideologie*, Zürich: Manesse, 1945, p. 52.
7 Ernst Cassirer, *The Philosophy of the Enlightenment* (trans. F. C. A. Koelln and J. P. Pettegrove), Boston: Beacon Press, 1955, p. 134.
8 Claude Adrien Helvétius, *Oeuvres complètes*, vol. 1: *De l'esprit*, Paris: Lepetit, 1818, p. 104 (my translation).
9 *Ibid.*, vol. 2: *De l'homme*, Paris: Lepetit, 1818, p. 566.
10 *Ibid.*, pp. 566–7 (my translation).
11 Claude Adrien Helvétius, *Neunundzwanzig Thesen des Materialismus*, Halle a. S.: Erlecke, 1873, p. 14 (my translation).
12 Helvétius, *De l'homme*, London: Société Typographique, 1774, p. 76 (my translation).
13 Helvétius, *De l'esprit*, Paris: Durand, 1776, p. 107 (my translation).
14 *Ibid.*, p. 169 (my translation).
15 Paul Henri Thiry Holbach, *Système de la nature*, pt 1, London, 1770, p. 200 (my translation).

16 Cf. *ibid.*, pp. 200–3.
17 Cf. Helvétius, *De l'esprit*, p. 75.
18 *Ibid.*, p. 97 (my translation).
19 Cf. *ibid.*, p. 96.
20 *Ibid.*, pp. 180–1 (my translation).
21 *Ibid.*, p. 182n.
22 Cf. Helvétius, *Oeuvres complètes*, vol. 2, pp. 211–12.

3 Elements of a sociology of ideas in the Saint-Simonian philosophy of history

Georg G. Iggers

The question has often been raised whether a sociology of knowledge existed in French thought before Marx. As a historian of early nineteenth-century French thought and a student, though not a disciple, of the Saint-Simonians, I have attempted in this paper to shed some light on the question.

The nonsociologist who approaches the literature of the sociology of knowledge is bewildered by the diversity of theories and methodologies. In a narrower sense, sociology of knowledge in the tradition of Marx and Mannheim implies the causal relationship of mental productions to isolable social factors and at least the theoretical assumption that the hypotheses of the sociology of knowledge must be empirically validated; in a wider sense, the only kinds of definitions offered for the sociology of knowledge which would include the theoretical efforts of men like Scheler, Sorokin, Durkheim, and others as well, seem to be the very broad ones such as 'primarily concerned with the relations between knowledge and other existential factors in the society or culture,'[1] with an analysis of the 'relationship between knowledge and existence,'[2] or with the study of 'the relatedness of knowledge and cognition to social existence.'[3]

Without going into the question of the point in time at which thinking about the relationship of ideas and society first constituted a sociology of knowledge (a problem on which there is little agreement in the literature) and without answering directly the inquiry whether the Saint-Simonian philosophy of society contained a sociology of knowledge, I shall restrict myself to tracing elements of a sociology of ideas in Saint-Simonian writings. As a theory of ideology which attempts to link ideas to the interests of specific social classes or groups in the Marxian or Mannheimian sense, it is very doubtful whether we can speak of a Saint-Simonian contribution except in a rudimentary sense. Nor is there, on the part of the Saint-

Simonians, any attempt at empirical validation of their hypotheses. As a matter of fact, the disciples of Saint-Simon—who are to be kept clearly distinct in this paper from their master, the Count Henri de Saint-Simon and from Auguste Comte—strongly question the utility of an empirical approach and stress the role of intuitional factors in the formulation of a science of society. But in a wider sense, the Saint-Simonian philosophy of knowledge is based on a concept of the social origin and social character of all cognition.

The Saint-Simonians had their two principal intellectual roots in the Enlightenment and in early nineteenth-century French counter-revolutionary Catholic thought. In a sense, the Enlightenment excluded a sociology of knowledge in its conception of natural law which rested on the assumption that certain universal ideas, e.g., the natural rights of man, were subject to human cognition following correct rational thinking independently of time or milieu.[4] In contrast, Catholic thinkers, like de Maistre, de Bonald, and Lamennais during his ultramontane period, emphasized the organismic character of society and the interconnectedness of social institutions and mental productions.[5] Despite their acceptance of an organismic view of society, both Henri de Saint-Simon in most of his writings and Auguste Comte at least in the *Cours de philosophie positive* assumed that fundamental to the history of civilization was the transformation of ideas from a conjectural to a positive state, which would at each stage of development express itself in corresponding changes in social institutions.[6] A basic distinction between the Saint-Simonian writers on the one hand and Saint-Simon and Comte on the other was the former's rejection of the assumptions that the history of man was essentially that of his enlightenment and that scientific ideas were isolable prime factors of social change.

Rather, for the Saint-Simonians, knowledge and ideas could at no point be isolated from their social context. Agreeing with de Maistre and Lamennais that the general ideas upon which society was based were religious in character,[7] the Saint-Simonians made it clear that they conceived of religion, 'the social link,'[8] as essentially referring to a reality immanent in society and nature rather than transcending it.[9] Thus 'any theological or metaphysical problem which does not originate from a conception of society and does not relate to society lacks any real basis, and any solution of a religious problem which cannot be translated into political terms is necessarily meaningless.'[10] Religion, although considered to be at the basis of society, was never viewed by the Saint-Simonians in abstract theological terms or, as in the case of Comte, as a pre-scientific theory of reality but rather as the 'general doctrine,' a *Weltanschauung* which determined the total pattern of social attitudes and their translation into institutional forms.[11]

All ideas, whether scientific, legal, aesthetic, economic, philosophic, religious, or literary were therefore understood in terms of two general factors: 'statically,' to borrow an expression from Comte, in terms of the type of society in which they arose; 'dynamically' in terms of the position of that society in the historical process. The history of mankind was conceived not as being in its substructure intellectual history as for Saint-Simon and Comte, but as primarily the development of human society from 'antagonism' and a stage of relatively little organization to the 'universal association, which is to say the association of all men on the entire surface of the globe in all spheres of their relationships,'[12] a society in which all aspects of cultural activity would be thoroughly organized and planned. Progress operated not unilinearly but in terms of an alternativity of two types of epochs or societies, 'organic' ones, in which the final, normative society was imperfectly mirrored, and 'critical' ones, arising from the inner contradictions of the organic ones which they were destined to destroy.[13] Organic periods were religious in nature and were marked by an attitude of faith and reliance on religious and intellectual authorities; critical periods, like those of post-Socratic Greece and Rome and post-Reformation Europe, were 'philosophic,' marked by doubt, individualism, and the rejection of authority.[14] All mental productions were either critical or organic in character and further reflected their relative location in history in the development from a military society based on the exploitation of man by man to the industrial society based on a systemic organized exploitation of the globe by man.[15]

The basic consequence of this conception of society and history was that knowledge could not be understood purely or even primarily in terms of truth. In the first chapter of the *Doctrine de Saint-Simon. Exposition,* the most important Saint-Simonian theoretical work, Bazard emphasized that the method of modern science since Bacon was not the only possible valid scientific method but merely one which corresponded to the analytical spirit of the critical age.[16] In organic ages, scientists relied much more heavily on intuition and particularly on the insights of genius.[17] According to the 'positivists,' the Saint-Simonians claimed, scientific method consisted in drawing an inventory of observed facts which if exact would present to the observing eye the law of the succession of all the facts. But this was not the case; there was no inherent logical relationship between two facts that could be established by empirical observation. Hence non-logical, non-empirical thought processes had to enter into the formulation of scientific laws.[18] Comte's law of the three stages, by which all sciences passed from a theological through a metaphysical to a positive stage, had to be rejected;[19] rather there was statically a critical, i.e., analytic or positive, science, in which scientists working in relative isolation amassed relatively uncorrelated data and held a mechanistic, atheistic conception of the nature of the universe,[20] and an organic, or theological, science in which scientists, guided by a general doctrine and organized as a body, systematized known knowledge into an encyclopedia or dogma.[21] Historically, the history of science, following the patterns of social organization from heterogeneity to homogeneity, did not witness the replacement of religion by science but rather a transformation of religious doctrines —understood in the wide social meaning of the term 'religion' as used by the Saint-Simonians—from fetishism, the belief in many causes, to the reduction of all phenomena to one cause.[22]

In an article several years before the publication of the *Doctrine de Saint-Simon*, Enfantin had already employed a theory of the social origin of political economy. All human conceptions at every epoch, as well as the different methods which had been successively used in the observation and the co-ordination of phenomena, had been related to the general idea of the civilization from which they proceeded. It was therefore incorrect to say that Adam Smith or any other man had founded a science. Yet the science of political economy was first developed in his time. It developed within a definite historical framework, within a civilization which had evolved as a revolt against the institutions and beliefs of the Middle Ages. Economic science was the protest against tutelage in the field of economics. Not only the origin but also the concepts of the science were socially conditioned, influenced to a large degree by the social relations that existed when the science originated.[23] The *Doctrine* itself pointed out that theories of property or of inheritance, 'generally considered to be sheltered from any moral or legal revolution,'[24] had always adjusted themselves to changes in the constitution of property as had conceptions of divine right, natural law, or utility invoked 'to consecrate the inviolability . . . of the existing organization of property.'[25] Similarly, legal thought, rather than deriving from an abstract conception of justice or of natural law, was always an expression of social conditions. Modern penology, punitive rather than correctional,[26] with its narrow definition of crime which excluded the economic and intellectual spheres from state control,[27] was an expression of the critical character of our society. Similarly such political concepts as the contractual theory of government,[28] the 'metaphysics of natural rights,'[29] and the doctrine of popular sovereignty[30] expressed the political sentiments of a critical age rather than the findings of a political science or the results of formal reasoning. If the non-objective element in political philosophy may readily be admitted, Bazard in an early article pointed out that historiography, too, rather than being an objective description of given facts, was basically interpretative and conditioned by social and historical factors.[31]

63

Aesthetics was regarded by the Saint-Simonians as a branch of social philosophy. Artistic creation was a social act which could be understood only within the framework of the social conditions which surrounded the artist. 'Every writer shared the sentiments of his time, the manners, prejudices, and opinions of the moment.'[32] The art critic of the Saint-Simonian daily, *Le Globe*, asked whether 'the artists who bemoan the destruction of the old cathedrals and castles have not understood that these buildings had to disappear with the social institutions for which they stood as symbols.'[33] Historically, art showed the steady displacement of military by industrial ideals, from pagan heroic epics to social realism.[34] Statically, art in organic periods represented collective work expressing the basic ideals of the collectivity as in the case of the Gothic cathedral or the epic,[35] while in critical periods theories of pure art emerged:[36] art became either a vehicle of social criticism or satire as in the eighteenth century[37] or, if detached from any conception of social responsibility, turned into impressionistic entertainment for the leisure classes[38] or into romantic despair.[39] Similarly, religion in critical periods, in so far as it survived, became 'mystic' in character, i.e., concerned with personal religiosity rather than with strengthening the feeling of social belonging.[40] Going beyond the analysis of the conditions of artistic creativity, the Saint-Simonians maintained that art appreciation, too, was determined by the two categories of history and society. The beautiful, always symbolic of an age and of a society, was strictly time-bound. Modern man, sharing in a different symbolism, could find no inspiration or true beauty in the art of the past which was technically and morally at a lower stage of development and which could only amuse.[41] Hence the interest in Shakespeare, 'a great poet doubtless but one who wrote in the infancy of dramatic art,'[42] was to be deplored. Modern literature to be meaningful must turn to bourgeois reality.[43]

In conclusion we may ask what was the significance of the Saint-Simonian endeavor in the study of the social relatedness of ideas. Doubtless there were elements of a sociology of knowledge. While basic Saint-Simonian concepts were shared closely with Henri de Saint-Simon, Comte, and some of the Catholic counterrevolutionary thinkers, the Saint-Simonians' unique contributions were (1) the thorough social conception of ideas as well as (2) the more extensive attempt to establish the social relatedness of various kinds of mental productions. On the other hand, it is still a far step from the Saint-Simonian explanation of the origin of all ideas in terms of vaguely defined and never proved *a priori* laws of progress or of the alternativity of two types of society to attempts to establish empirically validable hypotheses regarding specifically isolable factors in the production of ideas. While never losing their master's faith that empirical inquiry would bear out the lawful character of social change, the Saint-Simonians—at this point perhaps intellectually more honest than their rival Comte—admitted that their doctrine, like all great social theories, was not the outcome of empirical inquiry but was a fruit of intuition. Empirical inquiry, concerned with validation, never preceded but followed the insights of genius.[44] Thus their lack of knowledge of the details of oriental history did not prevent them from reconstructing its main outlines within the Saint-Simonian philosophy of history since subsequent archeological and historical discoveries would merely confirm what has already followed *a priori* from the doctrine.[45] Fundamentally thus the Saint-Simonian conception of society constituted a religious or philosophic *Weltanschauung* rather than scientific sociology.

Notes

1 Robert K. Merton, 'The Sociology of Knowledge' in Georges Gurvitch and Wilbert E. Moore (eds), *Twentieth Century Sociology*, New York: Philosophical Library, 1945, p. 366.

2 Karl Mannheim, *Ideology and Utopia: An Introduction to the Sociology of Knowledge* (trans. Louis Wirth and Edward Shils), New York: Harcourt, Brace & World, 1936, p. 264.

3 Ernst Grünwald, *Das Problem der Soziologie des Wissens*, Vienna and Leipzig: Braumüller, 1934, p. 2.

4 Grünwald, however, sees in what he calls the Enlightenment's 'theory of deception by the priests' (*Priestertrugtheorie*) one of the sources of the sociology of knowledge: *ibid.*, p. 5.

5 See particularly Joseph de Maistre, *Essai sur le principe générateur des constitutions politiques*, Paris: Société Typographique, 1814; and Félicité de La Mennais, *Essai sur l'indifférence en matière de religion* (4 vols), Paris: Tournachon-Molin et Seguin, 1817, and *De la religion considérée dans ses rapports avec l'ordre politique et civil* in *Oeuvres complètes de F. de La Mennais*, Paris: Bureau du 'Mémorial catholique', 1825, reprinted Frankfurt: Minerva, 1967, vol. 7.

6 Cf. Auguste Comte, *The Positive Philosophy* (trans. Harriet Martineau), London: Bell, 1896, vol. 1, p. 1 ff.

7 Cf. de La Mennais, *Essai*, vol. 1, pp. 30, 35 ff., 262 ff.; *De la religion*, p. 15; *Doctrine de Saint-Simon. Exposition*. Première année, 1829 (ed. C. Bouglé and Elie Halévy), Paris: Rivière, 1924, p. 199. An English translation of this work is now available: *The Doctrine of Saint Simon: An Exposition*. (First Year, 1828–9), (trans. with notes and an introduction by Georg G. Iggers), Boston: Beacon Press, 1958.

8 Eugène Rodrigues, 'Lettres' in *Nouveau Christianisme. Lettres d'Eugène Rodrigues, L'éducation du genre humain*, Paris, 1832, p. 138; cf. pp. 136–7; cf. Transon in *Oeuvres de Saint-Simon et d'Enfantin* (47 vols), Paris: Dentu, 1865–78, vol. 44, p. 16 (hereafter referred to as *Oeuvres*).

9 See the discussion of a dynamic in contrast to Spinoza's supposedly static pantheism in Rodrigues, pp. 130–1, 160; and *Oeuvres*, vol. 42, pp. 293, 308 ff.

10 *Oeuvres*, vol. 42, p. 298 (author's translation).

11 See *Doctrine*, p. 161: 'The most general fact in the growth of societies, the one which implicitly includes all the others, is the progress of the moral conception by which man becomes conscious of a social destiny. The political institution is the realization, that is, the putting into practice of this conception, its application to the establishment, preservation and progressive development of social relationships' (author's translation).

12 *Doctrine*, pp. 203–4.

13 *Ibid.*, pp. 127 ff., 412, and *passim*.

14 Cf. *ibid.*, pp. 128, 144, 196 ff., 224, 409–10, 440, 488, and *passim*.

15 Cf. *ibid.*, pp. 161–2, 203 ff., 223 ff. on the decline of exploitation; regarding the relation of religious ideas to this development, see pp. 227 ff., 429 ff., and the Second Year of the *Doctrine de Saint-Simon. Exposition*, in *Oeuvres*, vol. 42, pp. 151 ff.

16 *Doctrine*, pp. 132, 191. Regarding the possibility of other approaches to science than the rational method, see 'Troisième Séance. Conception. Méthode. Classification Historique,' *ibid.*, pp. 179 ff.

17 While critical periods amassed scientific data, only organic epochs would find scientists capable of synthesizing this material. Yet the great scientific hypotheses were never primarily the result of 'method' but of 'genius'. Cf. 'Troisième Séance', *passim*.

18 Regarding the limitations of positivistic method, see *Doctrine*, pp. 182–3. As to the similarity of the process of scientific thinking to that of artistic creativity, see *ibid.*, p. 190; for the assertion that all reasoning proceeds on nonrational foundations, *ibid.*, p. 449. Cf. p. 453: 'Indeed, progress in the political as well as the scientific order is due to the same faculty, to genius, to inspiration, to the love of order, of unity, that is to sympathy: for it is sympathy which binds us to the world around us and makes us discover the link among all the parts of this world in which we live.' See also *ibid.*, p. 488.

19 The 'Quinzième Séance' of the First Year of the *Doctrine* is devoted to the analysis of the law of three stages; *ibid.*, pp. 443–57. For a summary of the Saint-Simonian critique of Comte, see pp. 455–6. Cf. *ibid.*, p. 434.

20 Regarding the accumulation of unrelated data, see *Doctrine*, pp. 132 ff.; the multiplicity of scientific systems, *ibid.*, p. 198; the atheistic, mechanical character of the universe, *ibid.*, pp. 406 f., 436.

21 *Ibid.*, p. 197. Regarding the theological character of science in an organic age, see *ibid.*, pp. 436, and *Séances* IX and XI of the Second Year of the *Doctrine de Saint-Simon. Exposition*, in *Oeuvres*, vol. 42, pp. 321 ff., 357 ff.

22 *Doctrine*, p. 440; cf. pp. 481 ff.

23 *Le Producteur. Journal philosophique de l'industrie, des sciences et des beaux-arts* (Paris, 1825–6), vol. 4, pp. 373 ff.

24 *Doctrine*, p. 248.

25 *Ibid.*, p. 253.

26 *Ibid.*, p. 384; regarding the definition of economic and intellectual non-conformity as crimes in normative periods, see *ibid.*, pp. 387 ff. The codified law of imperial, 'critical' Rome was singled out particularly for criticism in *Le Globe*, the Saint-Simonian newspaper. In contrast, the law of the early republic, although the primitive expression of an age of conquest, was said to have possessed a highly religious, organic character (3 October 1831).

27 *Doctrine*, pp. 379, 390; cf. pp. 387 ff.

28 Cf. Georg G. Iggers, 'The Social Philosophy of the Saint-Simonians (1825–1832)' (unpubl. dissertation), University of Chicago, 1951, pp. 30 ff.; see also *Producteur*, vol. 3, p. 493.

29 Political theories regarding the natural rights of man and the needs of constitutional guarantees of individual liberties were regarded as expressive of the mistrust of authority which prevails in critical periods. See *Globe*, 30 January 1831; *Doctrine*, pp. 130 f.; *Producteur*, vol. 1, p. 410.

30 *Globe*, 30 January 1831; cf. *ibid.*, 2 October 1831.

31 'Considérations sur l'histoire,' *Producteur*, vol. 4, pp. 390 ff.

32 *Producteur*, vol. 1, p. 74.

33 *Globe*, 18 July 1831.

34 Émile Barrault, *Aux Artistes. Du passé et de l'avenir des beaux-arts* (*Doctrine de Saint-Simon*), Paris: Alexandre Mesnier, 1830, *passim*.

35 Cf. Barrault, pp. 16 ff., 40 ff., 73; *Producteur*, vol. 4, p. 195, regarding the social character of art in critical epochs.

36 Barrault, p. 75.

37 *Doctrine*, p. 144.

38 *Ibid.*, p. 131; cf. *Globe*, 26 September 1831.

39 Barrault, pp. 63 ff.; *Producteur*, vol. 4, p. 207; *Doctrine*, p. 198.

40 Rodrigues, pp. 125–6.

41 *Producteur*, vol. 4, pp. 189 ff.

42 *Organisateur, journal des progrès de la science générale avec un appendice sur les méthodes découvertes rélative à l'enseignement*, 7 November 1829.

43 *Globe*, 8 April 1832.

44 *Doctrine*, pp. 187 ff., 449.

45 Cf. *ibid.*, p. 174.

4 The conservative tradition in the sociology of knowledge

Werner Stark

It is a widely shared, if not indeed universally accepted, opinion that the sociology of knowledge as we know it today is in the last analysis an outcome of the great revolutionary movements which swept over Western society in the second half of the eighteenth and the first half of the nineteenth century. Marx is commonly regarded as its immediate, and Voltaire as its more distant progenitor. These two men fought the upper classes of their day not only on the political, but also on the intellectual plane, and they did so by showing, or trying to show, that many of the conceptions on which contemporary society was based, were not in fact what they pretended to be, namely the truth, but rather reflections of economic and power-political interests, i.e. 'ideologies'. Their whole approach and argument contained in this way, albeit in a crude and unscientific form, that vital reference to the social element in the genesis of ideas, which the academic sociology of knowledge has since been investigating in a more dispassionate and scholarly fashion.

There is certainly a good deal of justification for this interpretation of the origin of the branch of learning which goes by the name of *Wissenssoziologie* or sociology of knowledge; nevertheless, it conveys only half the truth and not the whole of it. It fails to notice the presence, in the inception and history of this study, of a second tendency, which comes from the political right, and not from the political left. Beside the revolutionary 'debunking' doctrine of ideology,[1] there is also a conservative tradition in the sociology of knowledge which has contributed no less, if not indeed more, to it than its opponent. This conservative tradition is often overlooked, and it is the purpose of the present paper to draw attention to it. Unless and until it is recognized that the subject has two tap-roots in the historical sub-soil, and not only one, it will remain impossible to understand its development and to appreciate its content and its bearings.

Before going any further, it is perhaps necessary to define more closely what the words 'revolutionary' and 'conservative' can mean in our present context. It would appear that two rather sharp dividing lines can be drawn between the hostile philosophies. The revolutionary approach is, first of all, based on a general belief in progress. According to Voltaire, history is the slow conquest of obscurantism by enlightenment and of error by the truth. Naturally, this progressivism was unacceptable to the protagonists of conservatism. They either maintained that primitive—'unspoilt'—man was nearer to the truth than modern man, or they asserted that truth, like custom, cannot be rationally produced, but must slowly and organically grow, so that it is more likely to be found in undisturbed communities with a continuous flow of history than in changing societies exposed to the shocks of discontinuity. Among Voltaire's great adversaries, Jean-Jacques Rousseau represented the former and Edmund Burke the latter variant. The second mark of distinction follows logically from the contrasting attitudes, characteristic of the two camps, to the phenomenon of class. The revolutionaries assumed that one class—their class—was nearer to the truth than any other. Voltaire, for instance, regarded the *grande bourgeoisie* as the seat of all enlightened opinion. The conservatives, on the other hand, insisted that a class point of view is by definition a partial point of view, while the truth, or at any rate the full truth, can only spring from a total vision. They either expected the truth from a total, unrefracted, internally harmonious kind of man (Rousseau) or from a total, unrefracted, internally harmonious kind of society (Burke); in other words, they followed in this matter, as in all others, the organismic or holistic conceptions on which their whole world-view was based.

In the years in which the social element in the genesis of ideas was for the first time discovered and tentatively investigated, that is to say, in the second half of the eighteenth century, both these doctrines, the revolutionary and the conservative, existed side by side and fought with each other for the mastery of the human mind. The revolutionary attitude was propagated by the Encyclopaedists, Voltaire, Diderot, d'Alembert and the rest, while the conservative position found its defenders among the German *Stürmer und Dränger*, the 'men of Stress and Strain', a group which included such brilliant figures as Herder and Goethe. A whole world divided the rationalists from these pre-romantics, but if they shared one thing, it was the awareness that the origin of our ideas cannot be fully understood unless it is seen in the light of the concrete social situation in which we find ourselves, and to which we owe, not only our daily bread, but also our cultural possessions.

Perhaps we can best see what the two schools had in common and what kept them apart, if we concentrate our attention for a moment on a significant detail. The 'ideologies' which Voltaire was most anxious to 'unmask' were the 'medieval superstitions' of the Church, *l'infâme* as he usually called her, and among them the account given in the Book of Genesis of the origin of the world seemed to him particularly objectionable. According to the Bible, God created the light on the first day, but the sun only on the fourth day. The assumption clearly is that there were three days when it was light, although the source of all light, namely the sun, was absent—a sheer impossibility. Voltaire concluded that we are confronted here with a prime piece of priestcraft. The priests, in their desire to enslave the masses and to live without labour, foisted on them this absurd fairy tale, and it is for the critical philosopher to show such fables up for what they are—rogues' tricks, born of class selfishness on the part of the privileged and tending to perpetuate their domination, and with it the exploitation of the underprivileged, for all time to come.

It is fascinating to see how the conservative forces answered this challenge. Johann Gottfried Herder's book, 'The Oldest Document of the Human Race', first published in 1774,[2] allows us to look deeply into their mentality and to discover in it the second—the conservative—root of the modern sociology of knowledge. Voltaire had treated the Bible story from an entirely unhistorical, severely abstract and logical point of view. He had condemned it above all because it was self-contradictory. Herder argued that this rationalistic approach would never reveal the true meaning of the Bible's teaching, and could in consequence never serve as the basis of a justifiable critique. In order to understand the contents of the 'oldest document of the human race', we must hold it, not against the canons of abstract logic, but against the backcloth of the concrete circumstances within which it originated. If it was interpreted in this way, it might appear, not illogical, but logical, not full of nonsense, but full of sense and truth.

The key that will unlock for us the true meaning of the Book of Genesis, so Herder points out, is the fact that it reflects and embodies the experiences of a pastoral tribe. In the life of the nomad who tends his flocks by night, there can be no greater impression than the breaking of the dawn. The breaking of the dawn will appear to him as a symbolical representation, or even as an actual repetition, of the breaking of the first dawn, the beginning of the world. While there is yet night, 'darkness' is 'upon the face of the deep', and the beholder can at best sense, feel, divine, a spirit or breath of life 'upon the face of the waters'. But then, as the light slowly rises in the east, everything springs, as it were, into existence. There is a new world after a spell of nothingness. Now, this coming to life, or coming to be, of the desert does not wait upon the actual appearance of the sun disk over the horizon. It takes place as soon as the eye can see in the half-light of the early hours. Hence, Herder concludes, to the Bedouin of today, and the Bedouin-like Jews of antiquity, the light is in effect *before* the sun, and therefore the Biblical account of the origin of the world is more than merely an absurd and stultifying old wives' tale. It is at least an understandable account, understandable from the genetic point of view.[3]

It is surely obvious that Herder's principle of interpretation is a genuinely sociological one. The ideas of the Jewish people are explained as reflections or mirrorings of the Jewish people's way of life: they appear, to put it in Marxian language, as an intellectual superstructure over a socio-economic substructure. It is impossible to deny that this is a first, and by no means hesitant, step in the direction of the sociology of knowledge.

If we have to allow, then, that Herder, as well as Voltaire, must be regarded as one of the founders of the sociology of knowledge, the question at once arises, which of the two traditions has contributed more to the development of the subject as a scholarly discipline. Without claiming that this difficult problem can be decided by a sleight of hand, it is perhaps permissible to point to three circumstances which would make it appear justifiable to rank Herder higher than his adversary as far as this branch of learning is concerned.

There is, firstly, the general spirit in which the study of the genesis of ideas is approached. Herder's attitude is a positive one, whereas that of Voltaire is purely negative. Voltaire wants to 'debunk', to destroy, Herder to understand, to explain. Voltaire looks for the nonsense in the opinions of the past, Herder for the sense in them. True, even Herder has an axe to grind, but his whole endeavour is nonetheless much nearer to the spirit of scholarship than the iconoclasm of M. de Voltaire.

Secondly, Voltaire missed a point of prime importance to the sociologist which Herder, for his part, fully appreciated, namely that every society, however class-divided it may be, is to a very large extent an intellectual unity. He operated with the over-simplified distinction between the rogues and the dupes, or the clever and the stupid, and assumed that the priests were often rationalists and even atheists while they preached an irrational religion to the people. This is hardly a permissible assumption. There have been societies, like that of ancient Egypt, where the priests had an esoteric philosophy of their own and kept the masses to a simpler exoteric creed, but the difference never amounted to a contrast between child-like belief on the one hand and cynical unbelief on the other. Esoteric and exoteric religion were always essentially variants of a common underlying metaphysic or style of thought, and it is doubtful whether a society with more radical, let alone irreconcilable cleavages in mentality could ever continue to function as a vital unity. Herder shows considerable superiority over Voltaire, not only in sociological insight, but even in common-sense, when he asserts that the priests are, as a rule, not more cunning and calculating than their lay contemporaries, but rather more tradition-bound, the preservers of an inherited lore.[4]

This leads us immediately to our third point. Voltaire's thinking suffers from the great, nay decisive weakness that it is largely unhistorical. The difference between the clever and the stupid, which plays so basic a part in his analysis, is no historical difference. It always existed and always will exist. But the prime task of the sociology of knowledge is precisely the elucidation of the dissimilarities in mentality between *succeeding* societies, the explanation of the *history* of ideas, and this can only be provided by a mind deeply aware of the realities of history. Voltaire's was not a mind of this kind; Herder's was.

In order to see how far Herder had succeeded in freeing himself from the narrow rationalism of the eighteenth century which still kept Voltaire in thrall and made him blind to the meaning and importance of many phenomena of the past, we must go beyond 'The Oldest Document of the Human Race' and consider also his essays, especially those on Ossian and Shakespeare. To Voltaire it was an axiom as firmly established as any proposition in Euclid that the primitive mind was, all along the line, inferior to the modern. Herder, on the other hand, sought to show that the difference between the primitive and the modern mentality was not a difference between immaturity and maturity, irrationality and rationality, or bad and good, but rather a difference between two dissimilar *modes* of thinking, each of which had its own inherent limitations and its own specific potentialities and excellence. He admitted that modern man was superior in all rational pursuits: he was for instance a far better mathematician and technologist than the nomad of the ancient world. But just because he was so proficient in the handling of abstract problems and propositions, he had lost the capacity for concrete experiences: the world, having become for him a tissue of quantitative facts, had lost all colour. The primitive for his part had a much simpler, a much more unsophisticated image of reality, but what he lacked in rationality, he gained in immediacy: he saw the world as it really was, in all its overwhelming variety. He had, above all, the invaluable gift of intuition, and this enabled him to grasp wholes *as* wholes in one great swoop of comprehension. If Herder had had at his disposal the commodious terminologies of today, he might have said that the primitive's mind was synthetic rather than analytic, the modern mind analytic rather than synthetic. We must be careful here not to claim too much for Herder:[5] even he was still a child of the eighteenth century. But it is not altogether fanciful to see in his speculations a first glimmering of the great insight which we are wont to connect with the name of Ferdinand Tönnies, namely, that there are fundamentally two types of society and culture, community and association, of which the one pre-disposes to a rational, quantitative and analytical, the other to a poetical, qualitative and holistic view of the world.[6]

Here again it will be best to watch the schools at work and see how they handle one or two points of detail. The rationalists asserted that there was, and could be, only one ideal of poetry which was binding on all times and countries: the lines of a poem, they demanded, should always scan exactly according to the metre chosen by the poet, the imagery employed should not only be striking, but also restrained, the verse should always be pure, and so on. From this point of view, much of the literature of the 'ruder' ages appeared worthless: the poems of the Edda, for instance, did not seem to scan at all well, their imagery was wild and exaggerated, and often the verse was impure or replaced by the 'impolite' technique of alliteration. The primitive bards, so the rationalists said, simply did not come up to the required standards of refinement. Herder, in reply, tried to show that it was foolish to judge the literature of two so utterly dissimilar societies as pre-historic Iceland and eighteenth-century France by the same canons. He sought to demonstrate that many features of early poetry which at first sight may appear meaningless and ugly, reveal their meaning and also their beauty if we see them in relation to the life from which they have sprung. Why do the ancient bards use alliterations instead of verses, why do they repeat the same phrases over and over again, why is their imagery crude and over-dramatic? Because they wrote, not for the refined *salon*, but for the village gathering, the camp fire and the march. Again, Herder's argument is entirely sociological: contrasting forms of art are not reducible to the same principles and not to be judged by the same tests because they are essentially the expression of contrasting forms of social life.[7]

A consideration of drama leads to the same result. The rationalists, ın their preoccupation with formal logic, insisted on the three classical 'unities'—unity of space, of time, and of action. On the basis of their ideal they condemned even Shakespeare, for he does not seem to care whether his scenes follow consistently from each other. He takes us freely from place to place and jumps over long stretches of time, and yet expects us to follow him without misgivings on this wild journey. He had not yet learned to discipline his mind, so the rationalists would say. Herder's counter-argument here is twofold, but both his thrusts are sociological in nature.

Firstly, he points out, the classical Greek drama, which provided the rationalists with their model and their norm, had an entirely different social origin from the Shakespearean play. The classical Greek drama, as Sophocles has shaped and Racine imitated it, grew out of the cult and therefore carried with it all the dignity and restraint of the temple. The Shakespearean play, on the other hand, stemmed from the fair ground, the scene of popular jollification, and there a certain indiscipline, nay riotousness, is not only allowable, but even entirely in style. To demand of Shakespeare that he should write like Sophocles or like Racine, is to demand the impossible. We must allow the dramatist to be himself, or rather to be what his society makes him,[8] for man is always 'the product of his estate, his occupation, his time and his place'.

Even more intriguing is the second line of argument along which Herder endeavours to move. He denies that Shakespeare's 'wild' poetic drama is entirely devoid of inner unity; on the contrary, he asserts that it has a unity, even a consistency, of its own—perhaps indeed a finer and firmer unity than the classical play. Going slightly beyond his words, though not beyond his thought, we can express his essential submission by saying that the dramas of Sophocles and Racine possess a merely mechanical, those of Shakespeare, however, an organic unity. Their unity, Herder explains, is not that of the measuring rod or the time piece, but it is a unity of *meaning*, and thus a deeper unity than any purely external or numerical unity can ever be.[9] We have called this argumentation intriguing because it points straight in the direction of Tönnies' dichotomy. A mechanistic conception and ideal of unity fits in with an associational life and culture, whereas a communal life and culture will naturally tend to produce the corresponding opposite conception and ideal of organic unity.

In view of these germinal ideas, in which much of the best sociological thought of the nineteenth and twentieth centuries is prefigured, it is not unjustified to place Herder above Voltaire in the prehistory of the sociology of knowledge. But we are speaking here, not of one man, however outstanding; we are speaking of a whole tradition, and so must pose the question whether there is a *chain* of thinkers which leads down from the period of 'Stress and Strain' to the present day. At the moment it is yet too early to attempt to write a comprehensive history of this intellectual movement; much preliminary spadework has yet to be done before this becomes possible. But we can at any rate mention a few of the names which would have to figure more prominently in such a survey of the conservative tradition as a whole.

After the French Revolution, the pre-romanticism of men like Herder gave way to the full romanticism of the Restoration, and in this period Louis de Bonald deserves our closest attention and study. 'De Bonald saw in literature and the arts an expression of society', writes Alexander Koyré,[10] paraphrasing a striking formula which de Bonald himself has coined. It would be a fascinating task to look in de Bonald's work for the passages in which this fundamental conviction is developed and applied. Around the middle of the century, an even stronger personality takes up the tradition and carries it on: Juan Donoso Cortés. His *Ensayo sobre el Catolicismo, el Liberalismo y el Socialismo* (1851), remarkable for the burning faith which informs it and far too little known, is conceived in a spirit distinctly opposite to that of Karl Marx, and yet in many ways curiously reminiscent of it. Donoso Cortés, like Marx, came from Hegel, yet he moved to the right, not, like Marx, to the left. He developed what one might call an idealistic conception of history: all depends on the relationship which a society establishes to God and the divine truths. Nevertheless, Donoso Cortés maintains that a society, a culture, is a unity and must be understood as a unity. Once a social pattern has formed, the modes of thinking arising within it will be of one piece with it, and their true meaning and bearing can only be found if we regard them as integral parts of that inclusive whole.

Both de Bonald and Donoso Cortés are colourful and commanding figures. But the central chapter of a history of the conservative tradition in the sociology of knowledge would have to be reserved for Max Scheler, if only because he consciously developed the subject and provided a consistent theory of it. Scheler's political pre-conceptions have never been systematically investigated, yet even a superficial reading will make it clear that his is essentially an aristocratic, even authoritarian outlook. Like Nietzsche, he reacted violently to the rising tide of democracy which the nineteenth century had unleashed and asserted that a culture which deserves its name is always the product of a small elite. The red thread which we are trying to trace thus runs to him and through him, and it leads on to those among our own contemporaries who are influenced by him. The name of Alois Dempf has to be mentioned here as particularly significant. Dempf's most interesting submission is that the irreducible multiplicity of metaphysical conceptions throughout history is due in the last analysis to the irreducible multiplicity of types of social organisation underlying them, and that in consequence only a perfect, i.e. organically integrated social order would be able to achieve a metaphysics acceptable to all men.[11] As can be seen, his approach is both sociological and organismic; in other words, it is akin to that of Herder.[12]

A searching history of the sociology of knowledge would have to discuss the doctrines of these men, and others who thought like them, in all due detail. But it would have a second and perhaps even more important task to fulfil, namely to show how the revolutionary and conservative traditions have impinged upon each other, and how out of their clash there has developed an ever richer and finer discipline. Even Marx, for all his revolutionary sentiment, was a disciple of Herder and de Bonald as well as of Voltaire and Condorcet. Several features of his thought can prove this. First of all, he was not a pure progressivist. He certainly believed that mankind would achieve a realistic world-view only after the revolution, when the truth-inhibiting and truth-destroying influence of the class-division of society was removed, but he also taught that his new realism would in a sense be a return to the old realistic world-view of the primitive class-less clan. Secondly, Marx repeated, if in a somewhat modified form, Herder's and de Bonald's main charge against modern thinking, namely that it is over-abstract, remote from direct experience. Whenever he complains of the 'divorce of theory and practice', he echoes conceptions characteristic of the 'Stress and Strain'. Finally, there is the remarkable fact that Marx's ideal man was similar to that of the pre-romantics and romantics—total, unrefracted man, man freed, not only from the limitations of class, but also from those of the division of labour. This is an aspect of Marxian thinking which is not very well known, but recent writers, such as Hans Barth and Georg Lukács, have underlined it, and the latter has expressly emphasised that it constitutes a link between Marx on the one hand, and Goethe (or Herder) on the other.[13] Thus even the so-called materialistic conception of history, i.e. the specifically Marxian doctrine of the genesis of ideas, was deeply indebted to the conservative tradition in the sociology of knowledge.

Notes

1 Those who are inclined to identify the sociology of knowledge *as a whole* with the doctrine of ideology, are referred to the author's book, *The Sociology of Knowledge*, London: Routledge & Kegan Paul, 1958, where the essential distinction between the two is explained and discussed in chapter 2.

2 *Älteste Urkunde des Menschengeschlechts*, cf. *Herders Sämtliche Werke* (ed. B. Suphan), vol. 6, 1883, pp. 193 ff.

3 Cf. *Werke*, vol. 6, pp. 258, 225 ff.

4 Cf. *ibid.*, p. 369.

5 One anticipation, however, is too interesting and striking to be passed over in silence. Herder, like Durkheim after him, explains the origin of our rational system of time-computing with reference to the alternation

between days of work and days of rest, or common days and sacral days. Cf. *ibid.*, pp. 294 ff., 340.

6 The main passages are the following: *ibid.*, pp. 266 ff., 403 ff., 415 ff., 437 ff., 444 ff.

7 Cf. *ibid.*, vol. 5, 1891, pp. 164 ff., 184 ff.

8 Cf. *ibid.*, pp. 209 ff., 217 ff., 249, 252 ff.; vol. 7 (1884), p. 103.

9 *Ibid.*, vol. 5, pp. 213, 219, 252.

10 Cf. *Journal of the History of Ideas* (January 1946), p. 56, footnote 3.

11 Cf. esp. *Selbstkritik der Philosophie*, Vienna, 1947.

12 On the other hand, Herder, like Marx, hoped and believed that mankind would, in the future, regain that 'natural' attitude to reality which it had once possessed in the past. Cf. *Werke*, vol. 7, p. 17, footnote (r).

13 Cf. Hans Barth, *Wahrheit und Ideologie*, Zürich, 1945, pp. 71 ff. and 122 ff., and Georg Lukács, *Geschichte und Klassenbewusstsein*, Berlin, 1923, pp. 153, 155 ff.

part three

Methodological and conceptual presuppositions

5 The theoretical possibility of the sociology of knowledge

Arthur Child

In the general concern over the problem of origin and validity as found in the sociology of knowledge, a far more basic problem has suffered relative neglect. This problem may be formulated as follows: is the sociology of knowledge, from a theoretical standpoint, even possible? If possible, then in what sense is it possible? And how, especially, can that possibility obtain a theoretical ground? These questions have received various and highly divergent answers. But, unless one can establish the legitimacy of the sociology of knowledge, there would appear to be little reason in discussing the problems that can arise only on the presupposition of its legitimacy.

As a matter of fact, the problem at hand is far wider than the mere sociology of knowledge: it concerns the legitimacy of all forms of the approach to thought in terms of a social matrix. However, the controversy over the theoretical possibility of this approach has proceeded almost entirely in reference to the sociology of knowledge. For its disowned and disowning parent, historical materialism, either has not cared or has not ventured to develop the problems involved in the assumption of the social determination of thought, and other variants on the social approach have similarly neglected the theoretical problems of the approach. Hence, in order to investigate the problem of the possibility of a social interpretation of thought, we cannot avoid considering the controversy as it has occurred in the peculiar context of the sociology of knowledge. As one might expect, points of relevance only to the sociology of knowledge mingle with points of wider relevance. For the most part, however, the debate concerns central issues, and the central issues belong not to the particular school of the sociology of knowledge but rather to the general mode of interpretation.

Here, therefore, we shall examine first the attacks, from various quarters, on the very existence of a sociology of knowledge and then the attempts of the sociologists of knowledge themselves to establish the theoretical legitimacy of their interpretative procedure. From this examination we hope to draw some conclusions of fundamental pertinence for the social mode of interpretation in general.

For the total rejection of the possibility of the sociology of knowledge we have found three important arguments: Julius Kraft rejects it on mechanistic grounds, Heinz O. Ziegler on vitalistic grounds, and Günther Stern on the basis of an analysis of the meaning of history.

The word 'sociology,' according to Kraft, can mean one of two things: either a theory about social phenomena or a theory that employs sociological categories. But in either sense sociology is futile:[1]

> For a consistent exposition of the first point of view, the application of specifically sociological categories is unnecessary and forbidden—i.e., the application of such categories as would not be reducible to the criteria of physical and psychological experience. They are unnecessary because the physical-psychological analysis extends to the elements of social phenomena; they are forbidden because only such an analysis can reach these elements. In the exposition of the second point of view, on the other hand, the very meaning of the science requires the application of sociological categories, which inevitably bear the character of fictions, since experience exhibits no irreducible social objects.

And as a presumed branch of sociology the sociology of knowledge falls, of course, under these alternative criticisms. But Kraft directs other criticisms at the sociology of knowledge specifically. He declares that in construing the knowing individual as dependent on a 'stratum,' the sociology of knowledge has meant to deny that men think and know. Or, if the notion of dependence on a stratum is intended solely as a metaphor, the sociology of knowledge merely states the platitude that, in so far as cognition depends on extra-mental conditions, it is not 'unattached.' And on this latter interpretation one must assume the sociology of knowledge to presuppose the objectivity of cognition, so that for a 'noological sociology of knowledge' there would remain no field of application.

> Moreover, from a strictly empirical point of view there can be no genuine sociology of knowledge in so far as one understands by this the reduction to social phenomena or to specific social essences (*Weseneinheiten*); for these reductions, in consequence of the psychical nature of knowledge and of the nonexistence of such 'essences,' must always be fictitious.[2]

Behind Kraft's rejection of the possibility of the sociology of knowledge lies the mechanistic assumption that all phenomena are reducible to—that is, can be explained without residue by reference to—physical entities or categories. There are no specifically biological categories, no specifically social categories, no specifically psychological categories. And if physical categories alone could explain social phenomena, the sociology of knowledge would be impossible indeed, for it consists in the interpretation of thought with reference to precisely the sort of categories that Kraft deems fictitious. But consider Kraft's main reason for denying the concrete results of the sociology of knowledge: that they are in principle impossible. And why? Because the sociology of knowledge violates the principles of mechanism! Although it is hardly practicable to undertake a refutation of mechanism here, we must point out that there are many and powerful arguments, from many angles, against the universal validity of the mechanistic interpretation. And not the least of these arguments consists in the actual contribution which the treatment of knowledge in terms of specifically social categories has made to the understanding of cultural history. It is, therefore, upon a dogma— and a precarious one—that Kraft's rejection of the possibility of the sociology of knowledge depends.

For the rejection of the sociology of knowledge by the 'psychological' school we turn to Heinz O. Ziegler, who complains that Karl Mannheim identifies being with meaning and refers 'all thought, all "mind" to historical being.'[3] And it is with reference to Mannheim's views that Ziegler criticizes the sociology of knowledge.

The sociology of knowledge would abolish what Ziegler regards as the proper and valid sociological mode of interpretation: the 'analysis of history into general, universally valid elements of human nature.' Thus the sociology of knowledge stands in opposition to the demand that 'the specific character of the sociological view of the social-historical world should be precisely the working-out of typical general structures.'[4] But if the understanding of individual meaning is the task of the sociology of knowledge and if, in Mannheim's words, 'only where there is meaning, does genuine history begin,'[5]

then *the social-historical world is apprehended, in the last analysis, in a purely idealistic manner*, and the concept of ideology receives a meaning wholly different from the meaning it has had heretofore. The doctrine of ideology is above all, for this historical manner of thought, the doctrine that the modes in which mind appears are exclusively determined by history. . . . Its task consists in imputing definite systems of world-views, taken as the unified expression of a 'mind,' to definite, unique constellations. But since this constellation itself can only be defined as a unity of meaning, 'mind' is really referred, after all, to 'mind.' If ideology means the situational determination of thinking and if, therewith, a real relation is ostensibly set up between two different spheres, nevertheless, in consequence of the fundamental philosophy of identity, this imputation of mental contents to 'existential' factors is nothing other than the reference of 'meaning' to itself.[6]

For Mannheim, therefore, ideology can be defined neither by the criterion of falsification nor by the criterion of service to special interests. Moreover,

there can be no question of 'correspondence,' for there are no factors alien to 'mind,' to which factors an ideology could be adequate or inadequate; rather every ideology is justified in itself . . . Above all, the absolutizing of this historical world into the sole reality is totally unfounded. And this point is the decisive one . . . If there are no existential relations, no forces, no modes of behavior which in principle transcend this sphere of historicity, then the historistic circle is really inevitable. Only with reference to an extra-historical—e.g., the religious— sphere or with reference to the identity of definite constants of human nature can history as such be classified and defined.[7]

But if there are no non-meaningful, extra-historical factors, Ziegler concludes, then there is no criterion by which to judge ideas either in reference to their truth or in reference to their situational correspondence.[8]

Ziegler himself holds, it is clear from the above, that mind is not determined by social being—by a reality which, because constituted by the relations of men to each other, must therefore undergo change —but that it is determined, on the contrary, by the eternal and fundamental drives of human nature, by forces beyond society and history. Yet, however earnestly, from such a position, one might desire to explain various ideas as rationalizations—for example, of the will-to-power—in point of fact one would find it impossible to do so. For if the sole determinant were a reality beyond society and history, as Ziegler claims, one could adduce no ground for the great diversity of these rationalizations. Why should rationalizations differ from time to time, from place to place, did these differences not result from differences in the social-historical situation? The fundamental drives themselves cannot change, according to Ziegler's theory, for they are postulated as unchanging; neither can they be conceived as expressing themselves differently under different conditions, for such a conception would admit, indirectly, that thought is determined by social-historical factors. The psychological theory of Ziegler himself, therefore, not only cannot function as a sociology of knowledge: it cannot even propound, logically, any explanation of thought at all.

Turning to Ziegler's criticisms of the sociology of knowledge as represented by Mannheim, we must affirm their singular ineptitude. They are based chiefly on Mannheim's statement that 'only where there is meaning, does genuine history begin.' But the meaning of the statement itself seems quite unobjectionable. If, in society, events repeated themselves in the same fashion year after year (as, to an extent and in a sense, in the realm of nature), if the life of a society, that is, went on and on without perceptible change, then one would have no occasion to record the happenings in that particular society; and in connection with such a society, one could not speak of 'history' in the ordinary sense of the term. The life of such a society would have no 'meaning.' But as Ziegler interprets the statement in question, Mannheim has identified being with meaning and has thus interpreted the social-historical world 'in a purely idealistic manner'! Ziegler's accusation depends, however, on the arbitrary assumption that the world is non-meaningful, irrational: if Mannheim absolutizes history, Ziegler absolutizes blind, naked drives. And on the assumption of the basic irrationality of the world, any interpretation of the world as meaningful, as logically comprehensible, would indeed appear to import meaning and logical connection into the world from the human mind. As we could not undertake to disprove mechanism in reference to Kraft, neither can we undertake here to prove that the world is neither arbitrary nor devoid of law nor alien to intelligibility. We can only point out the dogmatic character of Ziegler's rejection of the sociology of knowledge.

But even aside from the basic dogma of irrationalism, Ziegler's criticisms seem highly questionable. Ziegler complains, for instance, that by interpreting thought with reference to society, the sociology of knowledge refers mind to mind, meaning to meaning. This criticism, of course, rests on the accusation of idealism. Quite regardless of the issue of idealism however, why should one not refer mind to mind and meaning to meaning? It is perhaps not going too far to assert that, in some sense, meaning can *only* be explained with reference to meaning. But if so, then how can one justifiably criticize Mannheim, in the manner that Ziegler criticizes him, for interpreting thought with reference to intelligible social-historical structure?

And, finally, Ziegler is surely wrong in claiming that, without a realm beyond history, beyond process, beyond change, without a realm basic to, but itself untouched by, movement, there can be no criterion for judging either whether a judgment is true or false or whether it does or does not correspond to a given social-historical situation. It is difficult, if not impossible, even to understand what such a claim could mean. But perhaps Ziegler may be excused for this obscurity, inasmuch as meaning, on his account, appears to possess singularly little importance.

The third rejection of the possibility of the sociology of knowledge comes from Günther Stern. Stern believes that the reference of mind beyond itself to social-historical reality, to 'naked being,' necessitates an investigation as to the validity of the concept of universal historicity.[9] Thus, although sociology calls into question the validity of philosophy, its 'self-evident' premises give to philosophy a new impulse and in particular the impulse 'to determine the ontological character of that "being" by which even philosophy is said to be determined; and to examine the claim of this being to constitute the totality of being (*den Anspruch dieses Seins, das Sein darzustellen*).'[10] While Ziegler attacked the concept of universal historicity from the standpoint of an unchanging structure of human drives, Stern attacks it on the ground that man can lead a nonhistorical life, that there are nonhistorical and 'counterhistorical' epochs, that 'in spite of man's freedom in principle in regard to history, there are human existences and human worlds which are *unhistorical* and which, therefore, cannot be grasped historically.'[11] And in the case of nonhistorical subjects, consciousness cannot vary with a historical situation, so that the concept of universal historicity thus proves to be false.

Stern tries to make his contention plausible with an analysis of 'Today'; but since the analysis is long, involved, and obscure, we shall give merely a free paraphrase of its outcome. Stern appears, then, to be arguing somewhat as follows: Mannheim errs in the claim that all thought is determined by social being, that thought is a variable of social-historical situations, for basic to that claim is the theory of the omnipresence of history, the theory that men never exist save within the historical process—and this theory is false. In the first place, some men live (or men have sometimes lived) in very stable societies—societies in which life proceeds in the same manner from year to year, with the same activities, with the same modes of behavior; societies which encounter no unusual circumstances requiring an adjustment in pattern of life. But in reference to such societies one cannot speak of history. And, in the second place, different groups of men have different histories; and the life of these groups goes on with different traditions, different social relationships, different ideals. These different histories, then, have in common only the contemporaneity of the calendar or the interaction of war.[12] So in view of this counterhistorical situation, this 'extra-historical hiatus,' one cannot speak of thought as determined by History. There is no singular History, there are only plural histories. The sociology of knowledge stands convicted of error, therefore, in regard to its fundamental assumption of the universal social-historical determination of thought or consciousness.

Let us examine Stern's first contention—that thought cannot be determined by the historical situation because, in certain primitive and stable social forms, existence is not really historical. This contention, to begin with, is itself in all probability false. Probably never, so long as man has been man, have societies existed in which nothing—nothing at all—has occurred to break the routine of monotonous, everyday existence. In the life of every people (as witness the myths, the folk tales, the hero legends, which every people, even the most primitive, possesses) *something* occurs now and again which is deemed worthy of especial preservation in the oral literature of that people and which, therefore, in the sense in which Stern uses the term in his first criticism, goes into the making of 'history.' Even granting, for the sake of the argument, that there exist 'obstructive styles of thought . . . in which man lives in a state of pure repetition, with no anticipation of the possibility of existing in any other manner,'[13] this still would not prove that in such a state the existence of man is not historical: it could only prove that man is not always aware of the historicity of his existence. Thus Stern has mistaken a state of mind for a state of the world.

Moreover, Stern's argument rests on an ambiguity in the meaning of the term 'history.' On the one hand, history can refer to the ongoing, cumulative process which is the complex of man's activities; on the other hand, it can refer to events which possess some especial significance (and we must emphasize that whether or not an event possesses especial significance depends on the standpoint of the observer). Now, on the ground that there exist periods devoid of especially significant events (and, in consequence of our above observation, we must point out that the absence of significance depends on the standpoint of Stern himself), Stern asserts that there exist nonhistorical periods—periods, that is, in which there is no history at all. And from this premise follows, inevitably, the conclusion that in such nonhistorical periods thought cannot be determined by the social-historical situation. But this reasoning of Stern's is fallacious, for it neglects the other meaning of history as the process of human activity. Because of the ambiguity in the term, Stern can take his meaning of history as *the* meaning of history, whereas in the sociology of knowledge, in point of fact, history has quite another meaning.

Finally, however, even assuming with Stern that nonhistorical periods have really existed, the denial of the historical determination of thought would remain as unsubstantiated as before. For whether or not history goes on within a society, that society itself goes on within a history. In other words, the society in question differs from previous societies, and future societies will differ from it. Correlated with these social-temporal differences occur intellectual-temporal differences; and this correlation of social and mental differences allows the sociologist of knowledge to interpret varying conceptions as determined by varying social situations—as determined, that is, by historical factors. Thus the first ground on which Stern bases his denial of the possibility of the sociology of knowledge collapses altogether.

The second ground fares no better. To restate, this ground is as follows: thought cannot be determined by history because there is no such thing as History—there are only histories. However, the alternative of History versus histories has no relevance for the issue itself. The issue is simply this: assuming that there are only histories in the plural, assuming that every society possesses its own independent history which makes contact with other histories by means of the battlefield or on the calendar and in no other way—assuming this, is the principle of the historical determination of thought thereby disproved? Stern answers, 'Yes'; we must answer 'No.' For, by hypothesis, each of the many independent societies does have a history of its own: in each society things happen; the cumulative process of human activity goes on; the social-historical situation changes and, with it, all the multifarious minor situations out of which it is woven. And within each of these individual, monadic histories consciousness could develop a plenitude of successive and of coexistent forms in spite of its isolation from the consciousness of other societies. The 'counterhistorical situation' and the 'extra-historical hiatus' would appear, therefore, to be mere examples of a speciously profound terminology.

While Kraft, Ziegler, and Stern reject altogether the possibility of the sociology of knowledge, the second position maintains only that the sociology of knowledge is impossible as a *science*. Helmuth Plessner, for instance, adduces certain alleged assumptions which he believes to invalidate the sociology of knowledge as a science because of their supposedly metaphysical character. These alleged assumptions are as follows:

1. History, either as a progressive, teleological development or only as a continuous new creation and a perpetually unforeseeable occurrence, is the fundamental dimension of human life.
2. As regards knowledge, human life is primarily entangled in a consciousness in which nothing exists that has not been informed by subjectively conditioned categories.
3. True consciousness is not self-evidently true, for the self-

evidence of consciousness cannot be derived from the categorial correlation of subject and object. Man can only certify the truth of consciousness when he proves it by reference to an element beyond consciousness. This other element is practice.

4. The decisive sphere in the relation of consciousness to practice is the sphere in which and with which practice is alone possible. This is the vital sphere. As the decisive stratum, life has the role of the determining substructure.[14]

Inasmuch as the fourth of the alleged assumptions is no assumption of the sociology of knowledge, it can be dismissed immediately. The decisive sphere for the sociology of knowledge is not the vital sphere at all: as the very name of the school implies, the decisive sphere is the social sphere. Indeed, as we have already shown, the vitalistic theory of the determination of consciousness negates the very possibility of a *sociology* of knowledge.

While the second of the alleged metaphysical assumptions might be inferred from Mannheim's writings, it is not, we believe, a necessary assumption of the sociology of knowledge. For the thesis of the social determination of knowledge does not require that *all* contents of consciousness, without exception, should have been informed by socially determined 'subjective' categories. The thesis requires merely that *certain* contents of consciousness should be socially determined—those contents, namely, which are not bare perceptions but which involve interpretation. And for the sociology of knowledge, such a determination, far from being a metaphysical assumption, appears as a fact, and as a fact supported by a vast quantity of highly probable evidence.

The assertion of the third 'metaphysical' assumption seems rather extraordinary. For to criticize the sociology of knowledge for holding that true consciousness is not self-evidently true implies that true consciousness *is* self-evidently true. And if there is any assumption which is 'metaphysical,' that assumption is surely the assumption of self-evidence.

In regard to the first of the assumptions attributed to the sociology of knowledge—that 'history . . . is the fundamental dimension of human life'—it is hard to know what to say. Is Plessner doubting that human life is historical? But this is a 'self-evident' proposition if ever there was one! Of course the sociology of knowledge assumes that human life is historical, but so does everyone else—except, perhaps, for Plessner and Stern. But since we have already refuted Stern's arguments against historicity and since Plessner offers no arguments himself, we shall pass on from Plessner's first criticism content with pointing out its absurdity.

Plessner has also made a general criticism of the sociology of knowledge on the ground that 'for an empirical science of culture (*Geisteswissenschaft*), dependence on definite philosophical propositions is quite as intolerable as for natural science.'[15] Even, however, if the sociology of knowledge did proceed on the basis of certain empirically undemonstrable propositions—which Plessner, at least, has not shown to be the case—that fact still would not necessarily prejudice its scientific character. For the natural sciences, too, as has often been pointed out, make certain empirically undemonstrable or 'metaphysical' assumptions, as, for instance, the assumption of the uniformity of nature. Yet Plessner himself refers to the natural sciences as genuine sciences. We must conclude, therefore, that Plessner has not succeeded in impugning the character of the sociology of knowledge as a science.

Similar in outcome to the strictures of Plessner, but far more subtle and ingenious, is the position of Ernst Grünwald. Only Grünwald, in fact, has been able to offer any dangerous challenge to the scientific validity of the sociology of knowledge. In his view, for a preliminary summary, the sociology of knowledge is arbitrary, binding only upon him who accepts its fundamental postulates. Although for such a person, Grünwald concedes, the sociology of knowledge (together with all its specific implications) really is 'true,' this kind of 'truth,' obviously, is not the kind of truth with which science is concerned, for it is a truth relative not to the available facts but to the metaphysical postulates of the individual. We therefore term Grünwald's position a 'postulational skepticism.'

Showing that there are many possible 'transcendent interpretations' (as, for instance, the racial, the geographic, the climatic, in addition to the social), Grünwald holds that one can find no scientific justification for the preference of some particular transcendent realm as the exclusive determinant of thought. 'Science can point to no way out of this polytheism of absolute strata.'[16] Any transcendent interpretation becomes valid if—but only if—one ratifies, by 'an act of pure free will,' the metaphysical postulate that its particular realm constitutes the exclusive reality. 'The fundamental thesis, however, is scientifically undemonstrable and is also, therefore, scientifically irrefutable . . .'[17] And it follows that the social interpretation, like every other transcendent interpretation, is purely hypothetical. As a further result, the sociology of knowledge falls into error when it claims that it can discover real and objective relations:

> that it can show how a judgment is in fact a manifestation or a causal product of a social being of such and such a nature . . .
> For each of the possible transcendent interpretations of knowledge and cognition can advance the same claim with

precisely the same right; each one pretends that it—and it alone—is capable of disclosing real, existing relations. The truth is, rather, that the sociology of knowledge does not actually possess the possibility of establishing real relations of manifestation, real causal relations; it can only assert a possible causal nexus, a possible relation of 'expression.'[18]

The sociology of knowledge cannot prove that Kantianism, say, actually is the causal product of the interests of the German bourgeoisie at the end of the eighteenth century; it can only assert this proposition under the presupposition of its undemonstrable fundamental thesis.

The sociology of knowledge is therefore not a science, whose propositions are unconditionally valid for every thinking individual, but is only a possible schema for interpretation.[19] . . . With scientific justification it can only be stated—on the acceptance of the fundamental thesis, itself not scientifically demonstrable, that all thought and knowledge may be interpreted as a manifestation of social being—that a concrete judgment may appear as the manifestation of a concrete sector (*Ausgestaltung*) of social being . . . Only this and nothing more can the sociology of knowledge, when it rightly understands its own nature, mean by 'existential determination.' . . . Whether, by this restriction on the capacity of the sociology of knowledge, one calls into question its very character as a science, depends on what demands one is determined to make of a strict science.[20]

But it seems clear that as Grünwald interprets the sociology of knowledge it could not be called a science in any ordinary sense of the word.

Apart from Grünwald's own theory, however, he has here indicated a problem of the sociology of knowledge so central that it bears restating in simpler language. This problem results from the fact that, once thought is no longer interpreted solely in terms of thought, many different and radically incompatible modes of interpretation become possible. Within the conceptual realm itself, to be sure, many divergent interpretations of Kantianism are possible; but the resolution of the dispute involved in this situation is a matter (at least in principle) of sufficient evidence. But the case stands otherwise with the so-called 'transcendent interpretations.' It would appear that evidence does not count in the dispute between the various transcendent interpretations, for each interpretation flows from a 'fundamental premise' which the exponents of the other interpretations cannot accept. And if the adherent of the social or the vital or the racial or of any other possible basic principle holds fast by his particular principle, denying the validity of the other basic principles, then not all the evidence in the world could convince him of the truth of any other interpretation than his own. Precisely because of his own fundamental premise, he is bound to interpret away all evidence that might tend to contradict it. It follows, therefore, that for each of the various interpretations, one might claim the sole power of revealing the genuine objective determinants of thought.

In answer to this situation there are three courses which appear both to be plausibly defensible and actually to have been taken: one could deny altogether that thought is determined by anything beyond itself. Or one could maintain that each interpretation with reference to an extra-mental reality possesses validity for him who accepts its basic postulate. Or else one could attempt to prove, by some scientifically cogent means, that it is, in fact, some particular extra-mental reality—namely, social being—which alone determines thought existentially.

The first solution has offered for its own proof, in the main, nothing more substantial than a series of attacks on the sociology of knowledge. And the second solution expresses a thoroughgoing skepticism, for to say, in effect, that any interpretation is true provided one believes it to be true, is to deny both the existence and the meaningfulness of truth. But this position, so brilliantly presented by Ernst Grünwald,[21] cannot be refuted merely by calling it 'skeptical' or 'defeatist' or by employing any other nugatory criticism. That it does voice a despairing attitude toward the possibility of truth might, indeed, cause one to doubt its validity but could never prove definitely its invalidity. Turning to the third alternative, therefore, we must now consider the attempts at a positive establishment of social being as the extra-mental determinant of thought.

Two types of proof for the social determination of thought have been offered: Max Scheler strives to demonstrate the fact of social determination by deduction from a set of axioms, while Karl Mannheim seeks to prove its reality by induction. We take up first the deductive proof of Scheler.

Between knowledge and society, according to Scheler, there exist three possible fundamental relationships, and from these relationships follow the three chief axioms of the sociology of knowledge. The fundamental relationships Scheler presents thus:

> The knowledge that the members of any group have of each other and the possibility of their reciprocal 'understanding' is not, in the first place, something that comes *to* a social group but is rather something that *co-constitutes* the object, 'human society.' . . . To any 'group,' moreover, belongs some

knowledge, however vague, about its existence and also about
commonly recognized *values* and ends ... All knowledge and,
above all, all common knowledge about the *same* objects
determines, furthermore, the *specific characteristics* (*das Sosein*)
of society in *all* possible respects. But on the other hand, finally,
all knowledge is determined *through* society and *its* structure.[22]

And hence these principles or axioms: first, the knowledge that one
is a member of a society is not empirical but *a priori.* Second, one's
relation of participation in the experience of one's fellow-men is
realized in various ways, which are to be apprehended through ideal
types.[23] Third, 'in the order of the origin of our knowledge about
reality ... and in the order of the realization of the sphere of
knowledge peculiar to human consciousness and of the correlative
sphere of objects, there is a fixed law of order.'[24] These axioms,
furthermore, have certain important implications for the sociology
of knowledge:

It follows first that the sociological character of all knowledge,
of all forms of thought, intuition, cognition, is undubitable;
that although not, indeed, the *content* of all knowledge and still
less its objective validity, nevertheless the *selection* of the objects
of knowledge is co-determined according to the *ruling perspectives
of social interests*; that, furthermore, the 'forms' of the mental
acts in which knowledge is acquired are always and necessarily
co-determined *sociologically*, i.e., through the structure of
society. Since to explain always means to trace the relatively
new back to the known, and since society ... is always 'better
known' than anything else, we can now expect ... that both the
subjective forms of thought and intuition as well as the
classificatory *division* of the knowable world into categories ...
are co-determined by the division and classification of the
groups ... of which society consists.[25]

Observe, now, what Scheler attempts to do in the above. He tries
to prove, by deducing the thesis from a set of three axioms, that
social being ('perspectives of social interests' and 'the structure of
society') shares in the determination of knowledge. But anyone with
a rudimentary knowledge of logic knows that, no matter how
rigorously deduced a conclusion is, it remains no better than its
premises; and that, to prove the truth of the conclusion, the truth
of the premises must first be established. Has Scheler established the
truth of his premises, however? He apparently supposes that the
axioms—his premises—follow from the three fundamental relationships between knowledge and society, but he fails to show that they
actually do follow in their entirety. And even if he did show this, he
would still have to establish the relationships themselves as actual

relationships in the real world. But Scheler's method of proving the social determination of knowledge consists, first, in stating, with no attempt at genuine proof, a set of supposed relations between knowledge and society; then, in insinuating that the highest axioms of the sociology of knowledge derive from these relations; and, lastly, in deducing the social determination of knowledge from the axioms. The truth of the premises, however, remains unestablished.

And upon close inspection Scheler's argument reveals a still more incredible naivety of logic: he has performed no deduction at all. For consider the essential points of his argument in reverse order. The conclusion, *quod erat demonstrandum*, is that the sociological character of all knowledge is indubitable, etc. But from what is this basic principle of the sociology of knowledge deduced? From the proposition, comprehended in the third axiom, that 'the contemporary social sphere and the sphere of the historically past are *antecedent* to all other spheres (*a*) in reality and (*b*) in content and determinate meaning.'[26] And from what is the third axiom, in turn, deduced? From the third 'fundamental relation,' according to which all knowledge is determined through society and its structure. But where, we may ask, does any deduction occur? Is the first proposition deduced from the second, and the second from the third? Hardly: each statement merely expresses the identical idea in different words; and Scheler's earliest statement, in point of fact, is more precise and unequivocal than his later reformulations. Since Scheler's argument, therefore, is throughout dogmatic, it could never serve as a refutation of Grünwald's postulational skepticism.

In contrast to Scheler's supposedly *a priori*, deductive demonstration of social determination, Karl Mannheim attempts to establish it inductively and empirically. With great clarity he states the problem as follows:

> The existential determination of thought may be regarded as a demonstrated fact in those realms of thought in which we can show (*a*) that the process of knowing does not actually develop historically in accordance with immanent laws, that it does not follow only from the 'nature of things' or from 'pure logical possibilities,' and that it is not driven by an 'inner dialectic.' . . . This existential determination of thought will also have to be regarded as a fact (*b*) if the influence of these existential factors on the concrete content of knowledge is of more than mere peripheral importance, if they are relevant not only to the genesis of ideas, but penetrate into their forms and content and if, furthermore, they decisively determine the scope and the intensity of our experience and observation, i.e., . . . the 'perspective' of the subject.[27]

And to show that the 'existential factors in the social process' are 'of more than mere peripheral significance,' as also to show how they do 'penetrate into the "perspective" of concrete particular assertions,'[28] Mannheim adduces a number of examples of empirical evidence, although he refers to them simply as 'traits by which the perspective of an assertion may be characterized' and 'criteria which aid us to attribute it to a given epoch or situation.'[29]

In our opinion the characteristics of thought that Mannheim enumerates actually do characterize thought; moreover, they do seem to bear witness to the constitutive function of social reality in the intellectual realm. And no doubt there are a number of similar characteristics which one could also adduce and with which, added to Mannheim's, one could make out a good inductive case for the determination of thought by society. It might be objected by the postulational skeptic, however, that these facts only become evident or that they only exist or that they are only true upon the very supposition of what they purport to prove—namely, that society does determine thought. The skeptic might assert that on the assumption of another fundamental postulate, these social characteristics of thought would disappear, to be replaced by characteristics indicating the determination of thought by some other transcendent reality. It seems doubtful, therefore, that one could regard Mannheim's inductive proof as at all meeting the attack of Ernst Grünwald.

While no sociologist of knowledge has deliberately undertaken a study of the nature of mind with reference to social determinations, the 'vulgar Marxist,' Paul Szende, has come close to doing so. In his 'sociological theory of abstraction' he has attempted to describe not simply the result of social determination but also the mechanism, the mental process, through which social determination is effected.

Szende distinguishes between experience or sensory perception, on the one hand, and interpretation, on the other. The former being always veridical, it is in the latter that the ideological distortions, prompted by social interests, occur. And epistemology itself can be such an ideological distortion. Szende explains that

> experience, which always rests on immediate perception,
> preserves the connection with the external world; it gives
> information about its own requirements as well as about the
> changes occurring in the environment. In its elementary
> condition, sensory perception is unfalsified; to every man,
> without exception, it delivers similar, reliable communications.
> Without it, society would ossify. Therein consists its *democratic*
> feature.[30]

But the mind does not rest content with mere perception, mere experience: it operates upon experience. The basic operation of the mind on experience, in Szende's opinion, is the process of abstraction. Social interests guide this process. And it is in the process of abstraction that ideological falsification occurs, that interest-serving interpretations are developed out of the materials of veridical sense-perception. Abstraction, for Szende, consists in the neglecting of certain elements of a group of ideas and in the stressing of certain other elements, which are brought together into a concept.

> But what is neglected gradually falls into oblivion; the relation comes to be viewed as an independent being. This process of absolutizing becomes so much the more evident the thinner the content and the greater the compass of the concept, etc. .... At a primitive stage, man had already attained, little by little, the insight that a lasting influence on other men could best be achieved by producing in them the conviction that what *in reality is only the will and interest of a few individuals is properly viewed as in the interest of all.* Expressed in logical terms: A particular judgment, obtained by abstraction, is feigned to be universally valid. The relations, the motives, the particular interests from which one abstracted are utterly suppressed, the defective characteristics are laid aside.[31]

And Szende explains further that 'abstraction is a "purposeful-rational" act of choice, which takes place partly consciously, partly instinctively.'[32] The process of association he treats in a similar way.[33]

Szende thus carries the analysis of the theory of the social approach to thought a stage further than it is commonly carried. Not content with showing *that* sociological factors can be discriminated in the content of thought, he has also tried to show *how* the sociological factors actually do influence thought. Moreover (although we cannot afford the space for examples), he has applied his sociological theory of abstraction, in detail, to all the various disciplines from metaphysics and religion down through the sciences to statistics. It is true that Szende's work is altogether schematic, dogmatic, and unsupported by concrete research, as well as dubious in general outline. Nevertheless, Szende attempted to analyze mind as basically a social structure and process; while the sociologists of knowledge, who followed him, failed even to recognize the need for such an analysis.

Szende's analysis, however, does not yet go deep enough to escape the arguments of postulational skepticism. For, just as thought itself can be interpreted, alternatively, as determined by any of various transcendent factors, so the process of abstraction, too, can be interpreted as determined by race, climate, vital instincts, or what not, rather than by the interests of social classes. It would depend on one's 'fundamental premise,' as Grünwald says, which interpretation one would give to the process of abstraction. Thus, Szende has only described a manner in which social being may affect knowledge provided that social being does affect knowledge. In other words, while he has shown that the processes of the mind might be socially determined, he has not shown that they must be socially determined. And herein lies the chief weakness of Szende's analysis.

It appears, therefore, that if most of the refutations of the sociology of knowledge depend on dogma and confusion, the sociologists of knowledge, on their side, have thus far advanced no coercive ground for the objectivity of social determination. And such a ground alone could counter the arguments of postulational skepticism. But the theory of postulational skepticism itself, for all its brilliant ingenuity, is simply incredible. Since the incredible, however, is not necessarily false, we must consider this theory of Grünwald's anew.

And, after all, but little scrutiny reveals that Grünwald himself thinks in a highly dogmatic fashion: in his insistence that one must assume the determination of thought either by vital impulses or by race or by society, etc., Grünwald rejects the possibility that the disjunction might not be of an absolute and mutually exclusive type. He goes as far as to claim explicitly, in fact, that it is impossible for a thinker to assume more than one fundamental postulate at a time.[34] But why so? Without proof (and Grünwald offers no proof for this remarkable and basic claim) the assertion of the impossibility of a complex determination must remain itself pure dogma. Perhaps, therefore, the weakness of postulational skepticism lies in the elusive speciousness of its very clarity.

But Grünwald has undeniably presented a corrective to dogmatism —if in a dogmatic form—by calling attention to the multiplicity of factors that might determine thought. Let us consider the various possibilities of the situation, then, independently of Grünwald.

To begin with, no one with the slightest regard for the facts would deny that so some extent, in some fashion or other, thought does exhibit the influence of society. We shall therefore take this vague and indefinite sort of social determination as admitted; it is at least some kind of determination by a 'transcendent' factor. But can we deny that any other transcendent factor shares in the determination of thought? If we do deny this, we easily fall subject to Grünwald's criticism. But, after all, one cannot deny that other factors besides the social have some efficacy. Thought does seem to differ in certain respects with geography, with nationality, with race, and so forth. And such considerations would indicate the falsity of the claim that thought is determined by one extra-mental factor alone. In the second place, then, is thought determined by many factors acting individually? And again the answer would appear to be in the negative. For certainly some of the various factors do not act in complete isolation

ARTHUR CHILD

from one another: it is within highly particularized social-historical contexts that factors of geography and race, for instance, exert their hardly deniable influence on mentality. Indeed, it would seem precisely through social forms, through the reactions of man to environment in the quality of a social being, that the various nonsocial factors which transcend thought exert their peculiar influences on the realm of mind. Do these factors, finally, affect mind through the medium of one basic factor? The above considerations would point to this as the correct alternative. And that factor could hardly be other than the social, for the social alone appears always to be present in an effective and sufficient diversity of forms. If the last alternative could receive an adequate ground, therefore, as specified to the social, the arguments of postulational skepticism would be met, at last, in the measure and in the sense in which it is at all possible to meet them.

Thus it should be clear why the arguments of Scheler and Mannheim, apart from any logical deficiencies, fail to establish the possibility of the sociology of knowledge: their arguments contain nothing that could ground the primacy of the social determinant. It should also be clear why Szende's sociological theory of abstraction, apart from its naive conception of the process of abstraction, constitutes an especially significant attempt. For Szende perceived the central relevance of mind to the question at issue. But Szende dealt only with the functioning of mind; whereas, for an adequate grounding of the social approach to thought, the analysis must be conducted on a deeper level. The advocate of a social approach must show not merely how the mind might function: he must show also how it actually arises and what it is. For, if it can be established that both in origin and in constitution the mind is ineluctably social, then there will remain no doubt that knowledge is, in some sense and to some degree, expressive of a social determination.

Hence a social theory of mind, such as outlined in the social behaviorism of George Herbert Mead, becomes indispensable. For a social theory of mind provides the epistemological foundation without which, in the end, the interpretation of thought from a social standpoint cannot be critically defended against the traditional approach to thought, most ably maintained by Grünwald, as self-developing and self-inclosed. One need not accept in its entirety Mead's precise theory of the manner in which mind arises; many of the details, indeed, seem confused and contradictory. But the more general tenets appear quite susceptible of development into a theoretical foundation for the interpretation of thought from a social standpoint. If mind itself has a social origin—if, that is, it arises through the process of communication—and if thinking consists at bottom in the manipulation of generalized attitudes taken over from

98

the social group as a whole, then there can be no question of the social determination, in some sense, of knowledge and thought. And there can be no question, consequently, of the validity of the interpretation of thought from a social standpoint. Furthermore, if thought is indeed a social process, as Mead describes it, then neither can there be any question that, whatever transcendent determinants may exist besides society, they can determine mind only through the intermediation of social reality. Their function in respect to mind is but secondary; it is society which is primary and basic. And an adequate social theory of mind, therefore, would undermine the postulational skepticism of Ernst Grünwald.

But here we must make several qualifying remarks. The analysis of mind as social in origin and nature can provide no justification for the sociology of knowledge as a particular school of thought. The sociology of knowledge assumes many special and peculiar propositions which must also be justified in order to justify the sociology of knowledge as a school. For the sociology of knowledge, as we indicated at the beginning, is by no means identical with the social interpretation of thought. Second, the mere justification of the social approach leaves untouched the question of the meaning and the extent of social determination, as well as the problem of the interaction between this objective determination, the inherent logic of thought itself, and the spontaneous activity of the organically individualized mind. Third, while the general thesis of social determination may be true, it is quite another matter actually to discover and to establish that determination in concrete and specific research. The general theory can only justify the mode of investigation and ground the results of investigation; the results can in no sense be deduced from the general theory.

And there is a last, unavoidable reckoning with postulational skepticism—a reckoning, perhaps, which in a measure partakes of concession. For even if, in the view of social behaviorism, the theory of postulational skepticism has been undermined, the invincible skeptic might retort that social behaviorism itself appears only on the assumption of the social postulate. But we can argue with the skeptic no further: here, it would seem, we have come to one of those ultimate philosophical oppositions beyond which no additional analysis can avail. At such a point, indeed, the thinker must make a decisive and unambiguous choice as to the postulates from which his constructive reasoning will flow, as to his final—and only in that sense metaphysical—assumptions. It was precisely in the failure to reach any such point that the weakness of the various sociologies of knowledge lay. The strength of a more adequate theory for the social interpretation of thought will proceed, at least in part, from its conscious foundation upon assumptions that admit of no further reduction. And in such case, perhaps, by cogent reasoning upon those assumptions, one might hope to convince all who do not themselves build on postulates which, ultimately and irreducibly, stand in the most stringent opposition to the postulate of the intrinsic sociality of mind.

Notes

1 Julius Kraft, 'Soziologie oder Soziologismus?', *Zeitschrift für Völker-psychologie und Soziologie*, 5, Heft 4 (1929), 406.
2 *Ibid.*, p. 417.
3 Heinz O. Ziegler, 'Ideologienlehre', *Archiv für Sozialwissenschaft und Sozialpolitik*, 57, Heft 3 (1927), 689.
4 *Ibid.*, p. 690.
5 Karl Mannheim, 'Das Problem einer Soziologie des Wissens', *Archiv für Sozialwissenschaft und Sozialpolitik*, 53, Heft 3 (1925), 632.
6 Ziegler, *op. cit.*, p. 691 (emphases in the original).
7 *Ibid.*, pp. 691 ff.
8 *Ibid.*, p. 693.
9 Günther Stern, 'Über die sog. "Seinsverbundenheit" des Bewusstseins', *Archiv für Sozialwissenschaft und Sozialpolitik*, 64, Heft 3 (1930), 492 ff.
10 *Ibid.*, p. 494.
11 *Ibid.*, p. 499 (emphasis in the original).
12 'Die—eben bei Mannheim selbstverständliche—Voraussetzung, dass Geschichte immer weitergehe, die Voraussetzung, dass es eben Geschichte und nicht nur 'Geschichten' gebe ist selbst problematisch. Wo Geschichten aufeinander prallen, und ihre Vereinigung lediglich die Einheitsform des Kampfplatzes oder des gemeinsamen Kalenders erreicht, entsteht ein aussergeschichtlicher Hiatus' (*ibid.*, p. 501).
13 *Ibid.*, p. 503.
14 Helmuth Plessner, 'Abwandlungen des Ideologiegedankens', *Kölner Vierteljahrshefte für Soziologie*, 10, Heft 3 (1931), 168 ff.
15 *Ibid.*, p. 169.
16 Ernst Grünwald, *Das Problem der Soziologie des Wissens*, Vienna and Leipzig, 1934, p. 65.
17 *Ibid.*, pp. 65 ff.
18 *Ibid.*, p. 66.
19 *Ibid.*
20 *Ibid.*, p. 79.
21 Actually, Grünwald adheres both to the first and to the second positions; and, precisely because of his relentless development of the second position, he must be ranked also as the most persuasive exponent of the first.
22 Max Scheler, *Die Wissensformen und die Gesellschaft*, Leipzig, 1926, pp. 47 ff. (emphases in the original).
23 *Ibid.*, p. 48.
24 *Ibid.*, p. 52.
25 *Ibid.*, pp. 55 ff. (emphases in the original).
26 *Ibid.*, p. 53 (emphasis in the original).

27 Karl Mannheim, *Ideology and Utopia* (trans. L. Wirth and E. Shils), New York: Harcourt Brace Jovanovich, 1936, pp. 239 ff.

28 *Ibid.*, p. 243.

29 *Ibid.*, p. 244. For the seven traits that Mannheim discriminates, see *ibid.*, pp. 245–50.

30 Paul Szendf, 'Das System der Wissenschaften und die Gesellschafts-ordnung,' *Kölner Vierteljahrshefte für Sozialwissenschaften*, 2, Heft 4 (1922), 12 (emphasis in the original).

31 *Ibid.*, p. 10 (emphases in the original).

32 'Eine soziologische Theorie der Abstraktion', *Archiv für Sozialwissenschaft und Sozialpolitik*, 50, Heft 2 (1922), 420.

33 'Das System der Wissenschaften, etc.', pp. 11 ff.

34 Grünwald, *op. cit.*, p. 78.

6 Historicism[1]

Karl Mannheim

Historicism is an intellectual force with which we must come to grips willy-nilly. Just as in Athens Socrates was morally obliged to define his position *vis-à-vis* the Sophists, because the intellectual outlook of the latter corresponded to the socio-cultural conditions of the contemporary world and because their questions and doubts were a result of the broadening of the contemporary intellectual horizon, so we today are under a moral obligation to seek a solution to the problem of historicism.

Historicism has developed into an intellectual force of extra-ordinary significance; it epitomizes our *Weltanschauung* (world view). The historicist principle not only organizes, like an invisible hand, the work of the cultural sciences (*Geistewissenschaften*), but also permeates everyday thinking. Today it is impossible to take part in politics, even to understand a person—at least if we don't want to forgo present-day interpretive techniques—without treating all those realities which we have to deal with as having evolved and as developing dynamically. For in everyday life too we apply concepts with historicist overtones, for example, 'capitalism', 'social movement', 'cultural process', etc. These forces are grasped and understood as potentialities, constantly in flux, moving from some point in time to another; already on the level of everyday reflection, we seek to determine the position of our present within such a temporal framework, to tell by the cosmic clock of history what the time is. Our view of life has already become thoroughly sociological and sociology is just one of those spheres which, increasingly dominated by the principle of historicism, reflect most faithfully our new orientation in life.

Historicism is therefore neither a mere fad nor a fashion; it is not even an intellectual current, but the very basis on which we construct our observations of the socio-cultural reality. It is not something artificially contrived, something like a programme, but an organically developed basic pattern, the *Weltanschauung* itself, which came into being after the religiously determined medieval picture of the world had disintegrated and when the subsequent Enlightenment, with its dominant idea of a supra-temporal Reason, had destroyed itself.

Those present-day romantics who deplore the lack of a contemporary *Weltanschauung*, who have the slogan 'organically developed' constantly on their lips and who miss this 'organically developed' in present-day life, these romantics fail to notice that it is just historicism, and historicism alone, which today provides us with a world view of the same universality as that of the religious world view of the past, and that historicism alone could have developed 'organically' out of the preceding historical intellectual roots. In contrast to historicism, it is precisely romanticism—in so far as it propagates an earlier pattern of the world view as a standard for the conditions of modern life—which appears artificial, contrived, and merely a 'programme'.

All this does not mean that we should accept historicism as something given, as a fate which we cannot alter, as a higher and hostile power: historicism is indeed itself a *Weltanschauung* and hence is going through a dynamic process of development and systematization. It requires the philosophical labours of generations to help it mature and reach its final pattern. One would show little understanding if one were to accept any of its preliminary formulations as a final one.

If, then, one does not reject historicism out of hand but wishes to meet its challenge by going to its historic roots, then one must ask: 'what is the meaning of historicism, what do we understand by the term when we speak of it in this broader sense of a *Weltanschauung*?' It certainly is obvious that it does not connote historiography in general. Since Herodotus, history has been recorded in a multiplicity of different ways: as a plain chronicle of fact, as legend, as an edifying object of meditation, as a spiritual picture book, as rhetoric, as a work of art. We have historicism only when history itself is written from the historistic *Weltanschauung*. It is not historiography which brought us historicism, but the historic process through which we lived has turned us into historicists. Historicism, therefore, is a *Weltanschauung*, and at the present stage of the development of consciousness it is characteristic of *Weltanschauung* that it should not only dominate our inner reactions and our external responses, but also determine our forms of thought. Thus, at the present stage, science and scientific methodology, logic, epistemology, and ontology are all moulded by the historicist approach. Historicism exists only since the problems involved in the new ways of facing life—problems which found perhaps their most tangible expression in historiography—reached the level of self-consciousness.

The idea of *evolution* was undoubtedly the crystallization point, the philosophical axis of the new history as well as that of the new view of life. It is therefore the history of the idea of evolution that we may take as a starting point from which historicism may be most fruitfully and clearly understood. The idea of evolution is, however, only the most advanced component of this *Weltanschauung*; once we think and live through its implications we cannot stop short of building around it a comprehensive mode of living and a congruent system of thought.

The first approach to a historistic mode of thought and living lies, in any case, in the ability to experience every segment of the spiritual-intellectual world as in a state of flux and growth. We have become attuned to the doctrine of historicism only since there were written books about the evolution of institutions, customs, religions, psychic contents, etc. But so long as we confine ourselves to the mere registration of the 'mobility' of all these mental contents, so long as we are content with a simple feeling of eternal flux, we have still failed to grasp the full essence of historicism. It will be nothing but a new experience added to a variety of others, and if we carry on our philosophical reflection from this point, then we shall obtain nothing better than certain brands of relativism which are not too difficult to refute. The widely ramifying problems of dynamics arise only when one begins to realize that something more than a mere chameleon-like variation in the elements of life takes place in history. Historicism is more than the discovery that men were thinking, feeling, writing poetry, painting, and conducting business in different ways from one age to another. Historicist theory fulfils its own essence only by managing to derive an *ordering principle* from this seeming anarchy of change—only by managing to penetrate the *innermost structure* of this all-pervading change.

One can, however, work out this order from two directions: firstly, via an historical vertical analysis and secondly, via an historical cross-section. In the first case, one takes any *motif* of the intellectual-cultural life—an artistic form, a political idea, a certain mode of behaviour, etc.—and traces it back into the past, trying to show how each later form develops continuously, organically from the earlier. If one gradually extends this method to all the spheres of cultural life, then one will obtain, so to speak, a bundle of isolated evolutionary lines. Within each individual line of filiation, the merely factual, random nature of change disappears and we are able to observe the *law* of change. The different lines of development themselves, however, are still thrown together rather at random, without any recognizable law. This type of historicism is not completed until the second set of cross-sectional observations have been made; these are made to show how, at one temporal stage, the *motifs*, which have just been observed in isolation, are also organic-ally bound up with one another. The stream of ideas does not, then, flow and swell in separate channels (represented by the various spheres of life and culture). The separate *motifs* are, rather, mutually conditioning at the successive stages of evolution and are components and functions of an ultimate basic process which is the real 'subject' undergoing the change.

To work out the structure or the configuration[2] of this total process on the basis of a thorough examination of its separate elements is the final aim of historicism—a universal metaphysical and methodological principle which comes more and more to dominate the cultural sciences and now has become paramount in aesthetics, the science of religion, sociology, and the history of ideas. To extract out of the many-sided reality its slowly changing pattern and the structure of its inner balance, is the aim and at the same time the anticipated final vision of a fully developed historicism. At the present time even special historical investigations are, as far as is possible, undertaken with such an anticipatory vision of the totality of history in mind, and there are frequent attempts to explain the present in terms of these historicist concepts.

At this juncture, however, our historical researches and also our ways of experiencing the present become more than mere historio-graphy—they turn into a philosophy of history. We no longer wish to know merely 'what happened'. We are interested not only in the immediate 'why' (the immediate causal antecedents) of an event, but we also constantly ask ourselves: 'what does it mean?' As we inte-grate the element in question (the historical fact) into a totality, indeed a dynamic totality, and thence assess its meaning, our question becomes philosophical and the special science of history as well as the contemplation of life once again becomes philosophical. Whereas in the past it was a religious framework into which the various particular experiences were inserted so as to acquire a philosophical meaning, so now it is an historico-philosophical vision, which, increasingly refined and made more concrete in research, provides, with the help of the unifying principle of historicism, a philosophical interpretation for our world experience. It becomes increasingly clear that the hard-and-fast separation between history and the philosophy of history[3]—according to which the former appears as a rigidly specialized discipline—merely corresponds to the degree of insight, or, it may be, the lack of insight, of a particular epoch. At the same time it becomes increasingly clear that even the seemingly most specialized investigation of historical detail has its basis in the philosophy of history—for otherwise, whence would its problem be derived?

If, after what has been a period of maximum concentration upon isolated topics of specialized research, historical science increasingly seeks to put specialized investigations in a more and more comprehensive framework, and if, as a result, historical science is finally driven to work out its own outline, its foundations and presuppositions in the form of a philosophy of history, this only means that history becomes conscious of what up to now has been its unconscious driving principle. Historicism becomes a philosophy of history by extracting the implicit philosophy of historical description and consciously analysing the problems involved in the representation of the past. In this process, however, the life conditions which gave rise to historicism, and the historiography which received its impulse from the same life conditions, reach the stage of consciousness, the stage of systematic self-realization. Philosophical problems which had already *existentially* determined the strains and tensions of the living *Weltanschauung* now present themselves at the level of reflective consciousness.

New philosophies do not arise in the fashion that someone works out a system or secretes a new set of ideas; they come into being when the already existing, but largely unreflective, philosophical content of the new vital attitudes enters the centre of the field of vision. It is possible to show that even the apparently most extremely specialized methodological and logical problems arise as the result of the focusing of conscious attention upon, and the full development of all implications of, those premises which had already been present, though not explicitly expressed, within some new vital pattern. It is, however, a peculiarity of life and of living thought, that they do not, as it would appear from the point of view of the completed system, proceed from a generalized premise or systematic starting-point toward the concrete and particular, deducing the latter from the former. The process is rather something like this: the unreflective life is concerned at first with immediate, concrete experiences and starts *in medias res*. Only subsequently, at the reflective stage, are those premises abstracted which lie hidden within these stimuli. But just that which one perceives in 'phenomenological' immediacy, is, in fact, already shaped by the historical process; it is already permeated by the form-giving categories of a new 'reason', a new 'psyche'. In every event, then, there is something other than the event 'itself'. The event is moulded by a totality, either in the sense of a law of patterning or in the sense of a principle of systematization. Hence there are premises embedded in the unique event which can be unravelled. One may call this a 'miracle'; but it proves, in any case, that our unreflective creation of culture, our actions, our behaviour, and our perception, which carve new worlds in and around us, already possess definite categories and are mentally linked to reflective thought. These considerations show also that thought is only one of those organs we are using in groping our way ahead in the historical space surrounding us, taking possession of it, creating it, and, at the same time, accounting for it. Cognition is no pure contemplation—it approximates to this limit at most in certain specialized fields—it is no straight receptiveness, but is rather, like all sensory forms of organization, at one and the same time creative and receptive; it flows onwards, creating and receiving new forms in one continuous process.

We now undertake to pursue the present stage of historicism into its last philosophical implications—to disengage those factual, epistemological, and logical presuppositions which *are already contained in its non-reflective application.* Thus with the systematization of historicism itself, a destiny is fulfilled which historicism had to discover for all the past forms of the world process: that life has the constant tendency to ossify itself into a system.

At this stage of systematization of a new form of *Weltanschauung,* stresses occur which have to be brought into the focus of consciousness before we can proceed farther; such strains have existed ever since there has been a systematic, philosophical *Weltanschauung* at all. A conflict or tension arises between the ultimate conclusions and refinements which an earlier philosophy had obtained, by analysing an earlier stage of consciousness, on the one hand, and a different set of ultimate presuppositions which are derived from reflection upon the new socio-cultural reality, on the other.

If one wishes, therefore, to pursue the theory of historicism into its last philosophical implications, one has the peculiar task of viewing historically philosophy itself and of giving the historical character of all philosophy the status of a proposition within one's own philosophical system. Ultimately it is a matter of interpreting in terms of a systematic insight the proposition that even philosophy undergoes an organic change of pattern. This implies, however, the existence of some idea of the relationship which the philosophies of the different epochs bear to one another. That is to say, we must have some idea whether the different philosophies mutually destroy each other or whether they develop together, so to speak, in a supra-temporal division of labour as ultimate parts of a still unfinished system. Or, again, whether they are constantly constructed anew from still *more comprehensive new centres* in such a way that the old insights are incorporated in the new and invested with new significance. We believe that the last-mentioned conception is implied in the idea of historicism.

It would be, therefore, unhistorical simply to reject the conclusions of an earlier philosophy. They, too, derive from reflection upon a certain stage of socio-cultural reality which is itself part of the total dynamic process. One can say only that the conclusions of a past philosophy were obtained at a time when the new socio-cultural substratum had not yet emerged, so that no reflection could be directed upon it. But this is certainly no justification for an out-and-out rejection of the earlier conclusions and problems; what we have to do is rather to incorporate them in our own system. This means at the stage we have reached that the ostensibly universal significance of the earlier systems should be reduced to a partial, parochial one, and that its elements—in so far as they retain any validity at all—should be re-interpreted from a new systematic centre.

What is utterly impossible, however, is to negate a new philosophy, based upon the reflective analysis of a new stage of socio-cultural reality, *merely because this new system contradicts the ultimate presuppositions of an earlier system,* corresponding to an earlier stage. This is, however, just what is done by those who, imbued with the philosophy of the Enlightenment, reject *ab ovo* the gradually developing new insights of historicism. In this context, we mean by 'philosophy of the Enlightenment' those systems which in whatever form contain *a doctrine of the supra-temporality of Reason.* All the refutations coming from this quarter essentially amount to the charge of relativism, as allegedly implied by historicism. This slogan is thought to be sufficient to destroy the new challenger. In Germany it is mainly Kantianism that provides arguments for this type of refutation of historicism. The idea of the persisting identity, the eternal sameness, and the *a priori* character of the formal categories of Reason constitutes that kernel of Enlightenment thought which is challenged by the historicist approach, in so far as it has already developed.

What we have to show, as against Enlightenment, is that the most general definitions and categories of Reason vary and undergo a process of alteration of meaning—along with every other concept—in the course of intellectual history. It is rather questionable in general whether 'form' can be sharply separated from 'content'. We may always ask to what extent the particular content, which, after all, is unqualifiedly historical, determines the particular formal structure. If, however, one tries to evade the problems involved in historicity by assuming a timeless 'form as such', 'concept as such', 'value as such', and similar 'as such' structures, then it becomes impossible to say anything concrete in methodology at all. But even this self-immobilizing position may be shown to be historico-philosophically determined. Absolute formalism is limited to, and can only arise in, a socio-cultural environment in which all values in their concreteness have become doubtful and the abstract form of value as such alone remains credible. This, however, means introducing an abstract, artificial distinction into the indissoluble unity of the cultural products—a distinction, by the way, which has nothing to do with supra-temporal validity. It corresponds completely to a historico-philosophical situation, which manifested this 'formal impulse' in all spheres and hence was able to comprehend the intended state of affairs only within a very partial perspective. That, in fact, the form-content dichotomy which is at the basis of a static philosophy of Reason is completely devoid of universal applicability, that it merely fits a type of thinking one-sidedly oriented toward the manipulation of rigid thing-like objects, may be seen from the fact that actually, if not avowedly, such thinking always operates with lifeless models. When one speaks of formal categories or formal values, one thinks of containers or tubes in which liquids, say wine, can be constantly poured and where the vessels are thought of as permanent forms endowed with enduring identities. One obtains, however, a completely different correlation between form and content, when one starts out from models based on living and growing plants. Here, not only does the growing substance change, the sap rise and fall, but the form and the configuration (*Gestalt*) of the plant grows with and varies with the self-renewing 'content'. The farther we get away from the world of rigid 'things', the closer we get to the actual historical substratum of psychic and intellectual reality, the more we shall doubt the validity of such ostensibly supra-temporal attempts at splitting up reality which concentrate all change on one side and all permanence on the other. The questions of the possibility and adequacy of historical abstraction, generalization, and formalization arise once again at this point. We mention these problems, however, only to cast doubt upon the alleged self-evidence of the anti-historicist positions.

As a further argument against historicism, it has often been urged that logic and the theory of knowledge have a priority over the data of such special sciences as, say, psychology and history. It is maintained that the various genetic facts (i.e. the historical findings concerning the constant variation in the content of Reason, as it manifests itself in the special sciences), can in no way affect the assertions of principle made by those systematic sciences which provide a foundation for any knowledge.

What then, if it can be shown that the theory of knowledge of a particular epoch embraces nothing other than the ultimate assumptions of a thought pattern which happened to be the dominant one in that epoch? That the epistemologist and the logician in fact merely followed the lead provided by certain particular modes of experience (e.g. religious experience), or in scientific epochs, by the methodological peculiarities of certain special sciences which just came into the centre of interest? What if it can be shown—as is already clear today—that the ideal of an eternally identical Reason is nothing other than the leading principle of an epistemological system constructed *post factum*, a system that obtained its experiential foundations from the analysis of the conceptual structure of the exact natural sciences? It was in order to account for the exact natural sciences in the form in which they existed that one was obliged to construct a static Reason which would permit of eternal laws.[4] One would have reached a far different theory of knowledge if one had taken as a starting point the dynamic historical sphere. Indeed, the chief problem of the Kantian theory of knowledge, which was in the form: 'how is (exact natural science) possible?' suffices to show that although epistemology is supposed to provide a foundation for the various sciences, it is in fact dependent, both as to its own structural framework and as to its concrete historical content, on those spheres of knowledge which supply the material for its analyses.[5] Consequently, the fact that one starts out with certain postulates, discovered in the analysis of one field of knowledge, does not enable one simply to do away with those postulates which are derived from the observation of other fields of knowledge.

Finally, what if it can be shown that the accusation of relativism derives from a philosophy which professes an inadequate conception of 'absolute' and 'relative'; a philosophy which confronts 'truth' and 'falsehood' in a way which makes sense in the sphere of so-called exact science, but not in history, since in the latter there are aspects of the same subject-matter which can be regarded, not as either true or false, but as essentially dependent on a given perspective or standpoint which can co-exist with others?

In all these above-mentioned considerations, we have already confronted *the ultimate position of a static philosophy of Reason with that of a dynamic historical philosophy of life.* Here we are not concerned with details, but rather with showing to how great an extent the ultimate, logically decisive arguments of the two philosophies are supra-philosophical and pre-philosophical in origin. The fundamental problems: whether Reason is to be regarded as dynamic or static, whether the theory of knowledge possesses a structural priority over the philosophy of history, whether the final concept of truth, i.e. the distinction of the absolute and the relative, is conceivable only in one single form—and, in general, all the criteria which have a bearing upon this controversy—all depend on the attitude one takes toward reality and on the particular field of knowledge one prefers to invoke. The differences have extra-theoretical roots, and although one understands fully what the other means, one cannot achieve a theoretical mediation between these various pre-theoretical positions as long as one remains attached to them. This is what we have to show before everything else.

In one sense, historicism already possesses an unconditional superiority over its opponents; it can conceive the contrast not only in the antitheses of the *theoretical* systems, but can illustrate this contrast in terms of contrasting modes of practical behaviour. Up to now, it has been only in the field of theory that our analytic discernment, sharpened by controversies, was in a position to discover, whenever a dispute arose, the ultimate theoretical assumptions which were responsible for the fact that divergent assertions could be propounded concerning one and the same state of affairs. But now the historicist is in a position, and will be so in an ever-increasing degree, to point out what extra-philosophical and pre-philosophical attitudes of life and what dominant socio-cultural realities determine the choice of this or that set of axioms. In so doing, the historicist steps beyond the immanent exclusiveness of theory and becomes more or less an 'irrationalist' and 'philosopher of life'. But even this transgression of the boundaries of a particular sphere does not mean that he can be censured as a matter of course, as he is by those who have recourse to the autonomy of theory as something completely *a priori*.

We can discover in the doctrine of the *autonomy of the theoretical sphere* a further fundamental opposition between historicist and non-historicist philosophy. The doctrine of the autonomy of the theoretical sphere is generally put forward by its adherents with complete, unquestioning finality; the reason for this, however, is not that the thesis is beyond doubt, but merely that it is taken for granted as a seemingly self-evident axiom of this type of philosophy. This axiom (the doctrine of the autonomy of theory) has, however, its roots and ultimate foundation in a pre-theoretical soil. When this doctrine of the autonomy of Reason appeared in modern times, it did reflect a sociological relationship between different spheres that actually prevailed in the contemporary 'system of life and culture'. This relationship is, however, by no means timeless and eternal, but subject to historical variation, and this to such an extent that if one could describe how the relationship between the different spheres of life presented itself to immediate experience in different periods, one would get hold of the most fundamental index of cultural change. As evidence of the pre-theoretical foundations of the doctrine of the autonomy of theory, we may mention in passing the fact that for the Middle Ages, the subordinate, 'ancillary' relationship which philosophy and every other theory bore to theology, and to the religious sphere behind it, was something entirely beyond question. This was, however, in no way due to a narrow-mindedness, but was rather an ultimate formulation of that relationship between the different spheres of life which characterized the medieval world and dominated its mode of life. Just as, at that time, there did not exist any autonomous theory, so too, there was no autonomous ethics, no autonomous art, etc.; these were so embedded in the religious sphere that we cannot speak of them as autonomous in the same sense as we can with perfect justification when we deal with later periods. Only when the hierarchical determination of all the departments of life in the Middle Ages had lost its fulcrum in the religous sphere, only then do we see a process in the course of which the various spheres of life become independent of each other instead of being merged in unity. And in due course we encounter theories concerning the autonomy of these vital spheres as a reflection of the existential process of their separation. Art emancipated itself in the Renaissance and then went through that development which ultimately culminated in the idea of *l'art pour l'art*. Ethical action, which was primarily based in religious experience and in a metaphysical system adequate to it, tended towards value autonomy (*Selbstwertigkeit*). Exactly the same took place with philosophy and with the 'theoretical sphere' as a whole, which also emancipated itself from its ancillary position relative to the religious centre. It is in the Renaissance that the different spheres of life begin to emancipate themselves and achieve the autonomy of ethical action, artistic creation, and theoretical thought. The *doctrine* of the autonomy of the different spheres is only a reflective justification of that process which had already been completed and which only gained in depth and intensity as a result of philosophical reflection. Aesthetics, now constituted as a new science, ethics, with its doctrine of the autonomy of ethical valuation, and not least, the doctrine of the autonomy of the theoretical sphere over and against all other spheres—all these are now normative constructions and supra-temporal hypostatizations of this pre-reflective and historically determined relationship of the different spheres to one another. But it is just at this point that our own cultural outlook seems to be undergoing a transformation. We notice in all spheres (the 'ideological' is most conspicuous) that in contrast to these tendencies toward autonomy, atomization, and analysis (three fundamentally different tendencies, which nevertheless have something in common) there is taking place a movement toward synthesis. What historicism undertakes in the individual historico-cultural spheres, in art history, in the history of religion, in sociology, etc., in that it exhibits these different spheres of culture, not in their immanent exclusiveness, but as an integrative part of a totality—what historicism accomplishes here, is attempted also—to give one example out of many—in modern psychology. Here too, for example, the principle holds, that we should not only investigate the various sensory fields in isolation from one another, but should also explore the problems of the solidarity and unity of sensory experience. Here too, that analysing, atomizing, isolating tendency which dominated the other sciences as well, and which led to the endeavour to build up the most complex structures out of the most simple elements, is being supplanted by the recognition of 'complexes' and 'totalities' as primary and irreducible data, as given, for example, in perceptions of *Gestalt*. All these examples may be regarded as symptomatic of the fact that on the reflective ('ideological') side of the total process, one can find a number of parallel trends. This raises the question whether these phenomena do not represent a counterpart, at the level of scientific method, to the transformation process which is taking place in the social structure. If the atomizing, sectionalizing mode of thought may be regarded as corresponding to a social structure which allowed a maximum dissolution of the social bonds and which produced an economy consisting of liberalistically independent, atom-like units, then the present trend toward synthesis, toward the investigation of totalities may be regarded as the emergence, at the level of reflection, of a force which is pushing social reality into more collectivistic channels. It may very well be, indeed, that this newly developing impulse to restore a psychic and intellectual unity in the place of the separation of spheres brought about by the previous epoch, the levelling down of the sharp boundaries between them, corresponds to a general change in practical attitudes. Here too, therefore—so far as we can now see—the changed world situation is the basis for the emergence of a new theoretical superstructure. Here too, the doctrine of the autonomy of theory reveals itself to the eye of the sociologist of knowledge and the philosopher of history, in the same way as the earlier mentioned hypostatized non-temporal axioms of the philosophy of Reason, as *bound* to the historico-philosophical position and its corresponding 'life basis' (*Lebensunterlage*). By pointing out the basic connectedness of the theoretical premises of an epoch with the total structure of sociocultural reality, we do not intend to deny flatly that these doctrines have any lasting validity at all. For in the final analysis of these problems, one will have to examine the question whether the results of a structural analysis and a demonstration of the philosophico-historical and sociological determination of theory can in itself establish, or, if it be so, refute the straight systematic validity (*Geltungssinn*) of the theory itself. We were primarily interested in confronting the ultimate presuppositions of the two theories radically opposing one another today, a supra-temporal philosophy of Reason on the one hand, and a dynamically conceived historicist view on the other. Some of the points we sought to make were these: how the ultimate points of support of the possible arguments are organically bound up with the alternative of *static* and *dynamic*; how a static conception of the autonomy of Reason is bound up with the doctrine of the autonomy of theory; how, at the same time, the establishment of the primacy of epistemology leads to the same position from a different direction; and how this same position is connected with a

113

particularly rigid distinction—not tempered by historical considerations—between the 'absolute' and 'relative' as well as with a complete severance of all ties between the temporal and the supra-temporal. On the other hand, we wanted to show how all those positions, which in a static mode of thought consist of a system of mutually supporting propositions and as such are regarded as self-evident, become problematic in their very pre-suppositions for a dynamic mode of thought.

When one takes one's departure, not from a static Reason, but from a dynamically developing totality of the whole psychic and intellectual life as from the ultimately given, the place of epistemology as a fundamental science will be taken by the philosophy of history as a dynamic metaphysic; all problems as to how the various realms of thought and life are 'grounded' in one another become re-oriented around this fresh point of departure. What was formerly taken for granted thereby once again becomes problematic.

Notes

1 First published in *Archiv für Sozialwissenschaft und Sozialpolitik*, Tübingen: Mohr, vol. 52, no. 1 (June 1924), pp. 1–60.
2 The understanding of structure and of configuration is in no way the same thing. Alfred Weber has recently urged that there are two fundamentally different approaches to history ('Kultursoziologie', *Der Neue Merkur*, vol. 7, pt 3 (1923), pp. 169 ff.). He differentiates between a 'logical' and a 'configurational' (*Gestalt*) experience. At the present stage in this introductory section, where we are still describing historicism, we need not go farther into the difference between the two methods.
3 This interdependence of history and the philosophy of history has in our time been most impressively demonstrated by Croce. Cf. *Zur Theorie und Geschichte der Historiographie* (trans. Enrico Pizzo), Tübingen, 1905 (trans. Douglas Ainslie: *On the Theory and the History of Historiography*, S.A.S.). Cf. esp. ch. 4, 'Entstehung und begriffliche Auflösung der Geschichtsphilosophie', pp. 52 ff., also pp. 104 ('The Origin and the Conceptual Solution of the Philosophy of History').
4 This does not mean to say that this 'timeless' conception of Reason emerges as a matter of historic fact only with the epoch of the natural sciences; in reality, it was there much earlier. In the text above, we are primarily concerned with the *function* of this postulate in the thought system of philosophies oriented toward the exact natural sciences.
5 On the structural dependence of epistemology on the other sciences, cf. my study: 'Die Strukturanalyse der Erkenntnistheorie', *Ergänzungshefte der Kantstudien*, no. 57, Berlin, 1922.

7 Some social-psychological and political functions of ideology

Rolf Schulze

The purpose of this paper is to outline and examine a few basic functions which ideology performs for the individual and for society. In order to progress in this direction, it might help to agree on some basic conceptual definitions. To begin with, some effort must be made to arrive at a satisfactory definition of ideology, since that term occupies a rather central place in this paper.

It is recognized that the term (and concept) 'ideology' has undergone a number of changes in meaning from its probable inception during the French Enlightenment to its use by contemporary sociologists of knowledge. Scholars trace the recorded conceptual antecedents of the term 'ideology' from Greek antiquity through Francis Bacon (who recognized the influence of 'idols' on human affairs) to the French *philosophes* and Destutt de Tracy, most often credited with the creation of the term, *idéologie*, i.e., the study of ideas. From this initially neutral use of the term denoting the 'science of ideas,' the term gradually became associated with disparate and often derogatory connotations through diverse use by philosophers, politicians, laymen, and scholars.[1] The rather one-sided Marxian usage of ideology to denote the class-based *Weltanschauung* of the bourgeois 'enemy' was in time replaced by sociologists of knowledge with a more generic application of the term to a variety of politico-philosophical belief systems. It would appear desirable from the viewpoint of the researcher to define the term ideology in a rather universal manner, allowing him to apply the term to all types of belief systems.[2] The definition proposed below is designed to focus on those characteristics of ideology which are found among all groups of people regardless of their specific affiliation and type of belief system.

I propose we view ideology as a pattern of beliefs shared with other individuals and/or a group, which are held to be highly relevant to

ROLF SCHULZE

the group and individual, which are capable of generating high commitment, and which serve to justify and generate the particular values, norms, attitudes, and behavior of a group and its members.[3] More briefly, ideology is here defined as a pattern of beliefs characterized by a variable degree of commitment regardless of the type of content. The addition of the term 'content' to the latter definition deserves some comment. In order to enlarge the concept of ideology beyond mere classification and labeling, emphasis is here directed to the quantitative, ordinal, and empirically measurable aspects of ideology (such as degree of commitment) regardless of the particular label or content. In other words, it will be empirically more useful and more parsimonious theoretically to employ the single term 'ideology' for both political and religious patterns of belief, as well as for any other type of belief system.

Although typological models of ideology abound in the literature,[4] the more or less exclusive focus on differences in content robs the concept (of ideology) of its variable quality. Thus instead of fully exploiting this important social dimension we restrict ourselves to the relatively nominal and crude typological aspects of ideology. Mere labeling of individuals and groups as 'Catholic' or 'socialist' and the like is insufficient and deprives social scientists of at least one other useful, i.e., variable, aspect of the concept ideology, such as the above-mentioned degree of commitment to a particular ideology.

Despite the relatively long history of the use of the concept ideology in our discipline, only recently have attempts been made to focus on the quantitative aspects of ideology.[5] Cross-cultural quantitative and comparative work on ideology is either extremely rare or non-existent at this time.

Among writings on the functions of ideology of interest to our field, one may distinguish two major approaches: (1) the sociological (or socio-political-historical); and (2) the social-psychological. The former is exemplified by the majority of historians, anthropologists, political scientists, and sociologists, who utilize the classical division of ideologies by content, by core values, or by ascertaining a person's associational membership (without attending to quantitative dimensions of ideology).[6]

The second major mode of viewing functions of ideology may be classified as the social-psychological approach. Here the emphasis would be on the individual within his social milieu, on measuring the degree of commitment to any type of ideology, or on ascertaining the type and content of an ideology through interviews, questionnaires, or observation of the individual.

This social-psychological approach may be the only means of ascertaining the type, content, and degree of ideological commitment on the part of persons in a society who are formally unaffiliated,

116

unassociated, or otherwise estranged from the social system. It is unlikely that such persons are totally devoid of some personal belief system. Furthermore, as a consequence of their social position, i.e., as members of a particular social category, for example, as poor and black in a general affluent white society, they will not only develop an individual (negative) self-image but also a common set of beliefs about themselves as members of an indentifiable social group. In other words, social, situational factors influence one's social perspective and one's orientation toward others and society at large.[7] Not just formally organized associations but also members of social categories must possess some identifiable and measurable form of ideology—some pattern of beliefs, values, norms, and attitudes. But if they do not 'belong' (as is the case with much of our recently rediscovered poverty population), traditional sociological means of assuming the content of a person's ideology by classifying his major affiliation (church, party, union, or the like) will not work. Thus we must perforce rely on some social-psychological techniques.[8]

One of the implicit assumptions underlying any discussion of ideology is the well-established supposition of the universal need for ideology. Many scholars have devoted space to this notion, and thus I shall only summarize their major contentions. First, it is generally agreed that some cosmological ideology is found in every culture. Second, this cosmology is generally embodied in some 'religious,' i.e., supernatural belief system. Third, there is a learned need for some cosmology which is usually inculcated through the socialization process which includes the teaching (by the parents, religious,[9] and educational functionaries) and acceptance (by the person) of a particular ideology, e.g., Catholicism, Buddhism, socialism, or others.[10]

I think we may agree that there is indeed a universal need for some form of ideology, regardless of the origin of such need. This need is apparently based on the search for meaning, for ultimate meanings about the purpose of life and death, and the desire to justify and order the diverse experiences of a lifetime. Whatever the reasons for the universal existence and the postulated need for some ideology, a legitimate question might now be: does only 'religious' ideology satisfy this need or could a secular political ideology fulfill a similar function? An answer to this question is suggested by the data in the accompanying tables.

While Table 7.1 demonstrates a significant inverse relationship between degree of ideological commitment and meaninglessness-alienation (similar to the significant inverse relationship found between ideological commitment and normlessness, powerlessness, and self-estrangement), Table 7.2 illustrates the same relationship while dividing the total sample into members of primarily religious or

ROLF SCHULZE

political associations.[11] The results indicate that meaninglessness is significantly less among highly committed members of both political as well as religious associations. As a matter of fact, the relationship between degree of commitment (to the association and its ideology) and meaninglessness is somewhat stronger for the political groups than for the religious groups.

Thus, in respect to supply of 'meaning' both religious as well as political ideologies appear to be capable of functioning equally well. Additional results, not reported here, indicate that nondenominational respondents satisfied their need for meaning through political belief patterns, while denominational sample members drew meaning from their religious ideology. At a minimum, it appears that both religious as well as political ideologies can provide meaning and can reduce certain types of alienation.[12] Maximally speaking, perhaps commitment to any type of ideology has that effect. Thus in addition to providing cosmological meaning, ideology and ideological commitment fulfill some more prosaic, but nevertheless important, social-psychological functions.

The preceding discussion also bears on a topic which enjoyed a certain popularity a few years ago, namely, the 'end of ideology' theme supported by such scholars as Daniel Bell, S. M. Lipset,

TABLE 7.1 *Percentage of ideological commitment by meaninglessness-alienation**

IDEOLOGICAL COMMITMENT†	MEANINGLESSNESS-ALIENATION†				
	Low	*Intermediate*		*High*	*Total cases*
Low	16·2	27·5	53·3	64·4	170
Medium	42·5	47·8	36·3	26·0	168
High	41·3	24·7	10·4	9·6	88
Total %	100·0	100·0	100·0	100·0	
Total cases	80	138	135	73	426‡

$\chi^2 = 68·614$; d.f. = 6; P<0·001; C = 0·372; Gamma = −0·482.

* The sample of $n = 441$ was drawn from members in fourteen groups in five different cities of West Germany which represent several points (from 'left' to 'right') along the socio-religio-political spectrum.
† Items making up the index of Ideological Commitment and Meaninglessness-alienation are found on pp. 119–20.
‡ 15 cases undefined.

Edward Shils, and others. Ideology, far from being at an end, being in decline, or in danger of disappearing, has re-emerged as the focal point of major social concern in recent years. I have argued elsewhere that the old-line and traditional forms, patterns, and labels of ideology may have receded, but that simultaneously other patterns of beliefs, other ideologies, and new associations have taken their place.[13] For example, the American socialism of the thirties and forties has been replaced by the 'New Left' and a host of related social movements. Whether we adopt a macro socio-political viewpoint or a social-psychologically oriented stance, it seems clear that the need for ideology is relatively constant. There cannot be an ideological vacuum. When one major ideology fails (or is discredited), another form must take its place. After the demise of Nazism, Germany witnessed first a remarkable religious revival (including a variety of

TABLE 7.2 *Percentage of ideological commitment by meaninglessness by type of association*

POLITICAL GROUPS

| IDEOLOGICAL COMMITMENT | MEANINGLESSNESS-ALIENATION | | | |
	Low	Intermediate	High	Total cases
Low	12·1	24·1	51·3	62·2	96
Medium	40·9	48·3	34·2	31·1	109
High	47·0	27·6	14·5	6·7	69
Total %	100·0	100·0	100·0	100·0	
Total cases	66	87	76	45	274

$\chi^2 = 53\cdot352$; d.f. $= 6$; p$<0\cdot0001$; C $= 0\cdot404$; Gamma $= -0\cdot523$.

RELIGIOUS GROUPS

| IDEOLOGICAL COMMITMENT | MEANINGLESSNESS-ALIENATION | | | |
	Low	Intermediate	High	Total cases
Low	35·7	33·3	55·9	67·9	74
Medium	50·0	47·1	39·0	17·9	59
High	14·3	19·6	5·1	14·2	19
Total %	100·0	100·0	100·0	100·0	
Total cases	15	51	59	28	152

$\chi^2 = 14\cdot980$; d.f. $= 6$; p$<0\cdot025$; C $= 0\cdot300$; Gamma $= -0\cdot340$.

The index used to ascertain the degree of ideological commitment contains the following items:

(a) If someone verbally attacks our association, I feel I should defend the association.

119

ROLF SCHULZE

(b) Association members should vote only for those political candidates who are endorsed by the association.

(c) Whenever the association takes a stand on a particular issue, I usually support the official position of the association.

(d) One should never publicly criticize or attack the position of one's own organization.

(e) An association member's interests are fundamentally different from those of other associations or groups.

(f) I would prefer not to belong to this organization.

(g) I try as far as I am able to constantly improve our organization.

(h) I would like to get out of this group at the first, best opportunity.

The meaninglessness dimension was ascertained by means of the following items:

(a) I often wonder what the meaning of life really is.

(b) The future looks very dismal.

(c) I don't really know why I joined this group.

(d) I am completely aware of the aims of our association.

(e) Our association makes new members feel that it is very important to belong to this group.

The Guttman scalogram analysis yielded a coefficient of reproducibility of 0·93 and 0·90, respectively, . . . for the above indices.[14]

transient cults), followed and gradually replaced by the emerging and re-emerging political parties. Other similar examples may be cited.[15] One might even speculate about the ideological equivalent of the principle of the conservation of energy (first law of thermodynamics) which may be applied here to predict the existence of a relatively stable need for ideology and to indicate the need for a wide range of ideological expression in any social system.[16] If, for example, one type of left-wing ideology becomes obsolete, all former adherents of that belief-pattern cannot be expected to switch to right-wing or other opposite types of ideologies. Rather, we would expect them to look for, and if necessary to create, a new form of left-wing ideology which merely deletes those particular values believed to be useless, out-dated, or superseded.

Eric Hoffer's *True Believer* notwithstanding, I think that individuals who abandon one faith, e.g., the Catholic religious ideology, do not switch to a completely opposite type, but seek a religious ideology relatively similar to the one they have left. In other words, the Catholic who leaves his faith does not commonly switch to a radical Protestant denomination or to Communism, as some have claimed, but generally will enter a 'neighboring' ideology such as Episcopalianism or the like.[17] Disenchantment with an ideology does not mean discarding all values inherent in the belief system, but usually means discarding only one or a few major values. Thus an individual would switch to an ideology which includes most of the values of his former belief system with the exception of those to which he objected. The Catholic who comes to disbelieve in the infallibility of the Pope would not need to become a Communist to find persons who share this value. He would perhaps be able to find a close approximation to his new value arrangement among Episcopalians. He may or may not formally remain a member of the Roman Catholic Church. Associational membership or affiliation are thus often a poor indicator of ideological values. The empirical measurement of ideological content or commitment must therefore rely on a more social-psychological approach utilizing individual measurement and observation focusing not only on associational membership but also ascertaining the individual's specific array of values and his commitment to them.

The potential theoretical and explanatory utility of the concept 'ideology' can also be seen if one adopts a somewhat different view of ideology than has been common. As a first step we might break down ideology (or a belief-pattern) into component values. Thus any particular ideology is seen here as being divisible into core values, which in turn relate to specific norms, to attitudes, and ultimately to behavior (see Figure 7.1).

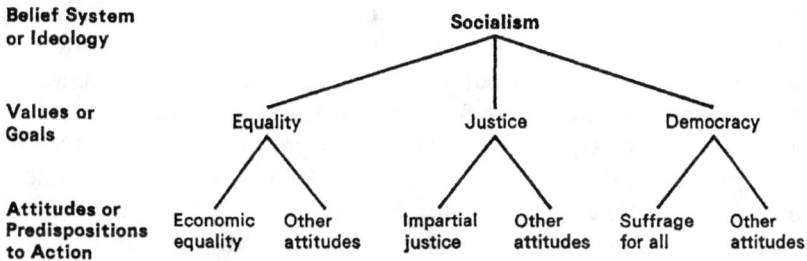

Belief System or Ideology				Socialism				
Values or Goals		Equality			Justice			Democracy
Attitudes or Predispositions to Action		Economic equality	Other attitudes		Impartial justice	Other attitudes		Suffrage for all — Other attitudes

Figure 7.1   Example of relationship between ideology, values, and attitudes

As Figure 7.1 illustrates, an ideology affects behavior through specific attitudes and norms, based on values which themselves are derived from the ideology, or better, which make up the ideology.

Now, the next progression may lead us to reexamine some traditional sociological variables. Take the concept of occupation, for example; it has long been considered an indispensable 'control' variable in our arsenal of must items in any empirical research instrument. Why do we use it? To do a better job of explaining and predicting human behavior? Ostensibly so; in part, because we were quick to recognize the statistical relationships and the amount of variance accounted for by this particular variable. Generalizations about the relationship of occupation, education, income, social status, prestige, etc., are unquestionably accepted. However, there is also another way to look at these major variables, that is, we may view them as indicators of underlying values, e.g., we may see occupation, not so much as an independent, but as an intervening variable, indicating one or more job or occupation-related values. In other words, to continue with this example, the white-collar occupation of physician may be viewed as more of an indicator of specific values (Hippocratic oath, service to man, professional ethics, AMA-related values etc.) than a direct determinant of behavior. It is the job-related values which directly influence behavior (through the value derived norms and attitudes)—not the occupation *per se*. If this assumption is correct, research utilizing such core values as basic data should have greater predictiveness than traditional approaches. The same could be said of such other standbys as religious denominational preference, sex, race, ethnicity, nationality, region, size of city, and so on. All these factors may also be viewed as intervening variables indicative of underlying values which may be ascertained more directly (but admittedly not as conveniently) by social psychological techniques.

Among the major functions of ideology is the presumed effect on the so-called integration or disintegration of a social system. The literature of the sociology of religion contains much material dealing with this particular aspect. Although, as most Latin American and European scholars would be quick to point out, American scholars have stressed the integrative functions to the comparative neglect of the disintegrative aspects of religious and political ideology, certain disintegrative episodes may have much to teach us. It is understandable, in light of the relatively quiescent American internal history and our comparative isolation, that stability and integration would be evaluated rather positively here (not that many Africans, Asians, Europeans, and Latinos wouldn't like a bit more stability).[18] Nevertheless, any discussion of the socio-political functions of ideology must be concerned with the issue of integration as well as disintegration. The historical record seems to indicate that wherever a single ideology predominates, persons adhering to a minority ideology (or ideologies) usually suffer various sanctions at the hands of an intolerant majority. Some examples coming to mind are the early Christians in Rome, the Huguenots in France, the Catholics in Northern Europe and the Protestants in Southern Europe, the Waldensians prior to the Reformation, the Armenians in Turkey,[19] the Jews in Europe, particularly in Nazi Germany, and many similar cases around the globe.

Certain exposures by the mass media and the publication of books like *Mississippi: The Closed Society*, by J. W. Silver, have amply demonstrated that America is by no means free of semi-totalitarian enclaves within which ideological opposition is severely sanctioned.[20]

There do seem to be a number of parallels between the Germany of the thirties and the America of today. A better understanding of both the genocide of six million Jews and the prospects for the American Negro might be achieved by taking another look at certain integrative and disintegrative functions of ideology. Let me try to illustrate this by starting with a personal experience.

At a party in New Haven, a Negro playwright predicted: 'The white man will kill us just as the Germans killed the Jews.' I have good reason to believe that he was serious about his statement. My reply was the standard one, 'It couldn't happen here.' But it rang hollow to both of us. I began to wonder: could it really happen here? What made it possible to kill six million human beings in a sup- posedly 'civilized,' modern nation like Germany? Could this happen again? Could genocide occur in Rhodesia, in South Africa, or in America? What this Negro feared was only what had occurred repeatedly in human history. The eventual elimination of minorities within a society by mass murder (or genocide), expellation, or assimilation. He apparently feared the former 'solution' (by genocide) because of recent European historical precedents; a not entirely unfounded fear. The liberal dream of the tolerant and egalitarian society seems to be just that, a utopian dream. World history is characterized more by forcible elimination of minorities than by peaceful coexistence between majorities and minorities. In cases where distinct populations live side by side in a pluralistic society, their mutual toleration is generally based on coercion and constraint, not on voluntary accommodation.

Race relations in the U.S.A., formerly quiescent only because of massive white coercion, now appear to be moving toward resolution by conflict. All the Negro playwright did was to recognize and verbalize his fear of the racial solution by murder, rather than expul- sion or assimilation. A solution by assimilation (through inter- marriage and full integration) seems less and less likely as ideological as well as structural polarization increases in our society. Thus the question remains—can genocide occur in America?

I am convinced a large part of the answer can be obtained through an examination of the role and functions of ideology. German Christians could justify the killing of Jewish men, women, and chil- dren by saying: 'Well, after all, they crucified Jesus Christ';[21] this type of ideologically justified statement differs little from the rationale of the Mississippi redneck who participates in the killing of a Negro because he regards the Negro as subhuman.

Though we may claim a fundamental distinction between Nazi Germany and the U.S.A. in terms of official policy, it is after all quite possible to imagine a change in our policy should the present 'racial' conditions change drastically. For example, a country which could justify the dispossession and internment of thousands of West-Coast Americans of Japanese ancestry during World War II could perhaps take similar measures toward black ghetto dwellers, especially if the black rebellion continues and the summers get hotter.

In such instances of minority mistreatment, and numerous others like it, our favorite explanatory variables, such as socio-economic status, economic factors, education, and still others, pale into insignificance next to such core values as may be contained in the ideology which not only makes such behavior possible but demands it. A comparison of the German ideological scene of the thirties and the present period in America may contain some answers to the preceding questions.

If we accept the notion that the Nazi ideology was a necessary condition preceding the genocide, then we must also ask why this particular ideology made such atrocities possible. Again, let us assume that the bulk of historians are correct and that an answer to this question is contained in the particular historical conditions of Germany, of the Nazi movement, and even of certain key personnel, notably Hitler, Goebbels, Rosenberg, Streicher, et al. But why was there no resistance, no counter-ideology, no significant protest? Whatever the answers, the absence of counter-ideology would seem to be a major key to such excesses, to such ideologically motivated atrocities. The lack of ideological balance or—if you will—its opposite, the presence of a condition of ideological hegemony, a situation, in other words, where there is no effective ideological opposition, is conducive to genocide. I am sure it is unnecessary, and it would be repetitious for me to rehash the historical facts of the Nazis' rise to power. However, the effective elimination, by various 'undemocratic,' illegal, and expeditious means, of virtually all potent opposition parties combined with the relative weakness and lack of opposition on the part of the two major Christian churches resulted in nearly complete ideological as well as practical domination of Germany by the Nazi party and its affiliated associations. This nearly total domination, once gained, then fortified by brute, coercive power and concentration-camp terror, and tacitly accepted by most Germans (as long as the fortunes of war were on their side), made it possible for the Nazis to carry out their designs with relative ease. It appears then, everything else being the same, that if one single ideology becomes preponderant in a social system, i.e., assumes a hegemonous position, ideologically justified and legitimate, political power accrues to the adherents of such an ideological association, which, when sufficiently great, is commonly used to eliminate all ideological opposition. This 'snowball effect' of an almost geometric increase of power has occurred repeatedly in recorded history. The descendants of Christians martyred in the Roman Coliseum in turn ruthlessly burned, tortured, and hanged their ideological opposition. Ideological and personal freedom and tolerance appear to be extremely rare in societies where one ideology (whether religious or political) predominates.

A single predominating ideology thus does not necessarily integrate a social system nor does the presence of more than one ideology disintegrate a society.[22] Rather, the existence of a broad range of religious as well as political ideologies, represented by various associations, appears to provide a fair chance for ideological balance. This in turn seems to be the best guarantee of social tolerance and, at a minimum, appears to be most often associated with a lack of disintegrating forces. At best, such ideological balance can produce integration around a common body of superordinate values, which may include values calling for toleration of ideological diversity.

Unfortunately, ideological intolerance is very common, even in societies where some reasonable ideological balance exists. However, it seems that only in situations where such intolerance is not opposed by relatively strong and competing ideologies does this intolerance find concrete and radical expression. Nazi Germany, Stalinist Russia, Inquisition Spain, Ross Barnett's Mississippi, 'apartheid' South Africa, and similar closed and semi-closed societal systems are examples of the disintegrative-destructive function of ideology. This disintegrative-destructive function of ideology is of great concern to the American Negro. The question is still: 'Can it happen here?' And the answer is not yet clear.

Notes

1 For a concise and insightful review of the history of the concept 'ideology' and its various conceptual associations to ideals, ideas, and class consciousness, see Gunter W. Remmling, *Road to Suspicion: A Study of Modern Mentality and the Sociology of Knowledge*, New York: Appleton-Century-Crofts, 1967, esp. pp. 111–14.

2 The adoption of a single term like ideology would obviate the need to use the term 'religion' to describe the fervency of political believers as Gerhard Lenski has done in *The Religious Factor*, Jules Monnerot in *The Sociology and Psychology of Communism*, Jerome Davis in *Contemporary Social Movements*, and still others who have used the more specific term 'religion' to refer to various religious characteristics of nonreligious belief systems.

3 This definition is largely based upon an early draft of my dissertation, 'An Analytical Comparison of Selected German Associations in Reference to their Belief Systems, Membership Alienation and Related Social Characteristics' (unpublished Ph.D. dissertation), East Lansing: Michigan State University, 1966.

4 See for example: Harry Bredemeier and Richard Stephenson, *The*

Analysis of Social Systems, New York: Holt, Rinehart & Winston, 1962, p. 251; Charles P. Loomis, *Social Systems*, Princeton, N.J.: Van Nostrand, 1960, p. 173.

5 As far as I know my attempts to measure ideological commitment to both religious as well as political associations and belief patterns (for my dissertation) are without direct precedent.

6 The writings of Henry Aiken, Ralf Dahrendorf, Rudolf Heberle, Karl Mannheim, Karl Marx, C. Wright Mills, Talcott Parsons, Max Weber, and many others are representative of this tradition.

7 It should not be necessary to declare my indebtedness to Marx and others who seek the origins of ideology in the social situation of a group or class.

8 Among sociologists who have pointed to the feasibility, even necessity, of ascertaining ideology in this manner are Reinhard Bendix, Ralf Dahrendorf, and Frederick Waisanen.

9 Under some circumstances (as in the Soviet Union) political functionaries may fulfill the role which religious functionaries occupy in the West and elsewhere.

10 It is recognized, of course, that such ideological socialization is relatively involuntary, i.e., the child commonly does not have a choice of the available ideologies. Adults usually have more knowledge of existing ideologies, but are rarely able to exercise complete freedom in choosing an ideology, e.g., various social and legal sanctions are applied to American Communists and Russian Christians.

11 The accompanying tables, as well as other empirical data, are based on material collected for my dissertation.

I am using Seeman's conceptual typology here. See Melvin Seeman, 'On the Meaning of Alienation', *American Sociological Review*, vol. 24, (December 1959), pp. 783–91.

12 Additional support for the contention that political ideology can fulfill most, if not all, of the functions traditionally ascribed to religious ideology may be seen in the very existence (and seeming viability) of the Communist political ideology in many societies, which apparently has managed to provide sufficient meaning to its adherents just as any 'supernatural' belief system would have done. Even though some observers (usually religiously affiliated and motivated Westerners who seem to engage in a certain amount of wishful thinking) of the Russian scene claim that on certain religious holidays many people crowd into the few remaining houses of worship in Soviet Russia, they also note that the majority of those in attendance are drawn from the older, almost prerevolutionary generation. This would seem to indicate the relative decline of traditional religious ideology in Russia and the seemingly successful substitution of a secular ideology. See also Lincoln Pettit, 'Atheism in the Soviet Union', *Michigan State University Magazine*, vol. 6 (May 1961), pp. 8–9, 28, 31.

13 Rolf Schulze, 'The Recession of Ideology?', *Sociological Quarterly*, vol. 5 (Spring 1964), p. 148.

14 Although these two indices met the criteria of scalability and unidimensionality established by Guttman, additional efforts to improve

both scales are proceeding. The scale of ideological commitment is being revised to remove all references to membership in (or allegiance to) associations and organizations. Instead, work is under way to construct a general scale of ideological commitment which is content-free, i.e., which can tap the degree of commitment to any set of beliefs regardless of specific content and allegiance to any association. Results from pretests of such a scale (and an improved index of meaningless-ness-alienation) are very promising.

15 The opposite type of substitution may also occur. Jackson Toby writes that 'insofar as traditional (religious) faith is shaken, secular commitments must be substituted'. Jackson Toby, *Contemporary Society*, New York: Wiley, 1964, p. 439.

16 A basic human need for ideology has sometimes been inferred from the existence of 'cultural universals' which include ideology (or facets of ideology). See George P. Murdock, 'The Common Denominator of Cultures' in Ralph Linton (ed.), *The Science of Man in the World Crisis*, New York: Columbia University Press, 1945, pp. 123–42. Others who posit the same basic and permanent need for ideology without resorting to cultural universals are David E. Apter in *Ideology and Discontent*, Bredemeier and Stephenson in *The Analysis of Social Systems*, Ralf Dahrendorf in *Gesellschaft und Freiheit*, Gerard DeGré in *Society and Ideology*, Louis Feuer in *Psychoanalysis and Ethics*, John Gillin in *For a Science of Social Man*, Will Herberg in *Protestant, Catholic, Jew*, and a number of additional scholars. Still others have disputed the position taken by members of the 'end of ideology' school and have vigorously denied the end or decline of ideology. More specifically in support of the point made above are Lenski and Tomkins who perceive the continued existence and need for such polar ideologies as 'conservatism and radicalism' or 'right and left'. Gerhard Lenski, *Power and Privilege*, New York: McGraw-Hill, 1966, and Sylvan Tomkins, 'Left and Right: A Basic Dimension of Ideology and Personality' in Robert W. White (ed.), *The Study of Lives*, New York: Atherton, 1966.

17 See also Gabriel Almond, *The Appeals of Communism*, Princeton, N.J.: Princeton University Press, 1954.

18 This is paralleled by the rather heavy emphasis among most structural-functionalists on stability rather than on social change. Non-American sociologists have been concerned with this ideological facet of domestic social science; cf. Ralf Dahrendorf, 'Out of Utopia: Toward a Reorientation of Sociological Analysis', *American Journal of Sociology*, vol. 64 (September 1958).

19 Marjorie Housepian has reminded us again that Franz Werfel's description of the Turkish massacre of Armenians (*The Forty Days of Musa Dagh*) is not pure fiction. See M. Housepian, 'The Unremembered Genocide', *Commentary*, vol. 42 (September 1966), pp. 55–61.

20 Several characteristics of totalitarian societies are also found in a few of our Southern states such as Mississippi and Alabama. The existence of a single 'official' party and its supporting ideology, a virtual monopoly over public communication media, terror tactics by the police and other organizations (Ku Klux Klan), and similar practices

which discourage dissent are characteristic indicators of a totalitarian milieu.

21 It was Pascal (1623–62) who wrote: 'Men never do evil so completely and cheerfully as when they do it from religious conviction.' Blaise Pascal, *Pensées*, Polemical Fragment, No. 894.
22 See also Allan W. Eister, 'Religious Institutions in Complex Societies: Difficulties in the Theoretic Specification of Functions', *American Sociological Review*, vol. 22 (August 1957), pp. 387–91.

part four

Karl Marx and the social determination of consciousness

8 On social existence and consciousness

Karl Marx

The subject of my professional studies was jurisprudence, which I pursued, however, in connection with and as secondary to the studies of philosophy and history. In 1842–3, as editor of the *Rheinische Zeitung*, I found myself embarrassed at first when I had to take part in discussions concerning so-called material interests. The proceedings of the Rhine Diet in connection with forest thefts and the extreme subdivision of landed property; the official controversy about the condition of the Mosel peasants, into which Herr von Schaper, at that time President of the Rhine Province, entered with the *Rheinische Zeitung*; finally, the debates on free trade and protection gave me the first impulse to take up the study of economic questions. At the same time a weak, quasi-philosophic echo of French socialism and communism made itself heard in the *Rheinische Zeitung* in those days when the good intentions 'to go ahead' greatly outweighed knowledge of facts. I declared myself against such botching, but had to admit at once in a controversy with the *Allgemeine Augsburger Zeitung* that my previous studies did not allow me to hazard an independent judgment as to the merits of the French schools. When, therefore, the publishers of the *Rheinische Zeitung* conceived the illusion that by a less aggressive policy the paper could be saved from the death sentence pronounced upon it, I was glad to grasp that opportunity to retire to my study room from public life.

The first work undertaken for the solution of the question that troubled me was a critical revision of Hegel's *Philosophy of Law*; the introduction to that work appeared in the *Deutsch-Französische Jahrbücher*, published in Paris in 1844. I was led by my studies to the conclusion that legal relations as well as forms of state could be neither understood by themselves nor explained by the so-called general progress of the human mind, but that they are rooted in the material conditions of life, which are summed up by Hegel after the fashion of the English and French of the eighteenth century under the name 'civil society'; the anatomy of that civil society is to be sought in political economy. The study of the latter, which I had taken up in Paris, I continued at Brussels, whither I immigrated on account of an order of expulsion issued by Mr Guizot. The general conclusion at which I arrived and which, once reached, continued to serve as the leading thread in my studies may be briefly summed up as follows: in the social production which men carry on they enter into definite relations that are indispensable and independent of their will; these relations of production correspond to a definite stage of development of their material powers of production. The sum total of these relations of production constitutes the economic structure of society—the real foundation, on which rise legal and political superstructures and to which correspond definite forms of social consciousness. The mode of production in material life determines the general character of the social, political, and spiritual processes of life. It is not the consciousness of men that determines their existence, but, on the contrary, their social existence determines their consciousness. At a certain stage of their development the material forces of production in society come into conflict with the existing relations of production, or—what is but a legal expression for the same thing—with the property relations within which they had been at work before. From forms of development of the forces of production these relations turn into their fetters. Then comes the period of social revolution. With the change of the economic foundation the entire immense superstructure is more or less rapidly transformed. In considering such transformations the distinction should always be made between the material transformation of the economic conditions of production, which can be determined with the precision of natural science, and the legal, political, religious, aesthetic, or philosophic—in short, ideological—forms in which men become conscious of this conflict and fight it out. Just as our opinion of an individual is not based on what he thinks of himself, so can we not judge such a period of transformation by its own consciousness; on the contrary, this consciousness must rather be explained from the contradictions of material life, from the existing conflict between the social forces of production and the relations of production. No social order ever disappears before all the productive forces for which there is room in it have been developed, and new, higher relations of production never appear before the material conditions of their existence have matured in the womb of the old society. Therefore mankind always takes up only such problems as it can solve, since, looking at the matter more closely, we will always find that the problem itself arises only when the material conditions necessary for its solution already exist or are at least in the process of formation. In broad outlines we can designate the Asiatic, the ancient, the feudal, and the modern bourgeois methods of production as so many epochs in the progress of the economic formation of society. The bourgeois relations of production are the last antagonistic form of the social process of production—antagonistic not in the sense of individual antagonism but of one arising from conditions surrounding the life of individuals in society; at the same time the productive forces developing in the womb of bourgeois society create the material conditions for the solution of that antagonism. This social formation constitutes, therefore, the closing chapter of the prehistoric stage of human society.

Friedrich Engels, with whom I was continually corresponding and exchanging ideas since the appearance of his ingenious critical essay on economic categories (in the *Deutsch-Französische Jahrbücher*), came by a different road to the same conclusions as myself (see his *Condition of the Working Classes in England*). When he, too, settled in Brussels in the spring of 1845, we decided to work out together the contrast between our view and the idealism of the German philosophy; in fact, to settle our accounts with our former philosophic conscience. The plan was carried out in the form of a criticism of the post-Hegelian philosophy. The manuscript in two solid octavo volumes had long reached the publisher in Westphalia when we received information that conditions had so changed as not to allow of its publication. We abandoned the manuscript to the stinging criticism of the mice the more readily since we had accomplished our main purpose—the clearing up of the question to ourselves. Of the scattered writings on various subjects in which we presented our views to the public at that time, I recall only the *Manifesto of the Communist Party*, written by Engels and myself, and the *Discourse on Free Trade*, written by myself. The leading points of our theory were first presented scientifically, though in a polemic form, in my *Misère de la philosophie*, etc. directed against Proudhon and published in 1847. An essay on *Wage Labor*, written by me in German, and in which I put together my lectures on the subject delivered before the German Workmen's Club at Brussels, was prevented from leaving the hands of the printer by the February revolution and my expulsion from Belgium, which followed it as a consequence.

The publication of the *Neue Rheinische Zeitung* in 1848 and 1849, and the events which took place later on, interrupted my economic studies, which I could not resume before 1850 in London. The enormous material on the history of political economy which is accumulated in the British Museum; the favorable view which London offers for the observation of bourgeois society; finally, the new stage of development upon which the latter seemed to have entered with the discovery of gold in California and Australia led

133

me to the decision to resume my studies from the very beginning and work up critically the new material. These studies partly led to what might seem side questions, over which I nevertheless had to stop for longer or shorter periods of time. Especially was the time at my disposal cut down by the imperative necessity of working for a living. My work as contributor on the leading Anglo-American newspaper, the New York *Tribune*, at which I have now been engaged for eight years, has caused very great interruption in my studies, since I engage in newspaper work proper only occasionally. Yet articles on important economic events in England and on the Continent have formed so large a part of my contributions that I have been obliged to make myself familiar with practical details which lie outside the proper sphere of political economy.

This account of the course of my studies in political economy is simply to prove that my views, whatever one may think of them, and no matter how little they agree with the interested prejudices of the ruling classes, are the result of many years of conscientious research. At the entrance to science, however, the same requirement must be put as at the entrance to hell:

Qui si convien lasciare ogni sospetto
Ogni viltà convien che qui sia morta.

London, January 1859

9 Marxism and Marxist sociology of knowledge

Gunter W. Remmling

The sociology of knowledge does not only aim at the discovery, analysis, and description of different thought styles. The discipline is more than that; it is also a theory of the relation of ideas and reality asserting the primacy of reality and the determination of ideas by reality.[1] Karl Marx developed a theory asserting the primacy of economic reality and the determination of ideas, or rather of the ideological superstructure, by this economic reality. It is more than a poetic gesture to call Marxism the 'storm center of the sociology of knowledge' because much of this sociology is a development of Marx's hypothesis and a struggle with the problems unleashed by his analysis of the order of things.

In historical perspective Hegel's work was the intermediary between Holbach and Marx: it provided Marx with the sophistication that he needed to elevate materialism to the rank of a scientific instrument capable of revealing significant interconnections in socio-economic and political reality.

Marx crystallized one aspect of the world: the economic structure of society, constituted by the material 'relations of production' which form the real foundation, on which develop legal and political superstructures and to which correspond definite forms of social consciousness. This historical materialism is at the center of Marx's system of thought, which is essentially a theory of social revolution.

Marx conceived of history as a process of the self-creation of man. This notion he derived only partially from Hegel, for whom the historical process was, after all, a movement and conflict of abstract categories, enacted in the heaven of pure thought; Marx found the 'sociological' thesis that social institutions change in the process of historical development in the political and historical works of late eighteenth-century authors; among them are the Scottish historian Adam Ferguson, whose *Essay on the History of Civil Society* appeared in 1767; the Scotsman John Millar, who published *The Origin of the Distinction of Ranks* in 1771; and the Frenchman S.N.H. Linguet, whose *Théorie des lois civiles* was first published in 1767. Marx, who was bent on writing an empirical work when he started his *Capital*, was a 'sociologist' largely opposed to Hegel's philosophy of history and political theory: his criticism of Hegel reveals the strong influence of the Scottish and French writers along with that of Saint-Simon.

Marx's work is also a new historiography: his earliest and dominating interest was in historical and social change. From his account he eliminated, however, 'any reference to forces or agencies beyond those of human beings living and working in society . . . His intention . . . was to give a scientific account of social change.'[2]

To begin with, Marx reversed Hegel's philosophy when he put *matter before mind*. Already in Paris, while writing for the *Deutsch-Französische Jahrbücher*, he concluded that 'legal relations as well as forms of state . . . are rooted in the material conditions of life, which are summed up by Hegel . . . under the name "civil society"; the anatomy of that civil society is to be sought in political economy.'[3] Marx continued the study of political economy—begun in Paris—after his expulsion to Brussels. There he arrived at a general conclusion which continued to serve as the leading idea in his further studies:

> In the social production which men carry on they enter into definite relations that are indispensable and independent of their will; these *relations of production* correspond to a definite stage of development of their material powers of production. The sum total of these *relations of production* constitutes the *economic structure of society*—the *real foundation*, on which rise legal and political *superstructures* and to which correspond definite forms of social consciousness. The mode of production in material life determines the general character of the social, political, and spiritual processes of life. *It is not the consciousness of men that determines their existence, but, on the contrary, their social existence determines their consciousness.*[4]

What exactly is the meaning of Marx's concept 'relations of production' (*Produktionsverhältnisse*)? They include the forces of production (*Produktivkräfte*) such as technology, existing skills, both mental and physical, inherited traditions, and ideologies. But it would be erroneous to identify the relations of production with the forces of production. The relations of production, furthermore, are not the same as the conditions of production (*Produktionsbedingungen*) consisting of such elements as population, climate, and the natural supply of raw material. Marx's central concept describes the way of economic production—the *entire* economic life of a society, the manner in which men's *social* activity *organizes* both the forces and conditions of production. These relations of production find their legal expression in property relations. Therefore, only productive or property relations may be called feudal or capitalistic. 'For Marx it is the relations of production, not the forces of production and not the conditions of production, which are the basis of the cultural superstructure.'[5]

Alienation: the loss of man

The *philosophes* had already realized that man's opinions and his education are determined by the social milieu. In the nineteenth century, the German idealist philosophers taught that the historical development of public opinion as all of history constitutes a lawful process. Now Marx declares in partial opposition to the idealist philosophers that the historical process is not determined by the 'spirit of the world' but solely by the material relations between men.

The *philosophes* meant to explain human history by reference to 'human nature.' They also used this concept to describe the qualities which an ideal state and society had to possess. The concept *human nature*, however, is settled with logical inconsistencies. If human nature is constant, we cannot refer to it in order to explain historical variation and cultural differences. If human nature, on the other hand, is variable, we have to ask what causes its changes?

The German idealist philosophers fully recognized this logical problem and located the hidden force behind the historical process outside of man, who consequently became a puppet in the hands of the spirit of the world. The spirit of the world, as the power behind the historical process, is, however, nothing else but one aspect of human nature which has been forced through the filter of logical abstraction.

Marx saw human nature as variable and combined this notion with the idea of a *meaningful* historical process, set in motion by man's intentions and activities. While man through his labor has important effects upon nature outside himself, he simultaneously causes changes in his own nature. The important difference between man and animal derives from the fact that man 'produces his life.' In contrast to animal species, man has to create the means of his subsistence and is always the product of his own activity. This 'production,' however, can only be carried out by a creature that sets its own goals and knows in advance what it wants to create. 'At the end of every labour-process, we get a result that already existed in the imagination of the labourer at its commencement.'[6] Significantly man projects himself outward, relinquishes what he designed—a part of himself: the products of his imagination and labor assume an independent existence.

137

This basic fact of human life begins to threaten man when a new element is added: the division of labor which establishes the mutual dependence of individuals and thus introduces the contradiction between the interests of the individual or the individual family and the common interest of all individuals. The collective work develops powers transcending those of man and finally 'each man has a particular, exclusive sphere of activity, which is forced upon him and from which he cannot escape.'[7] The division of labor in its complete form creates a situation where nobody any longer disposes over the means of his subsistence: now the relations of production and trade completely replace human relations; men no longer confront one another as men but as mere exponents of the anonymous and all powerful relations of production which separate and alienate one human being from the other.

This situation finds its expression in the writings of political economists who conceive of men's social life as forms of exchange and trade: Adam Smith views society as a commercial enterprise; every one of its members is a salesman. Political economy establishes, therefore, an alienated form of social intercourse as the true and original form of active human life.

On the nontheoretical level, human alienation finds its most striking expression in money. Money as such has no qualities; it is the indifferent power that makes everything and everybody available as an object of purchase. Since nobody has what he needs, everybody needs money to have anything: money 'is therefore the most eminent object.'[8] The other person becomes for all others whatever he can be in relation to money. What I am not, I can become through money which 'is the universal whore, the universal pander between men and peoples.'[9] It turns love into hate and hate into love, virtue into vice and vice into virtue, nonsense into reason and reason into nonsense. Money reflects the complete alienation of man from his true nature: from his nature as man.

While commodities relinquish their ultimate qualities in money, man relinquishes his in becoming a commodity: he becomes one as soon as his power of labor becomes useless unless it is sold. In society the worker is not a human being but merely the exponent of an abstract commodity—in selling it, he sells himself: the self-alienation of man has reached its ultimate form. The economic theorists of capitalism, therefore, view the proletarian—the man who, without capital or ground rent, lives entirely by his labor—as a mere worker, but not as a human being.[10]

The alienation of labor appears not only in its product but also in the process of production—in productive activity: here the worker experiences his labor as an external process which, instead of fulfilling him, makes him miserable; he does not develop a feeling of well-being but a nausea of physical exhaustion and mental debasement. For the worker the alienated character of labor 'shows itself in the fact that it is not his work but work for someone else, that in labor he does not belong to himself but to another person.'[11]

Marx rejected a human being which was nothing but a self-alienated producer of commodities and informed his collaborator Ruge that he had decided to 'make man into man.' The realization of man's true purposes, however, necessitated the liberation of life from its subservience to 'alien powers.' Man was no longer to be a product of the relations of production—these were to become a product of man; their power over man had to be terminated so that he could become the highest being for himself, his conduct toward others and toward himself motivated by nothing but his character as man. Only after his liberation from the external and alien conditions of his existence which adulterate all his true potentialities, as money does for example, can man fulfill his human possibilities: only then his ears will be free to receive music and his eyes will behold the beauty of form. Man must be freed from his slavery under the needs of material life to fulfill his real character: a being that determines himself.[12]

Marx's entire lifework was oriented around this central idea: the realization of man's true character and purpose. He crystallized it out of his differentiation from Hegel and Feuerbach; it motivated him to concentrate all his energies on the task of identifying the forces in the processes of reality that dissolve the contradiction between idea and reality. Consequently, Marx had to discover those elements in social activity that possessed the power to effect the breakdown of the existing relations and that would because of their own inner contradiction negate the general self-alienation in social life.

These elements, however, had to be found in the relations of active life itself; they were present in the relations which dominate as a nameless force the relations between men—that is in the economic relations wherein all self-alienation originates. The discovery of the laws of political economy was, therefore, at the same time the discovery of the conditions which had to be met in order to achieve the self-realization of man. This is the reason for Marx's tireless analysis of economic laws and their development as reflected in his *Capital* and similar writings.

Revolution and ideology

Like Hegel, Marx meant to embrace all of reality to offer a final answer to the question about the meaning and the course of human history. He combined this passion for totality with a ruthless determination to completely change the world: the material foundations of the world that he was born into had to be blown up in the grand revolution that he worked for; all the nonmaterial forces that were emanated by this doomed fundament had to be exploded along with the *economic* order. The destruction of nonmaterial culture was inevitable since all ideas were nothing but reflections of human existence as determined by the relations of production. The unavoidable overthrow of the economic order would automatically cause a change in intellectual reality.

Marx developed this theory of social and cultural change in his *Economic and Philosophical Manuscripts*, written in 1844, and immediately designated communism as the instrument that was to effect the radical transformation of economic, social, and cultural reality. First, however, 'true communism' had to be distinguished from 'false communism.' For true communism the expropriation of private property constituted merely one aspect of the general and overall appropriation of the world. Adherents of false communism, on the other hand, attacked the existing property relations in vain since they merely advocated a levelling of differences in property through raised wages or the equal distribution of wealth. These theoreticians—notably Proudhon—fostered only partial reform. In Marx's opinion they could neither effect a thorough change in human behavior nor could they halt the pernicious process that transformed the world of things into values by devaluating the world of man into things. False communism, if ever realized, would destroy everything that did not lend itself to be owned by all as private property. Instead of terminating the determination of man as a 'worker,' false communism would expand it over all of mankind, while capital would remain the general power dominating society. In contrast, true communism or humanism would lead to a repossession of man on the level of civilization attained under capitalism while simultaneously abolishing private property and thus human self-alienation.[13]

Fully comprehended communism would change, therefore, not only the social and economic relations but also the political, legal, moral, religious, and scientific behavior of man. Socialist man would own the world of objects not by having private, capitalistic possessions but by transforming all things into positive and concrete realizations of himself. In a world totally changed by communism—which is neither the aim nor the final form of human development—man produces man, himself, and then other men; his object which is created by the direct activity of his personality is his existence for other men, and their existence for him. Socialist man through his action makes the world his own since his mode of production does not lead to alienation but to self-assertion.[14]

Since Marx was convinced that the revolutionary overthrow of the existing order was the unavoidable consequence of the march of history, he immediately debunked all conservative ideas as false, as hopelessly out of tune with reality or the actual social configuration.[15]

To begin with, the relationship between existence and consciousness, that Marx postulates as basic, is destroyed as soon as the division of labor separates material and mental work. Now consciousness loses its connection with life; the fictitious idea arises that consciousness is no longer determined by existence. The division of labor, thus, causes our consciousness to replace life with its own creations. At this point man becomes unable to recognize that consciousness is nothing else but conscious existence. This development is aggravated through a further consequence of the division of labor: the producer loses his control over the product of labor which confronts him, henceforth, as an independent alien force in the shape of the automatism of the economic and political order. On this basis the ideological misinterpretation of existence arises: the world-market is confused with the spirit of the world.[16]

Traditional philosophy and theology explain law, political power, ethics, etc. as the manifestations of metaphysical principles, only because we can no longer grasp that such suprahuman powers, as God or the universal spirit, merely express man's self-alienation.[17] Thus man 'ideologically' deduces socio-political reality from omnipotent otherwordly forces because of his inability to control the relations determining his life. Against this background of the division of labor, Marx debunks as ideological the entire history of philosophy from Plato to Hegel and his followers.[18]

The death of truth

With the exception of the findings of the physical sciences all existing knowledge has now been debunked as ideological. Marx's total concept of ideology has suspiciously invaded truth and declared it dead: all existing ideas are *formally* parts of an ideological superstructure and *materially* the expression of a social reality mainly characterized by domination and oppression—by class struggles. Since Marx maintains that man's social existence determines his consciousness, he implies that his *total* world view is conditioned by the all-important criterion of interest-bound class position: the total concept of ideology calls into question man's total *Weltanschauung*— including his conceptual apparatus—and interprets it as a product of the collective life of which he partakes as a member of his class. Marx's forerunners did not expand the suspicion of ideology to the point of excluding the opponent—the victim of ideology—from intellectual discourse on the basis of a common theoretical frame of reference. The case, however, is different with the *total suspicion of ideology*. When we attribute, as Marx did, to almost all of history one intellectual world debunked as false and to ourselves another one, or if we assume that the bourgeoisie thinks in categories other than those of the proletariat, we refer not to the isolated cases of thought-content, but to fundamentally divergent thought-systems and to widely differing modes of experience and interpretation.[19]

Mannheim has pointed out that it was Marxist theory which first fused the particular and total conceptions of ideology.[20] Marx emphasizes the role of class position and class interest in thought. His approach, however, reflects at times the particular conception of ideology, i.e. a scepticism toward the ideas and representations of the ruling class which are viewed as more or less conscious disguises of reality, the true recognition of which would be harmful to the interests of this class. The distortions of reality which Marx suspects in the thought systems of the ideological spokesmen of the ruling class range all the way from deliberate lies to half-conscious and unwitting disguises—from calculated attempts to dupe the masses to self-deception.

In this light the ideological advocates of the existing social system appear as the fighting representatives of a certain political-social position and are accused of conscious or unconscious falsification of the true situation. As long as Marx operates with this particular conception of ideology, he uncovers distortion only on the psychological plane by pointing out the personal roots of intellectual bias. Hegelianism, however, enabled him to transcend this plane and to posit the problem in a more comprehensive, philosophical setting. Consequently the notion of a 'false consciousness' took on a wider meaning, implying the existence of the totally distorted mind that falsifies everything which comes within its range. On the basis of his theory of the *division of labor*, Marx begins to suspect that *inevitably* man's *total outlook* as distinguished from its details must be *distorted*. At this point the *particular conception of ideology merges with the total conception of ideology* and Marx discredits the total structure of man's consciousness, considering him no longer capable of thinking correctly.

Marx's total conception of ideology, however, was still limited or 'special' because of his decision to elect a collective guarantor of truth: the proletariat. Since Marx considered himself the spokesman of the proletariat he believed his particular philosophy safe from the charge of ideology. He, furthermore, limited his attack upon ideas to the 'prehistory of man.' For the Utopia that he sketched in his philosophy he assumed a reign of truth. The seriousness of his attack, however, must not be underrated as this prehistory of man covers almost all of history prior to Marx's Utopia. As soon as the belief in the saving powers of the proletariat and in the possibility of Marx's Utopia are not shared, the destruction of truth remains as the one stark fact.

We have to remember, however, that Marx's concept of truth differed greatly from that of traditional philosophers who defined a true idea as one that corresponds with the external environment. Marx was much closer to the American pragmatist thinkers than to his European speculative predecessors. What he represented may be described as a *political pragmatism*: 'In order to discover whether our ideas are true, we must act on them ... Whatever cannot be tested in action is dogma.'[21]

Marxism is both the theory and practice of social revolution; it is the class theory of the proletariat. The alleged nature of the historical process—an inevitable movement from capitalism through the dictatorship of the proletariat to a classless society—establishes the interests of the proletariat, however, as the interests of mankind. Here the hidden claim toward universality and absoluteness becomes obvious.

Marx's attempt to guarantee the truth and objectivity of his theory rests upon a syllogism: the premise that history is an inevitable process leads to the next that the class which accepts and carries this process knows truth. The reality of this historical process, however, is deduced from the assumptions that the proletariat has access to true reality and that consequently Marxism is true.

Marxist sociology of knowledge

The heritage left by Marx was so problematic that even his followers found it impossible to agree on a singular Marxist sociology of knowledge. Instead, there are several ranging from Max Adler's Kantian version to Emil Lederer's sociology of culture. In a manner of speaking we may, however, make a major distinction between a 'positivist' and 'historicist' branch of Marxist sociology of knowledge.

The historicists are informed by the earlier writings of Marx which intimately connect with Hegel's thinking. The positivists, on the other hand, stress the later scientistic Marx-Engels tradition; consequently they arrive at a narrow, empiricist attitude and deny the existence of everything but matter which exhibits its stubborn factness in the social world by economic relationships.

The positivist school

Bogdanov's writings are permeated by this emphasis on empiricist attitudes and the methods of physical science and he clearly belongs in the camp of the positivists or—as the historicists were fond of saying—'vulgar' Marxists. The Russian physician, philosopher, and sociologist Alexander A. Bogdanov was inspired by Ernst Mach's positivist-pragmatist system, Ostwald's energetic philosophy, and Avenarius' empirical criticism, and followed through with his own attempt to reduce history to an epiphenomenon of technological change. Bogdanov's sociology of knowledge is contained in the three volumes of his *General Theory of Organization: Tectology* (1925–9). The outlines of his position can, however, already be detected in his earlier works on sociology, *Psychology of Society* (1904) and *The Science of Social Consciousness* (1914). Here he maintains that social adaption and biological adaption are essentially the same. Variations in the social forms are due to changes in the natural environment. The few new social forms that manage to survive in the struggle for existence are adaptions. There are two main types of social adaption: technical and ideological, the latter being dependent upon the technical adaptions. All the ideological forms are 'organizing adaptions' of the technical forms.[22]

Transforming Marx's position into a naive and unsystematic dogmatism, Paul Szende argued that sense experience as such is reliable: only its interpretation is socially determined. These socially determined interpretations combine into an ideology which conceals reality in the interest of the ruling class.[23]

Otto Bauer made the attempt to develop an empirical interpretation of the genesis of world views. The reality factor determining the world view of a given class can be found in man's work experience: the members of the capitalist class are rooted in a working experience which consists essentially of the planning of work carried out by others. Therefore, they develop a world view in which the notion of an overall plan is paramount, i.e., idealism. The members of the working class, on the other hand, are determined in their thinking by a work experience which brings them into direct, physical contact with the forces of nature and the properties of matter—they arrive at a world view evolving around the same principles of force and matter: materialism.[24]

The historicism of Georg Lukács

An historicist version of Marxist sociology of knowledge was developed by the Hungarian Georg Lukács and, to some extent, by his Polish-born follower Stanislaw Warynski (Leo Kofler).[25] In as much as Lukács is an orthodox left-wing Marxist, who came to accept the Leninist interpretation of Marxism, this deviation into 'relativism' indicates that a measure of cerebral self-torture is not absent from the workings of the more subtle and creative minds in the totalitarian intellectual universe which is usually dominated by the naive and narrow thought-ways of lower-middle-class mental types. (Here Communists, Fascists, and American apostles of thought-control share, by the way, common ground.) This biographical datum also explains why the historicist element in Lukács' earlier writings is not something that meets the eye, but rather a subterranean current detectable only by intimate comparison of his thoughts with those of Marx. There are, of course, these more obvious facts: Lukács' book contributing to the sociology of knowledge and the sociological analysis of the ideology problem met with the disapproval of the Communist Party and he, in turn, abandoned eventually his objectivistic philosophy of history to regain the blessings of official doctrine.

Lukács' controversial book *History and Class-Consciousness* implicitly rejects all positivist and neo-Kantian attempts to construe Marxism as either positive or idealist historical and social science. In contrast to the vulgar Marxists, Lukács (1885–1971) returns to the specifically Hegelian ingredients in Marx's thinking and comes to use historical materialism as a *method* leading to a universal understanding of historical reality and the dialectic totality of the elements constituting this reality.

Lukács is convinced that the Hegelian conception of the dialectic guarantees the scientific value of Marxism. He proceeds to oppose both the limitation of the dialectic to the conceptual realm and its materialistic reconstruction. He arrives at a realistic version of the dialectic which is equally far removed from the idealist dialectic of the neo-Kantian Marxists, on the one side, and the dialectical materialism of the positivist Marxists, on the other. Turning directly against dialectical materialism, Lukács restricts his conception of the dialectic to the movement of historical reality; it is applicable to the social world only and serves no useful purpose in the interpretation of the physical universe. (Similarly, Karl Mannheim excludes the thought products of the physical sciences from his doctrine of the existential determination of knowledge.) For Lukács the dialectical movement of the historical process is *ens realissimum*, and in a typically Hegelian and historicist assertion he denies the existence of all supra-historical factors. Inevitably, there germinates in his thinking the notion that, as a method, historical materialism has to be applied upon itself, thereby becoming subject to historical and social relativization.[26]

Marx had never wavered in his conviction that all societies—ancient and modern alike—are under the mind-determining influence of the economic sphere; that, in other words, all societies have to be explained with the hermeneutic principle provided by historical materialism. In contrast, Lukács thinks that the economic conception of history is fully applicable only to the interpretation of modern capitalistic society and brings about the subtle, historical relativiza-

GUNTER W. REMMLING

tion of a principle that Marx had meant to be universally and eternally valid. It was correct, argues Lukács, to apply historical materialism unconditionally to the history of the nineteenth century. In the pre-capitalistic societies, however, the intensity of economic life which has been reached in capitalistic society did not yet prevail. Therefore, historical materialism cannot be applied to the pre-capitalistic social structures in the same way as to those forming part of capitalistic development. Here we need much finer analyses to reveal, on the one hand, what role the purely economic forces have played among the forces propelling society, provided such forces existed then in such 'pureness,' and on the other hand we need them to demonstrate how these economic forces acted here upon the other structural elements of society. The vulgar Marxists completely ignored this difference. Their application of historical materialism fell into the same error which Marx saw in vulgar economics; merely historical categories—in the first case categories of capitalistic society—were mistaken for eternal categories.[27]

His interpretation of historical materialism shows that Lukács was open to the suggestion that thought is existentially determined; he, obviously, realized that historical materialism had to be applied upon itself: in this view historical materialism stood revealed as the function, the expression of a determinate complex of social conditions. Yet at this exciting junction in the development of Marxist thought Lukács cautioned that this application upon itself neither leads to a complete relativism nor to the abdication of historical materialism as the right method. Following the dynamics of his initial reasoning Lukács concludes his observations, however, by saying that the truths contained in historical materialism resemble the truths which Marx saw in classical economics, in as much as they are truths within a given order of social life and production—only as such are they unconditionally valid. Societies may develop, however, wherein 'because of the nature of their social structure, validity will belong to other categories, to other contexts of truth.'[28]

In the historicist mood of his youth, Lukács did not only display impatience with 'eternal categories'—there grew in him the suspicion that the so-called 'hard facts,' i.e. the data furnished by experience, are, if seen in isolation, nothing but dead 'fetishes.' For the young Lukács the problem of truth appears in an entirely new light and in his Hegelian terminology he asserts that he sees 'becoming as the truth of being, process as the truth of things.' This leads to the historicist assumption that historical development is ontologically more real than the 'facts' of experience.[29] What Lukács wants to destroy is the methodological priority of facts. This he deems necessary to reveal the true nature of all phenomena which are essentially processes. For Lukács, all so-called facts are likewise constituted of

146

processes. Facts are nothing but 'artificially isolated and frozen *moments* of the total process.'[30]

Lukács contends, then, that facts are killed if they are isolated from the movement to which they belong in life. With this contention he also establishes the connection with a concept that is central to his thinking: *reification*. With this concept Lukács tirelessly attacks men's eagerness to abandon the flowing totality for the static system, their inability to see human relationships other than in the shape of relations between things, their tendency to transform the historical and the relative into the eternal and absolute. The disposition of men toward reification not only endangers the vitality of individual facts—this disposition threatens movement as such by destroying its meaning and, thereby, ruling out truthful statements about it. Like Marx, Lukács views the problem of commodities as the most typical manifestation of the phenomenon of reification (*Verdinglichung*). Relations among people take on the character of a thing (*Dinghaftigkeit*); they receive a 'ghostly objectivity' which makes them look like strictly closed systems operating on natural law principles. In this way there remains no trace of their true nature, namely that they were relations between human beings.[31]

As a historicist, Lukács claimed that the historical process is reality itself, as a relativist he announced that our loss of the sense for the historical movement as a whole prevents the apprehension of the truth of the world which we experience, and as a sociologist he saw the collapse of our cognitive apparatus determined by a social situation. As a Marxist, however, he identified this social situation in the bourgeois conception of the world and in the capitalistic mode of production.

In Lukács' view it is the capitalistic mode of production which leads to the substitution of things or fetishes for human relationships, to the functioning division between head and hand, between theory and action, and thus to the bourgeois conception of the world that postulates stability where it should discern movement. Reification is central to bourgeois thinking; the members of this class are divorced from reality. The bourgeois always tend to reify relations or conditions among persons—they are the true victims of the intellectual impasse created by the separation of subject and object, theory and practice and they are doomed to remain the prisoners of a social and intellectual situation which is of their own making. For the bourgeois —scholars and scientists are no exception—the essential quality of life is masked and what is warm and changeable freezes into cold, rigid forms: 'a mentality which can take in neither the human character of the social world nor yet its historical quality is manifestly condemned to miss the true meaning of reality and is in fact a mentality "every cognition of which is necessarily wrong." '[32]

The Marxists coined the term 'false consciousness' to convey the idea that there is a totally distorted mind that falsifies everything it touches upon.[33] Lukács uses this concept to penetrate the entire realm of mental activity. 'Bourgeois philosophy,' for example, is the degeneration of philosophical speculation into an exercise in shadow-boxing. The phantasmagoric, mythological, and metaphysical varieties of this philosophy stem from its false premise that true theory must be separated from practice, that only a contemplative attitude will produce valid philosophical ideas. Inevitably, the 'bourgeois philosopher' creates out of his deluded imagination the unrealistic division of thinking and being. Similarly, 'bourgeois historians' create out of their false consciousness a perversion of history; they distort history—the clearest expression of movement—into a frozen landscape, robbed of all depth, mutilated beyond recognition.[34]

For the bourgeoisie the cognitive catastrophe is total and there is no room for hope: this class is forever sunk in error, its conception of the world is of necessity unrealistic. The individual members of this class are inevitably deluded by false consciousness and, therefore, incapable of penetrating to an understanding of the real interconnection of things with totality. The bourgeois is barred from the view of truth by his particular position inside the process of production; this is a collective fate; because of their class position the members of the bourgeoisie are actually unconscious of their own position in the historical and social process. This limitation transforms bourgeois class-consciousness immediately into false consciousness; it is not an incidental, psychological limitation, but one that arises as the objective consequence of the economic structure of capitalistic society.[35]

Moreover, Lukács is convinced that truth is revealed in action, that reality can only be known by those who function inside it, who participate in the true historical reality which is the 'totality of the historical process.' Only those who have been called and who have the will to usher in the future, 'can see the concrete truth of the present.'[36]

The historical process which is reality becomes conscious of itself in the proletariat: the subject *and* object of history. The workers represent the first class in history which can have an adequate social consciousness.[37] The social consciousness of the working class is adequate because it is in harmony with the facts and movement of reality, but it is also determined by a social situation: the proletariat is capable of grasping the essence of capitalism and of the historical process leading to its destruction since—as a class—it occupies a social position in capitalistic society, where the naked and inhuman reality of this doomed order is directly experienced. The proletariat, Lukács maintains, holds in Hegelian fashion the key that will unlock the mystery of history: proletarian class-consciousness is the mentality which is ideally suited to the objective position of this class in society and history. The proletarian who is conscious of his class position understands life with its continuing, important struggles; he never loses his sense of the total historical process; he comprehends the truth of the future which he creates and which will be fully revealed to him at the moment of revolution when proletarian science and proletarian class-consciousness must achieve their full logical adequacy, since it will be in this instant of decision that consciousness is dialectically transformed into action, and theory into practice.

The proletariat, in recognizing itself, simultaneously achieves the objective recognition of society as a whole.[38] Only with the appearance of the proletariat does the understanding of social reality reach its completion: this class must fully understand its position in society in order to exist and to act; its class position becomes understandable only through the understanding of society in its entirety. This dialectical situation explains the unity of theory and praxis; because in the perspective of the proletarian self-recognition and recognition of the totality of history and society coincide: 'the proletariat is both subject and object of its own understanding.'[39]

Knowledge of truth spells ideological ruin as far as the bourgeoisie is concerned; for the working class, on the other hand, this knowledge is a weapon that must be wielded relentlessly to bring victory.[40] Class struggle is not an exclusively economic fight; class struggle is also a battle about the official interpretation of reality: bourgeoisie and proletariat complete for the 'consciousness of society.' The victor in this competition will not only emerge as the ideological ruler; his superiority will also offer him the chance to lead society.[41]

As soon as the bourgeoisie begins to realize that the ascending proletariat reveals truth, its false consciousness becomes 'a falseness of consciousness.'[42] Falseness moves from the noological to the psychological level: unintentional, unconscious object-inadequacy becomes intentional, deliberate concealment of a basically correct insight into reality; ideology changes into the lie and what started as a theoretical problem ends as a moral issue. Lukács believes that ever since the beginning of the nineteenth century the ideology of the bourgeoisie reflects its desperate fight not only against the understanding of a social system of its own making, but also against an awareness of its situation as a class.[43]

With a typically Leninist turn Lukács concludes that it is the task of the Communist Party—that 'sublime' expression and culmination of true proletarian consciousness—to educate the workers so that they will become in reality what they are ideally already: the true, empirical proletariat. It is the educative mission of this elitist party to induce the personal consciousness of individual proletarians to reach the level of the ideal, collective consciousness possessed by the proletariat as a class; this mission is consummated in the Revolution. In this process the party plays the star role; it embodies and safe-guards the class-consciousness of the proletariat; the party preserves the conscience of the workers' historical mission.[44]

Lukács the historicist, relativist, and sociologist was thus overcome by Lukács the Marxist-Leninist, who claims for the proletariat that it owns the future and is, therefore, able to see 'the concrete truth of the present.'[45] His attempt to guarantee absolute truth to one social class and especially to the Communist Party indicates that Lukács never battled the problem of relativism seriously. He raised the problem, but proceeded to limit the consequences by holding to account only the thoughtways of the bourgeoisie. Exempting the proletariat and the party elite from the charge of relativism, Lukács took a way that leads out of the impasse but not toward reason; instead it leads to the misty regions of myth and religion. Lukács refused to think through the challenge of relativism; he failed, in the end, to turn the critical probe inward, upon his own position and that of the working class; instead, he used the lever of faith to raise one privileged intellectual and social position out of the darkness of relativism: by a bold decree he declared it to be the absolute.

Of course, Lukács' attempt to settle the matter of relativism by escaping from the arena of reasoned and empirically anchored discourse is not remarkable as such; others, too, have sought refuge in those regions, where the scientific method of proof is overruled by the fit of faith. While the Communist Lukács found comfort believing in the messianistic role of the proletariat and the priestly aloofness of the party, the Catholic Scheler found his distant safety-zone in the imaginary world of Platonic essences.

Notes

1 For a detailed definition and discussion of the 'range of the subject matter' see Kurt H. Wolff, 'The Sociology of Knowledge: Emphasis on an Empirical Attitude', *Philosophy of Science*, vol. 10, no. 2 (April, 1943), pp. 107–9.
2 T. B. Bottomore and Maximilien Rubel, Introduction to Karl Marx, *Selected Writings in Sociology and Social Philosophy* (ed. with an introduction and notes by T. B. Bottomore and Maximilien Rubel; texts trans. T. B. Bottomore), 2nd impression, London: Watts, 1961, p. 21.
3 Karl Marx, *A Contribution to the Critique of Political Economy* (trans. from 2nd German ed. by N. I. Stone), Chicago: Kerr, 1904, p. 11.
4 *Ibid.*, pp. 11–12 (my emphasis).
5 Sidney Hook, *Towards the Understanding of Karl Marx: A Revolutionary Interpretation*, New York: Day, 1933, p. 134.

6 Karl Marx, *Capital: A Critical Analysis of Capitalist Production*, vol. 1 (trans. from 3rd German ed. by Samuel Moore and Edward Aveling, ed. by Freidrich Engels), 4th ed., New York: Appleton, London: Swan Sonnenschein, 1891, p. 157.

7 Cf. Karl Marx, Friedrich Engels, *The German Ideology*, pts I and III (ed. with an introduction by R. Pascal), New York: International Publishers, 1939, p. 22.

8 Karl Marx, *Nationalökonomie und Philosophie* (with an introduction by Erich Thier), Cologne and Berlin: Kiepenheuer, 1950, p. 227 (my translation; emphasis in original).

9 *Ibid.*, p. 229.

10 Cf. Karl Marx, 'Ökonomisch-Philosophische Manuskripte aus dem Jahre 1844' in Marx, Engels, *Historisch-Kritische Gesamtausgabe*, vol. I/3 (edited for the Marx-Engels-Institute Moscow by V. Adoratskij), Berlin: Marx-Engels-Verlag, 1932, pp. 45–6. (Referred to hereafter as MEGA.)

11 *Ibid.*, pp. 85–6 (my translation).

12 Cf. Marx, *Nationalökonomie und Philosophie*, p. 191.

13 Cf. MEGA I/3, p. 114.

14 Cf. *ibid.*, pp. 115, 119, 126.

15 Cf. Marx, *A Contribution to the Critique of Political Economy*, p. 12.

16 Cf. Marx, Engels, *The German Ideology*, p. 27.

17 Cf. *ibid.*, p. 21.

18 Cf. *ibid.*, p. 1.

19 Cf. *ibid.*, pp. 14–15.

20 Cf. Karl Mannheim, *Ideology and Utopia: An Introduction to the Sociology of Knowledge* (trans. Louis Wirth and Edward Shils), 7th impression, London: Routledge & Kegan Paul, 1954, p. 66.

21 Hook, *Towards the Understanding of Karl Marx*, pp. 103–4.

22 Cf. Alexander A. Bogdanov, *Die Entwicklungsformen der Gesellschaft und die Wissenschaft* (trans. I. Dursky), Berlin: Nike, 1924.

23 Cf. Paul Szende, *Verhüllung und Enthüllung*, Leipzig: Cl. Hirschfeld, 1922.

24 Cf. Otto Bauer, 'Das Weltbild des Kapitalismus' in O. Jenssen (ed.), *Der Lebendige Marxismus: Kautsky Festschrift*, Jena: Thüringer Verlagsanstalt und Druckerei, 1924. See also A. Fogarasi, 'Die Soziologie der Intelligenz und die Intelligenz der Soziologie', *Unter dem Banner des Marxismus*, vol. 4, no. 3 (1930).

25 Cf. Stanislaw Warynski, *Die Wissenschaft von der Gesellschaft: Umriss einer Methodenlehre der dialektischen Soziologie* (trans. Kazimierz Malecki), Bern: Francke, 1944.

26 Cf. Georg Lukács, *Geschichte und Klassenbewusstsein: Studien über marxistische Dialektik*, Berlin: Malik-Verlag, 1923. In 1953 Lukács' account of irrationalist philosophy, *Die Zerstörung der Vernunft*, appeared in East Berlin. Certainly Lukács had lost all appetite for even the slightest trace of relativism. Mannheim's sociology of knowledge figures in Lukács' reckoning with irrationalism as a 'relativist caricature' which denies that cognition can have any objectivity. (Cf. Georg Lukács, *Die Zerstörung der Vernunft*, *Georg Lukács Werke*, vol. 9,

Neuwied am Rhein, Berlin-Spandau: Luchterhand, 1962, pp. 549–50.)
A lessening of Lukács' doctrinaire attitude and a greater receptiveness
for some of the concepts of his earlier work are apparent, however, in
his more recent book, *Wider den missverstandenen Realismus*, Hamburg:
Claassen, 1958. It is possible that the change was occasioned by the
problems and conflicts which Lukács experienced when he participated
in the government of Nagy.

27 Cf. Lukács, *Geschichte und Klassenbewusstsein*, pp. 244–5.
28 *Ibid.*, pp. 234–5 (my translation).
29 Cf. *ibid.*, p. 198.
30 *Ibid.*, p. 202 (emphasis in original; my translation).
31 *Ibid.*, p. 94.
32 Werner Stark, *The Sociology of Knowledge: An Essay in Aid of a Deeper Understanding of the History of Ideas*, Chicago: Free Press, 1958, p. 308.
33 Cf. Franz Mehring, *Geschichte der deutschen Sozialdemokratie*, vol. 1, 4th ed., Stuttgart: Dietz, 1909, p. 386.
34 Cf. Lukács, *Geschichte und Klassenbewusstsein*, pp. 58–9 and 172–3.
35 Cf. *ibid.*, pp. 63–5.
36 *Ibid.*, p. 223 (my translation).
37 Cf. *ibid.*, p. 217.
38 Cf. *ibid.*, p. 165.
39 *Ibid.*, p. 34 (my translation).
40 Cf. *ibid.*, p. 80.
41 *Ibid.*, p. 234.
42 Cf. *ibid.*, pp. 77–8.
43 Cf. *ibid.*, pp. 78–9.
44 Cf. *ibid.*, p. 53. For Lukács, *history* is the genesis of *class-consciousness*, of that mentality that reaches its perfection and annihilation in the same flash of historical significance: the proletariat annihilates itself together with its opponent at the moment of revolution and at that same moment class-consciousness becomes totally real to immediately leave the stage of history, forever. (Cf. *ibid.*, pp. 62, 86, 89.)
45 *Ibid.*, p. 223.

part five

Émile Durkheim and the sociological theory of knowledge

10 The sociology of knowledge in the French tradition

Gunter W. Remmling

In a general and partial way, we may characterize the sociology of knowledge as a specialized area of modern sociological research which has made it possible for us to discern and describe the differences in human thought among different groups and at different times. Much like the historian of art who distinguishes different styles of art, the sociologist of knowledge distinguishes different styles of thought. In France Émile Durkheim, Lucien Lévy-Bruhl, and their followers established an important starting point for this type of sociological research when they revealed the system of logic peculiar to 'primitive tribes.'

The Durkheim school

Durkheim (1858–1917) went beyond the generalities of his predecessors who had taught that thought depends upon language, and language upon society; he took the next step when he tried to show in detail how both the forms of logical classification and the basic categories of cognition have been produced by society.

In collaboration with Marcel Mauss, Durkheim discussed the problem of classification and showed that the present concept of a 'class' does not go back beyond Artistotle: our modern forms of logical classification such as class and subclass, species and genus are not innate but based upon 'a hierarchical order for which neither the sensory world nor our own minds offer us a model.'[1] Durkheim and Mauss believed, however, that they had discovered the resemblance of such a model when their studies of the logical classifications of primitive men revealed that these classifications closely reflect the social organization of the tribe. Thus the hierarchical nature of logical classes was seen as the reflection of the hierarchical order of earlier (primitive) forms of social structure.

The Australian aborigines, for example, classify objects as belonging to different phratries: the moon may belong to one of two phratries, the sun to the other. Each of these primary tribal subdivisions may again be subdivided into two matrimonial classes; they in turn will serve as class categories for things. The first 'classes,' then, were classes of men and the importance of these 'social' classes was carried over to the non-social objects in the corresponding logical classes: all the objects and animals in the environment were classified as belonging to a certain tribal subdivision or kinship group. In this manner Durkheim and Mauss explain the social origin of logical relations: the tribe is the logical ancestor of the genus, the phratry the ancestor of the species. The association of certain objects with members of certain social groups originated the classification of these objects with these human beings—the hierarchy of tribe, phratry, and clan led to the hierarchy of genus, species, and class and from the unity of society we came to imagine the unity of the universe of things, the supreme logical whole.[2]

Furthermore, this primitive classification is not primarily conceptual, but has its basis in the emotional values inherent in all psychical, associative processes which involve elements of social life. Scientific classification emerges when social sensibility and sentiment diminish in importance and when conceptions having such emotional values are subjected to free and rigorous examination. But—concludes Durkheim in his arbitrary manner—contemporary scientific classification has its source in these emotional, mythological classifications based on collective representations: the mental habits which help us organize facts in groups (themselves hierarchically related) bear the indelible mark of a social genesis.[3]

This general argument is repeated with only minor modifications in Durkheim's daringly speculative work *Les Formes élémentaires de la vie religieuse* which introduces a sociologistic explanation of the categories of the understanding. By the analysis of the simplest religion known (the totemic practices of Australian tribes) Durkheim wants, first, to determine what are the elementary forms of religious thought and practice and, second, to demonstrate how the categories of the understanding have a religious (religion is itself the product of social causes) and, therefore, a social origin.

La Vie religieuse contains—mainly in the introduction—the rudiments of a sociological theory of knowledge which Durkheim develops with the hope of settling the dispute between empiricistic and *a priori* epistemology. He recalls that our judgments rest upon certain basic ideas which determine the nature and form of our intellectual activities. These are the general concepts which philosophers since Aristotle have called the categories of the understanding such as time, space, class, number, cause, substance, totality, etc.

The categories correspond to the most universal properties of things and provide the framework which makes the normal working of the intellect possible.[4]

The religious and consequently social origin of the categories may be observed, for example, in the category of time which was derived from social rhythms based on the concentration and dispersion of the social group; the divisions into days, weeks, months, and years correspond to the periodic recurrence of religious ceremonies and social activities—a calendar expresses the rhythm of collective life and simultaneously assures its regularity. The determination of these different moments and sequences of time is an entirely extra-individual affair, free from the whims and arbitrary decisions of any particular person. Individual man, to maintain his temporal relations with others, is forced to conform to this collective system of ideas and measurements.

Similarly the category of space was derived from the territory occupied by the society and the number of the fundamental regions of space varied historically with the variation in the fundamental number of clans. Next Durkheim explains the category of force as the logical formulation of the 'mana' of primitive man's practical cosmology, as an objectified collective force (social constraint) projected into things, as an efficient force upon which the category of causality depends. The all-inclusive category of totality is the logical expression of the totality most familiar to primitive man: the whole social group. Finally, Durkheim suspects that even the idea of contradiction is a function of given social conditions since the power of this principle has varied from one historical epoch and one society to the next. Durkheim concludes that all the variations undergone by the rules determining contemporary logic prove that 'far from being engraven through all eternity upon the mental constitution of men, they depend, at least in part, upon factors that are historical and consequently social.'[5]

In this manner Durkheim believes to have accomplished his objective; the negative aspects of the empiricistic and apriorist theory of the origin of the categories are eliminated while their viable elements are fused into his 'social origin' hypothesis: the categories are collective representations imposed upon the individual; they impress man as universal and necessary. Consensus about these basic modes of thought is of signal importance for co-operation and thus for the very existence of the group and this explains the uniformity of the categories *within a given group*. In the interest of survival each group must enforce this measure of logical conformity and impose the categories upon its members with 'a special sort of moral necessity which is to the intellectual life what moral obligation is to the will.'[6] The impression of necessity which the categories give is due to the fact that they are social representations with all the prestige bestowed by such an origin: the categories are therefore, for the individual mind, *a priori*, whereas their origin outside the individual mind satisfies the empiricist's positive desire to remain anchored in the objective universe of observable phenomena.

The categories are of religious origin, yet they remain at the foundation of man's intelligence; they appear now as 'priceless instruments of thought' which men created over many centuries and where they have accumulated their most valuable intellectual assets.[7]

Durkheim held, then, that religion furnished the early (primitive) intellectual and attitudinal framework wherein the categories were first elaborated. The religious attitudinal matrix he derived, however, from a wider complex of experience that incorporates the totality of social existence which consists of religious and secular elements. Durkheim found the real basis determining both the forms and practices of religious life and the forms and practices of intellectual life in the various factors constituting the structure of society: the stratification of groups, power relations, ecological and economic conditions, the division of labor, familial and kinship relationships, socially sanctioned moral imperatives, and so forth. When Durkheim revealed these social factors he also identified the objective patterns which make up the substructure molding the forms of knowledge during their inception. The forms of knowledge, however, cannot be derived directly from the social substructure; what must now come into play is a meaningful subjective element that is to inform and express the responses of human agents to the objective social conditions of their existence. This subjective element Durkheim found in the primitive attitudinal matrix wherein the universe appears as a plenum of supernatural forces. The ideas of religion, therefore, furnished the attitudinal structure which coalesced with the natural and social aspects of primitive life to determine both the emergence and early expression of the categories. Durkheim views the attitudinal structure—existing within the minds of individuals—as the product of collective experience. This structure is reflected by 'collective representations' which combine the experiences of many persons; it is the process of social interaction that makes these representations binding on all group members.[8]

Durkheim contributed to the sociology of knowledge—which is essentially the doctrine of the determination of cognition and knowledge by social reality—by describing the interaction between the structure of nonliterate societies, the complex of their religious attitudes, and the genesis of the categories of the understanding. Durkheim did more than most of the German sociologists of knowledge, who only posited the interrelationship between social structure and thought, because of his willingness to analyze 'the problem in terms of concrete historical material derived from the best empirical sources in the field of anthropology which were available to him at the time of his research.'[9]

Durkheim and his school were not preoccupied with political conflict and class struggles and the absence of any particular commitment enabled them to focus their attention upon social interaction in its entirety; therefore, these French sociologists emphasized from the onset the all-pervasiveness of social influences in the intellectual life of men in society.

The work of Granet

This emphasis is prominent in the approach of the sinologist Marcel Granet (1884–1940), who employs Durkheim's methodology in his works on Chinese language and culture. Granet recalls that all thinking is clothed in words; words are social formations, stemming from social interaction and, therefore, all thinking is rooted in and colored by concrete social life.

This observation led Granet to an attempt at the application of Durkheim's sociological theory of the categories. He published the results in 1934 in his book on ancient Chinese thought, *La Pensée chinoise*.[10] The work endeavors to reveal the rules and symbols governing Chinese mentality and opens logically with an analysis of Chinese language: although a written language has been extant in China since about 1800 B.C. it remained monosyllabic, restricted in phonetic scope, and dependent on word order for clarity and pitch for diversity when spoken. The grammatical apparatus of accidence and syntax is missing. Consequently, Chinese language is a poor vehicle for the communication of abstract and analytical forms of thought. This tongue is, however, rich in highly concrete images (emblems) conveying values and stimulating action. Chinese language is a powerful medium for the expression of sentimental, emotional attitudes and the suggestion of forms of conduct. As a moral, social, and ritualistic control device it expresses emotion, judges conduct as proper or improper, and assigns whatever is symbolized by the word to a definite place in the social order.[11]

Since this language opposes itself to all attempts at the economization of mental effort and the development of analytical and abstract thought, we are not surprised to find that the ideas which are directive of the operations of the Chinese mind are different from the categories determining the intellectual life of the occident. Being basic, these 'directive ideas' (*idées directrices*) still possess the value of categories—but they are synthetic and concrete, instead of analytic and abstract.[12]

Undoubtedly, Granet suggests a social genesis of the categories.

The Chinese conception of time, he argues, was deeply emblematical and reflective of the dynastic and feudal structure of ancient China. There, no thinker conceived of time as a monotonous duration constituted by repetition; time derived its meaning from a definite order of eras, seasons, and epochs; time was intimately associated with the notions of the calendar and of dynastic succession. Chinese time was not an abstract addition of quantitatively equal and qualitatively indistinguishable units. Each period of time was inseparable from a certain circumstance and occasion. Moreover, considerations of time were never separated from those of space which appeared as a complex of singular domains and climates extending into different directions. Chinese space was not abstract like Kant's pure and homogeneous medium; but, like time, it was highly heterogeneous and hierarchical.

For the Chinese, space was not extension as such; it was square and faded into four vague regions (the Four Seas) in or near which lived the animal-like barbarians—only the Chinese were human and lived in civilized space. At the center, space was densest and purest: here the group fully realized its diversity, hierarchy, and order. The site for this sacred, central square must be near the celestial palace; it must be a site where the convergence of rivers and of climates marked the genuine center of the world. To connect time and space and to ensure, thereby, celestial and social harmony, the chief must reside in various sections of the empire and he must reach each portion at a certain season to receive in audience the vassal from this sector. Traveling with the sun from the east, it took the sovereign five years to complete his tour of the empire.

This conception was the creation of a feudal society and since this society remained feudal, space 'never ceased to be imagined as a hierarchical federation of heterogeneous extensions.'[13] Together, the concrete ideas of space and time furnished an organon for the art of mastering, by ritual and symbol, the world and the society of civilized men at its center: they provided a framework for the mature art of ruling.

The Chinese combined an extreme respect for numerical symbols with an extreme indifference for all quantitative conceptions. Mere ordinal succession and quantity played almost no role in their thinking, apart from wordly trade and technology. For the Chinese philosophers numbers were manifestations of the structure of reality, means of arranging objects, actions, and people in hierarchies of essential value: these hierarchies were ultimately founded on the ranks of the feudal system and the power vested in the sovereign; they were, therefore, determined by social considerations. Numbers were important because of their polyvalence, as this made them remarkably suitable for efficacious manipulation. Numbers revealed the form or value of objects, because numbers symbolized the composition and power of social groups in relation to these objects which were associated with them. Therefore, the Chinese thinkers were able to 'represent with the help of numbers the protocol order that governs the universal life.'[14]

Numbers had a logical function which was classificatory. This function resided in the distributing of all things within the categories *Yin* and *Yang*. The classificatory usage of numbers, odd and even, connected with the other function of numbers: the protocol function. With the aid of numbers the sages were able to represent the protocol order which governed the life of the universe. Numbers established the etiquettes for the different groups they classified.

Yin and *Yang* are specifically Chinese categories which have a directive function and instill everything with a 'rhythm.' Granet assumes that they originated in the semi-annual ceremonies and the occupational divisions and cycles of the social structure which are determined by the principle of sex. Essentially, all that is masculine in nature may be classified under *Yang* and all that is of feminine nature under *Yin*. Like so many other Chinese 'emblems,' however, *Yin* and *Yang* are not principles of classification in an abstract sense—they emphasize and reveal concrete qualification and differentiation. What they emphasize are mainly alternating and contrasting social arrangements and segments such as the social division of labor and the occupational cycles of men and women which coincide with the changes in season.

The spring and autumn assemblies which play an important part in Granet's explanation of the genesis of these categories are sexual rites (*fêtes sexuelles*) which bring these social facts into focus: the male members of the group appear on one side of a river-bound valley, where they are revealed by the rising sun to the women who stand in the shadows, facing the men. These positions evoke essential attributes of *Yang*, such as the north of a river, the south of a hill, the sun, penis, and other attributes belonging to *Yin*, such as shady, the south of a river, cold, mysterious, vagina.

Between the men and the women has been divided the work during the year. The oncoming orgy will now bring into focus their complementary character in ritual form: men and women will fuse in sexual union and the emblems *Yin* and *Yang* will be evoked in all their rich meaning. *Yang* evokes the image of an open door, of generation, and of spring, when the men go out into the sunlit fields to produce the food that maintains life. *Yin* evokes the image of a closed door, of the hibernation of the time of winter when the women weave and do their share of the common labor. But now *Yin* and *Yang* are one, harmonizing as they are called back and forth, the cosmos of man and nature. Now time and space blend perfectly, because the site and the

161

occasion are perfect: there is order and harmony and there exists a unity between man and that universe of which he is a solid part.[15]

The two sexes have obeyed the command of an antithetical discipline; as rival groups they have communicated with emblem and deed: they have become parts of something larger than and embracive of all of life and time and space. Their close union under the domination of *Yin* and *Yang* has made men and women into a total and harmoniously related society focalized in a rite and this is projected mythically: *Yin* and *Yang* are *Tao*.[16]

'All *Yin* and all *Yang*, this is *Tao*.' *Tao*, the All-Encompassing, embraces all the other symbols; it is a total made up of two aspects which are totals themselves, because they are mutually substitutable. *Tao* is, however, not their sum, but the regulator of their alternance. Literally *Tao* means way or road, but its deeper meanings, contained in the classics, are always those of social and cosmic order, totality, responsibility, and efficacy. *Tao* is supreme. *Tao* is total efficacy, a center of responsibility, and finds its expression above all in the sovereign ruler who manages the world and animates it. *Tao* is the unique principle of all success and it is geared to the total art of ruling. According to Granet, *Tao* begins by evoking the image of the chief's journey which signifies the power of regulation and orderly efficacy vested in him.

The sovereign lord makes his tour of the empire, imitating the march of the sun and is considered by the Heavens as a Son. This unique man maintains the communication between the sovereign heaven and earth and, thereby, their felicitous harmony. This virtuous chieftain is the pivot of a great axis. Once more, Granet tries to reveal the essentially social character of a Chinese symbol: *Tao* is the concretion of notions evol vingaround the sovereign, his domain, the feudal hierarchy, the harmony of society and nature. *Tao* is the supreme emblem of social monism and the final assertion of man's oneness with the cosmos. Man's social arrangements, his ritual and etiquette, give expression to the all-pervading *Tao* in exactly the same way as do natural phenomena. He who knows the *Tao* of anything, knows the *Tao* of everything. The great of this world rule by the power of their 'saintly' wisdom: '*ce Savoir agissant, c'est le Tao.*'[17]

From Lévy-Bruhl to Halbwachs

Granet gives rise not only to the thought that the categories are socially determined but also to the suspicion that there exists a radical cleavage of categorial systems, that there are no common and universally valid denominators of conception and thought. A similar argument resides in Lévy-Bruhl's concept of the 'prelogicality' of the primitive mind. Prelogical thinking is said to follow 'affective categories' which are expressive of impulses and emotions. This primitive thinking is determined by the social group, and its connection with the world is largely a matter of 'mystic participations' and 'exclusions.' The primitive is alleged to have no clear idea of substance and attribute, cause and effect, identity and contradiction—his outlook is dominated by confused superstition. With Lévy-Bruhl (1857–1939) the continuity leading from 'primitive' to 'civilized' thoughtways becomes ruptured.[18]

Contemporary anthropologists have rejected the assumption that primitive mentality is basically different from modern, 'rational' mentality and argue to the contrary that the thoughtways which Lévy-Bruhl alleged to be typically primitive occur also among the members of developed societies. No matter how civilized and rational we may pride ourselves to be, we, as well, see the elementary threats—illness, death, insanity—through a vague emotional fog which becomes 'denser and more impenetrable as the fateful forms approach. It is indeed astonishing that "savages" can achieve such a sober, dispassionate outlook in these matters as they actually do.'[19]

Not only do civilized men exhibit traits of the primitive's mentality but 'primitives' also exhibit traits of civilized mentality and that to a significant degree. Bronislaw Malinowski claims that his observations among the Melanesian and Papuo-Melanesian tribes of Eastern New Guinea and the surrounding archipelagoes ('the classical land of magic') prove that there is knowledge of the rational and empirical variety 'among savages living in the age of polished stone.'[20]

The primitive does not only have one (prelogical, superstitious) domain of reality, but two. He has his everyday world of practical activities and this is directed by rational knowledge and experience. Besides this domain he has his region of belief and cult; primitive men use magic whenever they have to cope with mysterious and hostile forces, or with the 'great unearned increment of fortunate coincidence.'[21]

Malinowski is certain that his data prove that there are no irreconcilable differences between primitive and civilized mentality when *comparable* domains of thought and activity are considered. If we accept Malinowski's position we come to suspect that Granet is subject to a fallacy which is not unlike that of Lévy-Bruhl. Is it correct to compare—as Granet does—factual, technical-scientific concepts with conceptions that are not factual but traditional, not technical-scientific, but notions born of magic and ritual? Probably not and 'in a wide range of actual *practices*, the Chinese did not *act* on the assumption that "time is round" and "space, square." ' Granet, therefore, only 'demonstrated qualitative differences of concepts in *certain contexts*, but not within such comparable contexts as, say, that of technical practice.'[22]

A modification of Durkheim's position—especially by way of a psychological approach—was brought about by Celestin Bouglé and Maurice Halbwachs. Significant portions of their work are reminiscent of sociology of knowledge in the Durkheimian tradition—but in contrast to him they also proceed along the lines of primarily speculative social psychology.[23]

This injection of psychology, however, seems to have helped the acculturation of a sociology of knowledge derived from Durkheim in the United States. The germs of a peculiarly American sociology of knowledge are contained in the social behaviorism of G. H. Mead, which is a similar attempt to show the operation of those psychic mechanisms through which objective social constraints acting upon the individual become internalized within the private attitudinal complex of the person.[24] Soon American social psychologists developed experimental techniques that made it possible to empirically study the influence of group situations upon the individual's perception and judgment.[25]

The social psychology of G. H. Mead gives direction to the work of Florian Znaniecki, who wants to restrict the sociology of knowledge to the study of the carriers of knowledge—to the analysis of a certain complex of human interaction.[26] Znaniecki wants to demonstrate how men of knowledge orient themselves to special segments of society which have special criteria of validity determining what is 'important' knowledge. These segments of society which influence men of knowledge in their work, he calls 'the social circle.' The emphasis on the brain worker's 'audience' explains why this typically American variant of sociology of knowledge was destined to fade into the field of communications, public opinion, and propaganda analysis.

Notes

1 Émile Durkheim and Marcel Mauss, 'De quelques formes primitives de classification', *Année sociologique*, vol. 6 (1901–2), p. 6.

2 Cf. *ibid.*, pp. 9–13.

3 Cf. *ibid.*, pp. 66–72. Durkheim's attempt to make the logical powers of classification posterior to and dependent on the classificatory powers derived from the structure of the group is open to various forms of criticism—above all we may ask whether, if primitive men did not already possess at least a general power of classification, they could recognize human beings as constituting a class distinct from the animals or could arrive at such conceptions as phratry, clan, or family.

4 Cf. Émile Durkheim, *The Elementary Forms of the Religious Life* (trans. Joseph Ward Swain), 3rd impression, London: Allen & Unwin, 1954, p. 9. Durkheim explains that he calls time and space categories because he does not see any difference between the role which these ideas play

in the intellectual life and the role which falls to the ideas of class or cause.

5 *Ibid.*, p. 13.

6 *Ibid.*, p. 18.

7 Cf. *ibid.*, p. 19.

8 Cf. Gerard L. DeGré, *Society and Ideology: An Inquiry into the Sociology of Knowledge* (Ph.D. thesis), New York: Columbia University Bookstore, 1943, pp. 74–5.

9 *Ibid.*, p. 75. Kant had already tried to protect himself against attacks upon his universal, *a priori* view of the role played by the categories in the cognitive process when he rejected the psychological approach to epistemology. In our century it was especially Ernst Cassirer who fought most resolutely against all attempts to undermine the Kantian position by way of psychologistic, sociologistic, or historicistic reinterpretations. From a position that strives to retain the purity of Kant's basic question the categories appear as pure, formal concepts without any concrete content. As pure forms they have no relation whatsoever with an historically accumulated collective *experience*, or its counterpart. Those who claim an historical changeability of these pure forms simply confuse pure formal concepts with materially determined general concepts. Cf. Ernst Cassirer, 'Der Kritische Idealismus und die Philosophie des "gesunden Menschenverstandes"', *Philosophische Arbeiten* (ed. Hermann Cohen and Paul Natorp), vol. 1, no. 1, 1906. Also see Ernst Cassirer, *Das Erkenntnisproblem in der Philosophie und Wissenschaft der neueren Zeit*, 3 vols, Berlin: Cassirer, 1922–3.

10 This book is devoted to Chinese thought. It is, however, complimentary to *La Civilization chinoise* (1929), where Granet portrays the social and political system of the ancient Chinese. Cf. Marcel Granet, *Chinese Civilization* (trans. K. E. Innes and M. R. Brailsford), New York: Knopf, 1930.

11 Cf. Marcel Granet, *La Pensée chinoise*, Paris: Renaissance du Livre, 1934, p. 37.

12 *Ibid.*, p. 83.

13 *Ibid.*, p. 95 (my translation).

14 *Ibid.*, p. 297 (my translation).

15 Cf. *ibid.*, pp. 139–48. Cf. also O. Z. Fang, *Complete Chinese-English Dictionary*, quoted in H. G. Creel, *Sinism: A Study of the Evolution of the Chinese World-View*, Chicago: Open Court, 1929, p. 28.

16 Cf. Granet, *La Pensée chinoise*, p. 120.

17 *Ibid.*, p. 326. Cf. also C. Wright Mills, 'The Language and Ideas of Ancient China' in C. W. Mills, *Power, Politics and People* (ed. with an introduction by Louis Horowitz), New York: Ballantine Books, 1963, pp. 469–520.

18 Cf. Lucien Lévy-Bruhl, *How Natives Think* (trans. Lilian A. Clare), London: Allen & Unwin, 1926, and *Primitive Mentality* (trans. Lilian A. Clare), London: Allen & Unwin, 1923.

19 Bronislaw Malinowski, *Magic, Science, and Religion and Other Essays*, Garden City, N.Y.: Doubleday, 1954, p. 32.

20 *Ibid.*, p. 27.

21 *Ibid.*, p. 29.
22 Robert K. Merton, 'The Sociology of Knowledge' in Georges Gurvitch and Wilbert E. Moore (eds), *Twentieth Century Sociology*, New York: Philosophical Library, 1945, p. 388 (emphasis in original).
23 Cf. Celestin Bouglé, *The Evolution of Values* (trans. Helen S. Sellars), New York: Holt, Rinehart & Winston, 1926, and Maurice Halbwachs, *Les Cadres sociaux de la mémoire*, Paris: Alcan, 1925, and *La Mémoire collective*, Paris: Presses Universitaires de France, 1950.
24 Cf. G. H. Mead, *Mind, Self and Society*, University of Chicago Press, 1943.
25 Cf., for example, Kurt Lewin, *The Conceptual Representation and the Measurement of Psychological Forces*, Durham, N.C.: Duke University Press, 1938.
26 Cf. Florian Znaniecki, *The Social Role of the Man of Knowledge*, New York: Columbia University Press, 1940.

11 A sociological theory of knowledge

Edward L. Schaub

The key to Durkheim's interpretation of human experience, whether in respect of religion, morality, law, social relationships generally, or knowledge, is to be found in his contention of its duplicity. Man, he writes,

> is double. There are two beings in him: an individual being which has its foundation in the organism and the circle of whose activities is therefore strictly limited, and a social being which represents the highest reality in the intellectual and moral order that we know by observation—I mean society. In so far as he belongs to society, the individual transcends himself, both when he thinks and when he acts.[1]

Of the two beings, so far as cognition is concerned, the one is described as comprising sensations, images and individual representations. These are states of consciousness which result from the stimulation by objects and in all further respects are an expression of the psychical nature of the individual mind. They arise from our 'daily relations with external things' and concern themselves with the 'external and material world' as this presents itself to the individual.[2] As 'sensual representations' they are in constant flux. Moreover,

> a sensation or an image always relies upon a determined object, or upon a collection of objects of the same sort, and expresses the momentary condition of a particular consciousness; it is essentially individual and subjective. We therefore have considerable liberty in dealing with the representations of such an origin. It is true that when our sensations are actual, they impose themselves upon us *in fact*. But *by right* we are free to conceive them otherwise than they really are, or to represent them to ourselves as occurring in a different order from that where they are really produced.[3]

In the last analysis, they are immediately dependent upon the organism. Indeed, were man 'reduced to having only individual perceptions, he would be indistinguishable from the beasts.'[4]

Sharply distinct from these experiences are concepts. These, in their intrinsic nature, are 'outside of time and change,' 'immutable.' If they undergo alterations, it is only through our activity, in so far as we find them unsuitable. Even this change, indeed, they stubbornly resist. They are 'universal, or at least capable of becoming so.'[5] In further contrast to sensations, which can by no possibility pass from one consciousness to another, they are held in common or are least communicable—the latter by reason of the fact that they are essentially 'impersonal' representations. Conceptual thought does more than classify objects on the basis of common characteristics. It relates the variable to the permanent, 'the individual to the social.'[6]

Dominating all the details of the intellectual life are the categories. These are the most general of all concepts, such, for example, as those of time, space, class, number, cause, force, substance, and personality. 'They correspond to the most universal properties of things.'[7] 'They represent the most general relations which exist between things.'[8] 'They are applicable to all that is real'; 'not attached to any particular object, they are independent of every particular object; they constitute the common field where all minds meet.'[9] They 'dominate and envelop all the other concepts: they are permanent molds for the mental life.'[10] Like all concepts, they are in intent immutable (though not, as a matter of fact, unchanging) and, of course, universal. They are characterized by necessity, as well as by an authority which we are constrained to recognize. They impose themselves upon us *by right*: 'they have within them a sort of force or moral ascendency.'[11] They relate to 'an ideal world to which we attribute a moral superiority.'[12] In distinction from general ideas which scarcely enrich knowledge, in as much as they contain nothing more than the particulars from which they are derived, concepts and categories 'add to that which we can learn by our own personal experience all that wisdom and science which the group has accumulated in the course of centuries.'[13]

The characteristics just mentioned preclude concepts and categories from being merely abstractions from individual experience or 'the average of the corresponding individual representations.' 'Every time that we are in the presence of a *type* of thought or action which is imposed uniformly upon particular wills or intelligences, this pressure exercised over the individual betrays the intervention of the group.'[14] 'Collective representations are the result of an immense co-operation, which stretches out not only into space but into time as well; to make them, a multitude of minds have associated, united and combined their ideas and sentiments; for them, long generations have accumulated their experience and their knowledge. A special intellectual activity is therefore concentrated in them which is infinitely richer and complexer than that of the individual.'[15] Their origin is the *l'âme collective*, the *conscience collective*, and this has a distinctive nature and unique laws, markedly different from those of individual minds. It is *sui generis*.

The consideration upon which Durkheim relies in making his sharp distinction between the natures of collective and of individual minds is one which, in common with Bergson, he had learned from their teacher Boutroux.[16] Wholes, he was convinced, can be understood only in terms of themselves, of the qualities which as a matter of discovery alone they are found to possess, for they have a character irreducible to that of the component simples. The phenomena of life, for example, are not adequately describable in terms of physico-chemical laws. Sensation, though depending upon the brain because 'compounded out of molecular modifications,' is nevertheless 'something else because it results from a new synthesis *sui generis*, wherein those modifications enter as elements, but wherein they are transformed by the very fact of their fusion.'[17] Through the compounding of sensations, according to laws quite other than those of cerebral physiology or morphology, arise images and finally general ideas. This exhausts the nature of individual minds. There is, however, a higher psychical reality which arises through the convergence, association, interaction, and union of elementary, that is, of individual, consciousnesses. Its powers and characteristics are unique, for, though likewise engrossed in thinking, feeling, and acting, these functions diverge materially from the analogous ones of individual minds. True, the collective mind depends upon a material order and upon associated individuals, and it varies with the number of the latter, their geographical disposition, the nature of the means of communication, the stage of economic development, etc. Yet the synthesis by which it comes into being

> has the effect of disengaging a whole world of sentiments, ideas, and images which, once born, obey laws all their own. They attract each other, repel each other, unite, divide themselves, and multiply, though these combinations are not commanded and necessitated by the condition of the underlying reality. The life thus brought into being enjoys so great an independence that it sometimes indulges in manifestations with no purpose or utility of any sort, for the mere pleasure of affirming itself.[18]

To secure a definite conception of the role which Durkheim assigns to the collective mind in the knowledge process, one must examine the numerous, though somewhat scattered, suggestions which he makes concerning the meaning and the origin of various categories.

In his essay, '*De quelques formes primitives de classification*,'[19] he points out that we classify or order facts according to a hierarchical scheme, but that this cannot be accounted for in terms either of the contents of perceptual experience or of any characteristics of individual mind. True, vague feelings of resemblance attach to sense experiences as such, and similar representations are brought together in individual consciousness to form generic images. But the latter, it is contended, are entirely restricted in their content to the objects perceived. Hence they are incapable of originating the idea of a class, 'of a mold including the *whole* group of all possible objects which satisfy the same condition.' Indeed, it is contended that 'the mere observations of our interior life could never awaken' in us even the notion of a group. This latter notion and our modes of classifying sense objects are said directly to reflect the social group and its form of organization. 'Does not the word for "kind" (*genre*) designate originally a family group (γένος)?'[20] The hierarchy of tribe, phratry and clan became that of genus, species and class, and in this form it has survived in the most advanced thought, though the parent mode of social organization has long since changed. In support of his hypothesis, Durkheim cites numerous primitive methods of classification. He maintains, for example, that in the totemic culture of Australia, all objects of nature are regarded as 'a part of the tribe; they are constituent elements of it and, so to speak, regular members of it; just like men, they have a determined place in the general scheme of organization of the society.'[21]

A closely related category is that of totality. This likewise could never have arisen from individual experience, for, however we might extend and prolong the latter, it could never 'give a suspicion of the existence of a whole class which would embrace every single being and to which other classes are only coordinated or subordinated species.'[22] Fundamentally 'the concept of totality is only the abstract form of the concept of society'; in fact, the two, together with the concept of divinity, are conjectured to be only different aspects of the same notion. The South Australian savage, he quotes from Fison, 'looks upon the universe as the Great Tribe, to one of whose divisions he himself belongs; and all things, animate and inanimate, which belong to his class are parts of the body corporate whereof he himself is a part.'[23]

The category of space is similarly said to be underivable from the data of sense perception. In so far Durkheim is at one with Kant. Yet here again his characteristic position appears. If the data of sense are to be co-ordinated and things are to be arranged spatially, he argues, space cannot be conceived as an indeterminate, absolutely homogeneous medium whose parts are therefore qualitatively equivalent and interchangeable;

there must be a possibility of placing them differently, of putting some at the right, others at the left, these above, those below, at the north of or at the south of, east or west of, etc.—space could not be what it is if it were not—divided and differentiated. But whence come these divisions which are so essential?—All these distinctions evidently come from the fact that different sympathetic values have been attributed to various regions. Since all men of a single civilization represent space in the same way, it is clearly necessary that these sympathetic values, and the distinctions which depend upon them, should be equally universal, and that almost necessarily implies that they be of social origin. Besides that, there are cases where this social character is made manifest. There are societies in Australia and North America where space is conceived in the form of an immense circle, because the camp has a circular form; and this spatial circle is divided up exactly like the tribal circle and is in its image. There are as many regions distinguished as there are clans in the tribe, and it is the place occupied by the clans inside the encampment which has determined the orientation of these regions.[24]

In short, Durkheim contends that the spatial organization of our world of sense experience derives from the fact and from the character of the social organization.

Much the same is held to be true with respect to time. Individual representations or states of consciousness, to be sure, occur in a certain temporal order and may be reproduced accordingly in memory. Yet they cannot have engendered the category of time, for this implies 'a universal order of succession which imposes itself upon all minds and all events.'[25] It does not consist

merely in a commemoration, either partial or integral, of our past life. It is an abstract and impersonal frame which surrounds, not only our individual existence, but that of all humanity. It is like an endless chart, where all duration is spread out before the mind, and upon which all possible events can be located in relation to fixed and determined guide lines. It is not *my time* that is thus arranged; it is time in general, such as it is objectively thought of by everybody in a single civilization. That alone is enough to give us a hint that such an arrangement ought to be collective. And, in reality, observation proves that these indispensable guide lines, in relation to which all things are temporally located, are taken from social life. The divisions into days, weeks, months, years, etc., correspond to the periodical recurrence of rites, feasts, and public ceremonies.

> A calendar expresses the rhythm of the collective activities,
> while at the same time its function is to assure their regularity.[26]

Of collective origin is also the idea of force. It cannot have come from external experience: 'Our senses only enable us to perceive phenomena which coexist or which follow one another, but nothing perceived by them could give us the idea of this determining and compelling action which is characteristic of what we call a power or force.'[27] Nor can it represent an ejection or an extension to things of our experiences in the acts of making decisions and of restraining impulses. For the first forces conceived were not personal but anonymous, vague, diffused, and impersonal. Moreover, in contrast with the fundamental quality of self-experience, they were readily communicable, contagious and transferrable. These qualities are in themselves regarded as sufficient to indicate that the notion of force is a derivative of social experience. The earliest conception of force is that of mana, orenda, wakonda, etc.—the notion now very widely conceded to underlie, if not to antedate, animism, and to constitute the very basis of religion. Mana, however, Durkheim believes to be identical with the totemic principle, and thus to express the power and authority which group norms and representations, taboos, and religious requirements possess over the activities and lives of individuals.

The principle of causality involves the notion of force, but in addition the idea that

> every force develops in a definite manner, and that the state in
> which it is in every particular moment of its existence (cause)
> predetermines the next state (effect). The causal judgment
> affirms the existence of a necessary connection between these
> two moments for every force. The mind posits this connection
> before having any proofs of it, under the empire of a sort of
> constraint from which it cannot free itself; it postulates it, as
> they say, *a priori*.[28]

Neither individual habit nor instinct can afford a satisfactory explanation of such a conception. The feeling of regularity, being individual, subjective, and incommunicable, is vastly different from the category of causality by means of which we may so organize facts that we can understand one another in regard to them. The latter has its origin in primitive religious rites which all alike are compelled to observe.

> To prescribe that one must imitate an animal or plant to make
> them reproduce, is equivalent to stating as an axiom which is
> above all doubt, that like produces like. Opinion cannot allow
> men to deny this principle in theory without also allowing them
> to violate it in their conduct. So society imposes it, along with

172

the practices which are derived from it, and thus the ritual precept is doubled by a logical precept which is only the intellectual aspect of the former.[29]

Even so fundamental a principle as that of contradiction Durkheim suspects to be conditioned by social experience. He indeed avoids the extremes of M. Lévy-Bruhl, nowhere contrasting early thought with that of modern scientific culture in such a way as to suggest that the former possesses characteristics irreconcilable with the law of contradiction. Nevertheless he holds that the role played by the latter has varied with times and societies. Moreover, mythologies, whether the crudest or the most advanced, frequently 'set aside' the principle of identity or at any rate contradict it more often and openly than does scientific thought; for the latter, according to Durkheim, though observing the principle with exceptional scrupulousness, nevertheless cannot escape violating it.[30] In any event, the logical opposition of contradictories is the outgrowth of that form of opposition which found expression in the custom of taboo. Its origin, therefore, is social. The cleavage between the sacred and the profane is the source from which it sprang.

Remembering that Durkheim identifies the social with the religious in primitive culture, we are now quite prepared to understand his contention that religion 'has not confined itself to enriching the human intellect, formed beforehand, with a certain number of ideas; it has contributed to forming the intellect itself. Men owe to it not only a good part of the substance of their knowledge, but also the form in which this knowledge has been elaborated.'[31] The categories for Durkheim are social both in origin and in content; the point of view they create and the meaning they express are primitively and essentially social, that is, religious.

Their contents are the different aspects of the social being: the category of class was at first indistinct from the concept of the human group; it is the rhythm of social life which is at the basis of the category of time; the territory occupied by the society furnished the material for the category of space; it is the collective force which was the prototype of the concept of efficient force, an essential element in the category of causality.[32]

This view concerning the basis and the content of the categories renders acute the question relating to their validity. Shaped as they have been by the nature and the manifestations of society, more particularly at its totemic level of development, how can we, who have transcended the culture which regards all the universe as within its scheme of social organization, regard them as properly applicable throughout the entire range of experience? If we may be allowed to guess Durkheim's reply, it would be that at any rate it is only through these categories and related concepts that man is liberated from a point of view strictly relative to his biological existence and from an experience that is subjective in the sense of being merely individual. Only through them has man been able to reach the thought of a more or less stable order which is, on the one hand, the basis of corporate life and on the other the object of communication and of common thought. Collective representations, in the form of categories and concepts, reveal to individual minds a world other than that of merely personal experiences, a world by which thought and expression must be guided if they would lay claim to general acceptance—and, Durkheim would add, to truth. Truth, he writes, is characterized by stability and impersonality. It is therefore through the concepts which he receives as a participant in the social consciousness that the individual receives 'the first intuition of the realm of truth.' But Durkheim does not rest at this point. He does not identify truth with merely the socially accepted system of ideas. Nor does he define it pragmatically, as working capacity. He does indeed refer to categories as tools. But for him the analogy rests not in the fact that tools are instruments but in the fact that they represent accumulated capital. Moral experience, he holds, is irreducible to utilitarian considerations, and reason is improperly conceived when it is regarded as a mere servant to individual experience. Hence he never denies the legitimacy of the question whether the concepts and categories are capable of validly disclosing the nature of reality. On the contrary, he repeatedly suggests a reply, the upshot of which is that, even though society is but a specific reality, it is a part of nature, and the various parts of nature can scarcely be so diverse in fundamentals that what is true of society may be false in respect to other realities.[33] Moreover, the very fact that collective representations are held in common and maintain themselves with persistence, that they meet the various tests of individual experiences, is evidence that they are at least not wholly inappropriate. Nevertheless, all concepts and categories emanate from an experience which is itself in flux, and hence they bear the traces of the relative. Again, their acceptance and their status are conditioned by the fact that they harmonize with, or at least are not too greatly at variance with, the existing body of beliefs. Furthermore, individual minds must, in the last analysis, assimilate the concepts for themselves and this is never perfectly done. Each understands them in his own way and thus to a certain extent modifies them, whether through the omission of elements or through unclear or distorted understanding. These considerations justify the assertion that, according to Durkheim, no category or system of concepts may lay claim to being more than approximative in its objective significance, but that all are more than merely individual and that many are more than merely instrumental or even social in the narrow sense of the term.

In entire harmony with Kant and subsequent idealism, Durkheim refuses to sublimate the rational into merely associative or into any lower form of consciousness. He recognizes that human experience involves the presence of meanings and that these are of the nature of universals. The principles of unity characterizing rational experience, moreover, are described as distinctive and superior to those integrating data on the level of what is termed individual mind. It is a far step, Durkheim insists, from the feeling of resemblance which individuals may or may not experience in connection with sense data to the classification of objects on the basis of common characteristics and in such a manner as to promote intelligibility and co-operation between members of society; a far step from the spatial and temporal attributes of the sense data of individuals at particular points of space and time to the spatial order defining the relative position of objects in such a way as to hold good for all percipients, and to the temporal order in which objects receive a place, not duplicating or reflecting the co-existences or sequences in any individual consciousness, but constituting a system wherein all minds may meet and all events find inclusion. Temporal may not be equated with logical priority, nor mere sequence with necessary or causal relationship. If the first essential of a significant theory of knowledge is a clear recognition of the over-individual character of human experience and a refusal to discount this in the interests of ease or simplicity of explanation, Durkheim has admirably attacked his problem.

Unfortunately, he draws distinctions so sharply that a cleavage ensues between the individual and the collective mind. This fact may not be set aside as accidental;[34] for, as we have seen, it deeply affects his interpretation of the categories and of knowledge, as it does also his conceptions of morality and religion. It appears clearly in his theory of social causation, which declares that social processes of all sorts—legal, political, moral, religious, as well as scientific—are intelligible solely in terms of principles characteristic of the collective mind. Individuals, even those customarily regarded as epoch-making, are denied any originative activity: 'Every time that a social phenomenon is directly explained by a psychic phenomenon, one may be sure that the explanation is false.'[35] For Durkheim, as Gehlke has clearly shown, the genius 'has simply a finer cerebral endowment than the mediocre or inferior individual. His mental content, like that of the lowest member of the social group, is entirely derived from the social mind of the group. Whatever superiority he may seem to have is really only lent to him by the society in which he lived.'[36] Man, according to Durkheim, consists of body and soul. But what

175

is the soul and what is its origin? It is, he teaches, 'only a portion of the collective soul of the group; it is the anonymous force at the basis of the cult, but incarnated in an individual whose personality it espouses; it is *mana* individualized.'[37] The individualizing factor is the body.

> As bodies are distinct from each other, and as they occupy different points of space and time, each of them forms a special center about which the collective representations reflect and color themselves differently. The result is that even if all the consciousnesses in these bodies are directed towards the same world, to wit, the world of the ideas and sentiments which brings about the moral unity of the group, they do not all see it from the same angle; each one expresses it in its own fashion.[38]

Now 'if the *mana* is to individualize itself and break itself up into the particular souls, it must first of all exist, and what it is in itself does not depend upon the forms it takes when individualized.'[39] Hence it is that Durkheim distinguishes sharply between personality and the fact of individuation. 'It is not at all true,' he writes, 'that we are more personal as we are more individualized. The two terms are in no way synonymous: in one sense, they oppose more than they imply one another. Passion individualizes, yet it also enslaves. Our sensations are essentially individual, yet we are more personal the more we are freed from our senses and able to think and act with concepts.'[40]

In not a few connections, however, Durkheim is led to recognize a far more intimate and concrete relation of the individual to the collective mind. Thus, with far more of truth than of consistency, he writes: 'Just as society exists only in and through individuals, the totemic principle exists only in and through the individual consciousnesses whose association forms the clan. If they did not feel it in them it would not exist.'[41]

The converse of an hypostatization of the collective consciousness is a derogation of individual consciousness. Hence we find Durkheim maintaining that 'if man were reduced to having only individual perceptions, he would be indistinguishable from the beasts.' Gehlke ventures the assertion that 'so far as the individual appears at all in Durkheim's later theory, he has become only a body; he is no longer a soul (*âme*). His soul is the mind of society incarnated in his body. The social mind is all the mind that exists; and in this sense the social is the only real.'[42] But, as in the case of the collective consciousness, so here—Durkheim is not infrequently in advance of his basal contention. As a matter of fact, he endows the individual mind with more than a flow of sensations. These unite, according to laws of their own, into images (both anticipatory and memorial) and issue in general ideas. Individual minds, therefore, may look fore and aft, may even build up a certain order on the basis of experienced spatial and temporal connections and of relations to the organism, and these achievements are indeed superior to any which present psychological opinion is inclined to concede to even the highest of the animals.

Most commonly Durkheim thinks of mind in terms of content, rather than of activity, process or function. This leads almost inevitably to sharp separations and antitheses. The one mind is then identified with 'all the mental states which are related only to ourselves and to the events of our personal life. It is this that one would call the individual being.'[43] The relation of this being to the repository of representations called the collective consciousness then becomes analogous, as Durkheim himself points out, to that of the Platonic νοῦς to the realm of ideas. But again we would emphasize that the dualism is on occasion materially softened. Idealizations, religious experiences, and other social representations are referred to as expressions of heightened vital energies, especially active passions, and intense sensations. Again, the fundamental validity of religious experience is vindicated by way of a comparison between it and sense experience: as the latter 'corresponds' with an 'objective cause,' though this is not precisely as it appears to sense, so the former has an 'objective cause,' society, even though this has traditionally been misconceived.[44] This comparison implies that it is the living mind of the individual which fashions not merely its world of sense but likewise, upon the occasion of appropriate stimuli, the world of the ideal.

If we bear in mind that Durkheim conceives mind in terms of content, and also that in his last work he is concerned with the culture of a single, and that a primitive, people, we are enabled to understand why the cleavage between the individual and the social becomes more pronounced as we pass from his earlier to his later writings. In his first important book, *De la division du travail social*, he is concerned with a problem of social development. He recognizes that as society changes from the primitive segmentary to the organic type, the individual manifests increasing self-assertion and gains in rights and power; correspondingly, the control and authority of the group are laxed: repressive more and more gives way to restitutive law. In occupation, there is increasing specialization; in reflection, a heightened insistence upon the rights—indeed, even upon the duties —of personal judgment and conscience. It is in this wise that society advances and that truth and science prosper. Now the process just described is obviously one which may be read in terms of individual emancipation and development no less than in those of social growth and enrichment. Had Durkheim but drawn and steadfastly maintained this deduction, he would have reached radically different views concerning cognition. He would have recognized that even sense perception, so far from being either a product of the organism, or merely individual, is, as a matter of empirical observation, so thoroughly social that individuals only with difficulty and with developed scientific technique succeed in isolating the 'given' data or even in describing the 'fact'; and that, as a matter of logic, it is so thoroughly over-individual, that, apart from its relations and meanings, it would lack the credentials of any human experience. He would have recognized that sense perception from the very outset takes place in a social atmosphere, and that its objects are vested with all sorts of meanings derived from the attitudes of others toward them and from the names attached to them. Images, moreover, would have been detected as not infrequently imposing themselves upon us *de jure*.[45] But if individual representations have attributes described by Durkheim as characteristic of collective representations, the converse is no less true. Not all social ideas are authoritative; some social habits lack the prestige and power of early custom; and many prescriptions present themselves but as prejudices, constraining only as a matter of tragic fact. It is only because of his unswerving sub-servience to the notion of an independent collective mind as the source of concepts and categories, that Durkheim could have over-looked the findings of such writers as Wundt and Boas with respect to the high intellectual capacities of peoples of very primitive social life and organization, or the relatively rapid progress made by such peoples in comprehending the ideas belonging to a markedly different and superior civilization.

As a matter of fact, Durkheim reaches his notion of a collective mind largely through a method which contradicts the principles basic to it. The doctrine that complexes possess qualities not deduc-ible from those of their components and that they exhibit laws peculiar to themselves, demands, in consistency, a whole-souled empiricism with reference to the question as to what complexes actually exist and what their characteristics are. Durkheim fails to recognize the demand. On the contrary, he adopts a lofty *a priori* procedure. Without humble and searching observation of fact, he treats what he calls individual mind as though it were a chemical complex consisting of fused or compounded elements. Then, finding it hopeless thus to account for the more developed mental pheno-mena, he resorts to a further quasi-chemical process of fusion by which individual consciousnesses are said to unite into a different psychical reality called society. But does a sensation behave like a chemical element? Is a general idea a fusion of ideas? Is individual consciousness the sort of entity that may be compounded? Is there empirical evidence of any collective mind such as that which Durk-heim's *a priori* method leads him to accept?

Durkheim argues for the social origin of the categories, as against the traditional a priorism, on the ground that the categories vary with peoples and with levels of culture. If the categories thus change, Mr Webb has replied, 'this implies that the categories of space and time cannot themselves change in like manner, since it is in them that this change is said to take place.'[46] It is doubtful whether this objection will bear the weight which the writer supposes. In any event, as he himself recognizes and as we have seen in some detail, Durkheim's theory aims to guard against sheer irrationalism and to provide, in a certain sense and degree at least, for the objective validity of conceptual knowledge. But, as against Durkheim's argument based on the changes undergone by the categories, it is pertinent to marshal Durkheim's own objections to Lévy-Bruhl's view of a pre-logical mentality different in kind from that evidenced at higher stages of development. Durkheim himself repeatedly implies that the fundamental pattern of the logical is essentially constant, even though the extent to which it manifests itself in experience is conspicuously different. Moreover, even if the categories undergo a certain transformation, this is incomparably slower than changes in social organization and in the relation of individuals to one another and to the group. How can this be if the categories are products and components of a social mind?

Durkheim, as we have seen, himself freely concedes that the individual mind possesses feelings of resemblance as well as an awareness of spatial and temporal relations, and he attributes to it the possession of free images by means of which it may survey a wider field of fact than that immediately present to sense experience. He even admits that 'a complete analysis of the categories should seek these germs of rationality even in the individual consciousness';[47] 'undoubtedly the relations which they express exist in an implicit way in individual consciousnesses.'[48] Nevertheless, he maintains that categories do not exist until the various relations are regarded, not ego-centrically as it were—that is, by reference to the individual experience—but from a broader view possible and valid alike for all members of the group. Since this presupposes common action and communal experiences and ends, he describes the categories as social in origin. It would seem, however, that he might with equal propriety have emphasized the fact that, though growing into developed vehicles of knowledge only in the course of wide contacts with things and in association with like-minded and like-seeking individuals, they are ultimately rooted in instinctive responses and in sense experience. Remove one or two eggs from the nest of an absent bird, for example, and upon her return she will be aware, at the very least, of some alteration in respect to the contents of the nest. 'It can hardly, therefore, be denied,' writes Hastings Rashdall from whom we borrow the illustration, 'that something quantitative has found some kind of entrance into the animal's mind, in however obscure a form.'[49] As a matter of fact, the categories of Durkheim's descriptions really presuppose the categories. Take, for example, his description of the category of space. Its initial manifestation is said to be an arrangement of things valid for all members of the group and based on absolute demarcations according to sympathetic values accruing to them through association with divisions within the group. Obviously this rests on the fact that individual experience is itself characterized by spatiality. In so far as there is a difference between this spatiality and that involved in the concept of space, it would seem to be one of development and refinement. Or, if this is not granted, it is but a specific example of the process of generalization, and the category of space is left unexplained.

Such limitations as there may be in Durkheim's attempt to interpret cognitive experience by the aid of sociology are due, not to any blindness with respect to its general nature and range, but to his essentially intellectualistic psychology. Little or no recognition is given to those processes of trial and error, of forming and testing hypotheses, by which genuine advance is made. Hence the facts and concepts of development are not employed as they might be in the service of intelligibility. Instead of treating categories as active principles, functioning in the interests of rational interpretation, they are described as concepts, as contents—indeed, they are called collective representations. Regarded as such, they may be brought into sharp contrast with experiences or contents of a relatively immediate and simple sort, with the result that two separate consciousnesses seem necessary. Hence also it is that concepts are described as intrinsically immutable, as even resisting such pressure for change as may come from without. Instead, is it not the case that thought is dynamic, very much alive, self-examining and self-criticizing, self-changing and self-developing? Thought is a powerful, eventually an irresistible, principle of destruction and construction; it alters the very factors by which, in turn, its own life is conditioned. Hence it is that nothing which excludes thought is secure against its attacks, and that nothing which yields to its active lead is doomed to ultimate destruction.

To interpret as stages of a single process what Durkheim describes as separate realities would require a richer estimate of the native endowments of human individuals than is ventured by Durkheim and by many contemporary students of man and of society. In addition to an equipment in the way of tendencies to more or less adaptive reactions to external stimuli, man must needs have tendencies to become conscious, to establish connections, and to organize experiences in the interests of totality and consistency. That he possesses these tendencies, recent psychological analysis is making

180

increasingly clear. Given their presence, along with a high degree of plasticity, and given the further fact—obvious but too often slighted —that individuals are in relation with minds as well as with inert things, and one has all the essentials required for an explanation of the rational experience which individuals come to enjoy.

Generally speaking, theories of knowledge have been somewhat lethargic in profiting by advances in the special sciences. For Kant, knowledge meant that specific organization of facts which represents the aim and the achievements of mathematics and mechanics. Only gradually was it clearly recognized that there are other principles of interpretation and synthesis which are, if anything, even more significant because more concrete. Similarly, mind frequently tended to be regarded as monadic; or, if having windows, of admitting but external or foreign data to be more or less mechanically constructed into some sort of system. It but slowly became apparent that facts are not so plastic or so preordained for construction purposes as such a view implies; and that concepts and ideas are not so fixed and unadaptive. Autocratic theories regarding the relation of form and matter, ideas or concepts and data, have therefore yielded, even though but reluctantly, to the democratic notion of mutual adaptation, of a process of give and take. In the meantime, genetic and social psychology have revealed unsuspected facts with respect to the interdependence of minds and to the rôle played by fellow humans, no less than by physical nature, in the genesis of self-consciousness and the development of rational personality. Though significantly utilized by Royce, these discoveries have as yet received inadequate consideration in the camp of epistemologists and the task of reconstruction, or of revision, has been lagging. Durkheim's work will serve a valuable end if it adds weight to the query whether thought is not triadic, and whether the problem of knowledge, therefore, does not necessitate a consideration of the relation of mind to mind along with that of the relation of mind to its objects.

Notes

1 *The Elementary Forms of the Religious Life*, p. 16—a translation by Joseph Ward Swain of Durkheim's last and most extensive work, *Les Formes élémentaires de la vie religieuse*, published in 1912.
2 Cf. *ibid.*, p. 263.
3 *Ibid.*, p. 14.
4 *Ibid.*, p. 439.
5 *Ibid.*, p. 433. Universality is carefully distinguished from generality in the sense of degree of extension. By it is meant 'the property which the concept has of being communicable to a number of minds, and in principle to all minds; but this communicability is wholly independent of the degree of its extension. A concept which is applied to only one

object, and whose extension is consequently at the minimum, can be the same for everybody; such is the case with the concept of a deity.' *Ibid.*, p. 434, n. 1.

6 *Ibid.*, p. 439.

7 *Ibid.*, p. 9.

8 *Ibid.*, p. 17.

9 *Ibid.*, p. 13.

10 *Ibid.*, p. 440.

11 *Ibid.*, p. 437. It is for this reason, Durkheim suggests, that the highest functions of intelligence have always been regarded as specific manifestations of the soul—the soul being conceived in antithesis to the body and as an entity of a decidedly superior sort.

12 *Ibid.*, p. 263.

13 *Ibid.*, p. 435.

14 *Ibid.*, p. 434.

15 *Ibid.*, p. 16.

16 Cf. Boutroux's *Natural Law in Science and Philosophy* (trans. Fred Rothwell).

17 'Représentations individuelles et représentations collectives', *Revue métaphysique et de morale*, 6, p. 296.

18 *Religious Life*, p. 424. Confirmation of the last sentence of the quotation is found by Durkheim in his analysis of myths and of primitive religious rites. These analyses bring out convincingly to the present writer various limitations in pragmatic theories of religion, as he has pointed out in his paper, 'Functional Interpretations of Religion: a Critique', published in G. H. Sabine (ed.), *Philosophical Essays in Honor of J. E. Creighton*, Freeport, N.Y.: Books for Libraries, 1917.

19 Written in collaboration with Marcel Mauss and published as the first article in vol. 6 of *L'Année sociologique*.

20 'De quelques formes primitives de classification', *L'Année sociologique*, 6, p. 6.

21 *Religious Life*, p. 141.

22 *Ibid.*, p. 441.

23 *Ibid.*, p. 141.

24 *Ibid.*, pp. 11 ff.

25 *Ibid.*, p. 441.

26 *Ibid.*, pp. 10 ff. Cf. also pp. 11, 442, n. 1. On p. 441, n. 1, Durkheim—perhaps with Bergson in mind—objects to conceiving space and time 'as if they were only concrete extent and duration, such as the individual consciousness can feel, but enfeebled by abstraction.'

27 *Ibid.*, pp. 363 ff.

28 *Ibid.*, p. 366.

29 *Ibid.*, pp. 367 ff.

30 Cf. *ibid.*, p. 12, n. 4.

31 *Ibid.*, p. 9.

32 *Ibid.*, p. 440.

33 Cf. *ibid.*, pp. 18 ff., 19, n. 2, 437 ff.

34 According to G. Tosti, Gabriele Tarde accused Durkheim of reproducing 'the ontological delusion of mediaeval realism by conceiving society

as an essence or a transcendental unity.' Tosti thinks this criticism too severe and therefore qualifies it materially (cf. 'Suicide in the Light of Recent Studies', *American Journal of Sociology*, vol. 3, pp. 473 ff.). Durkheim, in turn, explained his position (*ibid.*, pp. 848–9), whereupon Tosti again took up the point in his article, 'Durkheim's Sociological Objectivism', *ibid.*, vol. 4, pp. 171–7.

35 Émile Durkheim, *Les règles de la méthode sociologique*, Paris: Alcan, 1895, p. 128.

36 *Émile Durkheim's Contributions to Sociological Theory*, New York: Columbia University Press, 1915, p. 99; see also pp. 64–87, 97–100. To this monograph the present writer acknowledges great indebtedness.

37 *Religious Life*, p. 264.

38 *Ibid.*, p. 270.

39 *Ibid.*, p. 267; see also p. 249. In a passage in *Les règles de la méthode sociologique*, pp. 12 ff. (quoted by Gehlke), Durkheim goes so far as to say: 'As for the forms which the collective states take, in being refracted in the individuals, these are things of a different sort. . . . They . . . take a body, a sensible form which is their own, and constitute a reality *sui generis*, quite distinct from the individual facts which manifest this reality.'

40 *Religious Life*, p. 272.

41 *Ibid.*, p. 249.

42 *Émile Durkheim's Contributions to Sociological Theory*, p. 86.

43 *Revue métaphysique et de morale*, 11, p. 46; quoted from Gehlke (p. 43), who has collated a number of passages bearing on this point.

44 Cf. *Religious Life*, p. 418.

45 Such a volume as James's *Varieties of Religious Experience* should make this amply evident. And is this not the usual story in the case of childhood and of youth? Upon awaking from his sleep one morning, the writer's boy of twenty-five months was convinced that there was a pig in his room. His dream evoked a belief not dispelled by the failure of repeated searches day after day to find the pig.

46 *Group Theories of Religion and the Individual*, p. 157.

47 *Religious Life*, p. 16, n.

48 *Ibid.*, p. 440.

49 *Is Conscience an Emotion?* p. 85. Professor Faris reports a significant experience which he had among the tribes of the upper Congo. He says: 'There is no formal drill in numbers, as there is no formal drill in anything, but I tried a lad once with the idea of discovering whether he could tell nine times nine. He took nine sticks and placed them on the ground, breaking the last one into nine pieces. He then placed one of these pieces on each of the other sticks, and found that he had eight whole sticks and one piece left over, so he announced that the result was—*eighty-one*.' ('The Mental Capacity of Savages', *American Journal of Sociology*, vol. 23, p. 615.)

part six

Max Scheler and phenomenological sociology of knowledge

12 Sociology of knowledge from the standpoint of modern phenomenology: Max Scheler

Karl Mannheim

Just as there are several different variants of historicism, it is possible to draw many different conclusions concerning the problem of a sociology of knowledge by starting from phenomenological premises; in our discussion, however, we shall not deal with phenomenological attitudes toward this problem that are possible in the abstract, but with the phenomenological outline of a sociology of knowledge recently published by Max Scheler.[1]

From the point of view we have adopted thus far, Scheler's study is particularly interesting as a striking illustration of our thesis that problems originally developed by a social opposition are taken over by conservative thinkers—and it also affords an opportunity to observe the structural transformation a problem undergoes when it is incorporated into the systematic framework of a theory based upon a different tradition. Here we have a concrete example of the final stage reached in the career of ideas first developed in a given social environment—a stage where, recognized as 'stubborn facts', they are taken up by the adverse movement and are transformed by it.

We may characterize Scheler's standpoint in a short formula by saying that he combines various *motifs* of the modern phenomenological school with elements of the Catholic tradition. We cannot say without qualification that phenomenology is a Catholic philosophy (although Catholic thinkers like Bernhard Bolzano and Franz Brentano are among its precursors); nevertheless, in many essential points it lends itself very well to bolstering up Catholic concepts of 'timelessness', 'eternity', with new arguments. By drawing an extremely sharp line between 'factual' and 'essential' knowledge, phenomenology offers concrete evidence justifying the Catholic dualism of the eternal and temporal—and prepares the terrain for the construction of a non-formal, intuitionist metaphysics.

Phenomenology holds that it is possible to grasp supra-temporally valid truths in 'essential intuition' (*Wesensschau*). In actual fact, however, we observe considerable divergencies among the intuitions achieved by different members of the school. These divergencies can be explained by the fact that intuitions of essence are always dependent on the historical background of the subject. Most impressive among phenomenological analyses are those based upon traditional Catholic values—our civilization, after all, is very largely a product of this tradition. It must be stressed, in so far as Scheler is concerned, that he has already dissociated himself from a number of Catholic tenets. This, however, is less important in the present context than the fact that he is still profoundly attached to the formal type of thinking exhibited by Catholicism.

The main point about Scheler and his new essay is that he has a far closer affinity to present-day reality, and takes the obligation to count with new cultural developments far more seriously, than the majority of those who interpret the world in terms of the Catholic tradition. As a philosopher of a restless and sensitive turn of mind, impatient of limitations and rigid formalism, he cannot rest satisfied with a line drawn once and for all between eternity and temporality; he feels impelled to account for the new cultural factors emerging in the world. Affinity to the present, embedded in conservative modes of thought and experience, produces extravagant tensions in the structure of his arguments, so that the reader is in constant fear lest the entire edifice blow up before his eyes, the building stones flying apart in all directions. Since we are stressing precisely the complex problems inherent in the interaction of various standpoints, we are mainly interested in the way in which a modern representative of an earlier intellectual and emotional phase comes to grips with the new factors of cultural reality—a configuration of real symbolic significance. For the essential richness of the historic-social world process stems largely from the possibility of such 'anachronisms' as this—attempts to interpret present-day world factors on the basis of premises which belong to a past stage of thought. There is, however, a particular strain in Scheler's treatment of the problem, because he not only seeks to incorporate new factors into an old framework but even tries to present the position of 'historicism' and 'sociologism' in terms of a philosophy of timelessness.

We shall deliberately limit our discussion to this structural side of Scheler's theory, and select from the bewildering wealth of his insights only those points which are relevant to our problem of the various intellectual 'standpoints'. We are not interested in detecting errors or inaccuracies, but only in tracing the line of historical determination which made this type of thought fatefully what it is.

The main characteristic of Scheler's essay is—as stated above—the great width encompassed by his argument: he tries to analyse the sociological from the point of view of timelessness, the dynamic from that of a static system. We encounter in his theory all the points enumerated in our description of the 'constellation' underlying the emergence of a sociology of knowledge: (1) thinking conceived as relative to being, (2) social reality as the system of reference in respect of which thought is considered to be relative, and (3) a comprehensive view of historical totality. In addition to this, we can also observe in Scheler the 'shift' from the original 'unmasking' tendency to an impartial sociology; this is not surprising, since this change is even more in line with a conservative attitude than with an oppositional one. The question we want to examine is to what extent a static systematizing approach can do justice to the dynamic and sociological—i.e. whether a 'timeless' philosophy can treat adequately those problems which arise from the present intellectual situation.

Scheler, according to whom the sociology of knowledge has up to now been treated only from a positivistic point of view, proposes to approach this problem from another point of view 'which rejects the epistemological doctrines of positivism and the conclusions drawn therefrom, and sees in metaphysical knowledge both an "eternal" postulate of Reason and a practical possibility' (Preface, p. vi). For him, the sociology of knowledge is part of cultural sociology which in turn is part of sociology—the latter being divided into 'real' and 'cultural' sociology. The former examines 'real' factors of the historical process, especially 'drives' such as the sex, hunger, and power drive, while the latter deals with the 'cultural' factors. Sociology as a whole, however, has the task of 'ascertaining the types and functional laws of the interaction' of these factors, and especially of establishing a 'law of succession' of such types of interaction. Thus, we have here, as in all sociologies of culture, a distinction of the 'substructure' and 'superstructure', but with the specific difference (this is the 'shift' characterizing Scheler's position) that (1) the 'substructure' consists of psychological factors (drives) rather than socio-economic ones, and (2) that there is a rather sharp line drawn between the two spheres, in contrast to the neo-Hegelian variant of Marxism. According to this latter view, the relation of 'substructure' to 'superstructure' is that of whole and part; both form an inseparable unity, since a certain 'ideal' configuration can emerge only in conjunction with a certain 'real' configuration and *vice versa*: a certain 'real configuration' also is possible only when the 'ideal' factors show such and such a configuration. Scheler, however, is unable to construct a historical theory of this kind, since he bases his 'cultural sociology' upon a theory of the drives and of the mind of *man* in general. This theory seeks to ascertain timeless characteristics of man, and to explain any concrete historical situation as a complex of such characteristics. And it also fails to establish a closer affinity with historicism when it examines in a 'generalizing' fashion the interaction of the 'real' and 'cultural' factors—taking it to exhibit a general law of succession, rather than a sequence of concrete, unique temporal phases. Although Scheler takes great pains to formulate a 'law' of the possible dynamic genesis of things embedded in an order of 'temporal efficacy' (p. 8), it is clear that such 'laws' can result only from the application of the generalizing categories of natural science. This sociology is merely consistent when it tries—after the fashion of natural science—to establish rules, types, and laws of the social process.

At this point, we should like to call attention to the fundamental difference between types of sociology which are possible today. The one continues the tradition of natural science with its objective of establishing general laws (Western sociology is of this type); the other harks back to the tradition of the philosophy of history (Troeltsch, Max Weber). To the former type, every historical individual is merely a complex of general, changelessly recurring properties, and the 'rest' which is not reducible to these properties is disregarded. The latter type, on the other hand, proceeds in the opposite direction. It considers historical individualities—comprising not only personalities but any historical constellation in its uniqueness—as the proper object of investigation. The individual, according to this conception, cannot be determined by a combination of abstractively distilled, unchanging characteristics; on the contrary, the historian must and can penetrate the psychic and mental core of a unique individual directly, without mediation by general properties, and then proceed to determine all characteristics and partial factors individually. This is how we proceed in grasping the physiognomy of a human face; we do not combine general characteristics (eyes, mouth, etc.) but the all-important thing is to seize the unique centre of expression and characterize the eyes, mouth, and other features in the light of this central insight. The school in question holds that this method, spontaneously employed in everyday life, has its application in science also and has in fact been unconsciously used by scientists; it is high time, then, to fix the methodological character of this type of knowledge. For it is not the case that the 'centre of expression', the particular physiognomy of a situation, the unique evolutionary line exhibited by a sequence of events can be grasped only by intuition and cannot be communicated or scientifically objectified. All such insight into wholes can be translated into controllable scientific knowledge, and the present revival of historico-philosophical modes of thought can be explained in our opinion by the desire to find a method of communicating what is unique in the historical process. In the sociology of culture, the attempt is made to analyse unique historical situations in terms of unique combinations of properties and factors undergoing a constant process of transformation—constellations which in themselves are phases in a genetic process the overall 'direction' of which can be determined.

Scheler himself seems to be aware of the fact that a sociology based upon a generalizing doctrine of the essence of man has already become a very problematic affair, since the general essences must always appear empty as compared to historical, concrete mental phenomena (one of the reasons why they can be sharply disjoined). Thus, he emphasizes (p. 13) that mind exists only in a *concrete multiplicity* of infinitely varied groups and cultures, so that it is futile to speak of a 'unity of human nature' as a presupposition of history and sociology. This means, however, that we cannot expect any essential illumination from the theory of essences, since it is now admitted that it can work out only the most general *formal* framework of the laws of intentional acts. Scheler, in fact, places himself in this fashion in the immediate proximity of Kantianism and of formal philosophy in general.

But why this summary rejection of the thesis of the 'unity of human nature', after Scheler himself proposed to base sociology upon such a highly general doctrine of the essence of man? The answer that the supra-temporal unity of man (to be treated in a general drive and mind theory) refers to the *essence* 'man', whereas the 'concrete multiplicity' merely deals with the *fact* 'man'—this answer, though expected, cannot satisfy us. To a human mind existing and developing only in a concrete multiplicity, only a *dynamic* essence 'man' can correspond; in our opinion, one cannot think in historicist fashion in factual research and remain static in essential analysis. If, however, one should nevertheless cling to such an 'essentialist' doctrine of the human mind and of intentional acts, inspired by 'supra-temporal' aspirations, then the problem still remains how one can attain concrete historical reality starting from this position. The questionable character of static generalizing and formalizing is not eliminated by restricting this mode of thought to 'essences'. Generalizing and formalizing are, in our opinion, valid 'technical' procedures and also have their uses in sociology, since they can be employed to control the multiplicity of data; for *concrete thought*, however—for the thinking of the concrete—they can serve merely as a springboard. Does, in fact, formalization not always lead to distortion, if we look at it from the viewpoint of the concrete? After all, a form is what it is only in conjunction with the concrete (historic) matter it in-forms, and it changes and grows together with change and growth of the matter. Those who engage in limitless formalization merely let themselves be guided—precisely in the sense of the distinction made by Scheler—by models and structural

KARL MANNHEIM

relationships prevailing in the dead, mechanized world of mere 'things', and the schemata so obtained obscure the peculiar nature of the living.

Thus, we are at this point in the presence of a profound conflict. On the one hand, Scheler propounds a doctrine of the 'timeless' essence of man; on the other, he is aware of, and feels responsible toward, the uniqueness of historic objects. This conflict is possibly the fundamental experience of our time (at least within the German cultural tradition).

Another thesis most characteristic of Scheler's doctrine concerns the 'law of the order of effectiveness of the real and ideal factors', already alluded to. The interaction of the two factors is described in the following way: mind is a factor of 'determination', not of 'realization'. That is, what works *can* be created by a culture is determined by mind alone, by virtue of its inner structure; but what actually *gets* created depends on the particular combination of the *real* factors prevailing at the time. Thus, the function of the real factors is to make a *selection* among the possibilities made available by Mind. Through this selective function, the real factors control the ideal ones. Both the ideal and the real factors existing at a given moment are, however, entirely powerless in face of those real factors which are in the process of emerging. Power constellations in politics, production control relationships in economy, follow their determined way in a robot-like fashion; they are subject to 'an evolutionary causality blind to all meaning' (p. 10). Human mind can at most block or unblock but never alter them.

What is fruitful in this way of looking at the problem is the fact that the peculiar phenomenological and structural character of the mental—which materialistic monism necessarily overlooks—is well seen here. Its one-sidedness, however, consists in our opinion in this, that Scheler does not go beyond the assertion of a phenomenological separation of the 'real' and 'mental'. As a result of this, the separation, and the abstract immanence of the 'mental', remain unchallenged even when at last an attempt is made to bring about a synthesis, clarify the mutual relationship of the two spheres, and answer questions concerning their genesis.

In order to illustrate the difference between Scheler's position and the one represented by us, we shall mention an example showing two possible conceptions of the mutual relationship between the actual and the possible, the real and the mental. One of these conceptions—toward which Scheler seems to lean to some extent—is expressed by one of the characters in a play by Lessing who says that Raphael would have become just as great an artist if he had been born without hands, since it is the artistic vision rather than the visible realization that matters. For such a theory, standing in the Platonic

192

tradition, in which ideas and models are considered as pre-existent, realization is something secondary. And it remains secondary even in Scheler's more moderate version of this conception. Obviously alluding to the example just mentioned, Scheler says: 'Raphael needs a brush; his ideas and artistic dreams do not create it. He needs politically and socially powerful patrons who commission him to glorify their ideals. Otherwise his genius cannot realize itself' (p. 10). Scheler stresses explicitly that he has no essential influence of the real factors in mind, as a result of which they would in part determine the substance of the works. This conception—which in its essence still harks back to Platonism—contrasts with another one specifically rooted in the modern attitude to life. This modern conception is expressed, for instance, in K. Fiedler's aesthetics. We may paraphrase Fiedler's theory somewhat freely in the following way: neither the creative process itself nor the work as a complex of meaning should be analysed by assuming that the artist sees models before his mind's eye before he starts working, and that he merely copies them afterwards as well as he can. The truth of the matter is that the work and its idea come into being *during* the process of creation. Every 'real factor', every line already drawn, every movement of the hand not only determines those that follow but also creates new possibilities not dreamed of beforehand. All real factors, such as the structure of the human hand and gestures, the particular texture of the material, the organic and psychic constitution of the artist are the source of meaning in this process. Their contribution to the work is not without effect upon the 'immanent' meaning it expresses. Hence, we should not merely say that the artist must exist as a man—and as this particular man—in order that an absolute possibility of the ideal world can gain shape (be realized) in the spatio-temporal world. What we should say is that the existence of the artist—determined as this particular existence—is itself a *conditio sine qua non* of the *meaning* and the idea embodied in the particular work. This new way of interpreting the correlation between 'idea' and 'reality' is also an essential component of our conception of the role of 'real factors' in cultural creation.

For us, too, there is a phenomenological separation between Being and Meaning; but this phenomenological duality can no longer be considered as fundamental when we come to examine both terms as parts of a dynamic genetic *totality*—a problem which surely has a meaning also within Scheler's system. When we reach 'existence' as an ultimate unity in which all phenomenological differences are cancelled, 'Being' and 'Meaning' appear as hypostatized partial spheres which are ultimately the 'emanations' of one and the same Life. For any philosophy or theory of culture or sociology (or whatever one may choose to call the ultimate synthesis in question) which seeks to transcend the abstract immanence of the various cultural products and to analyse them as part and parcel of an overall life process, the phenomenological duality cannot be more than a provisional device. One should not object at this point that the historian engaged in positive research is not interested in these metaphysical questions, since he need not go beyond the phenomenological separation of the spheres of 'Being' and 'Meaning' when he tries to give a historical account of the immanent evolution of ideas. This objection merely arises from a positivistic delusion which prevents us from realizing how deeply the supposedly pure scientist is engaged in metaphysics whenever he gives interpretations, establishes historical relationships, ascertains historic 'trends', or puts 'real' factors in correlation with 'ideal' ones. As soon as one attempts to explain a work in terms of facts in an artist's life, or of cultural currents of a period, and so on, he inevitably replaces the immanent 'meaning' of the works in the global framework of the life process, since he has deprived the works of their character as self-contained units and has been concerned instead with the central experience which determined the way of life and the cultural creativity of an epoch.

We have to recognize, in the light of the foregoing, that there is something true in the materialist conception of history, according to which it is Being, reality, that creates the ideal sector. The error of materialism consists merely in its wrong metaphysics which equates 'Being' or 'reality' with matter. In so far, however, as it negates the concept of the 'ideal' as something absolutely self-contained, as something that is somehow pre-existent, or unfolds itself within itself, merely on the basis of an immanent logic of meaning, or provides for historical or any other kind of reality the necessary stimulus that makes self-realization possible—in so far as it negates this concept of the 'ideal', materialism is right. And one cannot surmount this idealistic dualism if one proceeds like Scheler who combines with his idealistic theory a doctrine of 'the impotence of the mental', a thesis merely reflecting the transformation which German conservative thought underwent during the last phase of its development. Conservative thought in Germany increasingly drifted away from its humanistic origins since the inception of the trend of 'Realpolitik' and power politics, and at the same time abdicated more and more in the presence of the newly emerging social realities which did not favour the conservative aspirations. It is interesting to observe that the rising classes—whose aspirations are supported by the dominant 'real factors' of an epoch—consider *these* factors to be essential, whereas the conservatives, though they may acknowledge the importance of the real factors, can characterize their role and significance merely as a *negative* one.

In one word, as soon as we abandon the platonizing conception,

194

the phenomenological difference of the real and ideal factors will be subordinated to the genetic unity of the historic process, and we shall advance to the point of origin where a real factor is *converted* into a mental datum. From a merely phenomenological point of view (defined as one involving nothing but straight description of the given, disregarding all those aspects which are connected with its genesis) this 'conversion' of the real into the mental cannot be grasped, since according to this view the gap between bare 'Being' devoid of meaning on the one hand, and a 'meaning' on the other, cannot be bridged. Since, however, we as interpreting subjects are existent human beings, and have an immediate experience of our 'existence' in which real factors are converted into mental data, we are able to push our inquiry to the point where the two spheres of the ideal and mental meet. As regards this conversion, moreover, it should be noted that many factors classified as 'real' are by no means completely devoid of meaning and purely 'material'. One is often inclined, for instance, to regard economic and geographical data as belonging integrally to the 'material' and 'natural' sphere. We should not forget, however—to take up only the first example mentioned, that of economics—that only the physiology of the hunger drive belongs to mere 'nature', but that this physiological substratum constitutes an element of the historic process only in so far as it enters into mental configurations, for example by assuming the form of an economic order or some other institutional form. This should not be misunderstood. We do not want to deny the fundamental role of the drives—and it is by no means our contention that economy could exist without the hunger drive; but if something is a necessary condition of another thing, it need not be unconditionally equated with the latter. What matters for us is that the various forms of economic institutions could not be explained by the hunger drive as such. The drive as such remains essentially unchanged over time, whereas economic institutions undergo constant changes, and history is exclusively interested in these institutional changes. That excess over and above the purely physiological substratum which alone transforms the drive into a historical factor is already 'mind'. It is, therefore, not enough to say that economy would not exist without mind; it should be added that it is this *mental* element which makes *economy* out of mere drive-satisfaction. If, then, we constantly lower the limit of the 'natural' by refining our distinctions, so that the 'economic' turns out to be 'mental' rather than 'material', then we must recognize two 'mental' spheres, the mutual relationship of which is that of substructure and superstructure. The question will then be how one sphere affects the other in the total process—how a structural change in the substructure determines a structural change in the superstructure. Now to be sure, if two spheres of the 'mental' are distinguished in this fashion, then we are of the opinion that the mind-in-the-substructure—involving primarily the conditions of production, *together with all concomitant social relationships*—does in part shape and determine mind-in-the-superstructure. For we should not forget that mind-in-the-substructure is the more 'massive' factor, if for no other reason, then because it is the components of this substructure which create the enduring framework of the continuous existence of human beings—that which is generally called *milieu*. And since the 'conversion' of the real into the mental (the most mysterious event in the historical process) takes place within man as a living being, the greatest determining force is exercised by those categories of meaning in which the human being lives with the greatest intensity.[2] It is by no means the case, then, as Scheler seems to assume (if we understand him rightly), that a selection from among pre-existent mental forms takes place in the super-structure under the direct pressure of a purely 'natural' substructure,[3] but rather: that which is vaguely sensed as being 'nature' converts itself into the various 'mental' configurations of the substructure, and in this fashion shapes, first, men as existent beings, and then, cultural reality as a whole (in analogy of Fiedler's conception of the co-determining role of the real factors).

What we are reluctant to accept, then, is, first of all, the introduction of the 'natural' dimension of the substructure, as a supra-temporal, unchanging entity, in terms of which the historical process is to be explained in part. For a causal factor of this kind could give rise only to combinations of elements which are otherwise unchanging. To be sure, Scheler does speak of 'changes in the drive structure', but these can be interpreted in his system only as relative shifts, that is, mere quantitative modifications; thus, he suggests that it is the 'power drive' which predominates at one time, the 'racial instinct' at another, etc. In our opinion, however, 'natural' factors of this kind can be used as a dynamic principle of explanation of the historic process only if we assume that they undergo *qualitative* changes in the course of history. Such an assumption, in fact, is made plausible if we remember that the 'natural' on the various levels of its 'mental' transformations plays a different historical role every time.[4] At what time and in what form the so-called 'power drive' can manifest itself—in fact, whether it can do so at all—depends also on the total cultural constellation which the various generations find themselves confronted with in maturing. In this connection, too, there is no eternally self-identical 'power drive' as such which merely gets more or less repressed, but the identical expression 'power drive' covers a great variety of differently structured, differently experienced 'intentions of the will', having each time different objects as their correlates.

196

We are also reluctant to accept the positing of a mental world with an immanent logic of meaning *vis-à-vis* which the historical world with its 'real factors' plays only a selective role.

We also conceive the relationship within the 'possible' and 'actual' in a different way from Scheler. For us, too, there is at each moment that which is actual, surrounded by a horizon of possibilities; this horizon, however, is not the abstractly 'possible as such', but contains merely that which is possible in a given situation as a result of a certain constellation of factors. This 'horizon', in turn, is merely the starting-point of a new process leading to new actualities; this always involves the completely new, creative role of the moment and of the unique situation. For our conception of the world, then, it is not the abstractly possible that is higher; the value accent rests upon the emerging and the actual. The real is not, as in Scheler's system, an always inadequate selection from a transcendent treasure of forms, but a creative concretization flowing from historically unique constellations.

Only when we consider the actual *ex post*,[5] i.e. after it has emerged rather than *in statu nascendi*, as it would be seen from the viewpoint of the creative centre of the evolutionary process—only then can we view it as having the structure of an immanent, completely self-contained complex of meaning. Only those who focus their attention exclusively upon the actual, upon the finished product cut off from all functional relationships within the genetic process, can have the impression that what happened was the realization of something pre-existent, of a self-contained, absolute entity. Since, however, cultural sociology is primarily concerned with reconstructing the functional relationships between the 'actual' on the one hand, and the past genetic process on the other, it is in our opinion too risky for this branch of knowledge to adopt the premise of a 'pre-existent' world of ideas, even if only in the sense of a non-temporal genesis of pure 'meaning'. It seems to us that there can be an immanent logic of meaning only for the retrospective view of the analyst of structure: once they have become actual, all works of the mind display an intelligible, meaningful structure. We want to stress in this connection that it is one of the most important tasks to ascertain this intelligible structure of meaning of a set of actual, finished works.

We discussed Scheler's conception of the relation of the substructure and superstructure in detail, and gave a full account of our contrary position, in order to show that even apparently purely formal presuppositions of historical research depend on a valuational and social standpoint; we wanted to demonstrate in detail that in this field, too, the process of cognition, far from realizing step by step problems which already are there in 'pre-existent' form, approaches from different sides problems growing out of the living experience of groups belonging to the same society. Everything that distinguishes the static and dynamic view is somehow related to this central point—that of the relationship between the ideal and real. Since for Scheler the essential ultimate is something pre-existent, floating above history, the historic process can never achieve real essentiality and substantiality in his system in which the static, freely floating entities are not really 'constituted' but merely 'realized' by the historic process. Such a sharp dualism can never lead to a real philosophy of history; and the fact that methodological decisions also are connected with metaphysical and 'vital' orientations is nowhere more clearly visible than here. For we now can understand why Scheler decided in favour of a generalizing type of sociology when faced with the choice which sociology must make today— whether to proceed in accordance with the generalizing method or seek a renewal on the basis of historico-philosophical traditions. To be sure, the case of Scheler is not quite so simple. As we have seen, a tension arises in Scheler's system owing to the fact that although his basic doctrine is one of eternal values, he yet recognizes the dynamic as particularized in various 'standpoints' and wants to account for it in terms of the basic doctrine. Both the wide scope of his plan and the unresolved juxtaposition of static and dynamic elements in his doctrine can be well seen from the following passage in which Scheler says that he intends to 'hang up', so to speak, the realm of absolute ideas and values, corresponding to the essential idea of man, very much higher than all factual value systems thus far realized in history.

> Thus, we give up as wholly relative, as historically and sociologically dependent on the particular standpoints, all orderings of *goods, goals, norms* in human societies, as expressed by ethics, religion, law, art, etc., and retain nothing but the idea of the eternal Logos, whose transcendent secrets cannot be explored, in the form of a metaphysical *history*, by any one nation, any one civilization, any or all cultural epochs that have emerged thus far, but only by *all together*, including all future ones—by temporal and spatial co-operation of irreplaceable, because individual, unique cultural subjects working together in full solidarity (p. 14).

The tensions revealed by this passage illustrate the internal struggle between Scheler's doctrine of eternity and present-day historical consciousness; the important thing from our viewpoint is that Scheler tries to incorporate in his system, not only alien theses, but also alien systematic presuppositions. For the historicist, entities do not exist apart from the historic process; they come into being and realize themselves in it, and become intelligible exclusively through it. Man has an access to entities creating history and dominating the various epochs because, living in history, he is existentially linked to it. History is the road—for the historicist, the only road—to the understanding of the entities genetically arising in it. But the abyss between the temporal and eternal which Scheler's system assumes decisively affects his theory of the interpretation of history. The real entities are supra-historical; hence, contrary to what Scheler says, history cannot contribute anything relevant to their exploration, or, if there is a contribution which history as conceived by Scheler can make, it can only be a somewhat limited one.

History is in this system like a sea of flames surrounding the eternal entities. The flames may rise or subside; they may approach the entities or recede from them, and the rhythm of their movement, imposed by destiny, is shrouded in mystery; all we know is that some periods get closer to the entities than others. Fanatics of the Middle Ages, whose theory of history is based upon present-day romanticism, assert that the Middle Ages have marked the greatest proximity to the eternal entities, and they specify the culmination point within the Middle Ages at various moments, depending on the nature of their own subjective experience. Scheler marks a certain progress beyond this narrow glorification of one historical epoch, in that he maintains that each period and each civilization has a specific 'missionary idea' involving a close affinity to a certain set of entities which is different in each case.[6] But he still essentially cleaves to the static conception of entities, for in his view, too, the eternal entities remain cut off from the flux of historical life, their substance is alien to that of history. All that Scheler admits is a principle of 'access': some eternal entities are primarily accessible to just one cultural group, others to another. Historical 'synthesis', then, consists in a combination of all the essences discovered in the course of history. This way of looking at things, however, involves certain abrupt 'jumps' which we cannot square with our fundamental experience. Scheler's theory contains two such 'jumps'. He admits that concrete norm systems are historically and sociologically determined, and that at each moment man stands within history. But for him, all this applies only in so far as we are not dealing with an understanding of those 'entities' the realization of which is the 'mission' of mankind. In so far as these latter entities are concerned, historical man suddenly turns into a conqueror of temporality and acquires a superhuman capacity of shaking off all historical limitation and determination. This is one 'jump' in Scheler's theory. But we also may ask another question. How can we know in analysing history which of the entities proclaimed by various civilizations have been real, true entities? By what criteria can we judge that a certain civilization was mature enough to accomplish the 'mission' of humanity as regards one or the other entity? If we really want to assign such roles to all past epochs and civilizations, it is clearly not enough for us to have a valid, objective knowledge of our own entities; we must have supra-historical, superhuman intuitive powers to identify all entities, or at least those which have emerged thus far in the course of history. Thus, the historian of ideas in performing his essential intuition must twice transcend temporality: once when he identifies the eternal entities assigned to his own epoch, and for the second time when he interprets the past, trying to separate the genuine from the false, the real essence from mere subjective appearance. This, however, amounts to the postulation of an absolute intuition of essences—at least of all essences thus far discovered—at each moment in history; or at least the postulation of the absolute character of the present moment. But then, the idea of a collective 'mission' of *all* epochs and civilizations, which would have afforded a starting-point for a philosophy of history, becomes lost again; the historical process as such is given up as hopelessly relative, and all absolute significance is concentrated within the second 'jump' beyond temporality. Scheler tries to incorporate historicist ideas into his theory of timelessness, and even adopts the idea of 'perspectivic' vision. But his static conception of eternity never gets reconciled with the alien 'standpoint' of historicism with which he tries to combine it.

For anyone whose fundamental metaphysical experience is of such a (static) character, the sociology of knowledge—as well as of all other spheres of culture—must become a totally secondary affair. Accordingly, the real task of a sociology of thought—which in our opinion consists in discovering the overall line of development by following the genesis of the various 'standpoints'—is never formulated by Scheler.

One more objection must be made to Scheler's doctrine of essences. He forgets that any understanding and interpretation of essences (and hence also of the essences of past epochs) is possible only in perspective fashion. Both *what* is accessible to us of the essential intuitions of past epochs, and *how* they become accessible to us, depends on our own standpoint.

Notes

1 Cf. Max Scheler, *Probleme einer Soziologie des Wissens*, Munich and Leipzig, 1924. (Subsequent references to this work appear as page numbers in the text.)

2 Later on, we shall qualify this broadly 'economistic' theory from the point of view of a more comprehensive doctrine, that of historicism. It will then appear as something merely corresponding to one particular phase of the historical process—inasmuch as the 'vital centre' of man moves into different spheres of activity in different epochs, and each

epoch understands historical reality most clearly in connection with the sphere in which it lives most intensely. Thus, the economism which is predominant in Marxism is historically determined. Nevertheless, it must be recognized that the fundamental explanatory principle used by Marxism, the economic one, is rather powerful, because it characterizes the total process in terms of that factor which is the 'lowest' mental organizing principle of every social reality and hence lends itself very well to characterizing the structure of various epochs.

3 We do not assert that the doctrine of the pre-existence of ideas we attribute to Scheler has a *metaphysical* import, and still less that it should be interpreted in the sense of *temporal* pre-existence. All we want to indicate is that Scheler teaches a logical immanence of the ideal sphere, and thus a separate and independent givenness of the ideal as something apart from the real. The function of the latter consists merely in making a selection among the ideal data, rather than in creating them in part. However, it is impossible to carry through a thorough-going parallel between our position and that of Scheler, since we draw the line between 'mind' and 'nature' at a different place.

4 Thus a geographical fact, such as the insular position of a country, does not always have the same historical significance; its impact upon history will be different, according as we have to do with an 'early' historical epoch or with various stages of capitalistic evolution. The same natural factor performs a different function in different overall social and cultural situations; its 'meaning' for the cultural process changes accordingly.

5 It seems to be generally overlooked that the subject studying and understanding history can look at the latter from various 'standpoints' which make a considerable existential difference. Thus, as suggested above, it makes a great difference whether one surveys products of the mind retrospectively as finished products or rather tries to re-enact the process of their creation. In our opinion, however, it is a mistake to adopt the 'retrospective' standpoint, and to try to account for the structure of genesis in terms of the actual as an accomplished fact, when dealing with problems of a metaphysic of the genetic process. (On the other hand, the problem of the 'standpoint' of the subject studying history is not the same as the problem of 'standpoints' in the theory of historicism. All historicism teaches a determination of thinking by the 'standpoint' of the thinker, but such historicist theories may have a conservative or progressive slant, depending on whether they are conceived from a 'retrospective' or an *in statu nascendi* standpoint.)

6 Here, too, we can detect the essential difference between progressive and conservative thought. If a conservative thinker conceives an idea of humanity as a whole, his orientation is *cosmopolitic*, i.e. he calls for co-operation among different nations and civilizations, each conserving its peculiar identity. The progressive conception of humanity as a unit, however, involves *internationalism*, i.e. a negation of these national peculiarities. The conservative wants multiplicity, the progressive wants uniformity; the former thinks in terms of culture, the latter in terms of civilization.

13 Max Scheler's sociology of knowledge

Howard Becker and Helmut Otto Dahlke

Sociology of knowledge is a phrase which has so rapidly gained currency that it is on the verge of becoming a mere slogan. It therefore seems wise to begin this presentation of Scheler's sociology of knowledge with a few words of warning and definition.

Sociology of knowledge is not 'history of ideas in their social context,' 'social determination of thought,' 'dominance of material over non-material culture,' or anything remotely similar. Sociology of knowledge is the analysis of the functional interrelations of social processes and structures on the one hand and the patterns of intellectual life, including the modes of knowing, on the other. As long as sociology of knowledge remains *substantive*, logical priority is assigned neither to 'society' nor to 'mind.'

The problems embraced in terms such as 'social determinism' have been explicitly stated in a pseudo-dilemma; namely, that there are two mutually exclusive ways of interpreting ideas, intrinsically and extrinsically. An intrinsic interpretation is that in which a given product of 'mind' is handled as though its significance in form and content lies entirely within itself. Thus, for example, Kant's *Critique of Practical Reason* could be interpreted exclusively in terms of the logical interrelations of its parts, thus understanding it as the author himself would presumably have it understood. Contrariwise, extrinsic interpretation is that in which a set of ideas is referred beyond itself. Placed in a context it is relativized in such a way that the context exercises determinative power. Instance: Kant had a deeply religious mother, and grew up in Königsberg when kingly absolutism was the order of the day—*ergo*, the culminating formula in the *Critique of Practical Reason*, viz., the categorical imperative, is a mere derivative of moralistic precepts acquired at the maternal knee and a sense of duty pounded in by school, community, and professional life. The outcome is the equation, *Critique of Practical Reason* = the X of Prussianism+the Y of Pietism.

Intrinsic interpretations are those common in academic histories of philosophy; extrinsic interpretations are most popular among journalists. It should be clear, however, that neither horn of the dilemma need be grasped; any so-called intrinsic interpretation is framed within a large number of implicitly accepted and unanalyzed extrinsic items; any extrinsic interpretation presupposes the understanding of the idea-system as set forth by its originator. Like the famous induction *versus* deduction fallacy, the intrinsic *versus* extrinsic debate need no longer detain us.

Sociology of knowledge, then, represents the effort to state the sufficient social conditions of thought-forms without assuming that the full range of sufficient conditions is thereby exhausted, much less that 'society' determines 'mind.'

There are certain objectives which govern Scheler's approach to sociology of knowledge. First, he intends to show that there are no absolute, historically constant forms and principles of reason (not in the formal sense of reason, but in the subjective-categorical). Hence, for example, the Kantian modalities are considered merely as representative of European thinking rather than as categories valid for *all* peoples—particularly for preliterates. Second, he wants to discover the course of the development of knowledge and the various distinguishable forms taken throughout history. Third, he wants to overcome all mysticism, obscurantism, positivism, and the dogmas of the organized churches, thereby preparing the way for and validating real metaphysical thinking and knowing. Fourth, he wants to establish the factors in historical causation and to overcome the particularism of the naturalistic theories of history (Marxian economic determinism), as well as the ideological (Hegelian) and scientific or intellectualistic (Comtean) conceptions. Fifth and finally, he is concerned with the significance which the 'practical,' technological attitude of modern man directed toward the control and domination of the world and nature (in contrast to purely theoretical and contemplative attitudes) had and still has with reference to the starting points, goals, and categorical forms of knowing the world. The supreme end he envisages as a 'new culture of knowledge ... the union of knowledge useful in the material world (*Leistungswissen*) with knowledge which in the common sense makes the "cultured man" (*Bildungswissen*), and then the final union of both of these forms with, and under the aegis and guidance of, metaphysical salvation-knowledge (*Heilswissen*).'[1] In short, the aim is to synthesize the one-sided technological, pragmatic, activistic world view of occidental culture with the spiritualized culture of the East. Scheler valued highly what he held to be the oriental spirit of self-liberation and resigned acceptance of the world—a *Kultur des Duldens*—

'liberation from the accidents of existence . . . the ideas of scattered experience unified in the realm of ideas . . . the intuition of *essentia*—the basic procedure of metaphysics—. . . linked before all else with an attitude toward existing things which endures, "suffers".'[2]

Sociology of knowledge, for Scheler, is one of the means of achieving this attitude or end. As a science, however, it is subject to all the requirements of means-ends analysis,[3] and is part of general sociology, particularly of 'cultural sociology.'[4] This, together with the other main division, 'realistic' or 'real-factor' sociology, makes up the science. The sociology thus constituted is a non-normative science dealing with uniformities and types (average and 'constructed' or ideal-typical), though values and norms may be examined as causal factors. It is an analytical and causal examination of the objective and subjective content of human life.

The distinction between cultural and realistic sociology rests upon the intentions or purposes of the action, valuation, and thinking of man. In the former, the goal is 'ideal,' having reference to an ideal world. The artist, the musician, the 'pure' scientist may bring about changes in actuality, but only for an ideal purpose, not for a practical end. It is the converse for realistic sociology. The motivation is by drives or propensities—sex, power, hunger. Action is directed toward changes in actuality, such as production of goods. Consequently, a theory of mind is a necessary presupposition for cultural sociology, and a theory of drives for realistic sociology. The distinction between the two spheres is not merely methodological but ontological. The real factors (race and kinship, politics, economics) constitute a substructure, and the cultural (religion, philosophy and/or metaphysics, and science) a superstructure. The aim of sociology is to discover laws of interaction between these ideal and real factors in a given historical succession out of which, in every epoch, the unified whole of the life-content of a group constitutes itself. These are not laws of completed 'things' in chronological time, but laws of the possible dynamic becoming of things in the realm of existential or time-bound activity.[5] Scheler claims to have found one such law—but more of this later. Here it suffices to say that Scheler's law has to do with the interaction of the ideal and the real factors, as well as of the subjective human corollaries—namely, the mental and the drive structures. This interaction determines, within the limits of probability, what the net effect of these factors in socio-historical continuities will be.

Mind in either the subjective or objective senses, as 'individual' or 'collective' mind, determines only the *subsistence*—i.e., the essence or constitution—of all possible cultural objects, though not necessarily their *existence*. The realm of mind has its own immanent laws of development, but mind is not a realization factor; that is to say, an idea does not have an inherent power to become objective in the world. An idea as such is dead. The 'purer' the mind the more impotent it is. In order to be effective in life, it must be bound up with some interest, drive, or tendency, and thereby acquire power and indirect influence. Luther's tacking of the ninety-five theses on the church door at Wittenberg of itself would not have brought the Reformation. It was only with the support of the territorial princes that the Protestant Revolt could make any headway.

Negative factors of realization or positive factors of selection, which are the 'real' conditions of life, are determined by the drive structure (*Triebstruktur*). By this Scheler means the particular combination of real factors, viz., the conditions of power, the economic factors of production, the qualitative and quantitative conditions of the population, and the geographical and geo-political factors present in any given case. Rhythms of cultural creativity (renascences, for instance) follow a law of generation, a biological rhythm rather than an ideological or institutional-historical one. They are essentially youth movements. They become effective when a new structure of drives is developed, when the individual is released from the existing cultural inhibitions and norms.[6] This new drive structure is the ground for the selection and realization of the new cultural objects. The objective, real possibility of the development of a culture is never determined by ideal factors either existentially or subsistently, but only by antecedent real factors and their organization. Mind can have only a directive effect; it can bring about only a hindering or speeding up of the general trend of the real factors. Borrowing a term from Comte, Scheler concludes that the intellectual-cultural sphere expresses *liberté modifiable*, potential freedom and autonomy of action, 'modifiable freedom,' while the sphere of real factors expresses only *fatalité modifiable*, meaningless, blind, autonomous trends, 'modifiable fatality.'

The interrelations of the various factors of the mental sphere are not accidental or haphazard, but of determinate nature (*wesensgesetzlich*). Genetically and in essence these relations are of necessary character, and give rise to a general theory of the essence of human mind. All existential relations among the various cultural spheres empirically discoverable are anchored in this conception, according to which the laws (*Wesensgesetze*) of mind are not those of a real mind, either 'group' or 'individual.' On the contrary, there is a *plurality* of mind-structures, expressed in widely varying historical groups and culture-circles. There is consequently no uniformity of human nature as the proponents of the Enlightenment believed, nor is there, as Kant held, an innate universal set of categories. In short, there is a complete relativity which Scheler seeks to overcome by the presupposition of the subsistence of absolute ideas and values in a realm far removed from all historical systems of value. History is the approximation by various cultures of this norm or hierarchy of ideas and values:

> The historical mode of penetration into the metaphysical-absolute realm of values is through the sequence of various epochs and groupings, each with its own distinctive *ethos*. The value-hierarchy provides only the most formal, general, *a priori* makeup of any such *ethos*, but nevertheless their succession in time is integrally bound up with the essence of the realm of values and with its own timeless coming into being. Hence only the universal and solidary cooperation of all eras and peoples (including every future development) can fully evoke this realm of values—in so far as it is given to man to help in its realization at all.[7]

Because of unique constellations of conditions, different cultures as individualities grasp and develop certain aspects of this realm of ideas and values. They thereby become irreplaceable models or classical examples in certain things. The historical and sociological relativities of norms, purposes, and goods of society in religion, philosophy, law, and art is only a relativity of perspective in the absolute realm, for each represents a partial participation in the 'eternal and objective logos.' Given all cultures, past, present, and future, the logos may be expressed so fully that there is a total perspective, the varieties of cultures contributing, as Scheler says, to the 'meaningful unity of a magnificent painting.' In their totality they are a *unitas in multiplex* of the atemporal, absolute order of values and ideas. History as such is accidental existentiality.

The principle of the plurality of mind-structures is connected with the principle of an actual genesis of the subjective, functional, *a priori* categories of mind. Scheler rejects all theories which see in history only an accumulation of the achievements of man on the basis of a constant structure of mind, thus ignoring the development and transformation of man's psyche. 'For sociology of knowledge nothing is more important than this difference: whether the forms of thinking, valuation, perception of the world *themselves* undergo a change, or are merely applied differently to materials of experience which have been inductively and quantitatively expanded.'[8] As a consequence of Scheler's adherence to the first of these conceptions, there is for him no universal and constant view of the world such as 'the state of nature,' 'idealism,' or 'materialism.' There are only relatively 'natural' views of the world integrally united with particular societal groupings. Such a group-bound view is composed of all those objects of thought which are 'given' and 'accepted' without question, as matters of fact needing no proof or justification. These different pictures of the world penetrate into the very categorical structure of the given, so that for diverse groups at various levels of development they will be different. Examples: the biomorphic conception of the world prevailing in a sacred society, and the mathematical-mechanistic predominating in a secular society. It is therefore one of the tasks of sociology of knowledge to develop a theory of the laws of the transformation of these relative *Weltanschauungen*, their succession, parallel forms, interrelations.

Another problem of cultural sociology is that of the dynamics of culture, of which the shifts in the ways of knowing constitute a special case. There are three main problem-complexes. The first deals with the extent to which the content of culture outlives the groups which produce it or whether, on the other hand, they are so intrinsically bound together that the passing of the group is the death of the culture:

> In the same measure as enduring forms and patterns, precipitated as civilizations and cultures out of the dwindling number of history-streams, have their origin in spirit (*Geist*—which in its structure is always a concrete, never-repeated Present), they survive, in their earthly immortality, the existence of folk-units and governmental and economic institutions, and their objective meanings and value-content are capable of being revived in culture mixtures and Renaissances at any time. In the same degree, however, as they are 'manifestations' of the soul (*Seele*) and life of the group, as in sagas, folk-tales, folkways, custom, myth, etc., their value-significance perishes with the tribal existence which bears them—they are mortal.[9]

The second set of problems is concerned with those kinds of cultural diffusion, transmission, and acculturation which function so that the thought-forms involved are thereby incorporated in a new cultural synthesis.[10] Religion, philosophy, and art, as contents of cultural meanings, are interrelated and developed in this process of cultural synthesis, independently of the racial, political, and economic existences of the peoples who acted as their original bearers.

These two sets of problems are similar to those denoted by Alfred Weber's *Kulturprozess*. The third has to do with cumulative progress as exhibited by international co-operation and the like. 'Only the joint products of spirit and intelligence (in particular the positive sciences, engineering techniques, governmental and administrative forms, legal regulations) show a progress which cuts across the forms of culture and the existence-modes of peoples, and which steadily and cumulatively can and does become more international.'[11] It is directed toward the national domination and control of the world and/or nature and the development of the technical means to accomplish that end, and may be characterized as the continuous development of goods and methods, independent of the ethos of any given culture This store of rational knowledge and technique is transmissible to cultures ready to accept it when they have attained the stage where the means-ends relationship prevails. It is essentially an intellectual process, devaluating and building upon previous work, thereby illustrating a continuity, unity, and progress which the other two processes do not demonstrate. Its results are universally valid—*allgemeingültig*.

Two indispensable concepts for sociology of knowledge, says Scheler, are 'group soul' and 'group spirit.' These are not illegitimately reified entities; instead, they are essentially descriptive terms used to denote cultural growth and transmission on two levels—the unconscious and the conscious—and to define the culture content involved in each. The myth, tale, folk-religion, folksong, custom, and manners are typical cultural elements transmitted in this unconscious, automatic way, growing and active in all people, organic in the denotation of Romanticism. The relative natural view of the world corresponds to the 'group soul'—as an organic configuration. Changes are slow, and when they occur are essentially due to race mixture and/or culture borrowing.

Built upon the 'group soul,' unable to affect in it any deep-rooted change, and of a more 'artificial' character is the 'group spirit.' Its continuity rests upon a *creatio continua*; it acts consciously, and it is objectively oriented. The state, law, education, philosophy, art, and science are cultural elements of this nature. Such 'group spirit' appears only in the leaders or small groups of the elite; these are then followed by the rank and file. The effects of the 'group spirit' are exerted from above downward.

It has been mentioned that the central problem of cultural sociology is set by the question of the order in which the objective and real institutions (correspondent with the drive structure of the dominating elite) affect the production, maintenance, furtherance, or hindrance of the ideal world of meaning. The real factors determine the realization of the ideal at the point of the existing difference between the becoming (*das Werdende*) and what has become (*das Gewordene*). The actual transmutation of the ideal world into the actual is accomplished by the free act and will of the leaders, pioneers, elite. It is they who grasp the essences of the absolute world of values and ideas, which are then spread to the imitative masses. In the elite real and ideal factors converge into unity of structure and function.

Scheler vigorously proclaims that the fault of naturalistic conceptions of history has been to interpret or even to explain the ideal factors as determined solely by one or more of the real factors. Conversely, it has been the fault of all ideological, spiritualistic, personalistic interpretations of history to express all real occurrences and institutions as a unilinear unfolding of mind. Scheler does not accept any single determinant of thought-forms, as do the three most important naturalistic theories—race and kinship, political domination or the state, economic determinism—but proceeds with a conception of 'dominant motifs' in cultural integration in which one or another of these three factors prevails. There is no constant independent variable. When intrusive factors are excluded, however, there is a definite succession of these types of integration: (1) domination of blood or kinship ties (most preliterate groups); (2) transition to the predominance of political power (the state in particular); (3) the growing primacy of economic factors (as in modern times). Along with the style of cultural integration, types of social structure, or general forms of grouping—close-knit kinship units, secular and sacred societies, interest-groups—must be considered as variable factors in the determination of thought. With regard to the process of real history there is a two-fold function of human will and mind: (1) guiding, as primary function, i.e., holding forth an ideal value or goal; (2) directing, as secondary function, i.e., restraining and releasing the impulses which eventually realize the idea. Both of these functions are presumably exercised with reference to a determinate succession of automatic, blind, 'autonomous' (*eigengesetzlich*) events and conditions. This apparent paradox Scheler resolves, to his own satisfaction at least, by asserting that the meaning and content of the mind-structures is not determined by the fatality of real history, for it 'only opens and closes in determinate way and order the sluice gates of the stream of thought.'[12]

Apart from these more general considerations, we should take note of certain specific aspects of Scheler's sociology of knowledge. There are three possible and fundamental relations between knowing and society: (1) mutual understanding, or knowledge of inter-membership-character within a group, which is intrinsic to the nature of society; (2) all knowing or all collective knowledge about the same objects determines the haecceity or thisness (*Sosein*) of society; (3) societal structure determines all knowing. A series of axioms follows from these principles. First: knowledge of every person that he is a member of society is not empirical knowledge but is *a priori*, i.e., it precedes genetically the development of self-consciousness and self-value. There is no 'I' without a 'we,' and the 'we' is always filled with content earlier than the 'I.' Second: participation in the experience of others occurs in ways differing with the groups involved. One general type of participation is exemplified in identification—e.g., among certain preliterates, in crowds, and in the mother-child relation. Another is manifested in the inference from gesture, etc., to the existence of a 'subjective' experience in the other (*Analogie-*

schluss); this inference is most common in secular societies, where there is a great deal of 'strangeness.' Third: both as an axiom of sociology of knowledge and of epistemology, Scheler posits certain irreducible spheres of being which are simultaneously given with every human mind, of which the fundamental corollary for sociology of knowledge is that 'the social sphere of the contemporary age and the historical sphere of the past is prior to all spheres in this sense: (a) in reality; (b) in determinate content. "Thou-ness" (*Du-heit*) is the most fundamental existential category of human thinking.'[13] This is well illustrated by the thought of preliterate man, who is literally on 'speaking terms' with nature as a totality of 'thou-ness' in which he is immersed. In contradistinction to those theories in which the existence of others—*Du-heit*—is derived from empathy (*Einfühlung*) or from a conclusion derived from analogy with one's self (both types logically ending in solipsism), Scheler holds that selfhood and self-knowledge differentiate out of a previously amorphous stream of panpsychic experience (*aus dem Gesamtstrom des universellen Seelenlebens*)[14] or, otherwise put, upon the background of an evolving, all-encompassing consciousness which contains within itself the possibility of selfhood and experience.[15]

Meaningful total structures are initially given, and out of these the self arises in and through an objectifying, distancing process. Uniting all such parts within its cosmic wholeness is the all-life, a force much like Bergson's *élan vital*. Scheler says that it 'permeates all living things, from the least to the greatest organisms, that its course of development is the same as that followed by all other organisms, that it incorporates and stores up their experiences, that it enriches itself (*sich selber anreichert*) in order that the individual entities which later will issue from it may be richer and nobler.'[16] 'Thou-ness' is therefore the fundamental category, for it is the ground for the possibility of the 'I.'

The priority of society has several implications for sociology of knowledge. Foremost is the social character of all knowing. Second, the perspective of social interests determines the selection of the *objects* of knowledge only, not its content, and still less its validity (a point which Scheler continually stresses). Third, the structure of society determines in part the forms of the mental processes through which knowledge is reached, though he insists that all functional thought-forms are secured by grasping the essence—*Wesenserfassung*, not socially determined—of the objects themselves.[17]

Scheler then goes on to elaborate a sociologistic correspondence theory of knowledge *à la Durkheim*. Since explaining means relating the new to what is already known, and since society is always 'more known' than anything else, the arrangement of groups which compose a society determines the subjective forms of thinking and perception as well as the classification of the world in categories. As a consequence there is a structural identity of the world, of the soul, of God with the various degrees of societal organization, with the three fundamental ways of knowing (religious, metaphysical, and positivistic or scientific) at all levels of societal development. This identity, as has been pointed out, takes its sharpest expression in the elite. To trace this interconnection cross-sectionally and chronologically constitutes one of the most important tasks of sociology of knowledge. The sociologistic and, as such, essentially Durkheimian bent of Scheler's thinking in these connections becomes still more apparent when discussing the social forms of intellectual co-operation. He stresses their relation to the type-forms of human groupings, such as the closeknit kinship group, sacred and secular societies, and interestgroups. As a constructed type, for instance, the sacred society would exemplify the following characteristics: (1) truth and knowledge are traditional and given, the logic being an *ars demonstrandi*, not an *ars inveniendi*; (2) the method predominantly ontological and dogmatic rather than epistemological and critical; (3) the way of thinking realistic rather than nominalistic; (4) the system of categories organismic not mechanistic. This outline (taken from the opposite direction) also characterizes the main features of knowing in the secular society.

Not only is there this determination by the total societal structure, but even classes have different ways of thinking, perceiving, and valuing:

Subordinate Class	Dominant Class
1 Values regarded prospectively	Values regarded retrospectively
2 Things as becoming	Things as are
3 Mechanistic conception of world	Teleological conception of world
4 Realism (world predominantly as opposition)	Idealism (world predominantly as realm of ideas)
5 Materialism	Spiritualism
6 Induction, empiricism	*A priori* knowledge, rationalism
7 Pragmatism	Intellectualism
8 Optimistic view of the future, pessimistic retrospection	Pessimistic view of the future, optimistic retrospection
9 Thought-style seeking contradictions	Thought-style searching for identity
10 Thought related to environment	Thought related to heredity

These thought-modes of the class are not imperative, but are merely tendencies of thinking. Consequently, Scheler maintains that these class prejudices or even formal laws of class judgment can be overcome by every individual. To reveal these 'idols' of the class is one of the practical and pedagogical values of sociology of knowledge. Scheler presupposes, therefore, the existence of an absolute criterion of truth, and to further this distinction differentiates between pseudo-knowledge, i.e., ideology or rationalized interest of class, profession, estates, etc., and the higher forms of or real knowledge embodied in religion, metaphysics, and the sciences. Each of these three higher forms of knowing is valid in its own right.[18]

Religion as a constructed type has (1) its motive in the drive toward spiritual self-maintenance through salvation by holy, person-alistic world-guiding power; (2) its mental act (hope, fear, love, will) in recognition of the incompleteness of the world and its orientation toward something thought of as holy and divine; (3) its goal in the salvation of the person and group; (4) its personality types, the saint, the charismatic leader and, in the organized institution, the eccles-iastic; (5) its social form in the ecclesia, sect, cult; (6) its movement retrospective and completed.

Metaphysics as a constructed type has (1) its motive in the wonder that something be rather than not be; (2) its mental process, know-ledge of essences through direct envisagement (*Wesensschau*), not by observation and deduction; (3) its goal, the highest development of personality through wisdom; (4) its personality type, the 'wise man'; (5) its social group, the 'school' in the classical meaning; (6) its move-ment, the expression of individual creativity, not cumulative nor progressive.

Science as a type-form has (1) its motive in the desire to guide nature, society, and the psyche; (2) its mental process, observation, experiment, deduction, induction; (3) its goal, a world picture in mathematical symbols concerned only with functional relations, not with essences; (4) its personality type, the research man; (5) its social form, a sort of international scientific republic and its organizations (learned societies, universities, research institutes, etc.); (6) its move-ment, impersonal, use of the division of labor, continuous, inter-national, cumulative, progressive, with devaluation of previous achievements.

Among the manifold sources of Scheler's amazingly complex con-ceptions are: Comte, Alfred Weber, McDougall, Hegel, and Marx for cultural dynamics; Comte, Marx, and Durkheim for the relation of thought and societal structure. His main standpoint is pluralistic. There is the absolute world of essences as one pole and the constant, ahistorical biological substratum on the other. Between these two is historical culture, which from the point of view of mind is an acci-dental *existentium* of the absolute world and which receives its organic *élan vital* from the sphere of biological processes. Both are autonomous spheres so far as the nature and forms of movement are concerned. The gap between the two is overcome by their convergence and unification in an elite, another absolute. Scheler admits that without spirit and its normative direction there can be no state, no economy, etc. (implying thereby a very close, intimate relation between mind and 'real factors'), and that for the latter to *be* at all, they must be suffused with mind. As a result he has had to draw very close to the Hegelian conception that the fundamental evolution of culture is found in the dialectic interplay and progressive realization of ideas. But as soon as the fatal flirtation with Hegel begins, the view that ideas are dead, needing the resuscitative vigor of biological drives, becomes questionable. As a matter of fact, the theory that mind can guide a realm which by definition proceeds under its own power and laws is a patent contradiction. This whole way of handling the problem also leads to the treatment of mind or ideas as epiphenomenal, particularly in view of the emphasis upon the biological substratum as more 'real.' From this pluralistic position of autonomous spheres, it follows that the categorical determination of knowledge is not achieved by the societal structure, and that any functional interrelation is an accident or a miracle. The postulated autonomy and validity of the three fundamental ways of knowing also suggests freedom from societal determination.

In the end, therefore, despite the empirical evidence which serves to substantiate his contentions, Scheler lands in confusion and contradiction of his principles. The world as we know it is an accident, and for that reason stumbles befogged in a cosmos of irrationality. Aside from his ultimate principles, however, Scheler is correct in beginning with types of socio-cultural integration and the conception of a hierarchy of values, and then seeking to establish functional interrelationships of the component parts which, after all, are in every case of non-material character. He is also justified in his vigorous assertion that sociology of knowledge has no jurisdiction over questions of the *validity* of ideas, that its sphere of competence is that of a science, not of an epistemology or a philosophy. For all his penchant for sleight-of-hand and prophetic pronouncement, then, we may regard Max Scheler as among the greatest exponents of that *substantive* sociology of knowledge which is slowly winning its way among those who are tired of intrinsic *versus* extrinsic dilemmas.

Notes

For fairly full bibliographies listing the chief works of the main figures in the development of sociology of knowledge, see Barnes, Becker, and Becker, *Contemporary Social Theory*, New York: Appleton-Century, 1940, pp. 87–9, 892, 895–8.

1 Max Scheler, 'Future of Man' (trans. Howard Becker), *Monthly Criterion*, ed. by T. S. Eliot (February 1928), p. 20.

2 *Ibid.*, p. 20; cf. Nicolaas Diederichs, *Vom Leiden und Dulden*, Berlin and Bonn: F. Dümmlers Verlag, 1930.

3 Talcott Parsons, *The Structure of Social Action*, New York: McGraw-Hill, 1937, *passim*—use index.

4 Not in Alfred Weber's sense, nor in the usual American sense. The reader can best formulate his own definition after reading this paper and studying the chart on p. 211.

5 Max Scheler, *Die Wissensformen und die Gesellschaft*, Leipzig: Der Neue-Geist Verlag, 1926, pp. 5–6.

6 Scheler, *Wissensformen*, pp. 117–20. This compares interestingly with F. J. Teggart's discussion of 'transition' in his *Processes of History*, New Haven: Yale University Press, 1918.

7 'Die historische Form des Eindringens in die metaphysisch-absolute Wertewelt durch die Geschichte der Ethosformen der Zeitalter und der Gruppen, von der die Wertordnung nur die formalste, generalste apriorische Verfassung angibt, ist eine im Wesen dieser Wertewelt und ihres eigenen zeitlosen Werdens selbst angelegte, so dass nur die universelle und solidarische Kooperation aller Zeiten und Völker sie— mit Einschluss der je kommenden Geschichte—erschöpfen und im "Urseienden" mit-realisieren kann, soweit dies dem Menschen überhaupt zugeteilt ist' (Scheler, *Wissensformen*, p. 182).

    See also *ibid.*, p. 13; *Der Formalismus in der Ethik und die materiale Wertethik*, Halle: Niemeyer, 1921, 'Sinn des Satzes von der "Relativität" der Werte', pp. 272–8; and 'Historische Relativität der ethischen Werte und ihre Dimensionen', pp. 306, 329. Ernst Troeltsch, *Der Historismus und seine Probleme*, Tübingen: Mohr, 1922, pp. 605–8, p. 613.

8 Scheler, *Wissensformen*, p. 17.

9 Scheler, 'Future of Man', pp. 108–9.

10 Scheler, *Wissensformen*, p. 27.

11 Scheler, 'Future of Man'.

12 Scheler, *Wissensformen*, p. 31.

13 *Ibid.*, pp. 53–4.

14 Scheler, *Wesen und Formen der Sympathie*, 3rd ed., Bonn: Cohen, 1926, p. 289. See especially the discussion of 'die Fremd-Wahrnehmung', pp. 273–307.

15 *Ibid.*, p. 289.

16 Diederichs, *op. cit.*, p. 112. Pertinent also, pp. 51–66, 103–6, 111–15.

17 Scheler, *Wissensformen*, p. 55, n.

18 Scheler, 'Über die positivistische Geschichtsphilosophie des Wissens', *Moralia*, Leipzig: Der Neue-Geist Verlag, 1923, pp. 26–41; *Arbeit und Erkenntnis*, pp. 249–58.

part seven

Karl Mannheim and historicist sociology of knowledge

14 The significance and development of Karl Mannheim's sociology

Gunter W. Remmling

Ancient data such as the Code of Hammurabi, the Old Testament, the Confucian Classics, and Plato's *Republic* document that to a large extent social thought owes its origin and continuation to the dialectical interplay of the human desires for social order and social reconstruction. The relationship between stability and change, between social peace and social justice, was precariously balanced in the ancient and medieval systems of social philosophy, anchored as they were in tradition, values, and religion. Modern social theorists witnessed the revolutionary transformation of political, social, and economic institutions as well as the flight of the gods and the relativization of values. These experiences explain both the Machiavellian flirtation with anarchy and the Hobbesian romance with a totalitarian guarantee of social order.

The further development of social contract theory, especially the transition from John Locke (1632–1704) to Jean-Jacques Rousseau (1712–78), sharpened the confrontation between the guardians of order and the champions of change. By 1789 the scales were rigged heavily in favor of the desire for novelty and the Jacobinic mentality consummated its victory over the intellectual and social structures of the *ancien régime* in the chaos of revolution and terror.

Sociology arose as an attempt to transcend the alternatives presented to modern men by stability in conservative corruption and instability in radical disruption. Especially Auguste Comte (1798–1857), in naming the new discipline sociology, thought of it as an application of rational-scientific principles to social life; such application, he hoped, would harness the dynamics of change to a vehicle that was not hell-bent for chaos but followed the lodestar of order and stability.

Until the First World War Comte's optimistic equation of scientifically controlled evolution with orderly, unilinear progress retained a persuasive hold on the imagination of most sociologists with the notable exception of social Darwinist or Marxist conflict theorists. The business-class and working-class ideologists continued the Jacobinic confrontation: they either exploited evolutionism as a rationale for continuity of existing institutions or rejected evolutionary imagery in favor of revolutionary mystique.

The problems challenging the intellectual community as a result of the French Revolution were compounded by the devastating experience of World War I. By 1918 intellectuals were bedeviled not only by the tenuous relation of change and stability; most of them were compelled to admit that the barbarism of total warfare had debunked as illusionary the twin beliefs in evolution and progress.

Sharing the grievous disillusionment of their intellectual fellow workers most sociologists abandoned interest in the discovery of scientific patterning of developmental change. Instead they turned to an empirically delimited investigation of the operation of non-rational forces which were apparently stronger determinants of human behavior than rationality.

The chaos of relativities

The emphasis on the non-rational regions in social action and intellectual activity coalesced with the muscular force of ideological analysis to create a novel climate of opinion which achieved an historical dimension through the admittance of intellectual outsiders to a position of centrality. The fascination of Claude Adrien Helvétius (1715–71) and Paul Henri Holbach (1723–89) with the misuse of authority appeared as contemporary as Friedrich Nietzsche's (1844–1900) reduction of psychic and social life to the will-to-power and Karl Marx's (1818–83) economic determinism. The reexamination of traditional interpretations of reality proceeded along different lines. Sigmund Freud's (1856–1939) psychoanalytical theory devalued the conscious region of the mind and reduced social and cultural behavior to functions of instinctive mechanisms denuded of historical and spiritual significance. In similar fashion Vilfredo Pareto (1848–1923) emphasized the centrality of nonlogical social actions which manifest the bio-psychic qualities of residues; such actions are justified by non-logical theories which have their surface manifestations in derivations, that is, in pseudo-logical explanations of non-logical conduct.

Despite their substantive dissimilarities and notwithstanding their dependencies on a variety of intellectual antecedents, the Marxian, Nietzschean, Freudian, and Paretian paradigms combine to establish a co-ordinate system for the consciousness of twentieth-century men that achieves the quality of novelty because of the massive factuality of its givenness. In this new co-ordinate system cognitive acts directed towards cultural objectifications are deflected from the interpretation of objective meanings which are rooted in the structural principles of cultural objects themselves; instead cognition is directed to the understanding of what Karl Mannheim (1893–1947) calls 'documentary' meaning. Cognitive acts directed to the understanding of documentary meaning have a new intent: they interpret cultural objects as surface manifestations which 'document' the existence of deeper and larger complexes of reality.

Max Weber's (1864–1920) interpretative fusion of scattered items of documentary meaning in overarching general concepts such as 'spirit' and even more generally 'rationality' moves brilliantly in the space of the new system of co-ordinates. His analysis points away from and beyond the objective meaning of surface phenomena to underlying socio-cultural forces.

The new attitude to cultural manifestations brings with it a detachment of the cognitive act which forces the interpreter to remain largely 'without' the intended object so that its external connections with other realities will not be obscured by undue fascination for its internal complexities. The new 'extrinsic' interpretation of cultural objectifications is markedly similar to the optic of sociology which remains clear only as long as those who use it cut themselves off in thought—to use Herbert Spencer's (1820–1903) formulation—from all their relationships of 'race, and country, and citizenship.'[1] The spread of the novel mode of extrinsic interpretation provoked the growth of ideology-consciousness which stimulated logical positivists and semanticists to develop their peculiar form of language-consciousness while it drove Mannheim to his particular manner of intellectual self-consciousness.

Ever since Napoleon Bonaparte's use of the term ideology for aggressive purposes the realities of political conflict have been associated with the further development of this concept. The deployment of ideology as an intellectual weapon matured to deadly precision in the guerilla tactics of Marx and the Marxists who discredited the thinking of their adversaries as an anticipation of their unconscious interest, a distorted reflection of their existential situation. In mounting their counterattack the anti-Marxist forces answered in kind and contributed to the proliferation of ideological weapons and the escalation of political conflict.

Mannheim realized that the reciprocal unmasking of the unconscious roots of intellectual existence contributed to the erosion of man's confidence in thought as such. Surrounded by the political self-consciousness and cultural neuroticism of Weimar Germany Mannheim, however, permitted the thrust of his intellectual energy to carry him beyond the political confines of the ideological zone. He turned the weapon of ideological analysis against himself in the attempt to lay bare the social roots of all theories including his own.

In this process Mannheim not only developed his sociology of knowledge but also gave methodological precision to the time-honored search for the meaning of history. This search had lured German intellectuals before him into the luminous depths of histor-ism where all world views reveal themselves, in the words of Wilhelm Dilthey (1833–1911), as 'historically determined, therefore, limited, relative.'[2] From the historist philosophy of Dilthey also stems the insight that all intellectual workers who define their labors as relative modes of perceiving their objects within an historical horizon must face them as a 'chaos of relativities.'[3]

Mannheim seems to belong to those intellectuals who derive their creative strength from the act of standing close to an abyss. Arthur Schopenhauer (1788–1860) dared to think in the awareness that 'before us there is certainly only nothingness.'[4] Nietzsche was haunted by his knowledge of the limitless passion and drunken frenzy of Dionysian forces threatening to destroy all forms and norms in a fiery orgy of primitive life. Chaos is the name of the spectre that stalked Mannheim throughout his intellectual career. Continually he pitted the cunning of his reason against the growing shadows of mental and social dissolution.

Mannheim's encounter with the chaotic forces of dissolution and disorder occurred in two major ways. The first engagement was fought on the theoretical plane where chaos manifested itself in the 'gliding of standpoints' brought about by the dragon of relativity. Mannheim battled the intellectual chaos of relativities with a variety of conceptual weapons ranging from the restructuring of episte-mology to the construction of a 'consensus ex post' made possible by the synthesizing activities of the 'socially unattached intelligentsia.' The second engagement was fought on the empirical plane where chaos appeared in the guise of social disorder fashioned by the ogres of economic exploitation and social injustice. Mannheim opposed the threat to the coherence of modern industrial society with the double-edged sword of social planning.

Order and progress

The question concerning order and progress assumed a central position as soon as realistic analysis had persuaded a majority of people to accept as irreversible the great transition from feudal-theological society to industrial-scientific society. Feudal-theological society had bought order at the price of progress; industrial-scientific society wanted both order and progress. Since God had disappeared along with feudal-theological society philosophers were necessarily transformed from theologians into anthropologists. In a godless universe men were thrown back upon themselves; they were forced to exchange the metaphysics of spiritual transcendence for the rhetoric of the social contract. The first modern philosophers still straddled the old and the new world; among them Thomas Hobbes (1588–1679), convinced of the sinful nature of men, felt compelled to replace the needed but unavailable tyranny of God with the needed and available tyranny of the State. By the time of Rousseau the anthropological rhetoric of the social contract had become part of the revolutionary baggage of the *philosophes* and Jacobinists which disgusted Henri Saint-Simon (1760–1825) and his interpreters sufficiently to drag in the grab-bag of 'positive' philosophy as an antidote to the 'negative' philosophy of the pre-revolutionary and revolutionary intelligentsia.

Saint-Simon developed the principles of positivist philosophy to protect progress by restraining the corrupting egoism of the rich; at the same time he intended this philosophical rationale for the rule of a scientific-technological-industrial elite to safeguard order from the disruptive rebelliousness of the poor. There was to be no radical change in the basic structural arrangements of society; the task of equilibration was not to be performed by the hardware of revolution; the equilibrating principle had to be soft and Saint-Simon found it in a secular equivalent of religion, destined to grow into his *Nouveau Christianisme*. In his *Système industriel* there emerges the lofty ideal of brotherly love as the vehicle that would diffuse the agglutinant of moral unity across class lines, throughout society. Comte was even less willing to blame basic economic and political institutions for social evils which he saw originating in corruptive and insurrectionary ideas and manners. He, therefore, steadily moved toward a position from where the thrust of positive science could be directed to the task of establishing a new intellectual order justifying the imposition of the State as supreme moral authority between the leaders of society and the working classes.

Émile Durkheim (1858–1917) apparently conceived of his intellectual position as an uneasy balance between the extremes of Comtean and Marxian thought. Comte had been sufficiently close to conservative reactionaries such as Louis de Bonald (1754–1840) and Joseph de Maistre (1753–1821) to share their fear of the anarchic tendencies in the new division of labor spawned by the godless industrial-scientific order; this fear had persuaded Comte to champion the State as the means of effecting the necessary superimposition of moral unity. Drawing closer to Saint-Simon, Durkheim set out to demonstrate the possibility of an organic, non-authoritarian process for the development of a moral order appropriate both to the principles of stability and progress and the novel socio-technological conditions. This process allegedly resided in the industrial-scientific division of labor itself. Against the Marxian call to class struggle and, as he feared, anarchy Durkheim raised his own voice on behalf of the higher principle of 'organic' solidarity. In an ironically Marxian-like recourse to historical transcendence he saw the development and survival of his higher principle guaranteed by the movement of socio-technological reality itself. On the plane of implementation he relied heavily on the functional efficacy of allegedly non-authoritarian principles such as moral education and moral discipline. These principles were to facilitate the inevitable adjustment of individuals to industrial-scientific society which represents their unalterable destiny.

The feudal-theological order had died in the ashes of the French Revolution. After the passage of more than one hundred years the new industrial-scientific order showed no signs that the promises of its theoreticians were about to materialize. The promise of progress was no match for the unbridled insolence of bourgeois profiteering. The message of order was dwarfed by the growing shadow of working-class rebelliousness; it disappeared into the poisonous fogs of the First World War which catapulted Europe's hungry workers into the role change from industrial to military cannon fodder and from there into open revolt.

Saint-Simon and his disciples had promised order and progress; but their indifference to significant corrections of structural inequities explains why they merely provided ideological justification for the replacement of an old order by a new order. The old order had catered to aristocratic-clerical privileges. The new order served the interests of an industrial-capitalistic elite. Saint-Simon's principle of Christian brotherly love was to begin with an ethereal guarantor of progress inviting the kind of savage ridicule which Marx addressed to the bourgeois ideologists of his native Germany. Marx dismissed their halfhearted suggestions for reform as a 'bleating of sheep' which mirrors nothing but the wretchedness of social reality.[5] Comte, in his plan for social reorganization, had made it quite clear that the actual administration of the temporal power should be in the hands of businessmen and bankers. The leaders of business and finance were to maintain social control; they were to assure political, social, and economic justice and to sustain public morality. The sociological priesthood, on the other hand, was to be devoid of any material power to enforce their decisions and recommendations. Durkheim's 'progressive' conception of moral discipline surreptitiously pre-supposed that poverty recommended itself for its efficacy in the inculcation of moral restraint and the containment of anomie as his statistics on suicide rates seemed to indicate. These statistics after all had 'revealed' that regionally 'the more people there are who have independent means, the more numerous are suicides.'[6]

While the real estate profiteer Saint-Simon was preparing the positivist celebration of the emergent industrial-scientific establishment as the harbinger of a free and rational society, G. W. F. Hegel (1770–1831) joined the attack of German idealist philosophers upon the idolatry of factual reality. This attack began with Immanuel Kant's (1724–1804) move against the British empiricists; it had the objective of liberating men from their dependence on blind natural and social forces. Men were offered a new role: to be masters of their world and their own development. In a letter to Friedrich Schelling (1775–1854) the young Hegel celebrated the disappearance of 'the halo which has surrounded the leading oppressors and gods of the earth.' Hegel's Jacobinic opposition to the given state of affairs and the critical negativity of his dialectics attracted the attention of Marx.

Hegel's career as a radical intellectual was short-lived and ended with his co-optation by the Prussian Establishment. It was, therefore, left to Marx to activate the revolutionary potential of Hegel's fact-transcending conception of reason which had described reality as an historical process leading to ever fuller states of correspondence between existence and the potentialities of men. From such premises Marx drew the conclusion that the full development of mankind presupposed the complete, and of necessity revolutionary, transformation of the world. In its given factuality the world permitted only the kind of human impoverishment that Marx had meant to express in the phrase 'the less you *are*, the less you express your life, the more you *have*.'[7]

The drums of revolution

The sociological formula which Comte had suggested with his correlation of order and progress fell apart in the political conflicts of the early twentieth century. The theoretical fascination with the superstructure, with ideas and morality, distinguishing the sociological tradition stemming from Comte and Durkheim found its empirical correlate in the political behavior of the majorities in industrial societies. The common fascination with *order* led to alliances between established upper classes, emerging middle classes, and trade unionists among the working classes. On 4 August 1914 the German Social Democratic party's delegation to the *Reichstag* voted for the war credits; in France and Great Britain the majorities in the Social Democratic and Labour parties also supported the war efforts of their respective countries. On 10 November 1918 the German Social Democratic leader Friedrich Ebert (1871–1925) entered into an alliance with the Supreme Command of the Army and promised to support the aristocratic officers' corps so that the country be saved by the army from Bolshevism, disorder, and civil war.

The mystique of *progress* increasingly attracted the radical minority of Independent Socialists who shared Marx's fascination for the socio-economic substructure, taking his revolutionary call for sweeping structural change seriously. On 11 January 1919 the Spartacists—members of the newly founded Communist Party of Germany—took to the streets and the rooftops of Berlin tenements to fight a short-lived, bloody battle against *Freikorps* volunteers and regular army men who were directed by the former trade-union leader Gustav Noske (1868–1946).

The anarchy unleashed by the Berlin Spartacus rebellion—neither the first nor the last engagement fought by the champions of progress against the guardians of order—showed the serious dislocations brought about by the collapse of the order-progress formula: order was not progressive enough, progress was not sufficiently orderly. Anarcho-Communist experiments had bloody consequences in Bavaria where Noske's troops from Berlin liquidated the short-lived Republic of Soviets in late April 1919. In Mannheim's native Hungary a Communist revolt led by Béla Kun (1886–1939) brought down the new republic in March 1919. The Hungarian Communist republic in turn was crushed by Rumanian troops in August 1919, and in March 1920 Admiral Nicholas Horthy, leader of the reactionary Hungarian counterrevolution, restored the old order. The fugitive Béla Kun finally disappeared in the Russian purges of 1939, which accompanied Stalin's offensive against 'Trotskyism.' In the Soviet Union, too, the mystique of order had come to dominate the historical imagination and the cry for progress had turned into distant murmurs which fluttered forlornly in the cold winds sweeping across Stalinist labor camps.

Karl Mannheim—immersed in an empirical reality where the promise of progress and the assurance of order rode on sequential waves of terror—concluded that all ideas had been scandalized. This assumption informed the intellectual labor invested in his sociology of knowledge which took shape as the theoretical description and reflection of Weimar culture. Many exiles from the ill-fated German republic surrendered their lives to the feelings of futility and doom which overcame them in a Paris tenement, in a Brazilian hovel, or in the grey light of a New York hotel room; unlike them Mannheim found strength in his new English environment. This strength enabled him to gradually develop the outlines of a new synthesis which he believed capable of accommodating the twin desires of people for lasting order and progressive structural change.

The sociology of Karl Mannheim

Mannheim's intellectual development appears as a process involving the transition from relativist socio-cultural theory to instrumental planning theory, the subsequent reinterpretation of the functions of institutions and values, and the final attempt at a redefinition of military-political reality.

Strictly formulated Mannheim's thinking underwent four changes. These changes will be referred to as phases of his intellectual development: they are schematically approximated and briefly described in Table 14.1.[8]

TABLE 14.1   *The development of Karl Mannheim's sociology*

Stage of development	Major interest	Major work*
First Phase 1922–32	Sociology of Knowledge	*Ideology and Utopia*, 1929 (German ed.)
Second Phase 1933–38	Sociology of Planning	*Man and Society in an Age of Reconstruction*, 1935 (German ed.)
Third Phase 1939–44	Sociology of Religion Sociology of Values Sociology of Education	*Diagnosis of Our Time*, 1943 (English ed.)
Fourth Phase 1945–47	Political Sociology Sociology of Power	*Freedom, Power and Democratic Planning*, 1950 (posthumous, English ed.)

* English editions: *Ideology and Utopia* (trans. Louis Wirth and Edward Shils; preface by Louis Wirth), 1936.
Man and Society in an Age of Reconstruction (trans. Edward Shils), 1940.
German editions: *Diagnosis of Our Time* (trans. Fritz Blum), 1951.
Freedom, Power and Democratic Planning (trans. Peter Müller), 1970.

First phase: as a representative of the liberal, *avant-garde* intelligentsia of postwar Central Europe Mannheim accepts during the 1920s an absolute historism as the basis of his interpretation of socio-cultural reality. In the ideational force field generated by intellectuals of the Weimar republic and eventually in uneasy proximity to the Frankfurt *Institut für Sozialforschung* he develops his radical sociology of knowledge which claims, in contrast to Max Scheler's (1874–1928) moderate view, that all thoughts in the humanities and social sciences are determined in form and content by non-theoretical factors. An awareness of general ruthlessness in social-economic-political conflict and the desire of his generation to unmask the hypocrisy of established power positions combine into a personal motivational complex which drives him to expand the suspicion of ideology: he therefore widens Marx's total but special concept of ideology into his own vision of ideology which is not only total but also general. In Mannheim's radical optic the knowledge of all social groups appears as socio-existentially determined. In the brilliant flash of this epistemological explosion we witness the final shift of the intellectual seascape into contemporaneity: there are no longer any privileged social positions with regard to ideational truth or general intellectual reality-adequacy. In answer to the charge of relativism Mannheim develops a series of defensive arguments. These include the reconstitution of traditional, static epistemology on the basis of change-conscious modernistic dynamism, the reconceptualization of relativism as relationism, the accumulative effect of a *consensus ex post* in the non-partisan sifting of reliable knowledge and the related, well publicized function of the 'socially unattached intelligentsia.' This group, which Alfred Weber (1868–1958) singled out for special attention with the controversial concept *sozialfreischwebende Intelligenz*, has supposedly a more comprehensive vision of truth since its members are relatively free from the otherwise general attachment to specific socio-existential positions.

Second phase: in 1933 Mannheim joins the exodus of the German intellectual elite. Soon after his arrival in England his epistemological, ontological, and methodological theorizing that led to the formulation of his radical sociology of knowledge and to the global suspicion of ideology gives way to a novel interest in the crisis phenomena of the twentieth century. While the night of barbarism settles over Germany, Mannheim responds to the pragmatic and experimental openness of his English environment: he develops a theory of democratic social planning as his answer to the problems besetting advanced industrial societies. Significantly he demands that man himself be reconstructed to insure a lasting reconstruction of society. The achievement of these two interrelated goals depends to a large extent on the transformation of 'functional rationality' into 'substantial rationality.' Industrialization gave rise to functional rationality which is an elitist organizing force capable of relating the social actions of associated individuals to objective ends. The instrumental limitation of this form of rationality is to be overcome by substantial rationality which would enable the majority of people to grasp the interrelations of social facts and processes. Democratic social planning is expected to give rise to this substantial rationality which would, on the basis of individual insight into the interrelations of events, elevate interactional behavior to higher levels of autonomy and intelligence.

Third phase: the experience of World War II contributes to the lessening of Mannheim's fascination with rationality which had so far dominated his thinking. During the early 1940s Mannheim comes to believe that his earlier emphasis on rationality was one-sided and inadequate to the task of a fuller understanding of human personality. Moving closer to the complexities of psychic phenomena he integrates emotional and volitional variables into his hitherto predominantly rationalistic model of social planning. This change in intention leads to a novel focus of attention upon the social meanings of values and the functional significance of the institutions of education and religion. Values, religious behavior, and meaningful education are seen in close correlation with the human will and human feelings; they are therefore capable of enlisting the active support of men for the planned construction of a fundamentally and militantly democratic society. At this point Mannheim is mainly interested in the creation of a viable value system and the rejuvenation of public education and Christianity in the interest of social reconstruction.

Fourth phase: Mannheim's transition to this last phase coincides significantly with the end of World War II. As the chill of the cold war spreads over and beyond the ruins of Europe, Mannheim redirects his attention to the problems of political and military power. Although he retains his paradigm for social planning as ultimately developed in the third phase, he once more shifts his interest to a new field of inquiry and sets out to formulate his critical sociology of power as a unique presupposition for a realistic political sociology. This stage of intellectual development remained somewhat rudimentary as a consequence of his untimely death in 1947.

Notes

1 Herbert Spencer, *The Study of Sociology* (introduction by Talcott Parsons), Ann Arbor: University of Michigan Press, 1961, p. 67.

2 Wilhelm Dilthey, *Weltanschauungslehre: Abhandlungen zur Philosphie der Philosophie, Gesammelte Schriften*, vol. 8, Leipzig and Berlin: Teubner, 1931, p. 224 (my translation).

3 Wilhelm Dilthey, *Einleitung in die Geisteswissenschaften: Versuch einer Grundlegung für das Studium der Gesellschaft und der Geschichte, Gesammelte Schriften*, vol. 1, Stuttgart: Teubner, 1923, p. 413 (my translation).

4 Arthur Schopenhauer, *The World as Will and Idea*, vol. 1 (trans. R. B. Haldane and J. Kemp), 9th impression, London: Routledge & Kegan Paul, 1948, p. 530.

5 See Karl Marx, Friedrich Engels, *The German Ideology*, pts I and III (ed. with an introduction by R. Pascal), New York: International Publishers, 1939, p. 6.

6 Émile Durkheim, *Suicide* (trans. John A. Spaulding and George Simpson), London: Routledge & Kegan Paul, 1963, p. 245. See also Jack D. Douglas, *The Social Meanings of Suicide*, Princeton, N.J.:

Princeton University Press, 1967, p. 339: 'And the failure to see social meanings as problematic has led sociologists to read into statistics whatever forms of meanings fitted their preconceived explanations.'

7 Karl Marx, *Economic and Philosophic Manuscripts of 1844*, Moscow: Foreign Languages Publishing House, 1961, p. 119 (emphasis in original).

8 For a more detailed analysis of Mannheim's first phase see Gunter W. Remmling, 'The Radical Sociology of Knowledge and Beyond' in Gunter W. Remmling, *Road to Suspicion: A Study of Modern Mentality and the Sociology of Knowledge*, New York: Appleton-Century-Crofts, 1967, pp. 40–9. For the general problems of Mannheim's sociology see Gunter W. Remmling, *Wissenssoziologie und Gesellschaftsplanung: Das Werk Karl Mannheims*, Dortmund: Ruhfus, 1968. For the general structural context of the sociology of knowledge see Gunter W. Remmling, 'The Intellectual Heritage of Sociology' in Gunter W. Remmling and Robert B. Campbell, *Basic Sociology: An Introduction to the Study of Society*, Totowa, N.J.: Littlefield, Adams, 1970, pp. 25–57.

15 The epistemological relevance of Mannheim's sociology of knowledge[1]

Virgil G. Hinshaw, Jun.

In a recent issue of this journal a problem[2] was discussed that concerns the boundaries of a comparatively new discipline the subject-matter of which is, justifiably or no, of cogent interest to sociologist and epistemologist alike. The present article aims at approaching the same problem but from a different frame of reference, viz., that of scientific empiricism.

During the past century there has arisen an ever-increasing consciousness of the 'relativity' of various social phenomena. Much of such awareness has been both the direct and indirect manifestation of the growth of the scientific outlook. Discoveries resulting from actual attempts at application of the methods of science to fields wherein no such technique had previously been employed began to supplant not only blind superstition and adulatory adherence to authoritarianism but also perennial arm-chair speculation. Marx in his treatment of social institutions, Pareto in similar studies, Durkheim in his consideration of comparative religion, Lévy-Bruhl in his research concerning primitive societies, Westermarck in his inquiries into moral ideas—to mention but a few—have all shown conclusively the 'relative' nature of social institutions, habits, mores, customs, moral codes, and the like. Barring ideological components, the findings of such men have been gradually accepted into the body of scientific commonplace as well as into the general knowledge of the average educated individual, though time was when their claims were considered by the dominant lay and ecclesiastical groups to be little more than vicious radicalsim.

It is, however, this very ideological factor which colors the results of some of these men that is my chief concern in the present context. On the crest of the wave of emphasis on the relative character of much of what had been previously thought and held to be absolute in nature rode a vicious claim that knowledge *itself* was relative to particular contemporaneous historical and social conditions. Not only was it claimed that comparative studies revealed the relativity of certain social phenomena but also it was maintained that the content and validity of all knowledge was dependent upon, and hence relative to, the unique socio-historical context in which it arose. By some, history was claimed to be nothing more than a series of perspectivally biased projections while by others knowledge was held to be so inexorably relative that the search for anything like knowledge of an absolute character was considered but a quest for the will-o'-the-wisp. Among those propounding such theses of historical and epistemological relativism are to be found the names of Croce, Dilthey, and, of late, especially Karl Mannheim, though it is of interest to point out that neither of the latter two considered themselves relativists.

Closely identified, though sometimes erroneously, with this movement of historical and epistemological relativism has been the growth of one of the newest of the social sciences—sociology of knowledge. Springing ultimately from both French and German sources, *Wissenssoziologie* has only recently developed into anything approximating a science. Never having been free from internal strife and disagreement, it is little wonder that its progress has been so slow; and when this fact is realized, it likewise becomes clear just why there has been so much confusion from without concerning the nature and scope of the new discipline. Loosely one might distinguish and categorize two predominant, divergent strains within the sociology of knowledge. On the one hand there have been those who maintain that *Wissenssoziologie* is alone properly 'substantive.' According to this school,

> Sociology of knowledge is not 'history of ideas in their social context,' 'social determinism of thought,' 'dominance of material over non-material culture,' or anything remotely similar. Sociology of knowledge is the analysis of the functional interrelations of social processes and structures on the one hand and the patterns of intellectual life, including the modes of knowing, on the other.[3]

Associated with this group are such names as Rickert, Max Weber, Scheler, and others. On the other hand there have been those, particularly Mannheim, who have maintained that, in addition to this substantive phase, sociology of knowledge possesses an epistemological function. More precisely, Mannheim divides *Wissenssoziologie* into two main divisions: theory and an historico-sociological method of research. The former, theoretical branch is again subdivided into (1) 'purely empirical investigation through description and structural analysis of the ways in which social relationships, in fact, influence thought'; and (2) 'epistemological inquiry concerned with the bearing of this interrelationship upon the problem of validity.'[4] Revising this statement of the scope of sociology of knowledge, as a certain critic has recently done, one might make the simpler dichotomy of the problems 'of a substantive *Wissenssoziologie*, which includes the empirical and procedural aspects, and those pertaining to the epistemological relevance of the sociology of knowledge.'[5]

It is the main thesis of this paper that not only is there no epistemological branch of sociology of knowledge but also that if there are epistemological consequences of *Wissenssoziologie* their investigation belongs to the epistemologist, not to the sociologist of knowledge, who is properly a scientist. It is my contention that the claim to epistemological relevance of sociology of knowledge is largely based upon confusion—confusion, however, which is understandable in the light of the predominantly German philosophical background of *Wissenssoziologie*. My purpose throughout is to both indicate and examine as well as to attempt to clarify what seem to me to be Mannheim's basic confusions. This is not to say that the fate of his treatment of *substantive* sociology of knowledge goes hand in hand with that of his stress upon the epistemological relevance of *Wissenssoziologie*. On the contrary, as Mannheim himself admits, the substantive phase of sociology of knowledge is a self-contained discipline, actually neither implicating nor implicated by any claims of epistemological consequences, though until Mannheim's position is thoroughly examined and clarified such an acknowledgment on his part must seem paradoxical, to say the least. I am maintaining, then, that properly there is only a substantive sociology of knowledge, that a claim to an epistemological *Wissenssoziologie* is substantiated only by a confusion, and I shall attempt to indicate this confusion as well as to propose a clarification, using as an immediate approach to this task an investigation of Mannheim's epistemological emphasis.

A recent writer has well characterized Mannheim's rather ambiguous position as an epistemologically inclined sociologist of knowledge, particularly as exemplified in his *Ideology and Utopia*. In an attempt to reconcile what he considers the conflict between epistemological relativism and absolutism,[6] Professor E. W. Hall has outlined several major contentions of the German sociologist, which could be paraphrased in the following form: (1) The sociologist of knowledge claims that beliefs about complex sociological matters which explicitly involve values have relative truth-value, since actually one's whole epistemology is relative to—since existentially determined by—one's historical and social standpoint. That Mannheim is never clear as to just which spheres of 'thought' are to be subject to his theses concerning 'existential determination' is adequately pointed out by contemporary critics. In the words of one author,

> 'Knowledge' is at times used so broadly as to include every type of assertion and every mode of thought from folkloristic maxims to rigorous positive science; ... ethical convictions, epistemological postulates, material predications, synthetic judgments, political beliefs, the 'categories' of thought, eschatological doxies, moral norms, ontological assumptions and observations of empirical fact are more or less indiscriminately held to be 'existentially determined.'[7]

(2) The sociologist of knowledge claims that he is not alone concerned with the conditions of the occurrence of knowledge but also with the particularization of the scope and the extent of the validity of knowledge. (3) The sociologist of knowledge is not just concerned with the pointing out of the partiality of the assumed truth of a group or historical period. He claims that 'the social genesis of our ideas is relevant not merely to their occurrence, meaning, and scope, but to the ascertainment of their truth as well ...'; that 'the function of the findings of the sociology of knowledge lies somewhere in a fashion hitherto not clearly understood, between irrelevance to the establishment of truth on the one hand, and entire adequacy for determining truth on the other.'[8] (4) This last claim must not lead one to believe that the sociologist of knowledge is concerned just with the ascertainability of the truth of beliefs, while perhaps allowing that the 'truth in itself' is absolute. In Mannheim's words: 'we must reject the notion that there is a "sphere of truth in itself" as a disruptive and unjustified hypothesis.'[9] 'It is necessary,' he continues in another context, 'to raise the question time and again whether we can imagine the concepts of knowing without taking account of the whole complex of traits by which man is characterized, and how, without these presuppositions, we can even think of the concept of knowing, to say nothing of actually engaging in the act of knowing.'[10] (5) The sociologist of knowledge asserts that some social perspectives are cognitively better than others. 'As in the case of visual perspectives,' states Mannheim, 'where certain positions have the advantage of revealing the decisive features of the object, so here pre-eminence is given to that perspective which gives evidence of the greatest comprehensiveness and the greatest fruitfulness in dealing with empirical material.'[11]

Far from expressing the simple thesis of relationalism which Mannheim claims to be propounding, this hodge-podge of tenets seems to be indicative both of a potentially vicious relativism—since self-indicating—as well as of a definite encroachment upon a discipline not indigenous to sociology of knowledge proper, viz., epistemology. 'Relationalism,' Mannheim has informed his readers, 'states that every assertion can only be relationally formulated'—a thesis which seems hardly more than a truism. Since he expressly denies that he is fostering relativism by asserting that his conceptions entail a relationalism, one's curiosity is justifiably aroused in attempting to determine just how he manages to subsume the above tenets under this apparently trivial postulate. Furthermore, at the outset it can not be stressed too strongly that Mannheim's writings are beset with ambiguities as well as confusions, and attempts have been made by various writers to bring some type of order into the veritable chaos of his terminology. One of the best recent attempts is that of Professor R. K. Merton,[12] who has made an excellent case for the re-identification of Mannheim's position with that of Rickert and Max Weber, from which he had presumably departed. This re-identification accomplishes in an indirect and tacit way part of what I am attempting to do in the most direct and explicit manner possible. Since Rickert and Weber stress chiefly the substantive (and properly the sole) component of *Wissenssoziologie*, an identification with their position would entail an elimination of most, if not all, epistemological problems allegedly relevant to sociology of knowledge. This becomes abundantly clear when it is realized that this pair of sociologists tend to claim that although values are relevant to the formulation of scientific problems and to the choice of materials, they are quite irrelevant to the validity of the findings of the scientist. They do not deny the importance of the socio-historical perspective in so far as it determines what will be studied as well as the manner in which it will be investigated, but they are emphatic in denying that the perspective undermines the validity of any knowledge whatsoever.

While fully appreciative of Merton's brilliant analysis and cogent case for such an identification, I can not help feeling that his solution somewhat oversimplifies the actual state of Mannheim's thought. The Mannheimian tenets outlined above seem all-too-strong to be so gratuitously glossed over, especially since, taken as a whole, they lack the consistency of the Rickert-Weber position, let alone the question as to actual concurrence. Furthermore, and most important, I feel that Merton and most critics of Mannheim's epistemological phase of sociology of knowledge have completely neglected a most important analysis of his position—one which, I believe, affords us the correct solution to Mannheim's relativistic dilemma and general terminological confusion. Not only is it my contention that Mannheim is guilty of a general confusion regarding both the nature of truth and truth as it relates to knowledge, but also that to some extent other Continental sociologists of knowledge are suspect because of their similar philosophical background. In recapitulation, then, I am maintaining that either the function of the findings of the sociology of knowledge lies much closer to complete irrelevance to the establishment of truth than to entire adequacy for determining truth, or Mannheim, wittingly or no, is a victim of a confusion which is similar to that characterizing certain strains of pragmatist thought in America.

The answer and solution to the antinomy of vicious relativism and to the difficulties arising from lack of terminological precision lie in the recent clarifications elaborated upon by the scientific empiricists. It is under their leadership that there have been con-catenated the many separate contributions and findings of various men and groups concerning the study of language. Professor C. W. Morris, in his monograph, 'Foundations of the Theory of Signs,'[13] has compiled and reworked the results of three main groups, viz., the studies in social behavioristics, communication and semantics of the American pragmatists, the early contribution to formal logic of the Cambridge logicians, and the findings in logistics and linguistic study of the continental logisticians and epistemologists, particu-larly of the Vienna Circle. In his synthesis Morris distinguishes three dimensions of semiosis or the process in which something functions as a sign, viz., the syntactical, the semantical, and the pragmatical. With this modern philosophical school it is my firm belief that once subjected to this tridimensional analysis the dilemmas, confusions, and difficulties of Mannheim's 'epistemological sociology of know-ledge' immediately disappear. Consequently, to such analysis we now turn.

First, directing our attention toward the syntactical dimension of linguistic analysis, which deals with the relationships of signs to signs, or, more broadly, with the purely formal, structural features of a language—its logical syntax—one must distinguish the syntac-tical, metalinguistic predicate, 'analytic,' which with its correlative, 'contradictory,' can only be significantly predicated of logical sentences and mathematics. Simplification being appropriate to the non-formal treatment here, one may loosely assert that this concept of 'analyticality' can be completely characterized within a syntactical metalanguage, that is, a symbolism which refers only to the formal design or structure of the language and is not concerned with 'meanings' and 'truth' in their usual sense. Now in his concern with cutting the ground from under the 'prevailing idealistic epistemology,' which speaks of a realm or sphere of abstract truth, Mannheim tells us that 'there is no necessity to regard knowledge as though it were an intrusion from the sphere of actual happenings into a sphere of "truth in itself." '[14] Again, he speaks of the 'sphere of truth as such' or 'a sphere of truth which is valid in itself' as an offshoot of the doctrine of ideas.[15] Time and again he gives as the prototype of this so-called 'static theory of knowledge' the example, '$2 \times 2 = 4$.'

Although I believe that such normative remarks are not properly uttered by a sociologist of knowledge, and while I think that they are irrelevant to and far afield from his thesis of relationalism, two clarifications might be made in this regard. First, as many contemporary writers have sufficiently indicated, the so-called 'Problem of Abstract Truth', arising from the reification of contracted symbols, is a bogus problem, and only crops up when epistemologists make the quite unnecessary assumption of a universal truth because true propositions are every one of them true.[16] However, in spite of perennial confusion in this matter, it is worth while pointing out that even though I be a thorough-going Platonist, still I can hold to the relationalist's thesis that every assertion can only be relationally formulated, and with the best of relativists I can maintain without inconsistency with my position that my own socio-historical perspective will determine to a large extent just what assertions *I hold to be true*. Secondly, with the above mention of analyticality, which should be properly distinguished—and shall be presently—from semantical truth, the nature of mathematical and logical knowledge becomes clear, and Mannheim's confusions concerning the 'static prototype of knowledge,' exemplified by abstract, mathematical truths, are clarified. Mathematics is certain, or, if you like, 'static' knowledge because of its analytical or tautological character, not because of any reference to and actual correspondence with extra-mathematical states of affairs. Far from belonging to 'the realm of truth in itself,' Mannheim's example, '$2 \times 2 = 4$,' is but one of a vast number of tautologies, and is certain knowledge just because it has no referential aspect whatsoever.[17]

Turning to the semantical dimension of semiotic which is concerned with the relationship of signs to their referents, or, more broadly, to the referential or designative phase of all languages, we must distinguish the semantical, metalinguistic predicate, 'true,' which with its correlative, 'false,' can be defined only within the semantical metalanguage. In a non-technical sense these predicates reflect a correspondence between the descriptive sentences and the facts to which they refer.[18] Certain confusions disappear when it is realized that we never have complete verification in the scientific and usual sense of the word. To completely verify in these two senses, which differ only in degree, even the simplest statements would require an infinite number of tests, which we as human beings with finite powers in finite lifetimes, could not possibly consummate. Through sheer pragmatic limitation we could never effect a complete verification of this sort, and hence we must be satisfied with a vicarious process of gradually increasing confirmation. That such a process, involving in science successive approximations, proves adequate to the task and, moreover, is psychologically satisfying in everyday judgments should be self-evident, but this is far from saying that this clarification has always been recognized as platitudinous.[19]

The realization of this latter fact may help to clarify seemingly contradictory results in scientific progress. To the layman a possible source of confusion is always open with regard to such problems as the relationship of truth to hypotheses, to successive approximations, and the like. It is not at all absurd to imagine that a sociologist of knowledge, improperly delving into epistemology, might easily share in some of these confusions. Thus for one who uses the example of the 'destruction' of classical by contemporary physics as an indication of the purely relative character of all scientific truth and knowledge as well as an example of its socio-historical determination, one has but to point out, as one present-day author does, that 'It is incorrect to think that the theory of relativity and the quantum theory have destroyed classical physics. Classical theory has to be assumed to be a first approximation in order to define the experimental conditions under which relativity holds to a higher approximation.'[20] The 'problem' vanishes if one reads in Einstein's first paper on the special theory of relativity the statement, 'Let us have given a system of coordinates, in which the equations of Newtonian mechanics hold to the first approximation.'[21] Thus, far from proving the purely relative character of all scientific knowledge and truth and its perspectival determination, this instance of successive approximation, viz., that classical dynamics is a limiting case of relativistic dynamics, proves to be an excellent illustration of what might roughly be referred to as two independent indications of a correspondence with a factual state of affairs. It can not be overemphasized that the merely provisional character of all scientific theories—in the strict sense of the term 'theory' as it refers, for instance, to atomic conceptions—as well as the merely inductive character of all empirical laws must not be mistaken for a substantiation of a pragmatist theory of truth. In the main, the terminology within epistemological discussions refers to the two just mentioned features as the pragmatic aspects of all empirical knowledge, but to base upon them a pragmatic theory of truth is the exclusive privilege of the more superannuated forms of pragmatism.

No one will deny that *what is held to be* true and *what is considered to be* the knowledge of such and such a period are in part a function of the social and historical perspective, but this is a far cry from what Mannheim seems to be at times asserting—that the semantical truth of the knowledge of the day is determined by perspective or context. Surely successive approximations are not mere arbitrary techniques for juggling equations nor purely volitional decisions to manipulate experimental findings in such and such odd ways; they are rather successive approximations to determinate states of affairs, and sentences about approximations are, loosely speaking, true in so far as there is an actual correspondence between the sentence and its referents.

Completing the tridimensional linguistic analysis, we turn to the pragmatic dimension or aspect, which deals with language 'as a type of communicative activity, social in origin and nature, by which members of a social group are able to meet more satisfactorily their individual and common needs.'[22] More strictly, pragmatics is that level of language study which is concerned with the relationships of signs to their users, both intenders and interpreters.[23] Of the three dimensions of language analysis pragmatics—coupled with the inquiry concerning its interrelationships with and influence upon semantics and syntactics—is the sole legitimate discipline of *Wissenssoziologie*, and in so far as Mannheim claims, *qua* sociologist of knowledge, to be interested in either or both of the other two dimensions in themselves, just to that extent he is outrunning his function as sociologist of knowledge and has become an incompetent epistemologist. In the words of Morris:

> The psychoanalyst is interested in dreams for the light they throw upon the dreamer; the sociologist of knowledge is interested in the social conditions under which doctrines and systems of doctrine are current. In neither case is the interest in question whether the dreams or doctrines are true in the semantical sense of the term, i.e., whether there are situations which the dreams and the doctrines may be said to denote.[24]

However, it must be added that to correlate doctrines sociologically one has to know first which part or parts, if any, of such doctrines are actually cognitive in nature. Only after this has been done can the sociologist of knowledge determine whether the assertions with which he is concerned are either semantically true or false; and, most important, both of these tasks are necessarily prior to any of his other functions. As will be emphasized shortly, the almost inextricable union of the cognitive with the emotive in the typical ideology or Utopia makes for considerable difficulty and possible confusion in the consummation of this undertaking. Furthermore, the above contention of Morris does not lack corroboration from sociologists themselves. The promulgators of substantive *Wissenssoziologie* support an identical claim, as, for example, Scheler's many vigorous assertions 'that the sociology of knowledge has no jurisdiction over questions of the validity of ideas, that its sphere of competence is that of a science, not of an epistemology or philosophy.'[25]

The impact of this clarification is tremendous, and it seems a rather sad commentary in the history of recent ideas that such an elucidation should have been brought forth so late. Succinctly, the sociologist of knowledge is as regards truth properly concerned only with what is *believed in*, with what is *held or thought to be* semantically true. In very loose and inexact usage we might refer to his object of study as the 'correlate' in the pragmatical meta-language of semantical truth, but the drawing of such a parallel for the sake of symmetry is more likely to produce confusion than clarification. It should be, however, strongly emphasized that this study of 'truth'—in the sense of what is considered semantically true —in pragmatics by the sociologist of knowledge is in no way to be confused with the pragmatist's conception of truth. Schiller with his thesis that 'Truth is the useful, efficient, workable' and James with his doctrine that ' "The True," . . . is only the expedient in the way of our thinking' have been largely responsible for the usual notion of the pragmatist's doctrine of truth. The typical conception is epito-mized, for example, in the syllogism that since the belief that the earth is flat was useful, workable, and expedient for the limited explorations and observations of, say, the early Egyptians, therefore in point of fact the earth is flat, or, was 'flat for them.' This is not to say that Peirce and Dewey held to such a view concerning truth, or, for that matter, that James and Schiller reasoned quite so naively. Peirce is credited with having pointed out that an idea is not called true because it is satisfactory but is called the latter because it is true, and Dewey's conception of 'warranted assertability' is certainly an improvement upon earlier pragmatist notions of truth. However, despite their more sophisticated views both Dewey and Peirce— largely because of their emphasis upon context and inquiry—have tended to confuse the metalinguistic, semantical predicate, 'true,' with the actual process of verification.

That Mannheim in his latest work should have expressly admitted his agreement with many features of pragmatism is highly significant in understanding some of his confusions as sociologist of knowledge. It would certainly seem that his criterion for the cognitively best perspective, viz., that which 'gives evidence of greatest compre-hensiveness and greatest fruitfulness in dealing with empirical materials,' is subject to the same confused identification of semantical truth and empirical verification that is characteristic of certain portions of pragmatist thought. However, Mannheim's chief source of confusion comes from his very conception of the development of sociology of knowledge as a separate discipline, and a brief investi-gation of his notions in this regard is essential for complete under-standing of his confusion. His two key concepts, 'ideology' and 'Utopia,' play an all-important role in his conception of sociology of knowledge. On the one hand there is what he terms 'ideological thought,' which is considered distorted and untrue because of its perspectival determination. On the other hand what he calls 'Utopian thought'—in contrast with 'ideological'—is regarded as true rather than illusory since it in some sense 'transcends reality.' It is particularly with ideological thinking that Mannheim is concerned and he distinguishes both a 'particular' and 'total' conception of ideology. In contradistinction to the former, the latter conception entails an indictment of the entire system of thought of one's opponents as ideological, that is, as perspectivally distorted. Mannheim further distinguishes between the 'special' and the 'general' formulations of the concept of total ideology. It is the more comprehensive, general formulation which claims that 'the thought of all parties in all epochs is of an ideological character.'[26]

'With the emergence of the general formulation of the total conception of ideology,' Mannheim tell us, 'the simple theory of ideology develops into the sociology of knowledge. What was once the intellectual armament of a party is transformed into a method of research in social and intellectual history generally.'[27] It is in this statement and what it entails that the crux of Mannheim's confusion is to be discovered. If sociology of knowledge, as he claims, traces its heritage directly and immediately to the general theory of total ideology, then it is bound to be inextricably tinged with non-scientific, emotive elements. Moreover, this remains my thesis even with full cognizance of Mannheim's attempts at the elimination of certain extremely relativistic and propagandistic portions of early statements of sociology of knowledge.[28] Both the ideologist, panegyrist of the past, and the Utopian, harbinger of things to come, are primarily anti-intellectualistic. They are concerned with emotions, motivations, with the upholding or tearing down of standards, not with knowledge *qua* knowledge. Rather than a theory, both propound a rationale, a philosophy of life, an inseparable admixture of factionary bias and cognitive fact.

The denouement, the inevitable conclusion to be drawn, should be patent indeed. Despite Mannheim's rather feeble attempts at self-extrication from his dilemma of vicious relativism by introducing what Merton[29] has termed 'Dynamic Criteria of Validity' of historical judgments, 'Structural Warranties of Validity,' as well as the doctrine of 'Relationism' mentioned above, the upshot of this discussion is simply that the character of the object of his study has led him into serious confusions, the chief of which is the failure to distinguish between the scientific, the cognitive use, and the evocative, the motivational use, of language. This emotive usage is always present in the social context by virtue of the countless evaluations made explicitly and implicitly at every turn. The doctrines and systems of doctrines of both ideologist and Utopian, as has been sufficiently stressed above, fairly reek with evincive jargon, which, far from

239

having any semantical truth-value, usually have no cognitive meaning whatsoever. Party-lines of all factions have chiefly an evocative function, expressing emotions, attitudes, convictions, beliefs, intentions, for the general purpose of producing similar states in the prospective proselytes. Following Pareto's adumbration modern writers have sufficiently stressed the power of words, and no more than mention need be made of this psychological phenomenon here. Mannheim's confusion in trying to develop an epistemological sociology of knowledge lies precisely in his partial failure both to distinguish cognitive from non-cognitive aspects of 'knowledge' as well as to realize the vitiating influence of just this evaluative component in the 'knowledge' of any period. Attempts at piecemeal salvage of the semantically true from the untrue in the average doctrinal system is not only a thankless but also a hopeless task. At times it seems as if an all-or-none technique can alone possibly be employed, and it certainly is true that if one is seeking empirical knowledge, corresponding to semantical truth, one goes to the scientist, not to the ideologist or the Utopian.

Stripped of the duties of epistemologist which never properly belonged to him at all, the sociologist of knowledge still has a large and important role. As outlined above, *qua* behavior scientist, he will state the conditions under which his subjects entertain 'beliefs,' as well as indicate what they accept as verification for these 'beliefs.' He will report from his research that many such 'convictions' are entertained for numerous strictly meaningless theses, doctrines, and ideologies. Rather than semantical truth his discipline encompasses within its domain *what is held to be* semantically true. This latter object of study we loosely termed a 'correlate' in the pragmatical metalanguage of the semantical, metalinguistic predicate 'true.' Likewise, the sociologist of knowledge may be granted an additional function of making certain hypothetical studies concerning ideologies and conceptions of truth. Without taking sides or making normative judgments, he may, for example, be able to point out that a certain perspective A will be cognitively more adequate if a pragmatist conception of truth is current, whereas perspective B will be cognitively more efficacious if a correspondence theory of truth is held. This, of course, does not mean that he is properly epistemologist. Such a task is purely hypothetical and in contrast with some of Mannheim's procedures, the substantive sociologist of knowledge would be as disinterestedly scientific as any physicist engaged in thermodynamical research.

Furthermore, it is the sociologist of knowledge who emphasizes the complexity of the social as contrasted with the scientific situation. Not only are such factors as inadequate perception or incorrect knowledge of oneself abundantly present but also inability and unwillingness under some circumstances to report perceptions and ideas honestly are certainly ubiquitous as social phenomena.[30] With the recognition of the complexity of the life-situation there comes a poignant realization of the importance of the pragmatic aspect of linguistic give-and-take in the social milieu. As Louis Wirth puts it:

> In the realm of the social, particularly, truth is not merely a matter of a simple correspondence between thought and existence, but is tinged with the investigator's interest in his subject matter, his standpoint, his evaluations, in short, the definition of his object of attention.[31]

Thus, lastly, rather than becoming himself a victim of the pitfalls of emotive language, it is the function of the sociologist of knowledge to indicate in no uncertain terms just where and when any particular assertion or system of assertions is largely evocative in character. Here he is in his element, indicating rationales, showing the existential determination of many doctrines which have been and may be current, and emphasizing the quantities of 'non-cognitive knowledge' turned out by rightists, centrists, and leftists alike.

The threat, both actual and alleged, of epistemological relativism has proved a serious stumbling block particularly in modern social thought. Tracing the important recent attempts at confronting this difficulty, the historian of ideas would stress chiefly two movements; Continental social thought and Continental empiricist philosophy. During the past hundred years sociological thinking on the Continent has been distinguished, on the one hand, by considerable sophistication and understanding as well as keen comprehension of the vast number of functional interconnections of the social with other realms. On the other hand, these Continental social thinkers have been hamstrung by their metaphysical heritage, particularly by their grounding in Kantian thought, idealism, and phenomenology. One might almost say that this group is especially apt in becoming immersed in the hot water of relativism just because of the alleged or imagined conflict between their epistemological background and their social insights.

In contrast with this group Continental empiricists have up until very recently suffered from a relative lack of interest and sophistication in the social sciences, a trend which paradoxically enough can also be attributed to Kant.[32] It is true, though, that these Continental groups such as the Vienna Circle, the students of Poincaré, and the Polish logicians, have together with the students of Bertrand Russell performed logical and epistemological analyses with unprecedented precision. Their interest in language which grew out of this work has been further reinforced by their recent contacts with the social behaviorism of men like Pierce and Mead in this country. Out of this co-operation evolved the crucial distinction between the three dimensions of language. And here the empiricist strain of thought seems finally to have provided us with the tool to solve the problems of historical and social relativism to which the thinker of the idealist tradition knew no answer. The purpose of this paper has been merely to show how the results of the two different trends supplement each other. Modest as this task is itself, the phenomenon in question—the emerging integration of the new science and the new philosophy—is of deepest significance.

Notes

1 I should like to acknowledge my debt to the entire staff of the philosophy department at the State University of Iowa for their encouragement and help throughout the development of this paper.
2 Thelma Z. Lavine, 'Sociological Analysis of Cognitive Norms', *Journal of Philosophy*, vol. 39 (June, 1942), pp. 342–56.
3 H. Becker and H. Dahlke, 'Max Scheler's Sociology of Knowledge', *Philosophy and Phenomenological Research*, vol. 2 (1942), p. 310.
4 Mannheim, *Ideology and Utopia*, New York: Harcourt, Brace, 1936, p. 239; cf. also Merton, 'Karl Mannheim and the Sociology of Knowledge', *Journal of Liberal Religion*, vol. 2 (1941), pp. 130–1.
5 Merton, *op. cit.*, p. 131.
6 In his 'Knowledge as Knowledge and as Social Fact', a paper delivered at the meeting of the Western Division of the American Philosophical Association, Madison, Wisconsin, on 24 April 1942.
7 Merton, *op. cit.*, p. 134.
8 Mannheim, *op. cit.*, p. 256.
9 *Ibid.*, p. 274.
10 *Ibid.*, p. 267.
11 *Ibid.*, p. 271.
12 Cf. *op. cit.*
13 *International Encyclopedia of Unified Science*, vol. 1, no. 2.
14 *Op. cit.*, pp. 267–8.
15 *Ibid.*
16 Cf. C. K. Ogden and I. A. Richards, *The Meaning of Meaning* (4th ed.), New York: Harcourt, Brace, 1936, p. 95.
17 It seems to me that Mannheim becomes most unclear in his discussions of relativism, relationism, 'static theories of knowledge', 'truth in itself', and related topics. A case in point is his claim that relationism becomes relativism 'only when it is linked with the older static ideal of eternal, unperspectivistic truths independent of the subjective experience of the observer, and when it is judged by this alien ideal of absolute truth' (*op. cit.*, p. 270). As will become more and more obvious in the development of my thesis, such a statement either requires clarification or must be considered as exemplifying a rather strong tendency towards a position similar to that of certain types of American pragmatism.

A like judgment must be made with regard to his claim that 'formal knowledge' is unaffected by the social or historical context (*op. cit.*, pp. 150, 263), but since he leaves the term, 'formal knowledge', undefined, we are at a loss to know just what he means. In any event, I find him involved in the following dilemma: either he does not mean 'formal knowledge' in the same sense as I have used 'analytic knowledge' above, and hence his writings are fully as confused in this regard as I have made them out to be, *or* he does mean to identify his term with the category of tautologous knowledge. However, if the latter is the case, then considerable criticism is in order for his having fallen into needless confusions as exemplified by his unwarranted concern over 'abstract truth' and 'static theories of knowledge'. Another indication of his rather muddled thinking in this regard is, as Merton points out, his gratuitous imputation of a doctrine of 'absolute truth' to those who reject any extreme relativism. (Cf. Merton, *op. cit.*, p. 143.)

18 That 'true' and 'false' have been proved by the Polish logicians to be semantical rather than syntactical predicates not only reflects the essential invalidity of the coherence theory of truth but also presents the sole formally correct argument for the adoption of the correspondence theory, Russell's recently attempted analysis to the contrary.

It might also be pointed out that this proof can be considered as a 'projection' of realism, that is, as a feature within linguistic analysis which substantiates 'realistic tenets', though one must not lose sight of the fact that there can be no verifiable hypothesis of realism. On the other hand, if the formal isomorphs of 'true' and 'false' could be consistently defined in a syntactical metalanguage, this would come as near as possible to the formal projection of the so-called coherence theory of truth which is so characteristic of idealism.

19 It should be remarked that I have intentionally neglected any mention of the problem of basic sentences, a problem which is crucial in any technical epistemological discussion. Although it is true that consideration of this problem has repeatedly led to serious confusions, particularly with regard to perception and related questions, such epistemological refinements are quite irrelevant to the issue at hand.

20 V. Lenzen, 'Procedures of Empirical Science', *International Encyclopedia of Unified Science*, vol. 1, no. 5, p. 42.

21 Quoted from Lenzen, *op. cit.*, p. 42.

22 Morris, *op. cit.*, p. 10.

23 Though the distinction has no particular bearing upon the context in question, it might be well to mention in passing that Carnap has considered pragmatics in a broader sense. Accepting almost *in toto* Morris's analysis and terminology, Carnap and others have conceived of the pragmatical metalanguage as encompassing in its scope all of science as well as many of the traditional philosophical problems, in addition to the discipline outlined by Morris. That verification, in its usual sense, is included within the domain of pragmatics is perhaps the clearest indication that it is entirely divorced from the semantical predicate 'true'. Confusions concerning an identification of empirical verification with semantical truth will be considered presently.

24 *Op. cit.*, pp. 38–9.

25 Becker and Dahlke, *op. cit.*, p. 322. Cf. also the similar contention of *ten* representative critics of the sociology of knowledge that 'the sociological analysis of the elements of cognition be restrained from extension to . . . "validity" ' (Lavine, *op. cit.*, p. 342). In addition to the critics mentioned in the text of the present paper, Lavine makes reference to Alexander von Schelting, Maurice Mandelbaum, A. O. Lovejoy, C. I. Lewis, Gerard DeGré, Hans Speier, Talcott Parsons, and George H. Sabine. (Cf. *ibid.*)
26 Merton, *op. cit.*, p. 141.
27 *Ibid.*, p. 69.
28 Cf. *ibid.*, p. 130.
29 *Ibid.*, p. 141.
30 Louis Wirth, preface to Mannheim's *Ideology and Utopia*, p. xx.
31 *Ibid.*
32 Kant's epistemology was considered by himself primarily as an understructure of the physical sciences. It is fair to say, therefore, that the prevailing interest in mathematics and the physical sciences, which characterizes the continental empiricist tradition during the nineteenth century, can also be traced back to the influence of Kant.

16   Karl Mannheim and contemporary functionalism

Thelma Z. Lavine

In the growing self-consciousness of sociology as theory and method functionalism has emerged as perhaps the dominant interpretive approach among present-day American sociologists. It was inevitable, therefore, that the roots of the functionalist viewpoint be sought out and the effort made to determine the extent to which influential sociological theorists and social philosophers of earlier stages of sociological thinking may have been functionalists.[1] It is thus not surprising to find Mannheim revealed as a functionalist, e.g., by Werner Stark in his *The Sociology of Knowledge*,[2] who holds that 'the functionalist viewpoint is almost ubiquitous in his writings,'[3] or to find Ernest Manheim, in his introduction to Mannheim's *Essays on the Sociology of Culture*, being mindful to comment upon 'two terms which are basic to his point of view (for interpreting motives), namely *structure* and *function*.'[4]

Contemporary functionalism within the social sciences is the confluence of two distinct streams of nineteenth-century thought: (1) the organismic biological concept of organism, significantly characterized by the subservience of each of its parts to the maintenance of the whole and by their harmonious interdependence; utilized in divergent ways in the positivistic systems of Comte and Spencer for their conceptualization of society and its part-whole relationships; (2) the romanticist and historicist concept of the unity and uniqueness of the spirit, as manifested in a *Volk* or in world history, characterized by the vital functioning of each of its elements (e.g., custom, language, religion, law) in the total organic configuration and by their dialectical interdependence; utilized in divergent ways by Hegel and Marx for the conceptualization of the dialectic of metaphysical and historical reality, social groups and their historical development and relationships, and the range of mental productions. The failure of recent expositions of the development of the functionalist viewpoint[5] to recognize its romanticist and historicist sources impedes their understanding of those American as well as European contributors who are in some significant degree under these 'idealistic' influences.[6] In this latter category Karl Mannheim clearly belongs.

The present discussion will attempt (1) to examine the various meanings and usages of two key words in the language of functionalism, *structure* and *function*, as they appear in the writings of Mannheim; (2) to relate these meanings and usages in part to the dominance in Mannheim's thinking of a spiritual (*Geistige*) rather than a biological model of organic unity.

'Structure' and some related words[7]

As early as 1922, in his doctoral dissertation,[8] the word *structure* has assumed importance for Mannheim:

> To state our main contention right away: in our view primacy among logical forms belongs to systematization. The simpler forms can be understood, in our opinion, only in terms of this 'highest', 'all-embracing form'.[9]
>
> There can in fact be no mistaking that the trend which is becoming predominant today, at least in the cultural sciences, runs counter to the precept once given by Descartes to proceed, as it were, in atomizing fashion and explain more complex structures in terms of simple ones; the present trend is, on the contrary, to explain simpler structures in terms of more complex ones.[10]

The word 'structure' as he uses it here is still 'philosophical' in connotation and context, but the principle he advances of explanation of phenomena by reference to larger structures or systems and his attack upon 'atomism' and the Cartesian deductive mode of explanation are characteristic of the historicist and romanticist[11] forms of organismic thinking, which are never absent from his subsequent writing.

In the essay 'On the Interpretation of *Weltanschauung*'[12] his point is that, with regard to 'cultural products' such as works of art or religious systems, 'we can only understand the parts from the whole' which is the 'global outlook' (*Weltanschauung*) of each historical period. In the essay 'Historicism'[13] it is history itself which begins to be emphasized as the 'all-embracing' structure: 'The absolute itself is unfolding in a genetic process ... in categories which are molded by the unfolding of the material contact of the genetic flux itself.'[14] 'The historicist standpoint,' he argues soon after, '... eventually achieves an absoluteness of view, because in its final form it posits history itself as the Absolute; this alone makes it possible that the various standpoints, which at first appear to be anarchic, can be ordered as component parts of a meaningful overall process.'[15]

It is perhaps true to say that the historic process itself, as seen by historicism, is for Mannheim the paradigmatic case of 'structure': it is the ultimate 'all-embracing' reality to which any entity whatever must be referred for explanation; it is never static, but a process marked by ceaseless dialectical opposition; yet these conflicts are rendered meaningfully interdependent and harmonious in time; finally, the span of history, permitting of every type of social and cultural development in a vast, dynamic equilibrium, is the final arbiter of truth.[16]

By the time of *Ideology and Utopia*[17] Mannheim has 'transcended' this view of history by the aid of Marxist categories. He sees that he has been in the grip of 'Hegel and the Historical school' who have, however, offered the 'decisive, new element' that 'this unity [of the world] *is in process of continual historical transformation and tends to a constant restoration of its equilibrium on still higher levels.*'[18]

The sociological viewpoint that emerges clearly with *Ideology and Utopia* is ubiquitously expressed by Mannheim in explicit structural terms, as well as by implicit usage. The process of structural differentiation by which Hegel separated the concrete historical structure *Volksgeist* out of the abstract 'consciousness' or 'mind' of the Enlightenment, and by which in turn Marx differentiated 'superstructure' and 'substructure' out of the idealist unity of *Volksgeist*, must now continue with the further historico-social differentiation of 'substructure' and 'superstructure':

> By these [social] groups we mean not merely classes, as a dogmatic type of Marxism would have it, but also generations, status groups, sects, occupational groups, schools, etc. Unless careful attention is paid to highly differentiated social groupings of this sort and to the corresponding differentiations in concepts, categories, and thought-models, i.e., unless the problem of the relation between super- and sub-structure is refined, it would be impossible to demonstrate that corresponding to the wealth of types of knowledge and perspectives which have appeared in the course of history there are similar differentiations in the substructure of society.[19]

The central problems of Mannheim's sociology of knowledge revolve about the nature of the relationship between historically located 'structures' and mental 'structures.' An 'objective description of the structural differences in minds operating in different social settings'[20] is the task of the 'total conception of ideology.' The word 'ideology' belongs, of course, in the genus 'thoughtstructure.' The various meanings of 'ideology' and of the term 'Utopia' which is differentiated from it (subsequent to the dedifferentiation of Marx's ideology and class-consciousness into ideology) result from alternative methodological and substantive considerations regarding the relations between social structures and mental structures.[21]

Explanation within the sociology of knowledge remains, however, unwaveringly *structural*: by reference of a mental structure to a concrete social structure; or to a more comprehensive mental structure (e.g., a *'Weltanschauung'*); or to a more comprehensive social structure (ultimately to 'the social structure as a whole, i.e., the web of interacting social forces from which have arisen the various modes of observing and thinking');[22] or to an 'interdependent configuration' of 'social existence' and 'thought' in which 'the whole life of an historical-social group presents itself.'[23] All of these modes of structural explanation, it should be noted, are *historical* explanations; Mannheim frequently uses the hyphenated form 'historical-social' or 'social and historical' to characterize structure; where he uses only one of these, he ordinarily intends also the other; where he uses only 'structure' he ordinarily intends both (in *Ideology and Utopia*).

The problems of politics underlie all the major conceptualizations offered by the essays included in *Ideology and Utopia*. Given the conflicting perspectives of the various political parties, Mannheim asks what are 'the prospects of scientific politics,' i.e., is valid political knowledge possible? Mannheim offers two answers to this problem, both of which invoke the Hegelian view that the criterion of validity is synthetic comprehensiveness. The first hope of scientific politics is the 'fusion,' the 'dynamic reconciliation,' of the divergent political viewpoints into a comprehensive synthesis; this is the task of the sociology of knowledge. The alternative to this is the tendency towards the fusing of viewpoints which is latent within certain social conditions, processes, and groups: e.g., the socio-historic 'matrix' itself, political parties, the intelligentsia, education, group amalgamation.[24]

The word 'structure' appears infrequently in this context. It is implied, however, throughout. Clearly, for Mannheim synthesis of viewpoints is the ultimate in structural explanation; it is, in a given context at a specific time, the ideal 'all-embracing structure' in which the limitations and antagonisms of each partial structure are, for the time at least, transcended. It may be noted of Mannheim that in each of the areas of inquiry into which he ventures, synthesis of the prevailing interpretive structures is the norm by which his own contribution is guided.[25]

Already in *Ideology and Utopia* stirrings towards a more analytic conceptual apparatus are noticeable. The essay 'Towards the Sociology of Mind; An Introduction,'[26] written originally only two or three years after the publication of *Ideology and Utopia*, sternly advises that 'the patient assembly and critical use of data must supplement and check the play of intuition . . . Facts must be established and verified and factors isolated before the attempt can be made to fit them into a hypothetical pattern.' This 'Cartesian' method of procedure from the simple to the complex, repudiated at the height of his historicist commitment, is reflected also in his sketch of a general sociology which 'proceeds typically from elementary to complex phenomena.' This essay also contains a stern atomistic reminder that 'ultimate reality . . . attaches only to the individual.'[27]

What, then, has become of 'structure'? If we abandon, he says, 'the misconception of structure as a principle which inexorably unfolds itself,' we may 'still retain the structured meaning of historical change.'[28]

But these familiar words are now appearing on a new level of analysis which is indicated as soon as Mannheim raises the methodological question 'whether the structural interpretation of change leaves room for causal inquiries.'[29] His treatment of this problem entails the use of the following terms: 'system,' 'function,' 'functional scheme,' 'structurally relevant and irrelevant actions and motivations,' 'equilibrium,' 'functional relevance,' 'functional system,' 'functional meanings,' 'functionally necessary causes,' 'necessary role.'[30] Mannheim's systematic efforts have drawn him into the linguistic context of Anglo-American 'functionalism.'[31]

Mannheim does not speak of *functional* approach or mode of analysis, but synonymously of a 'structural account,' 'structural interest,' 'structural view,' 'structural interpretation,' 'structural perspective,' 'expository explanation,' 'interpretative approach,'

'interpretive method.'[32] Using this structural type approach we *interpret* the . . . occurrence if we detect its function in the equilibrium of the whole system in which it takes place. The conception of the system as an equilibrium is merely a heuristic device and is equally applicable to changing as well as to static structures. *The function of an event is its necessary role in a system, or, more specifically, it is the particular manner in which the heuristically assumed equilibrium of the system is conditioned by that event.*[33]

A structural interpretation of social change in terms of function is sharply distinguished from a 'causal' explanation. In a causal explanation 'we seek to *construe* an event through as many of its determinants as we are able to isolate. The final construct is largely an approximation of the actual event, and when the approximation is close enough for a given purpose we say the event is explained.'[34] Motivated action is one type of causative agency. However, such causes cannot throw light on a 'system' which has a 'functional scheme.' Mannheim offers the example of the capitalistic system 'of interlocking operations, such as production, distribution, the price mechanism, the credit system, the competitive stimulation of demand, the recruitment of the labor force, and so forth.'[35] He points out that were we to know 'the sum total of causal motivations' involved in modern capitalism, it would not 'explain the complete structure.' Only the structural interpretation can do that. Moreover, not all of this sum of motivated action is structurally relevant, i.e., 'necessary for the functioning of the capitalistic system.' It is the capitalistic system itself (which 'is functioning as if it had a blueprint') which 'not only outlines functions and roles which must be performed, but . . . also allocates motivations for the needed performances. Thus, to the investor on the commodity market local price differences present an opportunity for profit but at the same time he performs an economic function by equalizing the price level of grain.'[36]

In thus making what is now called, following Merton, the distinction between manifest and latent functions, and also in calling attention to 'structural inconsistencies (which) may resolve themselves in a system of wider scope'[37] Mannheim is, of course, drawing upon Hegel and the famous 'Cunning of Reason' concept. Mannheim confines himself in the present context to the knowing remark that 'this [the fact of structural inconsistencies] raises a problem of which Hegel had a keen appreciation.' In his earlier 'sociology of knowledge' stage, he had characterized this Hegelian concept as 'a doctrine of the "ruse of the Idea" according to which the subjective beliefs of men are mere tools to help real developments along.'[38]

The answer, then, to the question precipitating these analytic considerations concerning structure and function (namely, 'whether the structural interpretation of change leaves room for causal inquiries') is the succinct statement that 'social structure is the order in which causal sequences recurrently operate within a social system.'[39]

Mannheim sums up his argument by pointing out the complementarity of the 'causal' and the 'interpretive approach,' since it 'is clear that given structures require particular causal agents for their existence and that a structural change cannot take place without a corresponding shift in the necessary motivations.' Nevertheless, 'the structural interest focuses on the patterns which operate in a functional system. The latter is the aim of sociology . . .'[40]

The structural interests of sociology are more fully treated in the conference paper (presented in London in 1936), 'The Place of Sociology.'[41] Structural sociology has the task, he says here, 'of building up a simplified sketch of the circulation of events (*Kreislauf*) in different societies (in feudalism, capitalism, etc.).' He divides

250

structural sociology into statics and dynamics, the theory of statics being concerned with 'the problem of the equilibrium of all the social factors'; dynamics is concerned with 'those factors which are antagonistic in their respective tendencies . . . those principles which in the long run tend to a disequilibrium and thus bring out changes which transform the social structure.'[42]

What was to have been a comprehensive treatment of systematic sociology was left after Mannheim's death in the form of two sets of lecture manuscripts,[43] in one of which a lecture on 'Causality, Function and Structure Dialectics' had been planned, but not given. In it 'he intended to show that social structures correspond to the network of interaction of single causes.'[44] The little book containing these lectures is necessarily programmatic and somewhat disconnected. It represents a valiant but unsuccessful struggle to attain for sociology a vast methodological synthesis, a structure which would embrace the philosophical, speculative methods of German sociology and the empirical methods of American sociology; a 'generalizing' as well as an historically 'individualizing' method; the methods of Freudian and of behavioristic psychology, and the synthesis of both of these with the methods of sociology.

Further discussion of 'function'

Whereas Mannheim is singularly consistent in the meaning and use of 'structure,' with regard to 'function' he shows considerable ambivalence.

The word 'functional' pertaining to a method or a type of viewpoint is with few exceptions used by Mannheim in a pejorative sense. 'Functionalistic' is frequently coupled with 'mechanistic,' or 'atomistic' to denote a type of theory which reduces mind or society to discrete elements or to causal mechanisms. This type of theory 'fails, however . . . because it says nothing concerning the meaningful goal of conduct' or it may 'formally posit a purely technical, psychical, or social optimum condition, as, for example, the most "frictionless functioning." '[45] Sometimes the 'functionalistic' standpoint is contrasted with the 'romanticist,' or the 'morphological' or the 'organismic,' which are non-reductive and seek to preserve the older 'organic' ways of thinking against the 'technical' spirit: '. . . in the cultural sciences one must go beyond causal and functional analysis and combine it with a morphological approach.'[46] A similar usage is the distinction between 'functional rationality' and 'substantial rationality.' An act is substantially rational insofar as it 'reveals intelligent insight into the inter-relations of events in a given situation.' A functionally rational series of actions exhibits '(a) Functional organization with reference to a definite goal; and

THELMA Z. LAVINE

(b) a consequent calculability when viewed from the standpoint of
an observer or a third person seeking to adjust himself to it.' The
actor, in this case, need not have 'any idea as to the ultimate end of
his actions or the functional role of each individual act within the
framework of the whole.'[47] The deeply rooted antagonism of the
historicist orientation toward the term 'function' as part of the
vocabulary of natural-science 'technicians' suggests why Mannheim
does not use 'functional method' or 'functional analysis' to refer to
his own formalization of 'structure' and 'function.'

The word 'function' is used with considerable frequency especially
in Mannheim's 'sociology of knowledge' writings in a sense close to
the mathematical meaning of 'function,' i.e., as a variable dependent
for its value upon the value of one or more other variables. Mannheim's effort is, of course, to call attention by this formulation to the
fact that sociology of knowledge sees thought in a new light, i.e., as
dependent upon values assignable to existence, rather than in its
traditionally assumed independence of existence. Perhaps the most
familiar instance of this usage is near the beginning of the essay
'Ideology and Utopia': 'Both these conceptions of ideology [the
particular and the total] make these so-called "ideas" a *function of*
him who holds them, and of his position in his social milieu . . . These
are the two ways of analyzing statements as *functions of* their social
background.'[48] In 'The Problem of a Sociology of Knowledge' he
argues 'Once we have familiarized ourselves with the conception that
the ideologies of our opponents are, after all, just the *function of* their
position in the world, we cannot refrain from concluding that our
own ideas, too, are *functions of* a social position.'[49] This type of
viewpoint and its implementing methods he sometimes characterizes
as 'genetic' or as an 'investigation of the social determination of
knowledge' or as one which regards 'thought' as a 'product of' social
or 'existential conditions.'[50]

Does Mannheim explicitly or implicitly refer to thought as a
'function of' *need?* The word 'need' is rarely used by Mannheim,
explicitly or implicitly. Since he is operating with the Hegelian,
historicist conception of organic unity, rather than with a biologistic
conception,[51] the concept of biological need is irrelevant to his
thinking. Does the Marxist component in his historicist orientation
lead him to see a thought as a 'function of' *interest?* Although
Mannheim never makes a biological 'slip,' he does sometimes make
a Marxist one. However, he takes an explicit and firm stand against
'the method of "vulgar" Marxism [which] consists in *directly*
associating even the most esoteric and spiritual products of the mind
with the economic and power interests of a certain class . . . We
cannot relate an intellectual standpoint directly to a social class,'[52]
but only to its ' "intellectual motivation," which is expressed in its

252

commitment' to a *Weltanschauung* which in its 'style of thought' corresponds to the dominant interests of the group.

The meaning of 'function' as used in the 'structural approach' discussed above, as 'the necessary role of an event in a system' or 'the particular manner in which the heuristically assumed equilibrium of the system is conditioned by that event' is rarely explicit in Mannheim's writings apart from the few brief efforts at formal analysis indicated. Function in this sense of 'consequences for a system' is characteristically expressed by him in 'structural' terms, partly as a result of the depreciatory associations with a 'functional' viewpoint, partly because of the explanatory significance for him of 'structure.'[53] Implicit usage of function in this sense occurs often in the 'sociology of knowledge' writings in reference to variously designated thought-structures and their manifest and latent functions. Thus by 'Utopia' he means 'all situationally transcendent ideas ... which in any way have a transforming effect upon the existing historico-social order.'[54] Each Utopia has also, however, 'helped to mold the epoch in which it emerged.'[55] It may finally, be noted in *Man and Society in an Age of Reconstruction* the functionalist conception of planning is expressed almost exclusively in terms of 'interdependence,' 'system,' 'structure' and 'equilibrium.'

Does Mannheim make use of the concept of 'survivals' in the social Darwinist sense, or does he apply to thought-structures the analogue of the early view of functionalism in anthropology, that 'every custom ... fulfils some vital function?' If, on Mannheim's view, thought-structures are 'functions' of 'social structures,' then change in (the value of the variable) social structure, requires change in (the value of the variable) thought-structure. In the activist political context of *Ideology and Utopia* Mannheim frequently refers to viewpoints retained after the social structure which conditioned them has ceased to exist as 'antiquated,' 'invalid,' 'inappropriate,' 'obfuscating.' In the language of biologistic organicism, this is equivalent to calling these viewpoints 'survivals.' Yet the consistent stand taken by Mannheim on this point is the Hegelian one, that whatever is 'genuine' in any viewpoint arrived at in the history of thought is in a sense eternal. Even with respect to positivism, which he cannot accept, he holds that 'every metaphysics that will emerge after the supremacy of positivism will have to incorporate and "sublimate" in some form these "genuine" elements of positivism.'[56] 'Romanticism,' he points out in a subtle analysis, 'may be interpreted as a gathering-up, a rescuing of all those attributes and ways of life of ultimately religious origin ... which were for ever inaccessible to Enlightenment.'[57] However, 'this was by no means the original aim of Romanticism.' Every viewpoint, in its genuine components, he seems to be saying, retains always the latent function of conserving for the consciousness of mankind a segment of the comprehensive totality of experience and truth.

Mannheim and contemporary functionalism

An attempt has been made in this paper to show that the sources of Mannheim's functionalism lie in historicism rather than in the biologistic organicism which is conventionally assumed as the source of the functionalist viewpoint. The differences made in Mannheim's thinking by his historicist-romanticist orientation include: (1) his freedom from most of the biologistic difficulties that have plagued functionalism, e.g., with regard to need, change, adaptation, structure-function symmetry; and on the other hand (2) his involvement with an intricate set of metaphysical commitments that have imposed difficulties of a different order upon his meanings and his linguistic usage at every turn. Nevertheless, from this significantly divergent orientation, Mannheim abstracted the same set of analytical elements as did the biologically oriented sociologists: structure, function, system, interdependence, equilibrium, disfunction, disequilibrium. These are the analytical elements characteristically employed by contemporary sociological functionalism as formulated by Talcott Parsons and Robert K. Merton.

There remains only to point out that formal analysis is for the historicist, synthesizing, activist mind of Mannheim always an unstable position, seeking resolution in concreteness and in evaluative insight. His distance from the formalistic neutralism of contemporary sociological functionalism may be measured by his treatment of *equilibrium*. Equilibrium was for Mannheim only fleetingly a formal concept. He sought an evaluative meaning of equilibrium for our society based upon the historical development of consciousness and the interdependent findings of the special sciences. From this synthesis came his diagnosis for our time.

Notes

1 For example, Marx, Veblen, and Freud were classified as functionalists by Robert Merton in his 'Manifest and Latent Functions', *Social Theory and Social Structure*, Chicago: Free Press, 1949; Durkheim, widely classified as an early functionalist, has been subjected to re-examination in a recent essay which concludes that 'it would be erroneous to regard Durkheim as a functionalist in any of the commonly accepted contemporary meanings of the term'. Albert Pierce, 'Durkheim and Functionalism', in Kurt Wolff (ed.), *Emile Durkheim 1858–1917*, Ohio State University Press, 1960, p. 165.
2 Free Press, 1958, pp. 261–3.

3 *Ibid.*, p. 262.

4 London: Routledge & Kegan Paul, 1956, p. 9.

5 One example of this failure is the otherwise helpful essay by Walter Buckley, 'Structural-Functional Analysis in Modern Sociology' in Howard Becker and Alvin Boskoff (eds), *Modern Sociological Theory in Continuity and Change*, New York: Dryden Press, 1957. It is interesting to note a comparable point made by Kurt H. Wolff: 'Such a concept of consciousness [Mannheim's] is Hegelian-Marxian. Possibly for this reason it is absent from American preoccupations with the sociology of knowledge.' 'The Sociology of Knowledge and Sociological Theory' in Llewellyn Gross (ed.), *Symposium on Sociological Theory*, New York: Harper & Row, 1959, p. 577.

6 An adequate treatment of the history of the functionalist viewpoint must include the influences upon it of the biological and the spiritual forms of organismic thought, independently and interactively.

7 A detailed historical presentation of the meaning and use of these terms in Mannheim's entire published output will not be attempted here, but only what appears most significant for the purposes of this discussion.

8 *Structural Analysis of Epistemology*, Supplement no. 57, *Kantstudien*, Berlin, 1922; reprinted in Paul Kecskemeti (ed.), *Essays on Sociology and Social Psychology*, London: Oxford University Press, 1953, pp. 15–73.

9 *Essays on Sociology and Social Psychology*, p. 16.

10 *Ibid.*, p. 17.

11 For Mannheim's analysis of the romantic meaning of organism and organic thinking, see 'The History of the Concept of the State as an Organism' in *Essays on Sociology and Social Psychology*.

12 *Jahrbuch für Kunstgeschichte*, vol. 1 (XV), 1921–2; Vienna, 1923; reprinted in Paul Kecskemeti (ed.), *Essays on the Sociology of Knowledge*, New York: Oxford University Press, 1952, pp. 33–83. Cf. p. 82.

13 *Archiv für Sozialwissenschaft und Sozialpolitik*, Tübingen: Mohr, vol. 52, no. 1 (June 1924); reprinted in *Essays on the Sociology of Knowledge*, pp. 84–133.

14 *Op. cit.*, p. 172.

15 'The Problem of a Sociology of Knowledge', *Archiv für Sozialwissenschaft und Sozialpolitik*, Tübingen, vol. 3, no. 3 (April 1925); reprinted in *Essays on the Sociology of Knowledge*, p. 172.

16 Cf. 'The ultimate substratum which unfolds in time has its truth in its progress . . . This succession of steps in itself harbours truth.' 'Historicism', *loc. cit.*, pp. 130–1. In his introduction to *Essays on Sociology and Social Psychology*, p. 1, Paul Kecskemeti offers the following characteristics of structure for Mannheim, to which my discussion is indebted: '1. It was the most *comprehensive* feature of reality . . . 2. It was a *dynamic* entity . . . 3. It was an *intelligible* principle.'

17 F. Cohen, Bonn, 1929; reprinted as pts II–IV of *Ideology and Utopia*, Harcourt Brace, 1936.

18 *Ideology and Utopia*, p. 59. Italics supplied.

19 *Ideology and Utopia*, V, 'The Sociology of Knowledge', pp. 247–8;

originally published as Alfred Vierkandt (ed.), *'Wissenssoziologie'*, *Handwörterbuch der Soziologie*, Stuttgart: Enke, 1931.

20 *Op. cit.*, p. 51.

21 Cf. my 'Knowledge as Interpretation: An Historical Survey', pt II, *Philosophy and Phenomenological Research*, vol. 11, no. 1 (1950), esp. pp. 94–6.

22 *Ideology and Utopia*, p. 45.

23 *Op. cit.*, p. 278.

24 For a discussion of this see 'Knowledge as Interpretation: An Historical Survey', pp. 96–8.

25 This is itself of interest from a sociology of knowledge point of view.

26 Published in Ernest Manheim (ed.), *Essays on the Sociology of Culture*, London: Routledge & Kegan Paul, 1956.

27 *Op. cit.*, pp. 53–4.

28 *Op. cit.*, p. 72.

29 *Op. cit.*, p. 73.

30 *Op. cit.*, pp. 73–9, *passim*.

31 It should be noted that this essay was written, according to his editor, in Germany 'in the early thirties', prior to Mannheim's proscription by Hitler.

32 *Op. cit.*, pp. 73–9, *passim*.

33 *Op. cit.*, p. 76.

34 *Ibid.*

35 *Op. cit.*, p. 73.

36 *Ibid.*

37 *Op. cit.*, p. 74.

38 'The Problem of a Sociology of Knowledge', *loc. cit.*, p. 143. What is here translated as 'ruse of the Idea' is known to all readers of Hegel in English translation as the 'cunning of Reason', from the translation by J. Sibree, 1857, of G. W. F. Hegel, *The Philosophy of History*. It is interesting to see Mannheim in this paragraph note, although without reference to 'manifest' and 'latent', the use of the same logic by Freud.

39 'Towards the Sociology of the Mind: An Introduction', p. 73.

40 *Op. cit.*, p. 79.

41 *Essays on Sociology and Social Psychology*, pp. 195–208.

42 *Op. cit.*, pp. 206–7.

43 Published as J. S. Erös and W. A. C. Stewart (eds), *Systematic Sociology*, New York: Philosophical Library, 1957.

44 *Op. cit.*, editor's note, p. xxiv.

45 *Ideology and Utopia*, pp. 17–18.

46 *Essays on the Sociology of Culture*, p. 181. Here again is an instance of the Hegelianistic 'dynamic reconciliation' by the synthetic master-structure. Cf. also: 'The antagonism between these two types of thought (functionalist and romanticist) tends to become really bitter, but instead of taking sides we ought to try to understand the specific contribution which each of them has to make . . .' *Man and Society in an Age of Reconstruction*, p. 241; cf. also p. 169, n. 1. Mannheim believes that 'our society has been forced into planning' and that this requires us 'to think of things . . . once . . . passively accepted, in terms of func-

tion'. Planning, however, must be 'structural', a strategic 'reconstruction of an historically developed society into a unity . . .' Cf. pp. 242,
193.

47 *Man and Society in an Age of Reconstruction*, London: Routledge &
Kegan Paul, 1940, cf. pp. 53–4.

48 *Ideology and Utopia*, pp. 50–1.

49 *Essays on the Sociology of Knowledge*, p. 145.

50 Thus understandably giving support to the mistaken conception that
the relation between existence and thought for him is causal.

51 Cf. *Man and Society*, p. 126, n. 1.

52 Cf. *Essays on the Sociology of Knowledge*, p. 184.

53 Cf., however, *Ideology and Utopia*, p. 221: 'The concrete investigation
of the interdependence of the entire range of events from economic to
psychic and intellectual must bring together isolated observations into
a *functional unity* against the background of a developing whole.'
Also p. 85: 'Antiquated and inapplicable norms, modes of thought, and
theories are likely to degenerate into ideologies whose *function* it is to
conceal the actual meaning of conduct rather than to reveal it.'

54 *Ideology and Utopia*, p. 185.

55 'The Problem of a Sociology of Knowledge', *loc. cit.*, p. 176.

56 *Op. cit.*, p. 174.

57 *Essays on Sociology and Social Psychology*, pp. 89–90.

part eight

Contemporary sociology of knowledge: symbolic interactionism, phenomenology, quantitatism

17　Mannheim, Cooley, and Mead: toward a social theory of mentality*

Harvey A. Farberman

Louis Wirth[1] foresaw a convergence between social psychology and sociology of knowledge. Although the exact point of convergence was not yet visible, there is reason to believe it lies in the development of a social theory of mentality which ties together psychical and institutional process.[2] Our interest here is to show, (1) that Mannheim's analysis of the impact of external structural factors on mental production presupposes, but does not develop, a social theory of mentality, (2) that Charles H. Cooley's analysis of the emergence of self, which resorts to internal endowments, likewise, presupposes an externally derived cognitive structure, and (3) that the intersection of institutional and psychical process, which both sociology of knowledge and social psychology require, is given by George H. Mead, whose theory of mind and self, as symbolic interaction, makes social factors inevitably intrinsic to mentality.

Mannheim: the primacy of external factors

In his analysis of the conception of ideology, Karl Mannheim notes that:[3]

> The particular conception of ideology is implied when the term denotes that we are skeptical of the ideas and representations advanced by our opponents. They are regarded as more or less conscious disguises of the real nature of a situation, the true recognition of which would not be to his interests. (When we speak of the total conception), we refer to the ideology of an age as of a concrete historico-social group, e.g., of a class [wherein] we are concerned with the characteristics and

* I would like to thank Lewis A. Coser and Gregory P. Stone for helpful comments.

composition of the total structure of the mind of this epoch or group.

The element common to both conceptions, particular and total, is that neither allows reliance on the face value of what an adversary professes. Instead, we are directed to 'functionalize' the opponent's representations by asking under what situational conditions what is being said, is said. Assertions always are interpreted as functions of the structural conditions under which they appear. In both, an assumption is made concerning the conditional influence of situation on representation; however, where the particular conception directs our skepticism to the substance of a representation, the total conception does the same for the form of a representation. On the one hand, we are interested in discovering the disguised self-interest of the opponent, on the other, we are interested in the total formation of his mental character. The particularistic conception invites a purely psychological analysis which, as Robert K. Merton (1957) contends,[4] demands the imputation of motives with the understanding that, even if the opponent is lying, we can uncover that lie on the basis of some common criterion. Though our interests are different, we express them within a shared theoretical framework. Patently, this is not the case with regard to the total conception of ideology. Here the theoretical frameworks themselves are divergent and there is no common criterion for discerning validity. To the extent our mental frameworks themselves arise out of different collective matrices the very 'categories' of thought used are different.

Clearly, then, we are dealing with two analytically distinct phenomena. In one case, we are interested in discounting the deliberately managed deception to uncover the 'real' vested interests or self-prudential motives which lie behind the facade. In the other, we are interested in the structure and formation of the mentality which, to the extent it emerges from and is a representation of a given collective matrix, is conditioned by the time, place, problems, and history of that matrix. With the particular conception, we are interested in unveiling the *deflections* of reality foisted off through a particular rhetoric. With the total conception, we are interested in apprehending the general *reflection* of reality a given mentality represents in terms of existential conditions. In the case of deflection, we can speak of manipulatory vocabularies which are pragmatic and in bad faith. In the case of reflection, we can speak of matrix vocabularies which are *bona fide*.

Obviously what is missing in either case is any precise formulation of the exact relationship between existential conditions and deflecting or reflecting vocabularies. Nowhere does Mannheim tell us how existential conditions narrowly conceived as vested interests or self-prudential motives infiltrate a mentality so that it *deliberately* mis-construes reality in order to maximize advantage; or, how existential conditions broadly conceived as time, place, problem and history determine a socio-historical mentality so that it *unwittingly* construes a given reflection of reality.

If our major independent variable is existential condition or social organization (conceived narrowly or broadly), and our dependent variable is mentality (either deflecting or reflecting), we must begin to conceptualize mechanisms or processes which describe the linkages between them. To be sure, Mannheim is in need of a social theory of mentality. Some insight into why he did not develop one may be gained by placing his work in historical perspective.

The evolution of thought running from Descartes to Locke to Kant may be construed as an attempt to extricate the knowing subject from his social-historical context with the consequent attempt to search out the limitations on knowledge within the boundaries of the discrete individual.[5] In contrast to this kind of restricted, atomistic analysis, the modern approach which evolves in the work of Marx, Nietzsche, Scheler, Durkheim, Mead, Mannheim, and Schutz takes a more dynamic collectivistic turn which sees the knowing subject as part and parcel of a creative and determinative institutional process. As a result, where the classical approach strove to strip away the institutional biases from mentality, so as to uncover its inherent and necessary objectivity, the modern approach cannot conceive of thought as being apart from institutional involvement; hence, it is determined to search for the composition of mentality within the more or less resilient social process. Such shift in focus from the self-contained individual and his intrinsic processes to the collectively-construed individual and his inter-subjective experience means that those social-psychological efforts which seek to probe and discern the nature and forms which an inter-personal society exhibits set the boundaries within which questions of the composition of mentality can be formulated. In an important sense then, the possible relation-ships between the composition of mentality and social factors (processes) is a social-psychological query.

Social-psychological inquiry can get bogged down, however, by being either too individualistically or too collectivistically oriented. In Mannheim's case, it would appear that Hegelian and Marxian influence turned him toward a collectivistic emphasis. If we ask why Mannheim never explicitly discerned the social-psychological mechanisms which modulate social factors into mentality, it was owing to his predominant tendency to see men as reflections of institutional process. Mannheim did not, in any consistent sense, differentiate person from process. His work embodies what Karl Popper[6] (1962) labels a 'passivist theory of knowledge,' or a 'bucket theory of Mind,' where 'knowledge streams into us through our senses, and error is due to our interference with the sense given material, [consequently], the best way of avoiding error is to remain entirely passive and receptive.' This Hegelianized version of Kant's activist theory of knowledge appears to be reflected in Mannheim's conceptualization of man as a more or less indiscriminate reflector of institutional process. To the extent Mannheim did not *emphasize* man's selective, innovative capacity (as Kant originally did and as Mead subsequently does), he saw no great need to articulate a 'discontinuity' between man as a discrete social-psychological entity capable of 'selecting out' or 'indicating' to himself those factors which his own rationale makes relevant. Instead, his metaphor of man is an *imperium in imperio*, i.e., a resource in the service of institutional process. While we hardly question the revolutionary significance of placing man back into the ongoing social process and accordingly carry our probing of the composition of mind into that institutional process, we are inclined to look upon man as more discrete (in the sense of self-indicating) than Mannheim pictured him. We suspect that a careful sounding out of man as an *inter-personal agent*, as opposed to a *collectivistic agency*, will close the gap on the social-psychological mechanisms which Mannheim's sociology of knowledge obviously needs.

If Mannheim's work suffers from his inability to articulate a discontinuity between person and process, Cooley's work reveals a fundamental inability to achieve a continuity between person and process.

Cooley: the primacy of internal factors

Cooley locates the origin of self in an intrinsic, inarticulate, emotional endowment. In describing the emergence of self, as he observed it in his daughter, he wrote:[7]

> The self-feeling had always been there. . . . She had become familiar by observation and opposition with similar appropriative activities on the part of R. (her brother). Thus she had not only had the feeling herself, but by associating it with its visible expression had probably divined it, sympathized with it, resented it, in others. Grasping, tugging, and screaming would be associated with the feeling in her own case and would recall the feeling when observed in others.

By way of general formulation, Cooley says elsewhere:[8]

> The child gradually comes to notice the indications of self-feeling (the emphasis, the appropriate actions, etc.) accompanying the use of 'I,' 'me,' and 'my,' by others. These indications awaken

his own self-feelings, already existing in an articulate form. He sympathizes with them and reproduces them in his own use of these words. They thus come to stand for a self-assertive feeling or attitude for self-will and appropriation.

Presumably, the child has an instinctive self-feeling which is manifested in appropriative action itself set in the context of joint activity. Moreover, accompanying this appropriative activity is the expression of certain personal pronouns which apparently stand for those inner self-feelings being manifested. Thus, while the individual has inner feelings prior to interaction, they apparently require social experience for their behavioral manifestation. The significance of the appropriative aspect of activity is realized by the individual only when he sees their apparent representation of self-feelings in the visible gestures of others.

This process of recognition requires closer examination. We will break it into two phases: phase one consists of a recognition by the child of certain demonstrative gestures which are accompanied by the utterance of certain linguistic forms by others; phase two consists of a provocation of the child such that the child's own similar, but as yet inarticulate self-feelings become awakened, and in some manner associated and symbolically represented by similar linguistic forms. Now apparently underlying these phases are three hidden assumptions: (1) that the child 'understands' the demonstrative significance of the expressive gestures of others; (2) that the child can experience his own self-feelings; and (3) that he associates the visible representative gestures of others with his own self-feelings. With respect to these assumptions, two questions must be raised: (a) how can a child who gives no evidence of symbolic facility 'sympathize,' 'divine,' or 'understand' the significance of representative gestures of others and the linguistic forms which accompany them; and (b) how can he, lacking such facility, experience his own feelings? In effect, we are asking: how can a child grasp the experiential significance of these elements if there is no facility which allows them entrance into his world of experience? To postulate the emergence of feeling states as the base of self, if these feeling states have no way of entering experience, is to beg the question. It is implausible to assume that the child recognizes the representative essence of both appropriative activity and linguistic forms (in others) unless some cognitive faculty capable of handling symbolism is operative.

Both questions force us beyond the affective dimension in that any cogent answer must be predicated on the fact that the child is indeed experiencing the experiential world; that the child is indeed aware of the fact that he himself is a locus within, and to, which, the experiential world may be referred. Emergent inarticulate feelings are of no consequence unless experienced, and, in order for them to be experienced, some prior cognitive structure must be operative. Obviously, this prior cognitive structure presupposes an external symbolic medium which, when incorporated, is the foundation for such a structure.[9]

From this extremely brief review, we contend that the wide recognition Cooley is given for his conception of the social nature of self is somewhat misplaced. Cooley's core formulation is an example of a nominalistic position and, as such, falls short of an adequate theory of the social person. Indeed, his methodological prescription of imaginative introspection, which does not meet the methodological postulates of scientific social-psychology, confirms this beyond doubt.[10]

George H. Mead: primacy of the in-between

The inadequate positions of Mannheim and Cooley point toward some midway position which takes account of the social individual. The work of George H. Mead fits the bill. As C. Wright Mills remarks,[11] in Mead we find 'a theory of mind ... which conceives social factors as intrinsic to mentality' but, it should be added, realizes fully the selective character of mentality.

The major part of Mead's thinking revolves around a vigorous effort to shatter a deterministic conception of man, a conception which sees man marvelously but *mechanically* fashioned before the conditions and forces of an overwhelming universe. Mead's formulations point toward a model of man whose chief characteristic is precisely the ability self-consciously to reconstruct a universe better suited to his own interests. If the universe presents the 'thereness' of conditions, it is man alone who selectively indicates or 'picks out' those particular characteristics against which subsequent self-conscious response will be mobilized.

Two phases of man emerge: (1) that of man as a being who by selective perception 'slices out' and sustains a unique perspective of the universe, and (2) that of man who in the context of joint activity must appropriately adjust his own tested perceptions to those of others such that the business of communal living can proceed. If man is to be free and novel, provisions for the former must be allowed; if man is to be integrated under the rules of community and order, the latter must occur—there must be room both for relative percipient realities (i.e., the particular) and organized shared perspectives (i.e., the universal). Mead's problem is to account for both without sacrificing either.[12]

He attempts to negotiate the problem by assuming the correlative emergence of mind and self out of a communicative (social) matrix which itself is circumscribed by the (joint) functional act. Mead thus focuses attention on the communicative aspects of the ongoing social process; for it is here that self-conscious response emerges, and, as such, the common ground for freedom and order.

Accordingly, Mead spends much effort outlining the development of the significant symbol, for only through such a communicative mechanism can a universe of self-consciously shared meanings arise. Concern for the possibility of shared meanings is critical in that only as there are such meanings can mutual indication and presentation of stimuli take place. Only when those stimuli selected by one person are similarly meaningful and evocative to another person, can a relative identity of response be anticipated. As rational conduct is control over response, the essential condition for such conduct within an interactive situation rests in the organization of diverse and emergent perspectives into a single organized perspective, for only so far as there is such organization are mutually meaningful indications and expectations possible.

That Mead saw his central problem as one of reconciling emergent, relative, and unique perspectives into a single organized perspective, comes clear in his reaction to Cooley. In effect, Mead is searching for a sphere of experience which can support both the public and private and still be adequate to the methodological postulates of research science. Mead asks, 'are our selves psychical, or do they belong to an objective phase of experience which we set off against a psychical phase?' Clearly he recognized that, 'for social theory a great deal hinges upon the answer to the question whether society is itself psychical or whether the form of the psychical is a sort of communication which arises within primitive behavior.'[13]

How to account, then, for a structure whose hallmark characteristic is the ability to be aware of itself, but at the same time, tie it into a collection of other such structures. As already intimated, Mead attempted to explain the emergence of mind and self out of an already ongoing social process. With such an orientation, he opposed the notion that mind and self preceded social process. Indeed, he desired to reformulate mind and self in the light of behavioristic and pragmatic method which would see them as emergent agencies whose function it was better to establish more serene adjustments to the problematics of existence.

To conceive of mind and self as agencies which facilitate functional or purposive reconstruction of environment alters, in a most fundamental sense, a conception of man from 'thinker' to 'doer.' In this stroke reflections directed to the psychic dimensions of man turn from a study in metaphysics to a study in science, for if man is primarily a 'doer' then the ultimate unit of analysis is what he does, i.e., the act. Man's psychic dimension becomes connected to the empirical world via the behavioral act. Extreme importance is now attached to the

K

267

potential man has for reconstructively coming over against the elements in the larger evolutionary process of which he is one form.

This approach can be seen as a reactive synthesis emanating from three distinct traditions:[14] in response to Wundt's psycho-physical parallelism Mead rejects the assertion that mind is an entity prior to consciousness.[15] In opposition to Watson, Mead claims that it is the height of absurdity to preclude a recognition of specifically mental-istic or inner-processes;[16] in acceptance of James's objectification of consciousness, Mead nevertheless claims that no mechanism has been isolated to explain the emergence of mind and self.[17]

Correspondingly, Mead's effort rests on three developments: (1) to approach behavior as an ongoing activity which is observable; (2) to incorporate Wundt's isolation of language as a mechanism which could explain the internal transformation of objective experience into mind, self and other; and (3) to look at mind, self, and society as emergents out of this linguistic restructuring. Mead thus tries to bring together the methodologically impossible subjectivism of the introspectionists and the theoretically impossible objectivism of the early behaviorists.

For Mead, then, the central bridging formulation between the inner and the outer world is the 'attitude.' By conceptualizing the attitude as an 'incipient act' it becomes the initially unobservable phase of goal directed activity. This attitude can be considered an inner mobilization of energy which is preparatory to an external act. Such mobilization is not passive in response to a conditioning environment, but *selective* and sensitized to those aspects of the environment which are of interest to the purposes of the individual.[18] Only those parts of the environment to which the individual is attitudinally attentive become meaningful or relevant. All attitudes, therefore, carry with them the possibility of selective perception which facilitates purposeful behavior.

To this bridging concept of incipient action, Mead appends the concept of gesture.[19] He claims that some attitudes or incipient actions are actually observable, e.g., the clenching of a fist as a visible embodiment of a disposition to attack. Where incipient actions are observable, interaction between people is facilitated as each indi-vidual can make appropriate adjustive responses to others and, also, *anticipate* the adjustive responses of others—which means that an actor can react or respond to himself as do other people.[20] For this to happen, however, implies some sort of temporal organization of all interaction. Each individual in the interaction sequence must have some vague idea of where the action is going, or what the possible consequences of the action are, in order to be able to gain cognition of the other person's possible incipient actions. If the goals which are carried in the incipient action of the actor can be apprehended by other, then other can make some kind of approximation of how actor will behave since he will be able to hypothesize the controlling effects on that action of future goals. In a completely unmysterious way, Mead explicates the quasi-determinative relationship between imagining future consequences and goals and present action. That is, the future may serve to control or rationalize the act, but never actually determine it.[21] We see the emergence of a certain situational or action logic which, *in principle*, when understood by other, becomes the basis of meaningful response. From the point of view of the actor, Mead here depicts the essentially unrandom nature of action, i.e., it is rational in the sense that, to the extent an actor is able to imagine the future goals and consequences of his action, his present route of decision need not be undertaken blindly. Furthermore, it should be recognized that the organization of action through time is a primary requisite for communication, for only when an actor can respond to himself as others respond to him, can social life continue. If an actor has absolutely no idea of what the consequences of his actions are, and no idea of how people are likely to respond to him, there cannot be meaningful social organization. This requires no little imagination into an anticipated future. In fact, the assumptions which underlie the consensus that allows for social organization are the assumptions of other people's incipient or future actions.

Mead argues that this is possible only through the dynamics of symbolization. What this means is that individual 'A' is intrinsically endowed with similar possibilities for response as is individual 'B,' and further that individual 'A' has the capacity to respond to his own responses in the same way that 'B' does.[22] Of the sense mediums, language, by far, is central, for it enables us to hear what we are saying and as such allows us the possibility of responding to ourselves with the same kind of response to which others may react.[23] What is gained is that, in principle, and within the interaction situation, not only can we respond to ourselves as others do, but also deliberately mobilize those responses. Consequently, well in advance of the occurrences of action by other, we can in principle, and only approximately, anticipate it.

By way of symbolization, then, an individual gains the possibility of calling out the other person's perspective at the same time he calls out his own.[24] If we conceptualize the other person's perspective from a behavioral point of view as role, then the ability to take the role of the other person is, in fact, the operational functioning of mind. Mind is that emergent distinction which results when one person, in the course of responding to himself, is able to cognitively grasp the perspective of the other person and from the point of view of the reactions to his behavior implicit in that perspective, modify his own behavior.[25]

Once reflexiveness is achieved, the individual is able to incorporate through each social act the conditions of society. This can be carried on, and usually is, without any external movement at all. With the establishment of an 'inner-forum,' the individual is able to dialogue with himself concerning projected action. In the 'inner-forum,' the individual is not only responding to himself, but also to the incorporated expected responses of others. From this dialogue, a unification of perspective or common point of view can be arrived at even while the attitudes or expected responses of others are held only in imagination.

Mead has designated the 'me' as those incorporated responses of other, to the beginning of one's own acts. Through these incorporated responses others enter our world and influence our actions. He similarly designates the 'I' as those responses of ours which come over against the implanted reactions of others to our own initial phases of action.[26] Where the 'me' is the organization of attitudes of other which we incorporate, the 'I' is our response to the attitudes of others. In full, self is what arises as a result of the dialogue between the 'I' and the 'me.' An individual is forever initiating action, then taking into consideration the attitudes of others to that action, then revising or altering that action in the light of those attitudes.

In a sense interaction is a continual state of flux, for innovation can at any time emerge through our altered responses to other thus allowing the establishment of new forms of relations.[27] So, in effect, we do not adjust passively to the anticipated reactions of others but actively devise new strategies or forms in order to maintain the dialogue. Fresh perspectives may arise to completely alter the existing forms and nature of relationships. Further, to the extent *we can never really* predict the coming moment with anything like precision, interaction can always be a creative experience.

Finally, Mead speaks about the 'generalized other' which may be interpreted as the internalization of social organization.[28] Here Mead is recognizing the fact that an individual must alter his actions not only to singular other perspectives, but also to the general perspective. The individual must, to a greater or lesser extent, comprehend the divergent network of rules and roles of every individual and group he interacts with. By internalizing this entire variegated complex of rules and roles, the individual moves toward the development of a complete self.

In Mead's formulations, then, we see an attempt to overcome the methodological restrictions engendered with completely subjectivistic subject matter. By attempting to incorporate subjective states within the field of ongoing action, Mead has tried to deliver the subject matter of social psychology into a realm where operations can be devised for establishing propositions capable of inter-subjective testing.

In sum, Mead gives us more of a method than a full-blown substantive theory—the method is naturalistic, behavioristic pragmatism, i.e., research science. Both his theory of self and society conform to the objectivistic tendencies of this method: man as self is rooted in otherness; the focus of attention is definitely on what goes on *between* men; the stress is clearly on inter-personal communication. Social experience is the crucial phase of experience in that only by relating to others can an individual become distinctively himself. This is so, irrespective of the actual nature of the relationship; be it love or hate, co-operation or conflict, we are constrained to reorient our styles of interaction under the impact of other people. In every respect, then, the prerequisites for the emergence of unique selfhood are found in the matrix of social, plural, and objective experience. Indeed, that which we choose to call reality is identical with the organization of unique perspectives carried in social action. From the point of view of the individual, reality literally consists in the plurality or multiplicity of perspectives he can occupy—in fact, to exist or to be, is to know that one is in interaction.[29]

Notes

1 See 'Preface' in Karl Mannheim, *Ideology and Utopia* (trans. and ed. Louis Wirth and Edward Shils), New York: Harcourt, Brace & World, 1936, pp. ix–xxx.

2 Peter Berger and Thomas Luckmann, *The Social Construction of Reality*, New York: Doubleday, 1966.

3 *Op. cit.*, pp. 56–7.

4 Robert K. Merton, *Social Theory and Social Structure*, Chicago: Free Press, 1957, pp. 496–502.

5 See Wirth, 'Preface' in Mannheim, *op. cit.*; S. Taylor, 'Social factors and the validation of thought', *Social Forces*, 1, October 1962, pp. 76–82; Don Martindale, 'Max Weber on the sociology of culture', University of Minnesota, 1964, unpublished mimeo.

6 Karl Popper, *The Open Society and Its Enemies*, vol. 2, New York: Harper, 1962, pp. 213–14.

7 Charles H. Cooley, *Human Nature and the Social Order*, New York: Schocken, 1964, pp. 190–1.

8 Charles H. Cooley, *Sociological Theory and Social Research*, New York: Holt, 1930, p. 231.

9 Our analysis of Cooley's formulation is based primarily on one of George H. Mead's brilliant articles (note 13, *op. cit.*, pp. 693–706).

10 Cooley, *Sociological Theory and Social Research*.

11 C. W. Mills, 'Language, logic and culture', *American Sociological Review*, 4, October 1939, pp. 670–80.

12 Our social philosophical entree is due largely to the excellent rendition of Mead's work offered by Paul Pfuetze in *Self, Society and Existence*, New York: Harper, 1954, pp. 37–116.

13 George H. Mead, 'Cooley's contribution to American social thought', *American Journal of Sociology*, 35, March 1930, pp. 693–706.
14 For a comparable assessment of the traditions to which Mead responded, see Don Martindale, *The Nature and Types of Sociological Theory*, Boston: Houghton Mifflin, 1961, p. 354.
15 See note 13, *op. cit.*, p. 706.
16 Mead, *Mind, Self and Society*, University of Chicago Press, 1963, pp. 48–50.
17 *Ibid.*, pp. 3–5.
18 *Ibid.*, p. 173.
19 *Ibid.*, p. 5.
20 Mead, *The Philosophy of the Act*, University of Chicago Press, 1964, pp. 5–6.
21 *Mind, Self and Society*, pp. 42–3.
22 *Ibid.*, pp. 68–74.
23 Mead, *The Philosophy of the Present*, Chicago: Open Court Publishing, 1932, pp. 1–3.
24 *Ibid.*, p. 186.
25 *Mind, Self and Society*, p. 62.
26 *Ibid.*, p. 89.
27 *Ibid.*, p. 134.
28 *Ibid.*, pp. 172, 192.
29 *Ibid.*, p. 198.

18 Identity as a problem in the sociology of knowledge

Peter L. Berger

It is through the work of George Herbert Mead and the Meadian tradition of the 'symbolic-interactionist' school that a theoretically viable social psychology has been founded. Indeed, it may be maintained that in this achievement lies the most important *theoretical* contribution made to the social sciences in America. The perspectives of the Meadian tradition have become established within American sociology far beyond the school that explicitly seeks to represent them. Just as it was sociologists who 'discovered' Mead at the University of Chicago and diffused his ideas beyond the latter's confines, so the social psychology constituted on this foundation continues to be the one to which sociologists gravitate most naturally in their theoretical assumptions, a 'sociologist's psychology', despite the later competition from psychoanalysis and learning theory.[1] By contrast, the sociology of knowledge has remained marginal to the discipline in this country, still regarded widely as an unassimilated European import of interest only to a few colleagues with a slightly eccentric penchant for the history of ideas.[2] This marginality of the sociology of knowledge is not difficult to explain in terms of the historical development of sociological theory in this country. All the same, it is rather remarkable that the theoretical affinity between the sociology of knowledge and social psychology in the Meadian tradition has not been widely recognized. One might argue that there has been an implicit recognition in the linkage of social psychology, by way of role theory and reference group theory, with the psychology of cognitive processes, particularly in the work of Robert Merton, Muzafer Sherif and Tamotsu Shibutani.[3] In the case of Merton, however, the discussion of the cognitive implications of social-psychological processes occurs in a curious segregation from the treatment of the sociology of knowledge, while in the cases of Sherif and Shibutani there appears to be no conscious connection with the sociology of knowledge at all.

Understandable historically, this segregation is theoretically deplorable. Social psychology has been able to show how the subjective reality of individual consciousness is socially constructed. The sociology of knowledge, as Alfred Schutz has indicated, may be understood as the sociological critique of consciousness, concerning itself with the social construction of reality in general.[4] Such a critique entails the analysis of both 'objective reality' (that is, 'knowledge' about the world, as objectivated and taken for granted in society) and its subjective correlates (that is, the modes in which this objectivated world is subjectively plausible or 'real' to the individual). If these shorthand descriptions of the two sub-disciplines are allowed, then integration between them is not an exotic miscegenation but a bringing together of two partners by the inner logic of their natures. Obviously this paper cannot develop the details of such a project of theoretical integration, but it may indicate some general directions and implications.

Social psychology has brought about the recognition that the sphere of psychological phenomena is continuously permeated by social forces, and more than that, is decisively shaped by the latter. 'Socialization' means not only that the self-consciousness of the individual is constituted in a specific form by society (which Mead called the 'social genesis of the self'), but also that psychological reality is in an ongoing dialectical relationship with social structure. Psychological reality refers here, *not* to scientific or philosophical propositions *about* psychological phenomena, but to the manner in which the individual apprehends himself, his processes of consciousness and his relations with others. Whatever its anthropological-biological roots, psychological reality arises in the individual's biography in the course of social processes and is only maintained (that is, maintained in consciousness *as* 'reality') by virtue of social processes. Socialization not only ensures that the individual is 'real' to himself in a certain way, but that he will ongoingly respond to his experience of the world with the cognitive and emotive patterns appropriate to this 'reality'. For example, successful socialization shapes a self that apprehends itself exclusively and in a taken-for-granted way in terms of one or the other of two socially defined sexes, that 'knows' this self-apprehension to be the only 'real' one, and rejects as 'unreal' any contrary modes of apprehension or emotionality. Self and society are inextricably interwoven entities. Their relationship is dialectical because the self, once formed, may act back in its turn upon the society that shaped it (a dialectic that Mead expressed in his formulation of the 'I' and the 'me'). The self exists by virtue of society, but society is only possible as many selves continue to apprehend themselves and each other with reference to it.[5]

Every society contains a repertoire of identities that is part of the 'objective knowledge' of its members. It is 'known' as a matter 'of course' that there are men and women, that they have such-and-such psychological traits and that they will have such-and-such psychological reactions in typical circumstances. As the individual is socialized, these identities are 'internalized'. They are then not only taken for granted as constituents of an objective reality 'out there' but as inevitable structures of the individual's own consciousness. The objective reality, as defined by society, is subjectively appropriated. In other words, socialization brings about symmetry between objective and subjective reality, objective and subjective identity. The degree of this symmetry provides the criterion of the successfulness of socialization. The psychological reality of the successfully socialized individual thus *verifies* subjectively what his society has objectively defined as real. He is then no longer required to turn outside himself for 'knowledge' concerning the nature proper of men and women. He can obtain that result by simple introspection. He 'knows who he is'. He feels accordingly. He can conduct himself 'spontaneously', because the firmly internalized cognitive and emotive structure makes it unnecessary or even impossible for him to reflect upon alternative possibilities of conduct.[6]

This dialectic between social structure and psychological reality may be called the fundamental proposition of any social psychology in the Meadian tradition. Society not only defines but also creates psychological reality. The individual *realizes* himself in society—that is, he recognizes his identity in socially defined terms and these definitions *become reality* as he lives in society. This fundamentally Meadian dialectic makes intelligible the social-psychological scope of W. I. Thomas's concept of the 'definition of the situation' as well as of Merton's of the 'self-fulfilling prophecy'.[7]

The sociology of knowledge is concerned with a related but broader dialectic—that between social structure and the 'worlds' in which individuals live, that is, the comprehensive organizations of reality within which individual experience can be meaningfully interpreted.[8] Every society is a world-building enterprise. Out of the near-infinite variety of individual symbolizations of experience society constructs a universe of discourse that comprehends and objectivates them. Individual experience can then be understood as taking place in an intelligible world that is inhabited also by others and about which it is possible to communicate with others. Individual meanings are objectivated so that they are accessible to everyone who co-inhabits the world in question. Indeed, this world is apprehended as 'objective reality', that is, as reality that is shared with others and that exists irrespective of the individual's own preferences in the matter. The socially available definitions of such a world are thus taken to be 'knowledge' about it and are continuously verified for the individual by social situations in which this 'knowledge' is taken for granted. The socially constructed world becomes the world *tout court*—the only real world, typically the only world that one can seriously conceive of. The individual is thus freed of the necessity of reflecting anew about the meaning of each step in his unfolding experience. He can simply refer to 'common sense' for such interpretation, at least for the great bulk of his biographical experience.[9]

Language is both the foundation and the instrumentality of the social construction of reality.[10] Language focalizes, patterns and objectivates individual experience. Language is the principal means by which an individual is socialized to become an inhabitant of a world shared with others and also provides the means by which, in conversation with these others, the common world continues to be plausible to him.[11] On this linguistic base is erected the edifice of interpretative schemes, cognitive and moral norms, value systems and, finally, theoretically articulated 'world views' which, in their totality, form the world of 'collective representations' (as the Durkheimian school put it) of any given society.[12] Society *orders* experience. Only in a world of social order can there develop a 'collective consciousness' which permits the individual to have a subjectively meaningful life and protects him from the devastating effects of *anomie*, that is, from a condition in which the individual is deprived of the social ordering processes and thus deprived of meaning itself. It is useful to remind oneself of the linguistic base of all social order whenever one theorizes about the latter, because language makes particularly clear just what is meant by the social construction of an objectively real world. Language is undeniably a social invention and a linguistic system cannot be credited with an ontological status apart from the society that invented it. Nevertheless, the individual learns his language (especially, of course, his native language) as an objective reality.[13] He cannot change it at will. He must conform to its coercive power. Typically, he is unable to conceive of either the world or of himself except through the conceptual modalities which it provides. But this facticity, externality and coerciveness of language (the very traits that constitute the Durkheimian *choseité*, or thing-like character, of social phenomena) extends to all the objectivations of society. The subjective consequence is that the individual 'finds himself' (that is, apprehends himself as placed, willy-nilly) in the social world as much as in nature.

It is important to stress that the social construction of reality takes place on both the pre-theoretical and the theoretical levels of consciousness, and that, therefore, the sociology of knowledge must concern itself with both. Probably because of the German intellectual situation in which the sociology of knowledge was first developed, it has hitherto interested itself predominantly in the theoretical side of the phenomenon—the problem of the relationship of society and 'ideas'.[14] This is certainly an important problem. But only very few people are worried over 'ideas', while everyone lives in some sort of a world. There is thus a sociological dimension to the human activity of world-building in its totality, not only in that segment of it in which intellectuals manufacture theories, systems of thought and *Weltanschauungen*. Thus, in the matter under discussion here, the sociology of knowledge has an interest not only in various theories *about* psychological phenomena (what one may call a sociology of psychology) but also in these phenomena themselves (what one may then, perhaps impertinently, call a sociological psychology).

The relationship between a society and its world is a dialectic one because, once more, it cannot be adequately understood in terms of a one-sided causation.[15] The world, though socially constructed, is not a mere passive reflection of the social structures within which it arose. In becoming 'objective reality' for its inhabitants it attains not only a certain autonomy with respect to the 'underlying' society but even the power to act back upon the latter. Men invent a language and then find that its logic imposes itself upon them. And men concoct theories, even theories that may start out as nothing but blatant explications of social interests, and then discover that these theories themselves become agencies of social change. It may be seen, then, that there is a theoretically significant similarity between the dialectics of social psychology and of the sociology of knowledge, the dialectic through which society generates psychological reality and the dialectic through which it engages in world-building. Both dialectics concern the relationship between objective and subjective realities, or more precisely, between socially objectivated reality and its subjective appropriation. In both instances, the individual internalizes facticities that appear to him as given outside himself and, having internalized them to become given contents of his own consciousness, externalizes them again as he continues to live and act in society.[16]

These considerations, especially in the compressed form in which they have had to be presented here, may at first seem to be excessively abstract. Yet, if one asks about the combined significance of these root perspectives of social psychology and the sociology of knowledge for the sociological understanding of identity, one may answer in a rather simple statement: *Identity, with its appropriate attachments of psychological reality, is always identity within a specific, socially constructed world.* Or, as seen from the viewpoint of the individual: *One identifies oneself, as one is identified by others, by being located in a common world.*

Socialization is only possible if, as Mead put it, the individual 'takes the attitude' of others, that is, relates to himself as others have first related to him. This process, of course, extends to the establish-

ment of identity itself, so that one may formulate that social identification both precedes and produces self-identification. Now, it is
possible that the Meadian process of attitude- and role-taking occurs
between individuals who do not share a common world—for
instance, between Columbus and the very first American Indians he
met in 1492. Even they, however, soon identified each other within a
world which they inhabited together, or more accurately, they
together established such a world as they dealt with each other.
Socializing each other in terms of this world, they could then take on
the attitudes and roles appropriate within it. Columbus and his
Spaniards, being (like parents in this respect) the stronger party, had
the edge in this game of 'naming'—the others had to identify themselves in the Spaniard's terms, namely as *Indios*, while the Spaniards
were probably little tempted to identify themselves with the mythological creatures as which they in turn were first identified by the
others. In other words, the American Indian identified himself by
locating himself in the Spaniard's world, though, to be sure, that
world was itself modified as he became its co-inhabitant. In the more
normal cases of socialization, occurring between individuals who
already co-inhabit the same world, it is even easier to see how identification entails location in that world from the beginning. The parents
give their child a name and then deal with him in terms appropriate
to this identification. The literal act of 'naming', of course, is already
location in this sense (its exactitude depending upon the culture—
'John Smith' being less satisfactory as an 'address' than 'Ivan
Ivanovitch', 'Village-Idiot', and so forth). However, as the full
implications of the name and its location unfold in the course of
socialization, the child appropriates the world in which he is thus
located in the same process in which he appropriates his identity—a
moral universe as he identifies himself as a 'good baby', a sexual
universe as a 'little boy', a class universe as a 'little gentleman'—and
so on. One may expand the Meadian phrase, then, by saying that the
individual takes the world of others as he takes their attitudes and
roles. Each role implies a world. The self is always located in a world.
The *same* process of socialization generates the self and internalizes
the world to which this self belongs.

The same reasoning applies to psychological reality in general. Just
as any particular psychological reality is attached to a socially
defined identity, so it is located in a socially constructed world. As
the individual identifies and locates himself in the world of his society,
he finds himself the possessor of a predefined assemblage of psychological processes, both 'conscious' and 'unconscious' ones, and even
some with somatic effects. The 'good baby' feels guilty after a temper
tantrum, the 'little boy' channels his erotic fantasies towards little
girls, the 'little gentleman' experiences revulsion when someone

278

engages in public nose-picking—and this revulsion may, under the proper conditions, affect his stomach to the point of vomitation. Every socially constructed world thus contains a repertoire of identities and a corresponding psychological system. The social definition of identity takes place as part of an overarching definition of reality. The internalization of the world, as it occurs in socialization, imposes upon consciousness a psychological as well as cognitive structure, and (to a degree which has as yet not been adequately clarified scientifically) even extends into the area of physiological processes.[17] Pascal indicated the root problem of the sociology of knowledge when he observed that what is truth on one side of the Pyrenees is error on the other. The same observation applies to the good conscience and the bad (including the 'unconscious' manifestations of the latter), to the libidinously interesting and the libidinously indifferent, as well as to what upsets and what relaxes the gastric juices. And, of course, a French identity differs appreciably from a Spanish one.[18]

A third dialectic may be analysed if one now turns to the theoretical level of consciousness—that between psychological reality and psychological models. Men not only experience themselves. They also explain themselves. While these explanations differ in their degrees of sophistication, it would be difficult to conceive of a society without some theoretical explication of the psychological nature of man. Whether such explication takes the form of proverbial wisdom, mythology, metaphysics or scientific generalization is, of course, a different question. What all these forms have in common is that they systematize the experience of psychological reality on a certain level of abstraction. They constitute psychological models, by means of which individual psychological processes can be compared, typified and thus 'prepared for treatment'. For example, individuals in a society may have all kinds of visionary experiences. Both the individuals themselves and those with whom they live are faced with the question of what these experiences signify. A psychological model that 'explains' such occurrences allows them to compare any particular experience with the several species codified in the model. The experience may then be classified in terms of this typology—as a case of demon possession, say, or as a mark of sacred status, or as merely crazy in a profane mode. This application of the psychological model (the 'diagnosis') then permits a decision on what to do about the occurrence (the 'therapy') to exorcize the individual, to beatify him, or possibly to award him the role of buffoon and of menace to disobedient children. In other words, the psychological model locates individual experience and conduct within a comprehensive theoretical system.[19]

It goes without saying that each psychological model is embedded in a more general theoretical formulation of reality. The model is part of the society's general 'knowledge about the world', raised to the level of theoretical thought. Thus a psychological model that contains a typology of possession belongs to a religious conception of the world as such and a psychological theory of 'mental illness', as understood by contemporary psychiatry, is located in a much wider 'scientific' conception of the world and of man's place in it. *Psychological 'knowledge' is always part of a general 'knowledge about the world'*—in this proposition lies the foundation of what, a little earlier, was called the sociology of psychology. The import of this proposition can be conveyed by referring to the psychiatric concept of 'reality orientation'. A psychiatrist may decide that a certain individual is not adequately 'oriented to reality' and, therefore, 'mentally ill'. The sociologist may then accept this description, but must immediately ask, *'which reality?'* Just as cultural anthropology has been able to demonstrate that the manifestations of the Freudian 'pleasure principle' vary from one society to another, so the sociology of knowledge must insist on a similar socio-cultural relativization of the Freudian 'reality principle'.[20]

This sociological perspective has far-reaching implications for the analysis of psychological theories. As has been indicated, every socially constructed world contains a psychological model. If this model is to retain its plausibility, it must have some empirical relationship to the psychological reality objectivated in the society. A demonological model is 'unreal' in contemporary society. The psychoanalytic one is not. It is important to stress once again the matter of empirical verification. Just as the individual can verify his socially assigned identity by introspection, so the psychological theoretician can verify his model by 'empirical research'. If the model corresponds to the psychological reality as socially defined and produced, it will quite naturally be verified by empirical investigation of this reality. This is not quite the same as saying that psychology is self-verifying. It rather says that the data discovered by a particular psychology belong to the same socially constructed world that has also produced that psychology.

Once more, the relationship between psychological reality and psychological model is a dialectic one. The psychological reality produces the psychological model, insofar as the model is an empirically verifiable representation of the reality. Once formed, however, the psychological model can act back upon the psychological reality. The model has *realizing* potency, that is, it can create psychological reality as a 'self-fulfilling prophecy'. In a society in which demonology is socially established, cases of demon possession will empirically multiply. A society in which psychoanalysis is institutionalized as 'science' will become populated by people who, in fact, evince the processes that have been theoretically attributed to them. It should be clear that this self-fulfilling character of psychological models is grounded in the same dialectic of socialization that Mead first formulated with incisive clarity and which can be summarized by saying that men become that as which they are addressed.

The purpose of these brief considerations has been to indicate what theoretical gains might be expected from an integration of the approaches of social psychology in the Meadian tradition and the sociology of knowledge. This is obviously not the place to discuss the methodological issues or the numerous possibilities of empirical exploration arising from such integration.[21] Suffice it to say, in conclusion, that the theoretical viewpoint expressed here implies a serious reconsideration of the relationship between the two disciplines of sociology and psychology. This relationship has been characterized, at least in this country, by a theoretically unjustified timidity on the side of the sociologists and by a spirit of oecumenical tolerance that may have beneficial consequences for interdepartmental amity, but which has not always been conducive to clear sociological thinking.

Notes

1 On the 'diffusion' of Meadian social psychology among American sociologists, cf. Anselm Strauss (ed.), *George Herbert Mead on Social Psychology*, University of Chicago Press, 1964, pp. vii ff. For a critique of this Meadian 'establishment', from a psychoanalytically oriented viewpoint, cf. Dennis Wrong, 'The oversocialized conception of man in modern sociology', *Psychoanalysis and the Psychoanalytic Review*, vol. 39 (1962), pp. 53 ff.

2 Among American sociologists, the sociology of knowledge has remained rather narrowly associated with its conception by Karl Mannheim, who served as its principal 'translator' from the context of German *Geisteswissenschaft* to that of English-speaking social science. The writings of Max Scheler on *Wissenssoziologie* (the term was coined by him) remain untranslated today. American sociologists have also, in the main, remained unaffected by the development of the sociology of knowledge in the work of Alfred Schutz, not to mention recent contributions in the positivistic tradition (mainly by sociologists writing in German) and by Marxists (mainly in France). For the Mannheim-oriented reception of the sociology of knowledge in America, cf. Robert Merton, *Social Theory and Social Structure*, New York: Collier-Macmillan, 1957, pp. 439 ff., and Talcott Parsons, 'An approach to the sociology of knowledge', *Transactions of the Fourth World Congress of Sociology*, Louvain: International Sociological Association, 1959. For a conception of the sub-discipline more in the line of Scheler than of Mannheim (and with which the present writer

would not associate himself fully, either), cf. Werner Stark, *The Sociology of Knowledge*, London: Routledge & Kegan Paul, 1958.

3 Cf. Merton, *op. cit.*, pp. 225 ff.; Muzafer Sherif and Carolyn Sherif, *An Outline of Social Psychology*, New York: Harper, 1956; Tamotsu Shibutani, 'Reference groups and social control' in Arnold Rose (ed.), *Human Behaviour and Social Processes*, London: Routledge & Kegan Paul, 1962, pp. 128 ff.

4 This understanding of the scope of the sociology of knowledge, a much broader one than that of the Mannheim-oriented approach, has been strongly influenced by the work of Alfred Schutz. Cf. Alfred Schutz, *Der sinnhafte Aufbau der sozialen Welt*, Vienna: Springer, 1960; *The Problem of Social Reality*, The Hague: Nijhoff, 1962; *Studies in Social Theory*, The Hague: Nijhoff, 1964.

5 This dialectic between self and society can also be formulated in Marxian terms. Cf., for example, Joseph Gabel, *La fausse conscience*, Paris: Éditions de Minuit, 1962; and Jean-Paul Sartre, *Search for a Method* (trans. H. E. Barnes), New York: Knopf, 1963. For an attempt at integrating certain Marxian categories within a non-Marxian sociology of knowledge, cf. Peter Berger and Stanley Pullberg, 'Reification and the sociological critique of consciousness', *History and Theory*, vol. 4 (1965).

6 On the social structuring of conduct, cf. Arnold Gehlen, *Urmensch und Spätkultur*, Bonn: Athenaeum, 1956, where Gehlen proposes a biologically grounded theory of social institutions. On this very suggestive theory, which to date has remained practically unknown to American sociologists, also cf. Arnold Gehlen, *Anthropologische Forschung*, Hamburg: Rowohlt, 1961, and *Studien zur Anthropologie und Soziologie*, Neuwied/Rhein: Luchterhand, 1963.

7 Thomas's well-known dictum on the 'real consequences' of social definition was presumably intended, and has been generally understood as intending, to say that once a 'reality' has been defined, people will act *as if* it were indeed so. To this important proposition must be added an understanding of the *realizing* (that is, reality-producing) potency of social definition. This social-psychological import of Thomas's 'basic theorem' was developed by Merton, *op. cit.*, pp. 421 ff. The sociology of knowledge, as this paper tries to indicate, would extend this notion of the social construction of 'reality' even further.

8 Cf. Schutz, *The Problem of Social Reality*, pp. 207 ff.

9 Cf. *ibid.*, pp. 3 ff.

10 Cf. *ibid.*, pp. 287 ff. Also, cf. Ernst Cassirer, *An Essay on Man*, New Haven: Yale University Press, 1962, pp. 109 ff. The problem of language and 'reality', neglected by American sociologists, has been extensively discussed in American cultural anthropology; see the influence of Edward Sapir and the controversy over the so-called 'Whorf hypothesis'. It has been a central problem for sociologists and cultural anthropologists in France ever since the Durkheim school. Cf. Claude Lévi-Strauss, *The Savage Mind*, London: Weidenfeld & Nicolson, 1966.

11 On the maintenance of 'reality' by means of the 'conversational

apparatus', cf. Peter Berger and Hansfried Kellner, 'Marriage and the construction of reality', first published in *Diogenes*, vol. 46 (1964), pp. 1-25.

12 One may say that the Durkheimian theory of 'collective consciousness' is the positive side of the theory of *anomie*. The *locus classicus* of this is, of course, Durkheim's *Elementary Forms of the Religious Life*. For important developments of this (all of great relevance for the sociology of knowledge), cf. Marcel Granet, *La Pensée chinoise*, Paris: Albin Michel, 1950; Maurice Halbwachs, *Les Cadres sociaux de la mémoire*, Paris: Presses Universitaires de France, 1952; Marcel Mauss, *Sociologie et anthropologie*, Paris: Presses Universitaires de France, 1960.

13 The fullest evidence on the 'objectivity' of the child's language learning is to be found in the work of Jean Piaget.

14 The fixation of the sociology of knowledge on the theoretical level of consciousness is well expressed in the sub-title of the previously cited work by Stark—'An Essay in Aid of a Deeper Understanding of the History of Ideas'. The present writer would consider Schutz's work as essential for arriving at a broader conception of the sub-discipline. For a broader approach based on Marxian presuppositions, cf. Henri Lefebvre, *Critique de la vie quotidienne*, Paris: L'Arche, 1958–61. For a discussion of the possibility of using Pareto for a critique of pre-theoretical consciousness in society, cf. Brigitte Berger, 'Vilfredo Pareto's Sociology as a Contribution to the Sociology of Knowledge' (unpublished doctoral dissertation, Graduate Faculty, New School for Social Research, New York, 1964).

15 This problem is, of course, dealt with by Marx in his well-known conception of sub- and super-structure. The present writer would argue that, at least in Marx's early writings (as in the Economic and Philosophic Manuscripts of 1844), the relationship between the two is clearly a dialectic one. In later Marxism, the dialectic is lost in a mechanistic understanding of sub- and super-structure in which the latter becomes a mere epiphenomenon (Lenin—a 'reflection') of the former. On this 'reification' of Marxism in Communist ideology (perhaps one of the great ironies in the history of ideas), cf., for example, Joseph Gabel, *Formen der Entfremdung*, Frankfurt: Fischer, 1964, pp. 53 ff. Probably the most important work, within the Marxian tradition, which has tried to recapture the original dialectic in dealing with this problem is Georg Lukács's *Geschichte und Klassenbewusstsein* (1923), now virtually unobtainable in German, but available in an excellent French translation—*Histoire et conscience de classe*, Paris: Éditions de Minuit, 1960.

16 The overarching dialectic of socialization indicated here can be analysed in terms of three 'moments'—externalization, objectivation and internalization. The dialectic is lost whenever one of these 'moments' is excluded from social theory. Cf. Berger and Pullberg, *op. cit.*

17 For indications of the intriguing possibilities of such a 'socio-somatics', cf. Georg Simmel's discussion of the 'sociology of the senses', in his *Sociology*, New York: Collier-Macmillan, 1964, pp. 483 ff. Also, cf.

Mauss' essay on the 'techniques of the body', in his *op. cit.*, pp. 365 ff.

18 It is not intended here to propose a 'sociologistic' view of reality as *nothing but* a social construction. Within the sociology of knowledge, however, it is possible to bracket the final epistemological questions.

19 On the sociology-of-knowledge implications of diagnostic typologies, cf. Eliot Freidson, *The Sociology of Medicine*, Oxford: Blackwell, 1963, pp. 124 ff.

20 For a critique of the contemporary concept of 'mental illness', coming from within psychiatry itself, cf. Thomas Szasz, *The Myth of Mental Illness*, New York: Hosber-Harper, 1961.

21 Cf. Peter L. Berger and Thomas Luckmann, *The Social Construction of Reality*, London: Allen Lane, Penguin Press, 1967.

19   Existential phenomenology and the sociological tradition

Edward A. Tiryakian

A recent article observes that general theory in sociology is characterized by 'a perplexing multivariety of basic orientations' and that the
lack of a fundamental unity bars the 'integration of all or even most
of the existing sociological knowledge.'[1] The purpose of the present
paper is to re-examine the mainstream of sociology's theoretical
tradition, placing in relief the elements for a general theory whose
philosophical grounding is consonant with the broad movement of
existential phenomenology.[2] At the conclusion I shall suggest the
heuristic significance of this perspective and some of its methodological implications.

I shall not attempt to formulate a general theory of social existence,
for this would be entirely premature, but so far as it demonstrates
major areas of convergence in the sociological tradition which have
not been explicitly recognized, this paper represents an important
step in the direction of such a theory.

The phenomenological school in sociology

Although the history of sociology includes no accepted 'existential
sociology,' various writers of texts on theory[3] have shown an awareness of the phenomenological approach. Figures in this 'school,'
however, are usually treated as peripheral to the major sociological
currents underlying contemporary sociology. The original phenomenological school of sociology flourished in German-speaking areas
of Europe in the inter-war period; moreover, phenomenological
sociology was directly under the philosophical influence of Edmund
Husserl and Martin Heidegger. Underlying both German sociology
and phenomenology was a concern for the cultural crisis of European
society that had manifested itself in the upheavals of World War I.

The person most clearly recognized as a figure in phenomenological sociology is Alfred Vierkandt (1867–1952), who saw sociology as a radically formal study of social phenomena. Quite in keeping with the phenomenological method, he stressed the necessity of grasping directly the 'essential types,' 'ultimate facts' (including sentiments), and 'meaningful wholes' in the inner life of social interaction and social groups. The pure description of intersubjective bonds, of the 'spiritual' elements of collective life does not rely on an inductive approach to grasp the essence (*eidos* in Husserl's terminology) of the social phenomenon being considered. Because the direct apprehension of social essences cannot be achieved by means of analysis (in the sense of seeking to arrive at a whole by means of investigating component parts), Vierkandt gave primacy to understanding directly the integral wholeness of each society and social group, a wholeness manifested in the specific ethos, spirit, or way of life of distinct social systems.

Vierkandt hardly ranks as a major theorist today. Yet, his perspective on social phenomena as totalities in their formal structure is directly related to Gestalt psychology (also influenced by Husserl), on the one hand, and to the anthropological tradition of functionalism, which in its radical aspect stressed the total integration of culture as a unified whole, on the other. Ruth Benedict's well-known *Patterns of Culture*, which seeks to grasp the 'essence' of the cultural ethos of certain non-Western societies, has a distinct affinity with Vierkandt's methodological stand. Thus, formal sociology, Gestalt psychology, and functionalism share as a basic point of departure the acceptance of structural wholes as the fundamental units of investigation.

Better known figures in the phenomenological school are Max Scheler and Karl Mannheim, though they have not always been recognized primarily as phenomenologists. Spiegelberg in his excellent historical study of phenomenology[4] discusses the relation between Scheler and Husserl but omits Mannheim, while Timasheff in his survey of sociological theories[5] talks of the 'isolated' Mannheim in the philosophical school but leaves out Scheler in discussing phenomenological sociology. Mannheim and Scheler are usually identified as major writers in the sociology of knowledge, but their *Wissenssoziologie* is not widely understood as an integral part of their phenomenological approach to sociology. Their common concern in this endeavor was with the cultural crisis of their age, characterized in part by the fragmentation and relativization of knowledge. I shall discuss Mannheim and Scheler at some length in this context, since their contributions to sociological theory have not been given the attention they deserve.

Mannheim's studies of *Weltanschauung* (a global perception of social reality) reflect in part the influence of Wilhelm Dilthey on German sociology. Dilthey had raised the significance for the social sciences (*Geisteswissenschaften*) of grasping the integral perception of a culture's life situation and world view. Taking his lead from this suggestion, Mannheim made thorough empirical investigations of the social basis of *Weltanschauungen*, which as collective mental products or collective representations of reality (in Durkheim's sense) are among the cultural products found in human society. Mannheim's approach is distinctly phenomenological, as may be seen in his important 'On the Interpretation of "Weltanschauung." '[6] This is not surprising, for the notion of *Weltanschauung* implies the notion of *intentionality*, which plays a cardinal role in the doctrines of Husserl and his mentor, Franz Brentano.[7] Intentionality as an act of consciousness which directs the subject outward (i.e., consciousness is always relational, directed to something outside itself or as the phenomenologists state it, consciousness is always 'consciousness of' something) is a crucial tenet of the existential-phenomenological movement. Mannheim's studies of world views represent a sociological extension of this notion, for a *Weltanschauung* is an intentional psychological act of a collectivity of subjects, the apprehension of their collective world of lived experience perceived as a totality.

Mannheim's approach is phenomenological in other related aspects. His careful attention to the types of meanings[8] given in the phenomenal presentation of cultural objects reflects very much Husserl's stress on the 'meaningful' aspect of the intentional act: reduction to the essentials of a phenomenon involves unveiling successive layers of meaning, from the externally manifest to the core latent 'noematic' content.[9] For Mannheim the notion of 'structure' is cardinal and denotes the immanent unity of the social whole, a unity resting on the complementarity of conflicting social relationships and hence not fixed or 'static.' Not only is 'structure' akin to 'Gestalt' in psychology but it is also very much related to Husserl's notion of the 'constitution' of the objective field of consciousness. 'Structure' is not an empirical social object any more than 'constitution' is, yet it is a real object of the observer's perception. Without the presence of structure we could not perceive a meaningful region but only a disconnected series of unrelated (social) objects. It is the structure of things that gives us their meaning as wholes, and since there are various layers of structure, various strata of meaning, any phenomenon has a certain ambiguity in its relation to its ground. For the sake of brevity I shall not develop Mannheim's ideas further along this line, but it should be realized by now that this phenomenological approach to 'meaning' and 'structure' is at the heart of functional analysis, particularly as formulated by Merton in his distinction between 'manifest' and 'latent' functions.[10]

Mannheim's 'The Problem of Generations'[11] is also relevant, not so much as a seminal sociological study of structural sources of social change, but more, in this context, because it shows that Mannheim treated the spatial-temporal existence and historicity of social groups very much in the existential-phenomenological perspective. Inherent in this approach is the awareness that the existential space-time location of men and cultural objects does not coincide with an absolute space-time location; the latter is a construct derived from the world of experience (*Lebenswelt*). In this essay Mannheim refers to Heidegger, whose *Being and Time*, first published in 1927, has been a decisive influence in modern existential thought. He gives even more attention to Heidegger in 'Competition as a Cultural Phenomenon,'[12] where, after discussing Heidegger's description of the everyday world and the impersonal '*das Man*' or 'they' who act as the ubiquitous socializing agencies and manipulators of public knowledge, Mannheim comments,

> The philosopher looks at this 'They,' this secretive Something, but he is not interested to find out how it arose; and it is just at this point, where the philosopher stops, that the work of the sociologist begins.[13]

This remark indicates the grounds of a fruitful collaboration between existential phenomenology and sociological research; far from entangling sociology in the cobwebs of metaphysics, phenomenology can sensitize it to major aspects of social reality. But perhaps I should reserve the 'moral' of this article for the end, rather than making it in the middle.

For Mannheim, the sociology of knowledge as related to the study of *Weltanschauung* is not an abstract pursuit but an existential one, and this in a double sense. First, the methodology of the physical sciences is inappropriate for the sociology of knowledge because important items of knowledge are existentially determined in concrete historical situations, hence incapable of being measured quantitatively and interpreted on an absolute scale. We cannot assume that socio-cultural units are constant in space and time, and this raises the methodological problem of measurement (e.g., how can we quantitatively compare a conservative American *Weltanschauung* in 1965 with a conservative German *Weltanschauung* in 1865?). The phenomenological method, which is more appropriate than that of the physical sciences in studying problems of this sort, signifies that

> certain insights concerning some qualitative aspect of the living process of history are available to consciousness only as formed by certain historical and social circumstances, so that the historico-social formation of the thinking and knowing subject assumes epistemological importance.[14]

Second, not only does the sociology of knowledge uncover the existential relations of knowledge to social structure but also the task of *Wissenssoziologie* is itself an existential one, that of overcoming the relativism of the modern age. If knowledge is not absolute but rather determined by socio-historical processes, and if social groups presently have opposed world views, can a phenomenologically-based sociology overcome this fragmentation and thus prevent the dissolution of the modern world? Mannheim attempts to answer this existential question via his ideas of 'relationism' and 'socially unattached' intellectuals who can transcend conflicting perspectives.[15]

In this brief overview it is impossible to do justice to the richness of Max Scheler's phenomenological sociology[16] but some of its aspects may be rapidly indicated. Scheler's achievements of significance for sociology were (1) relating the intentionality of consciousness to specific forms of interaction, (2) phenomenological reductions of primary inter-personal psychological states, and (3) his attempt to arrive at ultimate, non-relative values. As a sociologist, Scheler is probably best known for his sociology of values, but his grounding affective intentionality in social structure is an important link in the development of existential phenomenology and the sociology of knowledge as well. An important theme of the existential-phenomenological tradition (from Kierkegaard to Sartre, Jaspers and other recent figures) is that human existence is disclosed in affective states: our existential self (*Dasein*) is always a sentient self (even indifference is a feeling), and the structure of our orientation to our situation is a spatial-temporal one of emotiveness. 'Rational man' is a useful construct but it is an abstraction from the integral self. Scheler deepened this insight into the affective nature of experience by suggesting the interdependence between affect and social structure (i.e., social bonds and roles have an affective structural basis reflected in personality). Scheler's phenomenological approach, therefore, uncovered a significant link between personality and social structure.

The phenomenologists Vierkandt, Mannheim and Scheler have not had many followers as such among contemporary sociologists. Georges Gurvitch, the foremost theorist in France, came in contact early with the phenomenological movement. Although his 'sociology in depth'[17] also reflects the influence of such sources as von Wiese and Mauss, and although Gurvitch has dissociated himself from formal phenomenology, his approach to social reality is very much an expression of existential phenomenology. His view of social structures as dynamic intersubjective realities is akin to Mannheim's notion of structure (and at odds with a notion of structure as a fixed entity that exists apart from a socio-historical process). Moreover, Gurvitch's rejection of social determinism and causality operating in social phenomena, his emphasis on the multiplicity of social times reflecting the multiplicity of social structures,[18] and his notion of the communal 'we' as a primary factor in the intentionality of consciousness (man experiences social reality as part of a 'we' no less directly than as an individual 'I')—all these reflect his early formative contacts with phenomenology.

To round out the contemporary scene, mention should be made of Chambard's article on the social experiential meanings of religious symbols in India,[19] which also contains an excellent general discussion of the relation of phenomenology to sociology. Though little explicit attention has been given to phenomenology in American sociology, contacts with Scheler did influence the late Howard Becker.[20] Perhaps the sociologist who has been most active in developing phenomenological sociology is Harold Garfinkel. His doctoral dissertation[21] investigated the significance of a person's imputing motives to others; it is a phenomenological study of the changing intentionality of social objects, including others as personalities given as 'wholes' in perception. In this work Garfinkel acknowledges the influence of both Husserl and Alfred Schutz, and the affinity with Scheler is also apparent. A later article[22] deals with the phenomenology of moral indignation as social affect, and more recently Garfinkel has presented data disclosing how individuals implicitly structure their situation *vis-à-vis* others.[23]

Existential phenomenology in the sociological mainstream

The phenomenological tradition in sociology is not limited to the above recognized figures, for much of the theory of sociologists who are not identified with the existential-phenomenological movement is in keeping with its presuppositions. In this section, therefore, I shall argue that a meaningful methodological convergence exists in the works of Max Weber, Georg Simmel, Emile Durkheim, William I. Thomas, Pitirim Sorokin and Talcott Parsons, and that this convergence points to a more comprehensive theory of social existence.

In relating Max Weber to phenomenology, mention must be made of the intellectual ferment in Germany in his formative years concerning the nature of investigation into 'cultural' phenomena. Wilhelm Dilthey had posited that the disciplines dealing with cultural phenomena or 'spiritual products' (the *Geisteswissenschaften*) were to be sharply differentiated from those dealing with physical matter (the *Naturwissenschaften*): the logical status of the cultural sciences was of a different order due to the nature of their objects of inquiry (that is, their objects are mental products of human consciousness). Thus, a causal interpretation along the lines of a mechanistic model is precluded in historical studies: the human spirit transcends any cadre of classification which enables the physical sciences to study their objects with precision, and furthermore, human behavior is permeated with value-orientations. The methodology of the natural sciences treats values as irrelevant for an 'objective' study of things and the dismissal of values limits the generality of positivistic methodology. Moreover, since the meaning we perceive in the world around us is grounded in the values we implicitly hold, social scientists and their studies are value-laden, which does away with an 'objective' interpretation of human events. Thus, runs Dilthey's argument, the precise, accurate measurements necessary to establish causal connections in the natural sciences are unavailable to the cultural disciplines. The latter, however, have a distinct methodological feature: since the observer is a human being studying other human beings, he has access to their inner world of experience. This direct access is 'sympathetic understanding' and 'intuition' by means of which the observer can view cultural phenomena 'from within.'

Weber was ambivalent concerning Dilthey's famous dichotomy. On the one hand, he felt that there is but one scientific logic, which applies equally to natural and cultural phenomena.[24] The construction of concepts is required for the empirical validation of statements concerning cultural as well as natural phenomena, and nothing in the nature of 'cultural' objects prevents one from constructing general concepts. The observer's values affect his sociological observations (e.g., in the selection of his theoretical problem), but he can make them explicit and go on to treat objectively the role of values in the socio-cultural phenomena he observes. Sociology should not accept the belief that the 'irrational' basis of human life manifests itself in the unique and thus assume the uniqueness of a cultural phenomenon. On the contrary, the initial presupposition should be that human behavior may be interpreted by means of a 'rationally consistent system of theoretical concepts.'[25] We first begin the analysis of specific historical phenomena, argued Weber, by constructing logical 'ideal types' on the assumption that actions are rational. Only when these ideal types *qua* categories of analysis are insufficient for the comprehension of an empirical course of events do we go on to look for 'irrational' factors, but even then we do not assume that there are noumenal 'things-in-themselves' which cannot be incorporated in a consistent theoretical framework.

On the other hand, Weber did accept important notions of the *Geisteswissenschaften*, notably the legitimacy of '*intuition* and 'understanding' (*Verstehen*) as modes of comprehending cultural phenomena which are in their nature irreducible to physical phenomena. Weber rejected a materialistic causal interpretation of history in terms of an economic determinism; he saw clearly that human behavior cannot be comprehended without reference to the motivation of human agents and to the subjective meanings they impute to their action.[26] This stress on the subjective meanings of the social situation is at the heart of Weber's sociology,[27] and it establishes a significant link between Weber and existential phenomenology.

Weber considered the intentionality of social action crucial for sociological analysis,[28] and this is entirely in keeping with the basic tenet of existential thought, originating with Kierkegaard, that 'subjectivity is truth' (namely, truth is always an experienced truth for the existent self). The latter proposition does *not* mean that the meaning a situation has for the subject cannot be communicated to others (which would make it truly 'irrational'). Certainly, as Weber forcefully stated in his well-known means-end schema, 'all interpretation of meanings, like all scientific observation, strives for clarity and verifiable accuracy of insight and comprehension.'[29] Thus, seemingly irrational conduct, which may be a significant causal agent in social change, as in the case of *charisma*, may nevertheless be emotionally understood and intellectually interpreted by the observer in terms of its meaning to the actors and its influence on subsequent social action.

Weber's methodology of *Verstehen*, thus, turns out to be upon closer examination an expression of existential phenomenology. It requires the sociological observer to uncover the subjective meanings manifested in historical phenomena and to relate one set of meanings to another (e.g., relating economic action to religious motivation). The major task of sociological investigation is to elucidate the dimensions of historical social structures; this is very different from trying to formulate causal social laws, which would imply a deterministic view of the social world.

Georg Simmel also reflects the influence of Dilthey in accepting the distinctness of socio-cultural phenomena. Simmel was as much a philosopher as a sociologist and wrote equally in both fields.[30] It is difficult to locate him in the history of sociology, though his is commonly taken to be a 'formal sociology.'[31] This is perhaps misleading, since Simmel did not take a 'formal' and distant approach to social phenomena but rather considered the description of pure 'social forms' as that which differentiates sociology from other disciplines. His analysis of specific structures of social life and the psychological processes they reflect (e.g., competition, subordination) is not germane here. It is important to note, however, the ties between Simmel and phenomenology.[32]

First, an important parallel exists between his distinction between the *form* and the *content* of social behavior, on the one hand, and Husserl's distinction between the *quality* of an intentional act and its *material* (or content). Second, although he diverged from Husserl in some respects, Simmel's study of social life may be viewed as an *eidetic one*, in the sense that he sought to reduce manifestly different concrete forms of social phenomena to their underlying essential characteristics ('forms'). Forms are revealed by means of an 'insightful look' at social life, grasping its essential psychological meanings as wholes; apparently heterogeneous contents may thus be shown to have a common form. The logic behind this is that the motivational factors in social life are emotional (affective psychological dispositions) which are adapted to specific types of social setting. A common nuclear 'meaning' underlies the repetitive aspects, the uniformities of social activity, and once the observer has grasped and described it (e.g., the meaning of the triad, the stranger, the cocktail party), its structural aspects will manifest themselves irrespective of the specific contents or occasions of the particular 'sociation' in question.

The affinity of Simmel's approach to phenomenological analysis is evident in the following interrelated elements of his sociology: (1) a pure description of social phenomena which (2) reduces them to their essential characteristics in terms of (3) meaningful core components of a non-social nature. Simmel was not interested in an empiricist, positivistic approach in which generalizations can only be made after carefully controlled experiments, but rather in a sophisticated direct 'understanding' of the forms underlying a variety of seemingly diverse phenomena. His investigations were mainly ahistorical, yet his methodology overlaps with Weber's for both gave primary emphasis to the subjective category of *Verstehen*.

Emile Durkheim seems, at first glance, at odds with an existential-phenomenological perspective, since his explicit methology is that of 'positivism.' The latter is commonly viewed as a repudiation not only of the 'subjective' perspective of existential phenomenology but also of the distinction between the physical and the socio-cultural sciences. Durkheim's positivism is indicated in his famous methodological dictum, to 'consider social facts as things.'[33]

Taken out of context, this statement might appear to make Durkheim antithetical to an existential-phenomenological viewpoint, but such a conclusion is unwarranted. On the contrary, 'consider social facts as things' has for Durkheim the same import and meaning as Husserl's dictum 'to the things themselves' ('*zu den Sachen*'). For Husserl,[34] valid phenomenological knowledge can only be obtained by an initial reduction from the 'natural attitude,' by bracketing the judgments about reality we make in our unreflective, everyday attitude of accepting things as they are perceived without questioning their foundation. But this phenomenological precept is exactly the counterpart of Durkheim's sociological rule!

Durkheim's positivism is grounded in accepting social facts as *sui generis* phenomena of intersubjective consciousness, as products of social interaction, which cannot properly be understood if reduced to a lower order of phenomena (physical or organic). They must be approached *naively*, that is, without preconceptions as to their nature or functions; this implies a suspension of the causal framework within which the positivism of the physical sciences operates. Since Durkheim's sociological analysis is really phenomenological, his studies owe their richness to a *radical description* of the interdependence of social phenomena rather than to the demonstration of causal principles operative in society. Indeed, I suggest that the spirit of Durkheimian sociology is profoundly akin to Heidegger's notion of *truth* as the dis-covery of being; namely, sociology must dis-cover what social facts really are and not what they are taken to be in the uncritical set of assumptions used by the public.

Durkheim's implicitly phenomenological approach, used to uncover successive layers of social reality from its overt manifestations to its covert essential characteristics,[35] is clearly illustrated in his famous study, *Suicide*. The 'surface' manifestations of suicide establish its presence as a social phenomenon; these objective, quantitative factors are then 'reduced' phenomenologically to underlying layers of the social structure in which the act of suicide occurs, and ultimately the meaning of the act is grounded in the psychological nexus between the individual and his social milieu (which is a subjective one). The 'depth' analysis leads Durkheim to perceive that sharp historical fluctuations in suicide rates are phenomenal 'surface' manifestations of much deeper, societal currents of a psychological nature, which presently lie outside the scope of scientific research. Thus, Durkheim casts sociological 'light' on what may initially appear to be an individual, irrational action.

I have treated Durkheim's relation to existential thought (as differentiated from phenomenology as a method) elsewhere,[36] but some summarizing remarks are appropriate here. In exactly the same spirit as the existential movement, Durkheim was primarily preoccupied with the moral crisis of modern society. Like the existentialist philosophers, he views man's existence as a 'co-existence,' as a 'being-in-the-world.' His analysis may logically be seen as an extension and enrichment of Heidegger's idea that the existential self (*Dasein*) is also a '*Mitsein*,' a 'being-with.' Durkheim always stressed that personality is constituted in society,[37] so that one's existence as 'being-in-the-world' may be said to be ontologically 'being-solidary-in-the-world-with-others.' Existence, then, is first and foremost social existence, grounded in solidarity. Hence, the breakdown in the normative consensus fundamental to social structure and in the consequent primacy of social obligations is, in Durkheim's eyes, the salient pathological feature of the modern world, and if it is left unattended it will injure both individual and society. The moral fragmentation of society (Durkheim's notion of *anomie* is the equivalent of today's 'pluralistic' society) and the fragmentation of personality are thus necessarily interrelated.

Existentialism and Durkheim's sociology are in spirit complementary, not polar, if Durkheim's perspective is seen as leading to 'social existentialism' and away from a narrower 'individual existentialism' from which no general theory of social order could be constructed. Durkheim's concern was the existential situation of modern society, and in particular how its moral dissolution was attended by a pathological weakening of the bonds of solidarity. His concern with modern society as an integral whole complements the existentialists' concern with man as an integral being. It is true that the existentialist ethic of Heidegger, Jaspers, and especially Sartre contains an individualistic bias: to fulfill his potentialities the individual must liberate himself from the yoke of impersonal society. But this does not mean that sociology and existential phenomenology are not complementary disciplines, for at the heart of the existentialist analysis of modern man is the idea that *freedom entails responsibility*, and that the liberation of the self from the routinized, banal, impersonal social world whose very appearance of objectivity and solidity conceals its existential ground, is a call not to anarchy or self-pity but to authentic inter-subjective social participation.

Recall that Durkheim emphasized that 'organic' society offers more potential freedom of action than 'mechanical' society, since it evaluates the individual in terms of personal achievement rather than by ascriptive status; the possibilities for freedom of action have historically been enlarged with the development of a differentiated but normatively integrated society. Yet, Durkheim also went on to criticize modern society *because* the normative or moral nexus between individuals has been so severely strained. What I wish to suggest is that Durkheim's critique of *anomic* society is highly congruent with the existential analysis of the *depersonalizing* effect of mass society; both have as their focal concern *inauthentic* social existence and its consequences.

In brief, Durkheim's sociology is no more 'anti-individual' than existential thought is 'anti-social,' and only a gross misreading could warrant such a conclusion. Durkheim, in spite of his Cartesian rationalism, always made a significant place for non-rational elements in his descriptions of social reality as well as in the process by which he arrived at such descriptions.[38]

Turning to American sociology, the problem is to select what should be taken for the mainstream of the American tradition. We have had various schools, but I suggest that the tradition represented until the present generation by Cooley, Mead, and W. I. Thomas has had the most lasting impact on sociological theory. Before seeing how Thomas's work in particular is related to existential phenomenology,

I would like to point out very briefly a key link between American social thought and the existential-phenomenological tradition. John Wild has recently pointed out that phenomenology owes much to the direct influence of William James, in particular to his stress on 'the relational structure of our lived experience.'[39] James treated the concrete experiences of life as a continuous process of becoming; his work, then, is an important bridge between the American pragmatic tradition and the European existential-phenomenological tradition. (Moreover, James acknowledged his major influence to be Charles Renouvier, the same French thinker who was Durkheim's teacher of philosophy!)

William I. Thomas was perhaps the major source of pressure to take sociology and social psychology out of the academic walls and into 'the field.' This impulse to see what is going on 'outside' and its rejection of academic abstractions is a major aspect of existential phenomenology. Thomas is well known, of course, as the author of the 'self-fulfilling prophecy,' but it is not so clearly realized that his theorem is a sociological formulation of the existential tenet that 'subjectivity is truth.'

Thomas's major works point out the subjective meanings of social action as basic reference points for sociological investigation. Objective social conditions have to be seen in the light of subjective components of social actors: their attitudes, their basic wishes, their definitions of the situation. Without an awareness of these subjective meanings, objective correlations are incomplete descriptions of reality.

Equally relevant is Thomas's more general perspective on the sociological endeavor, one which reveals a profound affinity with phenomenology. His conception of man is that he is meaningfully related to society, culture, and social others, and that in his activities he has an important element of conscious control. That is, the social actor is capable of organizing his social stage; he is capable of meaningfully relating himself in his consciousness to his social environment, though sudden changes in the environment (e.g., immigration) bring about disruptive crises. As Martindale points out, Thomas quite early held that the sociological endeavor should have as its object 'the phenomena of *attention*—"the mental attitude which takes note of the outside world and manipulates it." '[40] Although Martindale does not relate Thomas to phenomenology, the notion of 'attention' in the quoted passage is equivalent to the phenomenological notion of 'intention.'

If Thomas is a representative spokesman for the 'second generation,' Sorokin and Parsons are probably the most eminent contributors in the contemporary generation of theorists. Sorokin's sociology expresses a rapprochement to existential phenomenology more explicitly, perhaps, than any other discussed in this essay. First, he accepts the *Naturwissenschaften-Geisteswissenschaften* distinction, holding that socio-cultural phenomena have properties not accounted by psychological or bio-physical models of explanation.[41] Sorokin has repeatedly stressed that socio-cultural phenomena are interrelated by a realm of *meanings* imputed by social actors to these phenomena; such meanings (values, norms, aesthetics) transform the natural properties of objects.[42] The explanation of such phenomena involves a statement of interrelations at the level of meaningful wholes, which presupposes a socio-cultural space-time reality of a more fundamental nature than the physical sciences' abstract geometrical space and absolute time. Consequently, seemingly diverse socio-cultural phenomena may permit the sociological uncovering of integrated macro-sociocultural systems, characterized by fundamental premises that provide the basic orientation of these systems to reality.

Now, Sorokin's methodological approach is not only a more precise statement of the presuppositions underlying structural-functional analysis, but it also is phenomenological in spirit: his emphasis on uncovering meanings and 'reducing' macro-socio-cultural systems to their essential characteristics parallels Husserl's stress on intentionality and the reduction of phenomena to their core meanings (*noemata*). Sorokin' semphasis on an existential realm of socio-cultural reality apart from a physical conception of the universe is of fundamental importance for this paper. *This is one of the major foci of convergence in the sociological tradition being considered.*

The acceptance of a social reality qualitatively distinct from and more primary in experience than physical reality is the foundation of a general theory of social existence and an expression of *social realism*. Sorokin's approach is thus very similar to that of the Durkheimian school, and both may be regarded as part of an enlarged existential-phenomenological perspective. Durkheim, Mauss, and others of the 'sociologistic' school found that social space has properties different from physical space; moreover, Durkheim argued in *The Elementary Forms of Religious Life* that the scientific conceptions of space, time, and logical classes are derivatives of a primordial set of social existentials. This is a remarkable convergence with Heidegger's argument that the space-time continuum of modern science is not in itself reality 'out there' but rather a derivative of our existential being-in-the-world. Translated into the sociological tradition, Heidegger's notion of *Dasein*, the existential self as a being-in-the-world, should be treated as *intersubjective consciousness*. Sorokin and Durkheim implicitly concur with the existential stress on truth as a subjective reality, if this is extended to signify that socio-cultural systems and social groups perceive truth in the light of their existential social situations. The sociological tradition converges in the relational (but not relativistic) view that truth is an existential relation between the social actor and his situation; seen phenomenologically, truth and reality are binding for the actor who is always *engaged* in his situation. It is only for the *detached* observer that social truth appears to be an arbitrary or relative matter.

Sorokin's conception of sociology and social reality is congruent with existential phenomenology in two other major respects. First, his 'integralist' model is linked with the existential (and Gestalt) perspective of being-in-the-world as an integral whole. Just as phenomenal reality as a total process of *becoming* cannot be represented adequately, therefore, by a simplistic reduction to mechanistic models, for Sorokin (and Durkheim, Weber, Scheler, Mead, Thomas and the others discussed here), socio-cultural reality cannot be reduced to any form of material causation because a dialectic interaction takes place, in the world of experiences, between moral phenomena (ideas, values, beliefs) and physical phenomena. The world is *symbolically perceived* and not simply responded to physically, as empiricism and behaviorism would have us believe. Second, Sorokin shares a common agreement that modern society has lost sight of its moral basis, that the dissolution of the moral structure of the social world creates a normative crisis externally manifested in seemingly different symptoms, ranging from a crisis in epistemology to attacks on norms governing sexual behavior.

The work of Talcott Parsons is the hardest test case of this argument, for his general theory of action is in some major respects at odds with an existential-phenomenological perspective. Since I think that an action orientation is essentially congruent with such a perspective, I shall suggest briefly what the deviations are and what accounts for the divergence. First, unlike the basic existentialist evaluation that modern society is in a state of profound moral crisis (resulting in 'depersonalization,' 'objectification' and other features of mass society), Parsons's implicit orientation is much more one of 'rational optimism.' In his sociological writings, even the more recent ones, he gives very little attention to social problems as reflections of an underlying societal crisis;[43] this seems to indicate that he is unaware of the saliency of social conflict as a problematic structural feature of modern society. The 'equilibrium' model suggests that the ship of American society can be kept on its main course mechanically by means of an automatic pilot.

Second, and much more fundamental, Parsons makes implicit use of two quite different and basically antithetical models of human action. One of these models is based on a phenomenological perspective, but the other belongs to quite another tradition: broadly, that of utilitarianism, rationalism, nominalism, and behaviorism (the latter implying material determinism). This second model represents a later development in Parsons's approach to the action scheme, as Scott has cogently shown.[44] It is manifest in the hedonistic image of the individual actor in *Toward A General Theory of Action*, in the notion of 'need-disposition' and the statement that 'the personality may ... be conceived as a system with a persistent tendency toward the optimum level of gratification.'[45] Grafted onto this Tolman-influenced behavioristic-physiological view of the individual as an organism is the Freudian model of personality; the notions of 'internalization,' 'cathexis,' and 'mechanisms of defense' in *Toward A General Theory of Action* reflect the post-war influence of Freud on Parsons. The net effect of 'adopting' a Freudian model (and with it a deterministic, biologistic, object-relation psychology) is, as Scott has pointed out,[46] to undermine Parsons's own earlier voluntaristic scheme! The view of individual actions as the result of either primary libidinal drives or passive receptivity to socialization (via the unreflective mechanism of superego internalization), on the one hand, is basically incompatible with an emphasis on the individual's volitional organization of the situation and the omnipresent possibility of choice in selecting its configuration.

Since the voluntaristic perspective is basic to a theory of action and is clearly articulated with an existential-phenomenological *Weltanschauung*, it is important to examine Parsons's earlier *The Structure of Social Action*.[47] In this seminal study, Parsons noted a convergence in sociological theory which may be termed 'subjective realism.' Ends (goals, values) are not random or arbitrary; they are real, non-empirical (that is, not given by sensory perception), and extra-individual. Social action has a normative base and cannot be seen only as overt behavior; it is essentially the actor's subjective orientation to his situation in the light of his knowledge of the past, present and anticipated future.[48] Hence, scientifically valid (or positivistic, 'objective') knowledge of the situation does not exhaust all its significant elements, for these include subjective ones not accountable merely by reference to 'ignorance and error.'[49] The action frame of reference stresses the unfolding continuity of the actor's acts. 'Action is a temporal process,'[50] states Parsons, and he adds that the conceptual schema for analyzing this process 'is inherently subjective ... the normative elements can be conceived of as "existing" only in the mind of the actor.'[51]

This begins to suggest how closely the action frame of reference is consistent with a phenomenological perspective. Not only does it assume a *Naturwissenschaft-Geisteswissenschaft* distinction, in opposition to radical positivism,[52] but also, as Parsons explicitly acknowledges, 'the action frame of reference may be said to have what many, following Husserl, have called a "phenomenological" status.'[53]

As in Husserl's approach, emphasis is given to the *description* of the personality as a totality of unit acts. In going beyond description to a *causal* interpretation of acts by reference to motivational factors, Parsons's action perspective 'becomes, in Husserl's sense, "psychological." But its phenomenological aspect, as a frame of reference, does not disappear; it remains implicit in any use of the action schema.'[54]

This early and fundamental formulation of Parsonian 'action theory' is also very much in keeping with the existential side of phenomenology, with its stress on the actor's *freedom* and *becoming* as integral aspects of his social existence. As a recent reviewer of Parsons's sociological theory points out, action theory rests on an indeterminate element of voluntarism in the actor's orientation to his situation: 'Without this crucial element of freedom, denied in any closed, determinate system, action becomes mere behavior.'[55]

'Mere behavior' involves no element of volition on the part of the subject, no symbolic organization of the *environmental* elements into an existential *situation* which is a subjective reality and not just a set of physical objects. 'Action' implies interaction, or 'intersubjective consciousness.' This further implies that the subject is not passively socialized as an assembly-line product but that the actor (either individual or collectivity) is actively involved in the socialization process; the dialectic between individual and collective volitions suggests that 'there always remains some lack of congruence between individual and societal goals.'[56] The very conception of socialization as a continuous process of adjustment to social life is basic not only to an action frame of reference and to the sociological tradition noted here, but also to the existential perspective on reality as a *becoming* and not a fixed *being*. A Freudian model of personality development, however, is quite incompatible with such a notion of the socialization process, no matter how sociologically respectable one tries to render it.

In dealing with the personality as a system in the totality of action, Parsons has leaned heavily in recent years on the behavioristic-Freudian model. This model is so at odds with the earlier and more basic model that the term 'voluntarism' seems to have been shelved from the action theory vocabulary in recent formulations. And yet, when he analyzes the real world of experience, Parsons is far from having divorced himself from the mainstream under consideration. Thus, the 'pattern variables'[57] have a subjective reference, for they are a structural elaboration of Thomas's notion of the 'definition of the situation,' which is only meaningful from a subjective perspective. Moreover, one of the pattern variables, 'affectivity-affective neutrality' as a role dilemma, may be seen as an important refinement of Scheler's insight that affect is grounded in intersubjective consciousness; this and the other pattern-variables are certainly significant heuristic devices for any phenomenological investigation of social situations. The basic affinity between Parsons and existential phenomenology creates other continuities worth noting. As a feature of the American value system, for instance, Parsons includes 'instrumental activism' which is closely related to 'institutionalized individualism'; this, he notes,[58] must be sharply differentiated from a 'utilitarian' version of individualism. Why? Because the former stresses a moral obligation to achievement 'rather than an orientation to hedonistic enjoyment.'[59]

Here, then, is a very important return to the voluntaristic model of *The Structure of Social Action*. The voluntaristic model *is* one of 'instrumental individualism,' that is, its implicit view is that of socially given goals that each member of the social order is morally bound to implement; the actor's self-realization in a situation is instrumental to the self-realization of the community to which he belongs. Voluntarism, in other words, presupposes that the individual actor's situation is always defined in terms of a moral community, that the social world is not just cognitively but also morally ordered (and thus all social acts are to some degree morally evaluated). The world of the actor *qua* subject of action is a moral constitution that grounds the meaning of particular situations and particular objects (including social objects).

Parsons's phenomenological approach is also evident in his discussion of culture as a relational system of 'meanings' which are not properties of physical objects but rather a function of perception.[60] In its underlying form, then, the action frame of reference is a model of social existence emphasizing intersubjectivity, self-realization via an institutional moral order, the 'openness' of the actor to the world, the actor as a sentient being (and not a rationalistic creation). It is entirely consonant, therefore, with a conception of existential phenomenology as the philosophical underpinning of general sociological theory.

Conclusion

I have sought to show, in the course of this paper, that at the heart of the major intellectual sources of the sociological tradition is an underlying consensus which may be called 'subjective realism,' and that this view of the individual and society has a marked affinity with existential phenomenology. Subjective realism approaches social reality as it is phenomenally experienced by actors; it thereby avoids the pitfalls of both materialism and idealism. In the sociological tradition subjective realism manifests itself in various labels such as 'voluntarism' (related to 'personalism'[61]), 'pragmatism,' 'integralism,'

301

and 'sociologism.' The convergence with existential phenomenology leads to the possibility of a general theory of social existence. I have previously[62] suggested ways in which recognition of its affinity with existential thought may be fruitful for the development of sociology, but at that time I did not clearly realize the links with phenomenology. Consequently, I should like to expand these suggestions very briefly.

Sociologists will find very profitable the writings that provide significant bridges between existential phenomenology and the social sciences, in particular those of Maurice Merleau-Ponty[63] and Alfred Schutz.[64] From these and other sources may be gathered a number of 'sensitizing concepts' (to use Blumer's phrase), such as 'alienation,' 'care,' 'guilt,' 'authenticity,' 'horizon,' which can fruitfully be used to formulate new conceptions of empirical research that would make accessible social phenomena not amenable to a quantitative, external, object approach.

Existential phenomenology complements rather than entirely replaces the present typically positivistic approach to research; that is, it validates objective techniques of describing social phenomena, just as highly reliable quantitative propositions may be used to validate phenomenologically derived insights and interpretations of social reality. The methodology appropriate for the subjective realist frame of reference in sociology may be termed *transobjectivity*, to indicate that explanation goes beyond the object to a complex elucidation of the multiple perspectives and the social spatial-temporal dimensions of the social phenomenon. This methodology is, after all, at the heart of what Marcel Mauss proposed in his notion of the 'total social fact.'[65] The 'global' approach to social phenomena sees them as an actualizing (or in Heidegger's terminology, a 'temporalizing') set of events, since historicity is the ground of social actions; stated differently, social existence unfolds in social time.

Moreover, not only does sociological knowledge require both subjective understanding and objective cognizance[66] of the social situation (which should always be considered as a phenomenon of intersubjective consciousness), but it should also be seen as an essentially *radical description* of social reality. Existential phenomenology applied to sociology seeks the *roots* of social existence. This implies that it seeks to elucidate the existential nature of social structures by uncovering the surface institutional phenomena of the everyday 'accepted' world; by probing the 'subterranean,' non-institutional social depths concealed from public gaze, by interpreting the dialectic between the institutional and the non-institutional (e.g., the relation of charisma to the secular).[67]

At present, sociological theory is not doing justice to this unexplored realm of social existence; we are in a position roughly comparable to rationalistic psychology before the advent of depth psychology. Yet, the sociological tradition sketched out in this paper has already paved the way for a meaningful interplay between sociological theory and the existential-phenomenological perspective developed in modern philosophy (and spread in clinical psychology).[68] Sociological theory can remain true to itself and yet renovate its formulations by focusing on the existential horizon of social life. We know much more about the physical *universe* than about the social *world(s)* and its (their) elastic properties; we still have to investigate rigorously the interrelations of the two (e.g., the physical consequences of movement in social space), and this will in turn enable sociological theory to treat meaningfully the dialectic between the quantitative and the qualitative. In broad outline, these are the directions to which the sociological tradition points.

Finally, an existential awareness translated into empirical research will enable sociology better to appreciate and thereby cope with the seemingly 'irrational' discontinuities and large-scale upheavals of modern society. Far from abandoning sociology as a science, this is to restore its heritage, grounded in the sociological tradition, of utilizing its global knowledge for socially responsible ends.

Notes

1 Helmut R. Wagner, 'Types of Sociological Theory: Toward a System of Classification', *American Sociological Review*, vol. 28 (1963), pp. 735-6.
2 Space limitation obviates the explication of the philosophical background and central notions of existential thought and the phenomenological method; for purposes of the present discussion these will be treated as given. Good introductions to the major concepts, problems, and figures in this general philosophical movement are: John Wild, *The Challenge of Existentialism*, Bloomington: Indiana University Press, 1955; Pierre Thévenaz, *What is Phenomenology?*, Chicago: Quadrangle Books, 1962; Anna-Teresa Tymieniecka, *Phenomenology and Science in Contemporary European Thought*, New York: Noonday Press, 1962.
3 Theodore Abel, *Systematic Sociology in Germany*, New York: Columbia University Press, 1929; Nicholas S. Timasheff, *Sociological Theory, Its Nature and Growth* (rev. ed.), New York: Random House, 1957; Don Martindale, *The Nature and Types of Sociological Theory*, Boston: Houghton Mifflin, 1960.
4 Herbert Spiegelberg, *The Phenomenological Movement*, 2 vols, The Hague: Nijhoff, 1960.
5 Timasheff, *op. cit.*
6 In his *Essays on the Sociology of Knowledge* (ed. Paul Kecskemeti), London: Routledge & Kegan Paul, 1952, pp. 33-83.
7 See Franz Brentano, 'The Distinction between Mental and Physical

Phenomena' in Roderick M. Chisholm (ed.), *Realism and the Back-ground of Phenomenology*, Chicago: Free Press, 1960, pp. 39–61.

8 Mannheim, *op. cit.*, pp. 43–63.

9 Edmund Husserl, *Ideas*, New York: Collier Books, 1962.

10 Robert Merton, 'Manifest and Latent Functions' in *Social Theory and Social Structure*, Chicago: Free Press, 1949, esp pp. 61–5.

11 Mannheim, *op. cit.*, pp. 276–320.

12 *Ibid.*, pp. 191–229.

13 *Ibid.*, p. 199.

14 *Ibid.*, p. 194.

15 The convergence between Durkheim and Mannheim on some key points of their sociological perspective is striking. Durkheim's final perspective on morality in Armand Cuvillier (ed.), *Le Pragmatisme et sociologie*, Paris: Vrin, 1955; partially translated in Kurt H. Wolff (ed.), *Emile Durkheim 1858–1917*, Columbus: Ohio State University Press, 1960, pp. 386–436) is essentially one of relationism. Furthermore, Durkheim saw the role of the intellectuals and of education in the reconstruction of the moral basis of modern society in very much the same fashion as Mannheim. Both also felt that sociology must accept a role of social responsibility as its ultimate justification.

16 See Georges Gurvitch, *Les Tendances actuelles de la philosophie allemande* (2nd printing), Paris: Vrin, 1949, pp. 67–152; also the introduction by Werner Stark to Max Scheler's *The Nature of Sympathy*, London: Routledge & Kegan Paul, 1954.

17 Timasheff, *op. cit.*, p. 268.

18 Georges Gurvitch, *The Spectrum of Social Time*, Dordrecht, Holland: Reidel, 1964; also 'Social Structure and the Multiplicity of Times' in Edward A. Tiryakian (ed.), *Sociological Theory, Values and Socio-cultural Change: Essays in Honor of Pitirim A. Sorokin*, New York: Free Press, 1963, pp. 171–84.

19 Jean-Luc Chambard, 'Pour une Sociologie phénoménologique de l'Inde', *Cahiers Internationaux de Sociologie*, vol. 25 (1958), pp. 152–76.

20 Howard Becker, 'Current Sacred-Secular Theory and Its Development' in Howard Becker and Alvin Boskoff (eds), *Modern Sociological Theory in Continuity and Change*, New York: Dryden Press, 1957, p. 179.

21 'The Perception of the Other: A Study in Social Order', Harvard University, unpublished Ph.D. thesis, 1952.

22 'Conditions of Successful Degradation Ceremonies', *American Journal of Sociology*, vol. 61 (1956), pp. 420–4.

23 'Studies of the Routine Grounds of Everyday Activities', *Social Problems*, vol. 11 (1964), pp. 225–50. Garfinkel's imaginative research contains suggestive applications of Husserl's notion of *epoché* as a heuristic device, i.e., the 'bracketing' of the natural attitude to accept the world as solidly given. See Husserl, *op. cit.*, pp. 91–100 for a crucial chapter on the foundations of the phenomenological method.

24 For a comprehensive discussion of Weber's methodology and its relation to Dilthey's thesis, see Talcott Parsons, *The Structure of Social Action*, Chicago: Free Press, 1949, pp. 579–639.

25 *Ibid.*, p. 589.

26 This is reflected in his familiar definition of social action: 'In "action" is included all human behavior when and in so far as the acting individual attaches a subjective meaning to it.' Max Weber, *The Theory of Social and Economic Organization* (ed. and trans. Talcott Parsons and A. M. Henderson), New York: Oxford University Press, 1947, p. 88.

27 Abel, *op. cit.*, p. 124.

28 *Ibid.*, p. 123.

29 Weber, *op. cit.*, p. 90.

30 For a general study of Simmel as a philosopher, see Rudolph H. Weingartner, *Experience and Culture*, Middletown, Conn.: Wesleyan University Press, 1962.

31 This is the perspective on Simmel adopted by Abel, *op. cit.*, Martindale, *op. cit.*, and Raymond Aron, *German Sociology*, Chicago: Free Press, 1957.

32 For a discussion of the contacts between Simmel and Husserl, see Weingartner, *op. cit.*, pp. 23 ff.

33 *The Rules of Sociological Method*, Chicago: Free Press, 1950, p. 14.

34 N. 23, above.

35 Durkheim stops short of a 'transcendental reduction', in phenomenological terms, in that he does not seek to establish the universal essence of society. Either this would lead sociology into metaphysics, or else by its very generality such an essence would have no sociologically meaningful content.

36 *Sociologism and Extentialism: Two Perspectives on the Individual and Society*, Englewood Cliffs, N.J.: Prentice-Hall, 1962.

37 See in particular his 'Le dualisme de la nature humaine et ses conditions sociales', *Scientia*, vol. 15 (1914), pp. 206–21, trans. as 'The Dualism of Human Nature' in Wolff, *op. cit.*, pp. 325–40.

38 In his study of religion, for example, he does not arrive inductively at its essential characteristics as a social phenomenon but rather reaches them in a phenomenological 'intuitive' or 'insightful' manner (which of course is neither introspective nor arbitrary).

39 John Wild, *Existence and the World of Freedom*, Englewood Cliffs, N.J.: Prentice-Hall, 1963, p. 31.

40 Martindale, *op. cit.*, p. 348.

41 *Sociocultural Causality, Space, Time*, Durham, N.C.: Duke University Press, 1942. This methodological standpoint, so explicit in the European sociological mainstream (including Weber and Durkheim), is also characteristic of the American tradition under consideration. Note, for example, the dualism implied in the following statement by George H. Mead: 'The physical object is found to be that object to which there is no social response which calls out again a social response in the individual. The objects with which we cannot carry on social intercourse are the physical objects of the world.' *The Philosophy of the Act*, University of Chicago Press, 1938, p. 292.

42 *Society, Culture, and Personality: Their Structure and Dynamics*, New York and London: Harper, 1947, p. 49. Durkheim, of course, had opened up this sociological perspective in *The Elementary Forms of the*

Religious Life, New York: Collier Books, 1961, p. 364 and *passim*.

43 Thus, in 'Social Strains in America' (in Daniel Bell (ed.), *The Radical Right*, Garden City, N.Y.: Doubleday, 1963, pp. 175–99) he views the reactions of the political right as a temporary phenomenon in American society and not as a surface manifestation of a deeper social malaise and polarization of society. Whether such a malaise 'objectively' exists in American society is beside the point, which is that unlike the Continental tradition, Parsons's perspective is not a crisis-oriented one.

44 John Finley Scott, 'The Changing Foundations of the Parsonian Action Scheme', *American Sociological Review*, vol. 28 (1963), pp. 716–35.

45 Talcott Parsons and Edward A. Shils (eds), *Toward a General Theory of Action*, Cambridge, Mass.: Harvard, 1951, p. 121.

46 Scott, *op cit.*, pp. 725, 730.

47 *The Structure of Social Action*, Chicago: Free Press, 1949 (first pub. in 1937, New York: McGraw-Hill).

48 *Ibid.*, p. 79.

49 *Ibid.*, p. 81.

50 *Ibid.*, p. 732.

51 *Ibid.*, p. 733.

52 Radical positivism, empiricism, behaviorism, and materialism all are opposed to any dualistic view of reality.

53 *Ibid.*, p. 733.

54 *Ibid.*, pp. 750 ff.

55 Edward C. Devereux, Jun., 'Parsons' Sociological Theory' in Max Black (ed.), *Social Theories of Talcott Parsons*, Englewood Cliffs, N.J.: Prentice-Hall, 1961, p. 13.

56 *Ibid.*, p. 25.

57 *Toward a General Theory of Action*, pp. 76–91.

58 Talcott Parsons and Winston White, 'The Link Between Character and Society' in Talcott Parsons, *Social Structure and Personality*, New York: Free Press, 1964, p. 197 (first published in Seymour M. Lipset and Leo Lowenthal (eds), *Culture and Social Character*, Chicago: Free Press, 1961).

59 *Loc. cit.*

60 See his 'Introduction' to pt 4, 'Culture and the Social System' in Talcott Parsons *et al.* (eds), *Theories of Society*, vol. 2, Chicago: Free Press, 1961, p. 964. This, of course, is in direct agreement with Durkheim and Sorokin, n. 42, above.

61 See Albert C. Knudson, *The Philosophy of Personalism*, New York & Cincinnati: Abingdon Press, 1927; also Emmanuel Mounier, *Le Personnalisme*, Paris: Presses Universitaires de France, 1962; Paul Ricoeur, 'Une philosophie personnaliste', *Esprit* (December 1950), pp. 860–87; Edward A. Tiryakian, 'The Person as Existential Self' in Chad Gordon and Kenneth J. Gergen (eds), *The Self in Social Interaction*, New York: Wiley (forthcoming).

62 *Sociologism and Existentialism*, pp. 164–9.

63 *The Structure of Behavior*, Boston: Beacon Press, 1963; *Phenomenology of Perception*, New York: Humanities Press, 1962; *Signs*, Evanston: Northwestern University Press, 1964.

64 Maurice Natanson (ed.), *Collected Papers I: The Problem of Social Reality*, The Hague: Nijhoff, 1962.

65 In the crucial conclusion of his 'Essai sur le Don' (English translation: *The Gift: Forms and Functions of Exchange in Archaic Societies*, Chicago: Free Press, 1954); see the perceptive comments by Claude Lévi-Strauss in his introduction to Marcel Mauss, *Sociologie et anthropologie*, Paris: Presses Universitaires de France, 1960, pp. xxiii–xxx.

66 The intended distinction is reflected in the French *connaître* and *savoir*, or in the German *kennen* and *wissen*.

67 This depth analysis of the multi-layered meanings of social reality is, after all, in the spirit of structural-functional analysis. The reification of 'structure' has led its critics to assume that structural analysis is 'static', whereas in fact the existential reality of social structures renders their analysis more 'dynamic' than anything else.

68 Following the lead of Durkheim and Weber, the sociological formulation of a theory of social existence also requires codification of the comparative data in *space* provided by ethnology and those in *time* offered by historical studies. Such a background in the fundamental symbolic forms and historical processes of social experience (viz., the existential structure of societies) is of the utmost relevance to a sophisticated sociological understanding of non-random trends in contemporary large-scale societies. I am preparing a lengthy study of the modernization of sub-Sahara Africa which will seek, in part, to demonstrate the applicability of a social existential frame of reference to the sociological analysis of a concrete historical situation and type of society, namely 'colonial Africa'.

20 The sociology of knowledge and the nature of social knowledge*

David Martin

The sociology of knowledge may be divided into the discipline as traditionally understood, rooted in the Marxist notion of ideology, and the phenomenological exploration of the nature of our social knowledge. Both types of enterprise owe a great deal to the work of Scheler. It is therefore appropriate to begin by considering a new book on Scheler by John Staude, which is itself an exercise in the sociology of knowledge as usually understood. It will then be appropriate to develop the second major concern of Scheler in terms of the phenomenological understanding of social reality found in the work of Schutz and more recently in Berger and Luckmann.

To each of these two main objects of discussion there is attached a critical codicil based on the essays of Hayek. Hayek poses two contrasts. Like Scheler he accepts that the intellectual stratum is crucial but objects equally to the socio-analysis of ideas and to any notion that intellectuals have (so far) made use of privileged access to truth. As against Berger, Hayek defends the necessary density, opacity and even mechanical nature of some social phenomena against any attempt to bring all within the clear light of phenomenological understanding.

John Staude's perceptive essay in the sociology of knowledge describes Scheler's evolution, and sets it intelligibly in a social and personal context. He defines Scheler's problem as both the disunity of German culture, and the ambiguous position of the upper middle class in Wilhelmian Germany, where its economic success contrasted

* Review Article: *Max Scheler 1874–1928: An Intellectual Portrait* by J. Staude, New York: Collier-Macmillan, 1967; *The Phenomenology of the Social World* by A. Schutz, Evanston: North Western University Press, 1967; *The Social Construction of Reality* by P. Berger and T. Luckmann, London: Allen Lane, Penguin Press, 1967; *Studies in Philosophy, Politics and Economics* by F. A. Hayek, London: Routledge & Kegan Paul, 1967.

308

with political and social failure. The politically impotent upper middle class turned to personal rather than public goals and mixed public submissiveness with authoritarianism in the home.

Scheler admired the aristocracy as natural leaders and despised the middle class as a prey to *ressentiment*, especially the petty bourgeoisie. Hence his glorification of the feudal, the military, the chivalrous, the organic and the elitist (plus inevitably a penchant for eastern contemplative mysticism) and his disgust at individualism, restlessness, utilitarianism and the abstract reason. All his changes of allegiance—the German youth movement, Catholicism, even socialism—reflected his search for a social base from which the elite might exercise its leadership. His enthusiasm for the war derived from its capacity to unify Germany against the rationalism of France and the utilitarianism of England. His sociology of knowledge was an attempt to transcend and unify the varied tendencies and perspectives of post-war parliamentarianism. Yet throughout his Catholicism helped save him from the amalgam of pure intuition with blood and soil vitalism and racism found on the extreme right.

Scheler aimed to destroy science as the norm of all true knowledge. So he replaced the Comtean sequence of theological, metaphysical and positive by a concept of levels dealing with different types of question. These levels corresponded to personality types: the scientist would never replace the sage and the saint. He argued that the notion of a sequence only reflected the experience of the western European bourgeoisie.

Scheler's own sequence comprised societies based on kinship, the state and the market; and Marxist views were only true of those societies based on the market. Moreover, it was not so much relations of production as the interests of the elite which determined the actualization of ideas, releasing them from their eternal existence in a Platonic heaven. Actually Scheler takes Marx's notion about the ruling ideas being those of the ruling class and generalizes it for every period—just as Mannheim took Marx's notion of ideology and generalized it to include all thought. Only generalize Marxism enough and it is a potent intellectual tool of right-wing analysis. This does not make generalized Marxism always inferior to the version which gives ontological privilege to proletarian-based thinking and which ignores the continuous impact of an elite new class.

Unfortunately there is no space here to pursue Scheler's controversy with Lukács over the status of bourgeois science (especially economics) and his delineation of differing intellectual styles. His interpretation of the backward-looking, teleological intellectualist style of the upper class, with its emphasis on being rather than becoming, heredity rather than environment and on social harmony rather than conflict, would suggest an interesting comparison with the elements outlined in Mannheim's *Essay on Conservative Thought*.

For Scheler the sociology of knowledge overcomes the antagonism of thought-styles by bringing them into consciousness: a socio-analysis running parallel to psychoanalysis. Socio-analysis provides the appropriate point at which to introduce the first critical codicil based on Hayek, since nothing could be further from his whole intellectual procedure. No doubt Hayek would accept Popper's critique of the sociology of knowledge.[1] In a footnote he claims never to accuse opponents of anything worse than straightforward error, not even wickedness. Yet in common with Scheler and Mannheim he has a very high estimate of the intelligentsia both in terms of social impact and of the potential promotion of truth. What the intelligentsia believes today the wider society will believe tomorrow.

This is clearly not always the case, but it is a doleful thought for Hayek because in his view, whatever their potential, the intelligentsia has so far shown more capacity for disseminating fashionable nostrums than scholarly truth. Intellectuals are fairly able, generous people easily misled by their sympathies into overestimating the knowledge we can have about society and therefore into supposing that planning is always beneficial. These notions they derive from the 'constructivist rationalism' of Descartes. (Scheler did not like Descartes either, but mainly because the Cartesian cogito released the individual from the enveloping texture of society.) So they must be redeemed from error by argument: by showing that the Welfare State in certain aspects is the road to serfdom, that capitalism raised the standards of the working class (*pace* Ashton, Clapham, George) and not *vice-versa* (*pace* the Hammonds, Hobsbawm, Thompson) and that there is a moral element in capitalism because men must be free before there is any possibility that they may be moral rather than needing to be moral before they can be free. Society cannot be organized according to merit, still less according to needs; and the 'distortions' of the market are very often due to some previously privileged group striving to maintain its position. Government must be based on the three great negatives of peace, liberty and justice, without the intrusive adjective 'social' being inserted in front of justice. The immutable laws of economics are not what Lukács would describe as reifications unable to pass beyond themselves to the solution of the problems they describe but universal rules circumscribing what can be done socially without courting disaster.

Hayek's essays are dedicated to these themes and both his political philosophy (rooted in Mandeville, Hume, Adam Smith and Acton) and his scientific methodology relate closely to his economic liberalism. This relation can however be set on one side till the end of the whole discussion. It is his views on the intelligentsia which are most interesting here since the intelligentsia has played so crucial a role in sociologies of knowledge. He claims that the left, for all its talk about material interests and the proletariat, has acted as if it understood the key position of the intellectuals. These intellectuals are not the genuine experts but secondhand dealers in ideas, popularizers, makers of reputations. We are not so much the prey of experts but of people who decide between experts in terms of fashionable general ideas. These mediators are educated without having had experience of power or administration: 'knowledge without responsibility, the prerogative of the harlot throughout the ages', to adapt Baldwin's phrase about the *Express* to the *New Statesman*. Thus broadcasting systems, newspapers and universities, supposedly run by conservative cliques, disseminate socialism simply because of the convictions of their personnel: the divorce not of ownership but of content from control. These personnel are incapable of thinking or assessing evidence because their minds are pre-empted by general ideas. And why so? Because the highly intelligent who accept the social order choose the paths of influence and power or else care for scholarship disinterestedly, whereas those who reject the social order become intellectuals for whom teaching and research are less valuable in themselves than a means to promote their political dissatisfactions and resentments.

Turning now to the phenomenological aspect of the sociology of knowledge the role of the intellectual becomes much less salient. For Berger neither intellectuals nor the history of ideas are *that* important: the sociology of knowledge can also concern itself with everyday thinking. This is not the thinking of everyday people (which hardly anybody has yet investigated) but what Scheler called the 'natural' way of looking at the world. This area of interest is midway between the man on the Clapham omnibus and epistemology. It is not reality with the ultimate question-mark of epistemology against it but set in inverted commas or to be more exact in a mixture of phenomenological brackets and hyphens. It is the 'natural' way of being-in-the-world.

The development and analysis of the commonsense view of the world (for sociology) belongs to Schutz and those who want a brief exposition of his approach can do no better than turn to Part I of Berger and Luckmann. So this is perhaps the best point to summarize what is involved in Schutz, drawing on this section of Berger, on his own *The Phenomenology of the Social World* and on the helpful introduction to that work provided by George Walsh.

All conscious life is intentional but varies in mode as from one sphere to another, e.g. as between dreaming and waking. Everyday life seems peculiarly real, making it appear that its pattern of geographical, spatial and temporal relations and its technical modes are an objective datum. To go beyond the commonsensicality of the everyday to the world of aesthetic imagination, religious ecstasy or scientific objectivity requires a special transition. Men are creatures of the present, with a variable interest in their environment based on their pragmatic concerns and a variable tension between the momentum of their projects and the rhythm of their physical bodies and the objective socially established calendar—including historical events. Everyday life is shared with others, above all in face-to-face negotiations whereby people 'read' each other in a situation of mutual reciprocity. When they do this they understand each other better than they know themselves because self-understanding requires an act of retrospective reflection. Yet even the face-to-face relation takes place in terms of types (e.g. that the other is a jovial, friendly type etc.) which hold good until expressly contradicted. Outside such meetings there is a whole scale of relations involving varying degrees of anonymity, such as persons one only meets incidentally, those one meets frequently on a purely instrumental and momentary basis etc., not to mention predecessors and successors, with whom one may or may not have intense concern.

Humans express themselves in direct negotiations (smiles, nods, frowns) and in all kinds of other signs and symbols, above all language. Language transcends the face-to-face relation, stabilizing and objectifying our experience. It is an external coercive fact which constrains us and provides general categories and schemes of classification into which we subsume experience. (Here one can see the links between phenomenology, linguistic philosophy and one aspect of Durkheim.) Language also brings disparate worlds into contact (past and present, near and far) and translates symbols from one sphere to another (dreaming to waking).

In interacting with others we share a common knowledge which serves to locate the various participants, and suggests the way relations are to be handled, as well as providing sets of recipes, such as how to obtain a passport, use the phone. Beyond the limited pragmatic concerns of such recipes the world is more or less opaque.

In Walsh's introduction and in Schutz's own final chapter this is presented more abstractly, with some special reference to ambiguities in Weber's methodology, e.g. between meaning-adequacy and casual-adequacy, and to the general problem of deriving an objective science from congeries of subjective meaning. So an investigation of the structure of social action is called for. Action is an intention anticipating a point in the future when it will already have achieved its object: hence it is pluperfect as well as present continuous. To understand an action is to enter intimately into it, and to order it into categories of types of action, varieties of person, etc. Thus understanding is both more and less anonymous; similarly so in that it may include the comprehension of abstract laws with universal validity (such as those of economics) or of structures with a certain concrete particularity (such as the notion of Western capitalism). Another gradation between particularity and anonymity comprises that between I-Them relations and They—the Generalized Other as Mead would formulate it.

So here then we have a sort of grammar of the everyday, which is a form of life comprising present, past, future, pluperfect etc., I, you and they, and an apparatus of understanding ranging along a scale of abstraction from intimate signs to the comprehension of the most general laws of social science.

One cannot criticize Schutz himself *in extenso* but on almost every page one finds doubtful statements. It seems the elucidation of commonsense, however important in principle, involves a surprising amount of nonsense, just as demystification requires some remarkably mysterious mumbo-jumbo. He says we don't attach meaning to an action while performing it. Don't we? Again, he states that we share a common civilization and stock of knowledge with contemporaries not with predecessors. Not so: in most respects I share a world with Sir Thomas Browne rather than with Beatles or Trobriand Islanders. Again, it is not the case that I can finally clear up problems of inter- pretations with contemporaries but not with predecessors: Dallapic- cola is almost as problematic as Bach And the problem of freedom is *not*, except in a limited sense, a time problem simply because the past is completed and the future appears open.

In short the phenomenological approach as exemplified by Schutz shares with Sartre and Parsons a common subject matter, a common galloping verbal inflation, and a capacity for stringing truisms together unredeemed by the fact that they are at least all true. Yet this is conspicuously not the case in the phenomenological approach as developed by Berger and Luckmann. In their work one finds stylistic brilliance, consistent insight, a wide unified range of perspec- tive and reference, and humour.

The core of Berger and Luckmann is divided into two major sections: society as objective reality and society as subjective reality. Man is an animal largely without a species-specific environment whose plasticity is controlled by habits and institutions. Institutional- ization is 'the reciprocal typification of habitual action' by types of actors and it implies subjection to social control. Actions most likely to be typified concern the communication process, labour, sexuality and territory. As soon as habits and institutions acquire historicity their original, transparent, *ad hoc*, self-produced character becomes objectified. It is no longer the universe of the self-made man. Tradi- tion replaces biography and the deviant appears as one who realizes that 'this is none of I'.

The strain towards consistency of institutional spheres is genuine but not so much in terms of the logic of institutions as in terms of a reflective consciousness imposing logic on the institutional order. Like Homans, Berger and Luckmann are for 'bringing men back in'. This requires an investigation of what men 'know' about their socially-shared universes rather than an exposition of impersonal functional imperatives. It is language which simultaneously liberates us and abstracts our knowledge from concrete biography, turning it into the objective sediment of tradition.

Of course, roles involve typifications, whereby some varieties of action are appropriate to certain actors. Some roles are special in representing the total integration of society, e.g. monarchs and judges. The institutional order is real *only* insofar as it is realized in performed roles; and roles represent the institutional order which defines them—including their appendages of appropriate 'knowledge' (p. 96).

Berger and Luckmann discuss the appearance of socially segregated subuniverses of meaning based on the division of labour and an economic surplus. These universes may develop at differential rates and thus pose a problem for any attempted monopoly of reality-definition. Systems of legitimation try to order experience comprehensively, thereby holding incipient chaos at bay, and assuaging terror, even the terror of death.[2] These systems attempt a diagnostic therapy of deviants and 'annihilate' them by allowing them inferior ontological status, working them up as subsidiaries within the larger system.

Religion and ideology transmit bundles of contingent elements as necessary structures *tout court* by means of primary socialization. At this point the analysis is made in terms of Mead rather than Freud, i.e. the automatic identification with 'significant others'. However, rather than press this interesting phenomenological preference for Mead there is space to consider only the crucial issue of reification as presented on pages 106–8. Clearly the preference is based on a desire not only to humanize the external 'facticity' of society but also to humanize the external facticity of psychobiological determinism: a double extension of the human boundary.

Berger and Luckmann ask to what extent society is apprehended as a non-human actuality in which the consequences of human activity masquerade as facts of nature. For instance, marriage may be reified as theologically ordained, as biologically necessary, or as a functional imperative.

However, one must query to what extent there can be a proper reification based on external, constraining elements always confronting man. These never were part of any person's (or any two persons') biography, not even Adam and Eve, since *ab initio* they were confronted by a *rule*. Is not the model of two persons working out transparent *ad hoc* arrangements as much a piece of mythology as a model of a society run on socio-drama principles of freely-interchangeable roles? Surely society *is* in part 'a non-human facticity' and the attempt to eliminate this self-deluding and self-destructive. You cannot write genuine social history, as a collective biography on which no constraining, semi-arbitrary externality impinges.

In Berger and Luckmann's important last chapter they argue that phenomenology can be put at the *service* of a humanist approach. It can also evade the functionalist tendency to reify its concepts and its constructs even when claiming only to use them heuristically. However, in so doing they utilize the Marxist *aspiration* for a society where social relations are not external and constraining and the Marxist attack on all structures posing as immutable data, forgetting that they are only *more or less* mutable. Mutability is not malleability. The dense opacity and externality of social relations is inherent, amongst other things in terms of a functionalist analysis of the complexity of unintended consequences and either the determination of previous history or the stratagems required to try to eliminate that historical determination.

This is the point to turn to Hayek and to the second critical codicil, not of course for any defence of the functionalist penchant for a rigidifying, objectified and distorting conceptual apparatus based on an obsessive labelling of the universe, but for an understanding of the non-human complexities and 'arbitrary' mechanisms derived from the intended and unintended consequences of each man's choice, now as well as in the past. And this is not something to conjure away or to regret: historical determination is partly the obverse of necessary continuity, just as arbitrariness and constraining externality are partly the *result* of desirable freedoms. The alternative really *is* the road to serfdom. Total freedom from history and from 'repressive' society, and total lucidity, is the existentialist individual dream become a social nightmare: God incarnate not in man but in society —the paradoxical verification of Durkheim by his very opponents.

For Hayek functionalism is an extension of Hume and Adam Smith: society is a dense, opaque, partly impenetrable web informed by the recondite harmonies of the invisible hand. It is a system beyond the intentions of individuals lit only by highly specialized enclaves of scientific understanding. These are not total explanations of the system leading to comprehensive predictions about its course so much as angled shafts of light, often highly general in form, which illuminate the *limits* of our knowledge. The self-conscious direction of society, where all is understood, either intimately in the phenomenological manner or typically in laws, is not only totalitarian in its

315

proposed harmonization of essentially disparate individual ends, but also scientifically impossible. Hence Hayek's essays on the complexity of phenomena, the length of the rubric attached to sociological generalizations, the limits of prediction and the generality of the patterns we put forward. These are his best essays: well knit and beautifully written. Whether one thinks economics the reified reflection of bourgeois interests or unassailable scientific fact this cool rigour is stimulating. Reified it may be; mystifying not at all.

Notes

1 K. Popper, *The Open Society*, London: Routledge & Kegan Paul, 5th ed., 1966, vol. 2, p. 200.
2 Cf. Mary Douglas, *Purity and Danger*, London: Routledge & Kegan Paul, 1966; P. Berger, *The Sacred Canopy*, New York: Doubleday, 1967.

21 A quantitative study in the sociology of knowledge

Franz Adler

The basic question the present study is trying to answer is whether the sociology of knowledge must be dealt with in a speculative, philosophical manner or whether it can be approached in a way consistent with the present day approach to other problems of scientific sociology. The latter approach presupposes that the phenomena generally understood by the term 'knowledge' in such contexts, that is science, philosophy, religion, literature, be considered as part of the social and cultural activities of man, in no essential way different from his other activities. The task of a study in this field lies in determining relationships between activities of 'knowledge' and some other activities.

To fit into a framework of scientific sociology, the study has to proceed inductively rather than deductively. The induction has to be based on many observations rather than a few isolated cases. Preferably, it should be carried on by mathematical means. Furthermore, the study should lead to the possibility of prediction from one set of variables to others. No unnecessary burden of *a priori* assumptions should hamper its development.

The present paper describes the quantitative approach taken to a specific problem in the sociology of knowledge: how are types of epistemological thinking related to social and cultural change, individual freedom of action, and general security? A number of hypotheses, constructed on the basis of informally gained impressions, were set up to answer this question. To avoid repetition, they will be given together with the findings that modify them.

Method

Measurement of correspondence to types

In order to have a quantitative study of epistemological thinking, it

317

is necessary to develop a way of measuring such thinking. The present study attempts to measure the degree to which the thought of any given thinker corresponds to each of four types of epistemological thinking. Descriptions of the four types follow:[1]

Type A—Universalism, or 'realism' in the medieval sense

The thinker assumes identity of thinking and being. Reasoning is credited with the power to know the truth with the aid of given general concepts and to establish absolutely valid rules for the organization of human relationships in accordance with these concepts. Such concepts are divinely implanted or otherwise innate.

Type B—Nominalism

Thinking appears in terms of hypothetical concepts. The thinker considers all concepts as creations of the human mind, reached by grouping objects and impressions in accordance with their common characteristics. The mind is perfectly free in forming and defining general concepts in accordance with objectives these concepts are intended to serve. Knowledge and understanding of phenomena are held to be attained primarily by experience.

Type C—Organismic, or intuitional thinking

Wholes are constructed according to the organic principle. The whole is said to live in its members as the members live in the whole. Man as a member of a whole has direct insight into the nature of this whole which may be society, the state, nature, the universe. With the aid of some sort of inner light, the mind is thus able to form concepts and judgments, independently of the observation of particulars. It has the power to grasp the essential characteristics of complex phenomena in their totality and to segregate these characteristics from accidental and fortuitous features in order to arrive at insight into the true nature of events.

Type D—Dialectic thinking

The thinker assumes an ability of the mind to interpret all phenomena and events in their continuously changing aspects in terms of an evolutionary process which can be fully understood only when the fundamental concepts correspond to the trichotomous character of the process—thesis, antithesis, synthesis. He has a firm belief that the human mind is able to understand the universe, and hence to grasp the truth. The course of events is determined by the operation of antagonistic forces and must be understood with the aid of concepts adjusted to the contradictions logically represented by these forces.

For the purpose of measurement, the name of a thinker was submitted to a panel of philosophers or sociologists, presumably familiar with his work, who were asked to state which type he resembled most in their opinion. These judges were given the type descriptions with only their alphabetical designations, not the names of the types, so that differences in the subjective meanings of these names would not intrude themselves into the study.

It was hoped that a relation would prevail between the thought content on the one hand and percentages of judges' votes on the other. Thus it was assumed that the work of a man judged by 80 per cent of the judges to be most similar to type A would be more universalist in content than one judged only by 60 per cent to be most similar to this type, but less universalist than one judged by 95 per cent to resemble it most. Thus the percentage of the judges' votes serves as indirect measurement of correspondence to a type. The validity of this measurement cannot be proved, however, and is not claimed. Only when another, independent, method of measurement is tried, will it be possible to compare the results of this and the other. In the meantime, it will be well to remember that any statement made in this paper about degree of resemblance to a type of thought refers only to percentages of votes of judges.

Every thinker is thus characterized by four measurements, each indicating the degree of resemblance of his thought to that of one of the four types of thinking.

The other variables in this study are change, freedom of action, and security. While contemporary events could conceivably be measured directly with regard to these variables, this cannot be done for periods of the past. And if thinkers of the past are studied, it is obviously necessary to pair measurements of their epistemological type correspondences to measurements of change, freedom, and security of their own times. Thus it was decided to treat measurement of historical periods according to the named characteristics in a manner similar to that used in measuring correspondence to type.

Historical periods were submitted to panels of historians who were asked to check the following characteristics concerning each period:

a1 rapid change
a2 slow change
b1 change faster than in directly preceding time in the same area
b2 change at same speed as in directly preceding time in the same area
b3 change slower than in directly preceding time in the same area

c1 change directed toward more regulation of individual action
c2 change directed toward less regulation of individual action
c3 change not related to regulation of individual action at all
d1 time of general security
d2 time of general insecurity
e1 more secure than directly preceding time in the same area
e2 equally secure as directly preceding time in the same area
e3 less secure than directly preceding time in the same area

By counting all the votes of the judges received for each period and by determining the percentage that voted for a1 rather than a2, an indirect estimate of speed of change was obtained. The same was done for variables b, c, d, and e respectively. The logic of the procedure as well as the objections to it are essentially the same as with regard to the resemblance to types of thinking.

The next step was to correlate each of the variables A, B, C, and D with each of the variables a1, b1, b2, b3, c1, c2, c3, d1, e1, e2 and e3. The variables a2 and d2 could, of course, be omitted without loss of information.

Sampling

Four sampling problems arose in the course of this study. Samples of thinkers and samples of periods were to be studied, samples of philosophers and sociologists and samples of historians were needed as judges.

The universe of thinkers is hard to define. It seems that only such thinking is worthy of inclusion which has left or appears to be leaving a lasting mark on the history of thought. No complete list of such thinkers is available, and so it would be difficult to choose an unbiased sample from among them. Therefore it was decided to select a sample first and to define the universe as consisting of all those thinkers who might become part of such a sample whenever another one was wanted. The sample consists of the thinkers generally included in the author's course in the history of social theory. The universe represented by this sample is probably constituted by all the thinkers that are included or at some past or future date have been or will be included in somebody else's course of a similar nature.

The choice of historical periods, on the other hand, offered no difficulties once the question of what thinkers were to be included was settled. The periods of the sample are the approximate life times of the thinkers of the sample. The periods constituting the universe are the life times of all the thinkers in the universe. In times in which the life spans of many thinkers overlap, periods between important historical events combining several life spans or parts of several life spans were used instead of individual life spans.

The philosophers' panel of judges was taken from a membership list of the American Philosophical Association by a random method. The total panel of 600 was divided into five smaller panels of 120. Each of these smaller panels received a list of eleven thinkers to judge.

A panel of 120 sociologists was chosen randomly from those members of the American Sociological Society who, in the membership list of 1946, stated an interest in theory. The list of thinkers submitted to them contained twenty-one names.

A sample of 600 historians was taken from the membership list of the American Historical Association by a random method and subdivided into five panels. Each panel received a list containing nine or ten historical periods to be judged.

Thirty per cent of the philosophers, 34 per cent of the sociologists, and 41 per cent of the historians approached returned completed questionnaires.

Correlation

Scatter diagrams were prepared to discover the general types of relationship prevailing between each of the four types of thought and each of the eleven characteristics of periods. Of these forty-four diagrams, one half failed to show any discernible relationship: these were the diagrams representing organismic-intuitional and dialectic thinking. This seems to indicate a lack of relationship between these types of thought and chosen characteristics of historical periods. For the time being, this part of the study had to be dropped.

The other diagrams showed tendencies to curvilinear relationships and indicated that the use of types of thought as independent variables leads to better fitted curves than the use of characteristics of periods as independent variables. Second-degree parabolas were chosen to represent the relationships throughout.

Findings

Five hypotheses were considered. In the present section these are each stated in the original form in which they were conceived, along with the correlation results bearing on them. The final form of the hypotheses, after modification in view of the results, is then stated in each case.

Hypothesis 1

In its original form the hypothesis was: rapid change is accompanied by nominalist thinking, slow change by universalist thinking.

321

FRANZ ADLER

The curvilinear correlation coefficient, rho, measuring the relationship between universalism (A) and rapid change (a1), is 0·39, which differs significantly (on the 1 per cent level) from a zero relationship. The prediction formula which estimates rapid change from universalism is a1 = 82·9−0·29A+0·003A². This formula has a standard error of 18·5.

The rho which measures the relationship between nominalism (B) and rapid change (a1) is 0·228, which is statistically not significant. The equation by which rapid change may be predicted from nominalism is a1 = 60+0·77B−0·0063B². The standard error of estimate is 19·6.

The scatter diagrams further show that thought of the kind included in the sample whether universalist or nominalist does tend not to occur in periods judged by less than one third of the judges as rapidly changing.

Hypothesis 1 must, then, be modified to read: remarkable thinking of any description does not occur with slow change, but requires or brings about a minimum speed of change. Speed of change is inversely related to universalist thought content. There is a slight positive relationship between nominalism and speed of change—the highest speed of change occurs at about 60 per cent nominalism. The expected value for speed of change at 100 per cent nominalism is, however, higher than at 0 per cent.

Hypothesis 2

Originally, the second hypothesis of the study read as follows: increases in the speed of thought bring about increases in dialectic and organismic thinking. Decreases in the speed of thought bring about increases in universalism and decreases in nominalism.

In view of the appearance of the scatter diagrams, no equations for organismic or dialectic thinking were computed.

The correlation of universalism (A) with change faster than in the directly preceding period (b1) yielded a rho of 0·38, significant at the 1 per cent level. The equation of the curve is b1 = 81·09−0·46A+0·0035A². The standard error of estimate is 16·1.

Nominalism (B) and change faster than in the directly preceding period (b1) are correlated with a rho of 0·332, significant at the one per cent level. The prediction equation is b1 = 63·72+0·61B−0·0055B². The standard error of estimate is 16·97.

The relationship of universalism (A) and change at the same speed as in the directly preceding time in the same area (b2) produces a rho of 0·44, which is significant at the 1 per cent level. The equation describing the relationship is b2 = 10·37+0·68A−0·0068A². The standard error of estimate is 12·7.

The relationship of nominalism (B) to the same variable (b2) produces a rho of 0·285, significant at the 5 per cent level. The prediction equation is b2 $= 26\cdot49 - 0\cdot49B + 0\cdot0044B^2$. The standard error of estimate is 13·6.

Universalism (A) is related to change slower than in the directly preceding period in the same area (b3) with a rho of 0·37 which is significant at the 1 per cent level. The prediction equation is b3 $= 4\cdot14 + 0\cdot32A - 0\cdot0033A^2$. The standard error is 7·4.

Nominalism (B) is related to the same characteristic (b3) with a rho of 0·08, which is not significant. The equation is b3 $= 9\cdot60 - 0\cdot11B + 0\cdot00095B^2$. The standard error is 7·94.

The scatter diagrams show furthermore that remarkable thought of any kind is unlikely to occur in times considered by less than one-third of the judges as changing faster or by more than two-thirds of the judges as changing at the same speed or by more than about one-third of them as changing at a lower speed than preceding periods.

Thus hypothesis 2 assumes the following modified form: increased speed of change is negatively related to universalism. It is, in the main, positively related to nominalism, the highest increase occurring with about 50 per cent nominalism. Both, universalism and nominalism, occur with high degrees of increased speed of change and low degrees of unchanged or decreasing speed of change. No relation seems to exist between change in the speed of change and either dialectics or organismicism.

Hypothesis 3

The original hypothesis read: change directed toward more regulation of individual action occurs with universalist thinking; change directed toward less regulation of individual action occurs with nominalist thinking.

Universalism (A) is related to change directed toward more regulation of individual action (c1) with a rho of 0·19 which is not significant. The equation describing the curve is c1 $= 47\cdot52 - 0\cdot13A + 0\cdot0004A^2$. The standard error is 18·7.

Nominalism (B) is related to the same characteristic (c1) with a rho of 0·363, significant at the 1 per cent level. The equation is c1 $= 39\cdot09 + 0\cdot68B - 0\cdot0083B^2$. The standard error is 17·6.

The relationship of Universalism (A) to change directed toward less regulation of individual action (c2) produces a rho of 0·16 which is not significant. The equation is c2 $= 34\cdot47 + 0\cdot28A - 0\cdot0046A^2$. The standard error is 21·76.

The relationship of nominalism (B) to the same variable (c2) shows a rho of 0·335, significant at the 1 per cent level. The equation is c2 $= 23\cdot70 + 0\cdot40B - 0\cdot0018B^2$. The standard error is 20·77.

Universalism (A) is related to change not related to the regulation of individual action at all (c3) with a rho of 0·433 which is significant at the 1 per cent level. The equation is c3 $= 20\cdot38-0\cdot39A+0\cdot007A^2$. The standard error of estimate is 12·2.

Nominalism (B) is related to the same variable (c3) with a rho of 0·396 which is significant at the 1 per cent level. The equation is c3 $= 29\cdot4-0\cdot53B+0\cdot0047B^2$. The standard error is 12·4.

The scatter diagrams furthermore show that remarkable thought of the kind included in this study does not occur in times considered by more than two-thirds of the judges as unchanging with regard to regulation of individual action. It does not occur with times considered by more than 78 per cent or by less than 14 per cent of the judges as changing toward more regulation. It does not occur in times judged by more than 84 per cent of the judges as changing toward less regulation.

Modified according to these findings, the third hypothesis now reads: universalism is weakly negatively related to increasing as well as decreasing regulation of individual action. It shows, however, a significant positive relationship to change not related to regulation of individual action at all. Nominalism shows a mainly negative relationship to increasing regulation of individual action and a clearly positive relationship to decreasing regulation. Only small variations in change not related to regulation of individual action at all can be related to nominalism. A minimum of change toward or away from regulation is necessary for remarkable thought to occur. Change directed too strongly or not strongly enough toward more change does not occur with remarkable thought. Such thought is unlikely to occur in times too strongly directed toward a lessening of regulation of individual action.

Hypothesis 4

Originally, the fourth hypothesis of the study read: security is related to nominalist thinking, insecurity is related to universalist, organismic, and dialectic thinking.

In view of the appearance of the scatter diagrams, no computations were made for either dialectics or organismicism.

The rho measuring the relationship of universalism (A) and time of general security (d1) is 0·42, which is significant at the 1 per cent level. The prediction equation reads d1 $= 62\cdot46-1\cdot07A+0\cdot011A^2$. The standard error of estimate is 20·25.

The rho measuring the relationship of nominalism (B) to time of general security (d1) is 0·036, which is not significant. The equation is d1 $= 52\cdot03-0\cdot45B+0\cdot0061B^2$. The concave appearance of this curve is very probably due to chance. A convex curve would be expected, and the arrangement of most of the data on the scatter diagram confirms this expectation. However, a few stray data pull the curve down to its present shape. The standard error is 22·4.

The scatter diagrams show that thought of the kind included in this study is unlikely to occur below 10 per cent and above 87 per cent of security. The same is, of course, true below 13 per cent and above 90 per cent of insecurity.

Consequently the hypothesis was reworded to read now as follows: from zero per cent to about 50 per cent of universalist thought content, security shows a negative, from there on up a positive relationship to universalism. The opposite is true for insecurity. No statement with regard to nominalism should be made at present. With regard to dialectics and organismicism, the hypothesis must be regarded as rejected. It seems that both a minimum of security as well as a minimum of insecurity are needed for the occurrence of any remarkable thought of the kind included in this study.

Hypothesis 5

The original form of this hypothesis was: universalism, organismicism, and dialectics occur in periods which are less secure than preceding ones rather than in periods which are more secure. The opposite is the case for nominalism. The appearance of the scatter diagrams was such as to make any computations concerning dialectics and organismicism useless.

For the relationship of universalism (A) to time more secure than that immediately preceding time in the same area (e1), the rho is 0·345, which is significant at the 1 per cent level. The equation is $e1 = 42 \cdot 98 - 0 \cdot 67A + 0 \cdot 0077A^2$. The standard error is 15·4.

For the relationship of nominalism (B) to the same variable (e1) rho is 0·38, which is significant at the 1 per cent level. The equation is $e1 = 27 \cdot 36 + 0 \cdot 66B - 0 \cdot 0066B^2$. The standard error is 15·22.

For the relationship of universalism (A) and time equally secure as the immediately preceding period in the same area (e2), rho is 0·07, which is not significant. The equation is $e2 = 26 \cdot 35 + 0 \cdot 005A^2$. The standard error is 12·3.

For the relationship of nominalism (B) to the same variable (e2), rho is 0·23, which also is not significant. The equation is $e2 = 32 \cdot 13 - 0 \cdot 41B + 0 \cdot 0043B^2$. The standard error is 13·5.

For the relationship of universalism (A) to time less secure than the immediately preceding time in the same area (e3), rho is 0·3, which is significant at the 5 per cent level. The equation is $e3 = 30 \cdot 80 + 0 \cdot 65A - 0 \cdot 008A^2$. The standard error is 16·65.

For the relationship of nominalism (B) to the same variable (e3), rho is 0·093, which is not significant. The equation is e3 = 40·51 −0·25B+0·0023B². The standard error is 17·37.

According to the scatter diagrams, high degrees of stability of security (above 72 per cent) do not occur with important thinking. Periods judged by more than 74 per cent of the judges as having increased in security show absence of remarkable thought. The same is true about periods judged by more than 86 per cent of the judges as lessening in security.

In conformity with these findings, the fifth hypothesis was given the following modified form: universalism and increased security are in the main positively, universalism and decreased security are in the main negatively, related. For percentages of universalism below 40 per cent, the relationship is reversed. Nominalism and increased security are related in such a manner that the middle percentages (around 50 per cent) of nominalism tend to occur with higher degrees of security than either higher or lower percentages of nominalism. The relation of nominalism to decreased security shows the opposite pattern, but with a very much reduced difference between middle and extreme values. Too much stability seems to be unfavorable to remarkable thinking or *vice versa*. Remarkable thought seems not to occur with very high increases or decreases in security. No relation exists between organismic and dialectic thinking on the one hand and change or absence of change in security on the other.

Reliability and verification

When the answers from the philosophers, historians, and sociologists who served as judges began coming in, the first twenty of each panel were tabulated separately. Then all the answers from each panel, which arrived after the first twenty, and before the reminder letters were sent out, were tabulated separately. The answers which came in after reminder letters had been sent out were also tabulated separately. Thus there were three samples of answers for each thinker and for each period. These samples of answers were rarely identical, but a comparison of percentages showed that the number of significant differences between sets of answers was below the number which could have been expected to occur by chance if the samples had been drawn from identical universes.

Among the answers of the philosophers and sociologists, 0·24 per cent of differences among samples of votes concerning the same thinker were significant at the 1 per cent level, 1·7 per cent were significant on the two per cent level, and 3·7 per cent on the 5 per cent level.

Among the answers of the historians, 0·35 per cent of the differences among samples of votes concerning the same period were significant at the 1 per cent level, 0·9 per cent at the 2 per cent level, and 3·7 per cent at the 5 per cent level. Thus the method of measurement, if not demonstrably valid, is, at least, reliable.

At the outset of the calculation of the regression equations several cases were eliminated either because the number of votes cast concerning them seemed too small or because the lifetimes of the thinkers seemed to include several of the periods which were arbitrarily fixed for times in which many lifetimes of many thinkers overlapped. Seventeen of these cases were used to test the predictive efficiency of the equations. The predictions of characteristics of the periods from the resemblance of the thinkers to types A and B showed reasonably satisfactory results when compared with the measurements obtained for these periods by the votes of the historians.

Conclusions

On the basis of this study it can be said with some confidence that the sociology of knowledge is accessible by the same methods as the other parts of sociology, provided that the questions asked are of a nature that is suitable for scientific investigation. As in all other fields of knowledge, there are scientific and meta-scientific problems in sociology. The latter are open to philosophical speculation, the former to scientific inquiry. As far as scientific methods are applied, reliable knowledge is attainable. Where philosophical methods are applicable, aesthetic satisfaction may be achieved. It is pointless to argue the advantages of one over the other.

The method of measurement by votes of experts in its present, or more preferably, in an improved form may be applicable to a wide range of complex phenomena where direct measurement would be impossible or too time consuming. In any of these cases, types would have to be constructed, among which expert judges could choose in classifying observed or studied phenomena. The possibility of a transposition of the present method to a sociology of literature or art appears almost obvious. A sociology of international relations might use votes of military attachés, consuls, and ambassadors on various matters usually observed by them for the prediction of wars and other moves of international importance. The study of social movements might profit by the establishment of equations linking certain types of social, economic, and political processes as judged by newspapermen, with the rise of revolutions or reform movements as judged by the same kind or other kinds of observers. In other words, the method has practical promise as well as theoretical uses.

The specific hypotheses of the present paper need further study and further revisions. Additional hypotheses are needed to shed light on

327

the two types of thinking for which the present study has produced negative results only.

Note

1 These types and their descriptions are derived from Karl Pribram, *Conflicting Patterns of Thought*, Washington, D.C.: Public Affairs Press, 1949, pp. 1–49.

part nine

Applied sociology of knowledge

22 Mannheim's generational analysis and acculturation

Alex Simirenko

Studies of American ethnic communities of the past decade have provided us with new information on the descendants of immigrants of second and even third generations. These studies[1] reveal a complexity of the acculturation process never perceived by W. Lloyd Warner whose conceptualization of this process still remains a classic in the sociological literature.[2] A challenge to Warner's explanation of the acculturation process and a need for a new explanation is well underlined in the following succinct summary of findings by Nathan Glazer and Daniel Moynihan which contradicts Warner's proposition that each subsequent generation loses its ethnic profile as it passes into the American middle classes:

> In the third generation, the descendants of the immigrants
> confronted each other, and knew they were both Americans,
> in the same dress, with the same language, using the same
> artifacts, troubled by the same things, but they voted
> differently, had different ideas about education and sex, and
> were still, in many essential ways, as different from one another
> as their grandfathers had been.[3]

To account for the variability and the manifold complexity of the acculturation process it is necessary to abandon Warner, to whose ideas we shall return, and seek an explanation in Karl Mannheim's generational analysis.

Karl Mannheim's writing on generations forms one of the foundation stones in his sociology of knowledge.[4] This most original contribution to the problem of generations is found in his conceptual differentiation among various generational groupings. He maintained that simple generational separation performed on the basis of so many calendar years did not furnish a sound foundation for the analysis of social process and change. Mannheim distinguished between (1) the generation location, (2) the generation as actuality, and (3) the generation unit.[5] The generation location refers to the individuals who are located within the same generation simply by virtue of accident of birth and the biological rhythm. Individuals within it, however, can in turn be divided into separate actual generations when they participate 'in the common destiny'. An actual generation can be subdivided into a number of 'generation units' since different individuals while experiencing common social and intellectual fortunes may nevertheless respond to them in different fashion:

> Youth experiencing the same concrete historical problems may be said to be part of the same actual generation; while those groups within the same actual generation which work up the material of their common experience in different specific ways, constitute separate generation units.[6]

These generation units, of which there may be several at the beginning of their formation, tend to polarize into the dominant and the opposed types. Despite the fact that the dominant generation unit will impress its mark on the historical process of a particular age the opposed forces will still be there even if they are generally silent. It is very difficult for an individual to reject the dominant unit especially if this group 'happens to be rising in the social scale'.[7] Mannheim concludes that the individual who opposes the dominant movement has to have 'a very strong personality' and that the opposing generation unit which he joins is usually made up of persons who 'because of their "location" in an older generation, are unable or unwilling to assimilate themselves into the new entelechy growing up in their midst.'[8]

In the perspective of Mannheim's analysis Warner and his associates have paid a far greater attention to the dominant new generation entelechy and neglected the opposing generation units with their distinct responses to similar historical events. It will be recalled that in the study of the Yankee City ethnic groups,[9] Warner and Srole reveal that the acculturation of the members of an ethnic community tends to be related to their rise on the socio-economic ladder. Each ethnic group starts on the road toward acculturation to the American values as well as toward a socio-economic advancement as soon as it settles in an American city. The road toward a total assimilation may not always be even but unless the group is distinguished by some racial characteristic, it is doomed to be lost within the culture of the larger society. Warner and Srole observed the responses of opposition to this general trend, but these are not examined in any detail or explained. Thus they preclude the possibility of major cultural breaks within and between ethnic generational groupings by assuming that the economic attraction associated with the dominant response will break up any serious opposition. Following Mannheim's analysis, however, such an assumption is not warranted and should be made a matter of careful research.

To illustrate the usefulness of Mannheim's analysis, the paper reports partial findings of a considerably larger study of an ethnic community tracing the dynamics of its social and cultural change in which Mannheim's generational distinctions have been applied.[10]

The setting of the study

The study centred upon the Minneapolis Russian community which was formed in the 1880s by Slavic peasant immigrants from the former Austro–Hungarian empire who identified themselves with the Russian cause. The communal life is organized around the St Mary's Russian Orthodox Church located in the north-eastern area of Minneapolis. The group is divided into two adult generations: the original settlers and their children. The children of the old generation, however, while belonging to the same actual generation can in turn be subdivided into two distinct generation units. One generation unit continues to participate in the life of the ethnic community founded by their fathers, while the other unit has abandoned the community and pursues its goals within the wider mainstream of American society. We can classify the former as the colonists and the latter as the frontiersmen among the Minneapolis Russians for convenient identification of the two groups. Examined superficially members of both generation units have been acculturated to the values and symbols of the larger American society. They speak English at home, they received fairly similar public education and they appear to be dressed in indistinguishable fashion from the larger community. In short, they have lost the stigmas which identified their parents as aliens in the American society.

Procedure

In the course of the larger study, random samples were drawn from among the family units of the two groups and interviews were conducted with the wives in these families. Dues-paying members of the St Mary's Russian Orthodox Church were classified as colonists while its former members were classified as frontiersmen. Forty-two families in the colonist group and thirty-four families in the frontiersmen group were interviewed.[11] The interviews followed a schedule which gathered a variety of data on the family's social, economic, political and cultural position and activity.

TABLE 22.1 *Occupation of fathers of colonists and frontiersmen* (%)

Occupation	Colonists (n = 84)	Frontiersmen (n = 66)
Unskilled	47·6	47·0
Skilled or semi-skilled	38·1	43·9
Clerical or sales	2·4	4·5
Managerial or semi-professional	10·7	3·0
Professional	1·2	1·5

Since the two generation units of colonists and frontiersmen share the same generation location, their age profiles are similar. The women in both groups reported a median age between thirty-five and thirty-nine, while the men had a median age between forty and forty-four. The occupational profile of the fathers of the two groups is fairly similar, revealing their common social origins.

The common initial fortunes of the two groups are also revealed in their educational profiles which do not show significant statistical difference.

TABLE 22.2 *Educational profile of colonists and frontiersmen* (%)

Number of school years completed	Colonists (n = 84)	Frontiersmen (n = 68)
One to eight	7·0	3·0
Nine to twelve	62·0	60·0
Some college	31·0	37·0

$\chi^2 = 1·8$; 2 d.f. n.s.

Selected findings

There are many signs showing that despite their common backgrounds, the colonists and frontiersmen are pursuing their life according to different patterns. This can be seen in occupations performed by the men in the two groups.

The variation in annual family incomes of the two groups is not as great as their occupational differentiation, but is nevertheless significant. Comparatively few families among the frontiersmen (8·8 per cent.) live on an income under $5,000 in comparison to almost the third of the families in the colonist group (29·3 per cent.). Over half of the frontiersmen families (58·8 per cent.) are provided with an income between $5,000 and $7,500, while only a third of the families (34·1 per cent.) in the colonist group are found in this category. The income of $7,500 or more, however, is shared by 36·6 per cent. of colonists and 32·3 per cent. of frontiersmen.[12]

TABLE 22.3   *Male occupation of colonists and frontiersmen (%)*

Occupation	Colonists (n = 42)	Frontiersmen (n = 34)
Unskilled	9·5	2·9
Skilled and semi-skilled	57·1	35·3
Clerical and sales	16·7	8·8
Managerial, semi-professional, and professional	16·7	52·9

$\chi^2 = 11·3$; 3 d.f. $p < 0·02$

The north-east Minneapolis neighbourhood in which the Russian 'ghetto' is located is composed of well-kept single family houses or duplexes. Nevertheless there is a movement among the young generation to leave the area. The two groups of colonists and frontiersmen reveal distinct ecological distribution within these areas. Over half (57·1 per cent.) of the colonists continue to reside in north-east Minneapolis in comparison with one-fifth (20·6 per cent.) of the frontiersmen remaining in the same territory.[13] Ninety-three per cent. of the colonists and 97 per cent. of the frontiersmen own their homes. There was also no statistically significant difference between the cost of houses owned by the two groups.[14]

In the dawn of American sociology, Franklin Henry Giddings commented that 'a people can be judged and career can be predicted from the character of its pleasures, with more accuracy than from any

TABLE 22.4   *Type of music favoured by colonists and frontiersmen (%)*

Type of music	Colonists (n = 84)	Frontiersmen (n = 68)
Old-time	29·8	8·8
Popular	10·7	42·6
Semi-classical	51·2	27·9
Jazz	4·8	1·5
Classical	3·6	19·1

$\chi^2 = 38·1$; 4 d.f. $p < 0·001$.

other data'.[15] The character of pleasures of the two groups are not entirely distinct as yet since they are only one generation removed from their peasant past. In some of their activities and preferences, however, there is an indication that a shift is occurring in this area of life as well. Such was their response to the question of favoured type of music summarized in Table 22.4. Space permitting, one may have given varied interpretation of these figures, but the fact remains that musical taste of these groups tends to follow distinct patterns.

An important insight into the pattern of life organized by the colonists and frontiersmen is provided by their attitudes toward personal health. The colonists, located without any doubt in the less advantageous economic position, are much more concerned with their health than are the frontiersmen. Sixty-two per cent. of colonist families report yearly medical check-ups in contrast to only 35 per cent. of the frontiersmen families. The families who report seeing a physician only when some member of their family is sick include $28 \cdot 6$ per cent of colonists and $44 \cdot 1$ per cent. of frontiersmen.[16] It may may be argued that the economic rise of the frontiersmen has been effected at least partially by disregarding their health if we assume for the moment that there is no appreciative difference in the biological constitutions of the two groups.

Discussion of the data

The two groups of colonists and frontiersmen belong to the same actual generation and share similar ages as well as similar social backgrounds. Nevertheless they pursue a way of life distinct from each other. There is little doubt that Warner's data are reliable when he portrays the acculturated individual to have greater economic advantages than the less acculturated one. He neglects to see, however, that the less acculturated individual (in this case the colonist) is selective in the values that he accepts from the majority society, thus capable of forming a new sub-culture if he is numerically strong. The findings on education, musical tastes, medical check-ups, and even the data on ecological distribution of the colonists and frontiersmen cannot be explained within the conceptual framework of Warner and his associates.

Knowledge of social class differences unmitigated by ethnic factors would lead us to expect the frontiersmen who are placed in a higher class position to be better educated, which they are not, to prefer semi-classical music, which they do not, to seek greater medical attention, which they tend to ignore, and finally to live in houses which are at least more expensive than those of the colonists. Warner's framework can only explain successfully the data on occupational profiles of husbands in the two groups and the annual earnings of the families. This, however, is also anticipated in Mannheim's formulation and has been verified in many other studies, including one recently by S. Alexander Weinstock in his study of the Hungarian refugees.[17] Karl Mannheim's generational analysis can be utilized successfully to explain all the findings reported in the present paper and helps us to anticipate the rather startling fact revealing little or no difference in the educational profiles of the two groups. At the same time Mannheim's ideas account for the emergence of new cultural forms inadequately dealt with by Warner.

One basic question left open for us by Mannheim is still to be answered: what are the forces which give the opposing generation unit life and vitality, especially when the dominant new generation entelechy offers greater economic advantages to the members of an ethnic community? In other words, how do we explain the persistence of minority communities? This was one of the major questions which the larger study of the Minneapolis Russian community was directed to answer. While the full study cannot be summarized at this time, the data furnished here indicate that the colonists are quite capable but unwilling 'to assimilate themselves into the new entelechy growing up in their midst', to use Mannheim's phrase. If nothing else, their education should provide them with these opportunities. This, however, would force them to sacrifice other values which they cherish more than economic advancement.

Notes

1 See, for example, Judith R. Kramer and Seymour Leventman, *Children of the Gilded Ghetto: Conflict Resolutions of Three Generations of American Jews*, New Haven: Yale University Press, 1961; Solomon Poll, *The Hasidic Community of Williamsburg*, New York: Free Press, 1962; Herbert J. Gans, *The Urban Villagers*, New York: Free Press, 1962; Nathan Glazer and Daniel Patrick Moynihan, *Beyond the Melting Pot*, Cambridge: M.I.T. Press and Harvard University Press, 1963. For an excellent recent theoretical work on the subject, see Milton M. Gordon, *Assimilation in American Life: The Role of Race, Religion and National Origins*, New York: Oxford University Press, 1964.

2 W. Lloyd Warner and Leo Srole, *The Social Systems of American Ethnic Groups* (Yankee City Series, vol. 3), New Haven: Yale University Press, 1945.

3 Glazer and Moynihan, *op. cit.*, p. 14.

4 For a detailed discussion of Mannheim's contribution to the sociology of knowledge, see Robert K. Merton, 'Karl Mannheim and the Sociology of Knowledge', *Social Theory and Social Structure*, Chicago: Free Press, 1957, pp. 489–508; Don Martindale, *The Nature and Types of Sociological Theory*, London: Routledge & Kegan Paul, 1960, pp. 414–18; Werner Stark, *The Sociology of Knowledge*, London: Routledge & Kegan Paul, 1958; and Paul Kecskemeti, 'Introduction', Karl

Mannheim, *Essays on the Sociology of Knowledge*, London: Routledge & Kegan Paul, 1952, pp. 1–32.

5 Karl Mannheim, 'The Problem of Generations' in *ibid.*, pp. 276–320.

6 *Ibid.*, p. 304.

7 *Ibid.*, p. 318.

8 *Ibid.* It is unfortunate that Mannheim chose a vague psychological explanation when a sociological one could well have been advanced.

9 *Ibid.*, p. 311.

10 Warner and Srole, *op. cit.*

11 The findings are taken from the author's monograph entitled *Pilgrims, Colonists and Frontiersmen: An Ethnic Community in Transition*, New York: Free Press, 1964.

12 The sampling procedures are fully described in the above-mentioned publication.

13 χ^2 6·5 with two degrees of freedom, $p < 0.05$.

14 χ^2 15·0 with two degrees of freedom, $p < 0.001$.

15 Franklin Henry Giddings, *Democracy and Empire*, New York: Macmillan, 1900, p. 243.

16 χ^2 15·6 with two degrees of freedom, $p < 0.001$.

17 S. Alexander Weinstock, 'Motivation and Social Structure in the Study of Acculturation: A Hungarian Case', *Human Organization*, vol. 23 (Spring 1964), pp. 50–2.

23 Knowledge, power and the university: notes on the impotence of the intellectual

Robert G. Snyder

Since the latter part of the 1950s, liberal intellectuals (e.g., Daniel Bell and S. M. Lipset) have been celebrating the ascendancy of the university as the most important institution in modern society. Through its vital role as provider of knowledge and expertise, the university has been pictured as enabling the business and governmental sectors to survive and prosper in an increasingly complex technological society. The rise to pre-eminence of the university is viewed as resulting from the growing efficiency of the political and economic system and its ability to satisfy the economic and psychological wants of the vast majority of people and thereby to diffuse and remove the ideological content of political controversy. The function of the university is seen as having changed concomitantly to meet these new societal needs. Relinquishing its traditional dissident ideals of the 'house of intellect' (conservative) and the social innovator (radical), the university is now seen as providing the technical expertise to sustain fully the 'post-industrial' society. Rather than remaining at least partially independent of the Establishment as in the previous ideals, the university is currently described as actually being the lifeblood of the existing order. It is argued that because the great social problems of our age have been resolved or at least ameliorated to a tolerable level, there has resulted an 'end of ideology,' an end to the clash of total world views and an acceptance of the liberal welfare state as the form of government most efficacious to the needs of the people.

Within such a view of recent history, the political system in a modern Western democracy is seen as being largely utilitarian and pragmatic in nature—concerned with the distribution of resources within the limits of the given economic, political, and social system. No effort is made to question the underlying values of the system; they are assumed to be just. What is presumed to be important is convincing the people that they are happy with what they already have or that the consumption of more of the same will be satisfactory for their needs. Politics thus becomes the 'art of the possible,' the increasingly efficient and orderly operation of the productive system. Under such a view, *it is the workability* of the system that must be perfected, *not the ethics* of the system.

It is within such a context that the university has found itself a handmaiden to, rather than a leader of, the technological society. What has evolved since Eisenhower's warning about the dangers of the military-industrial complex has been the addition of a third force, the university, to make a tripartite power system. James Ridgeway, in his muckraking essay, has described the relationship between the federal government, big business, and the university as follows:

> The money flows out of the government down to the university, where someone hatches a utilitarian idea, and from there over to a company which either makes a product or designs a test. The object of the university game, then, is to control any two legs of the triangle, for by doing so, the university professor can establish the beginnings of power.[1]

Central to this view of the university is its growth as a power center within society. Clark Kerr, in his much-maligned classic, notes that the 'university's invisible product, knowledge, may be the most powerful single element in our culture.'[2] The reason that this is so, states Kerr, is that 'new knowledge is the most important factor in economic and social growth.'[3] Thus, he correctly characterizes the substantive work of the university as being a 'knowledge industry' which has the goal 'to serve as the focal point of national growth.'[4] Gunter Remmling, in his critique of the modern mentality, implies that the increase in technicist-managerial power is accompanied by a corresponding decrease in intellectual and ethical energy.[5] These large-scale processes, conceptualized as mental and ethical 'entropy,' have repercussions throughout the institutional configuration of industrial society.[6] They, specifically, affect the performance of professional roles and turning to sociologists Remmling argues,

> In similar fashion the so-called empirical sociologists operate within a field which is as narrow and fragmented as the interests of the bureaucracies and foundations paying for their expensive and inflated research apparatus. Here research problems are for the most part initiated by the commercial and administrative concerns of outsiders and independent scholars are replaced by research technicians for hire.[7]

William Birenbaum, a former provost at Long Island University who felt that the university should be a social innovator and was thus

340

dismissed for his incorrigible naivety, writes in his recent book of the nexus of power at which the university finds itself,

> The American university exerts a new kind of institutional power flowing from its possession of extensive properties and huge material wealth, from its capacity to withhold or to give strategic services, from its willingness or reluctance to respond to the pressures and problems besetting the other primary power centers, from the quality and character of its responses.[8]

Underlying the notion of power, then, is not merely an involvement in decisions affecting the allocation of resources but also an ability to affect the distribution of power in a conscious manner. In order to assert that the university is actually a power center or that intellectuals within the university are power brokers, one must first demonstrate the existence of two qualities of relationships between the university, the academics, and the rest of the system: (1) the existence of a direct relationship between knowledge and power—that knowledge is directly translatable into power on both the level of the university as an institution and on the level of the individual academic, and (2) a structuring of the university environment and its underlying values that encourages the emergence of an intellectual who will exercise his expertise in a socially conscious manner.

The relationship between knowledge and power

The university as power center

In the first instance, we will argue that the possession of knowledge does not yield automatic dividends in the accumulation of power. More highly specialized knowledge does not necessarily lead to equivalent accretions in power. Power is a social phenomenon. To yield it one must have an organization to translate individual will into social action. Knowledge must therefore have a social vehicle to transform it from potential power to active power. The university as an institution rarely acts as a catalyst for this transformation. Where the university does wield power, e.g., in its physical expansion, it usually does so much as a business firm might in furthering its financial self-interest. Indeed, it is ironic that the university as a corporate entity rarely uses its academic resources to help plan its own development. Instead, it uses its own bureaucratic expertise or engages outside consultants to gain specialized knowledge already available within its own institution. The essential point to be made here is that the university as an institution does not actively utilize knowledge as a lever of power.

It is true, though, that the university could exert a negative influence on the use of knowledge as power if it chose to curtail those ties with outside institutions for which the knowledge generated within the university provides an essential element. In some instances, notably military research and business recruitment, the university does play a great role in providing the expertise for the maintenance of these institutions. One can imagine what would happen if the university decided to deny the use of its facilities for ROTC programs, military hardware research, or business recruiting. The effects would be enormous. In these instances where a symbiotic relationship exists around the interests of money and expertise, it is, of course, unlikely that the university, under its present governing structure, would sever such mutually advantageous (as the power structure perceives them) ties.

In those areas which lie outside the direct commingling of financial interests of the university and its clients, e.g., most social science funding that comes from the government and foundations, the university as an institution does not act to constrain, nor does it presently have any interest in constraining, the production and use of the knowledge resources within the university. Rather, it is left to the discretion of the individual academic and his department to decide the uses to which this knowledge will be put. Let us now look at the relationship between knowledge and power on the individual level.

The academic expert as power broker

The equation of knowledge with power on the level of the individual academic is generally based on the concept of expertise. It is a commonly held belief that the productivity and growth of our culture is based on the technical knowledge of the expert. Because the development of our industrial society has led to increasingly complex and technical problems, knowledge—practical, not theoretical—has become highly differentiated and specialized. The university and its constituents have adapted themselves completely to this development. Largely discarding questions of theory, value, and historical development, the university has established an organization of knowledge which basically orients itself as a service industry to the government and business sectors. Knowledge is organized into discrete units; it is not treated as continuous and developmental. One studies a 'body of knowledge' rather than the process or forms that may lead to the discovery of knowledge. Knowledge is basically practical even when it reaches the level of 'model-building' or the discovery of so-called universal laws. Knowledge does not possess a *telos*; one does not ask: knowledge for what? beyond questions of efficiency for the operation of the given system. Because of the superabundance of knowledge and the scarcity of time, as Birenbaum points out, knowledge is organized into monopolies, select areas of vertical knowledge that remain inviolate to other members of the profession.

The secrecy and uncertainty generated by these knowledge monopolies define the area of power available to each academic. As Birenbaum succinctly puts it, 'A premium is placed on knowing a lot about a little. . . .'[9] Further, the academic marketplace seems to have its own version of planned obsolescence. Because of the seemingly limitless ability to make technical improvements over last year's model, the knowledge industry develops great wastes which must be discarded in favor of more up-to-date versions.[10] Thus the ever-alert expert preserves the impregnability of his mental sand castle from total obsolescence and outside attack by keeping his expertise one step ahead of the next person.

The durability of the expert's power obviously depends upon his ability to maintain a degree of uncertainty and, hence, unpredictability around his bailiwick of knowledge. The greater the monopoly of knowledge which the expert has in his field, the greater will be his ability to make demands on the system and, in turn, prevent the system from crushing him. And yet the expert must use his expertise or else it will be of no use to the system. And once this expertise is made part of the public domain, it is rationalized into the ongoing process of the system, thus eroding the expert's knowledge monopoly and, hence, his power. As Michel Crozier points out:

> the expert's success is constantly self-defeating. The
> rationalization process gives him power, but the end results
> of rationalization curtail this power. As soon as a field is well
> covered, as soon as the first intuitions and innovations can be
> translated into rules and programs, the expert's power
> disappears.[11]

Thus, the expert's power is being constantly eroded. In order that his services will be highly sought after, he must continue to pursue technical innovation, some sort of gimmick, or else his skills will become obsolete. He must specialize to greater and greater degrees lest he lose his corner on the market.

In this way, the expert becomes a prisoner of his own system. Because his area of specialization is so small, he can rarely branch out into another field where his worth as an expert is untested. In such an event he would have to begin with a new clientele whom he would have to convince of the value of his new expertise. Just as it takes money to make money in today's economy, an expert's changing his field would be like trying to make an investment with no capital or security; he would be starting from zero. Thus, there is a great incentive to the academic expert to stay within his field and not to experiment in other areas.

The structure of academia

Most importantly, however, it is the structure of the academic system and its dependence upon the economic-political system that locks the academic into his narrow field of specialty and prevents any venturing into the area of social criticism. The import of the 'end of ideology' movement was to ring the death knell of critical evaluations of the social system. They became unnecessary once the 'masses' were found to be in fundamental agreement with the efficacy of the liberal welfare state. Since liberal democratic theory, which is the major ideology in modern Western civilization, and its recent varieties of democratic elitism posit that the citizenry is to participate only in setting the general direction of the political-economic system, and since the direction of the system has already been agreed upon, the role of the people becomes obsolete and superfluous. The major decisions that remain are those of perfecting what is already extant. And improvement, here, is a job for experts, not philosophers.

The result of the acceptance of the 'end of ideology' theory has been the justification of the substitution of an elitist government for a democratic one, all the while maintaining the rhetorical trappings of democracy. The rise to prominence of the academic expert on the crest of this wave has signalled the removal of many problems from the realm of subjective public choice and their placement instead under the aegis of expert governmental problem-solving via their new definition as 'technical' problems. By defining a problem as being purely technical in nature, one can legitimize its removal from the sphere of public discussion and discretion. The expert comes to believe that his expertise may legitimately provide the solution to problems without public consultation because the solutions are perceived as being purely technical in nature and, therefore, subject to 'scientific' analysis.

Behaviorism and technique

The expert has come to believe that his expertness is founded on the scientific method he uses to pursue the solutions to his technical problems. The emphasis on scientific method, of course, has a long tradition in Western thought. Growing out of the liberal beliefs in an ethical relativism, an emphasis on the need for moderate rather than extreme solutions, and a desire to foster growth and preserve stability and order, the scientific method has molded scholars— today, including the social sciences—into a rigorous dedication to science as a series of procedures which will describe human behavior in terms of a set of easily replicable and quantifiable laws.

The reliance of the academic expert on method is founded upon the behaviorist tradition in the social sciences. Deriving from an extension of the assumptions of Newtonian mechanics to the social sciences, behaviorism seeks to discover some supposedly immutable, overarching, and determinate laws of *human* nature. In order to do this, the behaviorist must assume that man, singularly or *en masse*, does not possess either the self-consciousness to gain insight into his condition, the capacity for purposive behavior which would be the product of his insight, or the freedom to act in some way that would significantly alter either his own historically predetermined role or that of his society.[12] Instead, he must assume that man is but a passive actor in his social conduct, a Hobbesian social atom interacting impersonally with others in the pursuit of his self-interest. The individual is always *acted upon* by outside forces and is never considered to be the initiator of his own activity.

What is the quality of knowledge that develops from such an outlook? The 'methodist' perspective is succinctly described by Sheldon Wolin: 'The scientific form represents the search for rigorous formulations which are logically consistent and empirically testable. As a form, it has the qualities of compactness, manipulability and relative independence of context.'[13] One notes that the ability to achieve 'rigorous formulations which are logically consistent and empirically testable' depends upon an emphasis on man's external conduct, which is precisely measurable, and a discounting of personal values, intuitions, and goals. Thus, as Mannheim points out, it becomes 'more important . . . to be able to calculate the average behavior of the mass than to understand the private motives of individuals or to transform the whole personality.'[14]

The concentration of behaviorism on regularized determinate causes of human behavior has led to its preoccupation with the notion of 'objective' observations in the literal sense of the word; that is to say, that which is being studied is conceived as being a generic object—apart from any value which may inhere in the object, apart from the uniqueness which an environmental context might impart to the object, and apart from the predispositions which may affect the judgment of the observer. In particular, man the object is denied the importance of personal intuition, of consciously held purposes, or of an autonomous will. As Matson points out, for the behaviorist, man 'the robot can never be a *subject*, an end in itself; it acquires a simulated purpose, its artificial reason for "being," wholly from the outside.'[15]

A basic quality of methodistic logic is its anti-historical and anti-contextual bias. Underlying this characteristic is the assumption of the separation of fact and value. A fact must remain a fact regardless of its social or historical context. To admit otherwise would be to say that different contexts would yield different meanings of the same event, that interpretation would vary according to the time and place in which the event occurred. And to admit a developmental or contextual basis of knowledge would somehow mean denying the constancy of reality and the immutability of human behavioral laws.

Similarly, the behaviorist's subject/object distinction asserts a strict dichotomy between observer and observed as well as between the observer and his historical-cultural context. The behaviorist tries to accomplish this through his methodology which restricts his sphere of observation to purely externally measurable relationships. But clearly this omits a whole range of subject matter that is just as 'real' as the measurable data that the behaviorist seeks and just as relevant to one's understanding of reality. Mannheim, who was as concerned as any other social scientist with this problem, should be cited at length:

> In order to work in the social sciences one must participate in the social process, but this participation in collective-unconscious striving in no wise signifies that the persons participating in it falsify the facts or see them incorrectly. Indeed, on the contrary, participation in the living context of social life is a presupposition of the understanding of the inner nature of this living context. The type of participation which the thinker enjoys determines how he shall formulate his problems. The disregard of qualitative elements and the complete restraint of the will does not constitute objectivity but is instead the negation of the essential quality of the object.[16]

While the assumptions underlying methodism remain the same from problem to problem, the number of methods may vary widely according to the empirical hypothesis being tested. Thus, different tests may be used depending on the problem being studied, although the methodist perspective remains constant. As a result, different problems are treated as discrete areas of study which require specialized knowledge in order to deal with them. One becomes an expert in that area, but one is seldom able to assert expertise across other problem boundaries. The result is a chaos among interpretations of different problem areas. For while each part is explored with the highest degree of technical skill, there is no effort, either by prior design or *ex post* evaluation, to relate these individual findings to a comprehensive theory of behavior and development within a cultural-historical perspective. Disagreements arise over the purity of one's methods, not over the soundness of one's judgments. As noted earlier, such specialization leads to knowledge monopolies which are characterized by their obsolescent and, hence, self-consuming nature. The incentive, then, is to increase the rate and degree of specialization as shown by the sophistication of one's methods so that the academic may preserve his perceived area of personal power.

Another characteristic of methodistic or behaviorist knowledge is that it never seeks to prescribe, only to describe. As such, evaluations and judgments are never made to measure reality against a certain quality of performance. Since, according to the methodist, one can never arrive at a universally accepted standard of behavior, one must abandon all attempts to judge the quality of contemporary experience and must instead evaluate only in terms of its ability to encourage stability and order and to ensure the constant growth of the political-economic system.

As noted above, the behaviorist notion of objectivity is a specious and, indeed, spurious one since it leads to partial and misleading conclusions about the object of one's study. In the same way, the behaviorist assertion of value neutrality is deceptive since it hides its own underlying ideology. Behaviorism cannot be separated from the larger theoretical system of liberalism. Behaviorism's emphasis on ethical relativism, on a public realm based on the mechanism of functional rationality,[17] on its preoccupation with quantitative techniques, and on its narrowly utilitarian objectives is clearly derived from classical and more recently welfare liberalism. As Matson points out, behaviorism shares in common the purposes of the capitalist system: to shape, control, and manipulate the human organism to perform efficiently within the system. Further, it shares the same goals as the scientific management movement in seeking to eliminate disorder: to be materialistic, mechanistic, deterministic, and objective.[18]

While behaviorism's technicist bias generally disclaims affinity with political decision-making of any form, it has most vehemently of all rejected democratic processes of governance. Its distrust of the masses is based on a belief in the fundamental irrationality of man (an absence of what Mannheim calls 'substantive rationality') and the total determination of man's behavior by an imposed external system (implying that men can be considered rational only when viewed as functional parts of the larger system). The deterministic notion of human behavior of course permits no freely made choice among a variety of historical alternatives. The task of the behaviorist is seen as discovering the supposedly immutable and ineluctable laws of history and then bringing them to fruition. Behaviorism thus seeks to be not a passive observer but rather an active force in social control, a precision instrument of social manipulation.

Behaviorism, therefore, is not value-neutral but is instead a prosely-

ROBERT G. SNYDER

tizer of liberal-capitalist values of control of the public sector of
human life through a mechanized system of industrial efficiency and
technical proficiency. And it does so with all the moralistic fervor of a
political ideologue or religious cultist. Herein lies one of the great
paradoxes of methodism. As Matson states:

> On the basis of a rigorously value-purged objectivity—for which
> morality is irrelevant to the point of incompetence—the natural
> science of human behavior looks forward to a 'new and better
> world' suffused with the light of moral wisdom.[19]

A fundamental problem with the reliance on methods to provide
an analytic framework is that a method can never yield an insight.
A method can only test the verifiability of the assumptions that
underlie that method. It can never test the validity of competing
claims to truth. A method binds one to a particular view of reality;
it will never permit one to find new meanings in reality, nor new ways
of conceptualizing man's relationship to himself and to nature.
Indeed, methodism is the bane of scientific imagination as well as
traditional social theory. Creativity can only prosper in the absence
of methodological restrictions. As Wolin notes, some of the qualities
crucial to all theorizing include 'playfulness, concern, the juxtaposition of contraries, and the astonishment at the variety and subtle
interconnection of things.'[20] Methodism admits no such ambiguity,
permits no such variety. It demands knowledge that is 'economical,
replicable, and easily packaged.'[21]

External constraints

The quality of social science developed in the university depends,
quite naturally, on the structure of the academic environment,
including its relationship to the outside world, and the values that
inhere in that structure. To begin, one must return to Clark Kerr's
notion of the 'knowledge industry' as the 'most important factor in
economic and social growth' in this country. Increasingly, the
university and the academics within the university provide the stuff
on which the goods and services of this society are based. Complex
technological problems require complex technical solutions and a
stable and socially integrated society that will provide the climate
in which such technological advances can be made. Both the physical
and social scientist are therefore encouraged to provide the knowledge necessary to the pursuit of national growth. The structuring of
incentives toward this end come from both without and within the
university.

The external incentives that produce the academic technician are
rather common knowledge to most observers of the university. With

348

the financial squeeze making life more and more difficult in the university, outside grant money has become increasingly important. The greatest provider of such assistance is the federal government. But while it is true that the federal government is not always the insidious subverter of the truth that it is sometimes made out to be, it is nonetheless true that the government finances most (although not all) projects according to some criterion of worth that is generally related to its own notion of the 'national interest.' Further, grants are generally offered for proposals that have some tangible value, that can lead to practical consequences for the solution of technical problems.

The other major source of outside research money comes from the foundations. While many of these institutions do see their role as stimulating innovation, they are only willing to go so far in financing projects that may have outcomes contrary to government and business interests. Their sensitivity about keeping good public relations (which means not creating any controversy), governmental questioning of their tax exempt status, and their dependence on a healthy economy to bolster their own endowments are all constraints on their role as social innovator.

The business community, while it does not play a large role in financing research on campus, does exert great influence on the marketing of ideas produced in the university. Thus, the academic must be future-oriented in deciding which projects will be most lucrative on the open market. Furthermore, business interests are often contemporaneous with the financial interests of the university and are felt by the academic particularly when the university's trustees decide to become involved in planning the university's future.

In addition to financial considerations, both government and business exert great influence on the academic through their staffing policies. The university, of course, trains the major bulk of the manpower needed by the technological society. The academic himself, however, is becoming increasingly mobile between the different sectors. This growing interchangeability, while it may permit the academic to become more directly involved at the top managerial levels, nonetheless often increases his dependence upon these other institutions for their approval of his opinions and areas of study.

The effect of such research and personnel policies on the intellectual community is, of course, tremendous. Study at both the faculty and graduate-student levels is distorted toward those areas where money is available and therefore to those subject areas that government and business feel are important to fund. To both the graduate student and faculty member, the alternatives provided by these research opportunities are pseudo-choices. The fact that funds or jobs are available in a particular quantitative area and not in other quantitative or non-quantitative areas leads to a distortion of priorities: because a project is funded, it is somehow perceived as being more important than a non-funded area. Innovation is discouraged because the alternatives are already predetermined. To say that one has, as a last resort, the choice of not accepting a position or grant is to present a non-choice. Freedom comes from the ability to formulate alternatives, not merely to choose between predetermined alternatives. Thus, the academic becomes a prisoner of someone else's priorities. The role that the academic will play in social change as well as the standards set for judging his success or failure are therefore the results of external forces and not of the conscious choice of the individual academic.

The effect of such lucrative offers on the behavior of the academic, non-choices as they may be, is found in the development of the academic entrepreneur. More and more of the academic's time is spent thinking of ways to sell his services. Organizing projects, writing funding proposals, doing consultant work, or actually going to work for government or business are pursuits which call upon the academic to develop salesmanship skills which would rival those of the most adroit vacuum-cleaner or insurance salesman. The fast pitch, the neat packaging of the service or product, the promise of quick, practical, and economical results, and a heavy dose of showmanship are all skills that the academic entrepreneur must refine if he is to gain the best price for his service.

It is clear, however, that the manipulative values inherent in salesmanship are not those values most conducive to the intellectual endeavor. Trying to make the grant fit one's specialty or undertaking research or a job that is inimical to one's intellectual integrity often involves deception on the part of the academic of those to whom he is selling his service and, most importantly, deception of himself. What is most regrettable, however, is that the entrepreneurial emphasis basically implies a surrendering of the intellectual's freedom to choose those areas of study most relevant to the social issues of his time and to his own genuine interests. C. Wright Mills stated the consequence of this entrepreneurial activity with his characteristic brutal clarity: 'To sell yourself is to turn yourself into a commodity. A commodity does not control the market: its nominal worth is determined by what the market will offer.'[22]

The professional environment

Academic life in the university, however, is much more than a collection of unrelated entrepreneurs. The academic's action is severely structured by the requirements of his particular profession or discipline. The folklore of academia has often made much of the declassing influence of university life. From Karl Mannheim on

350

down to David Riesman, intellectuals have somehow felt that their special insight has enabled them to overcome the personal bias that is based on one's class origins and to allow them, in turn, to be detached and objective in their intellectual inquiry. But as Theodore Roszak has pointed out, 'if academic life *de*classes, it can also *re*class —into something that feels like and often pays like the great American upper middle class. . . .'[23] More importantly, academic life reclasses the individual into a profession that possesses a complete set of rules that govern conduct, status, and rewards. The academic discipline-profession often resembles a guild with a rigorous apprenticeship and standards of admission and behavior. The guild tends to be isolationist, conservative, and exclusionary. As Clark Kerr notes in discussing the university faculty: 'The guild view is elitist toward the external environment, conservative toward internal change, conformist in relation to the opinion of colleagues.'[24]

As important as the guild analogy, however, is the growing relationship of the academic discipline to the standardization of process and product and the specialization and differentiation of work so characteristic of modern bureaucracy. The effects of the scarcity of time and superabundance of technical knowledge were discussed earlier. Their effect has been to produce an academic expert who specializes in a narrow technical field of study to the exclusion of a broader perspective. Each academic organizes a knowledge monopoly around the area of his special technical proficiency. He protects his specialty by constantly increasing the degree of specialization and expertise necessary to understand his field.

The standardization of the study process is particularly significant. Pre-packaged curricula, large blocks of required 'sequence' or 'core' courses, standardized credit units of work and total hours needed to graduate, and the ranking of performance through the grading system are all devices used to standardize the process of education and its resultant product. Of further consequence as a structural incentive toward specialization and standardization is the increasing emphasis on methodology. More and more courses are required in methodology so that students will have marketable skills upon graduation. The emphasis on scientific technique is supposed to give the student the 'tools' with which to range across varied subject matter in order to arrive at putatively universal laws. While such 'laws' are indeed deducible, their range of conception is nonetheless limited to the positivistic outlook that underlies its view of history and human nature. It is the ultimate triumph of form over content.

The standardization of curricula is, of course, most evident at the undergraduate level. There, the neophyte student is supposed to absorb data and techniques and parrot them back to the professor or,

351

more likely, the graduate teaching assistant. This process may be learning but it is only a small part of education. Independent thinking is the last thing in the world that the student is asked to do. The goals of this system are to eliminate controversy and induce a routinized pattern of thinking and behavior. It is a socialization process that prepares the student for any number of technocratic jobs, including, of course, the academic profession. The graduate student in academia, now well on his way to the technocrat's longevity, is further reminded of his obligation to the profession: he must teach other people's courses with other people's curricula and he must do other people's research for use in the marketplace of the technological society.

If the individual academic seeks to monopolize a particular area of knowledge, then the professional discipline seeks to do the same on a larger scale. The profession, of course, acts as a service to those who comprise its ranks. It sets standards of qualification which anyone who seeks to become a member of that profession must fulfill. The profession serves the positive function of assuring that a high degree of intellectual integrity will be maintained and that charlatans who may pass off spurious goods on those unfamiliar with the nature and qualities of the discipline will be kept out.

But the major purpose of the discipline is to *legitimize* those techniques and areas of knowledge peculiar to itself. Like the individual academic, the discipline seeks to preserve an area of independence from all other areas and to protect itself from being consumed by the political-economic system of study. It does so by controlling the definitions of expertise and knowledge specific to the discipline, how those definitions will be used, and by whom those definitions will be used. In such a way the discipline keeps secret its workings and thus preserves an area of uncertainty around which it can demand public acceptance of its vital role.

Such professional standardization, however, may lead to unfortunate consequences for the intellectual vitality of the discipline as well as its quality of service to the public. By keeping the setting of definitions and standards of conduct to itself, the discipline may become insulated from the outside world to the point where it may lose any incentive toward being self-critical. Because the outside world (most importantly, the public at large) has little basis for evaluating the discipline in terms of its peculiar definitions, the discipline may be able to ignore broad public issues in favor of service to special interest groups. This, in fact, is precisely what has happened. The disciplines have so abstracted their expertise into areas of technical concern—Mills would call it 'abstract empiricism' —that they have removed themselves from public scrutiny and accountability, and substituted for it the goal of service to the political-economic elite. They have, in truth, become elitist, consciously bemoaning the ignorance of the masses while at the same time becoming increasingly abstract and secretive so as to deny the public access to the information and advice so vital for them to make intelligent decisions. The academic technicians then argue that they must make 'objective' (for the elite) evaluations as experts because of the very public ignorance which, in fact, was engendered by their own contrived and specious technical expertise. It becomes a self-fulfilling prophecy in which the efficiency of the integrative mechanisms of the political-economic elite is perfected at the expense of popular democracy.

Restructuring toward the goal of power

The direction that this paper has taken up to this point is not difficult to discern. A theme, if there is one to be found, is the circumscribing of any power that the academic might have by way of his expert knowledge by the cultural and structural forces that delimit his freedom to think and to act. Indeed, such knowledge as it is presently constituted, far from being posed as even a potential threat to the political-economic establishment, has instead been thoroughly co-opted for use by the system. The sources of cultural and structural constraint have been described in some detail throughout this paper. Let us briefly recapitulate their essence.

The cultural factors which have led to the academic's dependence upon, and interdependence with, the political-economic system derive basically from the increased (until recently) efficiency of the liberal welfare state. Combined with an 'end of ideology' ideology which is based on an ethical relativism, a reliance on moderate, pragmatic solutions, and an emphasis on efficiency, order, and growth, this welfare capitalism has developed into democratic elitism whereby a political-economic elite increasingly removes public issues from popular scrutiny and places them in the power of a technological elite which operates at their disposal. The goal has become one of achieving greater social integration within a system of differential power bases to be frozen in keeping with the existing political-economic elite. The means to this end has been the cult of 'scientism,' the almost metaphysical faith that Americans have in the redeeming qualities of science as a social purgative. The academic community, caught up in this bacchanal of technique, has developed a knowledge consumerism in which ideas, like goods and services, are to be consumed and then discarded as more fashionable models hit the market.

The structural constraints on the academic's independence derive basically from the academic's 'servant' status to the needs and demands of big government and big business. Dependence on outside support for both financial and personal well-being has meant that the academic has, of necessity, been in the position of selling his services in a market of virtually unlimited supply and very limited demand. The academic, instead of organizing to fight this control, has fallen willingly into line in adopting the position of selling his services to the highest bidder. With the overwhelming demand for technical skills, the academic disciplines have standardized the process and products of their educational programs through the emphasis on pre-packaged programs including, most notably, a rigorous training in methodology. Specialization takes place around trivial distinctions in subject matter as the positivistic criterion for truth undercuts any meaningful distinction that may be present. The economy and predictability of the academic product is achieved as the now-marketable skills of the academic are plugged into the rest of the system.

The import of such cultural and structural constraints would appear to lead one to the ineluctable conclusion of the impotence of the intellectual in today's university. The ability of the technological system to order the academic enterprise in the image of the existing concentration of power appears to be complete. To speak, then, as critics of the university often do, of the social responsibility of the intellectual, is to speak of a force with virtually no power. In the first place, the individual academic is in a highly dependent status with respect to the political-economic power system and its structural component, the professional discipline, on the campus. In the second place, and probably most importantly, the academic, given the commonality of interests he shares with the power structure as well as the efficient socialization process he goes through on campus, is highly unlikely to possess the social consciousness that is prerequisite to seeking organized political redress.

What exists on the campuses of our universities is what Mills has characterized as 'organized irresponsibility.' What can counteract this development is in 'organized responsibility,' and this can come only by searching for cultural and structural openings in the system in which innovation can take place around concentrated social action. To beseech the prodigal intellectual to use his conscience is not enough; he is, in fact, committed to the system as a matter of belief. When the system is successful in efficiently integrating all sectors of the society into its own interests, then one's consciousness and, thus, one's conscience are merged into the ongoing reality of the system.

What is needed, therefore, is to locate the cracks in the structural armor of the system so that innovation may be encouraged by the system as part of its adaptation to its own weaknesses. It is possible, in those areas of the political-economic system and the university where conditions have become fluid, to replace the stasis of normalcy with the dynamic of fundamental change. It is, of course, necessary that the intellectual recognize that the openings in the system exist, the need for constructive change, and the possibility of an organized effort that will protect him from the caprice of the system. Again, individual conscience is not enough. One must instead seek out opportunities presented by cultural and structural crises in the system: utilize those opportunities spontaneously created and promote new opportunities where weakness may be latent.

Both kinds of opportunities do exist in the system today and are becoming more common as time goes on. The basic reason for the development of structural fluidities has been the emergence of an over-all crisis of authority in the political-economic system. The seemingly inexorable tightening of the juggernaut of advanced technology has failed to eliminate sporadic breakdowns in the system or to mollify the mounting anxieties and frustrations extant in the vast majority of the citizenry. The inability of the federal government to eliminate poverty, to win a limited war, to prevent the ravaging of the environment, or to halt strikes by federal employees, as well as the inability of local government, especially in urban areas, to provide adequate services to its inhabitants in a deteriorating environment are all part of a pattern that is undermining the legitimated authority of the social, political, and economic institutions in America. It is these factors, more than any incipient revolutionary movement to date, that has begun to upset the existing political-economic equilibrium and to create openings where innovation may possibly develop. Indeed, one can generalize that it is not revolutionaries who make revolutions but rather the conditions engendered by the system itself.

What are some of the areas where structural fluidity may liberate the intellectual from his status as a glorified mechanic? In the broadest terms, it is possible that government agencies may find it necessary to ask advice on not merely the technical questions of *how* we get to some predetermined goal, but rather advice on what our goals *should be* in the first place. While such openings are unlikely in the highly ossified area of military research, it is nonetheless likely that open-ended projects may be financed in such socially relevant areas as education, ecology, consumer protection, and urban redevelopment. Such openings are valid opportunities to pursue creative research which may have some real effect on policy decisions at the national and local levels. The crisis in the state of the human condition may well have practical policy implications and it is here that the intellectual may find that his once-obsolete theoretical skills are now highly desired once again.

On the level of the university disciplines it is becoming increasingly clear that the major problems confronting this society know no disciplinary boundaries. It is clear, furthermore, that the disciplines are archaic structures which have long since seen their last creative idea and pulverized the majority of their members into unmitigated mediocrity and obeisance to the system. Such problems as poverty, race, social change, and peace do not fit into the knowledge monopolies of disciplines or individuals. They require new modes of analysis and conceptualization that even make the rather new notions of multi- or inter-disciplinary approaches look inadequate. The impetus for reform may come both from within and outside the university. As noted above, funding may well become available for supra-disciplinary projects from perplexed government agencies and foundations. The setting up of policy institutes, centers for advanced study and interdisciplinary programs are possible ways the university may be able to catalyze change in the system.

Certainly the most encouraging movement toward reform lies in the recent attempts by various elements within the university to restructure it with increased governing power residing in the faculty/student legislatures. Such a restructuring provides the possibility of creating an institution around which the 'organized responsibility' we spoke of earlier may develop. In the above examples of reforms, the intellectual could still be dependent for support upon the forces that were outside of his control. He would still be an individual versus giant social institutions. The university, in all instances, has played the sometimes passive, sometimes active role in permitting or encouraging the integration of interests between its constituents and the outside institutions.

The regaining of control of the university as an institution by the intellectual is an absolute prerequisite for rejuvenation of the intellectual as a social innovator. With such institutional control, the intellectual can shape his environment to suit his own needs: he may reform curricula, de-emphasize artificial regulations, overcome departmental obsolescence and even fulfill his major public service role which is to provide the knowledge to make an intelligent and self-conscious citizenry and to provide significant social, political, and economic alternatives from which people can choose.

Two objections will immediately be raised to such a course of action. The first is that no agreement could possibly be reached on questions of university policy by the intellectuals. The second is that such policy would hinder academic freedom. The first objection derives from the myth that because intellectuals are somehow supposed to be smarter and nobler than everyone else they should therefore find it necessary to reach total agreement on what is 'right' before they act, while political institutions at large do not have to do so. Such a myth should be dispelled. The existence of expertise in the university does not guarantee that there is greater wisdom or that agreement is any more achievable there than other places in society. The fact of the matter is, that, like any other institution, the university, either through passive or active commitment, is integrated into the over-all functioning of the system. The question is, therefore, not whether the university should be involved, but rather, in what way should it be involved. Intellectuals, as a community, can make decisions about the overall nature of their environment without unanimous consent and they must do so if they are to control the uses to which their knowledge is put.

This does not mean that thought control or curtailment of academic freedom for the minority will ensue. Those who wish to remain uninvolved may do so and those who disagree with overall policy may do so without fear of reprisal as long as they do not jeopardize the nature of the university meaning the return of the university to the service of a political-economic elite. But freedom means more than freedom from constraint. It means, most importantly, freedom to control what one is dependent upon, to formulate the alternatives from which one is to make choices. One can never escape necessity, but one can, through socially conscious thought and action, overcome necessity and turn it to one's own purposes. It is this act of overcoming that is the essence of freedom. And it is only n a university that can determine its own alternatives that the ndividual intellectual can be said to be free.

It is only in this way that the university can truly become a power center and its knowledge be given an organized base from which it can be put to useful social tasks. It is only in this way that the knowledge of the intellectual can be transformed into power and thereby require of the intellectual a responsibility for the implications of his thoughts and actions of which heretofore he has been relieved. No longer a mere technician, the intellectual will be required—by the direct consequences that his knowledge will have—to see the relationships between thought and action that he has previously neglected or rejected. The dichotomy between thought and action, between the contemplative and active lives, will be broken and their reunification will be a welcome advance in the study of political and social problems. As Roszak cogently asserts:

> Analysis and discussion, where they are politically relevant, become political *acts*—and it is this that we have specified, as the peculiar social responsibility of intellectuals. To think, to speak, to teach, to write: all of these *are* forms of doing. They ought properly to be seen as integral components of action and as an indispensable part of the political process.[25]

Those who wish to remain technicians, accept uncritically the values of outside forces, and act as servants of particular interests are

357

free to do so—but not within the university. They may seek employment from those to whom they feel so strongly committed. This does not mean that the university should become uninvolved. On the contrary, it should become more involved but not at the expense of becoming dependent upon outside special interests. The university must regain its objectivity, its ability to examine all the facts and meanings without having its decisions predetermined by prior commitments. But to be objective or disinterested is not to be indifferent. As Mills stated, 'I have tried to be objective but I do not claim to be detached.'[26]

Objectivity and commitment are not incompatible qualities: they are complementary ones. The generation of new ideas, their dissemination to the public, the achievement of an informed and self-critical public opinion, and the linking together of social theory and social action are all goals for which the university must strive. It is an educated and critical public that will ultimately offer the intellectual his only lasting protection from co-optation and abuse by powerful interest groups. *And it is only to the public, therefore, that the university owes any lasting allegiance.*

The university today lies at the nexus of past and future, at the point where old meets new in a dynamic and creative process. It is the university's and the intellectual's peculiar role to at once preserve the past and to create new beginnings from that past which will further human happiness and expand human freedom and reason. It is perhaps their unique promise to consciously make the present a continuous act of becoming: of affirmation, of renewal, of reaching out. For the intellectual, this process of becoming must be his ultimate goal, his ultimate responsibility.

Notes

1 James Ridgeway, *The Closed Corporation*, New York: Random House, 1968, p. 11.
2 Clark Kerr, *The Uses of the University*, Cambridge, Mass.: Harvard University Press, 1963, p. vii.
3 *Ibid.*, p. vii.
4 *Ibid.*, pp. 87–8.
5 See Gunter W. Remmling, *Road to Suspicion: A Study of Modern Mentality and the Sociology of Knowledge*, New York: Appleton-Century-Crofts, 1967, pp. 199–202.
6 See *ibid.*, pp. 4–10.
7 *Ibid.*, p. 109.
8 William Birenbaum, *Overlive*, New York: Delacorte Press, 1969, p. 70.
9 *Ibid.*, p. 97.
10 *Ibid.*, p. 17.

11 Michel Crozier, *The Bureaucratic Phenomenon*, University of Chicago Press, 1964, p. 165.
12 Floyd Matson discusses extensively these points throughout his excellent work, *The Broken Image*, Garden City, N.Y.: Anchor-Doubleday, 1966; see especially pt 1, pp. 3–113.
13 Sheldon Wolin, 'Political Theory as a Vocation', *American Political Science Review*, vol. 63, no. 4 (December 1969), p. 1070.
14 Karl Mannheim, *Man and Society in an Age of Reconstruction*, New York: Harcourt, Brace & World, 1940, p. 213.
15 Matson, *op. cit.*, pp. 43–4, 52 (emphasis in original).
16 Karl Mannheim, *Ideology and Utopia* (trans. Louis Wirth and Edward Shils), New York: Harcourt, Brace & World, 1936, p. 46. Mannheim, of course, is noted for his attempt—most would argue unsuccessful—to resolve the social scientist's dilemma of at once being detached and making value judgments through his notion of 'relationism'. See *Ideology and Utopia, passim*.
17 For the notion of 'functional rationality' as compared to 'substantive rationality', see Mannheim, *Man and Society in an Age of Reconstruction*, pp. 51–6. See also the following paragraph.
18 Matson, *op. cit.*, pp. 39–40.
19 *Ibid.*, p. 51. No more moralistic a view of the proper ordering of human behavior can be found than in the work of that quintessential behaviorist, B. F. Skinner. See his *Walden Two*, New York: Macmillan, 1948.
20 Wolin, *op. cit.*, p. 1073.
21 *Ibid.*, p. 1071.
22 C. Wright Mills, 'The Social Role of the Intellectual' in Irving Louis Horowitz (ed.), *Power, Politics and People: The Collected Essays of C. Wright Mills*, New York: Oxford University Press, 1963, pp. 301–2.
23 Theodore Roszak, 'On Academic Delinquency' in Theodore Roszak (ed.), *The Dissenting Academy*, New York: Random House, 1967, p. 25 (emphasis in original).
24 Kerr, *op. cit.*, p. 99.
25 Roszak, *op. cit.*, p. 34 (emphasis in original).
26 C. Wright Mills, *The Marxists*, New York: Dell, 1962, p. 10.

24 Ideology and utopia in South Africa: a methodological contribution to the sociology of knowledge

K. Danziger

Historical limitations of sociology of knowledge

Since the publication of Mannheim's major contributions to the sociology of knowledge the discrepancy between their epistemological promise and their actual fruit in terms of empirical research has become more and more striking. Mannheim's own tendency to over-rate the philosophical side of his work may have contributed to this development but the context of post-war sociological research is likely to have been of greater importance. Where the stimulus for research comes from 'direct market pressures and military needs'[1] there is not likely to be much interest in the problem of knowledge as a sociological category. Accordingly, the sociology of knowledge has been replaced by the analysis of 'mass communications', reflections on 'styles of thought' have given way to opinion polls, the relationship of social groups to ideas has been transformed into the relationship between 'audiences' and 'communication sources', and a concern with the social conditions for intellectual truth or error has been superseded by a more modern concern with the reliability of ratings. As interest in substantive problems wanes research procedure is converted into a set of administrative routines.

But these developments are closely related to wider social changes that would in themselves suffice to bring about the practical eclipse of the sociology of knowledge. Empirically, the strength of this approach lay in its ability to analyse and assign a proper place to socially transcendent ideas, that is to say, ideas which went beyond the present, actually existing, framework of social relationships and pointed either towards the past or towards the future. It is no accident that the sociology of knowledge was mainly restricted to an analysis of political ideas, for it is in political ideas that man's capacity to transcend the immediately given social framework receives its most

360

direct expression. Where ideas are not situationally transcendent they can be quite effectively studied by the ordinary methods of what Wright Mills calls 'abstracted empiricism',[2] but it is the failure of these methods in the face of utopian or ideological systems that requires the application of special methods of research.

Now, there seem to be strong reasons for thinking that the role of situationally transcendent ideas has suffered a considerable decline in Western societies, especially during the last quarter century. Mannheim was already aware of this trend and foresaw the possibility of a future world in which 'there can exist a condition in which thought will be utterly devoid of all ideological and utopian elements'.[3] More recently, other writers have furnished copious illustrations of the modern failure to develop positive images of the future, so that the future becomes either a frightful 'counter-utopia' (*1984*) or a mere repetition of the present which brings only technological but not human changes.[4]

Mannheim thought that these developments depended on a shift from the intellectual preoccupation with 'the problem of class relations' which had characterized an earlier generation, at least in Europe. As long as the relationships between social classes were unstable they were seen as a threat to the social system as a whole, and it is on this basis that positive speculation about the future of society flourished. But where the stability of existing class relationships was never in doubt, as in America, there was not the same 'drive for a total perspective', the social whole would take care of itself and the intellectual had to concern himself solely with problems of social technique and organization. Concern about the future of society as a whole introduces that dimension of historical time into human thought without which no situationally transcendent ideas, whether ideological or utopian, can develop. But under present conditions the threat to the whole of society comes not from the instability of class relations but from that 'military metaphysic' which is the modern counterpart of ideology. The sociological analysis of military and anti-military ideology would therefore constitute the most direct application of Mannheim's sociology of knowledge to the problems of the 'overdeveloped' society.

It is in the 'underdeveloped' countries of the world that class relations retain a degree of instability which casts doubt on the continuation of the existing system of social relationships as a whole. In many cases new groups of capitalists and old groups of landowners are rivals for the control of the machinery of the state, while the process of differentiation among the peasantry is greatly accelerated and wage workers begin to feel their potential power. Frequently, the relationships between these different social strata are in a state of violent flux and institutional channels for diverting the threat to the social whole are brittle or ineffective. Under these conditions, where the future of society as a whole is indeed in doubt, situationally transcendent ideas flourish as they once did in Europe, both in their ideological and in their utopian form, and the sociology of knowledge is faced with a magnificent field for empirical research. There is no lack of chiliastic, millenarian sects in modern Asia and Africa, and the range and variety of conservative ideology far exceeds the European contribution to this style of thought. On the other hand, one has to recognize the intense appeal which the rationalist utopias have for intellectuals from these societies. Ideas which transcend the framework of existing social relations can grow only where the continuation of existing relations is in doubt.

The South African context

There can be few societies where this doubt is more intense than in present-day South Africa. For a country which has established quasi-colonial relationships within its own borders[5] the world-wide collapse of the colonial system necessarily threatens the collapse of the existing framework of society. Moreover, large-scale industrial expansion has introduced new elements of instability into social relations which had previously enjoyed a measure of permanence. The effects of these sources of tension are greatly multiplied by the extraordinary rigidity of the existing system of social differentiation by race. This rigidity is partly due to the fact that 'race' has become a purely administrative concept and 'race relations' have been removed from the sphere of public policy to bureaucratic control.[6] The system as a whole therefore has the worst of both worlds. It suffers from the rigidity and organized irresponsibility of an efficient bureaucratic control of all important sectors of social life, but its leviathan is built on the tensions of a colonial society unable to satisfy the material or political aspirations of the majority of its population.[7] As the bureaucracy is dedicated to the preservation of the existing system, and not, as has happened elsewhere, to its change or even reformation, it can only have the effect of multiplying the disintegrative tendencies arising out of the basic tensions within the social system.

Small wonder that these conditions have led to widespread anxiety about the future of South African society as a whole. A considerable popular literature in both official languages has grown up dedicated to this problem,[8] and speculation about the fate of the existing system of social relationships is rife. Under these circumstances almost every segment of life becomes politicized—the individual cannot make a choice of sexual partner, take his seat in a bus or queue for his pension at the post office without involving himself in a political situation. That means that any questioning of existing administrative arrangements implies a questioning of the system as a whole. Not only do such conditions provide fertile soil for the growth of situationally transcendent ideas but the rigour of administratively imposed social divisions ensures that these ideas will develop into mutually impervious ideological systems between which no communication is possible.[9]

The colonial system produced four distinct national groups in South Africa:[10]; the indigenous African group, a numerically small group of Indians, a group of English-speaking Europeans and the group of Afrikaans-speaking inhabitants who are of very mixed ancestry. These groups are distinguished by language, culture, religion and partly by geographical location. Each of them is also internally differentiated in terms of social class and other factors which vary from group to group. For the African group divisions by tribal origin are important, for the Indians there are religious and language divisions; religious divisions also exist in the English-speaking group. The internal division of the Afrikaans-speaking group is essentially political; that is to say, there is a legal separation into dark-skinned 'coloureds' and fair-skinned 'Afrikaners'. The latter practically monopolize the bureaucratic power structure of the country while the former suffer all the usual forms of racial discrimination. Cutting across all other social divisions and supporting them lies the massive inequality in the distribution of political and economic power. While there are exceptions, economic power wielded through large industrial and financial organizations remains largely a privilege of sections of the English-speaking group, while political control of the vast administrative apparatus of the state has been an Afrikaner preserve for many years. The system as a whole is organized so as to secure the perpetuation of this existing pattern of privileges and the attitude to this pattern is the touchstone of the individual's political commitment.

The conflict of social interests arising out of this situation is given a special sharpness by the specific factors previously mentioned. Firstly, the existing distribution of social power is an anachronism in the post-colonial world; secondly, it is incompatible with many of the demands of a modern industrial system such as now exists in the country; and thirdly, the rigidity of the legal complex of *apartheid* ensures that no individual will be left out of the administrative net which forces quite personal aspirations to take on political forms. The fact that social antagonism takes on the form of a struggle on the issue of racial discrimination should not obscure the underlying threat to the existing pattern of class relationships which this antagonism entails. For the class composition of the main national groups is very uneven. There are few white workers who are not supervisors and there are even fewer Africans who have anything to sell but their labour. Where the terms 'white' and 'boss' are synonymous the antagonism between white and black cannot readily be separated from the antagonism between capitalist and worker. A threat to the system of race relations as a whole therefore readily implies a threat to the system of class relations as a whole. Under these conditions one might expect the development of a set of mutually exclusive systems of situationally transcendent ideas which are meaningfully linked to the contending social groups, a classical situation for the sociology of knowledge.

Methodological problems

In a preliminary study it was shown that crucial differences in 'styles of thought' could indeed be demonstrated as between intellectuals from privileged and from non-privileged groups in South Africa.[11] But before these findings can be extended some consideration of the methodological value of Mannheim's contributions to the sociology of knowledge is necessary.

What basically distinguishes the approach of the sociology of knowledge from the methods of latter-day empiricism is its concern with social totality. This concern first of all expresses itself in a sense of the interconnection of various types of political ideas so that each can only be studied and understood in relation to others which flourish in the same social context. From the point of view of empirical techniques of investigation the holistic approach means that less importance is attached to the content of specific attitudes than to the cognitive categories on which such attitudes are based. In an ideal typical sense these cognitive categories show a meaningful coherence so as to form distinctive Gestalt-like patterns, but in concrete individuals elements of different styles may co-exist. This suggests that an empirical sociology of knowledge would adopt an analytical approach which would firstly seek to describe the elements of each cognitive orientation and then attempt to assess the relative weight given to each of these elements in the mental productions of various individuals. Such an approach differs from that of the usual attitude survey in that it does not start with a collection of separate elements in order to arrive at the measure of the whole by their summation, but starts with whole patterns which are then analysed into constituent elements for purposes of identification.

This holistic approach is especially suitable for the analysis of the situationally transcendent, that is to say, the ideological or utopistic attitudes which require to be treated as wholes because they are themselves directed at the social whole. They arise, as has been indicated, where the future of the social whole is in doubt, and they have no other object than this whole. Their internal structure, if it is to be adequate to this object, must be correspondingly complex. Just as the essence of a social whole lies in the system of its constituent social relationships, so the essence of ideas about the social whole lies in the system of their interconnection. This system involves the operation of certain cognitive categories, above all, the categories of historical time, for these are the categories in which knowledge of the social whole is consciously presented. The cognition of the social whole involves the ordering of social events on a time scale, and the kind of ordering which is used determines the meaning which social events will have for the subject. The use of one or other system of temporal ordering enables the individual to assess the significance of isolated events for the social whole—one may see an event as a sign of slow social progress, another may see it as an indication that utopia is at hand. The elements of the cognitive styles which an empirical sociology of knowledge seeks to detect in ideas which transcend the existing social situation are therefore largely aspects of temporal orientation, the categories of historical time.

These categories are based on a certain dynamic orientation to the social process as a whole, a 'dominant wish', a basic motive with regard to the reality of social change. Out of this wish arise specific *Weltwollungen*, an 'intellectual motivation' to impose one or other system on the world, both cognitively and in action. These notions carry the strong implication that men are to be studied as the producers rather than as the 'consumers' of ideas. 'Social strata', says Mannheim, 'play a creative role precisely because they introduce new intentions, new directions or intentionality, new world postu-lates . . .'[12] This kind of approach differs sharply from the social psychological model of behaviourism, implicitly underlying modern attitude studies, according to which an attitude is essentially an 'implicit response' evoked by certain stimulus patterns and which is in turn 'drive-producing.'[13] In this case the role of the individual is essentially a passive one, and he is studied not as the producer of the world of stimuli which surrounds him but as its product. Thus, in an 'attitude inventory' or a survey question the *form* of the cognitive item is contributed by the investigator, while the subjects of the investigation function merely as selectors of items, accepting some and rejecting others. The very form of the research instrument makes it inevitable that the groups whose attitudes are to be studied should be treated essentially as audiences, as consumers of attitudes rather than as their producers. This approach has its uses in connection with certain practical problems. But the sociology of knowledge is essentially concerned with man as a producer of social orientations, with the cognitive forms that he imposes on the information at his disposal. Hence this discipline must be concerned with the analysis of cognitive response to unstructured material, and in the usual case it must restrict itself to those members of a group who have made or are likely to make some active contribution to the construction of a cognitive style, that is to say, the intellectual representatives of the group.

In the past, the sociology of knowledge has concerned itself almost entirely with historical material, leaving the investigation of contemporary data to the methods of the social survey or to anthropological methods. If an empirical sociology of knowledge is to make a contribution to the study of contemporary problems it is necessary for it to adopt certain modifications of technique so as to safeguard the objectivity of its findings. Thus, it is no longer possible to restrict one's analysis to the productions of a few systematic thinkers in the manner of the classical sociology of knowledge. In the first place such systematic thinkers may not exist in parts of the world where mental life has been decisively shaped by the colonial system with its emphasis on action and its contempt for intellectual values. Moreover, as soon as research deals with contemporary material the question of the representativeness of a given line of thought can only be answered by some form of sampling, whereas with historical material our knowledge of subsequent events can usually answer this question for us. This does not mean that it is necessary to seek that chimera of social research, the 'representative sample'. But it does mean that groups rather than individual intellectuals should be studied.

The use of groups of subjects and large numbers of protocols makes possible the application of quantitative methods which were excluded in the classical form of the discipline. But these innovations also make it necessary to take seriously the problem of reliability. Where it is a matter of analysing the intellectual premises of a single systematic thinker the social effects of whose thought are in any case known, the problem of the reliability of the interpretation hardly arises. But where one is dealing with a large number of individuals about whom one knows very little and who usually lack the self-consistency of great thinkers so that they may show elements of several styles of thought, the question of the reliability of the analysis can no longer be ignored. The way to deal with this problem is not to abandon the investigation of cognitive styles and to restrict the subject to simple yes-no responses which even a machine can score but to multiply one's human judges. By getting several judges of varying background to assess the mental product of each of the subjects of the investigation according to the same set of interpretive categories a measure of the reliability of the analysis can be obtained. This use of human judges cannot be avoided if cognitive styles are to be studied as part of a social totality.

The assessment of cognitive styles

The material used for the investigation of cognitive styles in South Africa consisted of several hundred essays written in response to the following set of instructions:

Essay: The future of South Africa
Please write a short essay of 2 or 3 pages on the history of South Africa projected into the future. Imagine you are a historian writing in the 21st century and giving a brief outline history of South Africa from 1960 to 2010. Do not write merely a description of South Africa in 50 years' time, but write an actual history of the intervening period.
  This is not a test of imagination—just describe what you really expect to happen.

These instructions were administered to groups of students in their class-rooms by their ordinary teachers. Subjects were told that the material was needed for purposes of social research and that all contributions were to be strictly anonymous. Forty-five minutes were allowed for the essay. The Afrikaans-speaking subjects wrote in Afrikaans and all other subjects wrote in English. The essays were collected during two periods: 1956–7 and 1960–2.

The subjects of the investigation consisted of 84 Africans, 51 Indians, 53 Afrikaans-speaking whites and 251 English-speaking whites. They were either university students or pupils in the last class of high school; a few of the African subjects were studying at a teachers' training college. The mean age of the white groups was about 19 years, that of the non-white groups about 21 years, but their overall educational level was comparable within the limits set by the South African system.

The essays were scored for elements of cognitive style by three independent raters, a psychologist, a sociologist and a historian. The cultural background of the raters was also rather varied, namely, British, Indian and German.

The raters were given the task of assessing the dominant type of historical orientation in each essay. For this purpose five types of orientation were distinguished: conservative, technicist, catastrophic, liberal and revolutionary. It will be seen that two of these, the conservative and liberal categories, correspond to two types of 'utopian mentality' distinguished by Mannheim. The other two Mannheim types, the chiliastic and the socialistic, were not found applicable to the South African data. As regards the latter, it was observed that while actual socialist ideas were almost completely absent in all the social groups covered by the present study, elements of the historical orientation which Mannheim attributes to this type of 'utopian mentality' were extremely common among the essays collected from non-white subjects. It was therefore decided to substitute for Mannheim's socialist-communist category a new category, named the *revolutionary* orientation whose characteristic temporal perspective was the same as that of the corresponding Mannheim type but which showed no socialist or communist content. When this was done it was found that it became very difficult to distinguish this new type from the chiliastic orientation; usually the two kinds of orientation seemed to merge in the same individual and assigning the essay to one or other of these two categories became a very arbitrary matter. No further attempt was therefore made to distinguish the chiliastic type of orientation and certain aspects of this orientation were included in the new 'revolutionary' category, notably the sharp differentiation between present and future and the voluntaristic conception of social causality. It is possible that this divergence from the patterns distinguished by Mannheim is due to the fact that his patterns were derived from the outlook of specific social groups at specific periods of European history which find little correspondence in the historical situation that is faced by the students who formed the subjects of the present study. They are neither workers nor peasants and yet, like so many others in the colonial world, they are driven to a revolutionary perspective by force of circumstances. It is only to be expected that their historical orientation should constitute a new type of organization which contains elements from both the chiliastic and the socialist utopia.

Mannheim's typology also requires to be amplified in other respects. His list of utopias is incomplete and does not take into account certain peculiar forms of the 'utopian mentality' which appear to have arisen in the twentieth century. One thinks here of the tendency for images of the future to become negative and frightening and also of the new genre of utopistic literature embodied in science fiction. The latter is an example of a general tendency to see the future essentially in non-human terms; machines have become independent of man and history becomes the history of technology. This arises out of an orientation which considers all problems solely from the point of view of technique, what Georges Friedmann has called the *technicist* orientation,[14] and it is not by any means limited to engineers. Time becomes entirely a matter of physics—historical time disappears, or rather it stops, for no perspective is as blind to changing human relationships as the technicist one. This kind of utopia usually means the projection of the social present into infinity. Concern with the remote future usually indicates passivity and helplessness in relation to the immediate future which is the effective range for constructive human action. It is under these conditions that the old split between present and future is replaced by the split between reality and illusion and that futurism takes on the non-constructive form of escapism.

But science fiction also provides a clue to a further pattern in which the 'utopian mentality' has manifested itself in recent times. The main theme of many of these stories is war and catastrophe, they exult in the description of terrible super-weapons and inter-planetary warfare; forecasts of the biological degeneration of man vie with predictions about the psychic control of the individual by means of advanced 'human engineering'; the theme of conquest of mankind by robots or machines has not entirely replaced more traditional phantasies of a Malthusian kind. The constructive aspect of utopistic thinking has here been replaced by a profound pessimism about the future so as to constitute what F. L. Polak calls a 'negative utopia', whose perspectives, one may add, are not by any means limited to science fiction (Aldous Huxley, Orwell). One is therefore dealing with a specifically modern type of historical consciousness whose main characteristics are the experience of the future as catastrophic and the use of the imagination for elaborate descriptions of the destruction of human values. Historical time has lost the rationality which it had attained in the classical types of utopian mentality and has regained some of the irrationality of chiliastic time. Instead of a rational progression linking present and future one gets a kind of detemporalization of their relationship so that the future either becomes the infinite prolongation of present agonies or else it is pushed into a remote area separated from the present by a temporal vacuum. Instead of the confident assertion of human hopes and human capacities one gets a profound conviction of human impotence. It is not inappropriate to refer to this type of perspective as the *catastrophic* orientation.

In order to transform the typology of historical orientation into a set of categories suitable for empirical application it is necessary to develop specific criteria for the differentiation of these categories. In classifying essays on the social future one requires more than general descriptions of the main types of historical orientation. It is necessary to distinguish these patterns in terms of a few major characteristics which will be recognizable in the empirical material. Four such criteria were in fact used by our raters, namely, (1) the attitude to and the interrelationship of the present and the future; (2) interrelationship of historical means and ends; (3) the conception of social change; and (4) the conception of social causality. On each of these criteria the essay was placed into one or more of the five categories of historical orientation, each orientation being considered independently of the others. The rater then assigned the essay as a whole to one or other of the five categories, depending on which category had occurred most frequently in his rating by means of the four criteria. Thus, an essay which had been rated 'conservative' on three of the criteria, 'liberal' on two and 'technicist' on one would simply get a final rating of 'conservative', this being considered the dominant orientation. Where no orientation emerged as dominant, the essay was classified as belonging to a mixed type. The following guide was used in making the ratings on each criterion:

(1) *Attitude to and interrelationship of the present and the future*

Conservative. The past serves as a model for present and future—the future consists of the carrying out of traditional policies.

Technicist. The historical present leads to the future via technological development, not via social change.

Catastrophic. The future is the catastrophic negation of present values.

Liberal. The present develops gradually and continuously towards the future which is expected to be socially different from and better than the present.

Revolutionary. There is much emphasis on present tensions which are removed by the eruption of the future at one or at a series of strategic moments.

(2) *Interrelationship of historical means and ends*

Conservative. The existing pattern of social power is both the chief end and the chief means of the historical process.

Technicist. Techniques tend to become goals themselves; great size, great power and large quantities are the indices of historical progress.

Catastrophic. There is a fatalistic acceptance of social violence and destruction leading to a negative goal.

Liberal. The goal is the improvement of the existing system by means of peaceful reforms voluntarily instituted from above.

Revolutionary. The complete and desired change of the social system requires violent means which are employed with strategic foresight.

(3) *Conception of social change*

Conservative. Denial of real change as possible or desirable; only temporary disturbances of the basic equilibrium of the system are recognized.

Technicist. Change is essentially quantitative and material, not qualitative and social.

Catastrophic. The present situation necessarily deteriorates until the final catastrophe is reached.

Liberal. Change is gradual and relatively smooth—conflicts are settled peacefully.

Revolutionary. Change occurs in terms of the violent development of irreconcilable conflicts.

(4) *Conception of social causality*

Conservative. The model is that of the organic functioning of an equilibrium pattern that has been established by tradition.

Technicist. There is a mechanistic emphasis on isolated causes, often of a chance nature, such as lucky finds and discoveries or exceptional individuals.

Catastrophic. This outlook is characterized by fatalism, a belief in the inevitability of decline.

Liberal. Enlightened self-interest and the spread of enlightenment provide the main social force.

Revolutionary. There is a voluntaristic emphasis on the role of the will for social change which is precipitated in political action.

Using this guide for the assessment of the essays the three raters agreed on the dominant type of historical orientation in the case of 384 out of 439 essays. The fact that only one essay in eight could not be reliably classified seems to indicate that this method of rating is potentially useful for purposes of empirical research. Moreover, there was no tendency for disagreements among raters to be significantly more frequent for certain groups of subjects or for certain types of orientation.

TABLE 24.1   *Percentage frequency of various types of historical orientation in essays from different social groups*

	Afrikaans	English	Indian	African
Conservative	30·3	20·2	7·8	13·1
Technicist	37·8	13·1	—	1·2
Catastrophic	18·5	31·8	2·0	4·8
Liberal	3·9	19·1	49·0	22·6
Revolutionary	—	2·0	31·4	46·4
Unclassified	9·5	13·8	9·8	11·9

The results of the assessment of the essays are set out in Table 24.1. Those essays on whose classification there was no agreement among the raters are shown as 'unclassified'.

The frequency of the various types of historical orientation conforms broadly to the position of the different groups in the social structure. Thus, the Afrikaans group which is at the head of the power hierarchy has the highest frequency of conservative types and the African group which constitutes the lowest caste has the highest frequency of revolutionary types. The high frequency of liberal types in the Indian group is probably connected with the extreme aversion to social violence that is characteristic of this defenceless minority group. Technicism as a historical orientation appears to be closely related to that attitude of political indifference which is found among groups which are politically unconcerned.

It seems, therefore, that social position determines the range of available historical orientations for the members of each social group. In each case there are two or three types of orientation which occur with some frequency in the group, but the relationship between social group membership and historical orientation is never unambiguous. It is possible for an African student to be a liberal or a revolutionary and for an English student to adopt a catastrophic or a liberal outlook. The outcome of the choice depends partly on the existing historical situation—but it must also depend on factors of a more personal sort.

When the content of the essays is examined in the light of their known historical orientation one is struck by the fact that there is one specific attitude which appears to be crucial in determining the choice of orientation, and that is the attitude to the underprivileged masses. This attitude appears to vary along two continua, active-passive and good-bad. At one extreme the masses are simply ignored—they remain, by implication, the passive objects of history. But if the masses intrude into historical consciousness this seems to involve a definite change in historical perspective, though to begin with they remain essentially passive and hence containable within the existing system. Thus, it was found that essays of the conservative type mentioned non-whites significantly more frequently than essays of the technicist type (2 per cent level of confidence). But when conservative and catastrophic types are compared one finds that the latter mention the non-white masses more frequently as independent political agents, while for the former they remain passive objects of administration (5 per cent level of confidence). Moreover, a similar difference exists between revolutionary and liberal types in that it is the former who see the masses as the crucial agent of historical change while the latter accord that role to the triumph of reason in the minds of the rulers. (The difference between liberal and revolutionary types in regard to mention of non-white masses as independently effective historical agents was significant at the 0·1 per cent level.) Finally, the crucial difference between catastrophic types on the one hand and liberal/revolutionary types on the other is obviously based on the benign significance which the masses have for the latter as contrasted with the fears that they arouse in the catastrophic type.

In other words, the individual's orientation to the social future appears to be a function of the manner in which he experiences the relationship between rulers and ruled. If he sees the latter as passive objects for administrative manipulation by the rulers in whose hands resides all effective social power and initiative, then his outlook will be a conservative one. If, on the other hand, he is convinced of the necessity of a violent clash of interests between rulers and ruled his outlook will be a revolutionary or catastrophic one. The degree of historical activity which is attributed to the masses depends on the extent to which the ideology of class conflict is openly accepted. The technicist type is furthest from this ideology, the revolutionary type nearest to it, whatever the specific embellishment which class ideology may receive in a caste society. While it is true that social caste sets severe limits to the individual's choice of ideological position, the positions he can choose from remain class positions, that is to say, they are essentially commitments on the basic issue of class conflict.

The problem of validity

It need hardly be stressed that no special significance attaches to the exact figures presented above. The subjects of this investigation were not intended to be representative of their respective population groups and no conclusions can be drawn from these data in regard to the actual frequency of, let us say, a conservative orientation in the Afrikaans group or a revolutionary orientation in the African group. However, it is clear that as far as student groups are concerned the differences found could hardly have been obtained by chance. But do differences on a set essay have any relation to the underlying differences of historical orientation that may exist among groups?

This question can only be answered by citing certain lines of evidence. In the first place, the observed differences on the essays correspond rather well to the known lines of political cleavage in the country. It is known that government policies which are based on a mixture of conservatism and technicism enjoy strong support from the Afrikaans section and partial support from the English section. It is also known that organizations which stress political gradualism receive some English and considerable Indian support. Finally, those illegal movements which rely on extra-constitutional action are based very largely on the African section of the population. These differences are clearly reflected in the essay material, though the actual percentages have little significance in themselves.

Another line of evidence which suggests that the essays yield more than accidental material on group orientations is derived from the replication of the investigation after an interval of several years. When essays were collected from comparable groups of African and Indian subjects in 1956/7 and again in 1962 it was found that the distribution of the various types of orientation in the two groups

373

remained remarkably constant; such minor differences as did exist between the earlier and the later sample were not statistically significant. This suggests that the distinctive cognitive styles of the essays are expressions of relatively stable types of historical orientation characterizing the various social groups.

In the case of the English-speaking group the original set of essays was collected in 1956/7 and a further set in 1960/1, in the period after Sharpeville and after the decision to leave the British Commonwealth. In this case there was one significant change—a decrease in the relative number of conservative types and an increase in the relative number of catastrophic types. This suggests that crucial historical events may produce a certain shift in the time perspectives of a section of the population. But the nature of this shift appears to be largely determined by the nature of the previous orientation. The fact that the commonest switch seemed to be from a conservative to a catastrophic and not to a liberal orientation suggests an interesting hypothesis about the nature of the catastrophic type. He may well be a conservative whose defences directed against the recognition of social change have broken down. He can no longer deny social reality, but still having a hierarchical view of social relations he reverses the perspective and anticipates the subjugation of his own group. As a result he suffers from a degree of personal alienation from the social process which the conservative does not know. The almost complete absence of catastrophic types in the non-white groups may be a reflection of their failure to adopt that 'jungle ideology' which is so prominent in sections of the dominant group.

In an attempt to test the generality of the cognitive framework expressed in the essays use was made of a method developed by Osgood[15] for the 'measurement of meaning'. This involved the administration of a list of adjectival pairs, such as, important-unimportant, negative-positive, good-bad, healthy-sickly, valuable-worthless, pleasant-unpleasant. A number of concepts then have to be placed on a five-point or seven-point scale running between each member of the adjectival pair. In the present investigation the concepts 'the past', 'the present' and 'the future' were used, and subjects had to rate each concept to decide whether 'the future', for example, seemed more good than bad, more negative than positive, etc. Fifteen pairs of adjectives, including the examples quoted above, were used to assess the overall positive or negative evaluation of these concepts, and there were also six adjectival pairs, such as, organized-disorganized, clear-hazy, transparent-opaque, which were concerned with the clarity of the concepts to be rated.

These scales were administered to seventy English-speaking white students, twenty-eight of whom had written essays that belonged unambiguously to the liberal type and forty-two of whom had written essays belonging to the catastrophic type. Several weeks elapsed between the essays and the scales which were administered as part of a psychological testing programme. On the basis of his responses to the adjectival scales each subject was then given six scores which represented his overall evaluation and clarity rating of the concepts 'past', 'present' and 'future'. It was found that the 'liberal' subjects consistently gave a more positive evaluation to 'the future' than to 'the past' or to 'the present', while the relationship was reversed for the 'catastrophic' subjects who evaluated 'the future' in a more negative manner. Similarly, the 'liberal' subjects accorded greater clarity to 'the future' than to the other concepts, while the reverse was true for the 'catastrophic' subjects. Three of the four differences between the two groups of subjects reached the 1 per cent level of statistical significance and one reached the 5 per cent level.

While it is not claimed that responses to adjectival scales can yield a valid measure of the meaning of concepts, it does seem that they provide a useful set of formal reactions whose peculiar abstractness makes them a suitable vehicle for the expression of underlying cognitive orientations. They provide an opportunity for assessing certain aspects of temporal orientation under conditions rather different from those of the historical essay. The fact that a clear correspondence exists between responses under both sets of conditions seems to suggest that the cognitive framework expressed in the essays is not an artefact of the method but has some general significance also for other situations.

Conclusions

On the basis of our empirical data it is possible to make certain suggestions about a few of the intractable problems that have troubled the sociology of knowledge for many years. What room does the sociological determination of cognitive style leave to individual choice? Where this problem is posed in terms of a rigid alternative no solution can be expected. In fact, no simple correspondence between one particular cognitive style and one particular social group appears to exist. Within the society as a whole there are a limited number of social orientations and these are unequally distributed among the various social groups composing that society. This means that the individual member of the group has a limited number of possible orientations open to him. Where two kinds of social orientation are about equally probable in a given group certain common psychological factors may well prove decisive in determining the choice. Thus, in one study it appeared that young women who were optimistic regarding the consequences of the last war were also relatively more secure in their relation to their parents and in their sex role.[16]

But where a certain type of orientation is highly improbable for a member of a given group only exceptional personal circumstances are likely to lead to its adoption. Moreover, it must be remembered that many individuals show a great deal of inconsistency in their orientation, and here too accidents of personal history may determine which type of orientation achieves a relative and limited predominance.

While the social determination of the range of available thought categories remains an incontestable fact, it is also true that the extent of this range varies for different groups at different times. Sometimes the range of available orientations may be extremely narrow and at other times exceptionally broad. It would be the task of future research to assess the social conditions determining the range of cognitive styles available at any particular time. Again, it is the so-called underdeveloped countries which provide the richest material for empirical studies along these lines.

Situationally transcendent ideas can be regarded as attempts at subjectively mastering the basic tensions in a society. They provide the individual with a method of dealing with social conflicts that might otherwise assume an overwhelmingly threatening significance. Where the social framework itself is in doubt these ideas therefore always have a role to play in the psychological economy of the individual—their significance is not merely sociological. But the individual also has to deal with internal conflicts of a more personal sort, and it would not be surprising to find certain parallels between his preferred methods of mastering internal, psychological, and external, social, conflict. Techniques which the individual has learned in the family situation may well predispose him to choose one rather than another of the social orientations which his group membership makes available to him. But the kinds of conflict resolution which the individual has experienced in the family will hardly be independent of the position which his family occupies in the social structure. The relationship between individual and social factors in the formation of social perspectives is therefore far more intimate than any abstract juxtaposition of social determination and individual freedom would suggest.

Nor can Mannheim's claim for the privileged position of the intelligentsia be supported. Without going over the well-known criticism of Mannheim's position[17] it need merely be pointed out that the data of the present investigation provide no support for the view that intellectuals have a special freedom to synthesize a more objective world view. The students covered by our investigation behaved in every respect as representatives of the wider social groups which had nurtured them, and their range of social orientations was correspondingly narrow. No trace of a common outlook or higher synthesis could be discovered. No doubt this is partly due to the exceptionally sharp nature of social conflicts in South Africa. But where the social whole is more stable the incidence of situationally transcendent ideas is low and the intellectual simply becomes a technician. Where the internal stability of the existing social framework is in doubt intellectuals are often concerned with utopian or ideological systems and their concern commands wide public interest; but under these conditions they invariably seem to act as the representatives of one or other of the main contending groups in society.

The non-privileged position of the intellectuals leaves Mannheim's 'perspectivism' without any social basis. In the South African case it would require an extraordinary intellectual feat to arrive at some synthetic perspective which combines the partial historical insights of Afrikaner nationalists, English liberals and African revolutionaries. Such a synthesis would simply constitute the philosophy of the bystander, the cognitive style of the socially uncommitted. But where the ubiquity of social conflict excludes the possibility of non-commitment the intellectual stance corresponding to it would simply become another version of *status quo* ideology. It would certainly fail to yield any superior insight into historical truth because it would be based on the negation of the essential element in the historical situation, namely, the incompatibility of the conflicting interests.

The fallacy of according greater truth value to the synthetic world view is based upon a failure to recognize the active role played by cognitive patterns in the historical process. Subjective views of the social process do not merely lead to meditation, they also lead to social action. Conservative or revolutionary ideology is not merely a matter of 'intellectual position', but of practical policies and social movements which seek to impose a certain image on the world. Under these conditions social truth is created, not contemplatively interpreted, and he is nearest to the truth whose situationally transcendent ideas represent the interests of social forces which are favoured by the historical process. Not that social position directly affects the truthfulness of propositions generated by a particular thought model. But it affects the kind of thought model which a given individual is likely to use.[18] The extent to which an intellectual model of society is able to generate truthful propositions depends upon the relationship between the interests expressed in this model and the actual trend of historical development. Where these two factors are as sharply opposed as in the case of the ideology of *apartheid* there arises the spectre of a totally 'false consciousness' whose every cognition must necessarily be wrong.

Notes

1 R. K. Merton, *Social Theory and Social Structure*, Chicago: Free Press, 1957.
2 C. W. Mills, *The Sociological Imagination*, New York: Oxford University Press, 1959.
3 K. Mannheim, *Ideology and Utopia* (trans. Louis Wirth and Edward Shils), London: Routledge & Kegan Paul, 1936.
4 F. L. Polak, *De Toekomst is verleden Tijd*, Utrecht: de Haan, 1955.
5 L. Marquard, *South Africa's Internal Boundaries*, Johannesburg: Institute of Race Relations, 1958.
6 L. Kuper, 'The control of social change: A South African experiment', *Social Forces*, vol. 28 (1949), 146–53.
7 C.W. De Kiewiet, *The Anatomy of South African Misery*, London: Oxford University Press, 1956.
8 A few representative titles may be quoted: A. M. Keppel-Jones, *When Smuts Goes: A History of South Africa from 1952 to 2010*, Cape Town: African Bookman, 1947; G. D. Scholtz, *Het die Afrikanervolk n' Toekoms?* (Have the Afrikaner people a future?), Johannesburg: Voortrekkerpers, 1954; B. B. Keet, *Suid Afrika, Waarheen?* (Whither South Africa?), Stellenbosch, Cape Province: Stellenbosch University Press, 1955; P. V. Pistorius, *No Further Trek*, Johannesburg: Central News Agency, 1957; P. J. Meyer, *Trek verder: die Afrikaner in Afrika* (Trek further: the Afrikaner in Africa), Cape Town: H.A.U.M., 1959; H. Spottiswoode, *South Africa: The Road Ahead*, Cape Town: Timmins, 1960; G. Allighan, *Verwoerd—The End; A Look-Back from the Future*, Cape Town: Purnell, 1961.
9 G. M. Carter, *The Politics of Inequality: South Africa since 1948*, London: Thames & Hudson, 1958.
10 L. Marquard, *The Peoples and Policies of South Africa*, London: Oxford University Press, 2nd ed., 1960.
11 K. Danziger, 'Self-interpretations of group differences in values', *Journal of Social Psychology*, vol. 47 (1958), 317–25.
12 K. Mannheim, *Essays on the Sociology of Knowledge*, London: Routledge & Kegan Paul, 1952, ch. 4.
13 L. W. Doob, 'The behaviour of attitudes', *Psychological Review*, vol. 54 (1947), 135–56.
14 G. Friedmann, 'Technological change and human relations', *British Journal of Sociology*, vol. 3 (1952), 95–116.
15 C. E. Osgood, G. J. Suci and P. H. Tannenbaum, *The Measurement of Meaning*, Urbana: University of Illinois Press, 1957.
16 R. N. Sanford, H. S. Conrad, and K. Franck, 'Psychological determinants of optimism regarding consequences of the war', *Journal of Psychology*, vol. 22 (1946), 207–35.
17 W. Stark, *The Sociology of Knowledge*, London: Routledge & Kegan Paul, 1958, pp. 300 ff.
18 C. W. Mills, 'Methodological consequences of the sociology of knowledge', *American Journal of Sociology*, vol. 46 (1940), 316–30.

25 Social classes in Ecuador: a study of the ideological distortion of social reality*

Gunter W. Remmling, Georg Maier, Elba Valdivia Remmling

In an immediate and general way the population of the Republic of Ecuador (1969 est.: 5,890,000) may be divided into two social groups. The co-existence of these groups has traditionally been marked by a high degree of social distance resulting from significant disparities in levels of participation in the national life of this—next to Uruguay—smallest independent country in South America which fully began its politically autonomous existence in September 1830.[1]

The first and dominant social group consists of Ecuadorians who in the main identify with the Hispanic European-oriented culture; the other group includes all those belonging to the indigenous Ecuadorian cultures. Hispanic Ecuadorian society which forms more than half of Ecuador's population is composed of the urban and most of the rural population of the coastal region, practically the entire urban population of the Sierra highlands, and a small percentage of the rural population of the Sierra region. The individual criteria for membership in Hispanic Ecuadorian society are adequate knowledge of the Spanish language, though not necessarily literacy, and western European style of dress usually including factory-made clothing and shoes. Indian physical features will bar easy rise in this social system, but are not sufficient to preclude entrance into the lower social strata.

The lower social ranks in Hispanic Ecuadorian society consist of people of mixed ancestry who are commonly referred to as mestizos or *cholos*; they can be distinguished from the indigenous Indian population largely because they exhibit a minimum of essential European characteristics. At times, especially in the army, an Indian will temporarily become *cholo*, subsequently returning to Indian

* With the support of grants from the American Philosophical Society, the Southern Illinois University Graduate School, and the Maxwell Graduate School of Citizenship and Public Affairs.

society—a fact which illustrates the vague and inadequate nature of this popular appellation.

Recent census data indicate that the coastal region between the Pacific Ocean and the western base of the Andes contains about 47 per cent of the country's population, the Sierra about 50 per cent and the Oriente which lies east of the Andes about 2·5 per cent. The remainder (about 0·5 per cent) of the population lives in the Galápagos Islands. Eastern Ecuador, that is, the Oriente assumed economic importance in 1967 with the development of the oil industry in that region; almost exclusively, however, the Oriente is thinly peopled by full-blooded Indians who have cultural affinities with the tribes of the Amazon basin rather than with those of the Andes. Among the warlike tribes of the Oriente the Jívaro are famous because of their custom of shrinking the heads of slain enemies and their use of blowguns and poisoned darts. The Galápagos Islands between 500 and 700 miles west of the coast of Ecuador became well-known when Charles Darwin visited them in 1835 as naturalist of the *Beagle*.

The tropical jungles of the Oriente and the volcanic Galápagos Islands are so thinly inhabited and culturally isolated that they have practically no relevance for the analysis of social structure and change. Of the three major physical divisions of Ecuador—tropical coastal lowlands, Sierra highlands, Oriente jungles—only the first two warrant attention in the context of this essay. Because of the absence of significant problems there will be no special analysis of the relations between coastal mestizos, who are products of a mixture of Spanish and Indian, and the Negroes, mulattos, and *montuvios* of the coast, who are individuals of Negro-Indian ancestry.

Class or caste?

An immediate and superficial observation may easily lead to the conclusion that Hispanic Ecuadorian society is stratified along lines of social class, while Indian society forms a caste separated by an impenetrable wall of social isolation from the class system of Hispanic Ecuadorian society. At first glance there seems to exist, furthermore, a tripartite division along ethnic lines: whites, *cholos*, Indians. Both the class-caste separation and the ethnic division conform, however, to the ideology of the ruling groups which favors social distance from Indian society and racial pride in white status. The actual interpenetration of all Ecuadorian social groups is, however, stronger—especially under conditions of incipient social change—than admitted by the ideology of the ruling groups; this ideology, therefore, takes the classical form of false consciousness.[2]

The unfolding class system

In an objective view Ecuador seems to develop a different kind of class system; the six social classes into which the population of Ecuador may be divided shape up roughly as in Table 25.1.[3]

TABLE 25.1   *Ecuadorian social stratification**

Class levels	Per cent distribution of population (estimated)	Class characteristics
Traditional upper class	0·2	Landed 'aristocracy'.
Moneyed upper class	1·5	Financial and commercial oligarchy (*nouveaux riches*).
Established middle class	8·3	Politicians, government officials, intellectuals, professional people, businessmen (European immigrants).
Emergent middle class	15·0	Skilled, unionized white-collar and blue-collar workers, small businessmen (taxi-cab drivers, barbers, retailers). Labelled *cholos* by the ideology of the upper social strata.
Assimilated lower class	35·0	Semiskilled workers, unskilled and migratory laborers, small farmers, common soldiers, servants, petty traders (bootblacks, street vendors). Also labelled *cholos* by the ideology of the upper social strata.
Semi-assimilated lower class	40·0	Servile laborers on the landed estates, subsistence farmers (rejected as Indians by the ideology of the upper social strata).

* Per cent distribution of population is estimated on the basis of responses by Ecuadorian sociologists to a questionnaire item eliciting information on social stratification. The estimates in Table 25.1 are rough averages taking into account responses to the questionnaire, results of personal interviews, field notes, and (comparatively) the stratification literature listed in note 3. Therefore, these estimates should be viewed as preliminary and merely approximate heuristic devices.

(1) *The traditional upper class*

The top level in the group which likes to think of itself as 'white' is occupied by the landed aristocracy of colonial ancestry. The members of the traditional upper class, representing about 0·2 per cent of the population, can be recognized by their *apellido* (family name). To have the right *apellido* in Ecuador is a virtual assurance of finding all doors open; a privilege which not even money or political aggressiveness can buy. The popular Ecuadorian saying that a Larrea speaks only to a Jijón Caamaño and a Jijón Caamaño only to God is an exaggeration but may serve as an example of the class lines which exist among the so-called whites. By an *apellido* a native Ecuadorian can tell what place is reserved for its bearer in society and identify his city of origin.

(2) *The moneyed upper class*

A somewhat less elevated status is occupied by the financial and commercial oligarchy of the *nouveaux riches*. Although economically and politically powerful, people in the moneyed upper class are socially slighted by individuals in the traditional upper class. A majority of persons belonging to the moneyed upper class lives at the coast—especially in metropolitan Guayaquil. As typical representatives of the moneyed upper class the bankers, exporters, and industrialists of the coast join forces with the landholders of the Sierra who represent the traditional upper class. The political interests of the two upper classes may be expressed by different political parties but their economic interests will always unite them; they represent less than 2 per cent of the population but possess privileges and power far exceeding their numerical significance—as long as their interests are preserved it does not matter who represents the government.

(3) *The established middle class*

This class which constitutes about 8 per cent of the population represents the lowest level of those Ecuadorians who like to think of themselves as whites; there is considerable social distance between them and the people immediately below them. The politicians, government officials, professional people, and businessmen who typically make up this group usually lack sufficient social and economic distinction to penetrate the two strata above them.

A representative of this group is the five-times president José María Velasco Ibarra who has the political success and desire but not the name or wealth to become a member of the 'in-group' which is made up of the two upper classes. The members of the 'in-group' tolerate him however because of his ability to lead the people and to win elections—and use him to achieve their own political goals.[4]

Velasco Ibarra had been elected president for the first time in 1933 as an official Conservative candidate; he was elected for the fifth time in 1968 as an independent candidate. Ecuador's socio-economic misery and political problems led to the event of 22 June 1970, when President Velasco Ibarra assumed dictatorial powers. He suspended Congress with the support of the armed forces and stifled student opposition to his regime by shutting down the universities in Cuenca, Guayaquil, Loja, and Quito. While the Army rounded up left-of-center politicians and student leaders, the police initiated a search for the former president, Carlos Julio Arosemena Monroy, and for Vice-President Jorge Zavalo Baquerizo.

A special position in the established middle class—that of the marginal man—is held by European immigrants who came to Ecuador during and after World War II.[5] The immigrants are primarily active in industry and commerce: they therefore favor political stability which insures their prosperity. They look back to the years of the Galo Plaza Lasso (1948–52) and the Camilo Ponce Enríquez (1956–60) administrations as the most stable; most immigrants vote for any liberal or conservative candidate as long as he does not represent the extreme wing of his party.

The recent European immigrants had no notable effect upon the population as a whole, but they have affected the composition of the established middle class; to become members of this class the newcomers assured themselves a measure of acceptance by emulating the standards and values of the upper classes which are revered by most people in the established middle class.

(4) *The emergent middle class*

Because of the reluctance of established middle-class individuals to unite in support of common interests with people of the emergent middle class the power of the upper classes has not been challenged by the middle classes; this situation has so far not been affected by the fact that the middle classes are becoming larger as Ecuador undergoes the transition from neo-feudal agriculture to semi-industrial capitalism.

The emergent middle class is composed of Ecuadorians whose life style represents a fusion of urban and Indian ways of life. Like the Indian, the *cholo* works with his hands, but unlike the Indian, he has enjoyed some sort of formal education which makes him aware of the social conditions which surround him. Not accepted by Ecuadorians who like to think of themselves as whites and too proud to side with the Indian, the *cholo* represents the expanding and socially most restless force in the country's life.

About 15 per cent of the population—labelled *cholos* by the ideology of the upper social strata—constitutes the emergent middle class. This group is made up of industrial workers, taxi-cab drivers, barbers, and the like; these people have become accustomed to industrial conditions and have usually two generations of experience in urban living. They have well-defined aspirations toward a better standard of living and improved education for their children. Most of the labor unions draw their members from this group.

(5) *The assimilated lower class*

This group consists mainly of so-called *cholos* performing semi-skilled, migratory and unskilled labor; it includes many migrants from the Indian hinterland who left the rural communities or *haciendas* to seek work in the cities. Quite a few of these migrants have become small traders or bootblacks, sellers of lottery tickets, street vendors, or professional crooks depending upon their initiative and their eagerness to 'strike it rich'; other members of this class work as household servants. The members of this class, representing about 35 per cent of the population, have developed little cohesiveness; from a political viewpoint this group constitutes the mass—an easy prey for demagogues like Velasco Ibarra who prefers to call them his '*sublime chusma.*'[6]

(6) *The semi-assimilated lower class*

The Ecuadorian Indians, comprising about 40 per cent of the national population, find themselves at the bottom of the social pyramid; many of them have *not* been assimilated to the national culture; some have been assimilated only superficially. The Indians are therefore semi-assimilated both as a *group* and as *individuals*.

The Indians exist in a tribal or village organization, largely uninformed and divided; some are entirely caught up in the tribal life and pre-agricultural economy of the undeveloped jungle areas of the Oriente; most of them toil as servile laborers on the landed estates of the Sierra, once the site of the high Indian cultures of the Andes. The cultural distance between the Indians of the jungle and the highland Indians of the Sierra is greater than the one which separated the Incas from their Spanish conquerors. Even so it may be said of the Indians in general that most of them have not developed any form or concept of ethnic unity and that they possess only a dim awareness of the Ecuadorian national superstructure. Although the cumulative output of self-contained independent and *hacienda* communities contributes substantially to the food supply of Sierra towns, most Indian peasants live on a marginal basis and barely obtain subsistence at levels below recognized dietary requirements. Thus, while the Indian in mass has impact upon the national economy, the Indian as an individual does not. Ecuador belongs to those low-ranking South American countries where the annual *per capita* income has so far not exceeded $250. This low average reflects insufficient economic development; it also reflects the concentration of wealth in the hands of a privileged minority and the poverty of the majority of the population which can afford only about one-half the daily intake of calories considered necessary by health authorities. The brunt of this poverty falls upon the agricultural laborers of the semi-assimilated lower class who receive daily wages which on the average amount to little more than the equivalent of 25 U.S. cents.

Most Indians are abjectly poor; living at bare subsistence levels they have nothing to lose but their misery. So far, however, most of the people in the semi-assimilated lower class have remained immune to the appeals of political movements. Cultural isolation, physical deprivation, and insufficient knowledge have combined into a deterrent which has kept Indian discontent from spreading across the Sierra. Most Ecuadorian political leaders of today do not even bother to reach the Indians; since large numbers of them are still illiterate they yield little voting power in a country where literacy is a qualification for voting. Even the Ecuadorian Communists who under their important leader, Ricardo Paredes, sought to make inroads into the native communities discovered their efforts dismayingly unsuccessful. Several observers have commented on the problems which middle-class agitators from Quito have encountered when they tried to teach the Indians that they were Communists. In 1951, for example, Professor John P. Gillin of the University of Pittsburgh became acquainted with the leading members of a group of 30,000 'Communist' Indians; they told him emphatically, ' "Yes, we are Communists." When I sat down to talk with them, I discovered that they did not know who Stalin was, where or what Russia was, or what Marx has said. But they did want their own pieces of land and were against the large landowners who, they felt, had abused them.'[7]

But the size of the Indian population and concern that it is gradually arousing hang like threatening clouds on the horizon of Ecuadorian politics.

What is true in Ecuador is true in all the nations of South America with large Indian populations. Buried under poverty and prejudice, the vitality of these nations is to be found with the Indians . . . The growth of Ecuador must be the growth of the Indians; as long as they are held in subjugation, the cultural and economic progress of the land will be retarded. The destiny of the Andes is a revival of Indian vitality that will open the doors to individual freedom and national unity.[8]

Social classes and ideology

The rigid class divisions which cut deeply into the tissue of Ecuadorian society have resulted in severe forms of social, political, and economic inequality. Outside influences and foreign ideologies have not managed to uproot this aspect of the *status quo*. If democracy entails 'general participation in political processes' and this in turn means 'awareness of the national political life, fluency in the national language, and presumable literacy' Ecuador could hardly be classified as a democratic country.[9] The permeation of Ecuadorian society with ideological thought styles—mostly in the shape of false consciousness—is not at all conducive to the development of such national political awareness: in a country like Ecuador the use of the designation *cholo*, even the application of the Indian label, must be considered an aberration into ideological thinking, since *cholos* or mestizos and, thereby, ultimately Indian blood have, in fact, permeated all social classes. This fact is either ignored or more typically denied as we move upward in the social pyramid: the ideological distortion of thought reaches its most obvious expression in the assertion of white status by upper-class Ecuadorians who display a marked admixture of Indian physical characteristics. The established middle-class mestizo is often equally undeterred by the facts of physical appearance when it comes to the assertion of white status.

In Ecuador, as in most Latin-American nations, the mixing of the races began in the sixteenth century, that is, in the first years of the conquest. Hardly any white women accompanied the conquerors on their adventurous journey into the New World. Furthermore, many of the *conquistadores*, who had Spanish or Portuguese wives and children waiting for them in Europe, married Indian women in the New World and established additional families. 'Many of the oldest aristocratic families of the Latin American countries owe their origins to such unions. Although later arrivals brought their Spanish consorts with them, the process of blood mixture of Spanish and Portuguese with the Indians went inexorably on through the next three centuries or more.'[10]

Since the conquerors mixed with the indigenous Indian population the search for the 'pure' Spaniard is academic; on the other hand we must recognize that the conquerors were the first to plant the seeds of contempt and disdain for the Indian civilizations which they did their best to destroy; the military arm of the conquest immediately set to work to establish a system of economic exploitation which transformed the Indians into water carriers and wood cutters for the ruling group forced upon the Indians by the conquest. The religious arm of the conquest represented by the missionaries was permeated by fanatics who devalued the often highly sophisticated achievements of the Indian civilizations as the devil's handiwork. Victims often have a tendency to identify with their oppressors; the Latin American Indians and their descendants of mixed blood were no exception; they began early to believe in the direct correlation between socio-economic power, and prestige and the degree of European ancestry.

White status ideology or the White Legend, as the Peruvian Eugenio Chang-Rodríguez calls this ideological element, is, therefore, of early origin; today this ideological thought style is evidenced by the full-blooded Indian who exchanges his indigenous life style for the urban way of life and who will immediately upon joining the mestizos adopt their disdainful attitudes toward the Indians.

The three variations of the Indian problem in Latin America

(1) *The absence of the problem*

The Indian problem does not beset social systems where the Indians are either numerically insignificant or where they have been obliterated and absorbed into the population. Argentina, Chile, and Uruguay represent the classical example of countries where the overwhelming majority of the population is of European extraction. Argentina and Uruguay may be called the creations of relatively recent arrivals from Europe; the Chileans 'solved' the Indian problem in a style which is reminiscent of the United States: the indigenous Indians were forced into reservations and kept from participation in the social and cultural development of the country.

Because of their numerical insignificance, if not virtual absence, the Indians do not represent a problem in countries such as Costa Rica, Cuba, and the Dominican Republic; however, some Latin-American social systems have racial problems in the form of tensions between whites, mulattoes, and Negroes (pre-Castro Cuba, and especially Haiti).

(2) *The solution and improvement of the Indian problem*

There are some Latin-American societies with strong Indian populations where attempts at the integration of the Indians into the national life are being made; these attempts at the solution or improvement of the Indian problem promise its eventual disappearance. In social systems of this type there is little or at least less evidence of white status ideology.

The recognition of the valuable contributions which Indian civilization has made to the national culture is relatively pronounced in Mexico: here the integration of the Indian population into society at large proceeds fairly rapidly. The example of Mexico seems to indicate that the emphasis on the Indian past is strongest in countries which have experienced a somewhat successful social revolution.

Guatemala and Venezuela have been less successful in their attempts at the solution of the Indian problem; since 1970 Bolivia has come close to a solution. The Indians of Peru have traditionally lived in great misery and poverty, but recently some improvements of their lot are in the making.

Peru, on the other hand, can look back to the proud intellectual leadership of Victor Raúl Haya de la Torre who was born in Trujillo, Peru, in 1895. In 1924 while in political exile in Mexico, Haya de la Torre formed the *Alianza Popular Revolucionaria Americana* which became widely known as the APRA or *Aprista* party. Despite persecution by the government and the military Haya de la Torre and his followers never wavered in their insistence that the Indian had to become an integral part of the social, political, and cultural life of Peru and Latin America in general; in this spirit the *apristas* opposed foreign imperialism and clamored for the unity of Latin America. Haya de la Torre, who ran for the presidency in the election of 1962—annulled by the military—is the author of political writings advocating the development of a distinctively Indo-American political system which finds its own way between the European and American models, scandalized as they are in the Latin-American view by their deterioration into imperialist adventures.[11]

Haya de la Torre's desire for a new political formula is reflected in his famous concept of Indo-America; this Peruvian intellectual rejects the term 'Spanish America' as an expression of the colonial period; he refuses to accept the term 'Latin America' because it mirrors the outmoded, reactionary republican period; he debunks the term 'Pan-America' as the expression of Yankee imperialism. 'Indo-America,' on the other hand, gives expression to the new revolutionary conception of a social system which will have a strong basis in its workers representing the tradition and the race of the exploited indigenous masses.

(3) *The Indian subculture of misery*

There are Latin-American societies with strong Indian populations which have so far isolated most of the Indians in a subculture of poverty, neglect, and non-participation in social, political, and cultural life; here we find the strongest evidence of white status ideology among upper-class and established middle-class individuals and the European immigrants who found this ideology convenient in their initial attempts at higher status identification. This situation prevails in Ecuador and to some extent in Colombia.

In Ecuador the intellectual opposition to white status ideology is represented by Jorge Icaza (b. 1906), author of the social protest novel *Huasipungo*, and Alfredo Pareja Diezcanseco (b. 1908).[12] Pareja Diezcanseco is one of Ecuador's leading writers and scholars who, like so many Latin-American intellectuals, suffered prison and exile. For him the spiritual health of Ecuador is in jeopardy as long as the welfare of the Indian is not assured; if Ecuador is to connect with the twentieth century and develop into a democratic society it must overcome the problems represented by its unintegrated population and the economic misery created by the outmoded latifundia system: the Indians are destined to play an important role in this future development, but their own status must first be improved by inter-marriage with individuals in other social classes. A first step in the direction of the solution of the Indian problem must be taken by im-proving the living conditions of the half-breed Ecuadorians—the *cholos*.

Roads to a solution of the Indian problem

The writings and political activities of intellectual leaders such as Haya de la Torre and Pareja Diezcanseco and the prevalence of the social protest novel as a literary genre indicate a significant consensus affirming that the development of Latin American societies depends to a very large extent on the successful integration of the Indian population into social, economic, political, and cultural life.

The importance of the Indian problem and the need for the integration of the Indians into society at large was already recognized in 1925 by the Mexican author José Vasconcelos (1882–1959) who advocated in his *La raza cósmica* the welding of a racial and cultural amalgam out of the diverse elements of the Ibero-American popu-lation: the other classical pronouncement of the racial and cultural future of an integrated Latin America came in 1927, when Vascon-celos published his *Indología*.

In 1935 another Mexican writer, Gregorio López y Fuentes (b. 1895), published his novel *El indio* which is not only a vivid and authentic description of contemporary Indian life but also a strong statement in favor of the Indian: the long-suffering victim of centuries of cruel exploitation. The full participation of the Indian is important for society and can only be restored to it by under-standing, education, and a just share in the products of his labor. With *El indio* and his other novels López y Fuentes joins the ranks of leading Latin-American intellectuals and writers who want to assist the transformation of their social systems from neo-feudal to modern nations. Like those of most other intellectuals the sympathies of López y Fuentes are on the side of the proletariat: the peon, the mestizo, the Indian. These sympathies were also expressed by the Peruvian writer and *aprista* Ciro Alegría (1909–67), the Guatemaltecan Nobel Prize winning (1968) novelist Miguel Ángel Asturias (b. 1899), and recently by the Mexican novelist Carlos Fuentes (b. 1928), and the Peruvian Mario Vargas Llosa (b. 1936), author of the prizewinning novel, *La casa verde*.[13]

Social mobility in Ecuador

Although serious preparation for incorporation of the Indian into national life is not in sight at present Ecuadorian society is not entirely rigid in its class structure: there are varying degrees of mobility.

Admission to the traditional upper class is only possible through recruitment by the elite group; the process is facilitated by the behavior of more affluent individuals who shun the classes below them and embrace the standards and value judgments of the traditional upper class. Established middle-class Ecuadorians disdain political and social agitation; they embrace political opportunism and support the position of the established ruling sections. Passage from the established middle class to the ruling groups is achieved most effectively, though not exclusively, through the armed forces, government service, the educational system, and the Roman Catholic Church.

Individuals in the emergent middle class and members of the assimilated lower class rely increasingly on the social elevator function of high-school training and, to a lesser extent, university education to penetrate the class levels above them.

Passage from the semi-assimilated lower class to the assimilated lower class is much more difficult; often it is only temporary. The first step usually involves the transition from rural to urban living. There are, however, numerous covert restraints which anchor the rural worker to the soil. Family ties and attachment to the tribal community restrain the Indian from leaving for the city; once he makes good his 'escape', he is bereft of these traditional defenses of the Indian. After his departure from the jurisdiction of his *patrón* the Indian goes through a critical period of transition; during this time he stumbles defenseless and bewildered through urban life until he achieves a minimal awareness of his rights as a citizen.

Factors affecting social mobility

(1) *Regionalism*

Ecuadorian regionalism deters social mobility; to some extent regionalism reflects geographical divisions. The Andes, running approximately from north to south in two fairly parallel ranges, divide the country into three regions: the coast roughly comprises the territory between the Pacific and the western slopes of the Andes; the Sierra nestles between the two mountain ranges; the Oriente is undeveloped, inhabited by Indian tribes, and, therefore, never played an important role in national politics or in political regionalism. Equally insignificant are the Galápagos Islands, 500 to 700 miles off the country's Pacific coast. Regional politics have, therefore, been an exclusive game between the coast and the Sierra; these politics have been affected by the gradual migration of people to the coastal area.

In 1950 more than half of the population (58 per cent) lived in the Sierra; less than half (42 per cent) occupied the coast, the Oriente, and the Galápagos Islands. Presently, however, population distribution is fairly even reflecting a demographic shift from the highlands to the coastal region.

This population shift was initiated by social and economic forces. The rural highland population lives on land which is maldistributed; for three centuries ceaseless and primitive exploitation has exhausted the soil; non-agricultural employment has absorbed only a small portion of the excessive population. Therefore life is beset by serious economic problems.

Industrial development, but especially the cultivation of export crops, place the coast in the forefront of the country's recent economic development. In 1963 bananas accounted for 56·1 per cent of the country's total agricultural production, cocoa for another 16·4 per cent.[14] In 1963 agricultural products represented 96·9 per cent[15] of the nation's total exports; in 1966 main exports were: bananas 47 per cent, coffee 22 per cent, cocoa 12 per cent. The people of the Sierra, on the other hand, grow crops like corn, potatoes, barley, wheat, and beans which are primarily used for domestic consumption.

The composition and role of the agricultural labor force further differentiate the coast from the Sierra.[16] The agricultural system of the Sierra is largely based on the neo-feudal exploitation of agricultural resources presupposing the oppression of the Indian and the colonial heritage of the *encomienda* system. In the coast the agricultural worker is not chained to the soil like the Sierra Indian; neither is his soul bound to the tribe nor his body to his *patrón*. The typical farmhand of the coastal region is a migratory laborer who moves from one harvest to another. In the coast the wage system early replaced the serfdom of the Indian which has retarded development in the Sierra.

Economic development in the coastal region has created a business and financial bourgeoisie which is relatively liberal in its political outlook. New political movements emerge in the coast, especially at Guayaquil where they are more successful than in the slow-to-change conservative Sierra, which is still dominated by the traditions of the landed aristocracy. The rapidly growing, progressive cities of the coast have also contributed to rural-urban conflict.

(2) *Rural-urban cleavage*

This cleavage amounts to a conflict between two different centuries; a gulf separates the two principal cities of Quito and Guayaquil from the rural regions of the Sierra. The cities have traditionally absorbed the talent of the interior, attracted most of the immigrants from Europe, and served as the headquarters of the upper classes. The landed aristocrats have traditionally furnished the principal connecting link between the country and the city: their social and political interests are in the city; their economic interests in the rural *haciendas*.

In sharp contrast to the traditional and indigenous rural world stands the urban community. The story of Ecuador is a tale of two cities: Quito and Guayaquil.[17] Quito, the nation's capital, is located in the Sierra; Guayaquil is the main seaport and financial center of the country. The other major cities—Cuenca, Riobamba, Ambato, Ibarra and Loja—rival neither the economic nor the political status of the two leading cities.

Quito with a population of over 500,000 is the political nerve center and conservative stronghold of the Sierra. Although Quito has experienced considerable industrial progress it is still primarily the center of the agricultural activity in the highlands; it is a city which has been changing gradually. The low acceptance of new ways of life and novel ideas resulted in a measure of political sophistication; it also produced stagnation.

Guayaquil, the 'capital' of the coast, is quite different; the seaport city has a population of over 700,000; it is rapidly developing, experiencing constant transformation. Traditionally a liberal stronghold, Guayaquil has always been a propitious place for the start of new political movements; its people are the least conservative, the most anxious to change, always looking for something new. This may explain, to a degree, the success which the extreme left, as well as popular movements such as the Concentration of Popular Forces (CFP) and *Velasquismo*, have enjoyed there.

Conclusion

This essay has sought to clear up some of the confusion surrounding the interpretation of social stratification and social mobility in the republic of Ecuador which represents those Latin-American social systems with large, insufficiently assimilated Indian populations. Traditional and common generalizations about the structure of Ecuadorian society emphasize distinctions which are based on racial criteria. Concepts which are popular with upper- and middle-class Ecuadorians separate the European-oriented Hispanic Ecuadorian society from the indigenous Indian subculture. In this view upper- and middle-class whites form a class system together with lower-class mestizos, while the Indians constitute a caste which is allegedly cut off from official society.

A key conclusion is that these loose, common generalizations reflect and support the ideology of the ruling groups asserting social distance from Indian society and racial pride in white status. The 'White Legend' is easily debunked by the fact that nearly all Ecuadorians regardless of their social status display an admixture of Indian physical characteristics; the interpenetration of this society with Indian and mestizo stock is likely to increase with the acceleration of social change.

Since the traditional, common interpretation of Ecuadorian social stratification is not reality-adequate an alternative paradigm distinguishing six class levels has been suggested as a theoretical model for further research. This paradigm permits the inclusion of the Indian population in the overall analysis demanded by the reality principle.

The rejection and socio-economic oppression of the Indians represent a fundamental contradiction in Ecuadorian society, since their historical and numerical significance entitles them to a more privileged social position. The discussion of the Ecuadorian Indian problem in cross-cultural comparison with other Latin-American societies led to the threefold distinction between societies without an Indian problem, those working at its solution, and social systems like Ecuador which suffer socio-economic retardation partially as a result of the unsolved Indian problem.

The Latin-American intellectual community has debated the Indian problem since the beginning of this century; most intellectuals advocate full assimilation of the Indians assuming that the transition from neo-feudalism to modern socio-economic and political circumstances presupposes the achievement of a fully integrated society.

The present direction of social change, however, does not favor the assimilation of the Indian population into the mainstream of the country's life. So far socio-economic development has been to the benefit of other population segments and Ecuador's semi-assimilated lower class is still waiting for the large-scale program that is needed to guide the rural masses through the difficult transition from neo-feudalism to economic modernism. The ideology of the ruling groups and their emulators which emphasizes social distance from the

'Indian' population and racial pride in 'white' status further retards the development of meaningful collective efforts on behalf of the poverty-stricken mass.

Notes

1 The 'first cry' of independence was raised on 10 August 1809, in Quito. This attempt at independence was as unsuccessful as the one of October 1810; freedom from Spain was brought by Simón Bolívar in 1822, when Ecuador joined with Colombia and Venezuela in the confederacy of *Gran Colombia*. Ecuador withdrew from Colombia in 1830.

2 This study is based on field notes which the authors collected during repeated travels in Ecuador and South America generally. Additional information was provided by one hundred South American sociologists who responded to mail drop or personal interviews. For the affiliations of Ecuadorian interviewees see Gunter W. Remmling, *South American Sociologists: A Directory*, Special Publication of the Institute of Latin American Studies, Austin, Tex.: University of Texas, 1966, p. 35.

3 For comparative perspectives on social stratification in Latin America see Richard N. Adams, 'A Change from Caste to Class in a Peruvian Sierra Town', *Social Forces*, vol. 31, no. 3 (March 1953), pp. 238–44; Ralph Beals, 'Social Stratification in Latin America', *American Journal of Sociology*, vol. 58, no. 4 (January 1953), pp. 327–39; Orlando Fals Borda, 'Estratos Sociales entre los campesinos colombianos', *Economía Colombiana*, vol. 5, no. 14 (June 1955), pp. 593–604; J. Halcro Ferguson, *Latin America: The Balance of Race Redressed*, London: Oxford University Press, 1961; Gino Germani, *Estructura social de la Argentina: Análisis estadístico*, Buenos Aires: Raigal, 1955; Gino Gerami, *Política y sociedad en una época de transición: De la sociedad tradicional a la sociedad de masas*, Buenos Aires: Paidos, 1962; Antonio M. Grompone, *Las clases medias en el Uruguay*, Montevideo: Ediciones del Rio della Plata, 1963; J. J. Johnson, *Political Change in Latin America: The Emergence of the Middle Sectors*, Stanford University Press, 1958; Joseph A. Kahl (ed.), *Comparative Perspectives on Stratification*, Boston: Little, Brown & Co., 1968; Louis Kriesberg, 'Entrepreneurs in Latin America and the Role of Cultural and Situational Processes', *International Social Science Journal*, vol. 15, no. 4 (1963), pp. 581–94; Gustavo Lagos, *International Stratification and Underdeveloped Countries*, Chapel Hill: University of North Carolina Press, 1963; William P. Mangin, *Las comunidades alteñas en la América Latina*, Mexico City: Instituto Indígenas Interamericana, 1967; Pan-American Union, *Materiales para el estudio de la clase media en América Latina*, 6 vols, Washington, D.C., 1950–1; Luis Ratinoff, 'The New Urban Groups: The Middle Classes' in Seymour Martin Lipset and Aldo Solari (eds), *Elites in Latin America*, New York: Oxford University Press, 1967; William C. Sayres, 'Social Evolution in Mestizo Philosophy', *Social Forces*, vol. 35, no. 4 (May 1957), pp. 370–3; Sakari Sariola, *Social Class and Social Mobility in a Costa Rican Town*, Turrialba, Costa Rica: Inter-American Institute of Agricultural

Sciences, 1954; Aldo E. Solari, *Sociología rural Latinoamericana*, Buenos Aires: Editorial Universitaria, 1963; Charles Wagley and Marvin Harris, 'A Typology of Latin American Sub-cultures', *American Anthropologist*, vol. 57, no. 3 (June 1955), pp. 433–7; Andrew Hunter Whiteford, *Two Cities of Latin America: A Comparative Description of Social Classes* (Anchor Books ed.), Garden City, N.Y.: Doubleday, 1964; Eric R. Wolf, 'Types of Latin American Peasantry: A Preliminary Discussion', *American Anthropologist*, vol. 57, no. 3 (June 1955), pp. 452–71; Eric Robert Wolf, *Peasants*, Englewood Cliffs, N.J.: Prentice-Hall, 1966; Juan Yepes del Pozo, 'Castas y clases sociales en el Ecuador', *Revista Forense*, vol. 42, no. 6 (December 1957), pp. 49–78.

4 Similarly Francisco Julião, former leader of some of the peasant leagues in the north east of Brazil, attempted to move into political power positions by using the social discontent of the landless, impoverished masses. See Anthony Leeds, 'Brazil and the Myth of Francisco Julião' in Joseph Maier and Richard W. Weatherhead (eds), *Politics of Change in Latin America*, New York: Praeger, 1964, pp. 190–204.

5 See Seymour Martin Lipset, 'Values, Education, and Entrepreneurship' in Seymour Martin Lipset and Aldo Solari (eds), *Elites in Latin America*, New York: Oxford University Press, 1967, pp. 26–7.

6 A term originally designating slaves and now more often applied to the *Lumpenproletariat*.

7 John P. Gillin, 'Some Signposts for Policy' in Richard N. Adams *et al.*, *Social Change in Latin America Today: Its Implications for United States Policy*, Vintage Books, New York: Random House, 1961, p. 20.

8 John Collier Jun. and Aníbal Buitrón, *The Awakening Valley*, University of Chicago Press, 1949, p. 196.

9 Martin Needler, *Latin American Politics in Perspective*, New York: Van Nostrand, 1963, p. 17.

10 Robert J. Alexander, *Today's Latin America* (Anchor Books ed.), Garden City, N.Y.: Doubleday, 1962, p. 47.

11 See Victor Raúl Haya de la Torre, *A dónde va Indoamérica?*, Santiago de Chile: Biblioteca América, 1936.

12 See Jorge Icaza, *Huasipungo*, Quito: Imprenta Nacional, 1934, and Alfredo Parejo Diezcanseco, *La lucha por la democracia en el Ecuador*, Quito: Editorial Rumiñahui, 1956.

13 See José Vasconcelos, *La raza cósmica* (1925), México: Espasa-Calpe, 1948; José Vasconcelos, *Indología* (1927), 2nd ed., Barcelona: Agencia Mundial de Librería, 1933; Gregorio López y Fuentes, *El indio* (1935), México: Novaro, 1955; Ciro Alegría, *El mundo es ancho y ajeno* (1941), 6th ed., México: Editorial Diana, 1963; Miguel Ángel Asturias, *Hombres de maíz*, Buenos Aires: Losada, 1949; Carlos Fuentes, *La región más transparente* (1958), 4th ed., México: Fondo de Cultura Económica, 1963; Carlos Fuentes, *Cambio de piel*, México: Editorial Joaquín Mortiz, 1967; Mario Vargas Llosa, *La casa verde*, Barcelona: Editorial Seix Barral, 1965.

14 Ecuador, *Programa de desarrollo agropecuario: Agricultura*, Quito: Junta Nacional de Planificación y Coordinación Económica, 1964, p. 72.

15 *Ibid.*, p. 141.

16 About 65 per cent of Ecuador's population is rural; in 1950 54·1 per cent of the population was active in agriculture; in 1962 the percentage increased to 55·2, revealing the comparatively slow rate of industrial growth (*ibid.*, pp. 28, 281). For more general observations concerning economic development, see William McCord, *The Springtime of Freedom: The Evolution of Developing Societies*, New York: Oxford University Press, 1965, pp. 10–13.

17 See George I. Blanksten, *Ecuador: Constitutions and Caudillos*, Berkeley, Cal.: University of California Press, 1951, p. 161.

26 The structures of doubt: reflections on moral intelligibility as a problem in the sociology of knowledge

Manfred Stanley*

Introduction

In recent years many social scientists have turned with renewed interest to perspectives such as symbolic interactionism, phenomenology, hermeneutics, and ethnomethodology. A variety of reasons may be assumed for this. One reason that has been frequently expressed, however, is a growing concern over the status in social science theory of the person as agent. It has occurred to many thinkers that certain trends in social science, notably structuralism and some forms of learning theory, seem to negate any reference to the person as a morally responsible participant in the construction and maintenance of the social world.[1]

It should be evident that questions of this sort are not merely of academic interest. Theoretical perspectives in social science exert both direct and indirect influence on social practices. Directly, theories can legitimate particular ways and negate other ways of looking at a social problem on the part of elites who wish to address themselves to problem-solving. Indirectly, theories can support or undermine particular religious and moral perspectives on what a human being essentially is and how he may be treated. For example, there are theories rooted in metaphors that encourage a view of persons almost exclusively as 'functions' of the operation of mechanical, organic, or cybernetic systems. When accepted and adapted uncritically to policy contexts, such theories can underwrite powerful

* This paper is part of an ongoing study of the theoretical foundations of pessimism among intellectuals regarding the impact of 'technique' upon what are commonly called humanistic values. The writer is pursuing this investigation as research associate with the Harvard Program on Technology and Society, and also as associated research fellow with the Educational Policy Research Center at Syracuse. I would like to acknowledge with gratitude the extensive comments on an earlier draft of this paper by Professor Robert Daly and Mr James Woods.

397

tendencies toward 'technicist' perspectives in policy formation and social control.[2] The pressing concerns of problem-solving can easily abort attention to a fine line of profound moral significance that must be drawn between two questions. The first is: *are* human beings and their works intelligible in terms of the assumptions underlying one or another metaphor that enters into social science theories? The second question is: is the history of some societies characterized by social processes and cultural assumptions that operate to produce human beings who are constrained to act in ways that make it appear *as if* they were so intelligible? To ignore the difference between these two formulations is to invite the technicist orientations that inevitably result when metaphors that should be used heuristically are reified into world views.

One may also note the practical significance of theories by observing the intellectual inadequacy of the protest perspectives that rationalize social movements against established institutions and their symbolic ramparts. The solipsism, gnosticism, and almost mystical drug-oriented egalitarianism that characterized so much of the protest of the 1960s are themselves a product of the institutions of government and industry whose hidden impersonal dynamics are often legitimated by theories that appear as gnostic in their mathematical opaqueness and distance from the feelings and experiences of ordinary men as do the cults of spontaneous revolt or privatistic self-indulgence that arise in opposition.

It has become an imperative for social science theory of some urgent practical significance that the search for a philosophically viable view of personal agency be rescued from the fruitless polemic between partisans of reified metaphors and partisans of solipsism who enthrone a mythically autonomous individual at the center of the social universe.[3]

Social theory provides few examples that illustrate more clearly the problematics of personal agency than the concept of legitimacy. Although often utilized today as if referring exclusively to rules of legal and political procedure, the concept of legitimacy summarizes those speculations that have classically addressed the general question of what it is that makes organized society possible other than the resort to physical force. As Professor Charles Taylor has usefully reminded us, no matter how political legitimacy is conceived,

> it can only be attributed to a polity in the light of a number of
> surrounding conceptions—e.g., that it provides men freedom,
> that it emanates from their will, that it secures them order, the
> rule of law, or that it is founded on tradition, or commands
> obedience by its superior qualities. These conceptions are all
> such that they rely on definitions of what is significant for men

THE STRUCTURES OF DOUBT

in general or in some particular society or circumstances, definitions of paradigmatic meaning which cannot be identifiable as brute data.[4]

Thus do 'we all know' (without normally being quite sure why) that it is possible for any given law to be experienced as morally improper even though legitimately accomplished in a purely legal sense. Only under certain imperfectly understood circumstances do laws seem to 'make' anything right or wrong. Normally, codified norms are subordinate to the influence of the larger social order of custom.[5]

For many years in American sociology the textbook account of legitimation has been cast in terms of 'socialization,' the introjection of society via learned norms, roles, and values into the inner domains of the psyche. In recent years debate has revived over what Dennis Wrong has called 'the oversocialized conception of man.'[6] As has been so often the case in intellectual history, it is largely the practical events of life that have compelled this reopening of theoretical questions about the meaning and sources of legitimacy. We may briefly review some of these here.

The widespread 'crisis of authority' in the Western world is now almost a popular cliche. The sense of erosion of common goals, the politicization and consequent ideological ambiguity of behavior that was once thought of simply as 'deviant' or even 'criminal,' and the rhetoric of generational conflict, are all symptoms of this alleged crisis.

A second example of the influence of practical events upon theories of legitimacy is the unforeseen unpredictability of how people actually respond to circumstances that bring pressure against norms and values which had traditionally been thought of as safely 'internalized.' The most glaring example of this, of course, is the capitulation of millions of people to the demands of totalitarian regimes.

Third, the concept of legitimacy, much like the notion of deviance, has itself come under severe ideological attack. Some argue that the concept of legitimacy is not scientific but inherently ideological, a tool of agents of the *status quo*. At its extreme this argument holds that the modification of the concept of legitimacy in the interest of tolerating a wide range of behavior heretofore under excommunication as 'illegitimate' expressions of human instincts will result in a utopian condition of liberation and happiness.[7] Theories of legitimacy thus continue to have unavoidable ideological implications as they become embroiled in the old and new social conflicts of our times.

One of these conflicts provides our final example of the influence of practical events upon questions of theory. This example cuts to the heart of the question of how the role of the person as responsible agent is to be understood in the context of concrete social processes. The example is the contemporary turmoil over the meaning of 'expertise.' In its most general sense, this turmoil pertains to the status of claims by aggregates of persons called 'experts' to dominance over other persons (laities) regarding legitimate access to the decision-making powers of society. It is pointless to belabor the now obvious fact that, in the United States at least, this conflict besets efforts to address almost every problem in public policy. It is more fruitful to formulate what this issue is about with reference to the goal of a social theory informed by an adequate respect for the role of personal agency.

We may distinguish two ways of defining how 'expertise' claims in social science get to be legitimated in a society. One way is to assert certain knowledge-claims about how society operates and to encourage people to accept as experts all those who are credentialed as having proficiency in such knowledge and its potential uses. When successful, this approach inevitably encourages people to assume that what specialized experts say and do reflects exclusive competence to define the phenomena that are under the alleged purview of their expertise. As was noted by both Adam Smith and Karl Marx, people seem to have a tendency to reify the division of labor. That is, they tend to identify the human person (his qualities, moral worth, and sometimes his authority over one's destiny) with that person's *function* in the structure of specialization. In a society that is highly differentiated in its division of labor, more and more of life comes under the domains of putative experts. Thus, just as I am ill because I have what the physician defines as my disease, or am nervous because I suffer from what my psychiatrist defines as my neurosis, so my national interests get to be what my government says they are, my enemies this year are those who foreign-policy specialists say have aggressive intentions toward my sphere of influence, and the level of my education is what my diploma says it is. To the degree that this assumption about the exclusive competence of ever-increasing numbers of experts legitimately to define reality is accepted by a population, to that degree we may speak of a technicist social organization.

It is clear that in some quarters there has arisen against this technicist tendency an assault upon the notion that any claims to expertise are possible, an assault rationalized by a kind of solipsistic debunking orientation that holds all knowledge to be ideology, and all authority disguised power. We will not seek here to disprove this view which seems to us manifestly false and itself a kind of dialectical overkill reaction to an increasingly impersonal social world. Rather we will for now only suggest that the test of an adequate social theory is its capacity to produce in practice (i.e. educational curricula, professional self-restraint, and public opinion) a non-technicist orientation to the legitimation of expertise. This orientation would be one in which people are led to understand (1) how the experts' pictures of the world came to *evolve* into what they are; (2) the philosophical *bases* of claims to expertise and the counter-claims of dissidents, and (3) the *continuities* between expert and non-expert ways of experiencing the world (e.g. how we *all* selectively rely on faiths, myths, doubts, assumptions, and convictions derived from common-sense experience).

With this review of the practical stakes in mind, this paper examines the concept of legitimacy in social theory. We distinguish between legitimacy and legitimation. Legitimacy is regarded here as a sense of the fitness (rightness and propriety) of the human world—
—the institutions, rules, and procedures in terms of which one discovers oneself to be related to society. We will be concerned with how one may analyze where this sense of legitimacy comes from. Legitimation is regarded here as a dynamic hermeneutic process—a struggle for meaning whereby an acceptable moral interpretation of the human world is actively sought for. We will be concerned with providing a partial account of why the human world cannot be definitively experienced as legitimate and hence why the struggle for legitimation is a permanent feature of what it means to be a person in the world.

This agenda determines the structure of the paper. Section 1 sets forth a definition of the sense of legitimacy and some strategies that have been used to account for it. Section 2 examines the sources of doubt that sooner or later besets persons about the legitimacy of their world. A basic account of such doubt is set forth in a model of the human world as a symbol economy of scarcity. This account develops the claim that doubt about the legitimacy of one's world is based on the fact that any imaginable solution to some existing condition of deprivation is inevitably fated to be replaced by a new experience of deprivation.

1

The concept of legitimacy

How may we, as scientific observers, speak of how persons experience something as legitimate when they are in that mode of reflection that phenomenologists call the 'natural attitude' of common-sense?[8] The analysis of common-sense perspectives and behavior is quite complex and, relatively, a newly articulated theme in the phenomenologically oriented sociology of knowledge. Systematic research designed to show just how social scientific models of aggregate behavior patterns can be reduced to the phenomenologically derived rules of common-sense experience in a given society is not equally urgent with respect to all kinds of social phenomena. But in the study of legitimation phenomena, the history of the present century suggests that our knowledge of these dynamics is far more inadequate than formerly assumed. On the one hand masses of people have unexpectedly capitulated to the wildest propaganda of totalitarian regimes whose demands were a living mockery of the most basic norms and values of 'Christendom' however regarded.[9] On the other hand, resistance to these demands occasionally emerges under conditions that are virtually unintelligible from the standpoint of ordinary social science theory.[10] As repeatedly pointed out by Schutz and other writers in a similar vein, what persons refrain from doing in a situation can be as sociologically important (i.e. may be a form of action) as what they observably do. In the study of legitimacy, this level of phenomenological insight into the rhythms of action is almost self-evidently important.

For persons to perceive something as legitimate (fitting, right or proper) or illegitimate is often a profoundly upsetting experience. In many situations to perceive something as legitimate or illegitimate calls forth a sense of obligation to act against one's immediate interests, to refrain from acting for the sake of one's interests, or in some other conflictful way to depart from one's ordinary activities. Thus, for example, social scientists must face questions like these: do people's acquiescence in a government's policy indicate a stance of support, of indifference, of ignorance, or of fear? does resistance to a policy or action reflect imputation of illegitimacy to the act or the perpetrator, or does it mean something else entirely? There are those who argue that such questions about the phenomenological contours of action are unimportant because we need know only what men 'do' about their perceptions, not what they 'feel' or 'think.' But apart from the false distinction between 'subjective' and 'objective' realms implied by such linguistic usages, this view neglects the whole problem of the temporal dimension of action. A person's failure to engage in observable action at any given moment in time can mean many things, as we have said. Some of the things it can mean include what to the person may appear as 'illegitimate' motives (cowardice, ignorance, insensitivity) that can lead to inner dialogues having manifest results only much later in time (such as sudden explosions of revolt, acts of reckless risk, dramas of 'unexpected' self-sacrifice, suicide,[11] or less dramatic events such as changes in 'public opinion' that, if widespread, can cumulatively produce what would appear as unanticipated patterns of behavior under given circumstances). Let us then examine in a very preliminary manner the notion of legitimacy from the standpoint of the 'natural attitude.'

One of the benefits of phenomenological analysis is that it is gradually forcing those acquainted with it to stop dividing everything that people do into the two categories of 'behavior' (observable motion) and 'attitudes' (subjective orientations imputed on the basis largely of verbal behavior).[12] Legitimacy is not just a subjective belief, opinion, or attitude 'brought to' an otherwise objective situation by a person. Legitimacy is, rather, a facet of the whole experience of an object itself. To begin simply, legitimacy is that about an object, phenomenon, or situation which makes it seem morally appropriate (in one or more of a variety of senses such as worthy, right, or proper). A complete phenomenological analysis of this experience would be difficult and complex, and this will not be pursued here. Rather we reduce the matter to two levels of reflection in the 'natural attitude,' or common-sense mode of awareness.

The widespread emphasis on the distinction between subjective attitudes and objective behavior has obscured the fact that on the simplest level of common-sense people experience many objects and events in an immediate sense as true, right, proper, reasonable, sensible, or their opposites. For example, it obviously is sometimes a question of personal disagreement whether a specific act of killing is definable as 'self-defense' or as 'murder,' and there may be no harm done by labeling some such quarrels as subjective differences of opinion. In the United States, as elsewhere, agents empowered to do so (judges and legislators) are given some latitude in defining the operational boundaries of terms like murder and justified homicide. However, it is most unlikely, if a legislature were suddenly to define the months of July and August an open season for the hunting of human beings for sport as what are now called 'game' are hunted, that this would be accepted by the American public as either legitimate because legal, or simply as a matter for disagreement on the level of subjective opinion.[13] Likewise, to take an example from the aesthetic domain, we do not—in the presence of a beautiful woman— tend to say, 'there stands a human female,' to which we then deliberately append statements like 'I personally, out of my subjective arsenal of assessment categories, add on my opinion that she is attractive, desirable, and elegant.' We do not respond like this for at least two general reasons. First, the structure of our percept is, on the naive pre-theoretical level, united to begin with, i.e. 'there is a beautiful woman.' On this level of perception, aesthetic, geometrical and other categories are often fused. Second, such categories as we call aesthetic, moral, and so forth are not in fact subjective attitudes. They are learned notions, just as much as anything else acquired through the socialization process.

What do these simple examples say to us? They suggest the following generalization: in every society persons perceive some objects, events, situations and so forth as *intrinsically* right or wrong, coherent or meaningless, necessary or optional. Of course, the word intrinsic here does not have any metaphysical connotations; no claims about ultimate reality are being made. Our use of intrinsic does imply, however, that there are certain things that are perceived by people in the common-sense mode as morally intelligible (or not) in and of themselves, not as a result of some conscious appeal to a subjective arsenal of assessment attitudes. To put it yet another way, phenomenologically speaking, the legitimacy of certain things for people is a property of the factual world 'out there,' not an opinion derived from 'within.' Of course, to uncover *what* is so experienced in a given society, by what sorts of people, and under what sorts of conditions, can never be a matter simply for speculation but should always be determined by empirical research.[14] The foregoing assertions inevitably meet with some confusion or resistance on the part of many people in liberal societies not so much because of the complexities raised, but because it happens that liberal societies define reality according to pluralistic, individualistic and utilitarian standards of cognition. But such standards, after all, are themselves part of a cultural environment into which people are born, and they are learned as 'legitimate' standards of cognition.

Let us now turn to the second level of common-sense reflection about legitimacy. We have said legitimacy is that about an object, event or situation which makes it seem morally intelligible. This formulation obviously begs some questions, in particular three that bear mention here.

1. In relation to whom does anything stand out in a context of moral appropriateness (as against a utilitarian or some other amoral context) and under what surrounding circumstances?

2. Under what circumstances in daily life does it seem to become important to make a consciously articulated issue of the moral appropriateness of something (plus on whose part and to what extent of reflective elaboration)?

3. What aspect(s) in particular is it about an object, event or situation that imbues the whole with moral intelligibility?

Consider an example of a situation in which all three questions clearly arise. As is well known, a good deal of minor tax cheating occurs among Americans without, in most cases, such acts being perceived by their perpetrators as in a moral context. Let us posit an adult married couple conversing on how best to evade reporting certain types of income. Now imagine their twelve-year-old son entering the room indignant at what he has overheard, ready to challenge the moral veracity of his parents. In the ensuing conversation it is not difficult to imagine the tax evasion issue as being transferred quickly from a utilitarian context to a moral one, as per question 1. Regarding question 2, the fact that it is their pre-adult and inexperienced son (rather than a close adult friend) who has thrown the gauntlet is intimately related to the level of conscious articulation to which this particular moral problematic will be driven in the conversation. And as regards the third question, one can easily imagine a conflict between legitimacy criteria emerging in this situation, the son insisting on the legality criterion for moral evaluation of his parents' action and the parents perhaps countering with a justification based on the government's alleged moral misuse of legally collected funds (e.g. waste, wars, welfare etc.). As anyone would quickly find who sought to link this particular hypothetical example to the three questions in a cohesive theoretical form, a very wide range of social science concepts and research material would be brought into play.

Space precludes exploring these three questions in the detail they warrant, except to point out the self-evident importance of phenomenologically oriented research for providing data capable of addressing them. However, a few more comments pertaining to the third question are in order because—whatever the circumstances that lead to the third question—once it is posed in a situation, persons are forced to move from the simplest level of the 'natural attitude' of common-sense to a somewhat more complex level (although still well short of theoretical reflection in any systematic philosophical or scientific sense).

The simplest level of constituting something as legitimate, as we have seen, is the orientation toward it as intrinsically right or proper. The subsequent level of reflection results from any form of challenge to this immediate naive perception. This next level is our third question as experienced by the actor in the situation: what in particular is it about X that imbues it with legitimacy for me? or, what is absent here that leads me to be so uneasy about X? or, what criteria of legitimacy are in conflict here that lead me to feel so ambivalent about X? (Obviously the phrasing is not meant to suggest everyday language but rather the phenomenological structure of the question, however expressed.) The second level of common-sense perception of anything as legitimate, then, is the recognition that it is not the whole object, event, or situation that is intrinsically legitimate, but some aspect of it. It becomes useful to speak of this, as we shortly will, as the 'irradiation' component of legitimacy.

We may review what has been said, then, by looking at legitimacy in terms of four points. First, an object, event or situation that is perceived as legitimate has certain features or aspects that, upon reflection, appear to impart legitimacy to the whole. Conceptually expressed, these features are values, institutions, concepts, laws, doctrines, and charisma. Second, these legitimating features stand in a relationship to the whole object, event, or situation such that the whole can be perceived as an integral moral unity. As a label for such relationships we will adopt Pitirim Sorokin's term 'logico-meaningful integration.' Third, when a person believes himself to have discovered the moral intelligibility of an object, event, or situation, that subjective attitude can be traced to four sources: (a) the logico-meaningful structure of the whole object; (b) the person's own interpretation of that structure in the light of his unique hermeneutical style (a blend of intelligence, knowledge, vocabulary, experience, cognitive sensitivities etc.); (c) the person's social location in the interest structures of his society; (d) the imperatives of the particular bounded setting of which the person and the object are both a part. Fourth and finally, all societies appear to have institutionalized criteria for distinguishing between more and less valid hermeneutical constructions. Cultivation of these criteria are in the domain of persons designated (by dint of birth, inspiration, study, magic, achievement or whatever) as competent in their use. Mindful of the generality of this term, we shall refer to such guardians of competence as the 'experts.'

Some brief elaborations on this approach to legitimacy may be helpful. First we address the effort entailed here to avoid the common trap of having to define something in terms either of an objective or subjective reference point exclusively (i.e. the tendency to define legitimacy either as observed behavior or as inferred attitude). This is followed by some comments on the phrase 'logico-meaningful integration.' Finally some relevant observations on the general notion of expertise are set forth.

1. Our phrasing is deliberately designed so as to avoid suggesting that legitimacy is purely in the eye of the beholder; that is, an attitude 'brought to' an otherwise objective (morally inert) situation. In the phenomenological perspective, the human world in which an individual discovers he is 'present' is already morally meaningful. The phenomenological notion that persons 'constitute' the world is *not* meant in the solipsistic sense that the world is in the eye of the beholder. Constituting the world does not mean inventing it, but interpreting what is already there. While interpretation is a creative act it has some invariants, and is certainly not creation in the sense of making a new product out of raw materials.[15] Although such matters are complex, there is nothing especially new about the issues they pose. The notion of hermeneutics itself emerged from the classical dilemmas of text interpretation which also entails achieving a balance between coming to terms with something that is clearly 'out there' (a written text) and yet having to interpret its layers of meaning. Indeed Paul Ricoeur has suggested that we may profit from regarding this situation as a paradigm for some of the methodological problems of interpreting social action.[16]

The approach taken here thus assumes there is much more to

legitimacy than a mere attitude.[17] However nothing is being said about the particular circumstances under which an object will be constituted in a moral context as against some other context. After all, people do not question the legitimacy of everything all the time. Likewise there is no reference here to the conditions under which an object will be constituted within one or another of the various moral sub-contexts of assessment (religious, legal, philosophical, aesthetic, etc.). Finally, no assumptions are made about the consistency of a person's response to an object, since it is possible to see an object as legitimate at a given time, illegitimate at another, or as morally irrelevant at a third time, depending upon the situational context of the relationship between oneself and the object in question. Problems of this sort provide important agendas for an empirical sociology of knowledge.

2. The second comment on our approach to legitimacy deals with the nature of the relationship between an object and that aspect of the object which seems crucial to the moral intelligibility of the whole.

The phrase we have used to describe that relationship is 'logico-meaningful integration.' This term is Pitirim Sorokin's.[18] It must be stated right away that this phrase applies to a much larger scope of criteria for intelligibility than just the moral context. Moral intelligibility, after all, is obviously not the only kind. However since Sorokin was grappling with the most generic problems of how to define intelligibility, we assume that moral intelligibility (whose boundaries with other modes of intelligibility are not always sharp) belongs in this larger context.

Sorokin distinguishes between four ways in which one can speak of cultural integration. These are (a) 'spatial or mechanical adjacency' or what he calls 'congeries'; (b) 'indirect association through a common factor'; (c) 'causal or functional integration'; and (d) 'logico-meaningful integration.' This last mode of integration is expressed by terms like 'consistent style' and 'harmonious wholes.' Sorokin describes the essence of the logico-meaningful method of cognition as 'in the finding of the central principle ... which permeates all the components, gives sense and significance to each of them, and in this way makes cosmos of a chaos of unintegrated fragments.'[19] It is relevant to our own discussion that Sorokin felt it necessary to point out that:

> Many such superlative unities cannot be described in analytical verbal terms; they are just felt as such, but this in no way makes their unity questionable. One cannot prove in mere words—no matter what they are—the inner consistency and supreme integration of the Cathedral of Chartres, or the Gregorian chant, or the musical compositions of Bach or Mozart or

Beethoven, or the tragedies of Shakespeare, or the sculpture of Phydias, or the pictures of Dürer or Raphael or Rembrandt, or many other logico-meaningful unities. But not being completely describable in terms of language, their supreme unity is felt by competent persons as certainly as if they could be analyzed with mathematical or logical exactness. All such unities are covered here by the term logico-meaningful, though many are not logical unities in the formal sense of the word logic.[20]

We are not quoting this passage in order to argue that logico-meaningful unities are incapable of being in some senses scientifically or logically analyzed. Neither Sorokin nor anyone pursuing the agenda of a social science would want to say that. Rather the point here is that logico-meaningful integration is a very fundamental property of the 'lifeworld' and yet is based on a diversity of connections that can exist between facets of the human world. These connections can be expressed in a wide variety of modes of discourse, not all reducible to each other. Sorokin never ultimately resolved the confusions such a term arouses, partly because he did not see it as his task to subject the notion to intensive phenomenological analysis. What he did want to say, I think, was that there is a type of integration or harmony in the world that cannot be reduced to the three other modes of integration mentioned earlier, and yet that humans are capable of perceiving it despite the great range of problems involved in defining the structure of such unities. We are using the term 'logico-meaningful integration' in our definition, despite all its inadequacies and unresolved ambiguities, because its complexities contain those pertaining to the concept of legitimacy itself. One of the implications of our approach to legitimacy is that those aspects of a culture that may be said to be the core of the legitimation experience (e.g. laws, constitutions, symbols, concepts, doctrines, myths) are not encountered as isolated 'traits.' Rather they are experienced as if they *irradiate* the objects around them (e.g. practices, governments, churches, bureaucracies) with a certain kind of moral significance (e.g. validity, propriety, coherence). What we take Sorokin to mean by 'logico-meaningful unity' is the structures and organizing principles of these irradiation effects. And we have adopted his term because, like Sorokin, we do not think that such irradiation effects can be finally reduced to mere spatial or mechanical adjacency, or to indirect association through a common external factor, or to causal or functional integration. Further, also like Sorokin, we think the problems of validly interpreting logico-meaningful unities require the engagement of the fullest range of human competencies that are now—from the standpoint of this task—irrationally deployed into the artificially specialized compartments of arts, sciences, and humanities. To put it another way, the present academic division of labor conceals the fact that logical, aesthetic, legal, casuistical, ontological and scientific competencies of thought are all needed to describe and interpret the structures underlying the vague unities of naive common-sense experience. This leads into the third comment pertaining to our definition of legitimacy.

3. In the quotation by Sorokin cited above, he refers to 'competent persons' as being those who successfully feel or intuit logico-meaningful unities. Certainly Sorokin's work as a whole suggests that he never meant the word 'feel' to be understood in this connection as a purely private, simply intuitive, experience. The word competent here means that a person, to interpret logico-meaningful unities, must already possess to some degree of cultivation the necessary requisites of a particular interpretive apparatus. (So, for example, one cannot argue a point of law without some command of the logic of legal discourse, which is to say, the techniques for separating legal criteria of assessment from other types.) One of the ironic results of the over-specialized academic division of labor is that, while on the common-sense level of experience these various criteria (legal, moral, philosophical, scientific, aesthetic) are all mixed together, many scholars—whose job it supposedly is to reveal the structures of these inter-connections—actually have a trained incapacity to accomplish this on the level of scholarly competence.[21]

What has just been described is an important feature of the problem of 'expertise' in modern complex societies. It underlies a certain tension between persons making knowledge-claims on the basis of the common-sense mode of experience, and those making claims on the basis of credentialed expertise. This tension is probably inevitable in any situation where expertise claims are grounded in specialized scholarly perspectives. This contradiction between the truncated discourse of specialized expertise and the integral but rudimentary experiences of logico-meaningful unities in the 'life-world' is one important source of cleavage between persons who define themselves as morally competent agents in the interpretation of the social world.[22]

There is another source of cleavage equally as important. It is rooted in a potential contradiction between 'experts' and everyone else with respect to a function that all persons defined as responsible agents actually must engage in as members of society. That function is also one of interpretation, but in the sense of translating abstract meanings (norms, ideals, commands etc.) into *situationally* relevant forms. Let us elaborate.

In the routine everyday world, as has been pointed out, we do not normally perceive with distinctness those aspects of an object, event, or situation which legitimize it; that is, place it in a moral context. Thus, when we encounter a 'good man,' an 'evil leader,' a 'beautiful painting,' a 'sacred place' or a 'reasonable argument,' we are not normally sure what these attributes of 'goodness,' 'evil,' 'beauty,' 'sanctity,' or 'reasonableness' are or where they are situated.[23] It appears to be a universal feature of societies that they have at least a rudimentary notion of technical proficiency in the recognition of logico-meaningful unities. Yet the work done by these masters of interpretation—the magicians, shamans, casuists, aestheticians, scientists, jurists—must also be done to some extent by all persons in the course of adapting to the contingencies of everyday life.

Those who claim the mantle of 'expert' must satisfy what appear to be three universal conditions of role legitimation. First, they must remain within certain (though not all) broad logico-meaningful unities that dominate the culture of which they are a part. (For example, in our own society, who would remain a 'competent scientist' for long who insisted on the truth of the Ptolemaic cosmology because it squares with divine attributes better than does the current cosmology?) Second, the experts must respect the range of the mainstream values and interests represented in the population, especially if these are articulated by other companies of experts. (For example, in our society, those scientists who believe in radical determinism of human behavior must yet function within a socio-legal system which recognizes the personal responsibility of the self as agent.) Finally, experts must seek to avert suspicion on the part of those who suspect them of invading everyman's right to that personal leeway for interpretation and decision that his society abstractly, and contingencies of circumstance concretely, allow him.

These tensions form some of the bases for the virtually universal mixture of veneration and fear directed toward the influence of expertise. With respect to our definition of legitimacy, these considerations suggest some of the important continuities as well as differences that exist between the common-sensical and the cultivated standards for interpreting, and acting within, one's world.

At this juncture it is perhaps worth stressing our concern that the argument regarding legitimacy as an objective phenomenon—i.e. moral intelligibility as something intrinsic to the world and its contents—not be mistaken for three other kinds of claims.

We are not suggesting that everyone is questioning the moral intelligibility of everything all the time. One must have a reason to gaze at something in terms of its specifically moral context of meanings.

Second, when we say that the legitimacy of something is perceived as intrinsic to that object, we do not want to have our use of the word 'intrinsic' confused with the notion of the temporally instantaneous. That is to say, it is not claimed that once a person does regard an object in a moral context he will then instantly experience a conviction about its legitimacy status. It is only argued that once he does arrive at a definite conclusion (he may remain stalled on the level of ambivalence), the object will be 'reconstituted' so as to appear intrinsically intelligible in a moral sense. Of course, this status may change again under new circumstances.

Finally, we claim that societies provide criteria for distinguishing between what can very broadly be labeled as valid versus invalid inferences about the moral status of an object. However, we are not suggesting by this that the application of such criteria leads inexorably to a single conclusion. Quite the contrary. Our discussion has been, for the sake of convenience, oversimplifying the experience of moral intelligibility by presenting it in terms of dichotomies such as right-wrong, proper-improper, etc. The application of criteria for validation of moral inferences is a process that can lead to conflicting *valid* conclusions. The basis for this generalization is the deeply ambiguous nature of social meanings as such. (This theme will be elaborated in section 2 of this essay.)

We have now reviewed some of the problems involved in discussing moral intelligibility in the common-sense context of experience. Nothing has been said about how scholars have tried to account for the experience of moral intelligibility in some kind of scientific explanatory framework. It is time to turn to this question.

Sources of legitimacy experience

Social scientists have tended to explain the sense of moral intelligibility by way of three sorts of strategies. For expediency of discourse we may call these: legitimacy as an intellectual product, legitimacy as a by-product of conformity, and legitimacy as world coherence. Let us discuss each in turn.

Legitimacy as intellectual product

According to such a view, moral intelligibility is the product of systematic reflective articulation—deliberate products of the intellect. Intellectually constructed justifications obviously have played and do continue to play an important role in society, although there is undoubtedly much variation by society and historical period in the degree to which such systematic articulations have proven functionally important. Many studies exist largely dealing with high-level intellectual formulations of this kind.[24] Rather few studies exist, however, of such processes among populations not defined as elites and intellectuals, that is, of what could be called the casuistry of everyday life. Phenomenologists have been somewhat active here and so have some sociologists influenced by them. In the United States a program of social research inspired (albeit in controversial ways) by the work of Alfred Schutz and stimulated by Harold Garfinkel at U.C.L.A. has taken hold among a number of social scientists and has already resulted in some significant contributions.[25]

Legitimacy as conformity

By conformity is meant, to put it simply, that one source of legitimacy is people's propensity to keep up with the Joneses most of the time, a propensity that is interrupted only occasionally by the need to ask why the Joneses do as they do. According to this argument it may be assumed that if a pattern of behavior is collectively sustained for a long period of time, people simply follow along because that pattern comes to appear as 'in the nature of things.' This type of argument is officially recognized in those legal systems whose intellectual articulations (statutes) are validated and modified at key points by appeals to 'precedent' grounded in customary norms (common law). Also, it is this type of argument that is appealed to by those social scientists who consider power and authority, when all is said and done, to be equated (except for the factor of time). If power is held strongly enough and long enough by a particular group, they argue, authority to hold that power will eventually be imputed to that group by the population at large almost as a kind of 'natural process' (habit, psychic corrections of cognitive dissonance, and so on). This claim is generally asserted to greatest effect against thinkers allegedly too intellectualistic in their theories in the sense that they make the assumption that people at large have to have the same standards of intellectual rigor, consistency, and justification that intellectuals like to insist upon for themselves.

It is fair to say that conformity as an explanatory principle is an important corrective to any over-zealous attitude toward intellectualistic criteria of moral intelligibility. But the conformity argument too begs many questions. For one thing, how much logical consistency and reasoned justification people need in everyday life is a highly under-researched issue. Since one cannot simply ask people such a question directly, there are methodological difficulties involved in designing appropriate research. Further, since the conformity explanation is undoubtedly more valid for some periods of time than for others, it is not enough to assert its occasional validity. One must be able to stipulate when such an explanation is of primary importance, and when it is of only secondary significance. Given the fact that so much of historical scholarship is still the record of elite productions and decisions, it is not surprising that our knowledge of such matters is not more advanced. Finally, the word conformity itself hides a host of conceptual problems that still require elucidation in social science. Most uses of the term conformity, when not referring to a socialization-as-introjection thesis, imply something like 'imitation' or 'habit' or 'reinforcement' hypotheses. But behavior outwardly defined as conforming by the scientific observer can conceal subjective participator-orientations as diverse as assent, reluctant acquiescence, and utilitarian expediency. Here again the potential usefulness of phenomenologically oriented social research becomes evident.[26]

Legitimacy as coherence

A third answer to the question about the sources of legitimacy has been based on the suggestion that there exist logico-meaningful unities (often confusingly called 'world views') of a scale capable of integrating cognitive standards, values, norms, and institutions into a pattern of experienced coherence characterizing the boundaries of whole socio-cultural periods. The methodological problems involved in defining such coherence structures are very complex. Scholars concerned with historical periodization are perhaps best aware of what these difficulties are.

Despite these difficulties we have separated our examination of this category of explanation into a distinctly emphasized sub-section because, in our view, it is here that the key issues of moral intelligibility begin. Our focus in this essay is predominantly on those crises of legitimacy on a scope associated with doubt about the moral intelligibility of major aspects of one's 'world.' We will argue later that however subjectively experienced, these crises cannot be understood without reference to logico-meaningful unities whose structures and dynamics are often remote from a population's subjectively relevant common-sense categories. What does this generalization mean? What are the referents and implications of the term 'world view'?

This is not the place to explore the full range of such macrophenomena of 'order' in any detail.[27] Rather, in order to illustrate the connections between these notions and the roots of moral intelligibility, we will found our subsequent remarks on a very important distinction which it is appropriate to introduce here.

The distinction has to do with how one goes about exploring the locus of any alleged orderliness that seemingly allows the human world to become a unit-object of moral reflection. One common answer that has been given is cast in terms of 'consensus.' This term can be used in two quite different senses, however. For present purposes we adopt Charles Taylor's vocabulary to distinguish them.[28] Professor Taylor argues that consensus could mean convergence of consciously held subjective attitudes about anything into some pattern of agreement. (Indeed he wants to restrict the term consensus to this sense.) If these 'common meanings' are highly inclusive in their range, they could add up to a shared world view. There is another approach to consensus, however, that is quite different.

As against 'common meanings' which are conscious in the minds of participants, there are also 'intersubjective meanings' which are not of necessity consciously available in the subjective lives of most or even any members of a population.

> When we speak of consensus we speak of beliefs and values
> which could be the property of a single person, or many, or
> all; but intersubjective meanings could not be the property of a
> single person because they are rooted in social practice.[29]

The key phrase here that distinguishes intersubjective meanings from common meanings is 'social practice.' Intersubjective meanings are constitutive assumptions that govern any pattern of social practice; that is, those norms, values and so forth which make that practice possible. Consensus about such assumptions and rules is not necessarily a matter of conscious agreement but of indirect acquiescence expressed through simple willingness to engage in a given social practice.

One good example is the practice of bargaining in liberal societies as against other forms of negotiation to be found throughout the world. 'Our whole notion of negotiation is bound up . . . with the distinct identity and autonomy of the parties, with the willed nature of their relations; it is a very contractual notion.'[30] Also presupposed in liberalism is a high degree of pressure toward separation between public and private domains of life, with as much of the volume of bargaining relationships left to the private domain as possible (i.e. free from public interference except for the enforcement of contracts themselves). Indeed one of the contradictions in liberal societies today that threaten their coherence is that interest-bargaining units have grown in size so far beyond 'human scale' that the original assumptions which legitimated the distinction between public and private life have become virtually irrelevant to the contemporary realities of the public-private distinction on the institutional level. (It is this realization that is expressed in phrases like 'private government' and 'corporate socialism.') To return to our example of bargaining in relation to intersubjective meanings; persons in our society who 'bargain in good faith' may thus not know that they have assumed the validity of certain meanings like the autonomous individual, the moral legitimacy of the will, the sanctity of contract, and the importance of utilitarian motives. But these meanings are brought to life in the everyday world by adherence to the *practice* of bargaining as it takes place in our society. This does not mean that persons do not bring attitudes of all sorts to the negotiation process. 'But what they do not bring into the negotiations is the set of ideas and norms constitutive of negotiation themselves.' Intersubjective meanings, then, are 'constitutive of the social matrix in which individuals *find* themselves and act.'[31]

The social science literature as a whole suggests a wide range of agreement that some such coherence patterns (beyond the sense of simple convergence among subjective attitudes) do exist. What is not a matter of agreement is the nature of these patterns. The search for them has given rise to some powerful and varied ideas in the social sciences, although there is considerable controversy between proponents of these ideas as to their relative validity.

One approach to this field of discourse has come to be called 'structuralism,' a loose label for a variety of themes whose complications preclude comment here.[32]

Other lines of inquiry that are moving into the ambit of social science interest because of their relevance to the investigation of intersubjective meanings include research into symbolism, root metaphors, and comparative mythology. A brief comment on the importance of all these for the proper explication of our topic in this present essay may be helpful.[33]

For our topic one of the more important approaches to symbolism has been the focus upon representative symbols. This designation refers to the symbols—linguistic and other—by and through which members of any aggregation try to do the following things: (A) define and experience themselves as communally bonded to each other; (B) distinguish between legitimate and illegitimate norms and actions; (C) differentiate themselves from other communities; and (D) relate themselves to some myth of transcendence. Examples of such symbols abound in the world: sacred books like the Bible and the Koran, the flags of nations, the cross of Christianity, and the white coats of the medical profession.[34]

Our usage of the phrase 'root metaphors' follows that of Stephen Pepper.[35] According to Pepper, root metaphors are really fundamental hypotheses about the world's basic metaphysical structure (the largest-scale logico-meaningful unit). Root metaphors begin as analogies from common-sense experience. They are elaborated by geniuses who see their philosophical possibilities for explanatory integration of observations, and are eventually systematized in the form of what Pepper calls 'world hypotheses.' Aside from animism and mysticism, which he considers inferior metaphors, Pepper expounds at length on four fundamental Western root metaphors, demonstrating their bases in common-sense, their metaphysical stages of construction, and their implied theories of truth. These metaphors are formism (Platonism), mechanism, organicism, and contextualism (pragmatism). The literature subsequent to Pepper's volume strongly encourages a view that the study of socio-cultural influences of metaphors is proving to be a most effective way in which the data of the humanities can be brought to bear upon a phenomenologically oriented social science.[36]

Myths are essentially various kinds of accounts which are believed —if the myths are 'live' in a population—to explain how the world and the society came to be. There are cosmogonic myths, myths of origin pertaining to particular social practices, myths of temporal structure (eternal return, cycles, linear progress), myths of sacred personages (messiahs, folklore saints and saviors, local gods). A very important facet of comparative mythology is the study of eschatologies—the mythologization of time with special reference to the future. American sociologists (as against anthropologists) have shown little interest in this area, despite the fact that close study of mythical thought structures soon reveals the difficulty of venturing any definitive distinction between secular and mythical thought.[37] Comte did not see himself as creating an eschatology when formulating his historical metaphysics of the three stages of progress, nor did Marx with respect to the classless society. With reference to social theories of our own day, Robert Nisbet has controversially subjected the whole category of 'development' theories (and by implication all alleged 'laws' of social change as such) to the charge that they are not scientific but mythical notions.[38]

The decline of vitality related to belief in some myth when that myth becomes non-credible is an issue very much present in modern secular societies. As Mircea Eliade says, 'Myth assures man that what he is about to do *has already been done*, in other words, it helps him to overcome doubts as to the result of his undertaking.'[39] Perhaps the central mythical theme of the modern West, shared by virtually all secular ideologies, is the image of man as artificer—in one way or another the fashioner of his world and his history. Many events have come to threaten this mythologized self-confidence. Aside from crisis phenomena like improperly assimilated technological innovations, wars, genocide, and conquests, there has also been the evolution of Western civilization itself into a stage of societal complexity that generates simultaneously available and competing world views *in the same society*. Sociologists of knowledge from Wilhelm Dilthey to Karl Mannheim began their work inspired by the significance of this fact, and almost all of them considered the simultaneous availability of multiple coherence structures in the same society as a major turning point in the cultural history of the human race. This pluralism is generally celebrated in liberal ideology. But since Nietzsche, another strain of Western thought has been marked in one way or another by the fear that this condition must end in nihilism, that is, the decline of coherence itself. Such decline is allegedly marked by the spread of a subjective sense of meaninglessness (amply reflected in the arts); that is, the sense that the only plausible basis left for legitimacy is force itself. The world comes gradually to be seen as 'up for grabs' and reality is reduced to a sense of 'anything is possible.'

In one of his books Mircea Eliade says this:

> It is not inadmissible to think of an epoch . . . not too far
> distant, when humanity, to ensure its survival, will find itself
> reduced to desisting from any further 'making' of history in the
> sense in which it began to make it from the creation of the
> first empires, will confine itself to repeating prescribed
> archetypal gestures, and will strive to forget, as meaningless and
> dangerous, any spontaneous gesture which might entail
> 'historical' consequences.[40]

We will not pursue the point, but in our view the technicist model of coherence and order is one fulfillment of such an ending of history.[41]

In concluding this section of the essay, two comments are in order. One is methodological in a somewhat specific sense, and the other has to do with the inappropriateness of the term world view.

Logico-meaningful unities of the sort comprised of intersubjective meanings are obviously important for the understanding of social structures. But it would be seriously fallacious to think of them in any sense as a 'cause' of social structures, or even as standing in any clearly definitive 'fit' in relation to social structures. The example of sub-Saharan Africa will be helpful in clarifying this point.

When we examine the socio-political structures of sub-Saharan traditional African societies we find that many of them shared a number of intersubjective assumptions in common. These included the efficacy of magic in social life; witchcraft beliefs; the importance of the power of ancestors in systems of social control; the absence of any doctrine of death as total spiritual annihilation; some degree of belief in what has been called the High God principle; and various assumptions about modes of psycho-physical therapy. Yet these same societies often varied radically in social and political structure. Some were dominated by kinship lineages, others had developed structures of political specialization. Some were hierarchical, others egalitarian. Some had age-grade stratification, others not. We see from this, then, that a pattern of intersubjective meanings can function as constitutive rules for more than one complex of social practice. Much will be made of this point in the second section of our essay.

Second, it seems to us clear from what has been said that 'world view' is a misleading term. This is first of all because we do not experience the coherence of the human world—insofar as that world

is comprised of intersubjective meanings—primarily as a passive
'view' or picture. The coherent world is *not*, in this sense, first of all
an object of reflection (hence of knowledge). Coherence in this sense
is the result of *action*—of commitment to social *practice*—because
it is through practice that abstract meanings are constituted into the
everyday world. These meanings, then, are not subjective attitudes
brought to the world. They are already out in the world because, as
we have seen, they are *presupposed* in structures of practice.[42]

We are now ready to proceed to the second major stage of our
reflections on the role of personal agency in the constitution of the
moral world. Up to now our concern has been with some dynamics
of the coming-into-awareness of one's presence in a human world
whose moral intelligibility is a problem subject to interpretation.
This process of discovery is mediated by the myriad conflicts over the
relative legitimacy of the rules and practices that make up everyday
life. Why can it not be said that the moral world, once constructed
(however done), remains legitimate forever, barring great disturbances of external origin? Why insist that everyone is a moral agent,
knowingly and willingly or not? To these questions we now turn.

2

The answers to the questions which closed the last section lie in the
very nature of what society is.

> To the ordinary person, reared in the tradition of Western
> empiricism, physical objects usually seem to exist 'by
> themselves' out there in time and space, appearing as disparate
> clusters of sense data. So, too, social objects appear to most of
> us as *things*: land, labor, capital; the working class and the
> employing class; the state and the superstructure of ideas,
> philosophies, religions—all these categories of reality often
> present themselves to our consciousness as existing by themselves,
> with defined boundaries that set them off from other aspects
> of the social universe. However abstract, they tend to be
> conceived as distinctly as if they were objects to be picked up
> and turned over in one's hand.[43]

Yet there are no stable objects in nature. Even stones are changed in
form eventually under pressure of the elements. Societies are not
stones. They are comprised of meanings whose boundaries can be
discerned to stretch from the remote world of 'once was' through the
seeming imperatives of the 'now' to the vague images of the 'might
be.' All of these times are co-present in the 'now,' which consists not
only of buildings, roads, rules, values and institutions but also of
nostalgia, hope, despair, memories, deprivation and desire.

Meanings, then, are abstract until interpreted, and they can not be said to be interpreted to the point of becoming relevant for the sociological analysis of the everyday world until applied to the contingencies of the most concrete 'now'—the mosaic of immediate situations. For a person to become conscious (on however rudimentary a level) is to 'awaken' into this field of meanings and to discover oneself an active agent of both the interpretation of meanings and of their practical organization in the common-sense world. In this sense, action can be avoided only by dying. To the extent that circumstances include episodes of choice in unpredictably contingent situations—and they always do—to live is indeed in a sense to be forced into freedom.[44]

It should be noted that this way of stating the point avoids the numerous criticisms that have been directed against the assumption that society is rooted in consensus based on successful socialization (i.e. the reproduction of society within the personality by way of introjection). In phenomenological terms, meanings may indeed be encountered by the person as located *within* himself as well as without. But this is a relative matter for empirical assessment, not an automatic assumption that it is safe to make with respect to any particular set of meanings. In any case, *wherever* meanings are encountered, they must be interpreted by the person with reference to situational applications and transactions (even if 'interpreted' is to mean the wholesale acceptance by the person of someone else's interpretations—this too is an interpretive act). In other words, meanings are viewed here not as introjected objects but as available patterns of rules, norms, values and so forth which provide fields of pressure and opportunity for the negotiation of motives, projects constraints, and legitimations among persons and groups.[45]

Lest our argument be misunderstood, it is well to reiterate at this point the observation that to say every person is a hermeneutical agent (i.e. an interpreter of the moral intelligibility of meanings) is not the same thing as saying that every person is free to constitute the world as he pleases. That is, no one can 'name' everything anew. As was established in section 1, the 'lifeworld' is already charged with sedimented meanings at the time that any one individual becomes aware of it. Thus, in our society, if we should happen to stumble across a large sum of money, we discover an already 'valuable' object and react accordingly. For this to cease to be true, the *whole interpretive horizon* (i.e. the economic and social organization of our society) would have to be altered in some way. This is what is so frightening about a phenomenon like 'runaway inflation.' In a money economy we experience the instability of currency in the social world much like we would an earthquake in the physical world. When the foundations shake, anything can happen.

419

MANFRED STANLEY

De-legitimation in social thought

Social thinkers have long been concerned with the sources of instability in the moral intelligibility of societies. In section 1 we reviewed three standard approaches to explaining the sources of legitimacy. These were deliberate intellectual constructions, conformity, and coherence through intersubjective meanings embedded in patterns of social practice. Some major theories of social change have been based on the converse of these three approaches to moral intelligibility. The continuities between theory and practice are illustrated by the fact that patterns of social control in the West have historically often been in the charge of varied categories of 'experts' on moral intelligibility.

Let us illustrate by looking at moral *un*intelligibility first as a felt *incoherence* in one's world, i.e. contradictions in intersubjective meanings. The threatening sense of incoherence has ever and again given rise in the West to philosophers of systematic metaphysics. The current influence of logical positivism vitiates the contemporary scholar's empathy with the dependence felt by previous generations of thinkers upon the assurances of order and meaning they derived from speculative metaphysics. After all, the philosophical system builders did not think in a vacuum. They were responding to the issues of their day. From Plato, through Augustine, Thomas Aquinas and Galileo, to Hegel, Marx, Comte and Spencer, the task of these men was to account for the world—its past, present and future. Their influence can be noted in the persistent interweaving of their free speculations with the dogmatic ideologies of both social control and revolution that are so marked a feature of Western institutional history.[46]

When free speculation moves from the philosopher's search for coherence to intellectually constructed legitimations *per se* for purposes of social control, we get phenomena such as dogmas and laws. The converse of such constructions are *heresy and crime*. These have ever been the province of officials, priestly and secular. The West has been particularly notable among civilizations for the production of dogmas and officials concerned with their maintenance, perhaps because of the emphasis on rigor and formalization that is so much a feature of Western thought. Be that as it may, from Socrates' judges to the House UnAmerican Affairs Committee the 'authorities' have protected against heresy the constructions of official legitimation. Likewise we have seen a persisting strain toward the formulation of legitimacy in legal-rational terms, as documented in the great sociological studies of Max Weber.[47] The gains achieved by such formalizations in the universalization of discourse across parochial boundaries are ever threatened by the strain toward

420

'legalism,' i.e. one form of imbalance in social practice between means and ends.[48]

With the advent of modern social science, the dogmas of Church and State were partially replaced by those of society itself, the converse of conformity to which is *deviance*. From Émile Durkheim to Talcott Parsons theorists have elaborated on the scientific principles of deviance as a source of social change. And from 'moral statisticians' to contemporary 'systems' engineers, the agents of social control have tried to measure deviance the better to control it.[49]

In some Western societies, notably the Anglo-Saxon ones, all three types of explanation for de-legitimation have come into some disrepute. Positivists no longer concerned with totalistic coherence have exiled metaphysicians to academic enclaves in which the latter address almost exclusively each other. Heresy is part of the bill of rights and officials everywhere are under contemptuous suspicion, having to rely ever more on power rather than authority. There is an increasing concern, as well, that behavior not be indiscriminately subjected to control through the criminal code (e.g. the debate over the regulation of sexual behavior and the use of some drugs). Finally, the concept of society itself has become so de-mystified in the years since Durkheim that sociologist-iconoclasts are even now dismantling the last rhetorical justifications for the scientific status of 'deviance' as a concept.

The secular millenialism of 'liberation'

The activities of personal agency in the constituting of the social world are obscured for those who uncritically accept explanations of de-legitimation such as just reviewed. This is because such explanations make it appear as if de-legitimation is just an episodic event, a departure from a normal and natural state of moral intelligibility. If moral unintelligibility is a matter merely of ignorance about some objective feature of the world, one is thus invited to turn to the metaphysicians and ask them to enlighten the agents of social control so that they may readjust their formulations of orthodoxy accordingly. If moral unintelligibility is due merely to violations of formalized norms, then let us stamp out heresy and crime by means of inquisitions and policy. And if de-legitimation is due to deviance, then bring in the social engineers and the behavior reconditioners. Such is the technicist mentality.

Before turning to a perspective on de-legitimation that avoids this orientation, a comment is in order about a view put forward by some as the final solution to the problem of technicism. It is a view that we cannot accept because, while it seems to rescue the notion of personal agency from annihilation through technicism, it does so at the price of trivializing all the moral ambiguities of choice inherent in the hermeneutical problems of legitimation.

In some quarters the decline of social controls based on metaphysics, dogmas, and theories of deviance has inspired some heady antinomian visions of liberation from virtually all institutions of social control. For some, this liberation will be marked by an ecstatic transvaluation ('polymorphous perversity' etc.) of most societally sponsored distinctions between legitimacy and iniquity. Underlying this millenial hope for many people is a notion of a limitlessly applied physical technology. When this notion is present the millenialism of liberation takes the form of a theory about 'the end of scarcity.'

The end of scarcity is as yet actually more of a theme than a theory, a will-o'-the-wisp of hope than a formula of the intellect. But it hovers as a thought between the lines of some writers on liberation (notably Marcuse) and as a sort of mental foam around the lips of the dionysian chemists who appear to feel that a culture of psychotropic drugs and cybernetic technology will render obsolete the hard problems of social organization and moral reasoning. The end of scarcity is a theme of the fullest eschatological stature. This is obvious once one recognizes that there are really only two final solutions to the ubiquitous problem of human desires. One is the oriental tradition, the striving toward release from the wheel of wanting. The other is the occidental way, the bending of nature itself to the demands of human will. What Nirvana means to the ego that would escape all desire, the end of scarcity means to the ego that would fulfil all desire. In one all is allowed because all is One. In the other, all is allowed because everything is possible.

Whatever else it may mean, as a sociological principle the end of scarcity is impossible. And because it is impossible, the cycles of legitimation, doubt, de-legitimation, and re-interpretation are generic and intrinsic features of society. They are aspects of what society essentially *is*.

No discussion of legitimation as the hermeneutical dimension of personal agency is possible without the help of a comprehensive conceptualization of scarcity. It is strange that so much of the explicit discussion of scarcity today should still rest on the notion of merely physical resource deficiencies. Not only have some of the important economists themselves repeatedly reminded us of the fallacies in such a materialistic starting point,[50] but most of the accepted orientations in the various social science disciplines point rather evidently away from such a restriction. Aside from its connections with the topic of moral intelligibility, there are at least three other compelling reasons why an adequate conception of scarcity is crucial for social thought at this juncture of history. We shall parenthetically note them here.

First, we are witnessing a planet-wide politicization of the concept of scarcity in connection with modernization and economic development problems. Superficiality of theory in this area can have practical consequences as social scientists increasingly become politically relevant agents of social change. Indeed, scarcity can be thought of as *the* core question in development theories if it is granted that the latter all basically derive from massive changes in people's sense of what they may legitimately expect from life and what they consequently experience as deprivations.[51]

Second, scientific innovation has made possible the nullification of many heretofore universal constrictions of material nature, thereby increasing the range of life-style options under conditions of material affluence. It is important to understand that this range is not infinite, and in what ways they all entail a price.

Finally, the concept of scarcity touches on the general problem of linkages between aspects of experience that are accessible to the immediate conscious awareness of average participants in everyday social life, and those aspects that are not thus accessible. This distinction between observer versus participant-models of reality remains an important issue in the philosophy of science. The persistence of scientific principles of explanation that transcend what participants are themselves aware of reflects the conviction of most scientists that unintended as well as intended consequences, latent as well as manifest functions, and causes as well as reasons remain valid concepts in social science. The way this general issue appears here is the distinction that must be drawn between what we will call the socio-cultural organization of scarcity structures (the observer's dialectical models of the socio-cultural order), and the contours of deprivation as experienced by a given population. To the extent that the experienced sense of deprivation is a generic feature of all social movements, an adequate formulation of scarcity is of obvious relevance for the study of collective behavior.

Before turning to our analysis of scarcity in detail, we may end this digression on the hopelessness of the libertarian millenium by citing the general reasons why the end of scarcity is an impossible resolution of the technicist fallacy. Society is experienced in terms of meanings such as norms, values, symbols, roles, and institutions. All meanings have the property of being abstract to some degree. That is, meanings carry implications beyond those that are concretized in patterns of social practice. Not all conceivable meanings, nor all implications of any given meaning, can be constituted in the reality-world of practice all at once. There is thus always a potential measure of relative deprivation built into the very nature of experience itself.

Furthermore, the interpersonal negotiations about the operative implications of meanings for concrete situations that form such an important part of the hermeneutics of legitimation must take place in a sedimented context of previously achieved agreements. For example, how can one bargain for one's interests in the absence of relatively stable intersubjective assumptions about what those interests are with which the negotiating parties identify themselves? Thus, while laws, social structure (the organization of roles and offices), and language itself, are all meanings subject to negotiation, they are not equally negotiable all at once. All achieved interpretations of moral intelligibility are therefore contingent on the outcomes of the never-ending mosaic of negotiations that comprises society itself. In all but the most integrated societies, moral intelligibility is not a stable phenomenon subject only to episodic exceptions. It is fluid, complex, and relative to social location and contingency. Nor, as we have seen, can the hermeneutics of legitimation be avoided by turning every object of desire into a free good through some salvational technology. For satisfaction is itself not an absolute but a relative state. To understand more clearly what this all means, we must now turn directly to the notion of scarcity itself.

The concept of scarcity

Scarcity may be defined for present purposes as a shortage of resources that are asserted as necessary to actualize any given end or intention in the form of action relevant to concrete social situations. An assertion that some such resource is scarce can be made by an 'expert' observer on the basis of an analysis derived from a theory about the relevant phenomena. The assertion of scarcity can also be made by someone who—as a participant in his society—applies his rules of common-sense interpretation to some experience of deprivation that appears to him as an objective 'lack' in his environment. (It should be clear that the social types we call 'observer' and 'participant' are analytic extremes. No social science commands any theory that is so pure in its comprehensiveness and separation from the categories of a parochial common-sense system as to make of the social scientist a pure observer. Likewise, all common-sense systems of thought have some theory content of an abstract propositional nature that the participant checks against his comparative experience. That makes him in part an observer, on however rudimentary a level.)

We should state right away that our concern with an adequate *concept* of scarcity will not be expressed here in any attempt to formulate a comprehensive *theory* of scarcity. A full-fledged theory of social change as (in part) the product of persisting strains toward de-legitimation would have to address three general issues. First, in what specific ways can a given society (viewed as a structure of meanings) be thought of as a field of *potential scarcities?* Second, under what conditions are such potentialities selectively concretized into *experienced patterns of deprivation* among particular sectors of the population? Third, under what conditions are these experienced deprivations linked to remedial social *action?*

These three general questions can be further disaggregated into at least five levels of reference that any comprehensive analysis of scarcity applied to historical cases would have to take account of. These levels of reference are the philosophical, the sociological, the social-psychological, the diagnostic-ideological, and the collective praxis aspects of scarcity. A brief word on each will be helpful prior to stating the relevance of all this to our larger concerns in this essay.

By the *philosophical* level we refer to the fact that all meanings can be subjected to dialectical analysis as to their potential implications. What such dialectical analysis can entail will not be entered into here. Professor Louis Schneider has recently contributed a helpful account of the relevance of dialectical operations to sociology.[52] The range of implications of any idea is neither singular nor infinite in scope. Dialectical analysis can be helpful, as we shall attempt to illustrate below, in laying open the abstract potentialities of any given meaning as regards how that meaning can come to be experienced in the everyday world.

By the *sociological* level we mean the patterns of concretization (roles, rules, institutions, organizations etc.) according to which meanings have become practically organized in any given society.

By the *social-psychological* level we mean the social distribution of relative deprivation experiences in the context of a given society.

By the *diagnostic ideological* level we mean those systematized hermeneutical accounts that, in the form of ideologies produced by intelligentsias, diagnose the moral intelligibility and directionality of the *status quo.* Such ideological formulations may or may not include recommended programs of action.

By the *collective praxis* level we mean those organized patterns of action embodied in social movements that evolve to rectify some ideologically diagnosed experience of deprivation.

In what follows we focus exclusively on the interaction of the philosophical and the sociological levels of analysis. Our intention is to show the way in which dialectical analysis of existing patterns of social organization can reveal—on the abstract level—scarcities that underlie potential experiences of deprivation. These abstract scarcities are the 'stuff' out of which trends toward de-legitimation and moral unintelligibility are made. These same abstract scarcities also are the foundations of the hermeneutical *reconstructions* that—

when translated into social action—point toward social and cultural change. *All persons are moral agents because all persons take part in the hermeneutical processes that result in the five analytically defined levels of reference set forth above.*This is true even of the person who, through ignorance or for some other reason, delegates his agency as interpreter of meanings to others (such as to 'experts'). *Such delegation is itself a moral act.*

This last generalization derives from the fact that since meanings are fluid because they are open (i.e. contain possibilities that stretch beyond accomplished experience), meanings must therefore be interpreted. Because no two persons can have exactly identical experiences, these interpretations—before becoming operational in social practice —must also be negotiated between parties whose co-operation is strategic to the smooth operation of some pattern of practice. This is clearly evident in the case of statutory norms. As we see with laws, interpretation consists—at the very least—of deciding whether a given situation is such as to fit under the criteria of a particular rule such that the rule is applicable to it (e.g. not all killing is murder). This necessary lack of fit between rules and situations is the ontological basis for the sociological understanding of human freedom. Freedom in this context of discourse means that every person is an interpreter of the meanings that comprise the social world, i.e. a hermeneutical agent. Indeed, social control essentially *is* the particular socio-cultural processes through which the fact of every person's moral agency is successfully *concealed* from particular categories of the population and differentially delegated to other sectors. (Such a definition must not be confused with a conspiracy theory of social control. Concealment, like awareness, is in part an aspect of evolutionary connections between consciousness and society.)

Some societies, then, are organized so as to restrict the distribution of important forms of moral agency to particular people or groups (ruling elites). Some societies officially define as 'free agents' all members of society considered as 'responsible.' In some societies, especially complex modern ones, certain people are designated as particularly authoritative agents whose mastery of a particular area of meaning officially entitles them to exercise their own interpretation as to when they may intervene in the freedom of other agents. Such people are normally called 'professionals' although, of course, not all professionals are equal in the power they are granted through such delegations of authority. Even in the case of the most powerful professions, however, the legitimacy of expertise must be negotiated if experts are to be accepted as authoritative.[53] These negotiations consist of everything from reasoned discussion, to propaganda, to mystification, and—where possible—the utilization of the police power of the state (impersonating certain experts is illegal in such societies). All this results in a polemical atmosphere surrounding experts which must be reduced by a relatively powerful legitimation of expert knowledge. This is usually accomplished if the meanings that constitute expert knowledge are reified, that is, if they can be made to take on in the 'lay' mind properties of false closure or misplaced concreteness. This combination of reification on the mental level and power on the social level lends the expert and his knowledge an air of non-negotiability—an important requisite for technicism on the level of popular consciousness.

For these reasons, authoritative experts can usefully be defined as 'functionaries of reified interpretations.' Once such levels of legitimation occur they are often self-reinforcing through what can be called 'secondary legitimation.' This results from the sheer placebo effects of expert-visibility such as the occasional anxiety generated by the mere presence of a policeman, the faith-healing phenomena characteristic of secular as well as sacred medicine, and the imputation of special knowledgeability about foreign cultures to persons introduced as 'foreign policy advisors.'

At this point a detailed example would be helpful of how the social scientist (and the moral philosopher) may proceed in detecting the potential scarcities inherent in the plenitude of implications that comprise society.

Plenitude and scarcity: an example

For the purposes of this example we focus on certain abstract principles of socio-economic integration that have been developed with reference to the analysis of whole societies by scholars interested in inter-societal comparisons. Specifically we adopt here the typology developed by Karl Polanyi and his co-workers who were building on the insights of Marx, Malinowski, Mauss and others.[54]

The typology distinguishes between three basic types of transactional structures of a scope capable of integrating whole economies. They are 'reciprocity,' 'redistribution,' and bargained 'market-exchange.' The growing literature on this typology is based upon the assumption that these terms refer both to different structural conditions surrounding social transactions, and to differing patterns of institutionalized meanings in terms of which such transactions are phenomenologically perceived by participants in the various social systems (e.g. the meaning of 'brideprice' is no longer considered by observers, as it once tended to be, an economic act of 'buying a wife').

Reciprocity denotes movements between correlative points of symmetrical groupings; redistribution designates appropriational

P

movements toward a center and out of it again; exchange refers here to vice-versa movements taking place as between 'hands' under a market system. Reciprocity, then, assumes for a background symmetrically arranged groupings; redistribution is dependent upon the presence of some measure of centricity in the group; exchange in order to produce integration requires a system of price-making markets.[55]

It must be understood that this is not psychological, but institutional analysis. For example,

Reciprocity behavior between individuals integrates the economy only if symmetrically organized structures, such as a symmetrical system of kinship groups, are given. But a kinship system never arises as the result of mere reciprocating behavior on the personal level.[56]

Symmetry need not be simply dualistic. Many groups may be symmetrical with respect to two or more axes. For example, kinship formations, neighborhood settings, totem groups, and city-states are historical instances of more or less permanent and comprehensive configurations within which there can form any number of smaller voluntary symmetrical associational linkages. Likewise, redistribution systems can have multiple appropriational and redistributive channels (e.g. special patronage groups, family-based insurance mechanisms, or voluntary welfare associations). Market societies too can contain multiple major loci for price and power bargaining, as was suggested some years ago by John Kenneth Galbraith in his theory of countervailing power.[57]

Finally, any society can contain all three modes of integration on various levels of subordination. For Polanyi himself, the 'Dominance of a form of integration is . . . identified with the degree to which it comprises land and labor in society.' This is not simply an arbitrary position. Land is, after all, in most societies, the major manifestation of the physical world and its constraints. Labor is men's major mode of expression of their active agency in the world. More than anything, it is how land and labor are institutionally defined that are the objective determinants of how members of a society will experience the meanings of their relationship to nature and to their own productive powers.

We will now use this typology to illustrate our notion of scarcity-by-implication by asking what sorts of experiences and frustrations would be facilitated by each one of these modes were it alone to function as a single, completely dominant, mode of societal integration. (We may ignore for present purposes the fact that such singular domination very seldom occurs in real societies.) It will be argued that reciprocity is logically correlated with that complex of values and norms historically associated with the notion of 'community,' redistribution with 'social welfare' mechanisms, and market-exchange with demand responsive 'innovation' capacities. Let us explore this further.

Reciprocity

The social structures characterized by reciprocity as a mode of integration have been associated ideologically with what has been called 'human scale' in that they allow for the symmetry of long-term interpersonal commitments, obligations, and the growth of emotional mutuality or identification. These themes are included among what has long been meant by community and, since the time of ancient Greek speculation, the concept has been correlated with the necessity for limitation in group size.

Despite these associations, however, there has clearly been a general evolution away from communities of reciprocity in the West for at least two basic reasons. First, the continuity of such structures has in the past largely rested on a combination of conformity and ascribed status placement. These have been experienced as restrictive to (i.e. depriving people of the opportunities for) initiative and personal freedom of choice. Second, such systems have also been associated with a certain lack of adaptability to social evolution because of the barriers they present to growth in organizational scale, complex division of labor, and impersonal functional rationality. It is this type of reasoning, for example, that underlies the frequent recommendations one hears from social scientists that traditional (especially primitive) cultures must be undermined if techno-economic development is to take place.[58]

Redistribution

As a mode of integration, redistribution is associated structurally with a tendency toward the centralization of power. It is an important basis for efficiency of resource allocation and, if the central authority is strong enough, for minimization of what would otherwise be endless conflicts of interest between diversified veto-groups.

However, redistribution obviously is also associated with the development of autocracy. Further, a society integrated exclusively by redistribution can produce an alienated and highly dependent population unaccustomed to participation in basic decision-making and responsibility for the management of societal processes.[59] And, as social critics in both socialist and capitalist societies have been pointing out, there is the possibility in redistributive systems for

429

exploitative social stratification through appropriation of resources by a privileged redistributive bureaucracy. Thus, redistribution implies a scarcity of resources relative to values of participation, decentralized 'grass-roots' skills, responsibility, and certain kinds of efficiency.

Market-exchange

Sociologically, the history of the utilitarian market-exchange principle has been associated with intensive techno-economic development via the appropriation of physical nature and of labor as factors of production, plus the mobilization of competitive energy for life in a society viewed as a commodity market. However, the institutionalization of the market economy has also been correlated with events perceived as conflicting with many religious convictions about human existence, and the values—however secularized—associated with these traditions. Such events include: (1) social-class formation based on accumulation of extensive wealth through the operations of the market; (2) societal and ideological rigidities in the face of human suffering due to resistance against change for any reasons other than greater market advantage; (3) the gradual transformation of all forms of value into the commodity criterion of marketability.

Further, it has been argued by some social critics that movements ranging from fascism through communism to extreme nationalism can be viewed in part as facilitating a kind of 'retribalization' of society. According to such arguments, totalitarianism should be seen as providing a mythologized 'functional-equivalent' to the communalism associated with the structures of reciprocity. It is assumed by thinkers holding such views that something as apocalyptic as totalitarianism can only be accounted for by a most extreme kind of deprivation—namely, deprivation of opportunities for the day-to-day expression of communal values and actions. This degree of deprivation must be closely connected with some central feature of the market-exchange principle of societal integration. From Saint-Simon to Robert Nisbet we do indeed find the explanatory emphasis in social thought being placed upon what to liberals has been the moral jewel of the market principle. This exemplary principle of market liberalism has been the modern view of society as an opportunity-structure for the fulfillment of an egoistic individualism. According to the critics, however, the result of this principle has been the destruction of community through its anomic reduction to theoretically atomistic egos related to each other only by the competitive struggle for life chances on the commodity market. The artistic, philosophic, and scientific literature centering on concepts like alienation and anomie has long been pointing to the moral effects of scarcities allegedly implied by the market principle relative to the values and norms of communalism. The literature of social planning from Comte through Karl Mannheim and, currently, the rhetoric of community development and the new towns movement (a kind of secular offshoot of nineteenth-century utopian communitarianism) obviously also bear upon these kinds of scarcities. And it is hardly necessary to point to the proliferating communities of the current counter-culture.

The purpose of this example, then, has been to illustrate the argument that any meaning has certain implications such that, once that meaning is made situationally operational in some way, particular problems appear solved for the moment. But meanwhile other implications of the same meaning constantly create possible new directions for experience that can make achieved experience appear wanting in some way. Discovery of this facet of life often results in episodes of nostalgia. Given the importance of nostalgia in social movements, it is strange that the topic has not received more attention from sociologists.

Nostalgia may usefully be defined as the perception of the past in terms of the phenomenology of present scarcities. Thus, in our example, the atomized member of the lonely crowd, descendant of the rebel who spurned conformity to the communities of reciprocity because of his desire for new horizons, now may look back upon the image of the community with romanticized longing. But it is a longing born not of historical experience with the object of his desire about which he may indeed know very little. Rather, the longing is the mirror image of the frustrations of his own time. Such nostalgia can find expression in forms ranging from popular art fads all the way to political and cultural movements of romantic reaction (a notable feature of nineteenth-century European anti-bourgeois conservatism.)[60] One should note, too, that nostalgia need not fasten upon a romantically redeemed past (retrospective nostalgia). It can also fasten upon a mythologized version of the original dream of liberation from the past associated with the founding ancestors of the present. In this context the present is turned into a result of a dream betrayed, and the nostalgia is pitched toward the future which becomes the time of the dream redeemed (prospective nostalgia).

If it be granted, then, that the human world that surrounds every person is charged with meaning, and that these structures of meaning are open (i.e. contain multiple possibilities for interpretation and action), the following question becomes appropriate. How do persons come to experience diverse implications of a meaning in everyday life?

The phenomenology of deprivation

What does a dialectical analysis of meanings accomplish? It helps us to understand the logic immanent in the values, norms, myths, symbols and so forth that comprise a human world. While such analysis is no guide to predicting how people will act, it does afford insight into the finite range of possibilities and constraints that are generated by meanings. These possibilities and constraints are not, of course, all equally available to the conscious awareness of participants in a given social world. To argue that the task of interpretation is purely a matter of looking at what people think they see because that is all that matters for what they do, is tantamount to adopting a solipsistic view of reality. On such grounds the observer's task reduces to pure ethnography.

The thrust of the present argument, however, is quite different. We have proposed instead the following. Meanings do have an immanent logic. Second, in any society some meanings are sociologically more important than others because they have become institutionalized in various ways as intersubjective presuppositions of practice. Third, while all persons interpret their world and negotiate these interpretations, any one person's efforts are limited by certain constraints. One of these constraints, as has been said, is the logic of those interpretations by past generations that have become institutionalized. There are many other constraints on new interpretations such as obstacles of secrecy, ignorance, competitive variety among interpretations, mystification of discourse, and so forth. One type of constraint, however, is of particular interest to us in this essay. That constraint is the logic *inherent* in a particular meaning.

At this point we should recall the important distinction to be made between the common-sense mode of interpretation and that of the scholarly level of reflection. In the pure common-sense mode, the person is concerned with carrying the interpretation of a meaning only to the point of imparting or restoring moral intelligibility to some practice in a concrete practical situation. The most abstract scholarly level of reflection is concerned with a much stricter range of validity criteria, those of philosophy.[61] The social scientific level of reflection is somewhere between that of common-sense and philosophy since social scientists are concerned with data that uncover the determinants of what people actually do, regardless of philosophically valid criteria. Some social scientists, however (this writer among them), are convinced by the argument that philosophical analysis (under the discipline of a phenomenological focus) is not just a game, but a source of clues to certain constraints on action that are inherent in the structure of meanings as such. While this is no place to explore such a claim in detail, it should be said that such clues are not conceived here as predictions. Rather they are coordinates of ideational trends that are aspects of the dialectical implications of meanings.

The dialectical analysis of potential scarcities latent in the structure of existing meanings is one way among many of engaging in the detection of cultural macro-trends. Trend analysis too is not prediction. It is really the narrowing of the range of plausible scenarios to sufficiently finite proportions to allow us to conceptualize sociological 'events.' The notions of 'past,' 'present,' and 'future' are themselves only socio-cultural meanings. The determination of 'events' and their connections (e.g. the rise of a social movement, the transformation of a regime, the decline of an ideology, the fall of a civilization etc.) is the way in which the scientific observer reckons (i.e. interprets) historico-social time. Events occur at varying rates, and thus many pasts, presents, and futures co-exist in the 'now.' Further, trend analysis is not prediction because what happens in society is based not only on scarcity structures but upon the dynamics of deprivation consciousness and collective behavior among populations. Here contingencies prevail. This would seem to be a realm appropriate for the skills of the historian who is well equipped to examine the filigree of contingencies in the life of societies. The sociologist's task, we suggest, is to provide models of macro-contexts from which micro-events derive their significance. Since macro-contexts (e.g. modes of socio-economic integration, root metaphors, myths, juristic systems, etc.) alter more slowly than do micro-contexts, it does not seem unreasonable to speak of long-range trends on the macro-level with multiple micro-directional possibilities. To get at these micro possibilities, social research must be designed to address situations. It is here that the agenda of phenomenological research must make its contribution. It is concerned with clarifying the connecting links between scientific observer-models of large scale socio-cultural systems, and the common-sense worlds of participants in such systems that form the contexts of alternatives, decisions, and acts on the micro-level of everyday situations.

At this point a short digression on the concept of 'situation' in social science will be useful, for our argument at this point can easily be misconstrued without it.

Our usage of 'situation' is inspired by a direction of research brought to fullest articulation in recent years by Professor Clyde Mitchell. What is meant here by 'situation' is not a 'case study' in the sense of what Mitchell quotes Gluckman as having called an 'apt illustration.' Situational analysis is not to be viewed as incompatible with macro-structural analysis. As Mitchell says, 'The typicality of the material is irrelevant since the regularities are set out in the description of the over-all social structure. In a sense the more atypical the actions and events described in the case history, the more instructive they are, since the anthropologist uses case material to show how variations can be contained within the structure.'[62]

Lest this seem misleadingly optimistic, however, a caveat is in order. Social science research oriented toward building integrated ladders of interpretation from the level of everyman to the most sophisticated strata of observer-interpretations based on comparative methodologies, is much more of a program than an accomplishment. And it is a program on whose validity there is by no means common agreement. Any close attention to how the term structure is used in the social sciences quickly reveals the controversies dividing observers who argue for different criteria of intelligibility in the ordering of macro-phenomena. The issues often boil down to conflicts over what sorts of observations should count as data to be utilized (as against excluded or de-emphasized) in the building of structural models. (As but one example in a long tradition, it is instructive to note how carefully Lévi-Strauss dissociates his notion of social structure from those of his peers and predecessors.) It would be very helpful if the more abstract conflicts over the meanings of macro and micro phenomena could be systematically shown to derive from the conflicting standards and requirements that scholars actually bring to the task of defining intelligibility itself. The sacred name of science can conceal the fact of membership in a morally ambiguous everyday world. The conflict between those who insist on attention to cognitive and intentional processes of humans as agents and those who consider such requirements as a lot of mysticism, is at least as much a conflict over a moral criterion for defining intelligible behavior as it is over a scientific one. Further, there are additional disagreements over how personal agency itself should be studied. For example, the overlaps and differences between the phenomenological styles of analysis of common-sense experience in the German and French traditions, situational and network analysis in British social anthropology, and American symbolic interactionism and ethno-methodology have yet to be traced for the benefit of progress in the sociology of knowledge.

In this present essay, the macro context on which we focus is not social structures but something broader (meaning structures) that includes those elements (norms, roles, institutions etc.) that are usually labeled as specifically social. We have proceeded in this fashion so as to be able to throw light on the interpretive, or hermeneutical, dimension of all social existence. Some differences between beginning with social structure and meaning structure may be sensed by looking closely at a comment by Edmund Leach made in defense of situational analysis.

In my view an anthropological structural analysis which appears comprehensive in that it narrowly defines *all* possible relationships is wrong in some rather fundamental way. I postulate that structural systems in which all avenues of social action are narrowly institutionalized are impossible. *In all viable systems there must be an area where the individual is free to make choices so as to manipulate the system to his advantage.*[63]

By looking at the human world as a total socio-cultural field of meanings and implications, the investigator is led to consider *all* action as based on a form of choice. This is because the essence of choice (i.e. the unavoidable element in it) is the person's necessary acceptance of *some* particular interpretation of the meaning of an act or event (whether this be his own interpretation or someone else's does not matter here—it is still a choice). Further, by focusing on the world as a meaning system, the notion of the personal 'advantage' in the name of which the individual is thought to manipulate the system cannot be confused with a merely subjective attitude factor. The notion of 'advantage' (including its referents and motivational status in a society) is itself a concept derived from a meaning system that is initially external to the person. It too must be learned abstractly and then situationally interpreted just like any other meaning.

How, then, may we use this mode of analysis to throw light on the actual ways in which persons can come to encounter scarcities by means of deprivation experiences?

We shall illustrate three ways of experiencing implications of meanings that are relevant for our understanding of the de-legitimation process. Depending upon which implications enter the interpretation, two or more meanings can be interpreted as in conflict with each other, as incompatible with each other, or one meaning may be experienced as directly implying the obsolescence of the other. While everyone interprets meanings, how they do this is properly a matter for empirical research and not speculation. Indeed it often happens that philosophers and scientists, because of an occupational bias toward intellectual consistency, perceive as incompatibilities what other people may see as simple conflicts to be reconciled by toleration or compromise into a state of at least morally intelligible if antagonistic co-existence. However if we refrain from seeking general 'laws' in such matters and confine ourselves to what insights the literature affords us with respect to particular kinds of threats to moral intelligibility, we are amply rewarded. Let us proceed to our examples.

Conflict

Our example will be one of conflict between two opposing normative interpretations of the same abstract values, and is taken from the history of Western political ideology.

Three values obviously part of the constitutive or intersubjective order of most Western European and North American societies are: sacredness of the human personality, high standard of living, and individual participation in the making of one's destiny. Related to these values are three institutionalized norms which, because of their general scope and evident direct relevance to the value criteria they represent, may be thought of as 'enabling norms.' Linked with the sanctity of the human personality is the norm that no man is to be treated as a means only, that is, he is never to be interpreted in purely instrumental terms. Linked with the high standard of living criterion is the norm of economic productivity and increasing equitability of distribution. Connected with the notion of individual participation in one's destiny is the norm of democracy.

If one attempts to translate these three norms into still more situationally specific policy directives, conflicting possible derivations emerge. Currently, two humanistic perspectives are competing for policy relevance: liberalism and Marxism. The major liberal policy derivation from the norm that no man is to be treated merely as a means was the proscription of chattel slavery throughout the Western world. Marxist humanists extend this interpretation to the eventual abolition of what they call 'wage slavery.'[64]

Likewise the norm of economic productivity is understood by liberal humanism to mean a high employment policy and the spread of consumption opportunities buttressed by welfare insurance mechanisms. But Marxist humanism stresses the hope for eventual liberation of all individuals from a struggle for material existence, from a reifying division of labor, and from the deprivation of resources needed to cultivate formerly aristocratic ideals of leisure and fulfillment.

Finally, the norm of democracy is understood differently. Liberalism conceives of it in terms of consumer sovereignty expressed politically through elected representatives, and expressed economically in market preference criteria for resource allocation and production. Marxists think of a necessary transition from ideological false consciousness to a non-alienated freedom based on the elimination of private property and its effects.

Such massive and seemingly abstract conflicts are nonetheless ultimately recognizable as rooted in the day-to-day variations of deprivation consciousness among individual human beings. Thus, people in a job-oriented market society who have been long unemployed and then find a job that enables them to support a family are likely to feel that dignity and freedom are no longer scarce in their lives. But persons who feel overwhelmed with desire for leisure to develop artistic or other propensities, and are employed eight hours a day to earn a living, are likely to experience this necessity as a form of slavery and may well come to question the institutions responsible for the deprivation of dignity and free leisure they regard as necessary resources for their fulfillment of being human. It may well be that the fluctuation of practical circumstances (e.g. business cycles, market conditions, foreign policy, personal talents) has led to co-existence between these two normative orientations in the form of alternating emphases between them. In the struggle for the right to interpret Western humanistic values, the practical philistinism of liberal humanism co-exists in dialectical tension with the inspiring but dangerously abstract moral sophistication of Marxist humanism.

Incompatibility

By incompatibility we mean conditions in which two sets of seemingly plausible interpretations are nonetheless experienced as incompatible with each other. Our example of such a possibility is taken from the literature of political development and has reference to cases of incompatibility between indigenous and externally imposed ways of defining what is a purely technological component of culture.

In 1952 there was published a case account of technological transference that has since become widely known in social science. It was a report of an almost pure case of incompatibility between two ways of experiencing an axe.[65] Toward the end of the nineteenth century in Australia, European implements began to diffuse widely into the paleolithic aboriginal cultures of Australia. Among these cultures was the Yir Yoront. Few implements were more welcomed by them than the imported short-handled steel hatchet that replaced their indigenous stone axe. From this innovation several unintended consequences ramified which eventually helped immobilize the entire society through self-destructive apathy. Sharp's essay traces these ramifications in detail.

Interested in such problems because of his own theoretically oriented field work in African societies, David Apter has tried to account for such cases by synthesizing a number of strands in social theory in an effort to relate two types of orientations toward values on the one hand to certain kinds of authority structures on the other. The distinction in orientations he calls 'instrumental' versus 'consummatory,' and these are terms that refer not to content of values but to the manner in which means and ends are related. Thus, instrumental value systems

> are those in which ultimate ends do not color every concrete
> act. If trade, new agricultural practices, or administrative

437

matters are introduced, the consequences are immediate, fragmentary and non-cosmological. Such systems can innovate without appearing to alter their social institutions fundamentally. Rather, innovation is made to serve tradition.[66]

Such systems are contrasted with consummatory types in which every significant social act is tied in with the socio-cultural order as a whole in such a way that the total web does not permit the legitimate instrumentalization of most of its parts.

As an example of Apter's point, we may take the case of Buganda, one of the African monarchies found by the British in East Africa.[67] The ability of some such societies to adapt to a wide range of modernizing stimuli has been of scientific interest for some years. With reference to our topic, if we are to ask how it was that Buganda developed an authority structure which permitted the instrumentalization of so much of its social and cultural life, it seems likely that the skills and data of the historian must be consulted. One clue, for instance, appears in an early historical study of Buganda by John Roscoe[68] in which he states that a nineteenth-century Buganda king (kabaka), upon being offered the accoutrements of the medium of one of the most important gods, refused them, whereupon another was appointed to that religious post. The result was that henceforth the office of king was separate from that of 'priest.'

Upon this basis, a more recent historian, D. A. Low, was led to surmise that

the fact that kabaka was not a priest of the traditional religion meant that he could take part in the ceremonies of any new one with which he might be intrigued, without conflicting with his traditional role, without breaking any tribal taboos, and without horrifying his people.[69]

Low's topic was the acceptance of Christianity into Buganda, but the implication for our problem is clear. The political history of the Buganda monarchy, including the decision mentioned by Roscoe, is directly related to the emergence of an authority structure in which a high degree of instrumentalization was possible, short of any threat to the monarchical principle itself.

In terms of our frame of reference, the major hypothesis that emerges from this example and the approach it represents is that consummatory systems tend to immobilize their components as resources to be turned to new ends. They resist the incorporation of new elements that might function as such resources. But as Apter's own work amply shows, the most credible formulations of such general hypotheses are those richly endowed with historical detail and qualification.

438

Obsolescence

By obsolescence we mean conditions in which one of two sets of implications seems to undermine the plausibility of (and hence render incredible to participants in the situation) the claims of the other set. Our example will be taken from the domain of representational symbols.

In a striking chapter in one of his books, Eric Voegelin presents an account of the struggle for symbolic representation in ancient Rome from polis to empire.[70] He rejects any analysis of the problem that is cast simply in terms of relative statistics of religious affiliation and argues that the real issue was the credibility of multiple and competing public representations of transcendent truth. His documentation consists of the writings of those figures who evidently understood the problem and addressed themselves to it at the various stages of ancient history, from Plato to Augustine. Based upon the work of a number of historians, Voegelin's account traces the transformations in the meanings of the gods, the soul, the community, and of time, as these impinged again and again upon the claims to legitimacy of the Roman political authorities. With this approach he is able to claim that part of the cultural vitality of Rome had to do with the manner in which various exogenous philosophical meanings were transformed by Roman thinkers into the Roman existential context. For example,

> the stoic idea that every man had two countries, the polis of his birth and the cosmopolis, [Cicero] transformed deftly into the idea that every man had indeed two fatherlands, the countryside of his birth, for Cicero his Arpinum, and Rome. The cosmopolis of the philosophers was realized in historical existence; it was the *imperium Romanum*.[71]

The story interweaves numerous variables such as the history of Roman political parties, the patronage system, and the changing ecology and demography of Roman imperialism to demonstrate the many reasons why the representational symbol order eventually became obsolete in the early centuries of our era.

The best example of the obsolescence of meanings that occurs in Voegelin's discussion is what happened after the Christians were granted toleration in A.D. 311–13. Perhaps because of the Christian behavior under persecution and their survival as a movement, it was apparently felt that the Christian God was worthy of respect and might retaliate against the persecutors of his people. He was therefore incorporated into the imperial system of divinity. Voegelin details the resulting legitimacy crisis foreseen already in A.D. 180 by the Roman anti-Christian philosopher Celsus. Celsus had understood that a radical theology of a de-divinized world and a monotheistic God would challenge the very essence of Roman civil religion, that is, the polytheistic basis of Rome's ability to integrate a plurality of ethnic and religious groups into a *pax Romana* symbolized by a divine emperor. The problem was never resolved, and 'The double representation of man in society through church and empire lasted through the Middle Ages.'

The point here is that when representational symbols become obsolete, that is, lose credibility, they cease to transmit the sense of existential coherence linking individual, community, and nature. Reality becomes sense-less, faith in truth claims regarding it are cast into doubt, and these scarcities of coherence and faith spell decline in the legitimacy of the logico-meaningful unity of the whole existing social order. The importance of such instances for our present topic is that they demonstrate that latent scarcities (in this case the threatened obsolescence of a symbol order with all that implies for politics, legitimacy, social control and public behavior), is not a matter which is amenable to rectification by simple fiat, however authoritative the source or vigorous the attempt. Part of the story is always the intrinsic logic of meanings and the adequacy of interpretations as revealed in the consequences of the policies to which they lead.

Conclusion

In this essay we have presented a perspective on how the problem of moral intelligibility may be approached in the sociology of knowledge. The initial assumption underlying the perspective is that one property of society itself is a persistent strain toward de-legitimation of its established routines.

After reviewing legitimacy as a general concept within a phenomenological frame of discourse, the notion of scarcity was appropriated from its more usual materialistic connotations and transformed into the fundamental dynamic through which de-legitimation occurs. Scarcities were regarded as growing out of a particular feature of society, the latter defined essentially as a mosaic of meanings. That feature is the capacity of all meanings to suggest to people, by means of implications, possibilities for operational concretizations *other than* those actually achieved up to a given point of time. Thus no actual state of affairs can ever be said intrinsically to satisfy the latent possibilities of meanings for persons who seek to fulfill them through action in history. All meanings are therefore open, pointing in some direction of the 'not yet.'

Since legitimation is an operation of closure (that is, discounting the value of pursuing further implications and protecting established interpretations by means of enforced social sanctions), legitimacy is always an unstable artifact of human interpretation—a dike against the never-ending trickle, flow, or stream of scarcities. Because no legitimations are such as to be self-evidently applicable to all contingent situations, the interpretation of moral intelligibility is a task that falls to everyone. In that sense every person is a hermeneutic agent, although societies evolve various ways of concealing this status from large portions of their populations.

The interpretation, negotiation, and legitimation of meanings—intrinsically unavoidable requirements for the maintenance of any human society—are within the capacity only of the human species. This is the basis for the claim that human beings confront a world different in kind than that studied by any other sciences than the specifically socio-cultural disciplines. One of the implications of our argument is that sociology and history are really interdependent parts of one discipline. The former looks at human action from the standpoint of environments experienced by people as sedimented products of cumulative past actions. These sedimented products (institutions, organizations, intersubjective meanings) are partial determinants of what people at any given time are likely to think, do, or hope for. History, by what still seems common consent, examines how human agents actually went about interpreting these environments through the creation of acts and agendas which—in the events that resulted—became part of the lifeworld of their descendents. Sociologists without historical awareness seem destined to reify the objects of their study, thus obscuring the varieties of human agency. Historians without the sociological perspective would have to invent it. For the sociological perspective *is* the effort to interpret social reality as something more than a haphazard sequence of 'happenings.'

Notes

1 Cf. the symposium edited by Samuel Z. Klausner, *The Quest for Self-Control: Classical Philosophies and Scientific Research*, New York: Free Press, 1965. This whole volume is organized around the problem of what social science research implies for classical Western notions of personal agency. In recent years a large corpus of literature has emerged in philosophy pertaining to the notion of 'action' and 'agency' that remains largely unintegrated with social science theories, despite the evident need for synthesis between such literature and the earlier writings of social thinkers like Cooley, James, Mead, Dewey and others. Cf. Robert McGowan and Myron Gochnauer, 'A Bibliography of the Philosophy of Action' in Robert Binkley et al., (eds), *Agent, Action, and Reason*, Toronto University Press, 1971, pp. 167–99. In this present paper we make no attempt to do justice to this range of writings. Neither do we incorporate the valuable empirical studies of moral

development that have been emerging in recent years, and are partly documented in C. M. Beck *et al.* (eds), *Moral Education: Inter-disciplinary Approaches*, Toronto University Press, 1971. Synthesis of this sort we intend to take up in future writings. In this present paper we focus primarily on the notion of legitimacy as concept and experience. Our purpose is to argue for a basic framework of assumptions about the topic of legitimacy—a framework that cannot be misused in the name of technicist notions of expertise. For another 'framework' effort somewhat along these lines, cf. Peter Berger and Thomas Luckmann, *The Social Construction of Reality*, Garden City, N.Y.: Doubleday, 1966.

2 Space precludes reviewing the notion of technicism at any length here. I have examined the literature and problematics of this concept in the following papers: 'Technicism, Liberalism, and Development' in M. Stanley (ed.), *Social Development: Critical Perspectives*, New York: Basic Books, 1972, pp. 274–325; 'Prometheus and the Policy Sciences' in Frank Johnson (ed.), *The Concept and Meanings of Alienation*, New York: Seminar Press, 1973 (forthcoming); 'Literacy: The Crisis of a Conventional Wisdom', *School Review*, vol. 80, no. 3 (May 1972). Suffice it to say here that a technicist society is not one that is merely characterized by sophisticated technology, or even by an inordinate faith in technological capacities. A technicist society is one in which human reason is bent to the service of *instrumental* rationality. In such a society the 'ends' or purposes of instruments are not likewise sub-jected to intensive rational analysis on the public level. Rather 'ends' are either taken for granted, left for private determination, or articu-lated on a level so platitudinous as to be nearly irrational. Technicism, then, is a radical disjunction between the application of reason to 'means' as against 'ends'. This formulation makes it clear that fear of technicism is not exclusively directed at physical machinery, but at social technology (e.g., bureaucracies) and some products of the intellect (e.g., scientific knowledge) as well. The call for a return to a democracy of the soil in the face of the modern impersonal division of labor, is not dissimilar to the yearning for a communal solidarity of the passions as against the refined sectors of intellectual specialization. If social scientific knowledge comes to be experienced as bereft of any resonance in common sense as physical technology often is today, then the legitimations for policy based upon such knowledge will also be threatened by serious neo-Luddite reactions. Ivan Illich has presented us with a valuable formulation of the problem of mass inaccessibility to the institutions and technologies of modern society in his essay on true and false utilities, 'Institutional Spectrum' in Ivan Illich, *Deschool-ing Society*, New York: Harper & Row, 1971, pp. 52–64. This present essay is based on our conviction that social science knowledge too can be presented in ways that facilitate true as against false utilities. The test of true utility is the degree to which social science knowledge reveals to those who master it the opportunities and limitations for personal agency in the legitimation or re-direction of the human world.

3 The urgency of this agenda is symbolized by the superficial straw-man construct of the 'autonomous individual' that provides the basis for

B. F. Skinner's assault upon 'the literature of freedom and dignity'; cf. B. F. Skinner, *Beyond Freedom and Dignity*, New York: Alfred Knopf, 1971.

4 Charles Taylor, 'Interpretation and the Sciences of Man', *Review of Metaphysics*, vol. 25, no. 1 (September 1971), p. 35.

5 For a discussion in the neo-primitivist vein that regards law as the virtual enemy of legitimation by custom, having been allegedly imposed by elites in the interests of taxation and other modes of social domination, cf. Stanley Diamond, 'The Rule of Law versus the Order of Custom', *Social Research*, vol. 38, no. 1 (Spring 1971), pp. 42–72.

6 Dennis Wrong, 'The Oversocialized Conception of Man in Modern Sociology', *American Sociological Review*, vol. 26 (1961), pp. 183–93.

7 This orientation has appeared in R. D. Laing's and other discussions of madness, in Herbert Marcuse's and Norman O. Brown's notions about the benefits of 'polymorphous perversity', and in the mainstream rhetoric of the drug and sex cults. For a general discussion of what all this implies for established sociological notions of 'deviance', see Irving L. Horowitz and Martin Liebowitz, 'Social Deviance and Political Marginality', *Social Problems*, vol. 15 (Winter 1968), pp. 297–310.

8 Cf. Alfred Schutz, 'Common-Sense and Scientific Interpretation of Human Action' in Maurice Natanson (ed.), *Philosophy of the Social Sciences: A Reader*, New York: Random House, 1963, pp. 302–46. Very much based on Schutz's analysis is Harold Garfinkel's essay 'The Rational Properties of Scientific and Common Sense Activities' in his volume *Studies in Ethnomethodology*, Englewood Cliffs, N.J.: Prentice-Hall, 1967, pp. 262–83. An essential work for understanding what this orientation to the study of the common-sense world means for social research methodology is Aaron V. Cicourel, *Method and Measurement in Sociology*, New York: Free Press, 1964. See also Lindsey Churchill, 'Ethnomethodology and Measurement', *Social Forces*, vol. 50, no. 2 (December 1971), pp. 182–90. It should be understood that the intent among such thinkers is not simply to reproduce the subjective reports of respondents uttered in common-sense terms. That would be nothing but crude ethnography. The intent, rather, is to incorporate models of common-sense experience into the models that the scientific observer generates from a more comparative data base, so that the categories of the scientist will have something to do with the way in which a given society is lived by its members.

9 Cf. the various works of Hannah Arendt whose recent career has been marked by efforts to rethink the problem of evil in the light of this century's experiences with totalitarianism.

10 For example see the virtually incredible account of the life and death of the Austrian peasant Franz Jägerstätter as documented in Gordon Zahn, *In Solitary Witness*, New York: Holt, Rinehart & Winston, 1964.

11 Cf. the masterful treatment of such matters in Jack D. Douglas, *The Social Meanings of Suicide*, Princeton University Press, 1967.

12 Cf. the comments by Charles Taylor on Lipset's approach to legitimacy, 'Interpretation and the Sciences of Man', pp. 36 ff. The works of

Schutz and of Merleau-Ponty should also be consulted with respect to this problem of the subject-object distinction in social research.

13 The existence of lynch mobs, vigilante groups and racial pogroms would seem to challenge this assertion. But it should be kept in mind that in United States experience, appeal to people's sense of the illegitimacy of these things has proven as important in keeping such phenomena in check as has the exercise of (what would often have proven insufficient) police power. It has, however, often been observed about Americans that illegality as a definition of illegitimacy is more likely to inspire consensus than any other way of defining illegitimacy.

14 The Calley case is an example in the United States. Polls have shown that in the order of eight out of ten Americans thought the sentence imposed on Calley after his trial was unjust. This statistic tells us virtually nothing. We need to know things like: what was the state of information about the case in respondents' minds? what were the influences of race thinking in relation to Vietnamese on perceptions of what Calley had done at My Lai? what were the multiple interpretations that were held of the meaning of the verdict itself? and so forth. Without such data we have no way of knowing what the public means by unjust.

15 This is what is so radically misunderstood by those who keep insisting that phenomenology involves nothing but introspective description of subjective states, and who mean by subjective 'private' (hence inaccessible) as against accessible 'public' data. All important writers in the phenomenological style who are of relevance to social science, such as Schutz and Merleau-Ponty, have taken great pains to insist that phenomenological analysis is not simple introspection, is not directed simply toward 'private' data, and is not subjective in the sense of a contradistinction to objective. Yet these arguments are still overlooked in even very recent publications that contrast behaviorism with phenomenology, as in John Finley Scott's *Internalization of Norms: A Sociological Theory of Moral Commitment*, Englewood Cliffs, N.J.: Prentice-Hall, 1971. Indeed Scott accuses phenomenology of being rooted in the world perspective of a morally well-socialized academic middle class whose members have difficulty imagining how morally diverse other people can be (pp. 21–32). Yet Alfred Schutz, for example, has rather little to say about morality in his classic treatise *The Phenomenology of the Social World*, Evanston: Northwestern University Press, 1967 (original ed. 1932). Instead, the conceptual axis of this work is the implications of Husserl's lectures on the phenomenology of inner-time consciousness for the analysis of social action. It is also strange that Scott should make this claim given that the empirical research most directly inspired by Schutz in the United States, namely the ethnomethodology of Harold Garfinkel and his associates, has virtually demolished the more traditional sociological approach to deviance, precisely by revealing the radical *pluralism* of moral perspectives and action in a society. Scott tends to lump together Parsonian structural-functionalism, phenomenology, and voluntarist philosophies generally in one great opponent of behaviorism. Of course, these remarks should not be taken to suggest any absence of fundamental

conflicts among writers in the phenomenological vein about the mission of the tradition they share. For example, cf. Dallas Laskey, 'Embodied Consciousness and the Human Spirit' in Anna-Teresa Tymieniecka (ed.), *Analecta Husserliana*, vol. 1, New York: Humanities Press, 1971, pp. 197–207. See also Gunter W. Remmling, *Road to Suspicion: A Study of Modern Mentality and the Sociology of Knowledge*, New York: Appleton-Century-Crofts, 1967, pp. 85-92.

16 Paul Ricoeur, 'The Model of the Text: Meaningful Action Considered As A Text', *Social Research*, vol. 38, no. 3 (Autumn 1971), pp. 529–62. Biblical hermeneutics has experienced for generations some of the conceptual debates now emerging in the social sciences. A very useful outline of these debates on an introductory level is available under the heading 'Biblical Theology, Contemporary' in *The Interpreter's Dictionary of the Bible*, vol. 1, New York: Abingdon Press, 1962, pp. 418–32. (The essay is by Professor Krister Stendahl, Professor of New Testament Studies at Harvard University.) A general review of the issues in greater detail may be had by perusing Claus Westermann (ed.), *Essays on Old Testament Hermeneutics*, Richmond: John Knox Press, 1963. A general introduction to the whole agenda of hermeneutics, its variations, and major figures, is available in the volume by Richard E. Palmer, *Hermeneutics*, Evanston: Northwestern University Press, 1969.

17 A similar position is taken by Philip Selznick in *Law, Society, and Industrial Justice*, New York: Russell Sage Foundation, 1969, esp. ch. 1.

18 Cf. Pitirim Sorokin, *Social and Cultural Dynamics*, revised and abridged in one volume by the author, Boston: Porter Sargent, 1957.

19 *Ibid.*, p. 14. In a later work Sorokin develops this classification in somewhat greater detail using slightly different terminology. Cf. *Sociological Theories of Today*, New York: Harper & Row, 1966.

20 Sorokin, *op. cit.*, p. 8. A profound effort to grasp the logico-meaningful unity of an architectural style is Erwin Panofsky, *Gothic Architecture and Scholasticism*, Cleveland: Meridian Books, 1957. Among historians, Jacob Burckhardt, Marc Bloch, and Johan Huizinga are noted for their efforts to define entire historical periods in such integral terms. On a more restricted level, the work of Edward Hall (and his disciples) in what has come to be known as 'proxemics' represents a serious commitment to the empirical unravelling of the 'social space' dimensions of the logico-meaningful unities of groups and cultures.

21 This is one basis for the difference between classical formulators of a major discipline who get to be recognized as geniuses and the workers in the vineyard who follow after. The founders usually possess an erudition untrammelled by definitions of academic specialization. Hence they work less with specialized disciplinary abstractions than with intellectual problems generated by the significant logico-meaningful unities of life experience. This is not, of course, solely because they possessed genius but because so many of these scholars had access to aristocratic standards of education.

22 It is not surprising, in this connection, that we see in modern Western societies the emergence of the notion of 'para-professionals'. This role presumably reflects an effort to combine the generalist skills of common

sense practice with some degree of the specialist skills of professional-ized scholarship. This is not to be interpreted as a trend toward lowering of competence standards, but rather as an attempt to combine two kinds of competence. One type is the result of cultivated specialism. The other type of competence is that which comes by way of a history of personal action in the lifeworld of common sense as such. The influence of para-professionalism will probably be limited, however, as long as the component of professional expertise that forms one half of the equation is itself so compartmentalized with respect both to other domains of professional expertise and to the phenomenology of the common-sense world. Medical para-professionals may serve as an example. On the one hand such personnel may actually come to be exposed to multiple professional perspectives (e.g. psychiatry, anthropology and sociology) more than full-fledged medical professionals. On the other hand, para-professionals may come to have more contact also with the pathogenic aspects of daily life (e.g. poverty, poor diet, psychic strains). If this proves to be the case, the influence upon orthodox professional medical practice and curricula that para-professionals could conceivably bring to bear might result in major changes of direction in these activities. This will not happen, however, if para-professionals are viewed as nothing but diluted professionals in street clothes.

23 This is so even in most examples that might at first sight appear to be exceptions to this generalization, as in the claim that a specific docu-ment—the Constitution—legitimates the whole United States govern-ment. But one requires only a reminder of the endless debates over the 'constitutionality' of a law or practice to be disabused of such a simplistic view.

24 For the concept of casuistry, see Sir Kenneth Kirk, *Conscience and Its Problems*, London: Longmans Green, 1927. For a study of the context in which 'conscience' became transmuted into 'interests' in liberal society see J. A. W. Gunn, *Politics and the Public Interest in the Seventh Century*, London: Routledge & Kegan Paul, 1969. For a doctrinal history of the legitimation of political acts by 'reason of state' see Friedrich Meinecke, *Machiavellism: The Doctrine of Raison d'Etat and Its Place in Modern History*, New Haven: Yale University Press, 1957. For two examples of studies focusing on individual thinkers who played an important role as intellectual brokers in adapting philo-sophical systems to the ideologico-moral problems of their times see Leonard Krieger, *The Politics of Discretion: Pufendorf and the Accept-ance of Natural Law*, Chicago University Press, 1965 and Melvin Richter, *The Politics of Conscience*, Cambridge, Mass.: Harvard University Press, 1964. The latter work is a study of T. H. Green's fusion of Hegelianism and pre-World War I British liberal theories of political obligation. Also relevant to the study of intellectual articu-lations of doctrine in the struggle over legitimation are Benjamin Nelson's study of the long conflict over the meaning of the deutero-nomic condemnation of usury among brothers, *The Idea of Usury*, 2nd ed., Chicago University Press, 1969, and C. B. Macpherson, *The Political Theory of Possessive Individualism*, London: Oxford University Press, 1962. In this work Macpherson argues that the 'market society' was

legitimated through the influence of seventeenth-century political theorists on the intellectual level who were themselves articulating the doctrinal significance of social organizational changes that had been forming in England for many generations. Historical studies of legitimacy crises always illustrate the dependence of events upon the deliberate fusing in real life of what has been called here legitimation by reference to intellectual constructions, legitimation by appeal to conformity and legitimation by reference to coherence. See, for example, Giorgio de Santillana, *The Crime of Galileo*, Chicago University Press, 1955, and Lewis Hanke, *Aristotle and the American Indians*, Bloomington: Indiana University Press, 1959. The investigation by de Santillana of the processes leading to Galileo's condemnation shows in many ways how things could have gone differently, depending always upon how interpretations of existing meanings were made at particular points. Galileo, for example, largely remained within the issues of theological interpretation, according to de Santillana, in defending the orthodoxy of his work. Yet the author shows how significantly other considerations bore upon the case. Among these were Pope Urban VII's strategic position in European politics; the struggle for control of elite education by the Jesuit order; the public relations problems of a thought police (the Holy Office of the Inquisition); and the anxiety of some theologians over any possible intellectual 'scandal' such as the conceivable unreliability of the Aristotelian sub-structure of Catholic dogma. Yet de Santillana does not neglect the intrinsic logic of the neo-Aristotelian principles of coherence itself as, for example, the sharp distinction between the earthly and the heavenly realms which Galileo's philosophy of nature seemed to be contradicting. Hanke's study describes the great debate between Sepúlveda and Las Casas in 1550–51 over the applicability of Aristotle's theory of natural slavery to the indigenous peoples found in Latin America. This debate was an official struggle between interpretations which, Hanke shows, was to have significant influence upon subsequent Spanish imperial policy for a long time. His account makes clear that while the humanistic and political interests represented in the debate are clearly understandable in our own day, the coordinates of interpretation were dominated by the coherence patterns and circumstances pertaining to sixteenth-century Spain. (It may be wondered why subsequent generations honor great intellectuals who contribute to the legitimation of some institution or policy. Reading historical studies of such efforts suggests at least one answer. Perhaps such men are honored because their efforts demonstrate personal potency in the face of situational challenges without threatening with mockery the persistent human striving after universal meanings that fulfill men's desire to experience history or nature as morally intelligible whatever their own momentary interests.)

25 Apart from the works of Schutz, see Maurice Mandelbaum, *The Phenomenology of Moral Experience*, Chicago: Free Press, 1955. In sociology itself there is a sort of intellectual movement called 'ethnomethodology' which has set itself the task of rectifying this dearth of studies on the construction of everyday life. The most important

sources growing out of this movement are as follows. Harold Garfinkel, *Studies in Ethnomethodology*, Englewood Cliffs, N.J.: Prentice-Hall, 1967; Aaron Cicourel, *Method and Measurement in Sociology*, New York: Free Press, 1964, and Cicourel, *The Social Organization of Juvenile Justice*, New York: Wiley, 1968; Douglas, *The Social Meanings of Suicide*, and Jack D. Douglas (ed.), *Deviance and Respectability: The Social Construction of Moral Meanings*, New York: Basic Books, 1970 and Jack D. Douglas (ed.), *Understanding Everyday Life*, Chicago: Aldine, 1970. In our opinion this literature is important precisely because it bears so basically upon the active, freedom-using capacities of human beings.

26 Schutz has some important things to say about Weber's use of the notion 'traditional behavior' in the course of which he clarifies for the benefit of all sociologists the necessity of the phenomenological analysis of sociological concepts he subsequently carries out, *Phenomenology of the Social World*, ch. 1. A more recent effort to cope in detail with the varieties of meaning the concept of conformity can have is J. G. A. Pocock, 'Time, Institutions and Action' in Preston King and B. C. Parekh (eds), *Politics and Experience: Essays Presented to Professor Michael Oakeshott*, Cambridge University Press, 1968, pp. 209–38. There have been various advances in the methodology of probing conformative behavior, including verbalization. For example, componential analysis techniques developed in linguistics have been used to study concepts like status and role, disease categories, and values. Much of this literature is gathered in S. Tyler (ed.), *Cognitive Anthropology*, New York: Holt, Rinehart & Winston, 1969. Clyde Kluckhohn has used the technique to study values in 'The Study of Values' in Donald N. Barrett (ed.), *Values in America*, Notre Dame University Press, 1961, pp. 17–45. There is no unanimity on the efficacy of techniques of this sort, as some of the essays in Tyler make clear. For some differences between approaches like ethnoscience, ethnomethodology, and phenomenology, see George Psathas, 'Ethnomethods and Phenomenology', *Social Research*, vol. 35, no. 3 (Autumn 1968), pp. 500–20. The sociology of religion has been rather fruitful in empirical studies that bear upon legitimation phenomena. Max Weber's studies in religion and society remain without peer as examples of how relatively scarce historical materials can be utilized in constructing a sociological account of legitimacy that includes a place for both persistence and change in mass behavioral regularities. The contemporary literature too contains some studies notable for their efforts to deal with similar problems. One might mention, for example, Kenneth Underwood's investigation of attitudes and behavior under conflict conditions in an American town, *Protestant and Catholic*, Boston: Beacon Press, 1957. Underwood is concerned with the empirical effects of Roman Catholic versus Protestant notions of legitimate authority and behavior. Also useful is Gillian Gollin's study of two communities of Moravian origin exposed to two radically contrasting national environments (Herrnhut in Germany and Bethlehem, Pennsylvania, in the U.S.), *Moravians in Two Worlds*, New York: Columbia University Press, 1967. An example of historical sociology in the structural-

functional ambiance applied to the problem of legitimation is Kai
Erikson, *Wayward Puritans*, New York: Wiley, 1966. A fascinating
study of constructed legitimacy in a formal organization whose bureaucratic hierarchy had no basis for authority is the investigation of the
American Baptist Convention by Paul M. Harrison, *Authority and
Power in the Free Church Tradition*, Princeton University Press, 1959.
In a somewhat related vein is this writer's study of the efforts of the
organizational elites of the Jehovah's Witness movement to maintain
simultaneously a culturally unpopular theological message and a
functioning social movement in the American urban environment
between 1880 and 1960; Manfred Stanley, 'Jehovah in the City of
Mammon' in H. Mizruchi and Paul Meadows (eds), *Urbanism, Urban-
ization and Change*, Reading, Mass.: Addison-Wesley, 1969, pp. 186–
207.

27 Cf. Paul G. Kuntz (ed.), *The Concept of Order*, Seattle: University of
Washington Press, 1968, Eric Voegelin, *Order and History*, 3 vols,
Baton Rouge: Louisiana State University Press, 1956–8, F. S. C.
Northrop, *The Meeting of East and West*, New York: Macmillan,
1950, for some approaches to the study of 'order' as principles of coherence in the structure of the world, of history, and of nature itself.
Also, cf. Philip Curtin, *The Image of Africa*, Madison: University of
Wisconsin Press, 1964, and Sir Thomas D. Kendrich, *The Lisbon Earthquake*, Philadelphia: Lippincott, 1955. These two studies are examples
of the sorts of work produced by historians that sociologists of knowledge can ill afford to ignore. Curtin traces the impact of world-view
themes (e.g. evangelicalism, 'natural man' theories, race doctrines,
evolution, and even specific physical theories like 'phlogiston') upon
the manner in which data from West Africa were received and interpreted by various social elites in Great Britain between 1780 and 1850.
With this investigation of refraction through world-view, Curtin is able
to account for many aspects of the subsequent style of British imperialism in Africa and its legitimation. Kendrick was interested in the
influence of world view themes upon specific reactions to the Lisbon
earthquake disaster of 1755. Finally, one of the few contemporary
attempts to analyze a significant issue of public policy from the standpoint of theories of world view is Theodore Geiger, *The Conflicted
Relationship*, New York: McGraw-Hill, 1967. Geiger's book is an
effort to apply some significant social theories bearing upon world
views and social change to the task of understanding the failures and
frustrations of the American foreign aid program.

28 Charles Taylor, 'Interpretation and the Sciences of Man'.

29 *Ibid.*, p. 28.

30 *Ibid.*, p. 23.

31 Both quotations from *ibid.*, p. 27; my emphasis.

32 Cf. Jean Piaget, *Structuralism*, New York: Basic Books, 1970; Michael
Lane (ed.), *Introduction to Structuralism*, New York: Basic Books,
1970; Jacques Ehrmann (ed.), *Structuralism*, Garden City, N.Y.:
Doubleday Anchor, 1970.

33 There have been very few attempts in American sociology to compose
systematic methodology texts that embody all these concerns. A notable

exception is Severyn T. Bruyn, *The Human Perspective in Sociology*, Englewood Cliffs, N.J.: Prentice-Hall, 1966.

34 One of the major sociological studies of representative symbols in American community life is by W. Lloyd Warner, *The Family of God*, New Haven: Yale University Press, 1961. Our sense of the concept of representative symbols is indebted to the formulation by Eric Voegelin, *The New Science of Politics*, University of Chicago Press, 1952.

35 Stephen Pepper, *World Hypotheses*, Berkeley: University of California Press, 1970 (original 1942).

36 Cf. Hugh Dalziel Duncan, *Communication and Social Order*, New York: Bedminister Press, 1962; Max Black, *Models and Metaphors*, Ithaca, N.Y.: Cornell University Press, 1962; Colin Turbayne, *The Myth of Metaphor*, rev. ed., Columbia: University of South Carolina Press, 1970. Those concerned with the misappropriation of metaphors for technicist uses should acquaint themselves with the work of the Scottish philosopher John Macmurray. In 1936 Macmurray published a volume, *Interpreting the Universe*, London: Faber & Faber, in which he wrote: 'We do not know how to represent our knowledge of the personal as idea. I have indicated my belief that this is the emergent problem of philosophy in our own day' (p. 142). Macmurray's Gifford Lectures entitled 'The Forms of the Personal' are the fruits of many years of effort to rectify this situation in philosophy. The results should be part of the education of all social scientists. Cf. John Macmurray, *The Self as Agent*, London: Faber & Faber, 1957 and *Persons in Relation*, London: Faber & Faber, 1961.

37 A notable exception to this generalization about American sociologists is Paul Meadows. Cf. 'The Metaphors of Order: Toward a Taxonomy of Organization Theory' in Llewellyn Gross (ed.), *Sociological Theory: Inquiries and Paradigms*, New York: Harper & Row, 1967, pp. 77–103.

38 Robert Nisbet, *Social Change and History: Aspects of the Western Theory of Development*, New York: Oxford University Press, 1968.

39 Mircea Eliade, *Myth and Reality*, New York: Harper, 1963, p. 141.

40 Mircea Eliade, *Cosmos and History*, New York: Harper & Row, 1959, pp. 153–4. Needless to say, the themes of exhaustion, silence, and apocalypse have been widespread in modern arts.

41 I treat this theme in my 'Technicism, Liberalism, and Development' in Manfred Stanley (ed.), *Social Development: Critical Perspectives*, New York: Basic Books, 1972, pp. 274–325.

42 A related position on the fallaciousness of the term world view is taken by Walter Ong who examines the misleading implications of the metaphor of vision when applied to the world experience of non-literate (oral-aural) cultures. Cf. Walter Ong, 'World as View and World as Event', *American Anthropologist*, vol. 71, no. 4 (August 1969), pp. 634–47.

43 Robert Heilbroner, 'Through the Marxian Maze', *New York Review of Books*, vol. 18, no. 4, p. 9.

44 The whole problem of choice from a phenomenological point of view is a very complex matter. For some of the issues, cf. Schutz, *Phenomenology of the Social World*, pp. 66–9.

45 For a view of motives along these lines, cf. Alan F. Blum and Peter

McHugh, 'The Social Ascription of Motives', *American Sociological Review*, vol. 36, no. 1 (February 1971), pp. 98–109.

46 On the interplay between theory and practice on the conceptual level, cf. Nicholas Lobkowicz, *Theory and Practice: History of a Concept from Aristotle to Marx*, Indiana: Notre Dame University Press, 1967. Cf. also Alvin Gouldner, *Enter Plato: Classical Greece and the Origins of Social Theory*, New York: Basic Books, 1965, for a view of social theory from Plato to today as a recurrent series of themes relating knowledge and social control.

47 Max Rheinstein, *Max Weber on Law in Economy and Society*, Cambridge, Mass.: Harvard University Press, 1954.

48 Cf. Judith Shklar, *Legalism*, Cambridge, Mass.: Harvard University Press, 1964.

49 For the moral history of statistics, cf. Jack D. Douglas, 'The Rhetoric of Science and the Origins of Statistical Social Thought' in Edward Tiryakian (ed.), *The Sociological Phenomenon*, New York: Appleton-Century-Crofts, 1970. For a discussion of some moral problems in the rhetoric of cybernetic systems engineering applied to social control, see my 'Prometheus and the Policy Sciences: Alienation as the Decline of Personal Agency'.

50 Cf. Lionel Robbins, *An Essay on the Nature and Significance of Economic Science*, London: Macmillan, 1946. For a discussion of the various meanings of scarcity in the history of economic thought, cf. Harold J. Barnett and Chandler Morse, *Scarcity and Growth*, Baltimore: Johns Hopkins Press, 1963. For a sophisticated and indeed beautiful treatment of scarcity in moral life, written by an economist, see Vivian Charles Walsh, *Scarcity and Evil*, Englewood Cliffs, N.J.: Prentice-Hall, 1961.

51 This argument is developed in my 'Social Development as a Normative Concept', *Journal of Developing Areas*, vol. 1, no. 3, (1967), pp. 301–17.

52 Louis Schneider, 'Dialectic in Sociology', *American Sociological Review*, vol. 36 (August 1971), pp. 667–78.

53 For a study of cleavages within the medical profession over conflicting legitimacy claims that reflect fundamental methodological and philosophical disagreements over what the profession is about, cf. Rue Bucher and Anselm Strauss, 'Professions in Process', *American Journal of Sociology*, vol. 66, (1961), pp. 325–34. Cf. also Eliot Freidson, *Profession of Medicine*, New York: Dodd, Mead, & Co., 1970. In another connection, cf. Harold L. Wilensky, *Intellectuals in Labor Unions*, Chicago: Free Press, 1956, and Harold Wilensky, *Organizational Intelligence*, New York: Basic Books, 1967.

54 Cf. Karl Polanyi *et al.*, *Trade and Markets in the Early Empires*, Chicago: Free Press, 1957; Marshall D. Sahlins, 'On the Sociology of Primitive Exchange' in Michael Banton (ed.), *The Relevance of Models for Social Anthropology*, New York: Praeger, 1965, pp. 139–236; Paul Bohannan and George Dalton (eds), *Markets in Africa*, Garden City, N.Y.: Doubleday, 1965.

55 Karl Polanyi, 'The Economy as Institute Process' in Polanyi *et. al.*, *op. cit.*, p. 250.

56 *Ibid.*, p. 251.

57 John Kenneth Galbraith, *American Capitalism*, New York: New American Library, 1952.

58 Cf. the essays in Stanley (ed.), *Social Development*.

59 As has been widely noted, this dependence and its consequent inefficiencies are probably related to the Soviet Union's efforts to introduce controlled market mechanisms into Russian life. Also cf. Percival and Paul Goodman, *Communitas*, New York: Vintage, 1960, pp. 188–218. They provide a proposal for a societal redistribution system designed in the light of modern technology but geared deliberately to avoid the creation of dependence. Whether one agrees or disagrees with their particular proposals, this is the sort of performance that distinguishes a fundamental social thinker from the typical technocrat in the field of planning.

60 Mircea Eliade develops a beautifully illustrative hypothetical argument between representatives of 'archaic' man and 'historical' man on the nature of freedom as they see it in the light of their respective phenomenologies of scarcity. Cf. *Cosmos and History*, pp. 154–9.

61 Cf. the essays cited in note 8. For an imaginative study very illustrative of the difference between the phenomenology of common-sense reasoning and technical legal reasoning in the area of juvenile delinquency, see David Matza, *Delinquency and Drift*, New York: John Wiley, 1964.

62 Foreword by Mitchell to J. van Velsen, *The Politics of Kinship*, Manchester University Press, 1964, p. xiii. Cf. also C. Clyde Mitchell, *Tribalism and the Plural Society* (*an inaugural lecture*), London: Oxford University Press, 1960.

63 Quoted by Mitchell in Foreword, *op. cit.*, p. xiii. Italics in original.

64 Marx expressed a modern version of a problem which C. B. Macpherson has shown to have a much longer history. The notion of wage slavery is rooted in the metaphysics of the will, of reason, and of freedom. In the seventeenth century, Macpherson points out, the issue of the franchise in the Leveller conception of freedom involved the question of whether being beholden to another man for one's livelihood did not deprive one of an important prerequisite for the vote, i.e. the proprietorship over the energies of one's own labor. Cf. Macpherson, *The Political Theory of Possessive Individualism*, pp. 107–59.

65 One accessible source for the essay by Lauriston Sharp, 'Steel Axes for Stone Age Australians' is in Edgar A. Schuler *et al.* (eds), *Readings in Sociology*, 3rd ed., New York: Crowell, 1967, pp. 750–69.

66 David E. Apter, *The Politics of Modernization*, University of Chicago Press, 1965, p. 85.

67 Buganda was the subject of one of Apter's field studies. Cf. David Apter, *The Political Kingdom in Uganda*, Princeton University Press, 1961.

68 John Roscoe, *The Baganda*, Cambridge University Press, 1911.

69 D. A. Low, *Religion and Society in Buganda, 1875–1890*, Kampala, Uganda: East African Institute of Social Research, Study no. 8, p. 4.

70 Eric Voegelin, *The New Science of Politics*, University of Chicago Press, 1952, pp. 76–107.

71 *Ibid.*, p. 91.

Further reading

Part one

Karl Mannheim, *Ideology and Utopia: An Introduction to the Sociology of Knowledge* (trans. and ed. Louis Wirth and Edward A. Shils), New York: Harcourt, Brace & World, 1936.

Gunter W. Remmling, *Road to Suspicion: A Study of Modern Mentality and the Sociology of Knowledge*, New York: Appleton-Century-Crofts, 1967.

Werner Stark, *The Sociology of Knowledge: An Essay in Aid of a Deeper Understanding of the History of Ideas*, London: Routledge & Kegan Paul, 1958.

Part two

H. Stuart Hughes, *Consciousness and Society: The Reorientation of European Social Thought 1890–1930*, New York: Knopf, 1958.

Karl Löwith, *From Hegel to Nietzsche: The Revolution in Nineteenth-Century Thought* (trans. David E. Green), New York: Holt, Rinehart & Winston, 1964.

Herbert Marcuse, *Reason and Revolution: Hegel and the Rise of Social Theory*, New York: Oxford University Press, 1941.

Werner Stark, *Montesquieu:Pioneer of the Sociology of Knowledge*, London: Routledge & Kegan Paul, 1960.

Part three

Irving Louis Horowitz, *Philosophy, Science, and the Sociology of Knowledge*, Springfield, Ill.: Thomas, 1961.

Hans Neisser, *On the Sociology of Knowledge: An Essay*, New York: Heinemann, 1965.

Kurt H. Wolff, 'The Sociology of Knowledge and Sociological

Theory' in Llewellyn Gross (ed.), *Symposium on Sociological Theory*, New York: Harper & Row, 1959, pp. 567–602.

Part four

Peter Berger (ed.), *Marxism and Sociology: Views from Eastern Europe*, New York: Appleton-Century-Crofts, 1969.

Georg Lukács, *History and Class Consciousness: Studies in Marxist Dialectics* (trans. Rodney Livingstone), Cambridge, Mass.: M.I.T. Press, 1971.

Karl Marx and Friedrich Engels, *The German Ideology* (ed. R. Pascal), London: Lawrence & Wishart, 1939.

Franz Mehring, *Karl Marx: The Story of His Life* (trans. Edward Fitzgerald), London: Allen & Unwin, 1951.

Irving M. Zeitlin, *Marxism: A Re-Examination*, Princeton, N.J.: Van Nostrand, 1967.

Part five

Gerard L. DeGré, *Society and Ideology: An Inquiry into the Sociology of Knowledge*, New York: Columbia University Bookstore, 1943.

Émile Durkheim, *The Elementary Forms of the Religious Life* (trans. Joseph Ward Swain), London: Allen & Unwin, 1915.

Émile Durkheim and Marcel Mauss, *Primitive Classification* (trans. Rodney Needham), University of Chicago Press, 1963.

Émile Durkheim *et al.*, *Essays on Sociology and Philosophy: With Appraisals of His Life and Thought* (ed. Kurt H. Wolff), New York: Harper & Row, 1964.

Part six

Max Scheler, *The Nature of Sympathy* (trans. Peter Heath with introduction by Werner Stark), London: Routledge & Kegan Paul, 1958.

Max Scheler, *Ressentiment* (trans. William W. Holdheim and ed. with introduction by Lewis A. Coser), Chicago: Free Press, 1961.

John Raphael Staude, *Max Scheler 1874–1928: An Intellectual Portrait*, New York: Free Press, 1967.

Part seven

Lewis A. Coser, 'Karl Mannheim 1893–1947' in L. A. Coser, *Masters of Sociological Thought: Ideas in Historical and Social Context*, New York: Harcourt Brace Jovanovich, 1971, pp. 429–63.

Karl Mannheim, *Essays on the Sociology of Knowledge* (ed. with introduction by Paul Kecskemeti), London: Routledge & Kegan Paul, 1952.

Jacques J. Maquet, *The Sociology of Knowledge; Its Structure and Its Relation to the Philosophy of Knowledge: A Critical Analysis of the Systems of Karl Mannheim and Pitirim A. Sorokin* (trans. John F. Locke), Boston: Beacon Press, 1951.

Gunter W. Remmling, *Chaos or Planning: The Sociology of Karl Mannheim; With a Bibliographical Guide to the Sociology of Knowledge*, London: Routledge & Kegan Paul (forthcoming).

F. Warren Rempel, *The Role of Value in Karl Mannheim's Sociology of Knowledge*, The Hague: Mouton, 1965.

Kurt H. Wolff (ed.), *From Karl Mannheim*, New York: Oxford University Press, 1971.

Part eight

Peter L. Berger and Thomas Luckmann, *The Social Construction of Reality: A Treatise in the Sociology of Knowledge*, Garden City, N.Y.: Doubleday, 1966.

Kenneth E. Boulding, *The Image: Knowledge in Life and Society*, Ann Arbor: University of Michigan Press, 1956.

Bukart Holzner, *Reality Construction in Society*, Cambridge, Mass.: Schenkman, 1968.

Alfred Schutz, *Collected Papers I: The Problem of Social Reality* (ed. with introduction by Maurice Natanson), The Hague: Nijhoff, 1962.

Gideon Sjoberg, 'Operationalism and Social Research' in Llewellyn Gross (ed.), *Symposium on Sociological Theory*, New York: Harper & Row, 1959, pp. 603–27.

Edward A. Tiryakian, *Sociologism and Existentialism: Two Perspectives on the Individual and Society*, Englewood Cliffs, N.J.: Prentice-Hall, 1962.

Part nine

Fritz Machlup, *The Production and Distribution of Knowledge in the United States*, Princeton University Press, 1962.

Karl Mannheim, 'Conservative Thought' in K. Mannheim, *Essays on Sociology and Social Psychology* (ed. with introduction by Paul Kecskemeti), London: Routledge & Kegan Paul, 1953, pp. 74–164.

Alfred von Martin, *Sociology of the Renaissance* (trans. W. L. Luetkens), London: Routledge & Kegan Paul, 1944.

Robert K. Merton, *Social Theory and Social Structure*, Part III:

The Sociology of Knowledge and Mass Communications, 1968 enlarged ed., New York: Free Press, 1968, pp. 493–582.

Elwin H. Powell, 'Beyond Utopia: The "Beat Generation" as a Challenge for the Sociology of Knowledge' in Arnold M. Rose (ed.), *Human Behavior and Social Processes: An Interactionist Approach*, Boston: Houghton Mifflin, 1962, pp. 360–77.

Larry T. Reynolds and Janice M. Reynolds (eds), *The Sociology of Sociology: Analysis and Criticism of the Thought, Research, and Ethical Folkways of Sociology and Its Practitioners*, New York: McKay, 1970.

Pitirim A. Sorokin, *Social and Cultural Dynamics*, vol. 2: *Fluctuations of Systems of Truth, Ethics, and Law*, New York: American Book, 1937.

Florian Znaniecki, *The Social Role of the Man of Knowledge*, New York: Columbia University Press, 1940.

Index

For Product Safety Concerns and Information please contact our EU
representative GPSR@taylorandfrancis.com
Taylor & Francis Verlag GmbH, Kaufingerstraße 24, 80331 München, Germany

www.ingramcontent.com/pod-product-compliance
Lightning Source LLC
Chambersburg PA
CBHW060127280326
41932CB00012B/1444